Artificial Intelligence and Machine Learning

Theory and Practice

Lyla B. Das
Sudhish N. George
Anup Aprem
Department of Electronics and Communication Engineering
National Institute of Technology Calicut (NITC), Kerala

NEW DELHI

Published by

Techsar Pvt. Ltd.
4435-36/7, Ansari Road, Daryaganj
New Delhi-110 002 (India)
E-mail: tech_info@techsarworld.com
Website: www.techsarworld.com

ISBN: 978-93-90620-09-8

Reprint 2025

Printed by Shree Maitrey Printech Pvt. Ltd. Noida

Artificial Intelligence and Machine Learning

Theory and Practice

Preface

Preamble

This book is meant to be an elaborate and comprehensive coverage of the most relevant topics in the field of Artificial Intelligence. The field is changing very fast and the many aspects of it will change with time. However, the basic algorithms and concepts will remain, and their relevance will not be surpassed for a very long time. Hence, learning has to start by acquiring a good grasp of the fundamentals. But without knowing where to apply and how to use these concepts, nothing will be gained. This book is meant to address these two aspects. Basic theory plus applications is the approach adopted in preparing the contents.

Artificial Intelligence (AI) is a very broad area of knowledge which has percolated into every aspect of human life. AI has algorithms catering to making machines work for us and thereby reduce physical and mental drudgery. What is generally referred to as 'machine learning' is considered to be a subset of AI. Machine learning has many branches of applications and also many ways for its use. First of all, there are the classical algorithms which have been around right from the 1950s and earlier. Because of their simplicity and efficiency, they are still very relevant. However, for problems which are complex and data intensive, deep learning is the solution. Both classical and deep learning are covered in this book. AI search algorithms which are also very old but very important, are also discussed.

The subdivisions of Machine Learning are Supervised, Unsupervised and Reinforcement Learning. All three are covered in sufficient depth. One very important and upcoming field of application is Natural Language Processing (NLP). A whole section of the book has been devoted to this.

Approach

There are three aspects to any topic in AI. They are 'theory, mathematics and coding'. This book will cover these three aspects for most topics. The point is that a user of the book will have the choice to use all the three aspects, or just the part he needs. A student who does not need the math portion can skip that and concentrate on just the theory and coding. Numerical examples and lucid explanations give the reader an easy entry into the world of AI and ML. It is not practical to insert all codes in the textbook. As such, a few codes will be included in some chapters. The remaining will be made available as part of the 'resources' of the book.

The aim of the book is to make the learning of these topics to be a joyful activity. The topics have been presented in a simple and clear way with interesting examples to make it student friendly. Every attempt has been made to include the latest developments in the field.

Prerequisite

This book is primarily focused on the students and practitioners of engineering (of any stream). Basic knowledge of Engineering math including probability theory, and some introductory experience of coding are the prerequisites for understanding the topics in the book. In the course of learning, coding in Python is expected to be done by the student and then only will they become masters. Executing projects based on the theory learned will lead to good expertise and confidence for a student.

Organization of the Book

This book is organized as 23 chapters. It is divided into four parts.

Part I, which has chapters 1 to 9 deals with the introduction, classical ML, mathematical chapters and AI search algorithms.

Chapter 1 introduces the terms Artificial Intelligence, Machine Learning and Data Science. To make the reader become aware of the potential of AI in tandem with other technologies, the self-driving car is discussed in some detail.

Chapter 2 is meant to build a solid basis for the machine learning process. The steps of ML, which are training, validation and testing are introduced. Types of ML and the meaning of terms such as regression, classification, overfitting, underfitting and the definition of the metrics used for evaluating models are all taken up in detail.

Chapter 3 takes up three of the classical machine learning algorithms in detail. The theory and mathematics of Linear regression, Logistic regression, Cost functions and gradient descent are taken up with rigor along with numerical and coding examples. Terms such are outliers, regularization, standardization and normalization are also discussed. The chapter concludes with a short description of Support Vector Machines.

Chapter 4 is the second chapter devoted to Classical machine learning. Supervised Learning Algorithms such as K-NN, Naïve Bayes, Decision Trees and ensemble methods are the topics in this. The chapter ends with an unsupervised learning technique named K—means clustering. Numerical problems for all these methods is the notable feature of this chapter.

Chapters 5 to 8 are the ones that cover the mathematical ground required to get a clear insight into all aspects of ML.

Chapter 5 concentrates on Bayesian Decision Theory and Linear Discriminant analysis. Chapter 6 includes topics such as Maximum Likelihood Estimation and Kernel Estimation Techniques. Chapter 7 takes up the task of unsupervised learning principles and discusses clustering techniques, one of which is explained in Chapter 4 as well. Chapter 8 deals with 'dimensionality reduction techniques' such as PCA, LDA and SVD.

Chapter 9 delves into search algorithms, the building block of solutions in AI. We begin by discussing basic search techniques, and then build more 'informed' search techniques. We consider the deterministic setting in this chapter; and the extension to stochastic setting.

Part II is about Deep Learning, its theory, and networks for important applications.

Chapter 10 starts by giving a good and clear insight into the basic theory of neural networks. It examines a single layer perceptron network and then proceeds to discuss multilayer perceptrons and a numerical calculation is used to explain backpropagation. This is followed with an analytical discussion of backpropagation. The second half of this chapter discusses the optimizations used when implementing deep learning. Aspects like batch, stochastic and mini-batch gradient descent are made clear. Further optimizations such as dropout, momentum, Adagrad, batchnorm, data augmentation, early stopping and gradient clipping are also explained. The chapter concludes with an overview of the popular activation functions such as Sigmoid, Tanh, ReLU and Softmax.

Chapter 11 is about convolutional neural networks and applications. It starts with a good introduction to image processing including convolutional filtering. This is followed by explaining the inside view of the stages of a typical CNN, with calculations of filter outputs and number of parameters. After this, standard CNNs such as Le Net, Alex Net, VGG Net. Resnet and Transfer Learning are covered. The last part of the chapter is a detailed discussion of Object detection with particular focus on YOLO.

Chapter 12 deals with sequential networks starting with the basic RNN cell, its theory and applications. After this, LSTMs and GRUs are taken up.

Chapter 13 is currently a hot topic of research and many applications are centred around it. To make the concept of GANs clear, many fundamental principles are used. One of these is the concept of 'latent space', Autoencoders, variational autoencoders, rationale behind GANs, training of GANs and their applications are the other topics covered.

Part III deals with Natural Language Processing (NLP)

Chapter 14 introduces the difficulties encountered in this field. It also explains the pre-processing to be used on 'text' before it enters the NLP pipeline.

Chapter 15 deals with 'N gram model' and 'POS Tagging'.

Chapter 16 talks about the frequency based methods to represent text. Here we get to know the 'bag of words' representation. The 'One hot vector' and 'TF-IDF' methods are covered. The other topics are 'document similarity' and 'sentiment analysis' which are very fundamental to the understanding of NLP principles.

Chapter 17 is of utmost importance as it deals with 'word embedding' which is the method used for text representation in all the latest NLP algorithms. A lot of effort has been done to make clear the two types of Word-to-Vec embedding, which are the CBOW and Skipgram models.

Chapter 18 takes up some very new concepts. The Seq2Seq network and Transformers are the latest building blocks of any NLP application and step-by-step coverage of both of them are included here. The list of important NLP applications are also mentioned.

Part IV deals with Reinforcement Learning

In Part IV, we look at Reinforcement Learning. Reinforcement learning is an active research area with important contemporary applications such as autonomous driving, robotics, 5G communication and Industry 4.0 applications. The history of reinforcement learning and applications are discussed in chapter 19.

Chapter 20 deals with fundamentals of sequential decision making and modeling of such problems using the Markov Decision Process (MDP). This chapter sets out the notation and concepts for the rest of Part IV and is a necessary read. The reader is introduced to the Bellman equation, a key idea for solution to decision-making problems, and some numerical algorithms based on the Bellman equation.

Chapters 21 & 22 form the core of modern reinforcement learning, where we discuss machine learning approaches to solving decision-making problems. In this book, we focus on reinforcement learning problems where the system dynamics are unknown. Chapter 21 broadly discusses approaches to learn the 'value function' given the real-world experience. However, in Chapter 22, we adopt the approach of learning the 'policy' given the real-world experience. In addition, in Chapter 22, we merge the two approaches to obtain 'Actor-Critic' algorithms. The rest of the chapter is dedicated to recent advances of 'Actor-Critic' architecture.

Chapter 23 introduces a decision-making model where the system dynamics are hidden, referred to as Partially Observed MDP (POMDP). We introduce a 'filtering approach' to infer and track the unknown dynamics and modify the Bellman equation in chapter 20 to accommodate the hidden dynamics. The rest of the chapter is devoted to reinforcement learning techniques approaches to POMDP.

Two appendices A and B are included. Appendix A is a basic introduction to Linear Algebra and Appendix B introduces Python Programming for Machine Learning.

Contact

Your feedback and suggestions for the improvement of this book are welcome. We have done our best to avoid errors. However, a few may still have managed to creep in. Kindly point them out to us. You can also write to us your feedback about the book and give suggestions. Our email ids are: lyla.das@gmail.com, sudhish@nitc.ac.in, anup.aprem@nitc.ac.in

Authors

Acknowledgements

This is my fourth major book and as I complete it, I would like to acknowledge all those who have helped me directly and indirectly in this Herculean task.

My previous books have been about Embedded Systems, Microprocessors and Microcontrollers (8051 and ARM). It has been only a few years since I started being interested in teaching Artificial Intelligence and Machine Learning. Right from the beginning of my entry into this exciting field, it has been my students who have motivated and inspired me to learn more because they wanted more. They also brought to me new and different views of looking at concepts, codes and applications. I am highly indebted to all the students I taught and guided projects in this field.

The people who helped me in preparing the manuscript directly are the following: Blesson Mathew who drew the diagrams and Anju C who did a lot of editing work. Nimitha U (Ph.D. scholar) and Sudeep PV (my colleague in the department) did a thorough review of many chapters and suggested changes. I acknowledge their contribution and express my thankfulness to them. Two students Saurabh Patel and Pratik Singh Thakur from NIT, Raipur worked as summer interns doing projects on ML. I am thankful to them for their enthusiasm in preparing the coding manual.

During the process of writing, I referred umpteen sources—research papers, blogs, videos and other kinds of online and offline content. I am thankful to the creators of those content—they gave me answers to many of my doubts and questions. I thank my family for being a source of solace. Last but not the least, I thank the Universe for making this possible.

Lyla B. Das

(lyla.das@gmail.com)

I have written the parts of the book which deal with some of the deeper mathematic concepts that are required for understanding the algorithms of ML. Teaching these principles usually come very easy to me, but writing it has been more tasking. However, at the end of it I feel very contented about my part in this project.

I would like to acknowledge my doctoral students Subodh Raj M S, Jobin Francis, Shanthini K S and Jithin Joseph for their active support in preparing the final version of the manuscript. My family, including my parents, have been the motivators for every aspect of my career pursuits. I thank God for being with me at every stage of my life.

Sudhish N. George

(sudhish@nitc.ac.in)

Writing this book (or parts of it) was harder than I thought and more rewarding that I imagined. Explaining the principles at an undergraduate level, the target audience for this book, while simultaneously including important recent developments was quite challenging. Writing this book enabled to me to develop a unique example-based teaching methodology for AI, which is incorporated in the textbook. I am deeply indebted to all my academic mentors who taught me, encouraged me and instilled in me a sense of curiosity and research. Through this book, it is my hope to share some of it with you.

Thanks to my parents, for their unconditional support and innumerable sacrifices; everything I am is because of you. A big thank you to my wonderful wife, for her love, support and encouragement; thank you for keeping me grounded and focused on finishing the manuscript. Above all, I thank the Almighty, for the blessings that He has showered on me which gave me the strength and power to sail through difficult times.

Anup Aprem
(anup.aprem@nitc.ac.in)

The Authors

Lyla B. Das is Associate Professor, Department of Electronics and Communication Engineering, National Institute of Technology Calicut (NITC), Kerala. Lyla B. Das graduated in 1981 specializing in Electronics and Communication Engineering from the College of Engineering, Trivandrum, Kerala after which she joined Keltron Controls as Deputy Engineer. She started her teaching career as lecturer in 1985 when she joined NITC (then Regional Engineering College, Calicut), and proceeded to complete her master's degree in digital communications from the same institute.

Over the period of the 37 years of her teaching career, she has taught a wide range of courses for undergraduate and postgraduate students, guided numerous projects and presented research papers in conferences and seminars at both national and international levels. Her areas of interest are AI and ML, Embedded Systems, Microprocessors and Microcontrollers, Digital Systems Design and Computer Architecture.

She started her writing career in 2010 when her book *The ×86 Microprocessors* was published by Pearson Education. This was followed by *The Embedded Systems –An Integrated Approach* in 2013 and the second edition of *The ×86 Microprocessors* in 2017. Her next book *Architecture, Programming and Interfacing of Low Power Processors –ARM 7, Cortex-M* was published by Cengage Publishers in 2018. This is her fourth book.

Sudhish N. George is Associate Professor, Department of Electronics and Communication Engineering, National Institute of Technology Calicut (NITC), Kerala. He obtained his B.Tech degree in Electronics and Communication Engineering from the M.A. College of Engineering (M.G. University), Kothamangalam, Kerala, India, in 2004, M.Tech degree in Signal Processing from the College of Engineering Trivandrum (Kerala University) in 2007, and Ph.D. in Multimedia Security from NITC in 2014. Since 2010, he has been a faculty in the Department. His current research interests include Image Processing and Computer Vision.

Anup Aprem is Assistant Professor, Department of Electronics and Communication Engineering, National Institute of Technology Calicut (NITC), Kerala. Prior to this, he was a postdoctoral researcher in the Applied Machine Learning Group at the University of Oxford. Anup holds a Ph.D. in Electrical and Computer Engineering from the University of British Columbia, Vancouver, Canada, an M.E. in Signal Processing from Indian Institute of Science Bangalore, and B.Tech in Electronics and Communication Engineering from College of Engineering Trivandrum (University of Kerala). Anup's research interests are broadly in Statistical Signal Processing, Stochastic Decision Making and Bayesian Machine Learning, with applications to social media, sensor and social networks and multi-agent systems.

B.2.3 Matplotlib

This is a library to do plotting in various forms, such as X-Y plot, scatter plot, histogram, pie chart, etc.

B.2.3.1 Plot 1

```
From matplotlib import pyplot as plt
plt.plot([1,2,3],[4,5,1])          # data for an X-Y plot
plt.show()                         # show (display) the plot
```

Contents

Part II: Deep Learning

Part I

Introduction, Classical ML, Mathematical Foundations and AI Search Algorithms

CHAPTER

1

Artificial Intelligence (AI) and Machine Learning (ML): An Introduction

In this chapter you will

- learn the definition and interpretations of Artificial Intelligence,
- evaluate the principles of Machine Learning,
- get introduced to the basic concepts of data science,
- analyze the features of a self-driving vehicle, and
- discover the applications of ADAS in vehicles.

1.0 INTRODUCTION

This chapter will give an insight into the meaning and relevance of the terms Artificial Intelligence (AI) and Machine Learning (ML). AI is a term that evokes a variety of visuals, some of which may be directly from movies and science fiction. We have seen movies in which machines seem to be able to do things, some of which we humans may also be able to do and some of which are beyond human capabilities. We see robots doing fantastic stunts and also having human level emotions and thoughts. Well, is this what AI is?

1.1 ARTIFICIAL INTELLIGENCE

Let us start with a more pragmatic view. Human beings are endowed with intelligence – it may vary in form and style between different people. No two people think, act or feel in the same way. But there are capabilities that define average human intelligence and we consider that as something natural. 'Intelligence' has the definition as the ability to respond appropriately and adaptively to external stimuli. When the word 'artificial' is prefixed to the word 'intelligence', we are actually thinking of creating a device—something 'artificial', to behave intelligently like humans. The artificial object is a machine/system which can do this. What is it that makes a physical object like a robot behave in a certain way? It is the series of instructions that has been embedded into the robot. We say it is an 'algorithm' stored in the memory of the robot that makes it behave intelligently—the robot also takes information from the external world through sensors and uses its actuators to act.

The level of intelligence a robot has is solely due to the algorithm running inside its processing device. Thus, AI is simply the result of using natural human intelligence to devise methods to make machines work in the way we want. The intelligence exhibited by these machines is therefore truly artificial. The machines that we talk about here are computing devices which do not have thoughts or feelings apart from what they have been designed for. They don't have the issues that human beings have. They don't get bored or frustrated doing repetitive work. That is the big plus point of using these 'intelligent' machines.

AI in action is very interesting. Whatever human beings can do intuitively and easily, is difficult for machines. But many things that humans find difficult, machines do wonderfully well. Computers are adept at doing complex calculations but it is not easy for them to recognise a person. The algorithm that runs inside a speech/face recognition system is not simple. But a human being can do it very easily. Seeing, observing, perceiving comes easily to human beings – but to make a machine do it requires a great amount of effort. The amount of effort that is put in, is indicated by the complexity of algorithms that run inside computing systems.

Thus, AI is aimed at reducing mental drudgery that human beings would like to be free of. We would like to have machines do things for us which we find difficult. Harnessing the power of algorithms in such a way as to get machines do things beyond human capability is also part of the AI scene. To define AI as trying to make machines 'think and act like humans' doesn't seem the right definition. In the current scenario, the aim is to make systems that 'complement' human intelligence. Automation of processes – both physical and mental, is the ultimate aim of AI.

Let us take a look at AI around us. There are many things that have been around us for long which we might never have thought as being as an AI application. Robots, handwriting recognition, face recognition, search engines, machine translation and recommendation systems are applications that we have been using for quite some time. They are applications of AI. Games played by computers is a very interesting application. When IBM's computer 'Deep Blue' defeated the world chess champion Gary Kasparov, it created quite a sensation. Now there are many other games in which computers outperform human players. It is the power of complex search algorithms which run in computers with high speed hardware, that has made this possible.

Now we see chatbots like Alexa and Siri and also domain specific ones of various business houses. They are relatively new applications of AI. Robotics is a field which is creating waves and ripples. Robots like Sophia, Asimo, Curiosity Rover. etc., have captured the imagination and interest of people worldwide. Some of them (like Sophia) are humanoid (of human shape) – others are not. An important application arena of robotics is the automotive industry where robots seem to be doing jobs faster, more efficiently and more effectively than human workers. Such robots have been designed for jobs like design, assembly and manufacturing of automotive parts. In a not so distant future, it is likely that most of the jobs in automotive plants will be handled by robots.

Thus, we see that AI seems to have percolated into all domains of human life. Now the application that is being anticipated by almost everyone in the AI field is a full-fledged 'self-driving car'. This idea which has been the stuff of science fiction and thriller movies is one that has been promised by many of the leading companies of the world. But it is still not in the stage of being an accepted and reliable application. Even though many stages of autonomy have been attained for this application, many more obstacles are to be circumvented before it becomes a truly autonomous vehicle. We will do a detailed discussion on the working and expectations regarding this in Section 1.4.

1.2 MACHINE LEARNING

In the previous section, we have tried to make sense of the term 'artificial intelligence'. Now let us take up the term "machine learning' which is sometimes explained as being a subset of AI. Let us try to make a distinction between these two terms. In both cases, machines are involved. When machines are made to perform actions intelligently, it is 'artificial intelligence'. When using the term 'machine learning', we focus on the word 'learning'. In this case, machines are said to 'learn'. Just as we humans learn from experience, machines learn from historical data. Machines look at historical data and make predictions or reach certain conclusions. Thus, having and using 'data' is a prerequisite and fundamental premise of machine learning. With more data comes better learning and better performance.

The question to be answered now is whether AI can function without ML. Can machines act intelligently without using data of the past? The answer is 'Yes'. Think of toy robots – they are simply programmed to perform actions. They don't need data of the past. They are rule based systems. Thus, all AI is not ML. Many chatbots are not designed using historical data. They are 'rule based'. There are many applications in which data of the past is not necessary. Search algorithms trying to find the shortest route and playing games, planning and scheduling algorithms, route finding methods – these are all AI applications in which data of the past is not involved and therefore they are not in the realm of ML, but are AI applications. As will be seen, this book is mostly about the machine learning aspect of AI. But there is a chapter discussing search algorithms, which is AI without ML.

1.3 DATA SCIENCE

These days the word 'data science' is in very common use. Let us try to discover its relevance. Extracting meaningful information from data is what data science is all about. Data is all around us. It has to be extracted, aggregated, cleaned and analyzed – from this, patterns will be observed, which can be used for deciding policies and making business decisions. To do this, statistical methods and/or machine learning will be required.

It is not mandatory for data analysis to use machine learning algorithms. Long before the time that the word 'machine learning' was coined, data analysis using statistical methods was already in use. But recently the amount of data that is available with business houses and governments is very large. To extract the necessary results, machine learning has become a valuable tool. This is where ML plays a role in the data science process. Also, a host of new applications have come up which harness data and give meaningful results. Thus, data is a very important resource. We will discuss this in greater detail in Section 2.1.

1.4 SELF-DRIVING CAR

Next, let us take a look at the self-driving car in some detail. We do this as an exercise to realize that an application such as this is a culmination of every aspect of technology and engineering. It is not a feat of just AI that can lead to the design of such a wondrous application. Right from sensors, actuators, embedded systems, IoT (Internet of Things), mechanical design, planning algorithms, machine learning–many fields of engineering are involved in its design. Some of the technical terms used in the next section may be new to you. Keep note of these new terms when you see them. Most of these terms will be the topics of study in this book.

Even though we use the word 'car', we only mean a vehicle that plies on roads – it could be trucks as well. Other terms such as driverless cars/vehicles, autonomous vehicles, etc., mean the same. In totality, we want a fully autonomous vehicle that can operate without human intervention in all kinds of terrain, in all weather conditions irrespective of whether it is day or night. What is the current state of the art for this application? Who are the key players in this segment? What are the promises made and how much of it has been realized?

It is mostly in the USA and some parts of Europe that the 'driverless' car technology is being researched with great enthusiasm. In India, two companies Tata Motors and Mahindra have started thinking on these lines but have not yet come up with a product. In the USA, some of the top players in this segment are Tesla, Waymo, Google, Apple, etc. There are companies who have successfully implemented driverless delivery trucks, there is also Uber trying out driverless taxis. Many more interesting and exciting things are happening.

In this section, our interest is in demystifying the concept of driverless driving. A 'self-driving vehicle' means that a human driver is being replaced by technology. A human being as a driver relies on his vision and power of decision making in eventless, eventful and critical situations. The driver will drive the car in all kinds of weather conditions and terrain. The driver is normally able to drive on roads with no lane markings, on dilapidated road conditions, the driver can make decisions in the most difficult situations. Can technology come close to this? This is the crucial question. In spite of many promises that have been made by many manufacturers, many more gaps are left to be filled before a full-fledged self-driving vehicle is made available to people at large. Still more time will be needed for people to accept that such a car is safe and reliable.

A driverless car aka self-driving car is one that can be driven without human intervention. This means that it can start, stop, accelerate, take turns, apply brakes, switch on lights, and reach a destination on 'auto pilot'. It can also find parking slots and do parking. A user has to give it information regarding the destination and maybe the route (using maps) and the car is expected to carry its passengers safely to that point. This sort of a car is also called a 'fully autonomous car'.

As of today, a fully autonomous car is not yet a reality. But many levels of autonomy have already been achieved. Note that many cars with drivers already have some levels of autonomy – for example, 'Adaptive Cruise Control' is one in which a car always maintains a fixed minimum distance from the vehicle in front of it. This is obviously a level of automation/ autonomy for the car. Many cars have been using it for many years. There are also cars with many automatic safety and reliability features. These are different 'stages' in the path to the development of a fully autonomous vehicle.

1.4.1 Levels of Automation

The Society of Autonomous Engineers (SAE) has defined a set of levels of automation which is elaborated in Table 1.1.

Table 1.1 Levels of automation defined by SAE

Level 0	**No automation:** The driver performs all the functions of driving and autonomy is zero.
Level 1	**Driver assistance:** The vehicle is under the control of the driver but there is some amount of automation for steering and acceleration.
Level 2	**Partial Automation:** Acceleration and steering may be autonomous but the driver monitors the vehicle and the environment continuously. This is the level at which ADAS functions.
Level 3	**Conditional Automation:** The vehicle has autonomy but the driver is necessary and his only task is to take control of the vehicle if and when necessary.
Level 4	**High Automation:** The vehicle is autonomous for the specified terrain and weather control. There is the option for a driver to take charge of the vehicle.
Level 5	**Full Automation:** The vehicle is fully autonomous for all weather and terrain conditions. There is the option for a driver to take charge of the vehicle.

This table is a reference to specify the level of autonomy that a self-driving car has achieved. No vehicle has achieved Level 5 as yet. Some automobile manufacturers have claimed to have attained Level 4, but not to the level that can satisfy safety, reliability and legal conditions. There are already vehicles operating in levels 1-3, but the aim is to reach level 5.

Now let us examine the requirements that a driverless car should fulfil.

(i) It should be capable of seeing the road, road signs, pedestrians, objects in its path, traffic lights and signs.

(ii) It should be able to see the surroundings which include the edge of the road and 'lane markings' on the road.

(iii) It must see objects very close to the wheels, like curbs and small objects on the road.

(iv) It must receive information from GPS satellites.

(v) The information from all sensors should be processed by a central computer which then gives the necessary signals for the accelerator, brakes and the steering mechanism. The central computer runs all the algorithms that are responsible for making it autonomous to the level for which it has been designed.

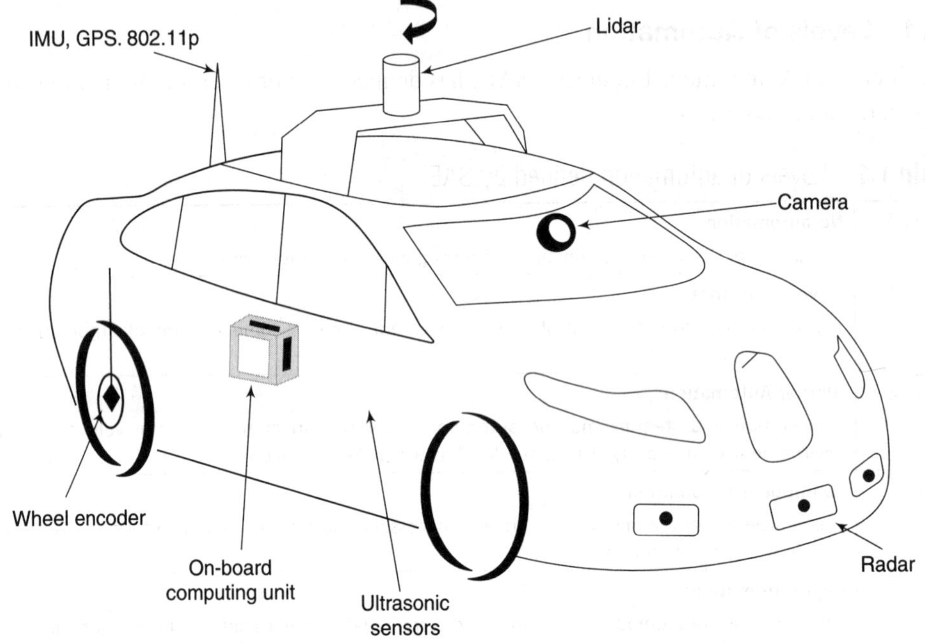

Fig. 1.1 Parts of a self-driving car

1.4.2 Parts of a Self-Driving Vehicle (SDV)

Figure 1.1 shows the important parts of a typical self-driving car. Let us find out what exactly is the role played by each of the parts marked in the figure.

1.4.2.1 Vision

This is implemented using lidars, cameras, radars and wheel encoders.

1.4.2.1.1 Lidar: This stands for 'Light Detection and Ranging'. Like a radar, this is also a distance measuring device – the difference is that 'light' energy is used in place of radio waves that a radar uses. Lidar is an active remote sensing device which generates its own energy. It has an infrared laser which sends pulsed light in 360° (three dimensions). This gets reflected from all the objects in the vicinity. The time taken for the pulses to return is used to calculate the distance from objects. Using this method, a 3D pattern of objects around the Lidar is obtained. Thus, all objects, big or small are identified. Lidars have high resolution and so even small objects can be identified. It gives precise readings in all weather and lighting conditions. Thus Lidar is the technology which is the major component of vision in most SDVs.

1.4.2.1.2 Radar: In Fig. 1.1, a set of radars are seen in the front of the vehicle. In many vehicles, radars are present in the side and back as well. This is for monitoring other vehicles closeby. Adaptive Cruise Control (ACC) which is present in SAE level 2 vehicles (Table 1.1) is based on signals from radars.

1.4.2.1.3 Cameras: This is an additional level of vision that aids in detecting traffic lights, road signs, other vehicles, pedestrians, obstacles on the road, etc.

1.4.2.2 Wheel Encoder

On the wheels, ultrasonic sensors are fixed. This is for detecting small objects close to the wheel. Curbs on the road and vehicles closeby in parking lots are detected using these sensors.

Most vehicles in the class of SDVs at some level, use lidars and radars for the major portion of vision. However, Tesla SDVs do not have lidars and radars The method used for vision in them is a set of eight cameras around the vehicle and a deep learning network which has been trained using all possible stationary and moving objects that may be encountered in a 3D vision of the vehicle. This involves a lot of data but Tesla seems to have done it to a certain level of accuracy. Still, many more loose ends are left to be tied up as the results are not foolproof. The deep learning network is a Convolutional Neural Network (CNN) with transformers.

1.4.2.3 GPS and IMU

These units are for getting the location and thus they are used for navigation of the vehicle. Location information is obtained from GPS satellites, but the satellite signal has the problem that it may be affected by weather conditions as well as by buildings and mountains. Thus a combination of GPS and IMU systems is the way location and navigation are managed. IMU (Inertial Measurement Unit) is composed of three gyroscopes and three accelerometers. Thus, measurement of acceleration and rotation in six axes is done. Based on this information and the initial position, the current location of the vehicle is obtained. Information from altimeters and tachometers are also used. When 'Inertial navigation' is used, measurements are not affected by the linear and rotational movements of the vehicle. The measurements are in the 'inertial framework' – just as if the vehicle is stationary (state of 'inertia').

1.4.2.4 802.11p

This is the IEEE standard for wireless internet for vehicles. With this, the car becomes internet enabled and it gets designated as a 'connected' car. The car is then connected through the internet to devices outside and inside the car. It can also be part of a Vehicle to Vehicle (V2V) network through which information may be shared – this maybe about traffic movement, road conditions, parking information, safety information and warnings. The term V2X (Vehicle to Everything) denotes the case when a vehicle can communicate with other vehicles and the surrounding infrastructure.

1.4.2.5 Computing Unit

This is the central computing system which processes the data obtained from sensors and servers (through internet) and satellites and makes decisions on acceleration, braking and steering the vehicle in the right path, in the right direction towards its destination. The path from the source to the destination is entered as an input into the vehicle computing system. Many planning, searching and route finding algorithms are involved in this.

Why is the SDV considered a product of AI?

A number of algorithms, many of which are considered products of AI are used for all the actions taken by the vehicle. Shortest route algorithms, path planning methods are some of them. Also, a lot of data is used to run machine learning algorithms. The manoeuvring of the vehicle is done based on the outcome of many such algorithms. Besides some of the classical algorithms, deep learning techniques are also used. It is true that an SDV is a product of the advancements in the fields of control systems, embedded systems, sensor and actuator technology, mechanical engineering and so on. However, it is the advent of AI and ML algorithms that has powered the thought that a full autonomous vehicle is a possibility, in a 'not so distant' future. It is the hope, desire and belief that 'artificial' intelligence can be brought close to natural human intelligence, that is leading the way in this direction. As such, we can definitely say that a fully autonomous car is an application of Artificial Intelligence (AI).

The question remains as to whether a fully autonomous vehicle is possible which is as good and reliable as one driven by a human driver. This question has not yet found a loud sounding 'yes'. It is true that a lot of driving on the roads may be made autonomous. This type of vehicle manoeuvring is already prevailing. Ships and aircraft navigate their pre-planned, pre-determined routes on 'autopilot'. This has been so for many decades. But for fine movements like landing of an aircraft and bringing a ship to port or cruising through narrow parts of the sea or rivers, manual control becomes necessary–someone who fulfils the role of a driver is needed.

For vehicles plying on roads also, this idea holds. On well-defined roads and highways, autonomous driving is not difficult. But to be able to steer the vehicle in difficult and unknown terrain, to take decisions in harsh and unexpected weather conditions, a human driver may still be needed. This is what many people think–though not everyone. Even though machines are able to do object detection and identification quite well, the vision capabilities and intuition of human beings far surpass the capability of machines. But with time and more efficient AI algorithms, things may change. That will be the time that all/most road traffic will become fully autonomous.

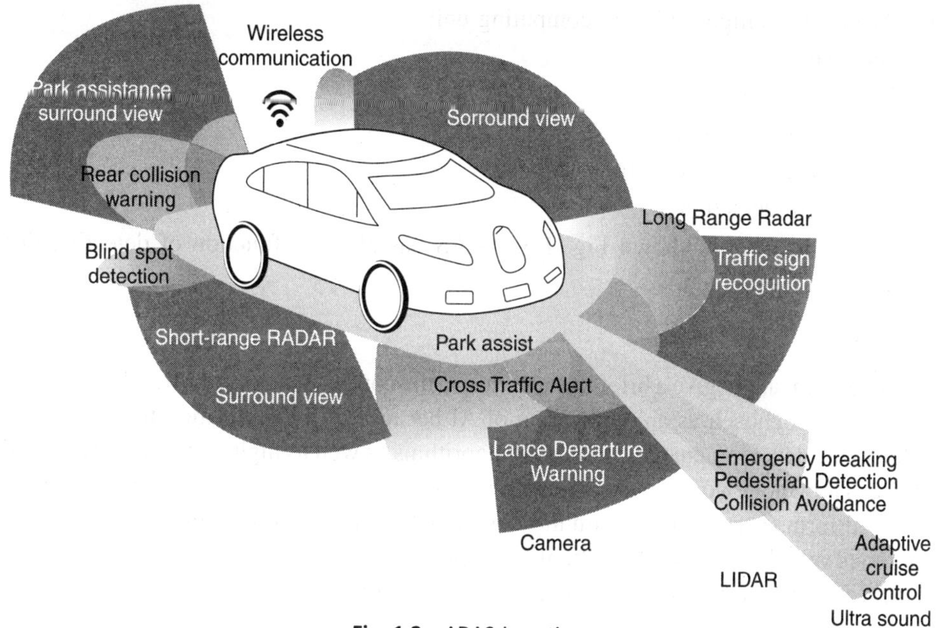

Fig. 1.2 ADAS in action

1.4.3 ADAS

This stands for Advanced Driver Assist System. Looking at Table 1.1, we find that ADAS corresponds to Level 2 of the SAE specification for autonomy. Let's take a look at what ADAS has to offer in terms of automation of vehicle functions. Figure 1.2 shows ADAS in action. A number of vision sensors (Lidar, radars, cameras, ultrasound) and wireless connectivity lead to the implementation of ADAS. There will be a central computing unit powered by AI to integrate the sensor inputs and the algorithms to provide the following functions as listed in Fig. 1.3.

(i) Automatic parking
(ii) Collision avoidance
(iii) Lane assistance

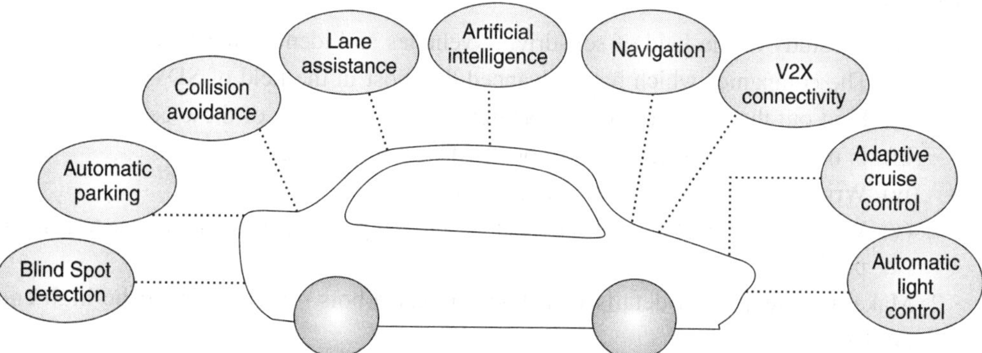

Fig. 1.3 Functionalities provided by ADAS

(iv) Artificial intelligence based computing unit
(v) Navigation
(vi) V2X connectivity
(vii) Adaptive cruise control
(viii) Automatic light control for headlamps
(ix) Blind spot detection

In addition to what is shown Fig. 1.3, ADAS has also the function of detecting driver drowsiness and issuing alerts.

Conclusion

This chapter is meant to give a brief introduction to the concepts of AI and ML. The self-driving vehicle has been chosen as an application of AI because of the realization that it is feasible only due to the development of high-end AI algorithms as well as high performance computing hardware. The whole world is looking with wonder and waiting to see this application in its full-fledged form. The fact that a country/company can develop something as advanced as an autonomous vehicle indicates its technological prowess. It is also an indicator of how artificial intelligence is seen to be making changes in the lives of ordinary people.

Questions

1. How is artificial intelligence to be defined? Explain with reasons.
2. What is the main feature of machine learning?
3. What exactly is the 'machine' which is implied in machine learning?
4. How can AI function without a 'machine learning' component?
5. Give a few examples of AI without ML.
6. Name a few applications of AI which may be listed as 'machine learning'.
7. Which are the different technologies used in self-driving vehicles for vision?
8. What is meant by 'Adaptive cruise control'?
9. What is the use of internet connectivity for vehicles?
10. What is the level of autonomy achieved so far in SDVs?

Exercise

1. Make a study of the field of self-driving vehicles and identify the following.
   (i) The companies which have advanced the most in the field of SDVs.
   (ii) Find out the level of expertise achieved by at least five of these companies.
   (iii) Is the Tesla car different from other SDVs? In what respects?
   (iv) Write a brief note on the history of SDVs.
   (v) What are the legal problems expected in making SDVs available for use to general public?
2. Make a writeup with details of a few famous robots which claim to be high-end products of AI.
3. Chatbots are considered to be products of AI. Find the history of Chatbots and write about a few of them.

CHAPTER

2

The Machine Learning (ML) Process

In this chapter you will

- learn the steps of the data science process,
- understand the different stages of machine learning,
- discover the difference between regression and classification,
- analyze the definition of loss/error,
- realize that machine learning creates models,
- identify overfitting and underfitting,
- recognize the necessity for validation, and
- memorize the definitions of the performance metrics used in ML.

2.0 INTRODUCTION

We have seen that 'Machine Learning' is considered to be a subset of Artificial Intelligence (AI). Even though machines are the fundamental entities in any AI process, when we use the term 'machine learning', we think of using machines that seem to be able to 'learn' from past occurrences which is essentially data of the past. Machines look at historical data and make predictions or reach certain conclusions. These 'machines' are actually certain algorithms which run on computers. One aspect of machine learning is that it is 'data dependent'. How well they perform is highly dependent on the type and amount of data they are trained with. Machine learning is also domain specific and it can perform only for the purpose for which the algorithm has been trained for. Since it has data as its basic component, let us bring in the term 'data science' and find the right slot for machine learning in the 'data science process'.

2.1 DATA SCIENCE

As was mentioned in Section 1.3, data is a very important resource. It comes in various flavours such as text, numbers, categories, images, videos, graphs, tables, data from sensors of electronic devices, etc. Our locations and web browsing history, our online purchases, our emails, chats, calls – in fact many of our transactions act as data for various applications. The steps in the data science process may be listed as:

(i) Data collection
(ii) Data preparation
(iii) Exploratory data analysis (EDA)
(iv) Machine learning
(v) Visualization

It is important to note that the fourth step, that is, machine learning – is not mandatory for the data science process. Only if the use of such algorithms warrants better results, do we need to use them. There are other statistical processes available to make sense of data. Thus, 'machine learning' may be considered as an optional step in the data science process. But many current applications mandate the use of advanced machine learning algorithms and produce remarkable results. Let's now try to understand all the steps in the data science process.

(i) Data Collection

Data is constantly being generated, but we collect only the data that we require. It is obtained from records of data as text, image, video, etc. Interviews, chats, reviews and recommendations are among the many forms of data that are collected.

(ii) Data Preparation

This includes data cleaning and data transformation and is a pre-processing step for data. Different kinds of data may need different pre-processing steps. The steps of pre-processing for text data and image data are different.

The data obtained may not be in the form that is possible to be accommodated by the next steps in the process. There may be missing data, irrelevant, duplicate and wrong observations, data expressed in wrong formats and so on. All this has to be set right and outliers (Section 3.4.3) have to be removed. Many steps of this process may have to be performed manually. All this amounts to 'data cleaning'.

Finally, the data should be in the correct structural form and should seem to 'make sense'. Feature engineering may have to be done. This is the process of taking the raw data and identifying the features which may be relevant for analysis. For example, for creating a 'face recognition' system, we have to be clear about which features of face images are to be employed. This is a very important and difficult step and automation tools are available for some parts of this data transformation step. Table 2.1 is the result of such a step.

(iii) Exploratory Data Analysis (EDA)

In the year 1970, American mathematician John Tukey came up with the philosophy of this new method which replaced the previous method of 'Confirmatory data analysis'. EDA is a formalisation of what we would do before we embark on a task. For example, a student who is planning to do higher studies in a foreign country is likely to do a thorough analysis of colleges, students, pattern of admission, statistics of placements, living expenses, weather conditions and many other aspects. He gets the data associated with all these factors, checks for patterns and makes inferences from it. He does all this before he makes his final decision. This is EDA employed for his personal matter.

EDA is a pre-assessment of the data and for that, analysis and visualization techniques are employed. Python and R are programming languages that may be used. This analysis helps to make a decision on the best method to be employed to get the answers that we seek from the data. In the process, patterns in the data are discovered, anomalies spotted, hypotheses are tested and assumptions checked. To get a full understanding of EDA, one needs to do it practically.

(iv) Machine Learning

In this step, one or more of the classical machine learning or deep learning algorithms are employed.

(v) Data Visualization

In this, the results of the work done on the data is put up as graphs or tables or metrics (Section. 2.6). Python libraries provide a number of visualisation tools which make this part quite easy.

Table 2.1 Features and labels of a set of T-shirts

T-shirt No	*Feature 1 (Length)*	*Feature 2 (Width)*	*Label (L/S)*
1	L_1	W_1	L
2	L_2	W_2	S
3	L_3	W_3	S
...	....	....	....
....	....	....	....
.....	....	....	....
n	L_n	W_n	....

2.2 MACHINE LEARNING

Now let's get started with the very important task of diving into the depths of 'machine learning'. The way machines are trained is in many ways similar to how humans are trained for a purpose. Consider how 'coaching' or 'training' is done in some (many) institutions for preparing students for various competitive exams. There, students are exposed to a large data base of sample questions and their answers. Over some time, the learners get familiar with this set. They get 'trained' to the concept of answering correctly to the questions in the data base. During test time, if similar questions are asked, they are able to give the right answers. The catch is that, if they are asked questions which they have not been trained for, the probability of answering correctly reduces drastically.

Many students may have knowledge other than what they have been trained in these centres. So they may be able to perform well even if they encounter unfamiliar questions. But when machines are trained with a dataset, they have knowledge only of information in that set. If they are tested for anything beyond that, they will not give correct results. Thus, training a machine with the 'right data' is the fundamental aspect of machine learning.

2.2.1 Supervised Learning

The type of machine learning that we have just talked about is called 'supervised' learning because the training data has questions with answers. In the context of machine learning, these answers are called 'labels'. If a machine is trained with the features of the samples along with their labels, we have supervised learning. In supervised learning, a teacher teaches the machine the right answers for each question. In ML terminology the questions are the 'features' and the answers are 'labels'.

A simple example will make it clear. (See Table 2.1). The length and width are the two features of a set of T-shirts and the labels are large (L) and small (S). The dimensions are given for 'n' number of T-shirts and the corresponding labels are also given. So a T-shirt may have the 'large' (L) label or the 'small' (S) label. This information is given in the last column and thus the labels for all the samples in the dataset is available.

The machine is trained with this dataset and the value of 'n' should be large. Once the machine is trained, it becomes capable of answering questions on this problem. After training, the machine is tested. In the 'testing' phase, the machine is given the features of say, another set of T-shirts. The machine should be able to say correctly whether the features correspond to the L class or S class. The machine should be able to 'classify' the test data correctly. This is the gist of the concept of supervised learning. Note that for this type of learning, the training data should have the features as well as the labels. It is like a trainer doing training on candidates to get them to acquire a specific skill.

2.2.2 Unsupervised Learning

We can try to understand unsupervised learning with the same example. If the machine is trained without giving it the 'labels' of the samples, then it is unsupervised learning. In the test phase, the machine will still be asked to classify the samples into the sets of large (L) and small (S). The machine must be able to do that. The machine may even be asked to classify the samples as large, medium and small – that makes it three classes. Or it may have to classify the samples as small, medium, large and extra large classes. The algorithm used here will cluster similar items and do the classification. The point here is that the training data does not contain any information on the labels. The ML algorithm attempts to find patterns in the data and clusters similar items into groups.

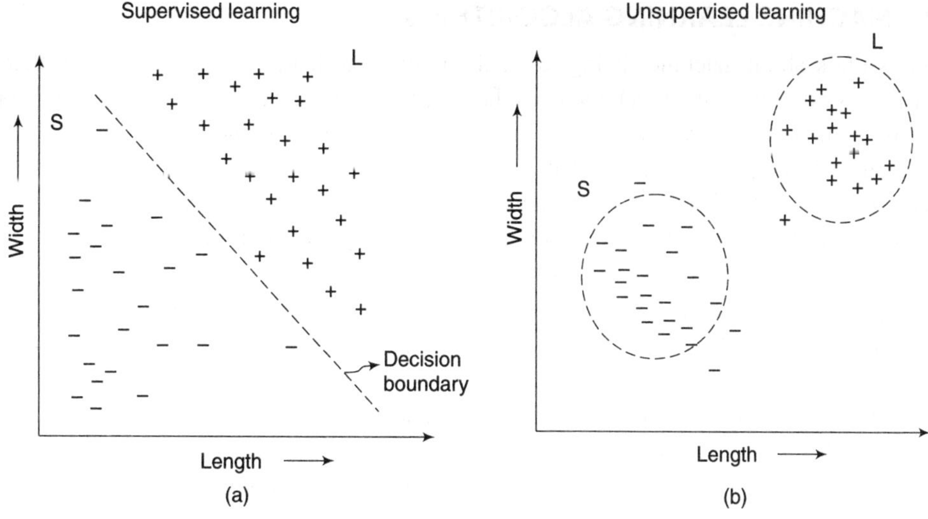

Fig. 2.1 (a) Supervised learning (b) Unsupervised learning

Figure 2.1 shows the plotting of the data corresponding to both these types of learning. For supervised learning (Fig. 2.1a), a decision boundary is to be obtained. For our example, the label for the samples above the boundary are classified as L and the samples below are classified as S. The symbol used for the L class is '+' and for the S class, it is '–'. In forthcoming chapters, we will discuss the important supervised algorithms.

In Fig. 2.1b, for the unsupervised case, the algorithm is able to find two clusters which can be assumed to be of S and L types as marked in the diagram. In this case, the algorithm does not do any labelling–it only creates clusters. K-means clustering, Gaussian mixtures, hierarchical clustering, spectral clustering, etc., are unsupervised learning algorithms. We will discuss one type of unsupervised algorithm in Section 4-5.

2.2.3 Reinforcement Learning

This is a slightly different method of machine learning. In this, the system works and moves forward based on a system of 'rewards'. Any action taken by the algorithm causes it to get a reward. A positive reward is given when the action taken leads it towards the goal. The reward will be negative (we can call it a penalty) for an action that leads it away from the goal. This is best explained by thinking of how robots work. A robot may have a goal of reaching a destination in a prescribed time. It can run or walk to reach that point. Running will take it faster to its goal, but there is the risk of falling down. If the robot falls, it is given a negative reward. The robot can simply walk to the goal comfortably without the risk of falling. But the rewards it gets along the path will not be high because of the slow movement. In reinforcement learning, the system of positive and negative rewards is what all algorithms are about. Maximizing the accumulated positive rewards on that path towards the goal is what spurs this method of learning. In this book, reinforcement learning is covered in detail in Part IV.

2.3 MACHINE LEARNING ALGORITHMS

When we talk about machines being 'trained' or 'made to learn', we actually mean that an algorithm is run (on a computer) that does the processes we are talking about. Thus, machine learning is all about the algorithms that are used for the different applications for which we need results. Depending on the type of data and the information or result that we want to extract from the data, different algorithms are available and have proved their efficacy over long periods of time. In Part 1 of this book, we discuss the most important and popular 'classical algorithms' that have been used from the 1950s onwards.

More recently, deep learning algorithms are in the forefront of machine learning. They are much more versatile and efficient than the classical algorithms. But they are data hungry and resource intensive. This means that their data requirement is very large. They don't give good results when the data available is meagre. They also need fast computers with GPUs (Graphical Processing Units which do parallel processing). Based on the performance we need and the resources available with us, one of these classes of algorithms may be chosen. In Part II of this book, deep learning techniques are covered.

One important point to keep in mind is that machines can only do work for which they have been trained for. If a machine is trained with a dataset composed of the images of faces, they can do biometric recognition only when the test images are faces. We should not expect them to recognize people based on fingerprints. In natural language processing, if the training set is composed of the works of Shakespeare, the system will give very wrong answers if tested for questions based on Vedas and Upanishads. The system will also be unable to recognize words which are currently in use in social networks. The learning that machines can accomplish is based on how well they are trained. Our goal in studying machine learning is to get the best out of the algorithms that are currently in popular use.

2.3.1 Classification and Regression using Supervised Learning

2.3.1.1 Classification

Machine learning is used to perform the function of prediction based on the data of previous events. We say that it creates a predictive model. In Section 2.2.1, we talked about classes of T-shirts and the algorithm is asked to do classification. Based on the values of the features of the samples, the system should say whether it is of class L or class S. This is a binary classification problem as the system has to decide between two classes only. If the system has three classes say large, medium and small, it is multinomial /multiclass classification as more than two classes are specified. But in both these cases, the problem is one of 'classification'. Classification is a very fundamental and common problem that machine learning is very good at. In a classification problem, the output takes on only discrete variables as outputs. In binary classification, we may use output variable names as Yes/No, 1/0, Positive/Negative, etc.

The number of features used in the example of Section 2.2.1 was just two – they were the length and width of the T-shirts. But in practical cases, the number of features may be much more than two. For example, consider the problem of deciding whether the given features correspond to fruit 1 or fruit 2. The features could be the following attributes of fruits:

(i) length, (ii) width, (iii) colour, and (iv) weight. The system should be trained based on these four features. Finally, when test data is supplied to it, the system should be able to say whether it is fruit 1 or fruit 2.

Classification can be done using images as well. We can have a system which has images of many animals as inputs. The system must be able to 'extract' features from the training images and finally classify test images as being that of animal1/animal2/animal3, etc.. 'Extracting features' automatically by the system is something that can be done only by deep learning techniques. In classical supervised ML, we should supply the features and labels for the training data.

2.3.1.2 Regression

In all the above examples, the ML system is asked to perform classification. There is something else that ML does and that is called 'regression'. In this case, the system produces a real number as the output. As an example, assume we have data of the income of farmers based on the area of farmland possessed by them. The question given is to predict the income of someone who has an area of land which is not in the training data. This is the test data, obviously. This is not a classification problem because the output is not a discrete/categorical variable. The result that the algorithm gives is a real number.

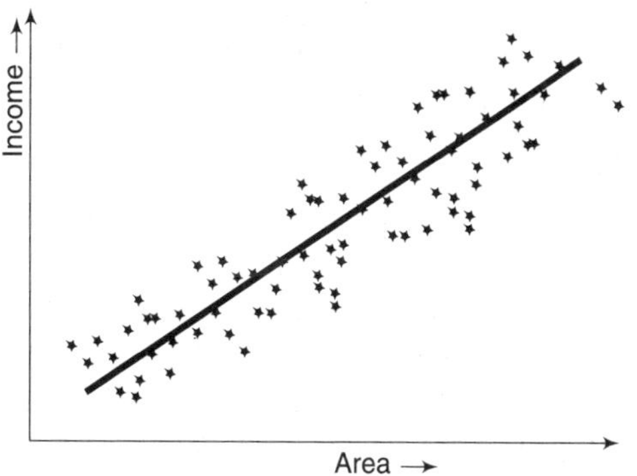

Fig. 2.2 A plot of linear regression

In Fig. 2.2, training data is fitted onto a straight line which is 'linear'. This is then called linear regression. If the training data is such that a polynomial of higher degree is needed to fit the training data, the term 'polynomial regression' is used. See Fig. 2.3 where a curve fits another dataset. This is a parabolic curve which is of degree 2. As a matter of fact, curves of higher degrees are also possible and this depends on the training data.

In Figs. 2.2 and 2.3, we used only one feature of the data, that is, the area of the farm. In practice, a number of features is the normal case. For calculating the income of the farmer, we can list a number of features which may be: type of crop, quality of the soil, geographical location, water resources, etc. If multiple features are used, we say that this is a case of multiple regression. In this case, the plot of income vs features cannot be plotted in a two-dimensional space. More on this and other aspects will be covered in later sections. In this introduction, the attempt is to understand the meaning of the terms 'linear/polynomial regression' and 'classification'.

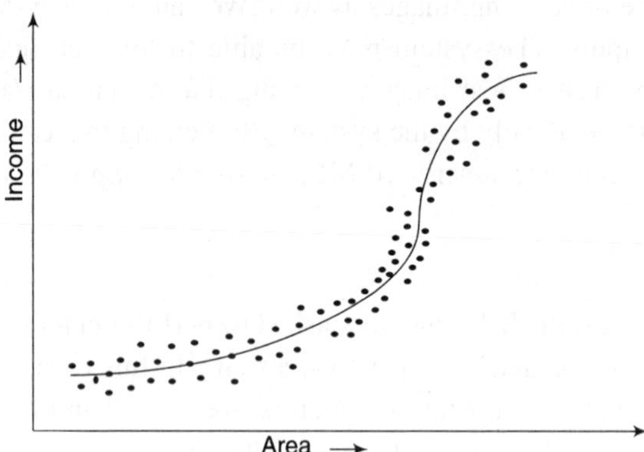

Fig. 2.3 A plot of polynomial regression

In addition, there is a model which is named 'logistic regression' which is a classification method. In truth, the data may be used like a regression model itself but for many applications, a threshold is brought into the picture by the use of a 'logistic' function and then it becomes a classification system. More on this is covered in Section 2.3.3.

2.3.1.3 Categorical Data

This term is likely to be encountered frequently. Let us see what is meant by it. The features that we used in our examples are all numeric values – the area of the farm and the length and width of the T-shirts. Actually most machine learning algorithms can handle only numeric data. But there can be data that belong to different categories, for example, if we talk about four colours say red, blue, green and yellow, it is categorical data. If the features are types of high-end cars, say, BMW, Mercedes, Audi, Rolls Royce – this is again, categorical data. How does the algorithm handle this non-numeric data? The answer is that this should be encoded into a numeric format. One hot encoding is a popular choice but is not the only type of encoding. There are algorithms which can use only categorical data. Examples are 'Naïve Bayes' model and 'Decision tree and its ensembles'. We will deal with these variations when discussing each specific algorithm.

2.4 MODEL CREATION

With this basic introduction, what is our conclusion regarding the action performed by a machine learning algorithm?

The answer is that it creates a model using training data. This model should be robust and when test data is applied to it, it must have the capability to give correct predictions. (See Fig. 2.4). In supervised learning, the model is created using labelled data. In the unsupervised case, it is unlabelled data that is used. The model that is created using training data should

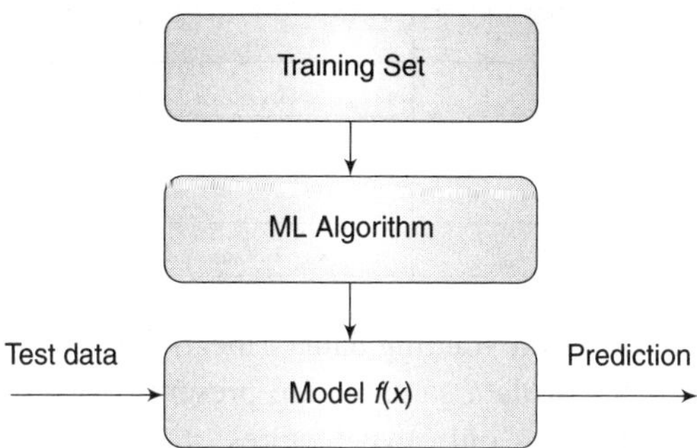

Fig. 2.4 The Machine learning process

approximate the input-output relationship as best as possible. But it is still an approximation. Let us delve deeper into the machine learning process.

2.4.1 Supervised Learning: Classification

The training data consists of input data $\boldsymbol{x}$ with its label y. The input samples and corresponding samples are represented as:

$$(\boldsymbol{x}_1, y_1), (\boldsymbol{x}_2, y_2), \dots \dots \dots .. (\boldsymbol{x}_i, y_i) \dots \dots \dots \dots (\boldsymbol{x}_n, y_n) \text{ where } \boldsymbol{x}_i \in R^d \quad ...(2.1)$$

R^d is a d-dimensional space. This simply means that each input sample $\boldsymbol{x}_i$ has d features. Each input sample $\boldsymbol{x}_i$ is a 'd' dimensional vector as shown in Table 2.2.

Table 2.2 A dataset with n samples of d-dimensional data and correponding labels

$\boldsymbol{x}_1 \rightarrow$	$x_{11}\ x_{12} \dots x_{1d}$	$y_1 \leftarrow$ label
...	... ...	...
$\boldsymbol{x}_i \rightarrow$	$x_{i1}\ x_{i2} \dots x_{id}$	$y_i \leftarrow$ label
...	... ...	...
$\boldsymbol{x}_n \rightarrow$	$x_{n1}\ x_{n2} \dots x_{nd}$	$y_n \leftarrow$ label

If it is a classification problem, the output y_i is a discrete variable. For binary classification, we create a model f which maps the d-dimensional space R^d into a set of two states which may be expressed as –1/+1, 0/1, Yes/No, etc. (See Eq. 2.2).

$$f : R^d \rightarrow \{-1, +1\} \quad ...(2.2)$$

Table 2.3 Training data for T-shirts classification

	Feature 1 (Length)	*Feature 2 (Width)*	*Label (L/S)*
$\boldsymbol{x}_1$	$x_{11} = L_1$	$x_{12} = W_1$	L
$\boldsymbol{x}_2$	$x_{21} = L_2$	$x_{22} = W_2$	S
$\boldsymbol{x}_3$	x_{31} = ...	X_{32}	-

	....	....	-
	....	....	-
x_i	$x_{i1} = L_i$	$x_{i2} = W_2$	-
	....		-
x_n	$x_{n1} = L_n$	$x_{n2} = W_n$	-

Table 2.3 shows the format of the training data of the T-shirt problem presented in Section 2.3.1.1. Note that '*n*' number of data samples are present. Each sample is a two-element vector. Since the training data has only two features, it can be plotted on the *X-Y* plane. For classification, the model should create a clear 'decision boundary' in which the data corresponding to the two classes is demarcated clearly. See Fig. 2.5 in which the L class is shown with a '+' sign and the S class with a '–' sign. Two cases of the 'decision boundary' are shown in Fig. 2.5. In one, the decision boundary is a straight line, in the other it is a curve. The ML algorithm should be able to model this decision boundary. Some of the popular algorithms for classification are support vector machines, neural networks, decision trees, K-nearest neighbours, logistic regression, etc.

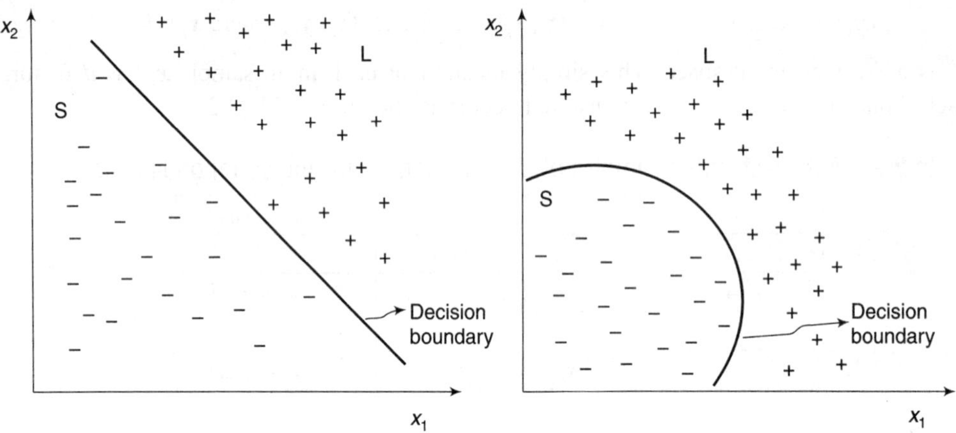

Fig. 2.5 Decision boundaries for classification (a) Linear boundary (b) Non-linear boundary

Using the process named 'training', we create a model $f(x)$ which approximates the training data $\boldsymbol{x}$ and its relation to its label y. The decision boundary is the result of creating the model. Since this model $f(x)$ is only an approximation, the label we get is called the 'predicted label' and it is notated as $\hat{y}$. The notation $\hat{y}$ is used for the predicted label, while y is the actual label. These two labels need not be the same even with the training data. With training data, if a sample is found to be in the wrong side of the decision boundary, then a training error is said to have occurred. Figure 2.6 shows two training errors. One '+' and one '–' labels are on the wrong sides of the decision boundary.

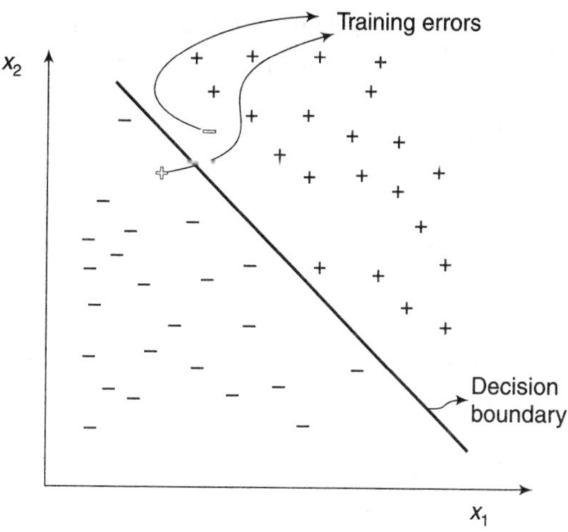

Fig. 2.6 Training errors

The next part of the machine learning process is called 'testing'. In this, we check how correct this model is, but for data which hasn't been seen so far by the model. Figure 2.7 shows correctly classified as well as, misclassified test samples. If y and $\hat{y}$ are the same, there is no error, while if they are different, it is counted as an error. For our T-shirt example, if the actual label for a T-shirt is S and if the system classifies it as L, an error is considered to have occurred. In Fig. 2.7, there are 2 misclassifications – these are counted as two test errors.

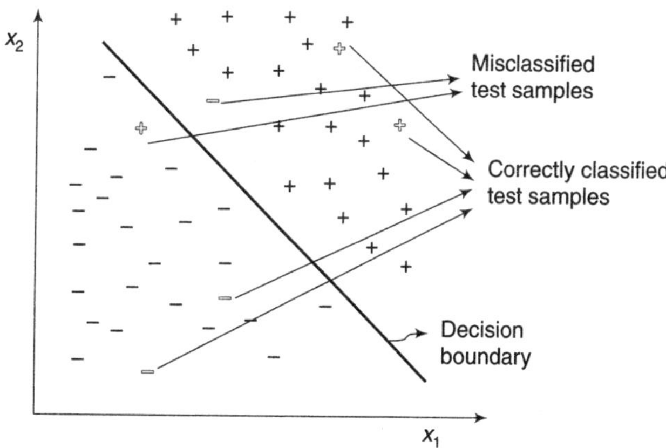

Fig. 2.7 The testing phase showing two test errors

2.4.1.1 Classification Errors

How is classification error computed?

When the actual label y and the predicted label $\hat{y}$ are different, it is an error. Counting the number of times this occurs is the method of computing classification error. The word 'loss' is also used for error. See Eq. 2.3 which defines the loss between the model $f(x_i)$ and label y_i

$$\text{loss}\ (y_i, f((x_i)) = \begin{cases} 1 \text{ if sign } (y_i) \neq \text{sign } (f(x_i)) \\ 0 \text{ otherwise} \end{cases} \qquad ...(2.3)$$

In Eq. 2.3, y_i is the actual label. $f(x_i)$ is the model created by the ML algorithm which gives the predicted label $\hat{y}_i$.

For classification to be correct, the sign of both these (y_i and label $\hat{y}_i$) should be the same. This means that if the actual sign is positive, the predicted sign should also be positive. This applies to the negative class as well. The same principle holds for multi-class classification.

The total training error is the sum of the errors accrued by the samples in the training set. The aim of any ML algorithm is to minimize this error. Equation 2.4 defines the total training error for n samples.

$$E^{\text{train}}\ (f) = \sum_{i=1}^{n} \text{loss}\ (y_i, f(x_i)) \qquad ...(2.4)$$

The test error is defined in the same way, for the samples in the test set. An efficient algorithm is expected to give low values for test and training errors.

2.4.2 Supervised Learning: Regression

Now let us try to understand the concept of regression in more detail. For a regression algorithm, the output should be a real number. Let us use our previous example of Section 2.3.1.2 to make this clear. Plotting of training data has been shown in Fig. 2.8. We find that many training data samples do not fall on the straight line which is used to fit the data. This means that there is training error corresponding to each of these points.

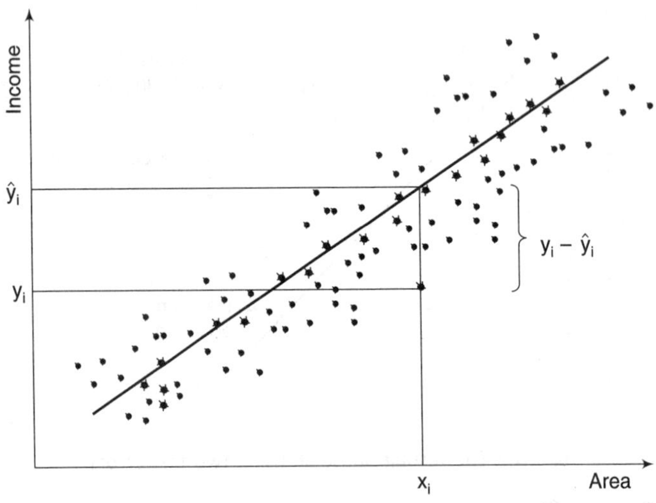

Fig. 2.8 Linear regression training errors

Let us look at Fig. 2.8. Consider the training sample x_i. The actual label for this input sample is y_i but the model has chosen it as $\hat{y}_i$ (on the line). The error for this sample is the difference between the two values, $|y_i - \hat{y}_i|$. There are similar errors for other samples of the training set. Thus, the total training error is the sum of all these values. Since the values may be negative or positive, usually the squared error is used as the error (loss) value. Note that $f(x_i)$ is the model created by the algorithm which gives the predicted value $\hat{y}_i$. See Eq. 2.5 which defines the squared error.

$$\text{loss}\ (y_i, f(x_i)) = (y_i - f(x_i))^2 \qquad ...(2.5)$$

Summing over all values of i, the total training error for n samples, is the sum of squared errors.

$$E^{\text{train}}\ (f) = \sum_{i=1}^{n} \text{loss}\ (y_i, f(x_i)) \qquad ...(2.6)$$

Test errors are also calculated similarly. Figures 2.9 and 2.10 show the case of the predicted $\hat{y}_t$ for a test data x_t for the cases of linear regression and parabolic regression. To get the test error, the actual values should be known from the data in the test set.

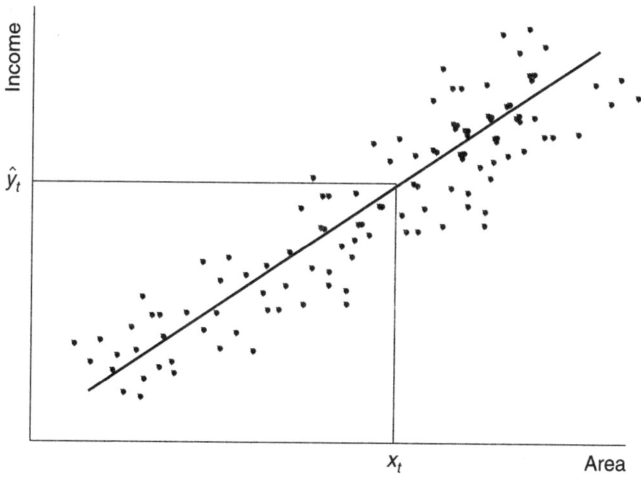

Fig. 2.9 Test data x_t and predicted lab $\hat{y}_t$ for linear regression

2.5 TRAINING AND TESTING

We have had a brief exposure to the machine learning process which consists of two steps, namely, training and testing. We started with the idea that machine learning is the process in which a dataset is used to create a model. Once created, this model needs to be tested for its robustness to perform correctly when presented with unseen data.

The dataset that is available to the ML developer is to be used to perform the actions of 'train' and 'test'. Given a dataset, it is divided into parts, Training : Test, in the ratio ranging from 90:10 to 70:30. This means that the bigger portion is used to create the model. The model is then tested with the remaining data which is expected to give an 'unbiased' evaluation of the model. Testing should be done with 'unseen and unknown' data. This simply means that the model should not have had any exposure to the data which is considered as the test set.

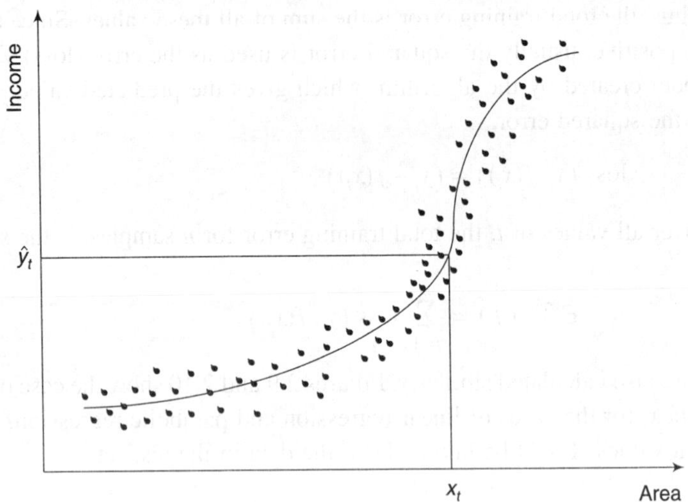

Fig. 2.10 Test data x_t and predicted lab $\hat{y}_t$ for polynomial regression

The data available for these processes should have some characteristics such that these processes are smooth. Let's delve into this matter.

2.5.1 Overfitting and Underfitting

These are two terms that are commonly seen in most machine learning literature. Let us start with an intuitive explanation.

Suppose we want to identify a lotus (Fig. 2.11) given the set of features of many flowers described in natural language. How do we describe this flower specifically? We could describe it very lightly specifying that it has a green stem and a few petals. This is a case of very little and very unspecific data. If we use this description, just any flower will be identified as a lotus. If we use this description as the features to develop a model, it will turn out to be a case of 'underfitting'.

Fig. 2.11 Image of a lotus

But we could describe it better saying: it has 15 petals, pink colour, pointed petals, yellow pistil, span of 8 inches. How will this fare? This will fare better because it describes a lotus but all lotuses may not fit this exact description as there are other colours, other span sizes, and the number of petals may not be 15 for all lotuses. With this set of features, many lotuses will be left out. This is because we made a stringent description of one specific sample of a lotus. This description if used, will be a case of 'overfitting'.

So how will ML models fare with these descriptions?

With underfitting, the model complexity is very low and is too general, and so the training and test errors will naturally be high. This is because most of the flowers in the set will be identified as lotus. In the case of overfitting, some specific lotuses with which we trained the model will be recognised correctly. So the training error will be low. However, when test data is given, the model will fare badly leading to high test error. We then say that the model does not 'generalize' well to 'test data'.

Figure 2.12 shows these two cases. The prediction error is plotted for training as well as test data. For underfitting, both training and test errors will be high because of the small amount of data which produced a low complexity model. In the case of overfitting, the model is complex and it fits the training data well. But because it has been trained with very specific data, it capability to generalize is lacking and so test error is high. The best fitting model will be one that neither underfits nor overfits. It should be a model of medium complexity. This idea is borrowed from the field of statistics but is applicable to ML because ML models are mathematically based statistical models.

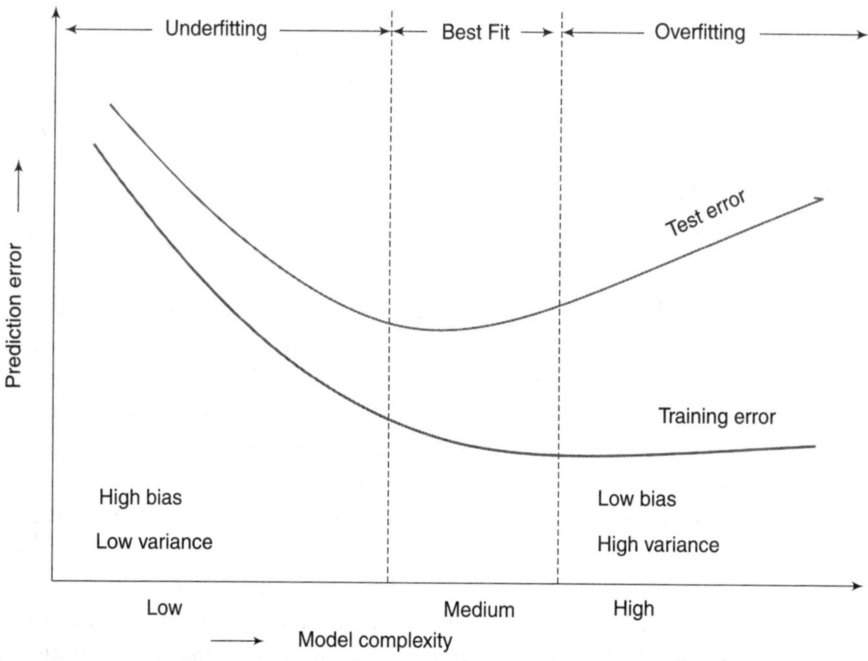

Fig. 2.12 Training and test errors vs model complexity

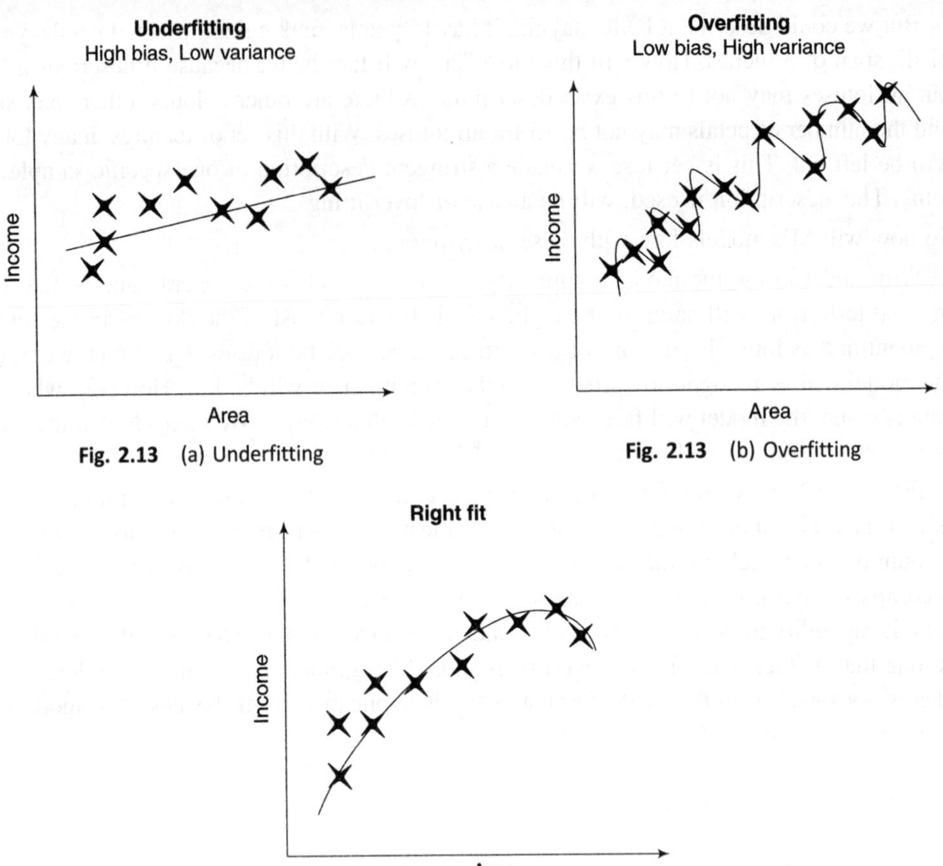

Fig. 2.13 (a) Underfitting

Fig. 2.13 (b) Overfitting

Fig. 2.13 (c) The right fit with medium bias and variance

2.5.2 Bias and Variance

In Fig. 2.12, the words bias and variance have been used. What do these words indicate in this context?

See Fig. 2.13 which shows three different cases of the plots of a regression problem. In Fig. 2.13a, the first case, a straight line has been used to fit the data points and we see that a lot of points seem to lie outside and far away from the line. This is because the algorithm we used does not seem to follow the pattern of the data. The algorithm seems to have had a preconceived notion that a straight line is good for fitting. We say that the algorithm has a 'high bias'. It is biased towards an idea and does not care about the trends in the data. It seems to ignore a number of data samples. This case can also occur if the number of data samples is not sufficient. There is high bias then also and this is a case of underfitting. There is low variance as well. This implies that even if the training data changes, the training algorithm does not follow the changes. This results in high training as well as test errors as was seen in Fig. 2.12. Figure 2.14 shows an extreme case of underfitting and high bias. Linear

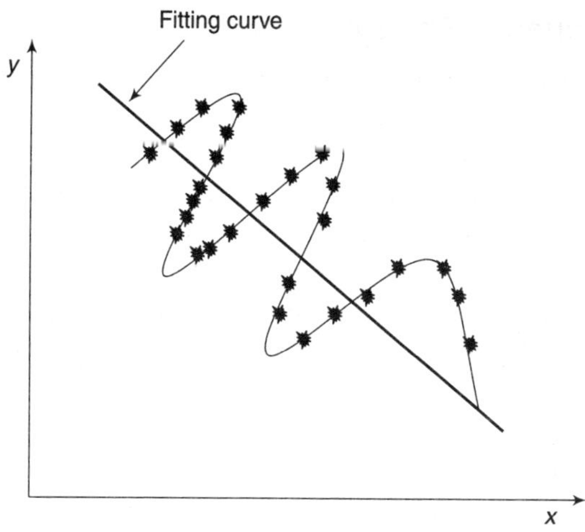

Fig. 2.14 Extreme underfitting

regression is the model employed but it is very poor fit for the data, the pattern of which follows a polynomial curve.

In Fig. 2.12, overfitting has been marked as having high variance. Variance is defined as how much a model changes with training data. In Fig. 2.13b, the model follows the training data exactly. If the data changes even slightly, the fitting curve will have to change. This is a case of overfitting because the model tends to fit exactly to this specific data. Naturally, training error is low. But if the data changes even slightly, the model will have to change. Noise will also cause the mode to change. Because of this, the model cannot generalize well and when unseen data comes during testing, it cannot perform correctly and thus the test error is high.

Variance indicates the amount by which the model $f(x)$ will change when using a different training set. This means that different models will have to be created for different training sets. This is not good for the case of predictions to be done for the same problem with slightly different training sets. An overfitting model is a 'high variance' model.

In Section 2.2, we talked about students who have been trained with a specific set of questions. Such students would have memorised all those questions and their answers. They will do well when questions from that question bank are presented to them. The training error is very low. But if they are given a test with different questions on the same set of topics, they will fare badly because they have been 'fit' with only specific questions. They are unable to generalize to other kinds of questions and so the test error is high. This is overfitting.

Figure 2.13c is a compromise between the two. The fitting curve is neither bound too tightly or too loosely to the parabolic curve which is used. This is only an example for understanding a case of best fit which will generalize well to test data. Also, note that when too many features of the data are used, overfitting will occur and conversely too little features may lead to underfitting as we saw in the case of the example of the lotus. In practical machine learning, we find that overfitting is a more frequently encountered problem than underfitting.

2.5.3 The Bias Variance Tradeoff

The above term is one that is commonly encountered in ML literature. Let us review once again the relevance and meaning of the words, bias and variance. Bias happens when the model makes simplifying assumptions which are erroneous. Naturally such a model cannot capture the pattern of the variation in the data. Variance is high when the model tries to capture every variation in the training data. It is sensitive to minor fluctuations in the data. In the case of regression problems, overfitting models may be high degree polynomials as in Fig. 2.13b. They tend to be high complexity models. In conclusion, we can state that for a particular set of training data, very simple models tend to be low variance, high bias ones. By increasing the complexity of the model, they become low bias, high variance models.

This discussion is meant to emphasise the fact that in many cases, a tradeoff may be required between bias and variance. Getting a 'low bias, low variance' the model requires extra effort. This also implies that for any given dataset, it may be necessary to do model selection, meaning that many models should be considered before finalising on one model. Let us discuss this matter starting with the concept of a validation set.

2.5.4 Training, Validation and Testing

In the machine leaning process, the functions of the training and test sets have already been covered. We know that the training set is used to train the selected model. The test set evaluates the model. The major chunk (70 to 90%) of the data is utilised for training and the rest is for testing. Now we should alter our thinking a bit to include a 'validation set' as well. This means that the dataset is divided into three sets—for training, validation and testing.

As mentioned, the major part of the dataset is used to train the model. The parameters of our chosen ML model are decided by the process of training. The test set is used only for evaluating the performance of the model and it is data which is hitherto 'unseen ' to the model. We can't be sure that the model we have created will do well on this test data This implies that the model has had no way to 'make corrections' to it before submitting itself to testing. To make any correction or change, there should be a feedback mechanism of 'evaluation and correction'. With that, we will be assured that our model will work to our expectations with respect to some chosen performance metric. To facilitate this, a part of the dataset is kept aside as a 'validation set' or 'development set (dev set)'. See Fig. 2.15 which shows that the major chunk of the data is still utilised for training, but small chunks are kept aside as 'dev set' and 'test set'.

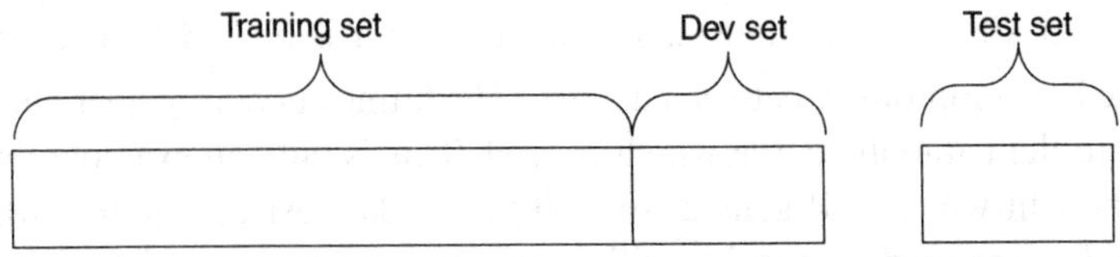

Fig. 2.15 The partitioning of the dataset

2.5.4.1 The Validation Set

This set of samples is applied to the trained model. The model is evaluated and then is fine tuned – this means that the validation set is used to modify the parameters and hyperparameters of the model. Note that the 'parameters' are those values which are iteratively obtained from the model during the time of training. For example, the 'weights' of a neural network are its parameters. In contrast 'hyperparameters' are to be specified by the developer before training. For example, the 'learning rate' which we will discuss in Section 3.5.2 is a hyperparameter.

In addition, validation is also used for model selection. The process of validation gives the developer a chance to check the performance of his model and apply changes to it. After all the changes are applied to the model, it can be declared to be the final model. Then the test set is applied to it to ascertain the performance of the model.

2.5.4.2 Model Selection

When a problem is to be solved, there are many ways to do it. There are different algorithms available. For example, if it is a classification problem, we can choose between algorithms such as logistic regression, SVM, Naïve Bayes, neural networks, KNN, decision trees and many others. If the problem is one of getting a continuous valued output, the choice may be between regression using lower or higher degree polynomial fitting. Thus, the validation set may be used for model selection. See the flowchart in Fig. 2.16. Each model may be tried out on a validation dataset and the best model may be chosen. This is another application of validation.

For model selection, many models are considered. How do we decide which one is best? We use some of the performance metrics (Section 2.6) on the validation set (also called the dev set). For example, if accuracy is the metric, then we select the one with the highest accuracy. For this to be meaningful, the size of the dataset should be big enough. For example, if the size of the development set is just 100, it may be unreasonable to conclude that a model with 90% accuracy is better than one that gives 90.1% accuracy. For that, a dev set which is large, say, with size above 1000 or more is required. In general, without large datasets, comparison between models will be difficult. At any rate, the developer should keep in mind that model selection is a highly iterative process and many models need to be considered before converging to a final decision. Also, in some cases, the set that we choose as the dev set may be biased with labels being predominantly

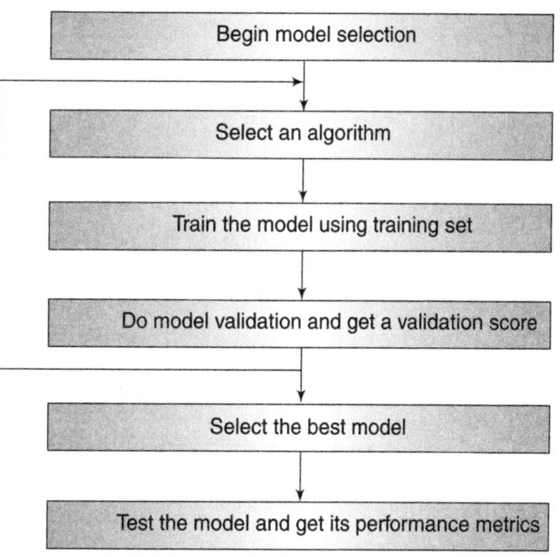

Fig. 2.16 The iterative process of model selection

positive or negative. All these necessitate the use of a validation technique named k-fold cross validation.

2.5.4.3 K-Fold Cross Validation

This is a method which is widely used. In this, the complete dataset contributes to both training and testing. There is no separate validation set. Let's discuss this method.

Assume a case of having 10,000 data samples. Let us use the value of $k = 5$. Thus, each subset has 2000 samples. The process is started with using one of the 5 subsets as a 'hold out set' which is actually a test set. Say, we use the set with $k = 1$ as the test set. Training of the model is done using the remaining 8000 samples. Testing is then done using the set that was the 'hold out set'. The accuracy is calculated for this set. Next, the second set with $k = 2$, is the hold out set. The remaining 8000 samples are used for training and the hold out set corresponding to $k = 2$, is used as the test set. (See Fig. 2.17). This procedure is repeated 5 times. Thus, every data sample gets a chance to be a training sample as well as a test sample. The average accuracy corresponding to the five test sequences may be taken as the model accuracy.

The downside of this method is computational complexity. For $k = 5$, the procedure is repeated 5 times. $k = 5$ and $k = 10$ are popular values for k-fold cross validation. Having higher values of k is not resorted to, unless the dataset is very small in size. In such cases, say when the dataset has only 15 samples, there is another method which is named as 'Leave out one cross validation'(LOOCV) in which one sample is 'held out' as the test sample. Training is done on the remaining 14 samples. The whole procedure is repeated for each of the 15 samples. This is also a computationally heavy procedure but may be resorted to, for very small datasets.

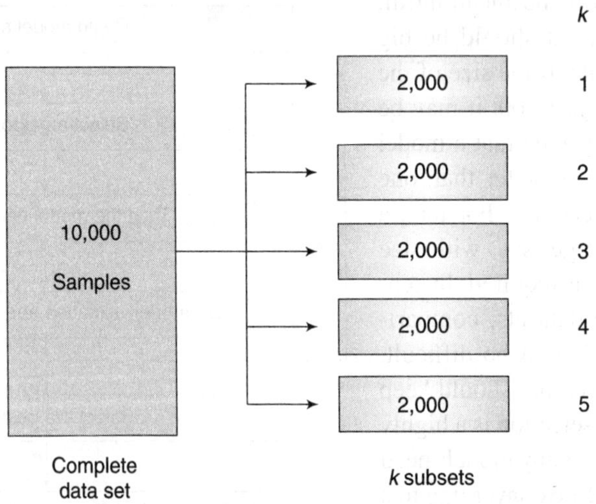

Fig. 2.17 Example of k–fold cross validation when $k = 5$

Now that we have understood that the machine learning process involves training, validation and testing, let us list out some salient points.

(i) 70% for training, 15% for validation and 15% for testing is a reasonable partition (this does not apply if *k*-fold cross validation or LOOCV is used.) If the total dataset is not very big, and we need bigger test and validation sets, 50:25:25 is a better split.

(ii) When the dataset is in the range of millions of samples, it is okay to have smaller percentages for testing and validation.

(iii) Validation is used for fine tuning the parameters and hyperparameters of the model.

(iv) The type of data chosen for validation and testing should be similar to the data expected in the field of deployment of the model.

(v) The validation (dev) set is used for evaluating the model 'before' it is made final. The test set is used for evaluating the model 'after' it is declared as final. Thus, both these sets should be from the same distribution. Otherwise, it will be difficult to evaluate what is wrong with the model if testing shows a bad performance.

(vi) The test set is used only after the model is trained, fine-tuned and is ready to go for deployment in the field.

(vii) Test data should be data which is 'unseen' to the model.

(viii) Overfitting is a more commonly known problem than underfitting. Regularization is a method to reduce it. (Section 3.4.1)

2.6 PERFORMANCE MEASUREMENT

Let us take the case of supervised learning only. In this, we have labels for each data sample. It is similar to saying that in a question bank, every question has an answer. The training data is used to train the model with the actual labels – that is, the right answers for each question. These 'actual' labels have names such as 'ground truth labels' and 'gold labels'.

During the process of testing, we get the labels that the system predicts. They are called predicted labels. But since the actual labels corresponding to the test set are also available, we are able to say whether the system has done a correct prediction or not. If the actual and predicted labels are different, there is an error. In Section 2.4, we have already defined errors for regression as well as classification.

		Actual label	
		Actual positive	Actual negative
Predicted label	Predicted positive	True positive (TP)	False positive (FP)
	Predicted negative	False negative (FN)	True negative (TN)

Fig. 2.18 The Confusion matrix for binary classification

2.6.1 Confusion Matrix

Now we discuss the performance metrics by which we can evaluate a classification model. See Fig. 2.18 which shows a 'confusion matrix' relevant for binary classification. In this case, a label will be either positive or negative.

Let's use an example. We have a dataset which contains the features of dogs and cats. Dogs is considered the positive class and cats the negative class. Then we can relate to the terms in Fig. 2.18 through which performance metrics are defined. (See Table 2.4). This means:

If the 'actual label' is Dog, and the system predicts it as 'Dog', we have a 'True Positive'.

If the 'actual label' is Cat, and the system predicts it as 'Dog', we have a 'False Positive'.

Similar is the meaning of the remaining two terms.

Table 2.4 Terms used in the 'confusion matrix'

Dogs – Positive Class, Cats – Negative Class		
Actual label	*Predicted label*	*Terms used*
Dog	Dog	True positive (TP)
Cat	Dog	False positive (FP)
Cat	Cat	True negative (TN)
Dog	Cat	False negative (FN)

Based on these definitions, we can define a few performance metrics as in Table 2.5.

Table 2.5 Definition of performance metrics for binary classification

Accuracy	$\frac{(TP + TN)}{(TP + TN + FP + FN)}$	The percentage of predictions that are correct.
Precision	$\frac{TP}{(TP + FP)}$	The percentage of Positive predictions that are correct.
Sensitivity (Recall)	$\frac{TP}{(TP + FN)}$	The percentage of Positive cases predicted as Positive
Specificity	$\frac{TN}{(TN + FP)}$	The percentage of Negative cases predicted as Negative

Looking at these definitions, accuracy seems to be the right indicator of the performance of any system since it predicts the percentage of correct predictions. The denominator is the total number of samples which accounts for all the different possibilities. In our example of dogs and cats, if there are 100 samples, and 90 of them are predicted correctly, the accuracy is 90%. That means that only 10 samples are wrongly predicted. This could be that dogs are predicted as cats, and cats as dogs.

If accuracy is a very good metric, why are there are other metrics?

We will see that there are situations in which accuracy is not a good indicator of the performance of a system. Let's see how that happens. When the data is not balanced, accuracy is not a good indicator. Imbalanced data means that the number of samples which are in one class is very small compared to that in the other class. Let's use an example.

Example 2.1 In a large population, the number of people afflicted with cancer is a small number. We have an ML system which detects cancer patients based on a number of features Let's take cancer patients as the Positive class, and healthy people as the Negative class. In a population of 100,000, if the number of cancer patients is 400 but the ML system detected only 100 of them, what is the accuracy? It also detected 200 healthy people as cancer-ridden. Note that totally 500 predictions are wrong.

Solution: Correct predictions are 99,500

Accuracy = 99,500/100,000 = 99.5%

The accuracy is found to be pretty high, but as a system which is meant to identify cancer patients, it is a failure because only 25% of the cancer patients have been identified. To evaluate this system, we need a better metric which gives an indication of correct predictions within a class. Recall (also known as sensitivity) and precision are better measures in this case. Their definitions are:

$$\text{Recall} = \frac{\text{True Positive}}{\text{True Positive} + \text{False Negative}} = \frac{\text{True Positive}}{\text{Total Actual Positive}} \quad ...(2.7)$$

$$\text{Precision} = \frac{\text{True Positive}}{\text{True Positive} + \text{False Positive}} = \frac{\text{True Positive}}{\text{Total Predicted Positive}} \quad ...(2.8)$$

For this case:

$$\text{Precision} = \frac{100}{(100 + 200)} = 33.67\%$$

$$\text{Recall} = \frac{100}{(100 + 300)} = 25\%$$

Which metric gives a better number to assess the capability of the system?

We see that 'Recall' assesses the number of right predictions out of the total 'truth' of the class.

Here we find that using recall as our metric gives us a better idea of the quality of the system since our intent is to identify the positives (cancer patients) in this large population. Since the recall is only 25%, we can clearly say that this system does not perform well for the purpose it is intended for, because it has detected only 25% of the total number in the Positive Class.

When is precision useful?

Precision is also called the Positive Predictive Value (PPV)

In spam detection, it is important to detect spam, but the more important thing is that normal mail should not get classified as spam. Let's consider such a system.

Example 2.2 Data is as given below.

Spam: Positive

Normal mail: Negative

Total size of data: 100,000

Spam: 200

150 spam correctly classified

100 normal mail classified as spam

Solution:

$$\text{Accuracy} = \frac{99850}{100000} = 99.8\%$$

$$\text{Precision} = \frac{150}{(150 + 100)} = 60\%$$

$$\text{Recall} = \frac{150}{(150 + 50)} = 75\%$$

The precision is only 60%.

A better system may be when only 20 normal mails are classified as spam. Then precision is higher.

$$\text{Precision} = \frac{150}{(150 + 20)} = 88.2\%$$

We see from the above examples that precision and recall are inversely proportional to each other. When precision increases, recall decreases and vice versa. Thus, it is necessary to have a balance between them and then we have a metric named as $F1$ score which is defined as in Eq. 2.9.

$$F1 = 2 \times \frac{\text{Precision} * \text{Recall}}{\text{Precision} + \text{Recall}} \qquad ...(2.9)$$

Example 2.3: Obtain the confusion matrix for the system for detection of images with cars. Total number of images : 10,000 actual number of images with cars (Positive class) is 425. Images with cars detected is 350. Images without cars detected as Positive class is 105. Draw the confusion matrix and calculate the accuracy, precision, recall, $F1$ score and specificity

Solution: Images with car: Positive class

Images without car: Negative class

Total size of data: 10,000

Actual number of images with car: 425

350 correctly classified, TP = 350

FN = 425 – 350 = 75

105 images without cars detected as positive class, FP = 105

TN = 10000 – 350 – 75 – 105 = 9470

Confusion Matrix:

	Actual Positive	Actual Negative
Predicted Positive	TP = 350	FP = 105
Predicted Negative	FN = 75	TN = 9470

Correct predictions = TP + TN = 9820

$$\text{Accuracy} = \frac{TP + TN}{TP + TN + FP + FN} = 9820/10000 = 98.2\%$$

$$\text{Precision} = \frac{TP}{TP + FP} = 350/(350 + 105) = 350/455 = 76.92\%$$

$$\text{Recall} = \frac{TP}{TP + FN} = 350/(350 + 75) = 82.35\%$$

$$\text{F1 score} = \frac{2 * (\text{Precision} * \text{Recall})}{\text{Precision} + \text{Recall}}$$

$$= 2*(0.7692*0.8235)/(0.7692 + 0.8235) = 79.542\%$$

$$\text{Specificity} = \frac{TN}{TN + FP} = 9470/(9470 + 105) = 9470/(9175) = 98.9\%$$

Conclusion

This chapter is intended to give an introduction to the basic precepts of machine learning. The whole machine learning process and the concepts of underfitting and overfitting have been taken up. In addition, performance metrics have also been covered. With this background, it will be a smooth transition to the important classical algorithms.

Questions

1. Distinguish between supervised and unsupervised learning. Use examples to explain the difference between the two.
2. What are the merits and demerits of classical machine learning over deep learning?
3. What is meant by saying that ML is domain specific?
4. With the help of examples, distinguish between classification and regression.
5. How does error occur in classification and regression models? You may use images and examples to make your point clear.
6. What are the factors to be taken into consideration when deciding the test dataset?
7. Using your own example, explain overfitting and underiftting. With the same example, explain what you have understood about bias and variance.

8. What are the specific points to be kept in mind when choosing a validation set?
9. How does cross validation help in the ML process?
10. Use examples to distinguish between 'True Positive'; and 'False Positive'.
11. In what cases, is 'accuracy' not the best metric for a ML system? Give an example.
12. What is the relevance of the word 'confusion' in the term 'confusion matrix' used for classification?
13. Is the confusion matrix used for regression problems?

Exercise

1. Draw a confusion matrix for a three-class system. Explain what it indicates?
2. Distinguish between balanced and unbalanced datasets. Give one example for each type.
3. We have a dataset where we are predicting number of people who have houses with area more than 2000 sq ft. Consider a dataset with 500 observations, i.e., $n = 500$

   Actual 'No' = 150, Predicted No = 190

   Actual 'Yes' = 350 Predicted Yes = 310

   Calculate the performance metrics.

CHAPTER

3

Classical Machine Learning Algorithms-I

In this chapter you will

- learn the mathematical formulation of regression,
- understand linear and polynomial regression,
- obtain the analytic solution for linear regression,
- analyze the gradient descent algorithm,
- derive the logistic regression concept intuitively and mathematically,
- discover the loss function for logistic regression,
- get introduced to the concept of regularisation,
- choose between standardisation and normalization,
- examine the relevance of terms such as outliers and dimensionality, and
- study the principle of Support Vector Machines.

3.0 INTRODUCTION

Now we start the important classical machine learning algorithms – both supervised and unsupervised. These algorithms which are discussed in this and the next chapter, will be taken up in an intuitive fashion, rather than with high mathematical rigour. However, mathematical support will be used wherever it is necessary to understand the concepts ingrained in the algorithm. Deeper mathematical concepts are given dedicated space in chapters 5 to 8.

3.1 GENERAL LINEAR MODEL

In Section 2.3.1, the concept of linear regression was introduced with an example. We will not repeat all that was covered there – rather, we continue from that point. In linear regression, the output of the system is a continuous variable.

3.1.1 Mathematical Representation

The input data is a set of vectors $\boldsymbol{x}_i$ with corresponding labels y_i.

$$(\boldsymbol{x}_1, y_1), (\boldsymbol{x}_2, y_2), \ldots \ldots \ldots .. (\boldsymbol{x}_i, y_i) \ldots \ldots \ldots \ldots (\boldsymbol{x}_n, y_n) \text{ where } \boldsymbol{x}_i \in R^d \qquad ...(3.1)$$

R^d is the space of d-dimensional vectors and R is the space of real numbers. Thus, the input data is a set of d-dimensional vectors $\boldsymbol{x}_i$ and the output is a real number y_i. (See Table 3.1).

Table 3.1 List showing '*n*' training samples of '*d*' dimensions and corresponding labels

$x_1 \rightarrow$	$x_{11}\ x_{12} \cdots x_{1d}$	$y_1 \leftarrow$ label
...	... ...	...
$x_i \rightarrow$	$x_{i1}\ x_{i2} \cdots x_{id}$	$y_i \leftarrow$ label
...	... ...	...
$x_n \rightarrow$	$x_{n1}\ x_{n2} \cdots x_{nd}$	$y_n \leftarrow$ label

The task involved is of creating a model $f(x)$ that maps the d-dimensional input space to a real number.

$$f : R^d \rightarrow R \qquad ...(3.2)$$

Let us start with the simplest case where $\boldsymbol{x}$ is a single dimensional ($d = 1$) vector. Also let's take the simple case in which the relation between the output y and input $\boldsymbol{x}$ may be expressed by a straight line as in Fig. 3.1. Since there is only one input variable x, this method is called 'univariate linear regression'. This also means that only one 'feature' of the input is used. The example (Section 2.3.1.2) in which the area of a farm is the only feature used to determine the income of a farmer is such a case. Now we have the task of finding a linear model $f(x)$ for this case. The model $f(x)$ will give $\hat{y}$ as the predicted output.

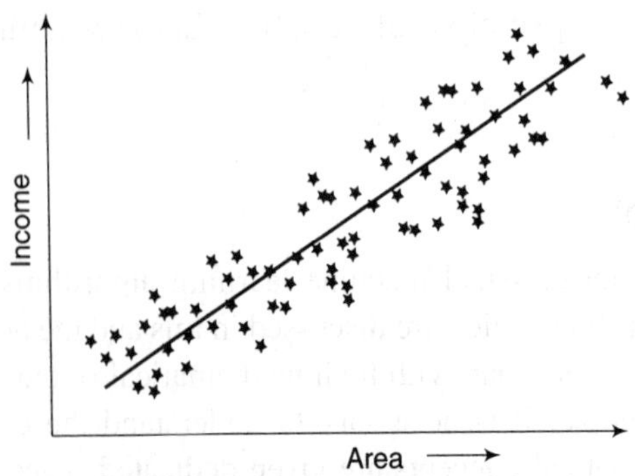

Fig. 3.1 Simple linear regression

$$f(x) \rightarrow \hat{y} \qquad ...(3.3)$$

A straight line approximation to model $f(x)$ may be written as

$$f(x) = \beta_0 + \beta_1 x \qquad ...(3.4)$$

where β_0 and β_1 are the parameters of the model. We should know that β_1 is the slope and β_0 is the y-intercept of the line. To find the exact line, our task is to get the values of β_1 and β_0. The squared error/loss for each data sample is, from Eq. 2.5, rewritten here as Eq. 3.5. For an input sample x_i, the actual label is and $f(x_i)$ is the predicted label which is the label obtained from the model. The squared error/loss is the square of the difference between the actual and predicted values.

$$\text{loss } (y_i, f(x_i)) = (y_i - f(x_i))^2 \qquad ...(3.5)$$

The loss summed over all n data samples is called the Cost function or Risk. We define it as

$$C = \frac{1}{2n} \sum_{i=1}^{n} (y_i - f(x_i))^2 \qquad ...(3.6)$$

When we want to find the line which maps the input to the output, it should be the one that minimises the average loss over all the n data samples as in Eq. 3.6

This Cost function is the Mean Squared Error (MSE). Equation 3.6 without the division by $1/2n$ has the name 'Sum of the Squared Errors (SSE)' or 'Residual Sum of Squares (RSS)'.

$$\text{SSE} = \sum_{i=1}^{n} (y_i - f(x_i))^2 \qquad ...(3.7)$$

Note: The total cost is divided by n, the number of samples. It is also divided by 2, which is used to cancel the 2 that we get when we do differentiation (in analysis), later. This is only for convenience in calculation.

We are trying to get the line that minimizes the Cost function. The line is defined by its parameters β_1 and β_0. Thus, the minimization of cost should be done with respect to these parameters. Using Eq. (3.4) in Eq. (3.6), we get

$$C(\beta) = \frac{1}{2n} \sum_{i=1}^{n} (y_i - \beta_0 - \beta_1 x_i)^2 \qquad ...(3.8\ )$$

Note that the Cost function is a quadratic function which is bowl shaped (parabolic) and the literature regarding it will tell you that it is a convex function which has only one minimum point known as the 'Global minimum' as shown as a 3D plot in Fig. 3.2.

Figure 3.2 can also be plotted as a contour plot. A contour plot is used for visualising a 3D plot in two dimensions. The third dimension is plotted as contours (constant slices). Figure 3.3 shows the contour plot for the 3D plot corresponding to Fig. 3.2. The numbers on each contour are the values of the Cost function for β_1 and β_0. At the centre, we have the minimum value of the Cost function.

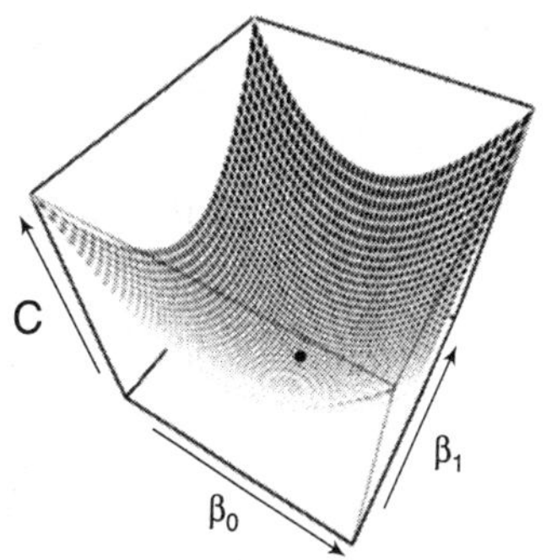

Fig. 3.2 The quadratic Cost function for linear regression

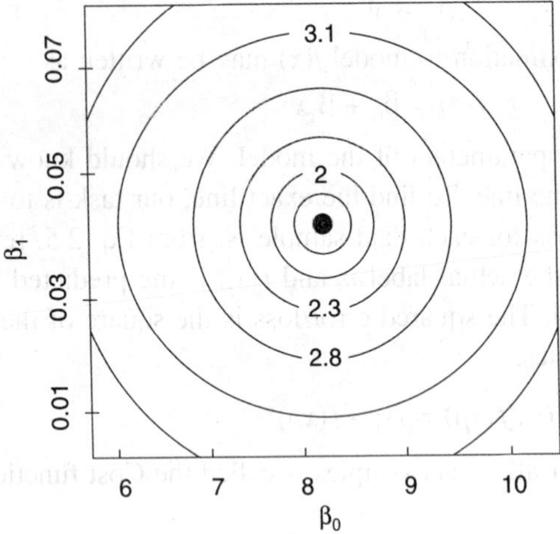

Fig. 3.3 Contour plot of the Cost function

So the aim of our minimization procedure would be to find β_1 and β_0 so that

$$\text{argmin}_\beta \frac{1}{2n} \sum_{i=1}^{n} (y_i - \beta_0 - \beta_1 x_i)^2) \quad ...(3.9)$$

Note:
argmin_β means 'find the value of βs such that the given function has the minimum' value. Here the function $C(\beta)$ has to be minimized with respect to β_1 and β_0.

To do this analytically, let us use our knowledge of calculus and partial derivatives. **Those who find it cumbersome may skip the derivation and use the final result.**

Minimize: $C(\beta_0, \beta_1)$, that is: $\frac{\partial C}{\partial \beta_0} = 0 \quad \frac{\partial C}{\partial \beta_1} = 0$ ...(3.10)

$$\frac{\partial C}{\partial \beta_0} = 2 \times \frac{1}{2n} \sum_{i=1}^{n} (y_i - \beta_0 - \beta_1 x_i) \times \frac{\partial}{\partial \beta_0} (y_i - \beta_0 - \beta_1 x_i) \quad ...(3.11)$$

$$\frac{\partial C}{\partial \beta_0} = \frac{1}{n} \sum_{i=1}^{n} (y_i - \beta_0 - \beta_1 x_i) \times (-1) = 0 \quad ...(3.12)$$

$$\beta_0 = \frac{1}{n} \sum_{i=1}^{n} y_i - \beta_1 \frac{1}{n} \sum_{i=1}^{n} x_i \quad ...(3.13)$$

$$\frac{\partial C}{\partial \beta_1} = 2 \times \frac{1}{2n} \sum_{i=1}^{n} (y_i - \beta_0 - \beta_1 x_i) \times \frac{\partial}{\partial \beta_1} (y_i - \beta_0 - \beta_1 x_i) \quad ...(3.14)$$

$$\frac{\partial C}{\partial \beta_1} = \frac{1}{n} \sum_{i=1}^{n} (y_i - \beta_0 - \beta_1 x_i) \times (- x_i) = 0 \quad ...(3.15)$$

$$\beta_1 \sum_{i=1}^{n} x_1^2 = \sum_{i=1}^{n} x_i y_i - \sum_{i=1}^{n} - \beta_0 x_i \quad ...(3.16)$$

Inserting β_0 in β_1,

$$\beta_1 = \frac{\sum_{i=1}^{n} y_i x_i - \frac{1}{n}\sum_{i=1}^{n} y_i \sum_{i=1}^{n} x_i}{\sum_{i=1}^{n} x_i^2 - \frac{1}{n}\sum_{i=1}^{n} x_i \sum x_i} \quad ...(3.17)$$

Let's use this result in a numerical example.

Example 3.1 Analytically find the linear regression line for the following data.

A heritage property needs to be modernized and for that, funds are required. It was decided that all the family members to whom the property belonged, should contribute. However, since the affordability of each member to contribute is different, it was decided that each one could contribute according to their personal wealth. The table shown below lists the details of five people's contribution based on their personal wealth. A sixth family member decided to use this data to decide how much he should contribute. His wealth amounts to ₹25 crore. Draw the linear regression line for the data in the table and suggest how much the sixth member should contribute.

Table 3.2 Wealth vs contribution data

Wealth in Crores of Rupees	20	1	35	5	10
Amount Contributed (Lakhs of Rupees)	38	2.5	80	8	30

Solution: The straight line approximation to model $f(x)$ is

$$f(x) = \beta_0 + \beta_1 x$$

Now consider, x = Wealth in crores and y = Amount contributed (in lakhs)

Table 3.3 Calculation of linear regression

Wealth in Crores of Rupees (x)	*Contribution in Lakhs (y)*	x_i^2	y_i^2	$x_i y_i$
20	38	400	1444	760
1	25	1	6.25	2.5
35	80	1225	6400	2800
5	8	25	64	40
10	30	100	900	300
71	158.5	1751	8814.25	3902.5

Using Eqs. 3.13 and 3.17,

$$\beta_1 = \frac{3902.5 - 0.2 \times 71 \times 158.5}{1751 - 0.2 \times 5041} = 2.2237$$

$$\beta_0 = 31.7 - 0.2 \times 2.2237 \times 71 = 0.122778$$

$$\hat{y} = \beta_0 + \beta_1 x$$

Hence for $x = 25$

$$\hat{y} = 0.122778 + 2.2237 \times 25 = 55.71.$$

For the given data, the sixth member should contribute ₹55.71 lakh.

The linear regression plot for this data is shown in Fig. 3.4.

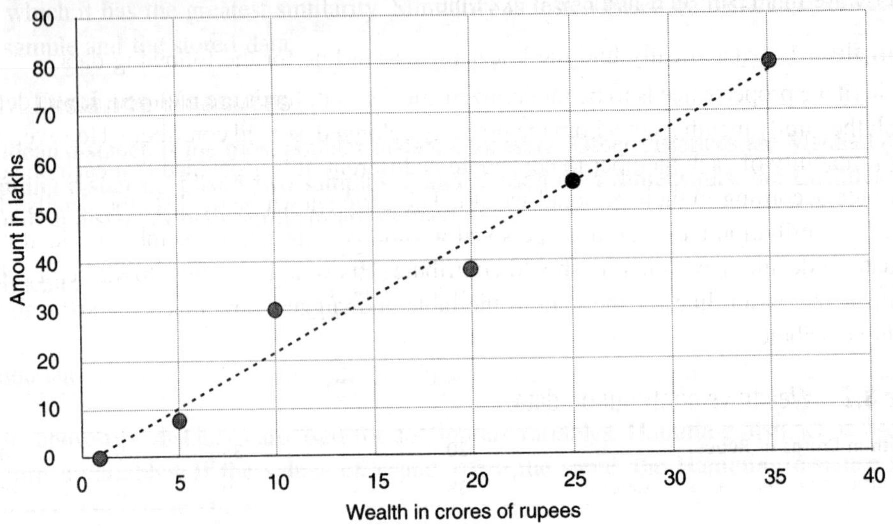

Fig. 3.4 The plot of wealth vs amount contributed

Code

```
import numpy as np
x=np.array([20,1,35,5,10])
y=np.array([38,2.5,80,8,30])
n=np.size(x)
x_mean=np.mean(x)
y_mean=np.mean(y)
nom=np.sum(x*y)-n*x_mean*y_mean
denom=np.sum(x*x)-n*x_mean*x_mean
b1=nom/denom
b0=y_mean-b1*x_mean
x=int(input('Enter the wealth of the sixth member (in crores): '))
#25 crore as per the Heritage property question
y_pred=b0+b1*x
print('He should contribute (in lakhs): ',y_pred)
```

//Code using Linear Regression functions of sklearn library

```
from sklearn.linear_model import LinearRegression
x=np.array([20,1,35,5,10])
y=np.array([38,2.5,80,8,30])
x=x.reshape(-1,1)
regression_model= LinearRegression()
regression_model.fit(x,y)
x6=np.array([int(input('Enter the wealth of the sixth member (in crores): '))])
#x6.append(input('Enter the wealth of the sixth member (in crores): '))
#25 crore as per the Heritage property question
x6=x6.reshape(-1,1)
y_pred=regression_model.predict(x6)
print('He should contribute (in lakhs): ',y_pred)
```

Example 3.2 For $f(x) = \beta_0 + \beta_1 x$

Assume $\beta_0 = 0$. So $(x) = \beta_1 x$. Draw a plot for $C(\beta_1)$ vs β_1 for the data x_i with label y_i given in Table 3.4.

Table 3.4 Values of x_i and y_i

x_i	0	0.5	1	1.5	2	2.5	3
y_i	0	23	30	37	40	47	50

Solution: The equation used is, from (3.6)

$$C(\beta) = \frac{1}{2n} \sum_{i=1}^{n} (y_i - \beta_1 x_i)^2$$

We find the Cost function to be a bell-shaped curve with a minimum value as is drawn in Fig. 3.5. Even though only one parameter is considered in this example, the idea of a 'bell shaped' Cost function with only one 'minimum' point is applicable to any number of parameters. This is the intuition to be gained from this example.

3.1.2 Gradient Descent: The Iterative Method

We have found the parameters β using numeric calculations. But there is an iterative method to find the minimum of the Cost function and that is the best method in practice. As is clear from Fig. 3.5, the Cost function is bowl shaped and has a single minimum point. If we could reach this point from any other point on the bowl-shaped curve, it would be ideal. And this is what the 'gradient descent' algorithm gets us to do. From any point on the parabolic Cost function, we can go down (descend) along the slope to reach its minimum at which the slope = 0. This is why it is called Gradient Descent algorithm.

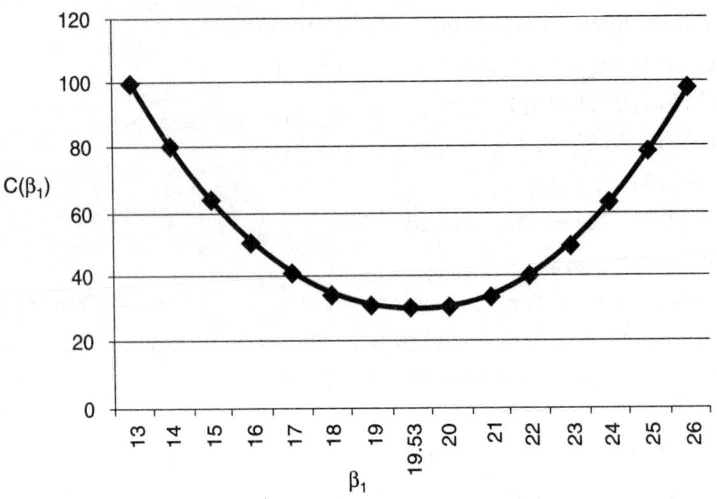

Fig. 3.5 The graph of Cost function vs β_1 for data of Table 3.4

How is this explained mathematically?

There are two update equations:

Update simultaneously β_0 and β_1

$$\beta_0 := \beta_0 - \eta \frac{\partial}{\partial \beta_0} C(\beta_0, \beta_1) \quad \text{...(3.18)}$$

$$\beta_1 := \beta_1 - \eta \frac{\partial}{\partial \beta_1} C(\beta_0, \beta_1) \quad \text{...(3.19)}$$

Note: the symbol ':=' indicates 'replace with'. Thus, at each iteration, β_0 and β_1 are replaced with their updated values.

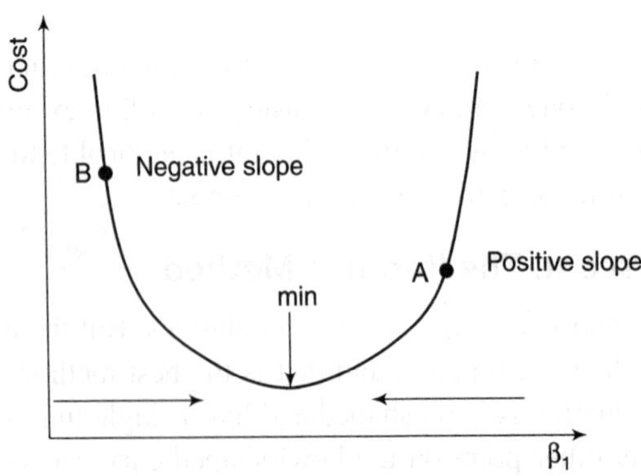

Fig. 3.6 Movement towards the minimum of the Cost function

The values of β_1 and β_0 are changed continuously (updated) until at the optimum values of these parameters, the Cost function is the minimum. The method is expressed by the two Eqs. 3.18 and 3.19. At each point corresponding to specified β_1 and β_0, subtract the slope of the Cost function (multiplied by η). η is named the 'learning rate' which determines how close together or farther away are the points that we choose. Note that the partial derivatives with respect to β_1 and β_0 correspond to the slope of the curve.

See Fig. 3.6, which is the Cost function with respect to β_1 (as $\beta_0 = 0$). It helps to understand the concept of gradient descent. Consider that at some time during the iteration, the Cost function has the value corresponding to point A. At this point of the curve, the slope is positive and so the subtraction in Eq. 3.19 reduces the value of β_1 and the next point in the iteration will be a lesser value of β_1. At another point B, the slope is negative, so the update equation 3.19 causes the values of β_1 to increase. This is the way β_1 moves to the left or right. In both cases, the minimum value of the Cost function is approached.

Note: Observe Fig. 3.6. If the function goes upward as we move right (on the X-axis), it is a positive slope, like at point A. That means we need to move leftward to reach the minimum. A negative slope is when the function goes down as we move right. At point B, the slope of the curve is negative. The minimum of the curve is reached by moving towards the right.

3.1.3 Learning Rate

η is called the learning rate and it is listed as a 'hyperparameter' which should be less than 1 ($\eta < 1$). It is a parameter that is within the control of the programmer. We are to specify the value of η when running the gradient descent algorithm. It is important to choose it optimally. It can have values as low as 0.001 or as high as 0.9. Too low a value causes the update to proceed very slowly – which means that the point moves downward in small, mini steps. A large value of η may cause the point to jump to and fro between both sides of the curve and may even prevent the algorithm from converging. See Figs. 3.7 a,b and c.

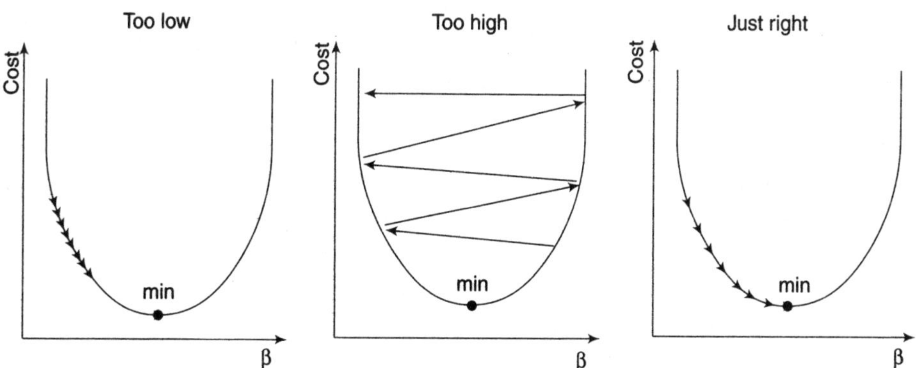

Fig. 3.7 Effect of the learning rate (η) on the rate of convergence

Note: We have discussed gradient descent with respect to linear regression. However, gradient descent is a very general algorithm that can be applied to find the minimum of any function which is differentiable.

3.1.4 Polynomial Linear Regression

This is the same as 'polynomial regression' mentioned in Section 2.3.1.2. Let us try to clarify why the word 'linear' is needed. A model is said to be linear when it is **'linear in parameters'**. Observe Eqs. 3.20 and 3.21.

$$f(x) = \beta_0 + \beta_1 x \quad ...(3.20$$

$$f(x) = \beta_0 + \beta_1 x + \beta_2 x^2 \quad ...(3.21)$$

Both are linear Eqs. with respect to β. We should actually write a general equation as

$$f(x, \beta) = \beta_0 + \beta_1 x + \beta_2 x^2 + ... + \beta_n x^n \quad ...(3.\ 22a)$$

This seems to be a non-linear function, but it is **linear in the parameters** β that we are out to estimate. But there is non-linearity between the input and output variables. Taking both these matters into consideration, Eq. 3.21 is referred to as 'Polynomial linear regression'.

The linear regression that we had talked about in Section.3.1.1 is called 'simple linear regression' where a straight line is used to fit the data. In that, the relationship between the input x and the output y is also linear. If the relationship between the input and output is non-linear, then a polynomial should be used to fit the data. We add higher degree terms to Eq. 3.20. For degree 2 non-linearity, the equation is as in 3.21. In this case, the fitting curve is parabolic.

A general equation for a regression model is written in vector notation as:

$$f(x) = \boldsymbol{\beta}^T \boldsymbol{x} \quad ...(3.22b)$$

where, $\boldsymbol{x}$ is a vector of input variables, $\boldsymbol{\beta}$ is a vector of parameters. Equation 3.22 means that $f(x)$ is the dot product of the $\boldsymbol{\beta}$ and $\boldsymbol{x}$ vectors.

The method of finding the parameters of polynomial linear regression is the same as what we did for simple linear regression. The iterative method is 'gradient descent'. Note that the cases we have considered so far are for 'univariate' data where only one feature of the data is used. But in practical cases, many features of the input being used is the more frequent case and the data is then said to be 'multivariate'.

3.1.5 Multivariate Linear Regression

We have discussed univariate linear regression but most practical cases are when data samples have more than one feature. In that case, we call it multivariate linear regression. In general, the linear regression model $f(x)$ is defined as in Eq. 3.23

$$f(x) = \beta_0 + \sum_{j=1}^{d} \beta_j x_j \quad ...(3.23)$$

For the case of two variables,

$$f(x) = \beta_0 + \beta_1 x_1 + \beta_2 x_2 \quad ...(3.24)$$

In this case, instead of a line, we will get a plane as the model. (See Fig. 3.8).

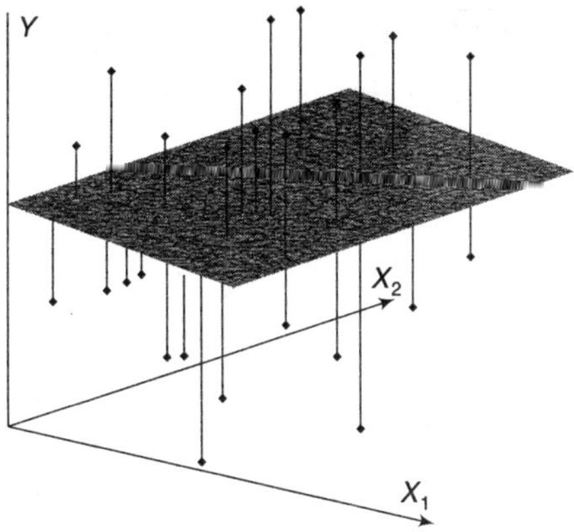

Fig. 3.8 A plane as the model when there are two variables

3.1.5.1 Normal Equation

When there are more features than two, the fitting plane will be difficult to visualise. But the procedure to find the parameters is the same as the univariate case. We just have to find the values of the parameters. The problem is formulated as follows:

Find β_j that minimizes the Cost function:

$$C = \frac{1}{2n}\sum_{i=1}^{n} (y_i - \beta_0 - \sum_{j=1}^{d} \beta_j x_{ij}))^2 \quad ...(3.25)$$

In this, '*n*' corresponds to the number of samples and '*d*' to the number of variables (features) of the input. Note that we think of '*d*' as the dimension of the input space.

For finding the parameters, let us rewrite Eq. 3.25 as

$$C = \frac{1}{2n}\sum_{i=1}^{n} (y_i - \beta_0 x_0 - \sum_{j=1}^{d} \beta_j x_{ij}))^2 \quad ...(3.26)$$

In this, we have just added x_0 as a variable with β_0 as its coefficient. $x_0 = 1$ always. This is done for the purpose of using a matrix representation for the model. Now we can use matrix notations.

Let *X* be an $n * (d + 1)$ matrix. Let **y** be the vector of labels of the training set. Let $\boldsymbol{\beta}$ be the vector of parameters that we want to estimate. (See Fig. 3.9)

Now we have the input variables for *n* samples expressed in matrix form and the labels and parameters as vectors. *C* is the Cost function to be minimized.

We want to find the $(d + 1)$ β's that minimize the Cost function. We write *C* as:

$$C(\beta) = \frac{1}{2n} ||(y - X\beta)||^2 \quad ...(3.27)$$

$$C(\beta) = \frac{1}{2n} (y - X\beta)^T (y - X\beta) \quad ...(3.28)$$

$$X := \begin{pmatrix} 1 & x_{11} & \cdots & x_{1j} & \cdots & x_{1d} \\ \vdots & \vdots & \vdots & \vdots & \vdots & \vdots \\ 1 & x_{i1} & \cdots & x_{ij} & \cdots & x_{id} \\ \vdots & \vdots & \vdots & \vdots & \vdots & \vdots \\ 1 & x_{n1} & \cdots & x_{nj} & \cdots & x_{nd} \end{pmatrix}$$

$$y := \begin{pmatrix} y_1 \\ \vdots \\ y_i \\ \vdots \\ y_n \end{pmatrix} \qquad \beta := \begin{pmatrix} \beta_0 \\ \vdots \\ \beta_j \\ \vdots \\ \beta_d \end{pmatrix}$$

Fig. 3.9 The matrix X and vectors x and β

$$\frac{\partial C}{\partial \beta} = -\frac{1}{n} X^T(y - X\beta) \quad \text{...(3.29)}$$

We have that:

$$\frac{\partial^2 C}{\partial \beta} = -\frac{1}{n} X^T X \quad \text{...(3.30)}$$

is positive definite which ensures that β is a minimum. We solve for

$$X^T(y - X\beta) = 0 \quad \text{...(3.31)}$$

The steps of this derivation are omitted but the solution is given below.

The unique solution is: $\beta = (X^T X)^{-1} X^T y$ ...(3.32)

This analytical solution is possible only if $X^T X$ is invertible. Equation 3.32 is called the normal equation and is the analytical method which may be preferred if the number of samples and the number of features is small. But for large datasets with many features, it is the iterative method using the gradient descent algorithm that will be better for practical applications.

Example 3.3 The total sales in a company is due to the sale of many products which are (i) consumer electronics, (ii) food items, (iii) clothes, (iv) furniture, and (v) real estate.

Write the equation for the model.

Solution: There are 5 features and hence we have 5 variables for this problem. We write this as

$y = \beta_0 + \beta_1 x_1 + \beta_2 x_2 + \beta_3 x_3 + \beta_4 x_4 + \beta_5 x_5$ where the variables are chosen as in Table 3.5.

Table 3.5

x_1	x_2	x_3	x_4	x_5
Consumer electronics	Food items	Clothes	Furniture	Real estate

Thus, we have 6 βs to be evaluated and this may be done analytically (Section 3.1.5) or iteratively (Section 3.1.2). We should get the model $f(x)$ that will give us the predicted label, $\hat{y}$.

Now that we have discussed the theoretical aspects of linear regression, let us make a note of its salient points.

(i) The input to a system of linear regression may be univariate or multivariate.

(ii) Simple linear regression is when we can model $f(x)$ as a straight line or plane.

(iii) Polynomial linear regression is when $f(x)$ is a polynomial in the variable x.

(iv) Analytical or iterative methods are available for finding the parameters of $f(x)$.

(v) The Cost function is the Mean Squared Error between the actual and predicted labels.

(vi) It is a convex function with only one minimum which is called the global minimum.

(vii) The gradient descent algorithm is one that attempts to find this minimum and through this gives us the method for finding the parameters of $f(x)$.

3.2 LOGISTIC REGRESSION

In Section 2.3.1.2 this term was referred to. Here we will discuss it in depth. We will see that the ultimate aim of logistic regression is binary classification and the way 'logistic regression' does this is by determining a decision boundary between two classes.

3.2.1 The Intuition

Let us try to get an intuitive understanding of this. In many cases, we will be unable to get a clear prediction of the occurrence of an event. But we can get a 'probability' value for that. For example, based on weather parameters, it may be possible to say that there is, say, a 70% probability that it will rain tomorrow, or be sunny the day after that. But probabilities are continuous variables, that is, real numbers. This sort of a prediction is not useful for many applications which are meant to do classification. It may be needed to declare that the prediction is Positive or Negative. For example, it may be needed to say categorically that a person has Covid/does not have Covid, or that a cancer is malignant/benign. These are examples of binary classification tasks. To get such an output, the probabilities should be converted to categorical (discrete) variables.

Suppose we want to know whether a bank will give a loan to a customer. Let's say that this will depend on his credit score. Then y, the output variable should be a Yes/No. The two cases are:

$$P(y/x) = \text{P(Loan Sanctioned)} = P(\text{Yes/Credit Score})$$
$$= \text{P(Loan Not Sanctioned)} = P(\textit{No/Credit Score})$$

Credit score is a real number. Only when the customer has a minimum credit score, will he be sanctioned a loan. Thus, a threshold has to be defined for the credit score above which the output variable 'y' is a 'Yes'. In logistic regression, this is the procedure involved. A new function will be introduced to convert the output probabilities into a binary valued discrete variable. Before we get into that, let us make a formal definition of classification. We will first consider binary classification.

3.2.2 Binary Classification

Given: $(x_1, y_1), (x_2, y_2), \ldots \ldots \ldots \ldots (x_i, y_i) \ldots \ldots \ldots \ldots (x_n, y_n)$ where $x_i \in R^d$ and $y \in Y$ ...(3.33)

$$Y \in \{-1, +1\} \quad \text{...(3.34)}$$

The function f maps the d-dimensional space to a space of two variables.

The training data has 'n' samples of 'd' dimensional input variables x_i, and corresponding label variables y_i.

y_i is a binary valued variable which may be expressed as 1/0, Yes/No, Positive/Negative, +1/–1 and so on.

The task to be done is to learn a classification function $f(x)$ as:

$$f(x) : R^d \rightarrow \{-1, +1\} \quad \text{...(3.35)}$$

The classification function $f(x)$ may be linear or non-linear. In Section 2.4, we talked about a decision boundary. The classification function defines that decision boundary.

3.2.3 Simple Logistic Regression: An Intuitive Derivation

Let us start with a very simple example in which x_i, the input has just one feature. A hospital has offered a free medical check-up for interested people. The data collected from those who registered for it shows a clear relationship to age. Those registered for this were seen to be above a certain age. Figure 3.10 shows the action of registering/not registering as *Yes/No*, depicted as 1/0. We want to predict whether a person (who is not in the training set) will take up the offer or not. The input feature for this example is only 'age'.

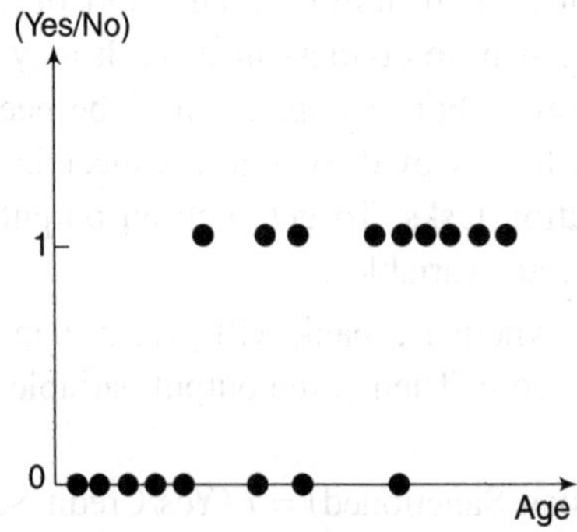

Fig. 3.10 Data distribution of Age vs Registered/not registered

Now we would like to fit this data onto a line to try to get a relationship between age and the probability of accepting the offer. The *Y* axis is now calibrated in terms of the probability of occurrence of the event. It is the 'predicted' probability of the occurrence of the event. So let us denote this probability as $\hat{P}$

See Fig. 3.11 in which a straight line is used for fitting this data. But using such a line seems to be fraught with problems. Most of the data does not fit on the line. The parts of the line above $\hat{P} = 1$ and $\hat{P} = 0$ does not make sense because probabilty values lie only between 0 and 1. So we remove those parts and get Fig. 3.12. This figure shows sharp transitions for the function at $\hat{P} = 0$ and $\hat{P} = 1$. Intutively we might feel that a function which is smoother will represent this case better. This leads us to Fig. 3.13.

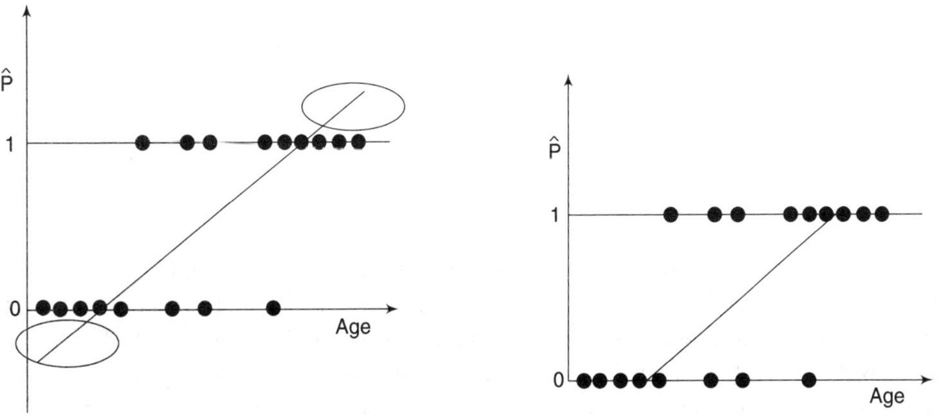

Fig. 3.11 Fitting the data on a straight line

Fig. 3.12 The straight line with unwanted parts removed

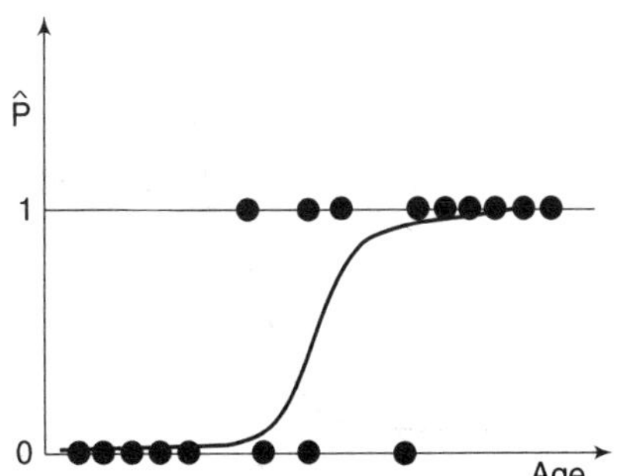

Fig. 3.13 Data fitted on a smooth curve

Figure 3.13 shows an S shaped curve which levels off at the top and bottom and seems to be a good fit to this data. Such a function is called a Sigmoid/logistic function which is as shown in Fig 3.14. Its equation is in Eq. 3.36.

$$g(z) = \frac{e^z}{1 + e^z} = \frac{1}{1 + e^{-z}} \qquad ...(3.36)$$

Note that

$$g(z) \to 1 \text{ when } z \to +\infty,\ g(z) \to 0 \text{ when } z \to -\infty \qquad ...(3.37)$$

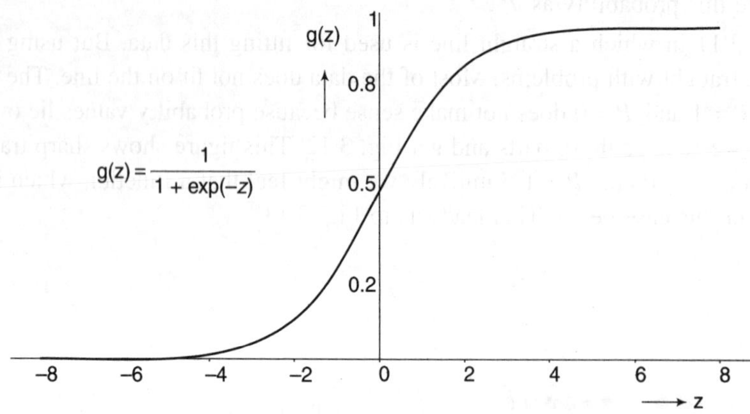

Fig. 3.14 The Sigmoid function

Let us now use the Sigmoid curve to fit our data. This has been done in Fig. 3.13. In this, the Y axis is the probability $\hat{P}(y/x)$ and it is a continuous variable. To make it a discrete output, we must fix a threshold. For this problem, let us fix the threshold as 0.5. This means that if $\hat{P}(y/x) >= 0.5$, the output $\hat{y}$ is considered Positive, otherwise it is Negative. Thus, $\hat{y}$ is now a categorical output variable. And we have a classification done here. (See Fig. 3.15).

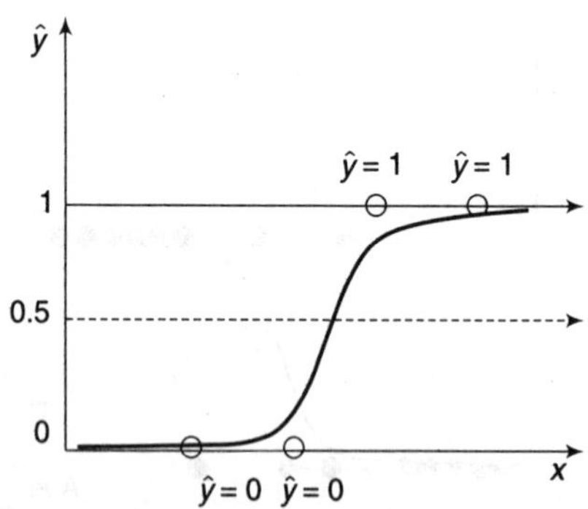

Fig. 3.15 Logistic regression with Sigmoid function

There can be many such Sigmoid curves, but the idea of logistic regression is to get the best fitting Sigmoid. How to find the exact Sigmoid curve? We must solve for the parameters of this curve. Let us examine the intuition behind this action. We had started with trying to fit a straight line to our data. The model $f(x)$ is thus a straight line with parameters β_0 and β_1

$$f(x) = \beta_0 + \beta_1 x \qquad ...(3.38)$$

But we replaced the simple straight line with the Sigmoid curve so as to fit the data. So we insert this equation into the equation of the Sigmoid (Eq. 3.36).

$$f(x) = g(\beta_0 + \beta_1 x) \qquad ...(3.39)$$

$$g(\beta_0 + \beta_1 x) = \frac{1}{1 + e^{-(\beta_0 + \beta_1 x)}} \qquad ...(3.40)$$

Once the values of β_0 and β_1 are available, the probability can be calculated and applying a threshold to that will give us the discrete variable $\hat{y}$.

Example 3.4

(a) Suppose $\beta_0 = -10.5$ and $\beta_1 = 0.006$. What is the probability that an applicant with a credit score of 900 will be sanctioned a loan?

(b) $\beta_0 = -1.65$ and $\beta_1 = 0.19$. Repeat the calculation with these values.

Solution: Let us take $\hat{y}$ = Positive, if the applicant gets the loan and $\hat{y}$ = Negative, otherwise.

Take $x = 900$

If $g(z) >= 0.5$, $\hat{y}$ is Positive.

Find $\hat{P} = f(x) = \frac{1}{1 + e^{-(\beta_0 + \beta_1 x)}}$

Case 1: $\beta_0 = -10.5$ and $\beta_1 = 0.006$

For $x = 900$, $\hat{P} = 0.00606$. This is below the threshold of 0.5 for $\hat{P}$. So the loan will not be sanctioned.

Now, to get a complete picture, observe Fig. 3.16.

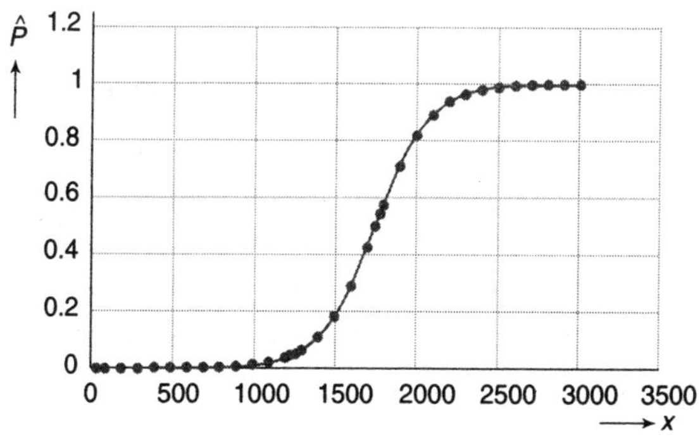

Fig. 3.16 The Sigmoid function for the parameters $\beta_0 = -10.5$ and $\beta_1 = 0.006$

We get the result that when the credit score is above 1750, $\hat{P} = 0.5$.

This is the threshold value for the credit score. For any score above 1750, the loan will be sanctioned.

Case 2:

$$\beta_0 = -1.65 \text{ and } \beta_1 = 0.19.$$

$$\text{For score} = 8,\ \hat{P} = 0.47 \text{ and for score} = 9,\ \hat{P} = 0.51$$

See Fig. 3.17 which shows the Sigmoid curve corresponding to these values of β_0 and β_1.

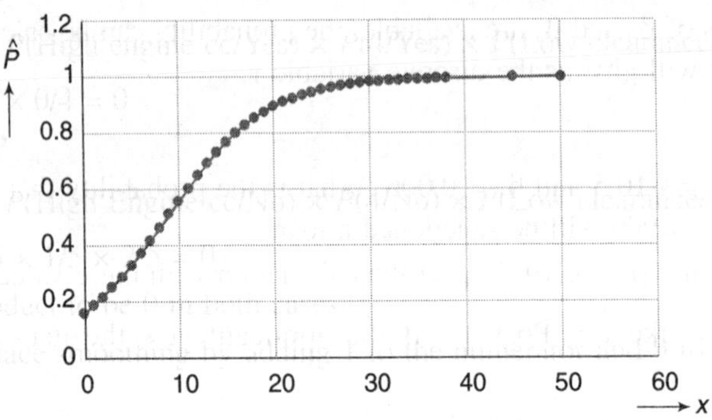

Fig. 3.17 The Sigmoid function for the parameters $\beta_0 = -1.65$ and $\beta_1 = 0.19$

What conclusion can we make about the parameters (β) and the threshold?

We see that the parameters of the fitting curve decide the threshold value of x. This is when there is only one feature for the data. For more than one feature (x), the parameters decide the decision boundary. But the parameters are obtained using the training data and more on this will be taken up in Section 3.3.5.

What if the number of input features is more than one, say three?

Then Eq. 3.40 is replaced with $\beta_0 + \beta_1 x_1 + \beta_2 x_2 + \beta_3 x_3$ for three input features. The algorithm is the same, though.

3.2.4 Mathematical Derivation of the Logistic Regression

We have seen an intuitive way of getting the equation for logistic regression. The goal of logistic regression is to get and estimate of 'P' for a linear combination of independent variables (which are the input features). We need a function that links this linear combination of input variables to a probability distribution (from 0 to 1).

Mathematically, this can be modelled as follows. If P is the probability of the occurrence of an event, $(1 - P)$ is the probability of non-occurrence of the event. The ratio $\dfrac{P}{(1-P)}$ is known as the odds of the occurrence of the event. The natural logarithm of 'odds' is named the logit of P, denoted *logit* (*P*)

$$\ln(\text{odds}) \Rightarrow \ln\left(\frac{P}{1-P}\right) \text{ is the logit (P)} \qquad ...(3.41)$$

This logarithm of odds may be equated to a linear function of independent variables. Taking the antilog of the *logit* function, let's get a regression function for the estimate of the probability *P*.

Taking a simple case of just one independent variable x_1,

$$\text{logit}(p) = \ln\left(\frac{P}{1-P}\right) = \beta_0 + \beta_1 x \quad ...(3.42)$$

Taking the antilog gives us

$$\frac{P}{1-P} = e^{\beta_0 + \beta_1 x} \quad ...(3.43)$$

From this, we get

$$P = \frac{e^{\beta_0 + \beta_1 x}}{1 + e^{\beta_0 + \beta_1 x}} \quad ...(3.44)$$

What we get by linear regression is the estimated value of probability, which we denote as $\hat{P}$, which is given below. So in Eq. 3.44., we replace *P* by $\hat{\hat{P}}$, divide the RHS by $e^{\beta_0 + \beta_1 x_1}$ and get Eq. 3.45 which is

$$\hat{P} = \frac{1}{1 + e^{-(\beta_0 + \beta_1 x)}} \quad ...(3.45)$$

The RHS is the equation for the Sigmoid function.

This is why we use the Sigmoid function for getting the estimate of the probability. Using a threshold, we then convert it into a binary variable and that is how classification is obtained. In Section 3.3.1, this was explained intuitively. Here we have derived it using the logit function. We arrive at the same result.

3.2.5 Decision Boundaries

We started with saying that logistic regression is meant to create decision boundaries. When the number of features is just one, this is easy to visualise. Take the case when there are two input variable x_1 and x_2. The input is a vector $\begin{bmatrix} x_1 \\ x_2 \end{bmatrix}$. A linear boundary is shown in Fig. 3.18.

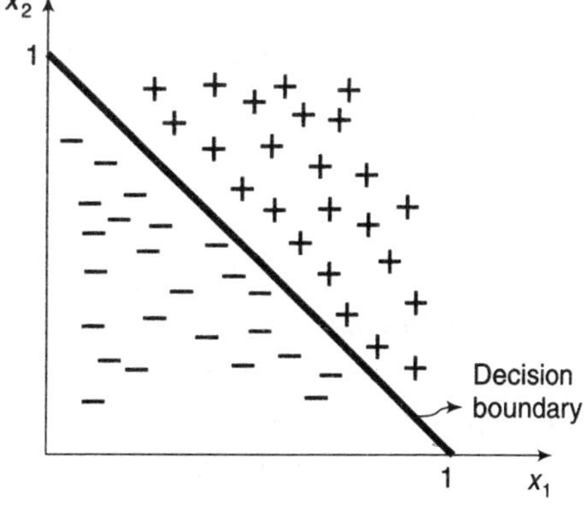

Fig. 3.18 Linear decision boundary for data with two variables

This is the decision boundary which we got by modelling $f(x)$ as $f(x) = \beta_0 + \beta_1 x_1 + \beta_2 x_2$.

Let's say we got the $\beta_0 = -4$ and $\beta_1 = 2$, $\beta_2 = 2$. Then as $f(x) = -4 + 2x_1 + 2x_2$. The boundary may be defined by transposing 4 to the right so as to get the equation as $2x_1 + 2x_2 = 4$. We can define the decision boundary by dividing the 2D plot into areas with $2x_1 + 2x_2 >= 4$ and $2x_1 + 2x_2 < 4$. This is how we get the linear decision boundary which is shown in Fig. 3.18.

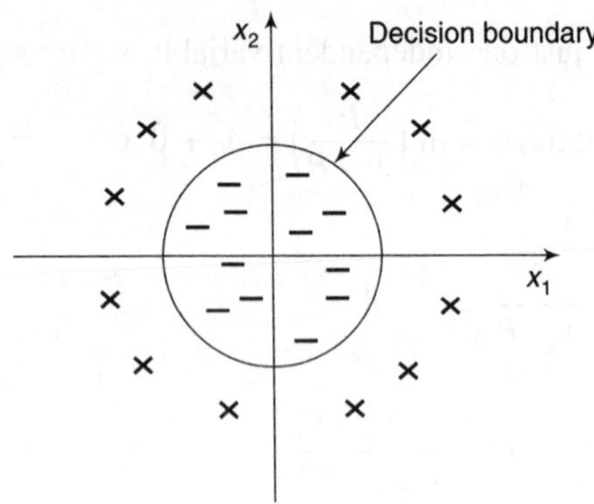

Fig. 3.19 (a) A circular decision boundary

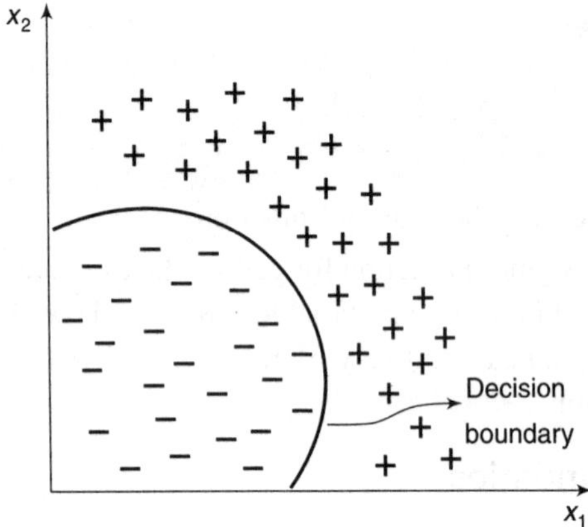

Fig. 3.19 (b) A quadratic decision boundary

For quadratic models with two features as in Fig. 3.19a, and 3.19b $f(x)$ is modelled as:

$$f(x) = \beta_0 + \beta_1 x_1 + \beta_2 x_1^2 + \beta_3 x_2 + \beta_4 x_2^2 \quad ...(3.46)$$

In Fig. 3.19c, a complex decision boundary is seen. That is obtained by choosing a model as a much higher degree polynomial.

The most important point to note is that the **'decision boundary' is defined by the parameters (βs) of the model and not by the training data**. The parameters of the model are obatined by the training data and the chosen model $f(x)$

3.2.6 Finding the Parameters of the Solution Iteratively

The method of finding the βs is the same as what we did in Sections 3.1.1 and 3.1.2 in the context of linear regression. Let us write that equation here. The Cost function is:

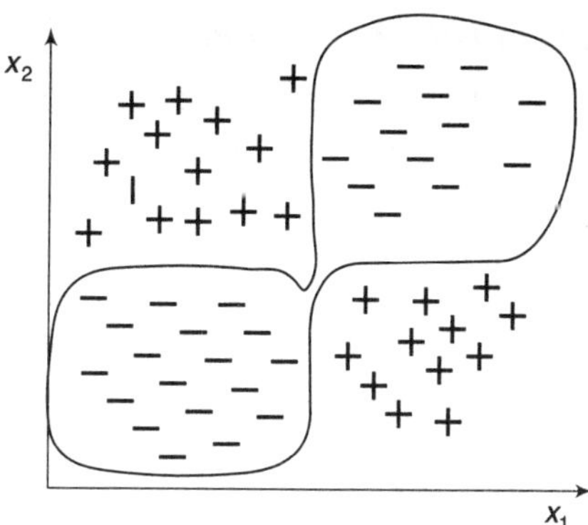

Fig. 3.19 (c) Complex decision boundary

$$C(\beta) = \frac{1}{n} \sum_{i=1}^{n} \frac{1}{2}(f(x) - y)^2 \qquad ...(3.47)$$

This is the same as what we used for linear regression. However, there is one 'major' difference here. The function $f(x)$ is not the simple line now. It is the Sigmoid function with an equation with an exponent and therefore $(f(x) - y)^2$ is not a simple quadratic function. It is a complicated non-linear function and $C(\beta)$ will turn out to be a non-convex function.

Recall that in Section 3.1.2, it was mentioned that a convex function has only one minimum and that the gradient descent algorithm could be used to find that minimum and thereby find the parameters of the function. This is not possible now because the Cost function is non-convex and has many minima which are called 'local minima'. It will be difficult to find the global minimum once the algorithm gets trapped in a local minimum.

The solution to this predicament is to find a better Cost function which will be a convex one. Another desirable property for the Cost function is that when a wrong prediction is made, the Cost function should have a high value. Thus, a wrong prediction should be 'sharply penalised'. Conversely, the right prediction should give zero cost.

Borrowing the 'Maximum Likelihood Estimator' from statistics, a Cost function is obtained which creates a convex space which is useful and friendly for optimization. Let us go into the details of such a Cost function which will be used to learn the β parameters using gradient descent.

3.2.7 Maximum Likelihood Estimation

We use a probabilistic framework named 'Maximum Likelihood Estimation'. In this, we assume a probability distribution for the output label and then a likelihood function is defined which calculates the probability of a given label for an input data. For the complete training dataset, this 'sum likelihood function' is to be maximized. The Bernoulli distribution is used to model our case. A Bernoulli distribution is a discrete probability distribution for a random experiment that has only two outcomes.

3.2.7.1 Cost Function for Logistic Regression

The probability of the output y with respect to the input x is notated as $P(y/x)$. Let us use y for the actual output and $\hat{y}$ for the predicted output.

Note: $\hat{y}$ is the same as $f(x)$ which is the model created/prediction made.

For a Bernoulli distribution, the probability distribution function is:

$$P(y|x) = \hat{y}^y (1 - \hat{y})^{1-y} \quad \text{...(3.48)}$$

This reduces to Eqs. 3.49 and 3.50 depending on the actual output.

If $\quad y = 1, P(y|x) = \hat{y}$ ...(3.49)

If $\quad y = 0, P(y|x) = 1 - \hat{y}$ ...(3.50)

These Eqs. correspond to the maximum likelihood estimation (MLE) which is well known in statistics.

Now let's do some operations on Eq. 3.48. Taking the log of both sides gives:

$$\log P(y|x) = \log[\hat{y}^y (1 - \hat{y})^{1-y}] \quad \text{...(3.51)}$$

$$= y \log y\, \hat{y} + (1 - y)\log(1 - \hat{y}) \quad \text{...(3.52)}$$

For a prediction, we want $P(y|x)$ to be maximized. Equation 3.52 is a function which is to be maximized. In general, it is best for optimizers to do 'minimizing'.

To turn it into a Cost function to be minimised, we add negative signs to Eq. 3.52

$$-\log P(y|x) = -[y \log \hat{y} + (1 - y) \log (1 - \hat{y})] \quad \text{...(3.53)}$$

The Cost function is therefore

$$C = -[y \log \hat{y} + (1 - y) \log (1 - \hat{y})] \quad \text{...(3.54)}$$

For N input samples, we sum from $n = 1$ to N and we get:

$$C(\beta) = -\frac{1}{N} \sum_{i=1}^{N} [y \log \hat{y} + (1 - y) \log (1 - \hat{y})] \quad \text{...(3.55)}$$

This is called the Log Loss function (also called the Binary Cross Entropy loss). We use the terminology $C(\beta)$ because we will be using this Cost function to 'learn' the parameters β.

Note: The natural logarithm is chosen.

The properties of the Cost function of Eq. 3.55 are listed in Fig. 3.20 a, b and c.

Cost $(\hat{y}, y) = -\log_e(\hat{y})$ if $y = 1$

$= -\log_e(1 - \hat{y})$ if $y = 0$

Case 1: If $y = 1$ and the prediction $\hat{y} = 1$, then Cost = 0

If $y = 1$ and the prediction $\hat{y} = 0$, then Cost $\rightarrow \infty$

Case 2: If $y = 0$ and the prediction $\hat{y} = 0$, then Cost = 0

If $y = 0$ and the prediction $\hat{y} = 1$, then Cost $\rightarrow \infty$

Fig. 3.20 (a) Properties of the Cost function

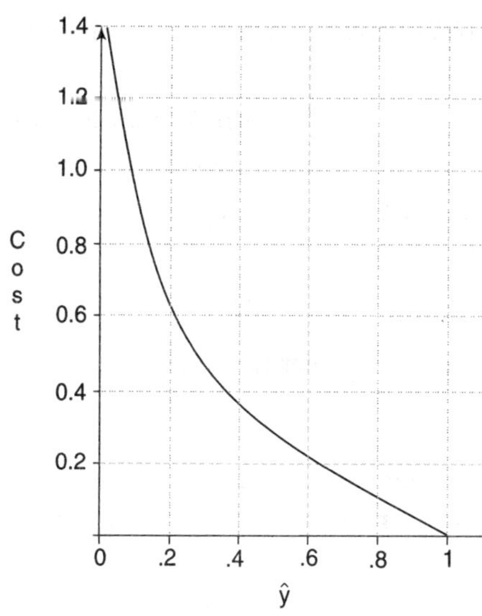

Fig. 3.20 (b) Case 1, when $y = 1$

Fig. 3.20 (c) Case 2, when $y = 0$

Note the important property of the Cost function which is evident from Figs. 3.20b and c:

(i) When the prediction is correct ($y = \hat{y}$), Cost = 0.

(ii) When the prediction is wrong(($y! = \hat{y}$), the Cost function is large and tends to infinity.

This means that the prediction is 'highly penalised' when it is wrong. This is a very desirable property for a Cost function and that is why this is a highly preferred Cost function for most classification problems. This is also the preferred Cost function in deep learning (Section 10.3).

This Cost function is used to perform gradient descent and get the parameters of the model. The gradient descent algorithm updates all the βs simultaneously and obtains the final value of the β*s* corresponding to the minimum point of the Cost function. (See Eq. 3.56).

Repeat {

Simultaneously, update for all β's

$$\beta_j := \beta_j - \eta \frac{\partial}{\partial \beta_j} C(\beta) \qquad ...(3.56)$$

}

With this, we end our discussion on logistic regression. Note that logistic regression is a **binary** classification method. For multi-class classification, this can be extended by using a 'One vs All' methodology.

Salient Points Regarding Logistic Regression

(i) It is binary classification method.

(ii) The Sigmoid function is used to convert the probabilities to binary discrete variables.

(iii) Mean squared error is not used as it leads to a non-convex cost function.

(iv) The log–loss function is convex and thus it is used as the Cost function for gradient descent.

3.3 FREQUENTLY USED TERMS IN MACHINE LEARNING

Now we will discuss some terms which we are likely to encounter frequently.

3.3.1 Regularization

In Section 2.5.1, overfitting was discussed and one solution to it was mentioned as using validation techniques. Another method is known are regularization. One reason for overfitting is that data is described by too many features.

If we are trying to fit a model using polynomial linear regression, it may have the form:

$$f(x) = \beta_0 + \beta_1 x_1 + \beta_2 x_1^2 + \beta_3 x_2 + \beta_4 x_2^2 + \beta_5 x_3 + \ldots \qquad \ldots(3.57)$$

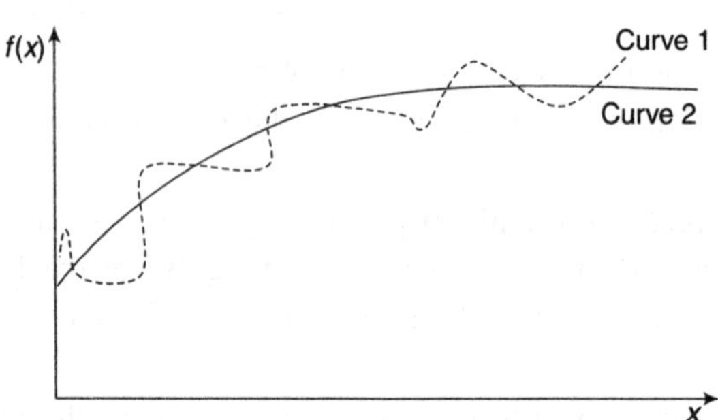

Fig. 3.21 Smoothing of high degree polynomials

Such a model could lead to a fitting curve such as the one marked as 'curve 1' in Fig. 3.21. This seems to be an instance of overfitting. How to tone it down to become somewhat like curve 2? The method should be to remove higher order terms from $f(x)$. That can be done easily by removing β_4 and β_5. But instead of 'removing' them, we can make their effect very small by shrinking their values. If we multiply those terms by a shrinkage factor, they will become very small and overfitting due to 'too many features' may be avoided.

In this case, we know that we would like to shrink those higher order terms. But in practical cases, we don't know what we are up against. As such, the method used is of shrinking all the parameters by using a regularizing term γ. Though the mathematics of this new idea is difficult to convince, in practice, it works very well and we get a smoother fitting model than one without regularization.

The concept used in regularisation is to add a term to the model $f(x)$ whereby the effects of the parameters are scaled down and then the relevance of the corresponding feature gets diminished. To the Cost function, we add a regularization term. There are two methods of doing it.

3.3.1.1 Ridge/L2 Regularization

In this method, the Cost function is modified by adding a shrinkage term in which the squared weight of each individual parameter β (except β_0) is scaled by γ. Therefore, the optimization function (Cost function) becomes:

$$C(\beta) = C(\beta) + \lambda \sum_{j=1}^{d} \beta_{j=1}^2 \quad ...(3.58)$$

3.3.1.2 Lasso (Least Absolute and Selection Operator) Regularisation

This is also called L1 regularisation

In this, the shrinkage term uses the absolute values of the parameters. Therefore, the optimization function becomes:

$$C(\beta) = C(\beta) + \lambda \sum_{j=1}^{d} |\beta_j| \quad ...(3.59)$$

λ is chosen such that neither overfitting nor underfitting occurs. Too high a value of λ, leads to underfitting. The more popular type of regularization is L2. Reasonable values of λ lie between 0 and 0.1.

Note: Regularization is applicable to logistic regression as well.

3.3.2 Standardization and Normalization

In cases where there are multiple features, it may be necessary to do some pre-processing on feature values. As an example, consider the case of four variables where x_1 represents the area in acres of a rubber plantation, x_2 represents the number of rubber trees, x_3 may be the number of water resources and x_4, the number of workers. We see from Table 3.6 that the range of the value of x_3 is very small compared to that of x_2. Feature scaling is needed so that the range of values of variables are the same, and that some features do not have more impact than the others. Two methods of feature scaling are discussed here.

Table 3.6 Data of a farm

Variable	*Maximum value*
x_1-Area of farm in acres	100
x_2-Number of trees	20000
x_3-Number of water resources	5
x_4-Number of workers	50

3.3.2.1. Normalization

In this, the re-scaled value of a variable x is given as

$$\acute{x} = \frac{x - \min(x)}{\max(x) - \min(x)} \quad ..(3.60)$$

This method is also known as Min-Max normalization and brings the value of x to the range 0 to 1.

3.3.2.2 Standardization

In this, the re-scaled feature is given as

$$z = \frac{x - \mu}{\sigma} \quad ...(3.61)$$

This method, which has also the name Z-score normalization is used such that the feature values will be a Standard normal distribution with mean $\mu = 0$ and standard deviation, $\sigma = 1$. The rescaled features are now in the range –1 to +1.

Note: Many practitioners use one of these two methods (sometimes, with some variations) and with experience in handling practical cases, one can decide which method is more suitable for what kind of data.

Example 3.5 Perform normalization and standardization for the variables of Table 3.7.

Table 3.7 Area vs Income data

Farmer	*Area of farm (in acres)*	*Monthly income in ten thousands of rupees*
1	8	15
2	5	12
3	6	24
4	6	17
5	7	10
6	9	23
7	6	20
8	8	17
9	5	14
10	8	19

Solution: Normalization

$$X' = \frac{x - \mu}{\sigma}$$

Area of land: min = 5, max = 9

Monthly income: min = 10, max = 24

Farmer	*Normalized area of land*	*Normalized monthly income*
1	0.75	0.357142857
2	0	0.142857143

3	0.25	1
4	0.25	0.5
5	0.5	0
6	1	0.928571429
7	0.25	0.714285714
8	0.75	0.5
9	0	0.285714286
10	0.75	0.642857143

Standardization

$$X' = \frac{X - \mu}{\sigma}$$

μ = Mean

σ = Standard deviation

Area of land:

$\mu = 6.8$

$\sigma = 1.398411798$

Monthly income:

$\mu = 17.1$

$\sigma = 4.53259798$

Table 3.8 Standardized and normalized values

Farmer	*Standardized area of land*	*Standardized monthly income*
1	0.85811633	−0.463310448
2	−1.287174495	−1.125182516
3	−0.572077554	1.522305757
4	−0.572077554	−0.022062402
5	0.143019388	−1.566430562
6	1.573213272	1.301681735
7	−0.572077554	0.639809666
8	0.85811633	−0.022062402
9	−1.287174495	−0.683934471
10	0.85811633	0.419185643

What is a hyperplane?

This word is likely to be seen very frequently. What does it mean? In simple terms, in geometry, it is a subspace with dimension one less than the ambient space. For instance, when we have a problem formulated in a 3D space, then hyperplanes are 2-dimensional –we call them 'planes' as in Fig. 3.8. In a 2D space, the hyperplanes are lines.

3.3.3 Outliers

The word 'outlier' is one that is relevant when handling data. The word has the dictionary meaning : *a person or thing situated away or detached from the main body or system*. This indicates that an outlier is a 'odd one out'—an entity that does not fit in the general scheme of things. If we find a data point far away, very much separated from the rest of the data, that could be identified as a possible outlier. See Fig. 3.22 which shows two points far away from the clustered data. These points are likely to be outliers. Outliers may be due to experimental errors during data collection or data entry. If a data point is identified as an outlier, it should be removed – otherwise, the algorithm may try to stretch its response to include this and the result of analysis will go wrong. There are visualising techniques as well as mathematical methods to identify data that may probably be an outlier. Analysts should use some of these methods to confirm it – then only that data should be discarded.

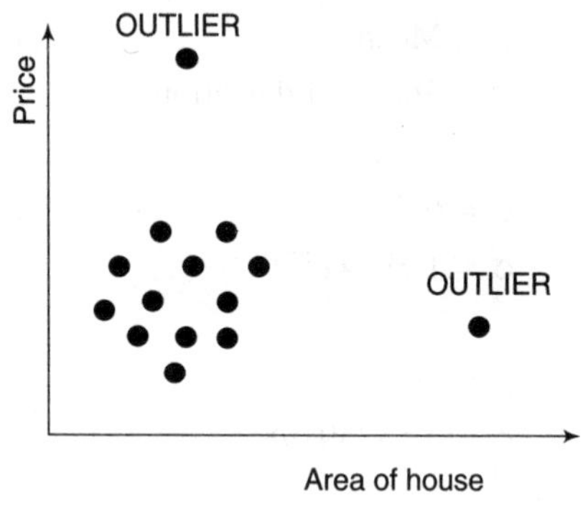

Fig. 3.22 Two outliers

In a typical case of the cost of houses in a particular locality, it may be that one or two houses are found to be priced too high or too low. There may be reasons why it is so, but for our analysis, we should consider them as outliers which need to be removed. Of course, we could develop a model to include these data samples, but it will then be an overfitting model which will give bad predictions.

3.3.4 Curse of Dimensionality

This is a term which may be encountered once in a while, in literature relating to machine learning. This term was coined in 1957 by R. Bellman in his book "Dynamic Programming". Let's examine the relevance of this term. Samples of data may be univariate or multivariate. Having more than one feature is the rule rather than the exception. But the question about how many features are sufficient for a good prediction is debatable. It depends on the actual case and the application for which it is envisaged. More number of features means more dimensions for the input data.

For predicting house prices, which are the most relevant features? The area, number of bedrooms, number of bathrooms, number of balconies, area of the land around, geographical location, etc., are relevant features. This accounts for a 6-dimensional data. Should we add features like, number of schools close by, number of hospitals close by, distance to the beach, etc. If we do, each data sample now has 9 dimensions. The question is whether adding the last three features will improve the accuracy of predictions.

There is confusion about whether more dimensions add or reduce the accuracy. It is obvious that the complexity of the algorithm also increases accordingly. Up to a certain point, the accuracy of predictions does improve as more dimensions are used, but after that, the performance levels off. Those who are aware of the 'Law of diminishing returns' in Economics will be able to relate well to this idea.

Also, higher dimensional spaces have the possibility of adding more noise and less information. Thus the possibility of error increases when dimensions are very high. Most of the available data analysis tools cater to low dimensional spaces. When there are too many features, overfitting also does happen. One solution is to use dimensionality reduction techniques which are discussed in Chapter 8.

3.4 SUPPORT VECTOR MACHINES (SVM)

SVM is, like, logistic regression, intended only for binary classification. This algorithm was propounded in the year 1992 and it became very popular. The classification methods we have seen so far do not perform very well with complex data. In such cases, SVM is a good solution. In this chapter, an intuitive explanation of the method will be presented.

3.4.1 The Maximum Margin Classifier

We know what a decision boundary is. For two-dimensional data, it is a line, for three-dimensional data, it is a plane. For higher dimensional data, it is a hyperplane which is difficult to visualize. Let us start with the case of a linear decision boundary in the case of training data having just two features. The decision boundary is a straight line as in Fig. 3.23a.

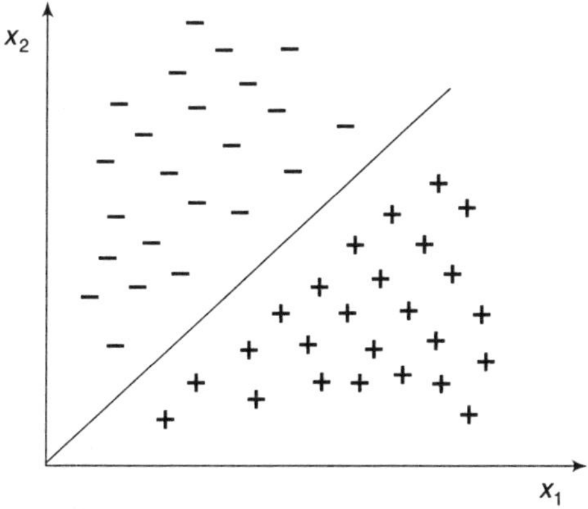

Fig. 3.23 (a)

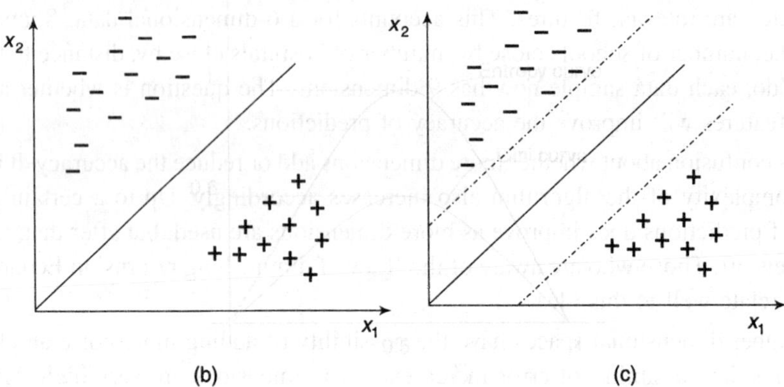

Fig. 3.23 (a) Linear decision boundary for data with two features (b) Space on either side of the decision boundary (c) Maximum margin shown

In Fig. 3.23b, we find a lot of space on either side of the decision boundary, with no training data. The word used for this space is 'margin' (Fig. 3.23c) and when a classifier chooses a decision boundary with the maximum possible margin, it is called a maximum margin classifier. To understand the relevance of 'maximum margin' take a look at Fig. 3.24. All the five lines are candidates for the decision boundary. Which of the five lines is a better choice? Is should be logical to think that a line with a largest margin is likely to be better. This is because it is likely to give a better chance for unknown test data to be on the correct side of the boundary. Thus, the optimization problem to choose the decision boundary is one of getting a separating line with the maximum margin. This is the concept behind the term 'maximal margin classifier'.

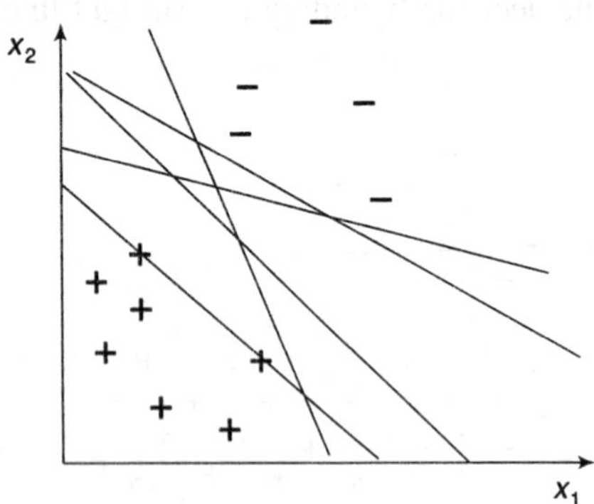

Fig. 3.24 Finding the best decision boundary

Now observe Fig. 3.25. We see that the margin on either side is defined by the training data points which are closest to the decision boundary. These data points are named 'support vectors'. Note that the margin is defined only by these vectors. None of the other training data has anything to do with the margin. This is the reason why this method has the name Support Vector Machine.

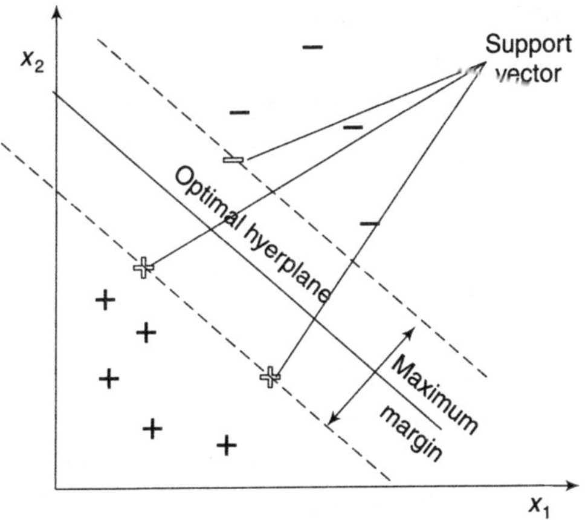

Fig. 3.25 Support vectors defining the boundary

It is clear that support vectors are the critical vectors of the training set that would change the decision boundary, if they are removed. In a '*d*' dimensional space, the problem of finding the optimal hyperplane is an optimization problem that could be solved analytically by using Lagrange multipliers.

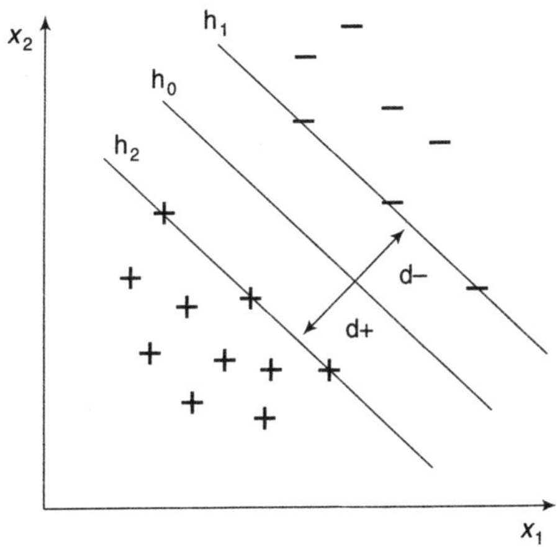

Fig 3.26 Defining the decision boundary by the width of the margin

For a two-dimensional case where there are only two features, the equations for the decision boundary h_0 shown in Fig. 3.26 is:

$$\beta_0 + \beta_1 x = 0 \quad ...(3.62)$$

For h_1 and h_2, the equations are

$$\beta_0 + \beta_1 x > = 0 \quad ...(3.63)$$

$$\beta_0 + \beta_1 x < 0 \quad ...(3.64)$$

The optimization problem is one of finding three hyperplanes such that the margin is maximized.

For '*d*' dimensional data, the corresponding equations are

$$\beta_0 + \beta_1 x_1 + \beta_2 x_2 + \dots\dots\dots + \beta_d x_d = 0 \quad ...(3.65)$$

$$\beta_0 + \beta_1 x_1 + \beta_2 x_2 + \dots\dots\dots + \beta_d x_d < 0 \quad ...(3.66)$$

$$\beta_0 + \beta_1 x_1 + \beta_2 x_2 + \dots\dots\dots + \beta_d x_d >= 0 \quad ...(3.67)$$

The solution of the problem lies in getting the values of β so that our hyperplanes are defined. This is done using training data. For test data, the problem is of finding 'which side of the hyperplane' the data is to be assigned to. We use the values of $x_1, x_2 \dots \dots \dots \dots, x_d$ in Eq. 3.68 and find the sign of $f(x)$. Accordingly, we can say whether it is a Positive or Negative class.

$$\hat{y} = \beta_0 + \beta_1 x_1 + \beta_2 x_2 + \dots\dots\dots + \beta_d x_d \quad ...(3.68)$$

3.4.2 The Hyperparameter, c

So far, we have seen that the aim of the SVM algorithm is to get a decision boundary which clearly demarcates the training data and also gives the maximum margin. This means that there should not be any data points in the space defined as the 'margin'. Getting this is, at best, an ideal case. In practical situations, many outliers may upset this ideal case. There may be positive data samples which are found on the negative side of the hyperplane and vice versa.

In practice, there is hyperparameter 'c' which can be used to get a tradeoff between the margin and correctness of classifying training data. It is seen that margin width and c are inversely related such that:

When c is large ⟶ small margin
When c is small ⟶ large margin

Let's try to understand what this implies.

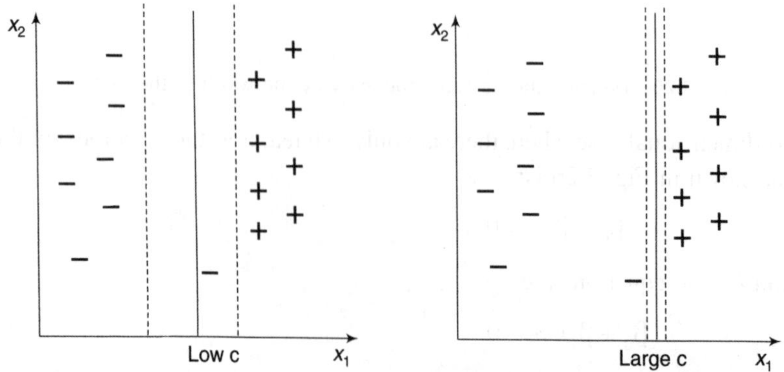

Fig. 3.27 The tradeoff between c and margin (a) Low c (b) Large c

The parameter '*c*' indicates the amount by which the algorithm can opt to allow misclassification of the training data. For small *c*, it will choose a large margin, but some misclassification is allowed. For large values of *c*, the algorithm will choose a smaller-margin hyperplane if that hyperplane does a better job of doing correct classification on the training data.

See how the margin width is affected by the value of *c*. In Fig. 3.27a, a low *c* gives a large margin, but a negative sample is on the wrong side of the decision boundary. In Fig. 3.27b, the decision boundary is changed such that misclassification is avoided, but the end result is that the margin is very small.

We see that when we have a small *c*, the margin is large and there is less chance of misclassification for test data. The real importance of *c* will show up in the test data which is the future data but which we don't have a clue to, during the time of training. A classifier which allows a small amount of misclassification for training data is referred to as a soft margin classifier. Figure 3.27a exemplifies this situation.

3.4.3 Non-linearly Separable Data

If we look at Fig. 3.28 we note that the data is not separable by a line. We say that it is 'non-linearly separable' in a two-dimensional space. To deal with it, SVM has a method which is referred to as the 'Kernel trick'. Figure 3.28 shows that it can be separated by a plane. This has been done by projecting the data onto a higher dimensional space using a 'kernel'. One simple kernel is shown below.

$$X_1 = x_1^2 \quad \text{...(3.69)}$$

$$X_2 = x_2^2 \quad \text{...(3.70)}$$

$$X_3 = \sqrt{2}\, x_1\, x_2 \quad \text{...(3.71)}$$

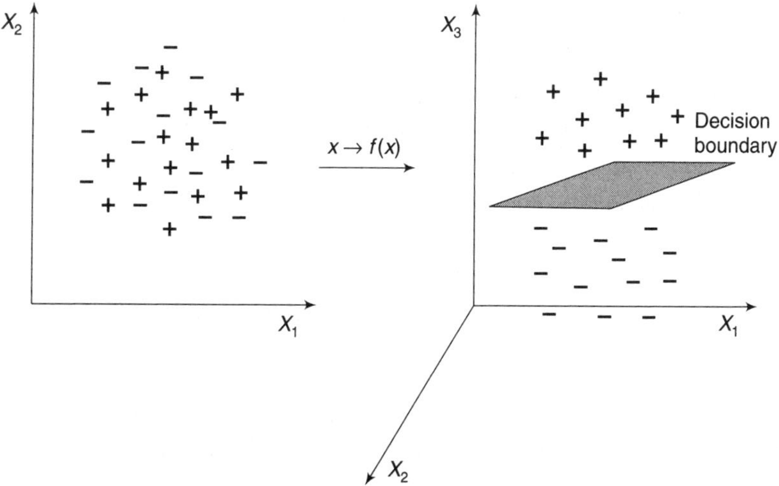

Fig. 3.28 Non-linearly separable data projected to higher dimensions

Pros of SVM

- For linearly separable data, SVMs work amazingly well.
- For data that's almost linearly separable, SVMs can still be made to work pretty well by using the right value of *c*.
- For data that's not linearly separable, we can project data to a space where it is perfectly/almost linearly separable. We typically don't define a specific projection kernel for our data. Instead, we pick from available kernels, tweaking them in some cases, to find one best suited to the data.
- But we can as well define our own kernels.
- Most SVM libraries already come pre-packaged with some popular kernels like *Polynomial, Radial Basis Function (RBF)*, and *Sigmoid*

Conclusion

In this chapter, we have discussed three of the classical machine learning algorithms. One of them is a regression method while the other two are used for classification. These algorithms are very important in order to understand the basic concepts of machine learning. Many of these concepts form the basis for deep learning as well.

Questions

1. Distinguish between MSE and RSS.
2. Is there a difference be the definition of loss and Cost function?
3. Explain the concept behind the gradient descent algorithm.
4. What is the relevance of the word 'linear' in the term 'polynomial linear regression'?
5. How is probability converted to a discrete variable in logistic regression?
6. How does the logit function play a role in logistic regression?
7. What is meant by MLE? Explain.
8. For multi-class classification, can logistic regression be used? Why or why not?
9. Give an example of outliers and some methods to remove them.
10. Why is regularisation done?
11. Why is 'dimensionality' considered a curse if it is high?
12. Define an outlier. Give an example to prove its negative impact on ML.
13. What is the logic behind the term 'support vectors'?
14. How can non-linearly separable data be handled by SVM?

Exercise

1. In machine learning, there is an IID (Independent and Identically Distributed) assumption. Find out what this means. An example should be used to explain this concept.
2. Why is the IID assumption relevant for machine learning?

3. Table 3.9 provides tabulation of the rent obtained per day, for a company that has different types of rooms. Use this data in linear regression and get the parameters of the line used to fit the data. **Observe the data carefully before starting the calculations.**

Table 3.9 Data of rent vs no. of rooms

Store No.	*No. of rooms*	*Rent per day (Rupees)*
1	17	3680
2	15	3990
3	28	6655
4	35	9540
5	12	3310
6	22	5560
7	13	4500
8	3	35650

4. Distinguish between odds and odd ratio by explaining each of them with examples
5. Implement the following algorithms using Python coding.
   (i) Gradient descent with different values of the learning parameter. Show with the help of simulated figures, how convergence rates change with the change in the learning rate. Show this with the help of a simulated figure. Use, say 10 to 12 values of x and corresponding y. For example see this:

   X = [0, 0.18, 0.26, 0.57, 0.48, 0.62, 0.44, 0.55, 0.89, 1.0, 0.92]

   Y = [0, 0.12, 0.44, 0.21, 0.44, 0.32, 0.20, 0.53, 1.0, 0.60, 0.63]

   Note: Don't use this set of data. Make your own data and calculate the Cost function for different number of iterations at different learning rates and make plots for convergence (getting the minimum).

   Note: Figure of gradient descent with different values of the learning parameter are to be shown.

   (ii) Linear regression with small (say, around 20) and large data sets. Use test data and find the Mean Squared Error.

   (a) one parameter-plot the curve

   (1) don't use the function for LR which is available

   (2) use the functions for LR

   Note: As an example, you can make your own data for say, years of experience vs salary.

   This is only a tip. Use your creativity for other data.

(b) more than one parameter–use LR function and a large data set. Scatter plot may be useful.

(iii) Logistic regression: Find the confusion matrix and performance metrics for the data given in Table 3.10.

Table 3.10 Data of placement vs CGPA

CGPA	*Placed = 1, Not Placed = 0*
5	0
5.25	0
5.5	1
5.75	1
6	0
6.5	1
7	1
7.5	0
8	1
8.5	1
8.75	1
9	0

CHAPTER

4

Classical Machine Learning Algorithms-II

In this chapter you will

- learn the K-NN method,
- analyze the Naïve Bayes formulation,
- identify the methods for creating decision trees,
- perform arithmetic calculations for these algorithms,
- discover the advantages of ensemble methods, and
- study one unsupervised learning technique.

4.0 INTRODUCTION

In this chapter, we will take a look at a few more of the classical algorithms. Those that are covered here are intuitive, simple and easy to formulate. Let us start with a very simple one.

4.1 K-NEAREST NEIGHBOURS (K-NN)

This algorithm may be used for both classification and regression, though it is more popular for classification problems. It is also referred to as a lazy algorithm. Deeper mathematical concepts will be found in Section 6.2.2.2. This is a very simple algorithm and one speciality of this is that no model is built. The training data is stored with its labels and when a new data sample comes in, it is assigned to one of the several classes therein.

Assume you are going for a party in your college where parents, students and faculty have been invited. You are late and when you reach there, you find most other people have already reached. As you go in, you find people clustered in different groups. Which group do you join? Not the faculty group or the parents group, for sure. You will mentally search for the friends group with which you have the greatest similarity based on a number of criteria. And then you join that group.

This is the idea behind the K-NN algorithm. The training data is already available with features and labels and when a new test sample is presented, it searches for the class label with which it has the greatest similarity. Similarity is tested based on distances between the new sample and the stored data.

4.1.1 Distance Measures

Euclidean distance is the most popular distance measure. Other distances are Manhattan and Hamming distances. Given two samples x_i and x_i' each of d dimensions, the Euclidean and Manhattan distances between them are defined as:

Euclidean $$\sqrt{\sum_{i=1}^{d} (x_i - x_i')^2} \quad \text{...(4.1)}$$

Manhattan $$\sum_{i=1}^{d} |x_i - x_i'| \quad \text{...(4.2)}$$

The above two distances are used for continuous variables. Hamming distance is used for categorical variables. If the values of x_i and x_i' are the same, the Hamming distance D_H is equal to 0. Otherwise $D_H = 1$.

$$x = x' \Rightarrow D_H = 0$$

$$x \neq x' \Rightarrow D_H = 1$$

$$D_H \neq \sum_{i=1}^{k} \left| x_i \oplus x_i' \right| \quad \text{...(4.3)}$$

4.1.2 The K-NN Method

In Fig. 4.1, we find data that has already been categorised as Class 1 and Class 2. This is the training data which is available as feature values and labels. A new data then comes in. It has

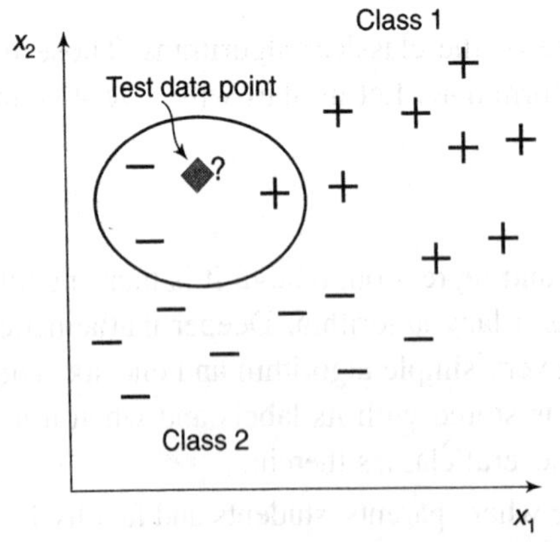

Fig. 4.1 (a) K-NN technique for $K = 3$

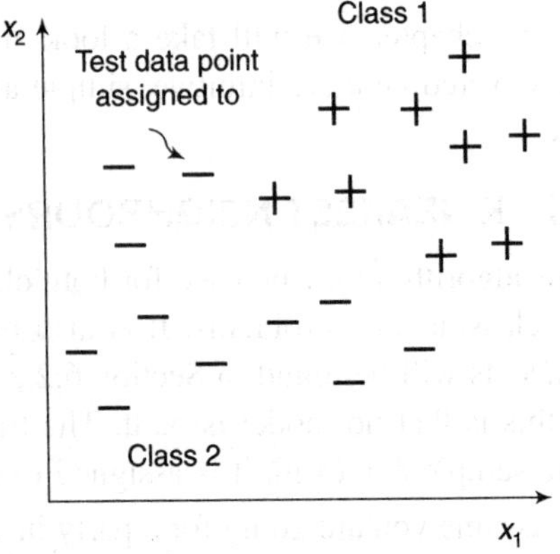

Fig. 4.1 (b) Test data assigned to Class 2

to be assigned to one of the two classes. If $K = 3$, three training data points with the least distance from the test data are to be identified. These are said to be the '3-nearest neighbours' of the test data. In Fig. 4.1a, the three nearest neighbours are shown in a circular box. Two of the nearest neighbours belong to Class 2 (with 'minus sign' symbol). Thus in this example, the new data is categorised as belonging to Class 2. See Fig. 4.1b.

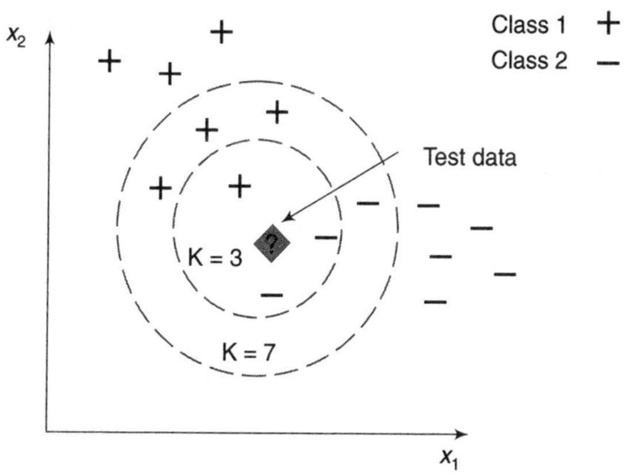

Fig. 4.2 The algorithm for $K = 3$ and $K = 7$

In Fig. 4.2, two values of K are considered – one with, $K = 3$ and another with $K = 7$. With $K = 3$, out of three nearest neighbours, two belong to Class 2. Hence, the test data is assigned to Class 2. But with $K = 7$, we find that out of the seven nearest neighbours, four belong to Class 1. So now, we have to assign the test data to Class 1. This shows that choosing the right value of K is important.

The steps of the K-NN algorithm are:

(i) Select the number K

(ii) Calculate the Euclidean/Manhattan distance of the test data from all the available data.

(iii) Identify the K-nearest neighbours using this calculation.

(iv) Count the number of the neighbours in each category.

(v) Assign the new data point to that category for which the number of nearest neighbours is higher.

4.1.3 Choosing the Value of *K*

There is no defined rule for choosing the value of K. If K is small, the stability of the decision is questionable, If K is very high, the computational cost outweighs the simplicity of the algorithm. Choosing $K = \sqrt{n}$ is suggested by some practitioners. However, it is best to do computations with different values of K, plot it against accuracy and choose the best value.

4.1.4 Pros and Cons of the K-NN Algorithm

Pros: It is simple as no model needs to be built.

Cons: When the number of dimensions increases, the computational complexity becomes too high. Then the algorithm begins to slow down significantly as the training data sample size also increases.

Example 4.1 Data of three breeds of dogs and two features (in inches) are given in Table 4.1, Using $K = 3$ and 5, identify the breed of a dog with features given as: Ear flap length = 6.3 inches, Ear flap width = 3.1 inches.

Table 4.1 Data of dog breeds

Sl No.	*Ear flap length*	*Ear flap width*	*Breed No.*
1	6.3	3.6	1
2	6.6	2.6	3
3	8.6	3	2
4	6.5	3.3	1
5	6.3	3.2	1
6	6.5	3.4	1
7	8.8	2.8	2
8	7.3	2.6	3
9	6.3	2.4	3
10	7.2	2.6	3
11	7	2.9	2
12	7.6	2.2	3
13	6.2	3.7	1
14	7.7	2.3	3
15	8.7	2.9	2

Solution: We calculate the distance between the test data and each training data. Let us use both Euclidean and Manhattan distances and find the rank of the distances of the test data with respect to each training data. (See Table 4.2.)

Table 4.2 Calculation based on Euclidean and Manhattan distances

Training Data				*Calculations using Manhattan distance*		*Calculations using Euclidean distance*	
S. No.	*Ear flap length*	*Ear flap width*	*Breed No.*	*Manhattan distance*	*Rank*	*Euclidean distance*	*Rank*
1	6.3	3.6	1	**0.5**	**3**	**0.5**	**4**
2	6.6	2.6	3	**0.8**	**5**	**0.58**	**5**
3	8.6	3	2	**2.4**	**10**	**2.3**	**13**

4	6.5	3.3	1	**0.4**	**2**	**0.282**	**2**
5	6.3	3.2	1	**0.1**	**1**	**0.1**	**1**
6	6.5	3.4	1	**0.5**	**3**	**0.36**	**3**
7	8.8	2.8	2	**2.8**	**12**	**2.517**	**15**
8	7.3	2.6	3	**1.5**	**8**	**1.118**	**10**
9	6.3	2.4	3	**0.7**	**4**	**0.7**	**7**
10	7.2	2.6	3	**1.4**	**7**	**1.029**	**9**
11	7	2.9	2	**0.9**	**6**	**0.728**	**8**
12	7.6	2.2	3	**2.2**	**9**	**1.581**	**11**
13	6.2	3.7	1	**0.7**	**4**	**0.608**	**6**
14	7.7	2.3	3	**2.2**	**9**	**1.612**	**12**
15	8.7	2.9	2	**2.6**	**11**	**2.408**	**14**

Test Data: Ear lobe length = 6.3 inches, Ear lobe width = 3.1 inches.

Sample calculation for one training data (6.3, 3.6)

Euclidian distance; $\sqrt{\sum_{i=1}^{d} (x_i - x_i')^2} = \sqrt{(x_i - 6.3)^2 + (x_i - 3.1)^2}$

$$\sqrt{(6.3 - 6.3)^2 + (3.6 - 3.1)^2} = 0.5$$

Manhattan distance = $\sum_{i=1}^{d} |(x_i - x_i')| = |(x_i - 6.3)| + |(x_i - 3.1)|$

Sample calculation for one training data (6.3, 3.6): $|(6.3 - 6.3)| + |(3.6 - 3.1)| = 0.5$

Similar calculations are done to find the distance between all the training data and the test data. The results are:

With Manhattan distance, the first 5 nearest neighbours' breeds are (1, 1, 1, 1, 3)

- For $K = 1$, the breed no. is 1
- For $K = 3$, the breed no. is 1
- For $K = 5$, the breed no. is 1

With Euclidean distance, the first 5 nearest neighbours' breeds are (1, 1, 1, 1, 3)

- For $K = 1$, the breed no. is 1
- For $K = 3$, the breed no. is 1
- For $K = 5$, the breed no. is 1

In this problem, we find that the solution we get is the same for the three values of K that have been used.

4.1.5 K-NN for Regression

The following example is a case where K-NN is used for regression.

Example 4.2 A company conducts an interview and announces the salaries of the selected candidates. The salaries are fixed based on the age and a score based on their skills. The score is between 7 and 10. The monthly salary in thousands of rupees is shown in the fourth column of Table 4.3. Find the salary that should be fixed for a person with age 38 and score = 8.2. Use K-NN with $K = 3$.

Table 4.3 Data of salary and scores

Sl No	Score	Age	Salary
1	7.5	45	78
2	7.6	26	46
3	8.4	31	56
4	8.9	34	59
5	7.2	40	74
6	8.7	36	60
7	7.9	24	40
8	8.7	28	62
9	8.3	23	45
10	8.4	32	59

Solution: Test Data: Score = 8.2, Age = 38

Sample calculations for one training data: (7.5, 45)

Euclidian distance = $\sqrt{\sum_{i=1}^{d}(x_i - x_i')^2} = \sqrt{(x_i - 8.2)^2 + (x_i - 38)^2}$

E.g: $\sqrt{(7.5 - 8.2)^2 + (45 - 38)^2} = 7.035$

Manhattan distance = $\sum_{i=1}^{d} |(x_i - x_i')| = |(x_i - 8.2)| + |(x_i - 38)|$

E.g: $|(7.5 - 8.2)| + |(45 - 38)| = 7.7$

Table 4.4 Calculation based on Euclidean and Manhattan distances

Training Data				*Calculations using Manhattan distance*		*Calculations using Euclidean distance*	
Sl No.	*Score*	*Age*	*Salary (K)*	***Manhattan distance***	***Rank***	***Euclidean distance***	***Rank***
1	7.5	45	78	**7.7**	6	**7.035**	6
2	7.6	26	46	**12.6**	8	**12.015**	8
3	8.4	31	56	**7.2**	5	**7.003**	5
4	8.9	34	59	**4.7**	3	**4.06**	3
5	7.2	40	74	**3**	2	**2.236**	2

6	8.7	36	60	**2.5**	**1**	**2.062**	**1**
7	7.9	24	40	**14.3**	**9**	**14.003**	**9**
8	8.7	20	62	**10.5**	**7**	**10.0125**	**7**
9	8.3	23	45	**15.1**	**10**	**15**	**10**
10	8.4	32	59	**6.2**	**4**	**6.003**	**4**

With $K = 3$, The shortest distance is between Sl nos. 6, 5, 4:

Take the average of their salaries: (60 + 74 + 59)/3 = **64.33 K**

With $K = 5$, The shortest distance is between Sl nos. 6, 5, 4, 10, 3:

Take the average of their salaries: (60 + 74 + 59 + 59 + 56)/5 = **61.6 K**

Example 4.3 During the time of recession, a company decides to lay off a number of employees. The decision was made based on their age and monthly salary (listed in rupees). The list is given is Table 4.5. What will be the fate of an employee with age 48 and salary ₹1,42,000? Use K-NN with $K = 5$.

Table 4.5 Data of employees laid off based on salary and age

Sl No.	*Age*	*Salary in Rupees*	*Laid off ? Y/N*
1	24	42,000	N
2	36	59,000	N
3	46	81,000	N
4	20	20,000	N
5	41	1,22,000	N
6	53	20,000	N
7	22	98,000	Y
8	39	65,000	Y
9	60	1,01,000	Y
10	49	2,30,000	Y
11	32	1,60,000	Y

Solution: This problem is best solved after normalization because the age and salary data are on different scales (another way would be to express the salary in 1000s as in Example 4.2). However, let us use the normalization method here.

Normalized values: $$X_N = \frac{X - \text{Min}}{\text{Max} - \text{Min}}$$

$$\text{Min age} = 20, \quad \text{Max age} = 60$$

$$\text{Min salary} = 20{,}000, \quad \text{Max salary} = 230000$$

Sample calculations for one training data: (24,42,000)

$$\text{Normalized age} = \frac{X - 20}{60 - 20} = \frac{24 - 20}{60 - 20} = 0.1$$

$$\text{Normalized salary} = \frac{X - 20000}{230000 - 20000} = \frac{42000 - 20000}{230000 - 20000} = 0.105$$

Table 4.6 Normalized data

Training Data							
S. No.	*Normalized age*	*Normalized salary*	*Laid off? Y/N*	*Manhattan distance*	*Rank*	*Euclidean distance*	*Rank*
1	0.1	0.1	N	1.0763	10	0.766	10
2	0.4	0.177	N	0.6953	7	0.497	7
3	0.65	0.277	N	0.341	2	0.295	2
4	0	0	N	1.281	11	0.909	11
5	0.525	0.46	N	0.27	1	0.200	1
6	0.825	0	N	0.706	8	0.594	8
7	0.05	0.327	Y	0.86	9	0.683	9
8	0.475	0.204	Y	0.592	6	0.430	6
9	1	0.368	Y	0.495	5	0.358	3
10	0.725	0.954	Y	0.444	3	0.420	5
11	0.3	0.636	Y	0.489	4	0.408	4

Test data: Age = 48, salary = ₹1,42,000

With $K = 5$, The shortest distance is between Sl nos. 5, 3, 10, 11, 9 (Manhattan):

The company's decision for lay off is (N,N,Y,Y,Y). *Therefore, the employee is be laid off.*

With Euclidian distance, 5, 3, 9, 11, 10 with lay off decision: N,N,Y,Y,Y. *Therefore, the employee is be laid off.*

With the three example calculations, the exact way of using the K-NN algorithm should be very clear. Next we move on to another simple and popular classification method.

4.2 NAIVE BAYES CLASSIFICATION ALGORITHM

Here we talk about a very popular classification algorithm which is widely used in many tasks and specifically in Natural Language Processing. The popularity stems from its very simple and fast computation. The word 'naïve' which means 'inexperienced in the ways of the world' indicates that the assumptions made by the algorithm are 'not really correct'. Nevertheless the algorithm performs pretty well. Detailed mathematical coverage of Bayesian decision theory is available in Section 5.1.

This technique belongs to the 'generative' class of algorithms, in contrast to the 'discriminative' class of algorithms that we have used so far. Let us make ourselves clear about these terms.

4.2.1 Discriminative Algorithms

Recollect the concept used in the 'logistic regression' classification model we have learnt (Section 3.3) In it the whole idea was centred around creating a 'decision boundary' which models $P(y/x)$ directly and separates the two classes. It discriminates between Positive and Negative samples. It then looks at the test data x and finds a label y which is most likely for it – that is, the test sample will find itself on one or the other side of the decision boundary. Note that here, $P(y/x)$ is modelled directly.

4.2.2 Generative Algorithms

They work in a different manner. We know the Negative and Positive samples in the training set. This means we know $P(y)$.

We also know $P(x/y)$, that is, we know:

(i) For which values of x, is y = Positive
(ii) For which values of x, is y = Negative
(iii) We then:
  (a) Model $P(x/y)$
  (b) Model $P(y)$
  (c) Use Bayes rule to get $P(y/x)$

We build two models based on y = Positive and y = Negative. When a test sample comes, we try to match it with one of these models and see which comes out best. The probabilities that we use are $P(x/y)$ and $P(y)$. The first is a conditional probability. The second is called a 'prior'. Using these two, we get the class for a test sample.

See Fig. 4.3. In it, two sets are shown enclosed in circles–one circle contains values of x which cause output y to be Negative and another contains the x values which cause y to be Positive. Note that the two sets shown in the figure are: the samples of x for y = Positive and for y = Negative. When a test sample x_{test} comes, we must be able to find the set it belongs to. This is done using the Naïve Bayes rule which we will formulate now and is also discussed in Section 5.1.4. Note that the Naïve Bayes algorithm is a generative algorithm.

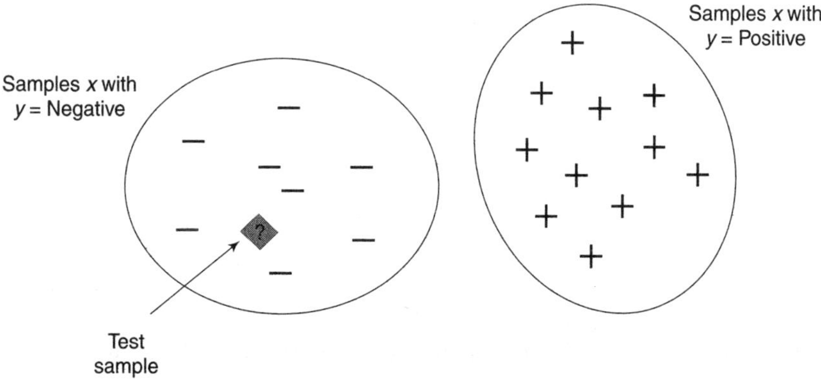

Fig. 4.3 Data corresponding to each class label y and a test data

4.2.3 Naïve Bayes Formulation

The Bayes rule of conditional probability for the variables X and Y is given by the following set of formulas.

$$P(XY) = P(X/Y)\,P(Y) \quad \text{...(4.4)}$$

$$= P(Y/X)\,P(X) \quad \text{...(4.5)}$$

From Eqs. 4.4 and 4.5, we can write

$$P(Y/X) = \frac{P(X/Y)\,P(Y)}{P(X)} \quad \text{...(4.6)}$$

Equation 4.6 is the 'Bayes rule'.

Here:

(i) $P(Y)$ is called the prior.

(ii) $P(X)$ is called the evidence.

(iii) $P(X/Y)$ is called the posterior.

(iv) $P(Y/X)$ is called the likelihood.

Our aim is to get the likelihood for a certain evidence.

For our classification problem, where x is the input data and y is the label, the steps are:

1. Model $P(x/y)$ and $P(y)$
2. Use Bayes rules (Eq. 4.6) to get $P(y/x)$
3. Find $\text{argmax}_y P(y/x)$ $= \text{argmax}_y \frac{P(x/y)P(y)}{P(x)}$ ...(4.7)

$$\approx \text{argmax}_y\, P(x/y)\,P(y) \quad \text{...(4.8)}$$

Let's model it:

Our classification framework is:

Given: Training data:

$$(\boldsymbol{x}_1, y_1), \dots \dots \dots \dots (\boldsymbol{x}_n, y_n)/x_i \in R_d \text{ and } y_i \in Y \quad \text{...(4.9)}$$

Task: Learn a classification function

$$f: R^d \to Y, Y = \{+1, -1\} \quad \text{...(4.10)}$$

We have the training data $(\boldsymbol{x}_i, y_i)$ where $\boldsymbol{x}_i$ is a feature vector and y_i is a discrete label. $\boldsymbol{x}_i$ has d features and there are n number of samples. A new sample $\boldsymbol{x}_{new}$ comes in. It has features $(a_1, a_2, \dots \dots \dots a_d)$.

We want to find the label y_{new} of this new sample. Using Eq. 4.7,

$$y_{new} = \text{argmax}_{y \in Y} \frac{P(a_1, a_2, \dots, a_d|y) * P(y)}{P(a_1, a_2, \dots, a_d)} \quad \text{...(4.11)}$$

The label (Positive or Negative) is one which has the maximum value for $P(y|a_1, a_2, \dots, a_d)$. The denominator of Eq. 4.11 corresponds to a sample x_{new} with feature values $(a_1, a_2, \dots \dots \dots a_d)$.

The denominator can be ignored as is done in Eq. 4.8 to get

$$y_{new} = \text{argmax}_{y \in Y} P(a_1, a_2, ..., a_d|y) * P(y) \quad ...(4.12)$$

This is our final equation.

What is the difficulty in evaluating the two terms in Eq. 4.12?

In the equation, the second term is $P(y)$ which is easily obtained from the training data. The first term denotes the probability of getting a particular label y for a specific **combination of features** which are $(a_1, a_2, \ldots \ldots \ldots a_d)$. This is very difficult to identify and extract from a training set. The solution is to make a simplifying assumption that each feature is independent. So we can use the probability of 'individual features' which give a specific label. This is, we find $\rightarrow P(a_1/y), P(a_2/y) \ldots \ldots \ldots \ldots P(a_d/y)$.

This 'untrue assumption of independence' is why this method is referred to be 'naïve', which implies 'innocent' or 'lacking in judgement'. Based on the assumption of independence of the features, we can write:

$$P(a_1, a_2, ..., a_d|y) = P(a_1/y) \times P(a_2/y) \times \ldots P(a_d/y) \quad ...(4.13)$$

Naive Bayes classifier formulation is:

$$y_{new} = \text{argmax}_{y \in Y} P(y) \, \Pi \, P(a_j|y) \quad ...(4.14)$$

Steps of the method:

(i) Estimate $P(y)$ for each y (by counting the number of occurrences of the label)

(ii) Estimate $P(a_j|y))$ for all $j = 1$ to d

(iii) Use Eq. 4.14 to get y_{new}.

We will find that the implementation for this method is very simple. A numerical example will clarify the method

Example 4.4 A kennel club has a number of puppies for sale. They have the sales record of the puppies which were highly in demand and which got adopted within the first three months of their age. Table 4.7 gives this list of pups and their features. Use the Naïve Bayes method to answer the following questions:

Will the puppies with the following features be adopted?

(i) Brown colour, extra long ears, curly fur

(ii) Cream colour, straight ears, thick fur

Table 4.7 Sales data of puppies

	Colour	*Ear Flap*	*Fur*	*Adopted Yes/No*
1	Brown	Folded	Curly	Y
2	White	Straight	Thick	Y
3	White	Folded	Thick	Y
4	Cream	Folded	Curly	Y
5	Cream	Extra Long (EL)	Curly	N

(Contd.)

6	Brown	Folded	Thick	N
7	Brown	Straight	Thick	Y
8	Cream	Straight	Curly	N
9	Brown	Extra Long (EL)	Thick	Y
10	White	Extra Long (EL)	Curly	N
11	White	Extra Long(EL)	Thick	Y
12	Cream	Folded	Thick	N
13	White	Folded	Curly	Y
14	Brown	Straight	Curly	N
15	White	Straight	Curly	Y

For this problem, we do the counting of data to get the required probabilities.

Solution:

Case 1: Brown colour, Extra long ear flaps, Curly fur

Note that the features for the test data are:

a_1 = Brown colour, a_2 = EL ears, a_3 = Curly fur

The method is to use Eq. 4.14 for both the labels, which are Yes and No

Find $y_{new} = \text{argmax}_{y\ (yes,no)}\ P(y) \times P(\text{Brown}/y)) \times P(\text{EL}/y) \times P(\text{Curly}/y)$

Let's find the 'priors' first.

$P(\text{Yes}) = 9/15$; out of the 15 labels, 9 are 'Yes'

$P(\text{No}) = 6/15$; out of the 15 labels, 6 are 'No'

(i) Conditional probabilities for the label **Yes** are as follows, for the test sample

$P(\text{Brown/Yes}) = 3/9$; For the feature 'colour', out of the 9 'Yes' labels, 3 are 'Brown'

$P(\text{EL/Yes}) = 2/9$; For the feature 'Ear flap', out of the 9 'Yes' labels, 2 are 'EL'

$P(\text{Curly/Yes}) = 4/9$; For the feature 'Fur', out of the 9 'Yes' labels, 4 are 'curly'

Calculating:

$P(\text{Yes}) \times P(\text{Brown/Yes}) \times P(\text{EL/Yes}) \times P(\text{Curly/Yes}) = 9/15 \times 3/9 \times 2/9 \times 4/9 = \mathbf{0.019}$

(ii) Conditional probabilities for the label **No** are as follows, for the test sample

$P(\text{Brown/No}) = 2/6$; For the feature 'colour', out of the 6 'No' labels, 2 are 'Brown'

$P(\text{EL/No}) = 2/6$; For the feature 'Ear flap', out of the 6 'No' labels, 2 are 'EL'

$P(\text{Curly/No}) = 4/6$; For the feature 'Fur', out of the 6 'No' labels, 4 are 'curly'

Calculating: $P(\text{No}) \times P(\text{Brown/No}) \times P(\text{EL/No}) \times P(\text{Curly/No}) = 6/15 \times 2/6 \times 2/6 \times 4/6 = \mathbf{0.029}$

We find that the greater value of y is for the label 'No'.

$$\mathbf{y_{new} = No}$$

We conclude that the puppy with the features listed will not be adopted.

Case 2: (ii) Cream colour, Straight ear flaps, Thick fur

Calculating:

For Label Yes:

$P(\text{Yes}) \times P(\text{Cream/Yes}) \times P(\text{Straight/Yes}) \times P(\text{Thick/Yes}) = 9/15 \times 1/9 \times 3/9 \times 5/9 = 0.01234$

For Label No:

$P(\text{No}) \times P(\text{Cream/No}) \times P(\text{Straight/No}) \times P(\text{Thick/No}) = 6/15 \times 3/6 \times 2/6 \times 2/6 = 0.022$

We find that the greater value of y is for the label 'No'.

$$y_{new} = \textbf{No}.$$

4.2.3.1 Laplace Smoothing

One problem in the method in Example 4.4 is that in Eq. 4.14, any probability term could be zero and then the whole product becomes zero. To avoid this possibility, the solution is to use 'smoothing'. Out of the many methods of smoothing that could be used, let us choose 'Add one Laplace Smoothing' which is quite a simple and popular formulation. In this, each conditional probability is modified by adding the number '1' to the numerator and the count of the training data in the denominator. This can be made clear using a numerical example.

Example 4.5 See Table 4.8 which shows the features of cars for which a car showroom found to be highly preferred or not (Yes/No) by customers. The features used are: Engine cc, number of seats and ground clearance.

The test data is the set of the following features: High engine cc, low clearance, 4 seater. Is this a highly preferred car or not?

Table 4.8 Data of highly preferred/not preferred cars

	Engine cc	*No. of seats*	*Ground clearance*	*Preferred –Yes/No*
1	High	7	High	Y
2	Medium	5	Medium	N
3	Medium	4	Medium	Y
4	Low	4	Low	N
5	Low	5	Low	N
6	Medium	5	High	N
7	Medium	7	High	Y
8	Low	5	Medium	N
9	Medium	7	High	Y

Solution: We use the Naïve Bayes formulation

Test data: High engine cc, low clearance, 4 seater

$$P(\text{Yes}) = 4/9$$

$$P(\text{No}) = 5/9$$

Let us use Eq. 4.14.

For the label 'Yes'

$y_{test} = P(\text{Yes}) \times P(\text{High engine cc/Yes}) \times P(\text{4/Yes}) \times P(\text{Low clearance/Yes})$

$4/9 \times 1/4 \times 1/4 \times 0/4 = 0$

For the label 'No'

$Y_{test} = P(\text{No}) \times P(\text{High Engine cc/No}) \times P(\text{4/No}) \times P(\text{Low clearance/No})$

$= 5/9 \times 0/5 \times 1/5 \times 2/5 = 0$

We find the product to be 0 in both cases.

So we use Laplace smoothing by adding 1 to the numerator and 9 to the denominator of both cases.

For the label Yes: $y_{test} = P(\text{Yes}) \times P(\text{High engine cc/Yes}) \times P(\text{4/Yes}) \times P(\text{low clearance Yes})$

$$= \frac{4}{9} \times \frac{(1+1)}{(4+9)} \times \frac{(1+1)}{(4+9)} \times \frac{(0+1)}{(4+9)} = \mathbf{0.000809}$$

For the label No: $y_{test} = P(\text{No}) \times P(\text{High engine cc/No}) \times P(\text{4/No}) \times P(\text{low clearance/No})$

$$= \frac{5}{9} \times \frac{(0+1)}{(5+9)} \times \frac{(1+1)}{(5+9)} \times \frac{(2+1)}{(5+9)} = \mathbf{0.00121}$$

We find that the greater value of *y* is for the label 'No'.

$$y_{\text{test}} = \text{'No'}$$

We find the label is 'No' .

Note: As the number of features increases, the product corresponding to Eq. 4.14 becomes smaller and smaller until it becomes too small for the computer to handle correctly. This creates an 'underflow' error. To avoid this, the method is to convert each term into a logarithm and then the product becomes a summation. This is covered in Section 16.5.1.

4.3 DECISION TREES

Our next important algorithm is decision trees. Decision trees are widely used in ML as well as in statistics and they have popular names such as ID3, C4.5, CART and regression trees. There are minor differences between them, but all of them work on the concept of information gain. Classification and regression are possible with decision trees. Here we concentrate on examples for classification only.

4.3.1 Flowchart

It is very easy to visualize a decision tree because it is essentially like a flowchart which all of us have learnt in computer programming. But a flowchart shows the tasks in a process and many decisions are taken along the path, whereas a decision tree is expected to make a single classification decision. In machine learning there are well-defined criteria used to reach the decision-making process. An ML problem usually has data with a large number of features. The right features to use for each node of the tree have to be evaluated using the concept of Information gain/Gini index. We use decision trees in a greedy, top down manner.

Let's start with a very simple tree just to understand the flow of our reasoning. What we see now is essentially the 'flowchart' which is familiar to all of us.

Example 4.6 Consider the case of many graduates of the ECE stream. Some of them are good in hardware, others are experts in software. When job offers come, they choose jobs according to their preferences as well as salaries. See Fig. 4.4 which shows the job and salary statistics of last year's placement. There were 60 students who were placed. The first split is the preference of hardware (HW) vs software (SW). For those who preferred HW, the next decision is about the domain. We see that 20 students got placed in the HW domain and 40 in the SW domain. 4 students were selected for the analog domain which paid an average salary of ₹20 lakh per annum. The remaining got an average of 15 LPA in the digital domain. Similarly, there is a split of choice in the software domain as well. The salaries are shown in the 'leaves' of the tree.

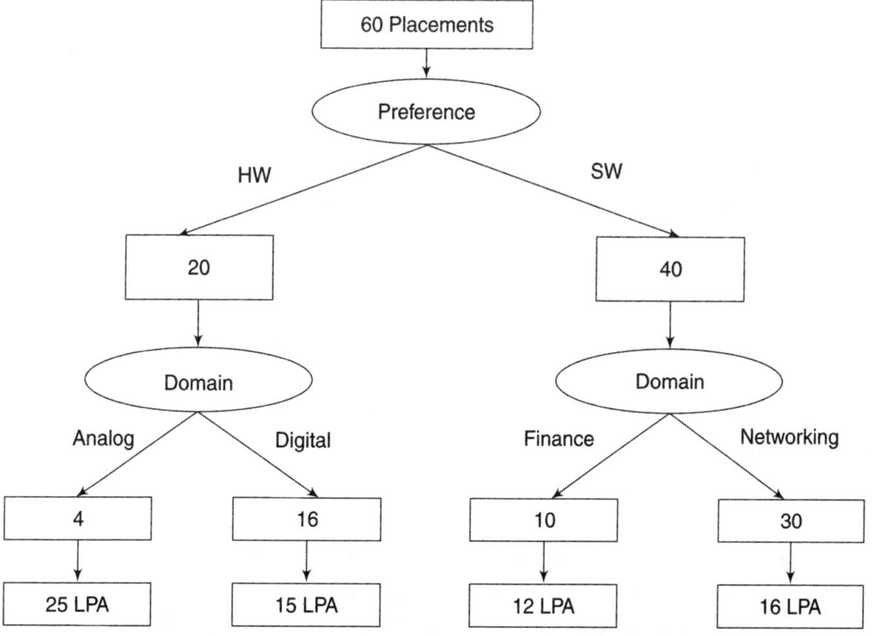

Fig. 4.4 Flowchart of last year's placement

If a student of the current final year sees this flowchart, he can make an evaluation of the choices he has and the salary he will get based on his choice. This is how this flowchart will be useful for him. From this example, it is clear that a flowchart represents the processes on the way to make decisions.

This example tree is simple and has a hierarchical decision making criteria. The first split is based on whether the job domain is hardware or software. The next splits come hierarchically under each of these decisions. Thus, the analog and digital job domains come under the hardware decision, while the 'network' vs 'finance' domains come under the software domain.

This tree may grow with new branches according to the variety of new data. For example, after the decision of taking a software job in the finance category, more choices can be included like: bank vs stock market. In the digital category of hardware jobs, a split maybe made at the node as embedded domain vs VLSI domain. Thus, the tree will become bigger as more subsets of decision making come it. Finally, this tree will become very large, with many nodes and lots of data.

What we see in Fig. 4.4 is a flowchart that we have always been using mentally for our decision making and also for academic problems like writing an algorithm to solve a problem. Now let's see how we use this kind of thinking in making decision trees in ML applications. Keep in mind that 'classification' is the aim. We will start with defining certain important terms relevant to this topic.

4.3.2 Node Purity

The first point to understand in decision trees is the way to choose the feature at each node. What should be the splitting criteria for each node? In Fig. 4.4, the root node split was based on the feature of hardware vs software. We got a split of 20:40 for the data. This node is not 'pure'. Its purity is 66.67% because that percentage of data is on one side and the remaining is on the other side. In our example, the data is of 60 students. If all of them had chosen an SW job, then the node would be 100% pure because the split caused all the data to belong to one class only.

Take another case. 100 students of ECE were asked if they wanted jobs after B.Tech or wanted to go for higher studies. Assume all of them said they wanted jobs now. Since the split caused all the data to be on one side of the node, this node is said to be 100% pure. This is the best case when deciding the criteria for splitting. We get a clear decision boundary here and maximum information gain.

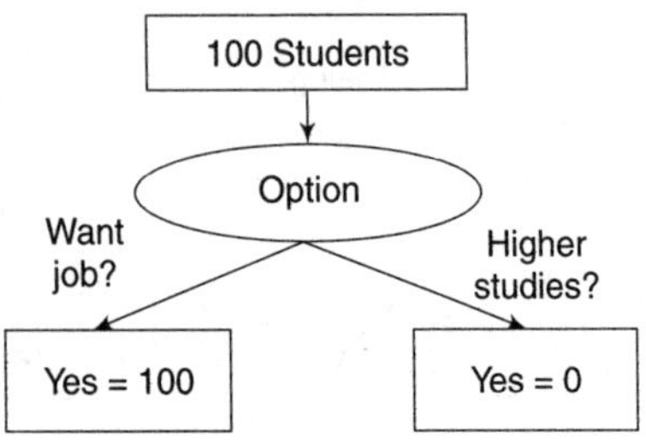

Fig. 4.5 A pure node

At a three-way splitting at a node, if the division of data for classes A, B and C are 60%, 30% and 10%, the purity is denoted as 60%. For a two-way split which divides data into two classes of 50% each, the **impurity** is 100%. This means that a 50% split is not preferred. See Fig. 4.6 which shows pictorially, the gradation of purity for data. If the node is pure, all the data is in one class. In practice, many features will be available for data and therefore we may need to find which feature is best for splitting the data such that each node has maximum purity. These points will become clear soon.

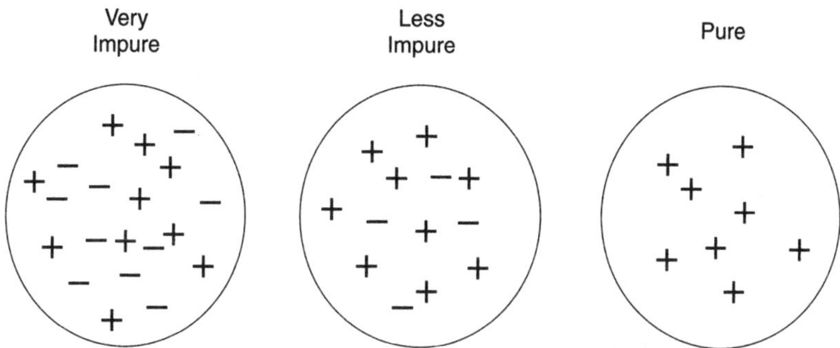

Fig. 4.6 Gradations of node purity

4.3.3 Information Gain at Each Node

In the decision tree methods named ID3 and C4.5, information gain is used as the splitting criteria for each node. We will go into the details of this.

Information gain is based on Entropy which is well known in the field of 'Communications'.

Let us start with the concept of Entropy. For a binary class, with P_1 and P_2 as the probabilities, the definition of Entropy for a set of samples S is

$$\text{Entropy}(S) = -P_1 \log_2 P_1 - P_2 \log_2 P_2 \quad ...(4.15)$$

For C classes

$$\text{Entropy} = \sum_{i=1}^{C} -P_i \log_2 P_i \quad (4.16)$$

See Figure 4.7 in which we see that maximum Entropy is when $P_1 = P_2$. This happens when there is 100% impurity for the node.

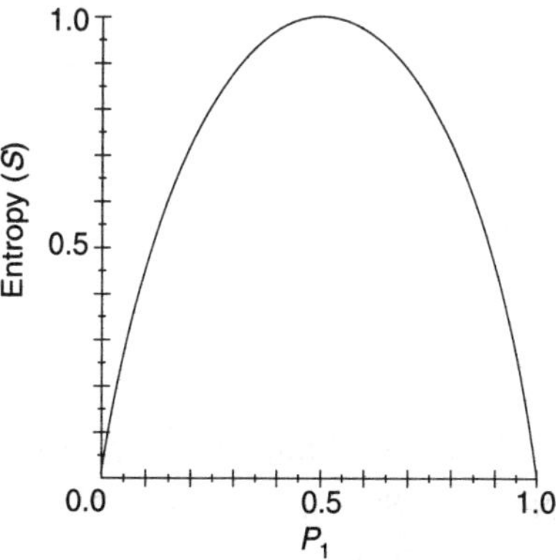

Fig. 4.7 Entropy vs probability P_1

What if all the data belongs to one class?

The probability of that class = 1.

Then Entropy = $-(1 \log_2 1) = 0$

Example 4.7 Calculate the Entropy if there are three classes and $P_1 = \frac{1}{4}, P_2 = \frac{3}{8}$

Solution: $P_1 = \frac{1}{4},\ P_2 = \frac{3}{8}, P_3 = 1 - \left(\frac{1}{4} = \frac{3}{8}\right) = \frac{3}{8}$

$$\text{Entropy} = \sum_{i=1}^{C} -P_i \log_2 P_i = -\frac{1}{4}\log_2\frac{1}{4} - \frac{3}{8}\log_2\frac{3}{8} - \frac{3}{8}\log_2\frac{3}{8} = 1.5612$$

Now that we know about Entropy, we can define Information gain. It is a measure of how much information is provided by a feature about a class. This measure is used to determine the order of the features used in the nodes of a decision tree. The root node is named the parent node, and the sub-nodes are child nodes. At a node,

$$\text{Information gain} = E_{\text{parent}} - E_{\text{children}} \quad \text{...(4.17)}$$

This means that that at any node, information gain is the difference between the entropies of the parent and children. There may be many children, so E_{children} is the average entropy of the children. Information gain measures the expected reduction in entropy caused by partitioning the examples according to the given feature. We need an example calculation to help us visualise this.

$$\text{Gain}(S, A) = \text{Entropy}(S) - \Sigma_{v \in \text{Values}(A)} \frac{S_v}{S} \text{Entropy}(S_v) \quad \text{...(4.18)}$$

S = Samples in the set

Gain (S, A) = Information gain of set S for attribute (feature) A

Entropy (S) = Entropy of parent node

$\frac{S_v}{S}$ = Proportion of samples in the specific child node

Example 4.8 Now let us use the same data in Table 4.7 for which we had used the Naïve Bayes formulation. We can use a decision tree for the same data. We use the data to build a decision based on 'Information gain' as the splitting criteria. This decision tree is used to answer the question:

Given the following features, will these puppies be adopted?

(i) White colour, Extra long ears, Thick fur

(ii) Brown colour, Folded ears, Thick fur

Solution: The data is:

Y – 9, N – 6

Colour → Brown, 5, Y – 3, N – 2 → White, 6, Y – 5, N – 1 → Cream, 4, Y – 1, N – 3

Ear → Folded, 6, Y – 4, N – 2 → Straight, 5, Y – 3, N – 2 → EL, 4, Y – 2, N – 2

Fur → Curly, 7, Y – 5, N – 2 → Thick, 8, Y – 4, N – 4

Entropy of the parent: Entropy (9,6) = $\sum_{i=1}^{C} -p_i \log_2 p_i = -\frac{9}{15}\log_2\frac{9}{15} - \frac{6}{15}\log_2\frac{6}{15} =$ 0.971

Case 1: Feature - Colour

→ Brown, 5, Y – 3, N – 2

$$\text{Entropy (Brown)} = -\frac{3}{5}\log_2\frac{3}{5} - \frac{2}{5}\log_2\frac{2}{5} = 0.971$$

→ White, 6, Y – 5, N – 1

$$\text{Entropy (White)} = -\frac{5}{6}\log_2\frac{5}{6} - \frac{1}{6}\log_2\frac{1}{6} = 0.65$$

→ Cream, 4, Y – 1, N – 3

$$\text{Entropy (Cream)} = -\frac{1}{4}\log_2\frac{1}{4} - \frac{3}{4}\log_2\frac{3}{4} = 0.8113$$

$$\text{Gain (S, Colour)} = \text{Entropy}(S) - \Sigma\frac{S_v}{S} \times \text{Entropy}(S_v)$$

$$= \text{Entropy}(S) - \frac{S_v}{S}\text{(Brown)} \times \text{Entropy (Brown)} - \frac{S_v}{S}\text{(White)} \times \text{Entropy (White)} - \frac{S_v}{S}\text{(Cream)} \times \text{Entropy (Cream)}$$

$$= 0.971 - \frac{5}{15} \times 0.971 - \frac{6}{15} \times 0.65 - \frac{4}{15} \times 0.8113 = \mathbf{0.171}$$

Case 2: Feature - Ear Flap

→ Folded, 6, Y – 4, N – 2

$$\text{Entropy (Folded)} = -\frac{4}{6}\log_2\frac{4}{6} - \frac{2}{6}\log_2\frac{2}{6} = 0.9183$$

→ Straight, 5, Y – 3, N – 2

$$\text{Entropy (Straight)} = -\frac{3}{5}\log_2\frac{3}{5} - \frac{2}{5}\log_2\frac{2}{5} = 0.971$$

→ Extra Long, 4, Y – 2, N – 2

$$\text{Entropy (Extra Long)} = -\frac{2}{4}\log_2\frac{2}{4} - \frac{2}{4}\log_2\frac{2}{4} = 1$$

$$\text{Gain } (S, \text{Colour}) = \text{Entropy}(S) - \Sigma\frac{S_v}{S} \times \text{Entropy}(S_v)$$

$$= \text{Entropy}(S) - \frac{S_v}{S}\text{(Folded)} \times \text{Entropy (Folded)} - \frac{S_v}{S}\text{(Straight)} \times \text{Entropy (Straight)} \frac{S_v}{S}\text{(Extra Long)} \times \text{Entropy (Extra Long)}$$

$$= 0.971 - \frac{6}{15} \times 0.9183 - \frac{5}{15} \times 0.971 - \frac{4}{15} \times 1 = \mathbf{0.0133}$$

Case 3: Feature - Fur

--> Curly, 7, Y – 5, N – 2

$$\text{Entropy (Curly)} = -\frac{5}{7}\log_2\frac{5}{7} - \frac{2}{7}\log_2\frac{2}{7} = 0.8631$$

--> Thick, 8, Y – 4, N – 4

$$\text{Entropy (Thick)} = -\frac{4}{8}\log_2\frac{4}{8} - \frac{4}{8}\log_2\frac{4}{8} = 1$$

$$\text{Gain (S, Fur)} = \text{Entropy } (S) - \Sigma\frac{S_v}{S} \times \text{Entropy } (S_v)$$

$$= \text{Entropy } (S) - \frac{S_v}{S}\text{ (Curly)} \times \text{Entropy (Curly)} - \frac{S_v}{S}\text{ (Thick)} \times \text{Entropy (Thick)}$$

$$= 0.971 - \frac{7}{15} \times 0.8631 - \frac{8}{15} \times 1 = \mathbf{0.0349}$$

The information gain for the three features is tabulated in Table 4.9

Table 4.9 Information gain (at the root node) for the three features

Feature	*Information gain*
Fur	0.0349
Ear flap	0.0133
Colour	0.171

We find that the feature 'Colour' is a better feature for splitting at the root node, because the information gain is higher than that for the feature 'Ear flap' and 'Fur'. So we use the feature 'colour' at the root node and get Fig. 4.8.

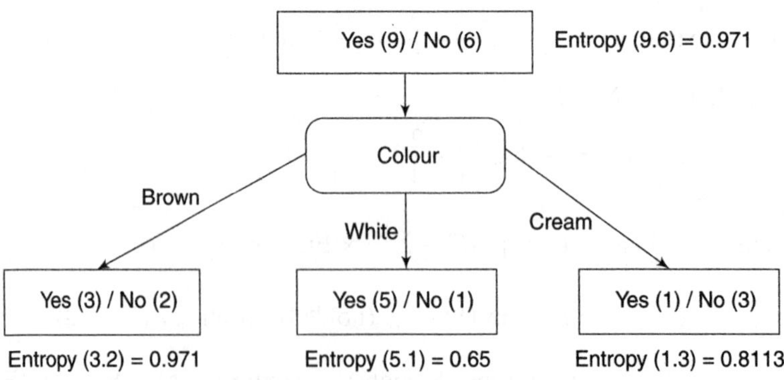

Fig. 4.8 Splitting of the root node with 'colour' as the feature

Then we re-start the process at the children nodes (the colours Brown, White and Cream) to split the tree further and then reach a final decision. Now, by fixing the feature 'Colour' as the first decision node, we will proceed further by considering the remaining attributes for each colour.

For Colour 'Brown'

Case 1: Ear flap

→ Folded – 2, Y – 1, N – 1

$$\text{Entropy(Folded)} = -\frac{1}{2}\log_2\frac{1}{2} - \frac{1}{2}\log_2\frac{1}{2} = 1$$

→ Straight – 2, Y – 1, N – 1

$$\text{Entropy(Straight)} = -\frac{1}{2}\log_2\frac{1}{2} - \frac{1}{2}\log_2\frac{1}{2} = 1$$

→ Extra Long – 1, Y – 1, N – 0

$$\text{Entropy(Extra Long)} = -\frac{1}{1}\log_2\frac{1}{1} - 0 = 0$$

(Refer Fig. 4.8)

$$\text{Gain }(S_{\text{Brown}}, \text{Ear flap}) = \text{Entropy}(S_{\text{Brown}}) - \Sigma\frac{S_v}{S_{\text{Brown}}} \times \text{Entropy}(S_v)$$

$$= \text{Entropy}(S_{\text{Brown}}) - \frac{S_v}{S_{\text{Brown}}}\text{(Folded)} \times \text{Entropy (Folded)}$$

$$-\frac{S_v}{S}\text{(Straight)} \times \textit{Entropy}\text{ (Straight)} - \frac{S_v}{S}\text{(Extra Long)}$$

$$\times \text{ Entropy (Extra Long)}$$

$$= 0.971 - \frac{2}{5} \times 1 - \frac{2}{5} \times 1 - \frac{1}{5} \times 0 = 0.171$$

Case 2: Fur

→ Curly – 2, Y – 1, N – 1

$$\text{Entropy(Curly)} = -\frac{1}{2}\log_2\frac{1}{2} - \frac{1}{2}\log_2\frac{1}{2} = 1$$

→ Thick – 3, Y – 2, N – 1

$$\text{Entropy(Thick)} = -\frac{2}{3}\log_2\frac{2}{3} - \frac{1}{3}\log_2\frac{1}{3} = 0.918$$

$$\text{Gain }(S_{\text{Brown}}, \text{Fur}) = \text{Entropy}(S_{\text{Brown}}) - \Sigma\frac{S_v}{S_{\text{Brown}}} \times \text{Entropy }(S_v)$$

$$= \text{Entropy}(S_{\text{Brown}}) - \frac{S_v}{S_{Brown}}\text{(Curly)} \times \text{Entropy (Curly)} - \frac{Sv}{S}$$

$$\text{(Thick)} \times \text{Entropy (Thick)}$$

$$= 0.971 - \frac{2}{5} \times 1 - \frac{3}{5} \times 0.918 = 0.020$$

Table 4.10 Information gain at node 'Brown'

Feature	*Information gain*
Fur	0.020
Ear structure	0.171

For the child node 'Brown', Table 4.10 shows that *the information gain is higher for the feature 'Ear flap', it will be used as the decision criteria in this stage.*

For Colour 'White

Case 1: Ear flap

→ Folded – 2, Y – 2, N – 0

$$\text{Entropy (Folded)} = -\frac{2}{2}\log_2\frac{2}{2} - 0 = 0$$

→ Straight – 2, Y – 2, N – 0

$$\text{Entropy (Straight)} = -\frac{2}{2}\log_2\frac{2}{2} - 0 = 0$$

→ Extra Long – 2, Y – 1, N – 1

$$\text{Entropy (Extra Long)} = -\frac{1}{2}\log_2\frac{1}{2} - \frac{1}{2}\log_2\frac{1}{2} = 1$$

Refer Fig. 4.8

$$\text{Gain } (S_{\text{White}}, \text{Ear flap}) = \text{Entropy } (S_{\text{White}}) - \Sigma\frac{S_v}{S_{\text{White}}} \times \text{Entropy } (S_v)$$

$$= \text{Entropy } (S_{\text{White}}) - \frac{S_v}{S_{\text{White}}}(\text{Folded}) \times \text{Entropy (Folded)}$$

$$- \frac{S_v}{S}(\text{Straight}) \times \text{Entropy (Straight)}$$

$$- \frac{S_v}{S}(\text{Extra Long}) \times \text{Entropy (Extra Long)}$$

$$= 0.650 - \frac{2}{6}\times 0 - \frac{2}{6}\times 0 - \frac{2}{6}\times 1 = 0.317$$

Case 2: Fur

→ Curly – 3, Y – 2, N – 1

$$\text{Entropy (Curly)} = -\frac{2}{3}\log_2\frac{2}{3} - \frac{1}{3}\log_2\frac{1}{3} = 0.918$$

→ Thick – 3, Y – 3, N – 0

$$\text{Entropy (Thick)} = -\frac{3}{3}\log_2\frac{3}{3} - 0 = 0$$

$$\text{Gain } (S_{\text{White}}, \text{Fur}) = \text{Entropy } (S_{\text{White}}) - \Sigma\frac{S_v}{S_{\text{White}}} \times \text{Entropy } (S_v)$$

$$= \text{Entropy } (S_{\text{White}}) - \frac{S_v}{S_{\text{White}}}(\text{Curly}) \times \text{Entropy (Curly)}$$

$$- \frac{S_v}{S} \text{(Thick)} \times \text{Entropy (Thick)}$$

$$= 0.650 - \frac{3}{6} \times 0.918 - \frac{3}{6} \times 0 = 0.191$$

Table 4.11 Information gain at node 'White'

Feature	Information gain
Fur	0.191
Ear structure	0.317

For the child node 'White, *Table 4.11 shows that the information gain is higher for the feature 'Ear flap', it will be used as the decision criteria in this stage.*

For Colour 'Cream

Case 1: Ear flap

→ Folded – 2, Y – 1, N – 1

$$\text{Entropy (Folded)} = -\frac{1}{2}\log_2\frac{1}{2} - \frac{1}{2}\log_2\frac{1}{2} = 1$$

→ Straight – 1, Y – 0, N – 1

$$\text{Entropy (Straight)} = 0 - \frac{1}{1}\log_2\frac{1}{1} = 0$$

→ Extra Long – 1, Y – 0, N – 1

$$\text{Entropy (Extra Long)} = 0 - \frac{1}{1}\log_2\frac{1}{1} = 0$$

Refer Fig. 4.8

$$\text{Gain } (S_{\text{Cream}}, \text{Ear flap}) = \text{Entropy } (S_{\text{Cream}}) - \Sigma \frac{S_v}{S_{\text{Cream}}} \times \text{Entropy } (S_v)$$

$$= \text{Entropy } (S_{\text{Cream}}) - \frac{S_v}{S_{\text{Cream}}} \text{(Folded)} \times \text{Entropy (Folded)}$$

$$- \frac{S_v}{S} \text{(Straight)} \times \text{Entropy (Straight)} - \frac{S_v}{S} \text{(Extra Long)} \times$$

$$\text{Entropy (Extra Long)}$$

$$= 0.811 - \frac{2}{4} \times 1 - \frac{1}{4} \times 0 - \frac{1}{4} \times 0 = 0.311$$

Case 2: Fur

→ Curly – 3, Y – 1, N – 2

$$\text{Entropy (Curly)} = -\frac{1}{3}\log_2\frac{1}{3} - \frac{2}{3}\log_2\frac{2}{3} = 0.918$$

→ Thick – 1, Y – 0, N – 1

$$\text{Entropy (Thick)} = 0 - \frac{1}{1}\log_2\frac{1}{1} = 0$$

$$\text{Gain }(S_{\text{Cream}}, \text{Fur}) = \text{Entropy}(S_{\text{Cream}}) - \Sigma\frac{S_v}{S_{\text{Cream}}} \times \text{Entropy}(S_v)$$

$$= \text{Entropy}(S_{\text{Cream}}) - \frac{S_v}{S_{\text{Cream}}}(\text{Curly}) \times \text{Entropy (Curly)} - \frac{S_v}{S}(\text{Thick}) \times \text{Entropy (Thick)}$$

$$= 0.811 - \frac{3}{4} \times 0.918 - \frac{1}{4} \times 0 = 0.123$$

Table 4.12 Information gain at node 'Cream'

Feature	*Information gain*
Fur	0.123
Ear flap	0.311

For the child node 'Cream',

Table 4.12 shows that the information gain is higher for the feature 'Ear flap', it will be used as the decision criteria in this stage.

From the above calculations, it can be noted that for all the three colours, next splitting criteria is the feature 'Ear flap'.

Further, the presence of a few pure nodes can be observed directly from Table 4.7. They are leaves of the tree.

- Extra Long ear under Brown colour → Y
- Folded Ear under White colour → Y
- Straight Ear under White colour → Y
- Straight ear under cream colour → N
- Extra Long ear under cream colour → N

Since there is only one more feature remaining for finalizing the decision, no more calculations need to be done. Instead, by observing the table the following pure nodes can be identified.

They also become the leaves of the tree.

- Folded ear under Brown colour → Curly Fur → Y
- Folded ear under Brown colour → Thick Fur → N
- Straight ear under Brown colour → Curly Fur → N
- Straight ear under Brown colour → Thick Fur → Y
- Extra Long ear under White colour → Curly Fur → N
- Extra Long ear under White colour → Thick Fur → Y
- Folded ear under Cream colour → Curly Fur → Y
- Folded ear under Cream colour → Thick Fur → N

Based on the calculations and observations made above, the decision tree is obtained as in Fig. 4.9.

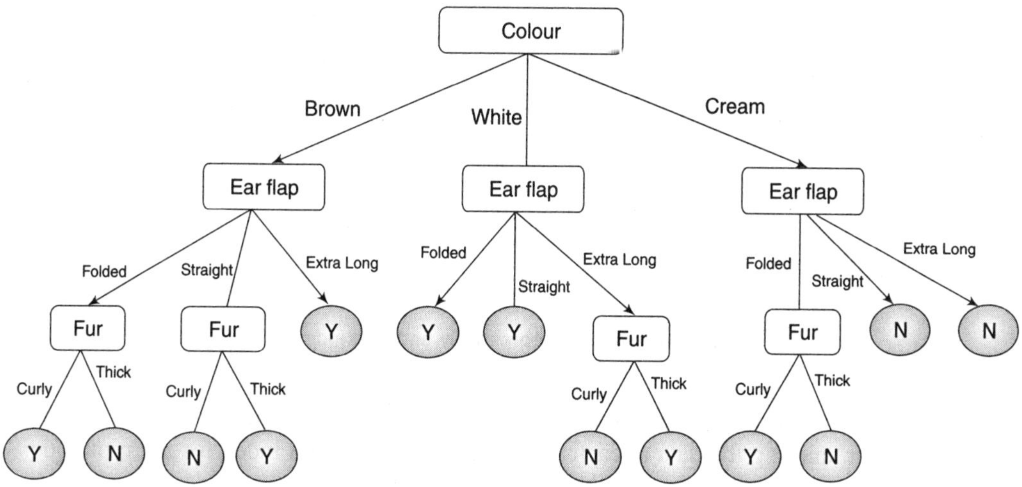

Fig. 4.9 The complete decision tree

Test data:

Moving from the root downwards, the adoption possibilities of the puppies with the following features are given below:

(i) White colour, Extra Long Ears, Thick fur → Y

(ii) Brown colour, Folded ears, Thick fur → N

4.3.4 The Gini Index

Tthere is another index to decide the splitting of data at the nodes of a decision tree. This is called the Gini index. Because this does not involve a 'logarithm' term, there is less computation and so it is the preferred index in many standard decision tree models. In CART (Classification and Regression Tree) and in many Python toolkits (Sci-kit, for example), the use of the Gini index is the default method.

The Gini index also called Gini impurity is calculated by summing the squares of the probabilities of each class and subtracting this sum from 1. Figure 4.10 shows the comparison of the variation of this index as well as Entropy (refer Fig. 4.7) for a binary probability P_1. Note that when node impurity is maximum with $P_1 = P_2$ (each equal to 0.5), Entropy = 1, whereas Gini = 0.5.

$$\text{Gini} = 1 - \sum_{i=1}^{C} P_i^2 \qquad ...(4.19)$$

when there are C classes.

When Gini indices are compared for deciding the splitting criteria, the feature corresponding to the lowest value of the index is to be chosen.

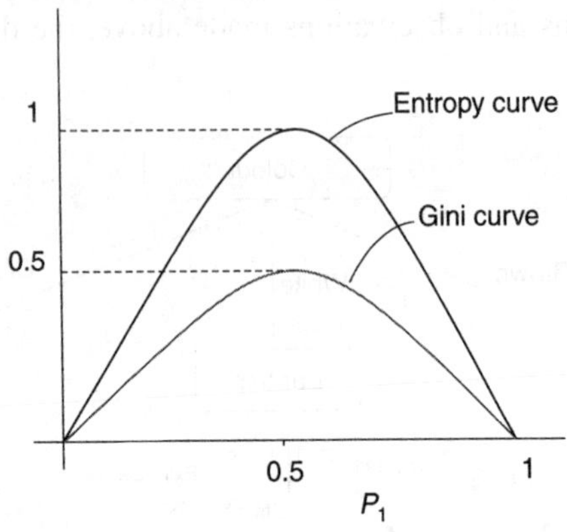

Fig. 4.10 Comparison entropy and Gini index

Example 4.9 Let us use this method for the same data of Example 4.6. We need to find the best feature for splitting the data at each node. Let us use the Gini index for the root node.

Solution:

Case 1: Feature - Colour

Table 4.13 Gini index calculation for the feature 'colour'

	Count	*Yes & No*	*Gini index calculation*
Brown	5	Y – 3, N – 2	Gini = $1 - \left(\left(\frac{5}{6}\right)^2 + \left(\frac{1}{6}\right)^2\right)$ = 0.2779
White	6	Y – 5, N – 1	Gini = $1 - \left(\left(\frac{5}{6}\right)^2 + \left(\frac{1}{6}\right)^2\right)$ = 0.2779
Cream	4	Y – 1, N – 3	Gini = $1 - \left(\left(\frac{1}{4}\right)^2 + \left(\frac{3}{4}\right)^2\right)$ = 0.375
Gain for the node with feature 'Colour', weighted by the fraction (of each colour) of the total data: : $\frac{5}{15} \times 0.48 + \frac{6}{15} \times 0.278 + \frac{4}{15} \times 0.375 = 0.3712$			

Case 2: Feature – Ear flap

Table 4.14 Gini index calculation for the feature 'Ear flap'

Ear	*Count*	*Yes & No*	*Gini Index calculation*
Folded	6	Y – 4, N – 2	Gini = $1 - \left(\left(\frac{4}{6}\right)^2 + \left(\frac{2}{6}\right)^2\right)$ = 0.4445

Straight	5	Y – 3, N – 2	$\text{Gini} = 1 - \left(\left(\frac{3}{5}\right)^2 + \left(\frac{2}{5}\right)^2\right) = 0.48$
Extra Long	4	Y – 2, N – 2	$\text{Gini} = 1 - \left(\left(\frac{2}{4}\right)^2 + \left(\frac{2}{4}\right)^2\right) = 0.5$
Gain for the node with feature 'Ear flap', weighted by the fraction (of each Ear flap) of the total data: : $\frac{6}{15} \times 0.445 + \frac{5}{15} \times 0.48 + \frac{4}{15} \times 0.5 = 0.4708$			

Case 3: Feature – Fur

Table 4.15 Gini index calculation for the feature 'Fur'

	Count	*Yes & No*	*Gini Index calculation*
Curly	7	Y – 5, N – 2	$\text{Gini} = 1 - \left(\left(\frac{5}{7}\right)^2 + \left(\frac{2}{7}\right)^2\right) = 0.408$
Thick	8	Y – 4, N – 4	$\text{Gini} = 1 - \left(\left(\frac{4}{8}\right)^2 + \left(\frac{4}{8}\right)^2\right) = 0.5$
Gain for the node with feature 'Fur', weighted by the fraction (of each fur type) of the total data: : $\frac{7}{15} \times 0.408 + \frac{8}{15} \times 0.5 = 0.4570$			

The results of these calculations is tabulated in Table 4.16

Table 4.16 Comparison of Gini index for the three cases

Feature	*Gini index*
Fur	0.4570
Ear flap	0.4708
Colour	0.3712

The lowest Gini index is of colour. So we choose this feature for splitting at the root node.

Therefore, we should split the root node as in Fig. 4.8. Similar calculations may be done for the next level to get the final decision tree which will be the same as Fig. 4.8.

With this, we conclude our discussion on simple decision trees and go on to a technique which uses decision trees in a different way.

4.4 ENSEMBLE METHODS

The word 'Ensemble' (pronounced 'on-sombl') means "a group of items viewed as a whole rather than individually'. The intuition behind the method is that decisions made collectively by a large group of people are better than that of an individual even if that person is considered to be an expert. In fact, in practical life, we follow this principle regularly. For example, we never depend on one doctor's opinion when planning a serious medical procedure. We take second and third opinions from other doctors. We may also consult friends and people who had done such a procedure earlier. When planning to watch a movie, we check reviews and ask friends too. In short, we use ensemble methods as a natural process of decision making.

This same principle is used in machine learning and such methods are named 'Ensemble methods'. We then avoid the risk of having to rely on the result of a poorly performing ML system. We combine the results of many ML systems to get a final prediction which is likely to be better. High variance and high bias are some of the problems associated with ML. Ensemble methods help in reducing this. High bias is reduced by the technique of boosting and high variance by bagging. We will see these techniques in the forthcoming sections.

4.4.1 How are the Results of Multiple Systems Combined?

4.4.1.1 Majority Voting

Let's start with the classification scenario. Assume we have many classifiers for tackling a problem. How do we decide which is the correct classification result? There will be 'ties' because all classifiers need not give the same prediction. The solution will be to take a 'majority vote'. The steps are:

- Multiple models are used to make predictions.
- The prediction by each model is considered a 'vote'.
- The prediction we get from the majority of the models is used as the final prediction.
- In some methods, different weights are assigned to each classifier. The prediction of those classifiers with higher weights will have a higher impact on the final result.

4.4.1.2 Averaging

Suppose we ask friends to rate a movie, on a scale of 1 to 5. Then, the average rating could be taken. As an example, the average of 5 ratings is:

- (5 + 3 + 3.5 + 4 + 2.5)/5 = 3.6

4.4.1.3 Weighted Averaging

- This is an extension of the averaging method.
- For instance, if two of your colleagues are professional movie critics, while others have no prior experience in this field, then the ratings of these two friends are given more importance as compared to the others.
- For example, the result is calculated as [(5*0.3) + (3*0.24) + (3.5*0.18) + (4*0.18) + (2.5*0.10)]/5 = 3.82

4.4.2 Types of Ensemble Methods

Most of the important ensemble methods use the same ML model. This means that many versions of the same classifier are modelled for the same dataset which is manipulated in such a way that it seems that different datasets are available to each classifier. The most popular type of classifier used in ensemble methods is the decision tree. Many decision trees are used with different data, different number of nodes, etc. Each of them is named a 'weak learner/ base learner'. The ensemble algorithm strengthens the weak learners in such a way that better results are obtained from the 'ensemble' than from a single decision tree. We will show how these methods work. These methods may be divided as sequential and parallel.

4.4.2.1 *Sequential Methods*

In this, different models are created sequentially. In the first iteration, a number of weak learners are used. In the next iteration, these learners are strengthened and training data is selectively 'weighted', based on the misclassified examples of the previous iteration. This sequential process is repeated until the best results are reached. The Adaboost algorithm is a popular method of this type which produces spectacular results. Error rates as low as 3% have been shown to be produced by Adaboost, for the same dataset for which a standard decision tree gave an error of around 25%. Gradient Boost and XG Boost are other sequential ensemble methods.

4.4.2.2 *Parallel Methods*

In this, weak models are generated in parallel. The data is manipulated in such a way as to give the illusion of independence between models. 'Random Forest' is a popular method of this category.

4.4.3 Adaboost

This was developed by Freund and Shapire and their team for a competition, in the year 1997. Let's go into some detail of this method.

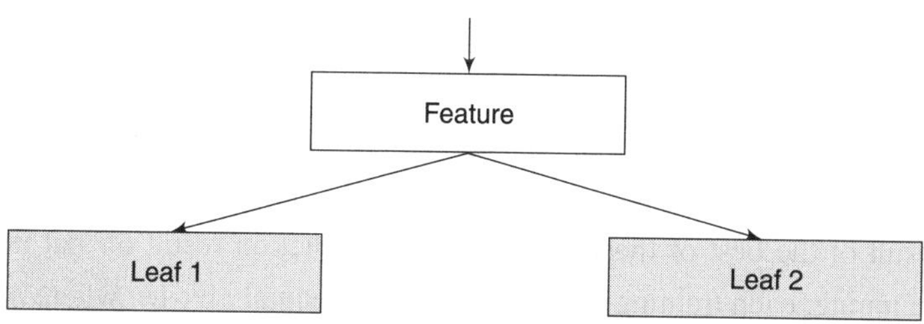

Fig. 4.11 Decision stump

This is a sequential method in which boosting is applied to data and weak learners after every iteration. What is a weak learner? It is defined as a classifier which performs better than random guessing but is still poor in action as a classifier. A decision stump is used as a base (weak) learner in Adaboost. A stump is a decision tree (Fig. 4.11) with just one node and two leaves. This means that only binary classification can be done by this stump and it can use only one feature. The Adaboost algorithm uses a large set of stumps which is then called a 'forest of decision stumps'. This algorithm has two important actions:

(i) Weighting of data samples
(ii) Weighting of the classifiers

Figure 4.12 shows these two aspects. We consider binary classification only. At each of the M iterations, the classifier's error is noted. Based on that, data is modified by 'weighting' the data to get 'modified' data. This process is repeated until the last iteration. The classifier G_m, $m = 1$ to M of every iteration is also given a weight. At the end of the whole process, the final result is decided by a majority vote of the predictions done by all the classifiers, but note that each classifier's weight has an impact on the final prediction.

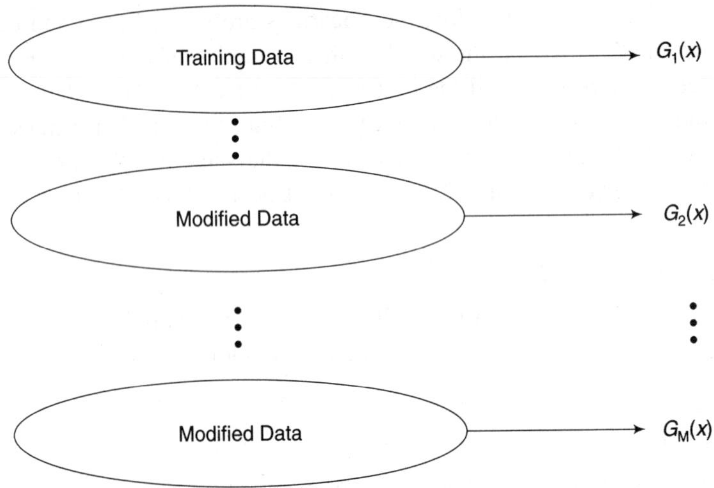

Fig. 4.12 The sequential process in the Adaboost algorithm

At each iteration, the attempt is to reduce the errors of the previous iteration. The steps are listed as:

- Use the training data to train M number of classifiers in a sequential fashion. A classifier consists of a number of decision stumps, one for each feature of the data. The classification result of the best of these stumps is the prediction result of that iteration.
- In the beginning, each training sample is weighted equally by $1/n$ where n is the number of training samples.
- Find the misclassified samples.
- Calculate error err_m using Eq. 4.20 which is just the definition of classification error.

$$err_m := \frac{\sum_{i=1}^{n} w_i 1\{y_i \neq G_m(x_i)\}}{\sum_{i=1}^{n} w_i} \qquad ...(4.20)$$

- Then find α_m from Eq. 4.21

$$\alpha_m = \log\left(\frac{1 - err_m}{err_m}\right) \qquad ...(4.21)$$

$$w_i = w_{i-1} * e^{+/-\alpha_m} \quad ...(4.22)$$

- In the next step, the misclassified training samples are 'weighted' as in Eq. 4.22. w_{i-1} is the weight in the previous iteration.
- This new set of samples are used to train the classifier in the next iteration.
- Figure 4.13 shows the relationship between err_m and α_m. Note that:
  - For a stump with no errors, $err_m = 0$, α_m is large and positive.
  - For a stump with $err_m = 0.5$, $\alpha_m = 0$.
  - For a stump with more than 50% error, α_m is a large negative value.
- Misclassified samples get a higher weight (Eq. 4.22). Due to this, in the next iteration the algorithm pays higher attention to these samples. Correctly classified cases are scaled down correspondingly and so they get reduced attention.
- The error that one classifier makes influences how the next tree is created (because it is a sequential process).
- This sequence of iterations is continued until misclassification reaches a minimum.
- The final prediction $G(x)$ is decided by a majority vote of these M classifiers. But the 'importance' assigned to each classifier is different and that is taken care of by weighting each classifier by α_m. In effect, a more accurate classifier has a higher impact in the final prediction. Note Eq. 4.23.
- Output $G(x) = \text{sign}\left[\sum_{m=1}^{m} a_m G_m(x)\right]$ ...(4.23)

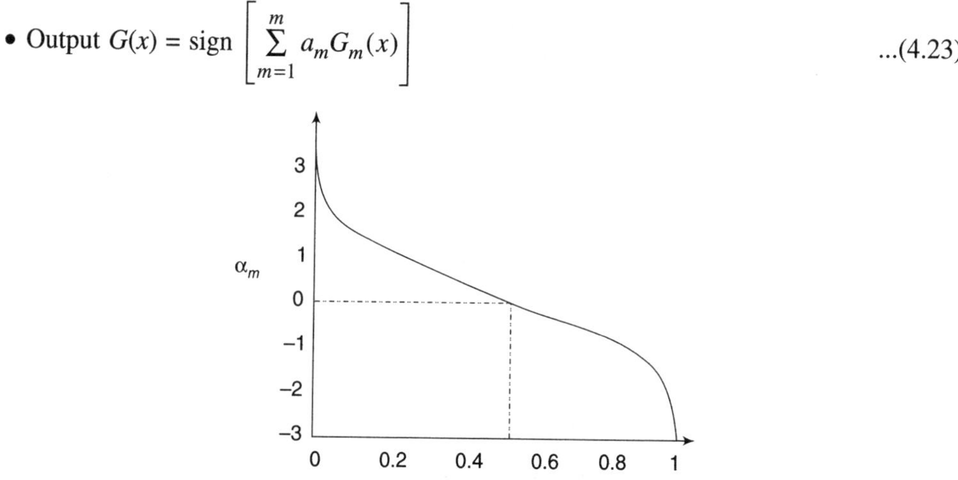

Fig. 4.13 Relationship between err_m and α_m

4.4.4 Bagging

Now we will examine the parallel types of ensemble methods. The first term we encounter here is 'bagging' which stands for 'Bootstrap aggregation'. So we need to know the meaning of the word 'bootstrap' in this context.

What is bootstrapping in the context of bagging?

Bootstrapping is a re-sampling method. The original training dataset is distorted by re-sampling and converted to multiple datasets. The sampling is performed with replacement (a popular technique in statistics). This means that the same data is allowed to occur more than once in the target dataset. In the bootstrapped dataset, some data from the original set may be repeated and others may be left out. See Figure 4.14 which shows that the original set has 4 samples. By using different combinations of these 4 samples, we get 'm' datasets. In the figure, $m = 3$.

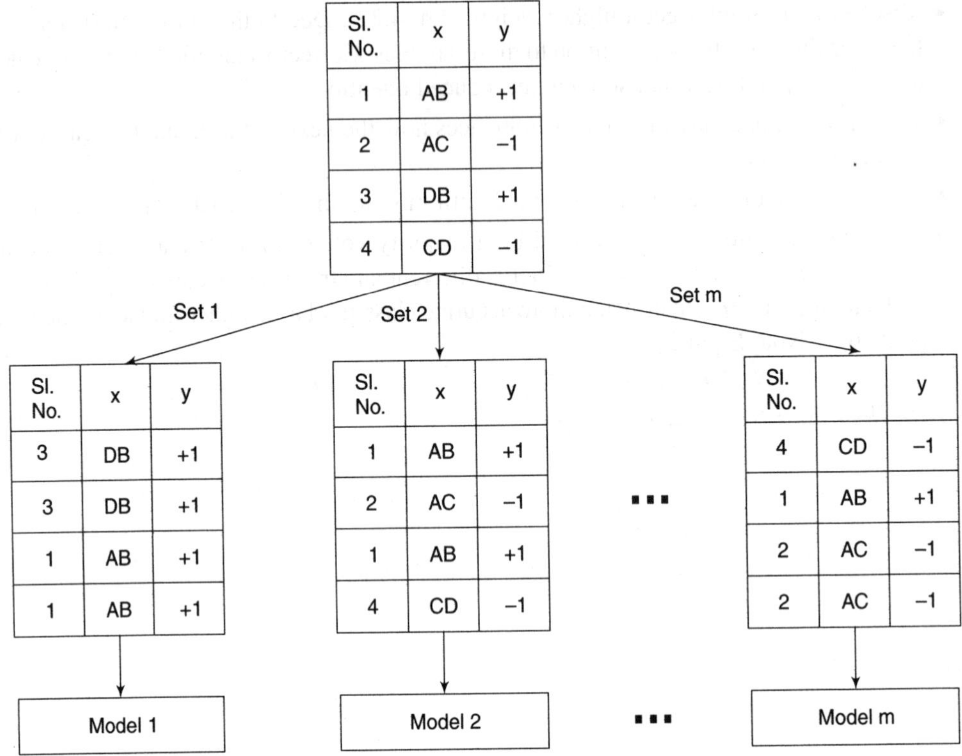

Fig. 4.14 An example of 're-sampling with replacement'

When these 'm' different training sets are applied to 'm' different classifiers and their results are aggregated, we have bagging. Note that all the new subsets have the same size. Decision trees are the most popular of these 'base classifiers'. The final result is taken from the individual classifiers by using majority voting or averaging or weighted averaging.

Steps in the Bagging algorithm:

- Bootstrapping is done by creating random subsets from the original dataset.
- All features of the original are included in the subsets.
- A base classifier (usually a decision tree) is fitted on each of these subsets.
- Predictions from each classifier are combined to get the final result.

4.4.5 Random Forests

This is a popular bagging technique with a slight difference with respect to the bagging that we just talked about. The salient points regarding it are:

- A number of decision trees (a forest of trees) are used.
- At each node in the decision tree, only a 'random' subset of features are considered, to decide the best split. If the number of features in the training set is d,$\sqrt{d}$ is a suggested count for the number of features of each tree in the algorithm.
- The difference between 'Bagging trees' and 'Random Forest' is that in the former, all features of the data are considered for making the different trees. In the latter, only a subset of the features are considered for each tree.

See Figure 4.15 which shows a Random Forest algorithm with '*m*' decision trees. Every tree is trained with the same data but because the feature used for each tree is different, the trees turns out to be different. The final prediction is majority voting (weighted or unweighted).

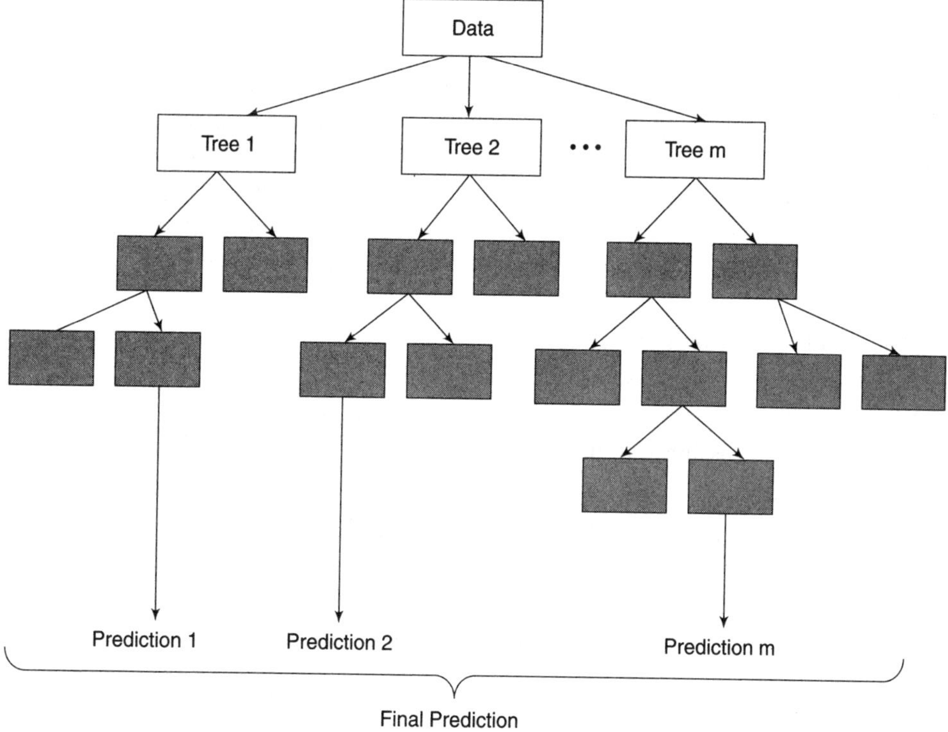

Fig. 4.15 A example of 'Random Forests'

4.5 UNSUPERVISED LEARNING

Unsupervised learning was touched upon briefly in Section 2.2.2. Here we will go into some depth of one unsupervised algorithm. Before that, let us discuss the important applications of this class of methods.

Unsupervised learning is one which deals with data which has no labels. This means that the features of samples are given, but the classes they belong to is not part of the dataset. The algorithm is expected to find inherent patterns in the data and output that as the result. It has a similarity to how human beings learn on their own without any teacher or trainer giving them guidance or prompts.

The applications of this method are many.

(i) When we do internet search for some topic, we get many instances of the same topic from many sources. If you search for the topic 'Himalayas', you will get stories from many news feeds. The technique of 'clustering' is the method used.

(ii) Recommendation engines use the technique of association to tell you about sales trends regarding the items you have purchased or searched for. Messages like "Customers who bought this, also bought this", is because of this method. Movie recommendations based on the movies you have seen earlier is another application.

(iii) Medical imaging is an important application because patterns which may be the symptoms of a disease can be identified using unsupervised learning.

K-means Clustering

Clustering is an unsupervised learning technique in which no labels are given 'a priori'. Let's discuss the K-means clustering algorithm which is very simple and intuitive. The idea behind clustering is that similar items tend to cluster together. Similarity is based on some distance measurement. Euclidean distance and Manhattan distance are popular. When the distance between two items is small, they are assumed to be in the same cluster, and vice versa.

In the K-means clustering, it is necessary to specify the number of clusters (the value of K) we want to get. The steps are listed as:

(i) Start with K centroids taken randomly.

(ii) Each centroid is to be associated with a specific cluster.

(iii) Find the distance between each input sample x_i and the centroids.

(iv) Each sample is assigned to the cluster with which it has the minimum distance.

(v) This is the first iteration.

(vi) Using the samples which are now in each cluster, find new centroids.

(vii) Perform steps iii and iv.

(viii) This set of iterations is to continue until centroid values do not change any more.

(ix) Alternatively, the number of iterations may also be specified.

Example 4.10 A number of people have registered to go for a trip. The organizers want to have two groups based on age. We use K-means clustering for this. The age data is:

15, 15, 16, 19, 19, 20, 20, 21, 22, 28, 35, 40, 41, 42, 43, 44, 60, 61, 65

(a) Find the two clusters starting with centroids $C_1 = 16$, $C_2 = 22$

Solution: Age is the only feature – thus data is single dimensional. Let us start with two centroids: $C_1 = 16$, $C_2 = 22$.

Let us use Manhattan distance which is the magnitude of the difference between two values. The distance between the each x_i and both the centroids are calculated. In Table 4.17, $D1$ is the distance between the corresponding x_i and the first centroid and $D2$ the distance form the second centroid. Whether a sample is to be assigned to cluster 1 or cluster 2, is based on whether $D1$ or $D2$ is the smaller value. This is the first iteration.

The first iteration

After getting the two clusters, the mean of the values in each cluster is taken as the new centroid (as seen in the fifth column of Table 4.17).

Table 4.17 Calculation of second centroid

Age	D1	D2	Cluster	New centroid
15	1	7	1	
15	1	7	1	15.33
16	0	6	1	
19	3	3	2	
19	3	3	2	
20	4	1	2	
20	4	1	2	
21	5	1	2	
22	6	0	2	
28	12	6	2	36.25
35	19	13	2	
40	24	18	2	
41	25	19	2	
42	26	20	2	
43	27	21	2	
44	28	22	2	
60	44	38	2	
61	45	39	2	
65	49	43	2	

Second Iteration; C1 = 15.33, C2 = 36.25

Table 4.18 Calculation of new centroid after the second iteration

Age	D1	D2	Cluster	New centroid
15	0.33	21.25	1	
15	0.33	21.25	1	
16	0.67	20.25	1	
19	3.67	17.25	1	
19	3.67	17.25	1	
20	4.67	16.25	1	
20	4.67	16.25	1	18.55
21	5.67	15.25	1	
22	6.67	14.25	1	

(Contd.)

28	12.67	8.25	2	
35	19.67	1.25	2	
40	24.67	3.75	2	
41	25.67	4.75	2	
42	26.67	5.75	2	
43	27.67	6.75	2	
44	28.67	7.75	2	
60	44.67	23.75	2	45.9
61	45.67	24.75	2	
65	49.67	28.75	2	

We find that after the first iteration, we get new centroids. After the second iterations (Table 4.18) centroids change again. The iterations are to be continued until centroids do not change any more. The algorithm can also be handled by fixing the number of iterations to be done.

Example 4.11 A farmer has a number of teak trees in his farm. He wants to cut and sell them. The buyer told him that two sets are possible—the ones with lesser volume of wood would be used for doors and windows of houses, and the ones with more volume would be used for furniture. A clustering algorithm is used for this to be done automatically. Only two clusters are needed. Use Euclidean distance as the metric. The data is two-dimensional – height and diameter of the trees (Table 4.19). Initial centroid C1(x, x') 12, 75 C2(x, x') = 30, 50. This information is shown in Fig. 4.16.

Table 4.19 Data of trees

No	*Height in metres (x_i)*	*Diameter in cm (x')*	*Euclidean distance From C1*
1	10	100	25.07
2	20	150	75.42
3	30	170	96.69
4	12	75	0
5	35	140	68.94
6	12	80	5
7	22	120	46.09
8	22	90	18.02
9	8	85	10.77
10	28	110	38.48
11	19	140	65.37
12	21	75	9
13	10	65	10.19

14	25	50	28.17
15	11	40	35.01
16	16	45	30.26

Table 4.20 Calculation of new centroids after one iteration

No.	*Height in meters (x)*	*Diameter in cm (x′)*	*Euclidean distance From C1*	*Euclidean distance from C2*	*Cluster*	*New centroid*
1	10	100	25.07	53.85	1	(19.15, 107.69)
2	20	150	75.42	100.49	1	
3	30	170	96.69	120	1	
4	12	75	0	30.80	1	
5	35	140	68.94	90.13	1	
6	12	80	5	34.98	1	
7	22	120	46.09	70.45	1	
8	22	90	18.02	40.79	1	
9	8	85	10.77	41.34	1	
10	28	110	38.48	60.03	1	
11	19	140	65.37	90.66	1	
12	21	75	9	26.57	1	
13	10	65	10.19	25	1	
14	25	50	28.17	5	2	(17.33, 45)
15	11	40	35.01	21.47	2	
16	16	45	30.26	14.86	2	

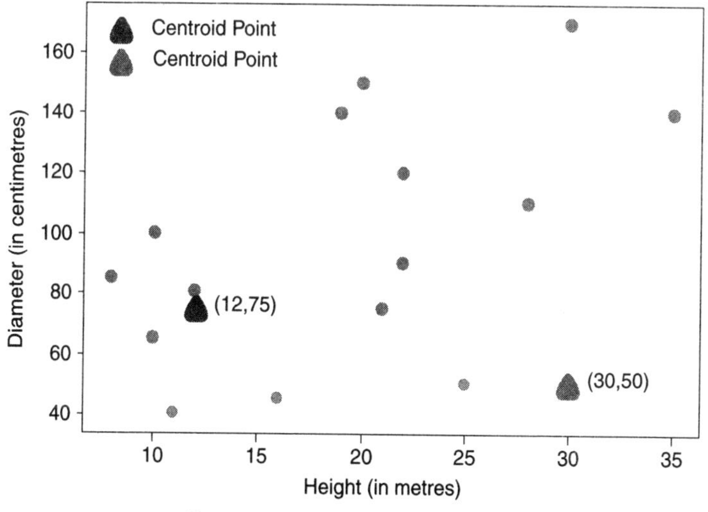

Fig. 4.16 Data and initial centroids

Now we do the 2nd iteration with centroids obtained from the previous iteration (Table 4.21)

Table 4.21 Calculation of new centroids after second iteration

No.	Height in metres (x)	Diameter in cm (x′)	Euclidian distance from new centroid (C1*)	Euclidian distance from new centroid (C2*)	Cluster	New centroid
1	10	100	11.95	55.48	1	(20.6, 118.5)
2	20	150	42.31	105.03	1	
3	30	170	63.24	125.64	1	
4	35	140	35.98	96.62	1	
5	12	80	28.60	35.40	1	
6	22	120	12.63	75.14	1	
7	22	90	17.91	45.24	1	
8	8	85	25.28	41.07	1	
9	28	110	9.14	65.86	1	
10	19	140	32.30	95.01	1	
11	25	50	57.98	9.15	2	(15.83, 58.33)
12	12	75	33.46	30.46	2	
13	11	40	68.18	8.06	2	
14	21	75	32.74	30.22	2	
15	16	45	62.77	1.33	2	
16	10	65	43.66	21.30	2	

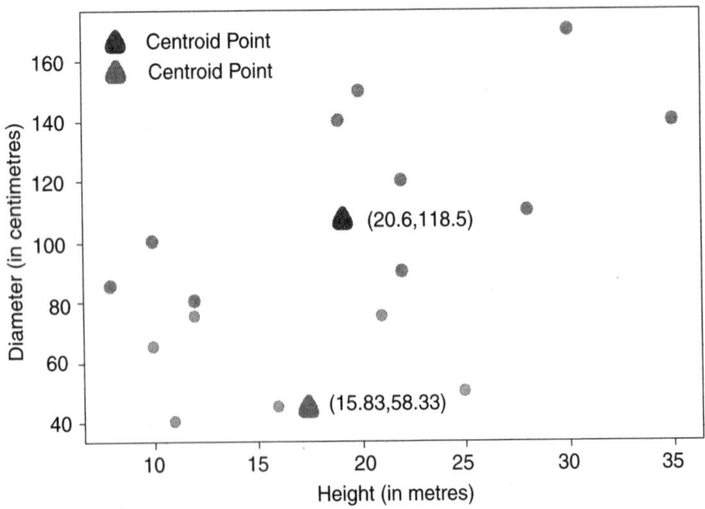

Fig. 4.17 New centroids after 1st iteration

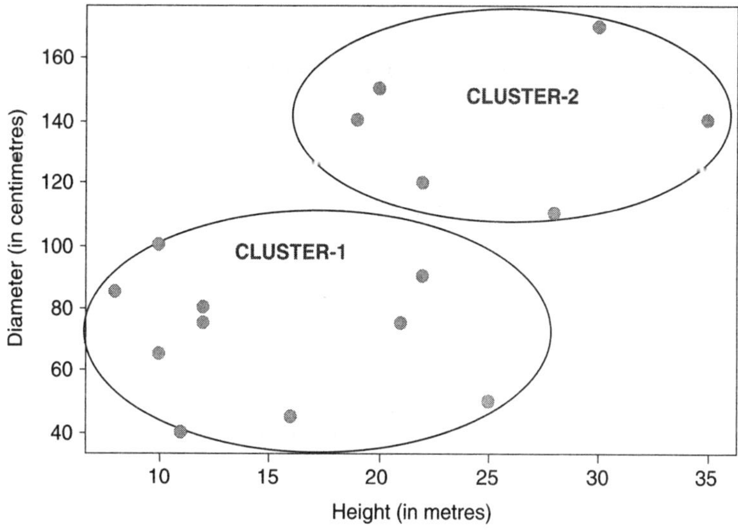

Fig. 4.18 The clusters after the convergence of the algorithm

Table 4.21 and Fig. 4.17 show the new centroids after the second iteration. Figure 4.18 gives two clusters after the convergence of the algorithm.

Conclusion

With this, we come to an end of the most popular classical machine learning algorithms. Codes for all of them will be taken up separately.

Questions

1. How does the 'curse of dimensionality' affect the K-NN algorithm?
2. How is the value of K selected?
3. Why is the Naïve Bayes formulation included in the 'generative' class of algorithms?
4. What is the simplification done in the Naïve Bayes method? Is it a realistic simplification?
5. Define information gain as is used for creating decision trees.
6. Why is the Gini index preferred over the entropy based method for creating decision trees?
7. What is the difference between bagging and boosting?
8. How is a 'weak learner' defined?
9. How does Random Forest differ from ordinary bagging?
10. What is the principle used in K-means clustering?

Exercise

1. For Naïve Bayes and decision trees, the features used in this chapter are categorical. How will the algorithm manage if the features are numeric? Give an example to prove your point.
2. What are the pros and cons of (i) K-NN, (ii) Naïve Bayes, and (iii) Decision trees?
3. Use the K-means clustering algorithm to cluster the following 8 examples into 3 clusters. [4]

   Note: Use Euclidean distance as the metric. **Perform three iterations**

   A1 = (2, 10), A2 = (2, 5), A3 = (8, 40), A4 = (7, 5), A6 = (6, 4), A7 = (6, 4), A7 = (1, 2), A8 = (4, 9).

   The initial seeds are A1, A4 and A7.
4. A family living in Kerala plans to spend their summer vacation in Goa. They look for a house to stay. Table 4.22 shows the data about the features of houses and whether they are highly preferred by customers or not.

Table 4.22 Data of houses in Goa

Name of locality	*Rent <40K ?*	*Area>2000 Sq ft ?*	*Hospital nearby ?*	*Beach nearby ?*	*Preferred ?*
Anjuna	Y	N	N	Y	Y
Old Goa	N	N	N	N	N
Candolim	N	N	Y	N	N
Calangute	Y	N	Y	N	Y
Morjim	N	N	y	Y	N
Siolim	N	N	N	Y	N
Margao	Y	Y	N	Y	Y
Mormugao	N	Y	N	Y	N
Canacona	Y	N	N	Y	Y
Aldona	Y	N	y	N	N
Vasco	N	N	y	Y	N
Colva	N	N	y	Y	N
Mapusa	Y	N	N	Y	Y
Chorao	N	N	Y	N	N
Dona Paula	N	N	y	Y	N
Miramar	N	N	N	Y	N
Palolem	N	N	N	Y	Y
Vagator	N	Y	N	Y	N
Divar	Y	N	Y	N	Y
Benaulim	N	Y	N	Y	N

Use this data and the Naïve Bayes formulation to determine whether a house with the following attributes is highly preferred or not.

Rent <40K	*Area>2000 Sq ft*	*Hospital nearby*	*Beach nearby*	*Preferred?*
Y	N	Y	N	

5. Fourteen cars as listed below have been classified as P (plus) and M (minus) based on a few attributes. A decision tree is to be fitted on these data. Do the relevant calculations for deciding the best divisions of the decision tree. Find the complete tree and find the class of the car with the following data:

   Colour: Blue, Type: Minivan, No of doors: 2, Tyre : JK

   (i) Use information gain (ii) Use Gini index

	Colour	*Type*	*No of doors*	*Tyre brand*	*Class*
1	RED	SUV	2	JK	P
2	BLUE	MINIVAN	4	JK	M
3	GREEN	HATCHBACK	4	JK	M
4	RED	MINIVAN	4	CEAT	M
5	GREEN	HATCHBACK	2	CEAT	P
6	GREEN	SUV	4	CEAT	M
7	BLUE	SUV	2	CEAT	M
8	BLUE	HATCHBACK	2	JK	P
9	RED	SUV	2	CEAT	M
10	BLUE	HATCHBACK	4	CEAT	M
11	GREEN	SUV	4	JK	P
12	RED	HATCHBACK	2	CEAT	P
13	GREEN	SUV	2	CEAT	M
14	GREEN	MINIVAN	4	JK	M

CHAPTER

5

Bayesian Classifier

In this chapter you will

- learn the fundamentals of classical Bayesian decision theory,
- understand the conditions form minimum-error-ratmmme classification,
- study the essence of discriminant functions, and
- familiarize with the popular Naive Bayes classifier.

5.0 INTRODUCTION

In this chapter, we will discuss the popular Bayesian decision theory which is considered the classical form of classifier in machine learning. It is the fundamental statistical approach for classification problems and is considered the backbone of most of the advanced classifiers available today. This classical classifier is based on the assumption that all probability values are known in prior. This assumption holds when enough samples are available or the analytical model for the feature construction is ready.

5.1 BAYESIAN DECISION THEORY

Suppose we have an l-class classification problem with classes $\{C_1, C_2, ..., C_l\}$. Let $\mathbf{x}$ be any arbitrary sample in the sample set. The aim of this classifier is to fit the correct class among the given classes for the sample $\mathbf{x}$ by exploiting the statistical properties of the samples. The informal representation of Bayes formula can be represented as follows.

$$\text{Posterior} = \frac{\text{Likelihood} \times \text{Prior}}{\text{Evidence}} \quad ...(5.1)$$

Now, our goal is to define each of the terms mentioned in Eq. 5.1.

- *Prior:* It is a priori probability defined for each class of the particular classification problem. Let $P(C_i)$ be the prior for the ith class. These prior probabilities define our prior knowledge how likely an event (corresponds to a particular class) occurs before it actually occurs.
- *Likelihood:* It is also known as class-conditional probability density function We consider the feature vector, **x** is a continuous random variable whose distribution relies on the characteristics of different classes and is expressed as $p(\mathbf{x}/C_i)$ (for i^{th} class). It is simply the probability of a certain observation given the classes.
- *Posterior:* Suppose we know the class-conditional probability density function and prior. Then, by using Bayes rule, we can formulate the reverse conditional probability $P(C_i/\mathbf{x})$ as follows.

$$P(C_i/\mathbf{x}) = \frac{p(\mathbf{x}/C_i)\, P(C_i)}{p(\mathbf{x})} \qquad ...(5.2)$$

  This conditional probability density function is known as posterior or aposteriori probability density function. It is the probability of a certain class given our observations.
- *Evidence:* $p(\mathbf{x})$ is the evidence term. We can define it using total probability theorem as follows.

$$p(\mathbf{x}) = \sum_{i=1}^{l} p(\mathbf{x}/C_i)\, P(C_i) \qquad ...(5.3)$$

  The evidence factor is merely considered a scale factor which guarantees that the sum of posterior probabilities is one.

5.1.1 Bayes Decision Rule

If we have an observation (feature vector), **x**, our aim would be to map **x** to the correct class by exploiting the statistical properties. In that scenario, we can calculate the posterior probability for all classes based on the input observation **x**. Then, we can naturally decide that the true class for **x** is the class with maximum posterior probability, $P(C_i/\mathbf{x})$. Mathematically, it can be represented as

$$C^* = \max_i P(C_i/\mathbf{x}) \qquad ...(5.4)$$

where, C^* indicates the true class for the observation **x** with maximum posterior probability. For a two-class problem, the Bayes decision rule is defined as

Decide C_1 if $P(C_1/\mathbf{x}) > P(C_2/\mathbf{x})$; otherwise decide C_2 ...(5.5)

Equivalently,

Decide C_1 if $P(\mathbf{x}/C_1)P(C_1) > P(\mathbf{x}/C_2)P(C_2)$; otherwise decide C_2 ...(5.6)

Since the evidence term is merely a scaling factor, it is not considered in Eq. 5.6. Thus, the evidence term is unimportant for a decision making. We can formulate the following inferences based on Eq. 5.6.

1. If $p(\mathbf{x}/C_1) = p(\mathbf{x}/C_2)$ for some $\mathbf{x}$, the decision making will completely rely on the prior probabilities.
2. If $P(C_1) = P(C_2)$ (classes are improbable in nature), then the decision will only depend on the likelihood values.

Thus, both the factors such as likelihood values and prior probabilities have important roles in decision making. In Bayesian decision theory, both these factors are combined to achieve maximum classification accuracy. The probability of error whenever we make a decision is an important parameter and is portrayed in the following section.

5.1.2 Probability of Error

The dual of the process of maximizing the posterior probabilities is the minimization of probability of error. Thus, we can formulate the Bayesian decision rule, either by maximizing the posterior probabilities or minimizing the probability of error in the decision making. Both of these processes serve the same objective. For a two-class classification problem, the probability of error is

$$P(\text{error}) = \min\ [P(C_1/\mathbf{x}), P(C_2/\mathbf{x})] \qquad ...(5.7)$$

Then, the average probability of error is

$$P(\text{error}) = \int_{-\infty}^{+\infty} P(\text{error}/\mathbf{x})p(\mathbf{x})d\mathbf{x} \qquad ...(5.8)$$

Thus, we can reformulate the Bayesian decision rule by using Eq. 5.7. This is because of the fact that for every $\mathbf{x}$ we ensure that $P(\text{error}/\mathbf{x})$ possesses the least value as per Eq. 5.8.

> Thus, decision making relies on both the priors and the likelihoods and Bayes Decision Rule combines them to achieve the minimum probability of error.

5.1.3 Loss Functions

In classification problems, instead of directly allowing the classification, we generally allow some actions. These actions allow us the possibility of rejection in close cases. We can measure the cost of these actions by using *loss functions*. A loss function helps us to convert a probability determination into a decision.

Suppose an l-class classification problem with categories or classes, $\{C_1, C_2, ..., C_l\}$ and k possible actions, say $\{a_1, a_2, ..., a_k\}$. Then, the informal definition of loss function is the function $L(a_i/C_j)$ which defines the loss occurred while taking the action a_i when the true class is C_j. One of the classical examples for the loss function is zero-one loss function and is as follows.

$$L(a_i/C_j) = \begin{cases} 0 & i = j \\ 1 & \text{otherwise} \end{cases} \qquad ...(5.9)$$

Thus, it assigns no loss to a correct decision ($i = j$ indicates the correct decision) and uniform unit loss to an incorrect decision.

Suppose **x** is our observation and we consider the action, a_i for it. Then, for the true category (class), C_j, the loss function is $L(a_i/C_j)$ Now, the expected loss or conditional risk associated with the action a_i is by definition,

$$R(a_i/\mathbf{x}) = \sum_{j=1}^{l} L(a_i/C_j)P(C_j/\mathbf{x}) \qquad ...(5.10)$$

Thus, we can minimize the expected loss by choosing a suitable action that minimizes the expected loss or conditional risk for an observation **x**.

By considering the zero-one loss function as given in Eq. 5.9, the zero-one expected loss or conditional risk is

$$R(a_i/\mathbf{x}) = \sum_{i \neq j} P(C_j/\mathbf{x}) = 1 - P(C_i/\mathbf{x}) \qquad ...(5.11)$$

Here, we consider $l = k$ and there is a one-to-one mapping between the classes and the actions.

Decision Rule

Now, our aim is to formulate a decision rule that minimizes the risk in an l-class classification problem. It is a function that guides us which action is the best suitable one for every possible observation. Thus, this function, say $a(\mathbf{x})$ suggests us one of the a_i for every observation **x** which minimizes the overall risk. The overall risk is the expected loss or conditional risk for a given decision rule. For any possible observation, **x**, it is defined as,

$$R = \int R(a(\mathbf{x})/\mathbf{x})p(\mathbf{x})d\mathbf{x} \qquad ...(5.12)$$

Clearly, we want the decision rule, $a(.)$ that minimizes $R(a(\mathbf{x})/\mathbf{x})$ for all possible **x**. Thus, Bayes decision rule gives us a method for minimizing the overall risk. We must select the action that minimizes the conditional risk and can be mathematically represented as,

$$a^* = \min_{a_i} R(a_i/\mathbf{x}) \qquad ...(5.13)$$

$$a^* = \min_{a_i} \sum_{j=1}^{l} L(a_i/C_j)P(C_j/\mathbf{x}) \qquad ...(5.14)$$

The resulting minimum risk is known as the Bayes risk, R^* and is the best we can do.

Two-Category Classification Example

Let us consider a two-class classification problem with two actions, a_1 when the true class is C_1 and a_2 for C_2. The equations for conditional risk as per Eq. 5.10 are:

$$R(a_1/\mathbf{x}) = L(a_1/C_1)P(C_1/\mathbf{x}) + L(a_1/C_2)P(C_2/\mathbf{x}) \quad ...(5.15)$$

$$R(a_2/\mathbf{x}) = L(a_2/C_1)P(C_1/\mathbf{x}) + L(a_2/C_2)P(C_2/\mathbf{x}) \quad ...(5.16)$$

Even if there are many ways for making the decision rule, the fundamental decision rule is to

$$\text{decide } C_1 \text{ if } R(a_1/\mathbf{x}) < R(a_2/\mathbf{x}) \quad ...(5.17)$$

$$\text{if } L(a_1/C_1)P(C_1/\mathbf{x}) + L(a_1/C_2)P(C_2/\mathbf{x}) < L(a_2/C_1)P(C_1/\mathbf{x}) + L(a_2/C_2)P(C_2/\mathbf{x}) \quad ...(5.18)$$

On rearranging, we may write it as

$$\text{decide } C_1 \text{ if } (L(a_2/C_1) - L(a_1/C_1))P(C_1/\mathbf{x}) > (L(a_1/C_2) - L(a_2/C_2))P(C_2/\mathbf{x}) \quad ...(5.19)$$

Thus, now the decision rule depends on both the posterior probabilities and the loss differences. We must scale the posterior probabilities with the loss differences (which are generally positive).

On expanding Eq. 5.19 via Bayes rule, we can write it as

$$\text{decide } C_1 \text{ if } (L(a_2/C_1) - L(a_1/C_1)p(\mathbf{x}/C_1)P(C_1)$$
$$> (L(a_1/C_2) - L(a_2/C_2))p(\mathbf{x}/C_2)P(C_2) \quad ...(5.20)$$

and otherwise, decide C_2.

Under the reasonable assumption that $(L(a_2/C_1) > L(a_1/C_1))$, we can rewrite Eq. 5.20 as follows.

$$\text{decide } C_1 \text{ if } \frac{P(\mathbf{x}/(C_1)}{P(\mathbf{x}/C_2)} > \frac{(L(a_1/C_2) - L(a_2/C_2))P(C_2)}{((L(a_2/C_1) - L(a_1\ /C_1))P(C_1)} \quad ...(5.21)$$

and otherwise, decide C_2.

The LHS of Eq. 5.21 is called the *likelihood ratio*.

Thus, we can say the Bayes decision rule says to decide C_1 if the likelihood ratio exceeds a threshold that is independent of the observation **x**.

5.1.4 Naive Bayes Rule

If the dependency among the features in the feature vector, $\mathbf{x} = (x_1, x_2, ..., x_d)^T$ in the d-dimensional feature space are not known, we may consider that the features are conditionally independent of each other. Thus, our posterior probability density function becomes,

$$P(C_k/\mathbf{x}) = \prod_{i=1}^{d} p(C_k/x_i) \quad ...(5.22)$$

In such cases, the Bayesian classifier becomes

$$P(C_k/\mathbf{x}) \propto \prod_{i=1}^{d} p(x_i/C_k) \quad ...(5.23)$$

This equation circumvents the issue of dimensionality in case of higher dimensional feature vector. This classifier is known *as Naive Bayes classifier* or *idiot Bayes classifier*. It performs surprising good accuracy even in cases violating the underlying independence assumption. Because of its simplicity and reasonable accuracy, Naive Bayes classifier acts as simplest surrogate for conventional Bayes classifier.

5.2 RECEIVER OPERATING CHARACTERISTICS

One of the fundamental ways of analysing a classifier is signal detection theory. It is basically a measure of distance between two Gaussian distributions and has great role in radar signalling and similar applications. Consider the following experimental setup as an example.

Suppose we are interested in detecting a single pulse. We may read an internal signal x. We may assume that the signal is distributed about mean μ_1 when no external signal is present and around mean μ_2 when an external signal is present. We assume that the distributions have same variance, say σ and possesses Gaussian distribution, $p(x/C_i) \sim N(\mu_i, \sigma)$. Generally, the classifier (detector) uses some threshold, $\bar{x}$ to decide if the external signal is present. In many cases, we may not have the idea about the value of $\bar{x}$ and even the means and standard deviation of the distributions. In that scenario, the term discriminability characterizes how difficult it will be to decide if the external signal is present without knowing $\bar{x}$. One form of discriminability is

$$d^* = \frac{|\mu_2 - \mu_1|}{\sigma} \qquad \text{....(5.24)}$$

Even if we do not know μ_1, μ_2, σ or $\bar{x}$, we can find d^* by using a receiver operating characteristic (ROC) curve, as long as we know the nature for some experiments. We consider the following four probabilities for defining the ROC curve.

1. *Hit:* A hit is the probability that the internal signal is above $\bar{x}$ given that the external signal is present.

$$P(x > \bar{x}/x \in C_2) \qquad \text{...(5.25)}$$

2. *Correct Rejection:* A correct rejection is the probability that the internal signal is below $\bar{x}$ given that the external signal is not present.

$$P(x < \bar{x}/x \in C_1) \qquad \text{...(5.26)}$$

3. *False Alarm:* A false alarm is the probability that the internal signal is above $\bar{x}$ despite there being no external signal present.

$$P(x > \bar{x}/x \in C_1) \qquad \text{...(5.27)}$$

4. *Miss:* A miss is the probability that the internal signal is below $\bar{x}$ given that the external signal is present.

$$P(x < \bar{x}/x \in C_2) \qquad \text{...(5.28)}$$

We can experimentally determine these probabilities, if sufficient number of trials are available for our experiment. We can plot a two-dimensional graph, i.e., false alarm versus hit for a fixed value of threshold, $\bar{x}$. The basic idea is to assume our densities are fixed (reasonable) but vary our threshold $\bar{x}$, which will thus change the false alarm and hit rates. Thus, the receiver operating characteristic plots the hit rate against the false alarm rate as shown in Fig. 5.1. Form this figure, we can understand that any pair of hit and false alarm rates passes through only one ROC curve. Thus, we can determine the discriminability, d^* from these rates. From Fig. 5.1, it is clear that $d^* = 3$ gives us the best shape for the curve as it gives the least values for false alarm rate and highest values for the hit rate.

In practice, we can simply vary a control parameter for the decision rule and plot the ROC curve and it helps us to formulate the best decision rule. We can simply extend the concept of ROC curve for multidimensional distributions.

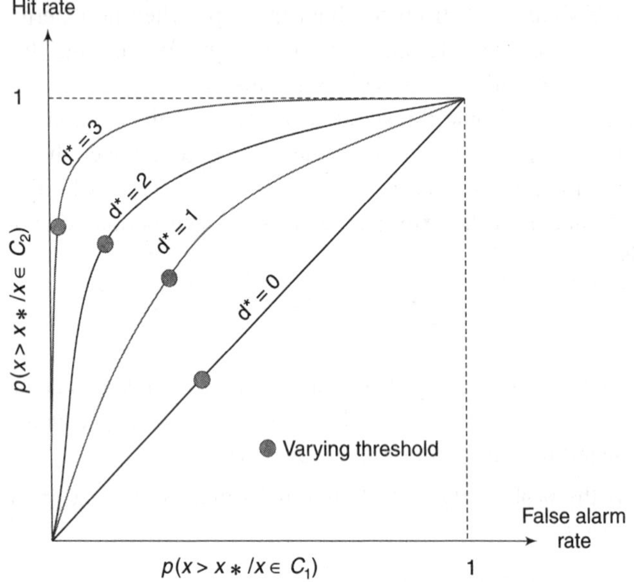

Fig. 5.1 Receiver operating characteristics (Ref: Duda et. al., *Pattern Classification*)

5.3 DISCRIMINANT ANALYSIS

We can represent the classifiers in different ways. One of the most popular and useful methods is in terms of discriminant functions. In this case, we use a set of functions say, $g_i(\mathbf{x})$, $i = 1, 2, ..., l$ for an l-class classification problem with an arbitrary feature vector (observation) $\mathbf{x}$; where i points the ith class. Let's say $g_i(\mathbf{x})$ is a discriminant function for the ith class.

The decision rule for a multi-class classifier can be formulated as

$$\text{decide } C_i \text{ if } g_i(\mathbf{x}) > g_j(\mathbf{x}); \quad \forall i \neq j \qquad ...(5.29)$$

or, equivalently

$$i^* = \max_i g_i(\mathbf{x}); \quad \text{decide } C_i \qquad ...(5.30)$$

Discriminants as a network

We can view the discriminant classifier as a network (for l classes and a d-dimensional input vector) as shown in Fig. 5.2.

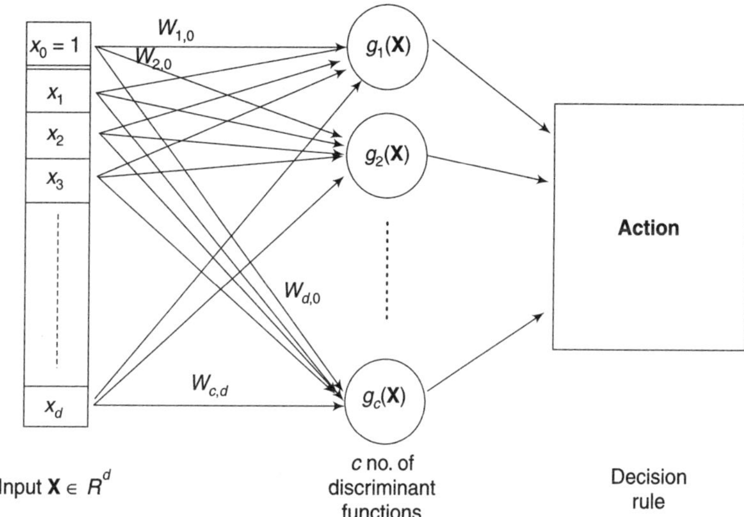

Fig. 5.2 Discriminants as a network

Figure 5.2 describes the functional structure of a general statistical pattern classifier which consists of d input features and c discriminant functions corresponding to c-classes. The arrows in the figure show the direction of the flow of information. The subsequent steps determine which of the discriminant values is the maximum, and categorizes the input pattern accordingly.

Minimum Conditional Risk Discriminant

Since the minimum conditional risk corresponds to the maximum discriminant, we can formulate a relationship between the conditional risk and discriminant function in the following manner.

$$g_i(\mathbf{x}) = -R(a_i/\mathbf{x}) \qquad ...(5.31)$$

$$= -\sum_{j=1}^{l} L(a_i/C_j)P(C_j/\mathbf{x}) \qquad ...(5.32)$$

This means that the minimum conditional risk corresponds to the maximum discriminant. Thus, in the case of zero-one loss function, the Bayes discriminant function can be further simplified into:

$$g_i(\mathbf{x}) = P(C_i/\mathbf{x}) \qquad ...(5.33)$$

Uniqueness of Discriminants

Is the choice of discriminant functions unique?

No! The following operations can be performed on discriminant functions without influencing the decision.

- Multiply by some positive constant.
- Shift them by some additive constant.
- For monotonically increasing function $f(.)$, we can replace each $g_i(\mathbf{x})$ by $f(g_i(\mathbf{x}))$ without affecting the classification performance.

Thus, we can prefer any discriminant function for minimum-error-rate classification in such a way that it must be simpler to understand or to compute than others. Some of the examples for discriminant functions are listed below.

$$g_i(\mathbf{x}) = P(C_i/\mathbf{x}) = \frac{p(\mathbf{x}/C_i)\mathbf{P}(C_i)}{\sum_{j=1}^{l} p(\mathbf{x}/C_j)P(C_j)} \quad ...(5.34)$$

$$g_i(\mathbf{x}) = p(\mathbf{x}/C_i)P(C_i) \quad ...(5.35)$$

$$P(C_i/x) = \ln p(\mathbf{x}/C_i) + \ln P(C_i) \quad ...(5.36)$$

where, ln represents the natural logarithm.

Decision Regions

The effect of any decision rule is to divide the feature space into decision regions. One decision region corresponds to one particular class; say i^{th} class corresponds to i^{th} decision region R_i. The decision rule in terms of the decision regions and discriminant functions is reformulated as,

$$\textit{If } g_i(\mathbf{x}) > g_j(\mathbf{x});\ \forall i \neq j, \text{ then } \mathbf{x} \text{ belongs to } R_i \quad ...(5.37)$$

The *decision boundaries* separate the regions; where ties occur among the largest discriminant functions.

$$g(\mathbf{x}) = g_1(\mathbf{x}) - g_2(\mathbf{x}) \quad ...(5.38)$$

where, $g_1(\mathbf{x})$ and $g_2(\mathbf{x})$ represent the discriminant functions corresponding to class-1 (C_1) and class-2 (C_2) respectively for the observation $\mathbf{x}$. The corresponding decision rule for dichotomizer is,

$$\text{decide } C_1 \text{ if } g(\mathbf{x}) > 0; \text{ otherwise decide } C_2 \quad ...(5.39)$$

If $g(\mathbf{x}) = 0$, then $\mathbf{x}$ lies on the decision boundary and can be assigned to either class. Some examples for such manipulations of the discriminant function are,

$$g(\mathbf{x}) = P(C_1/\mathbf{x}) - P(C_2/\mathbf{x}) \quad ...(5.40)$$

$$g(\mathbf{x}) = \ln \frac{P(\mathbf{x}/C_1)}{P(\mathbf{x}/C_2)} + \ln \frac{P(C_1)}{P(C_2)} \qquad ...(5.41)$$

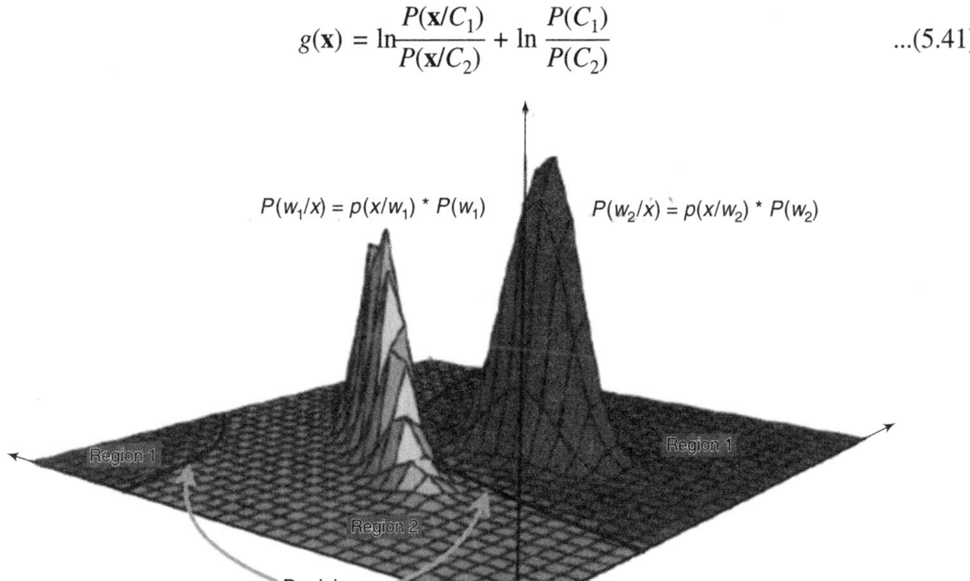

Fig. 5.3 Decision regions of a two-class classification problem

5.4 LINEAR DISCRIMINANT FUNCTIONS

Linear discriminant functions are the discriminant functions that are either linear in the components of **x**, or linear in some given set of functions of **x**. They are popular because of their easiness in computations. Generally, they can be optimal, if the sufficient conditions for distributions are met. Even if they are not optimal, we can make some compromises on the performance in order to utilize the benefits of their simplicity in operations.

There are two important methods to estimate the discriminant functions. First one, the *generative* approaches estimate the discriminant function by first estimating the probability distribution of the patterns belonging to each class. Second one, the *discriminant* approaches estimate the discriminant function explicitly, without assuming a probability distribution. In this section, we assume that we know the proper forms for the discriminant functions. The problem of finding a linear discriminant function is considered as a problem of minimizing a criterion function such as sample risk or training error.

5.4.1 Linear Discriminant Functions for Two-class Category Case

As mentioned earlier, the more common form of discriminant functions for two-class problems is to use a single discriminant function (dichotomizer) instead of two:

$$g(\mathbf{x}) = g_1(\mathbf{x}) - g_2(\mathbf{x}) \qquad ...(5.42)$$

A *linear discriminant* as dichotomizer has the following form (discriminative approach):

$$g(\mathbf{x}) = w^T \mathbf{x} + w_0 = \sum_{i=1}^{d} w_i x_i + w_0 \qquad ...(5.43)$$

where, **w** is the weight vector and w_0 represents the bias or threshold weight. This forms the following decision rule:

$$\text{Decide } C_1 \text{ if } g(\mathbf{x}) > 0; \text{ and decide } C_2 \text{ if } g(\mathbf{x}) < 0 \qquad ...(5.44)$$

As per Eq. 5.43, the decision rule can be interpreted as the observation **x** is mapped to the class C_1 if the inner product, $\mathbf{w}^T\mathbf{x}$ is greater than the threshold $-w_0$ and class C_2 otherwise. The illustration of a simple linear classifier is given in Fig. 5.4.

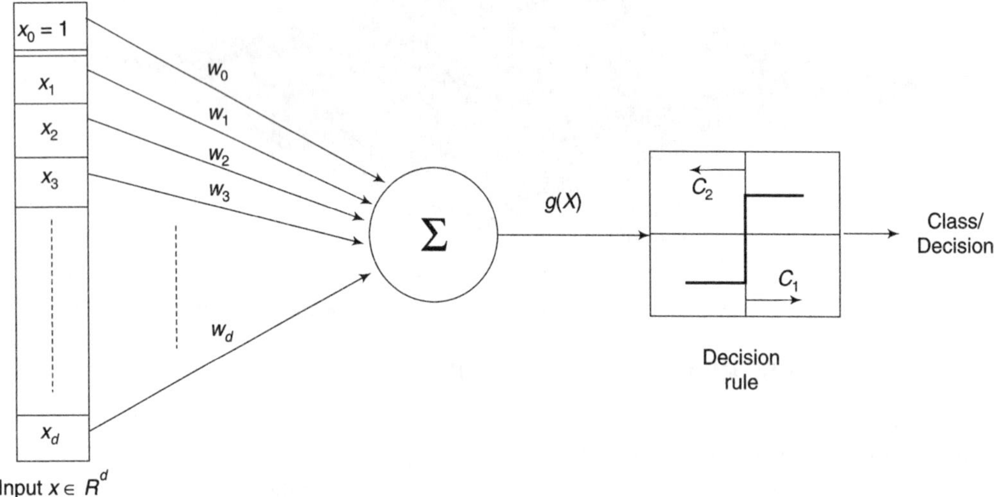

Fig. 5.4 A simple linear classifier having *d* input units, each corresponding to the values of the components of an input vector. Each input feature value x_i is multiplied by its corres-ponding weight w_i; the output unit sums all these products and emits +1 if $w^T\mathbf{x} + w_0 > 0$ or −1 otherwise.

> The equation $g(\mathbf{x}) = 0$ represents the decision boundary between the classes C_1 and C_2. When $g(\mathbf{x})$ is linear in nature, the decision surface is a *hyperplane*, H and its orientation depends on the weight vector **w** and its location by the bias $-w_0$.

Hence, **w** is normal to the hyperplane (decision surface) and if $w_0 = 0$, the hyperplane passes through the origin.

Now, the task is to estimate **w** and w_0 using a set of training examples $\mathbf{x}_i$ for obtaining the exact decision boundary. The solution can be found by minimizing an error function. Training error or empirical risk is one of the most commonly used error function, which is

$$J(\mathbf{w}, w_0) = \frac{1}{n} \sum_{i=1}^{n} [z_i - \hat{z}_i] \qquad (5.45)$$

where, n represents the total number of samples. The quantities z_i and $\hat{z}_i$ are the true class label and predicted class label respectively. The true label is defined as

$$z_i = \begin{cases} +1, & \text{if } \mathbf{x}_i \in C_1 \\ -1, & \text{if } \mathbf{x}_i \in C_2 \end{cases}$$

and the predicted labels are

$$\hat{z}_i = \begin{cases} +1, & \text{if } g(\mathbf{x}_i) \in C_1 \\ -1, & \text{if } g(\mathbf{x}_i) \in C_2 \end{cases}$$

We can use proper "learning" algorithms to minimize this error function.

Geometric Interpretation of g(x)

$g(\mathbf{x})$ gives an algebraic measure of the distance of $\mathbf{x}$ from the hyperplane (decision boundary), H. Then, any arbitrary observation $\mathbf{x}$ can be represented as,

$$x = \mathbf{x}_p + r\frac{\mathbf{w}}{||\mathbf{w}||} \quad \text{...(5.46)}$$

where, $\mathbf{w}_p$ is the normal projection of $\mathbf{x}$ onto the hyperplane, H, and r is the desired algebraic distance which is positive if $\mathbf{x}$ is on the positive side of H and negative if $\mathbf{x}$ is on the negative side. $\frac{\mathbf{w}}{||\mathbf{w}||}$ Indicates the direction of r. Figure 5.5 shows the geometrical interpretation of $g(\mathbf{x})$.

When we substitute $\mathbf{x}$ in $g(\mathbf{x})$, we get,

$$g(\mathbf{x}) = \mathbf{w}^T\mathbf{x} + w_0 \quad \text{...(5.47)}$$

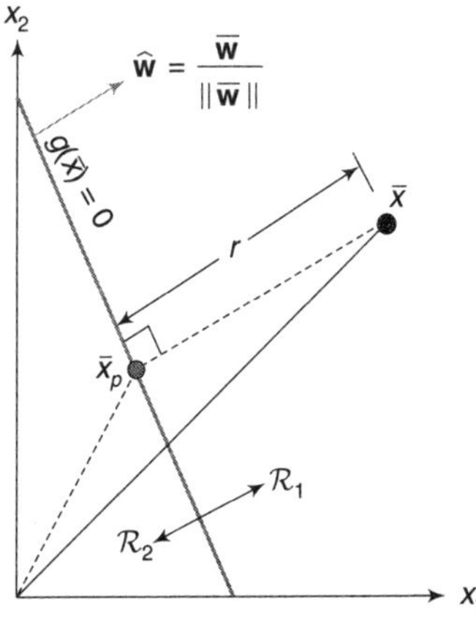

Fig. 5.5 The linear decision boundary H, which separates the feature space into two regions R_1 (where $g(\mathbf{x}) > 0$) and R_2 (where $g(\mathbf{x}) < 0$)

$$g(\mathbf{x}) = \mathbf{w}^T\left(\mathbf{x}_p + r\frac{\mathbf{w}}{\|\mathbf{w}\|}\right) + w_0 \qquad ...(5.48)$$

$$g(\mathbf{x}) = \mathbf{w}^T\mathbf{x}_p + r\frac{\mathbf{w}^T\mathbf{w}}{\|\mathbf{w}\|} + w_0 \qquad ...(5.49)$$

$$g(\mathbf{x}) = r\|\mathbf{w}\| \qquad ...(5.50)$$

$$\because \qquad \mathbf{w}^T\mathbf{w} = \|\mathbf{w}\|^2 \text{ and } \mathbf{w}^T\mathbf{x}_p + w_0 = 0.$$

Thus, the distance of **x** from the decision boundary is

$$r = \frac{g(\mathbf{x})}{\|\mathbf{x}\|} \qquad ...(5.51)$$

In fact, the distance of hyperplane, H from the origin is $w_0/\|\mathbf{w}\|$. If $w_0 = 0$, then $g(\mathbf{x})$ is in the homogeneous form $\mathbf{w}^T\mathbf{x}$, and the hyperplane passes through the origin.

In short, a linear discriminant function as a dichotomizer divides the feature space of the classifier by a hyperplane into two decision regions. The orientation of this hyperplane is determined by the weight vector **w** and the location of the surface is determined by the bias w_0. The dichotomizer is proportional to the signed distance from **x** to the hyperplane.

5.4.2 Linear Discriminant Functions for Multi-class Category Case

The extension of two-class classification problem to the multi-class classification can be achieved in many ways. One of the examples is the "one against the rest" method. In this case, we reduce the l-class classification problem into $(l - 1)$ two-class classification problems. In a second example, "one against another" approach uses $l(l - 1)/2$ linear discriminants, one for every pair of classes. However, both of these approaches have some "*ambiguous regions*" (where the classification is undefined), which is a hindrance to the efficacy of these approaches.

To avoid the problem of ambiguous regions, we consider l linear discriminant functions such that

$$g_i(\mathbf{x}) = \mathbf{w}_i\mathbf{x} + \mathbf{w}_{i0};\ i = 1, 2, \ldots, l \qquad ...(5.52)$$

and assign **x** to C_i if $g_i(\mathbf{x}) > g_i(\mathbf{x})$ for all $i \neq j$. Such a classifier is known as "*linear machine*" as shown in Fig. 5.6.

Thus, the linear machine divides the entire feature space into l-regions, say R_i and $g_i(\mathbf{x})$ will give the maximum value if **x** belongs to i^{th}-class which corresponds to region R_i. Suppose R_i and R_j are two nearby regions. Then, the boundary between them is a hyperplane, H_{ij} when $g_i(\mathbf{x}) = g_i(\mathbf{x})$. This boundary is defined by,

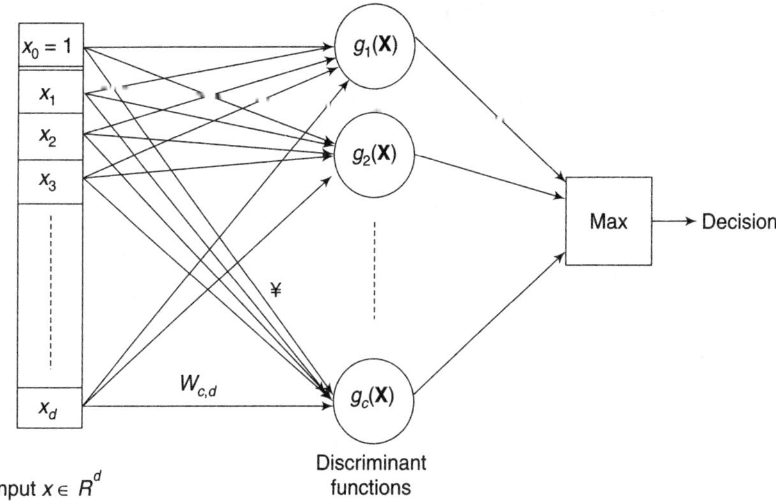

Fig. 5.6 The linear machine

$$(\mathbf{w}_i - \mathbf{w}_j)^T \mathbf{x} + (w_{i0} - w_{j0}) = 0 \qquad \text{...(5.53)}$$

The inference from Eq. 5.53 is that $(\mathbf{w}_i - \mathbf{w}_j)$ is normal to the hyperplane H_{ij} and the distance between the observation $\mathbf{x}$ and H_{ij} is

$$r = \frac{\left(g_i(\mathbf{x}) - g_j(\mathbf{x})\right)}{\left|\|\mathbf{w}_i - \mathbf{w}_j\|\right|} \qquad \text{...(5.54)}$$

Thus, the linear machine considers the difference between the weight vectors instead of merely weight vectors and divide the feature space into l-convex decision regions. Although there are $l(l - 1)/2$ pairs of regions, there are typically less decision boundaries, since they need not all be contiguous.

5.4.3 Higher Order Discriminant Functions

The expanded form of the linear discriminant function for d-dimensional feature space is given as:

$$g(\mathbf{x}) = w_0 + \sum_{i=1}^{d} w_i x_i \qquad \text{...(5.55)}$$

where, x_i denotes the components of the feature vector $\mathbf{x}$ and w_i represent the corresponding components of the weight vector. We add more terms in Eq. 5.55 which involves the product of different components of the feature vector x. The advantage is that we shall obtain more complex-adequate decision boundaries which can improve the classification performance.

Quadratic Discriminant Functions

By adding the terms which involve the product of pair of components of the feature vector x in the generalized equation of linear discriminant functions, we shall get the *quadratic discriminant functions*. The generalized equation of quadratic discriminant functions is

$$g(\mathbf{x}) = w_0 + \sum_{i=1}^{d} w_i x_i + \sum_{i=1}^{d} \sum_{j=1}^{d} w_{ij} x_i \, x_j \qquad ...(5.56)$$

The decision boundary of such functions (where $g(\mathbf{x}) = 0$) is a hyperquadric surface. Such surfaces are important while we deal with multivariate Gaussian distributions.

Polynomial Discriminant Functions

If we add more in the form of product of components of $\mathbf{x}$ like $w_{ijk} x_i x_j x_k$, we can formulate another type of discriminant functions. For example,

$$g(\mathbf{x}) = \mathbf{w}_0 + \sum_{i=1}^{d} w_i \, x_i + \sum_{i=1}^{d} \sum_{j=1}^{d} w_{ij} \, x_i x_j + \sum_{i=1}^{d} \sum_{j=1}^{d} \sum_{i=1}^{d} w_{ijk} \, x_i x_j x_k \qquad ...(5.57)$$

Even though the complexity of operations is increased, the polynomial discriminant functions have the capability of providing increased accuracy level.

5.4.4 Generalized Linear Discriminant Functions

An alternative definition for linear discriminant function is drawn as follows (we assume $x_0 = 1$).

$$g(\mathbf{x}) = \mathbf{w}^T \mathbf{x} + w_0 = \sum_{i=1}^{d} w_i x_i + x_0 w_0 = \sum_{i=0}^{d} w_i \, x_i = \boldsymbol{\alpha}^T \, \mathbf{y} \qquad ...(5.58)$$

Thus, the d-dimensional feature (parameter) space is extended to $(d + 1)$-dimensional feature space. This is called *augmented feature space,* where $\mathbf{y}$ is the augmented feature vector and $\boldsymbol{\alpha}$ represents the augmented weight vector.

$$\mathbf{x} = \begin{bmatrix} x_1 \\ x_2 \\ \vdots \\ x_d \end{bmatrix} \xrightarrow{\text{Augmented weight vector}} \mathbf{y} = \begin{bmatrix} x_1 \\ x_2 \\ \vdots \\ x_d \end{bmatrix} \text{ and}$$

$$\mathbf{w} = \begin{bmatrix} w_1 \\ w_2 \\ \vdots \\ w_d \end{bmatrix} \xrightarrow{\text{Augmented weight vector}} \boldsymbol{\alpha} = \begin{bmatrix} w_1 \\ w_2 \\ \vdots \\ w_{d+1} \end{bmatrix}$$

Thus, the discriminant function $g(\mathbf{x}) = \boldsymbol{\alpha}^T \mathbf{y}$ separates the points in $(d + 1)$ space by a hyper-plane which passes through the origin.

The corresponding decision rule for a two-class classification problem is

$$\text{If} \quad \alpha^T \mathbf{y}_i > 0 \text{ assigny } \mathbf{y}_i \text{ to } C_1; \text{ otherwise decide } C_2 \qquad \text{...(5.59)}$$

Generalized Discriminants

A generalized discriminant can be obtained by first mapping the data to a space of higher dimensionality.

$$d \longrightarrow \hat{d} \quad \text{where} \quad \hat{d} << d$$

This is done by transforming the data **x** through properly chosen functions, $i = 1, 2, ..., \hat{d}$ (called ϕ functions).

$$\mathbf{x} = \begin{bmatrix} x_1 \\ x_2 \\ \vdots \\ x_d \end{bmatrix} \overset{\Phi}{\Rightarrow} \begin{bmatrix} x_1(\mathbf{x}) \\ x_2(\mathbf{x}) \\ \vdots \\ x_d(\mathbf{x}) \end{bmatrix}$$

Thus, the generalized discriminant is defined as a linear discriminant in the $\hat{d}$-dimensional space. Mathematically, it is

$$g(\mathbf{x}) = \sum_{i=1}^{d} a_i x_i \overset{\Phi}{\Rightarrow} \sum_{i=1}^{d} a_i y_i (\mathbf{x}) = \alpha^T \mathbf{y} \qquad (5.60)$$

Finding the value of α can be performed by using different learning algorithms. Some of the examples for such techniques are gradient decent algorithm, Newton's method, perceptron rule, etc.

Conclusion

This chapter concludes our discussion of Bayesian classifier theory which is a probabilistic model and which has wide ranging applications in the field of machine learning. The concept of linear discriminant analysis has also been covered. The applications of these mathematical formulations in machine learning have been taken up in Chapters 3 and 4.

Questions

1. Explain Bayes decision rule. Explain how it can be used for two class classification.
2. Why Bayes classifier is optimal?
3. Explain loss function? How can it be factored into Bayes decision theory?
4. Give the expression of a multivariate Gaussian distribution explaining all parameters.
5. For a Bayesian classifier, obtain the discriminant function and decision surface for multivariate Gaussian distributions having same covariance matrix and distinct means.
6. Prove that a Bayes classifier is equivalent to a minimum distance classifier, assuming that the feature vector is Gaussian.

7. It is estimated that 50% of emails are spam emails. Some software has been applied to filter these spam emails before they reach your inbox. A certain brand of software claims that it can detect 99% of spam emails, and the probability for a false positive (a non-spam email detected as spam) is 5%. Now if an email is detected as spam, then what is the probability that it is in fact a non-spam email?
8. Discuss the principles of Naïve Bayes classifier. Discuss the shape of the decision surfaces obtained using a Naïve Bayes classifier.
9. The minimum error rate classification can be achieved by the use of discriminant functions $g_i(x) = \ln p(x|\omega_i) + \ln P(\omega_i)$. The densities $p(x|\omega_i)$ are assumed to be multivariate Gaussian. Determine the discriminant function for (i) $\Sigma i = \sigma^2 I$, (ii) $\Sigma i = \Sigma$, and Σi = arbitrary. Discuss the nature of decision surface in each case.
10. How does Naïve Bayes treat numerical and categorical values?

Exercise

1. Assume a two-class problem with equal a priori class probabilities and Gaussian class-conditional densities given as follows:

$$p(x|\omega_1) = N\left(\begin{bmatrix} 0 \\ 0 \end{bmatrix}, \begin{bmatrix} a & c \\ c & b \end{bmatrix}\right) p(x|\omega_2) = N\left(\begin{bmatrix} d \\ e \end{bmatrix}, \begin{bmatrix} 1 & 0 \\ 0 & 1 \end{bmatrix}\right).$$

where, $a \times b - c \times c = 1$.

(a) Find the equation of the decision boundary between these two classes in terms of the given parameters, after choosing a logarithmic discriminant function.

(b) Determine the constraints on the values of a, b, c, d, and e, such that the resulting discriminant function results with a linear decision boundary.

2. Let $p(x|\omega_i) = N(\mu_1, \sigma_2)$, for a two category one-dimensional problem with $p(\omega_1) = p(\omega_2) = \frac{1}{2}$

Show that the minimum probability of error is given by:

$$P_e = \frac{1}{\sqrt{2\pi}} \int_a^\infty e^{\frac{-u^2}{2}} du \text{ where, } a = \frac{\mu_2 - \mu_1}{\sigma}.$$

3. Suppose we are given the following dataset, where A, B, C are input binary random variables, and y is a binary output whose values we want to predict. How would a Naive Bayes classifier predict y given an input $A = 0$, $B = 0$, $C = 1$. Assume that in case of a tie, the classifier always prefers to predict 0 for y.

A	B	C	y
0	0	1	0
0	1	0	0

1	1	0	0
0	0	1	1
1	1	1	1
1	0	0	1
1	1	0	1

4. Suppose we have a two-class problem (A, ~ A), with a single binary valued feature (x, ~ x). Assume the prior probability $P(A) = 0.33$. Given the distribution of the samples as shown in the following table, use Bayes rule to compute the values of posterior probabilities of classes.

	A	~A
x	248	167
~x	82	503

5. Consider a two-class classification problem with the loss matrix given as $\begin{pmatrix} \lambda_{11} & \lambda_{12} \\ \lambda_{21} & \lambda_{22} \end{pmatrix}$

   Note that λ_{ij} is the case for classifying an instance from class j as class i. At the decision boundary, what will be the ratio $p(\omega_2/x)/p(\omega_1/x)$ in terms of the loss-function?

CHAPTER

6

Parametric and Non-Parametric Estimation Techniques

In this chapter you will

- be introduced the popular parameter estimation techniques such as maximum likelihood and Bayesian estimation, and
- be equipped with non-parametric techniques for density estimation.

6.0 INTRODUCTION

In the previous chapter, we learnt how to design an optimal classifier using Bayesian decision rule. Even if Bayesian classifier guarantees optimal classification performance, it could use only if the prior probabilities and class conditional probabilities are known to us. However, in most of the practical applications, such complete information is rarely available. In this chapter, we will address such scenarios. Firstly, we assume that some partial knowledge about the statistical properties of the data is available such as number of parameters, and probabilities and probability densities. Such applications belong to the category of "parametric estimation" techniques where parameters like, mean, variance, etc., must be estimated from the available training samples. Even if, a number of parametric estimation techniques are available, this chapter introduces two popular estimation techniques such as "Maximum Likelihood (ML) estimators" and "Bayesian estimators". Secondly, we consider the scenarios where the knowledge about the probabilistic structure of the problem is unknown. One approach to tackle such a problem is to estimate the unknown probabilities and probability densities using the available training samples in supervised classification problems, which are known as "Non-parametric Estimation Techniques". This chapter also introduces some common non-parametric estimation methods such as "Histogram Density Representation" and "Kernel Density Estimation".

6.1 PARAMETRIC ESTIMATION TECHNIQUES

Although the performance of ML estimators and Bayesian estimators is almost similar, these techniques are conceptually different. ML estimators assume that the values of the parameters are fixed but unknown. However, Bayesian estimators assume that the parameters are random variables with known apriori distribution.

6.1.1 Maximum Likelihood Estimation

Maximum Likelihood (ML) estimation techniques are popular because of their implicity compared with their counterparts and good convergence property as the number of training samples increases. Consider an l-class classification problem and we assume that we have l sets of samples, say, D_1, D_2, ..., D_l, where D_i represents the set of samples corresponding to i^{th} class. We say such samples are *i.i.d.* - independent identically distributed random variables and the class conditional probability $p(\mathbf{x}/C_i)$ for class - C_i has a known parametric form with unknown parametric values. Let $\boldsymbol{\theta}_i$ be the parameter vector for the ith class. For example, $\boldsymbol{\theta}_i$ consists of two components say mean μ_i and covariance matrix Σ_i. In addition to this, we assume that the parameters for the different classes are functionally independent.

Suppose a set D of training samples drawn independently from the probability density $p(\mathbf{x}/\boldsymbol{\theta})$ to estimate the unknown parameter vector $\boldsymbol{\theta}$ and assume D consists of n samples, say $\mathbf{x}_1$, $\mathbf{x}_2$, ..., $\mathbf{x}_n$. Then, the likelihood of $\boldsymbol{\theta}$ with respect to these samples is defined as,

$$p(D/\boldsymbol{\theta}) = \prod_{i=1}^{n} p(\mathbf{x}_i/\boldsymbol{\theta}) \qquad \text{...(6.1)}$$

As per the definition, the maximum likelihood estimate of θ is the value of $\hat{\theta}$ which maximizes $p(D/\theta)$ such that

$$\hat{\boldsymbol{\theta}} = \max_{\boldsymbol{\theta}} p(D/\boldsymbol{\theta}) \qquad \text{...(6.2)}$$

To simplify the computational bottleneck of likelihood function, it is easier to work with logarithm of likelihood function. Since the logarithm is monotonically increasing, the $\hat{\boldsymbol{\theta}}$ that maximizes the log-likelihood also maximizes the likelihood. Thus, we define the "log-likelihood" function as,

$$l(\boldsymbol{\theta}) = \ln p(D/\boldsymbol{\theta}) \qquad \text{...(6.3)}$$

Hence, the maximum log-likelihood estimate of $\boldsymbol{\theta}$ is the value of $\hat{\boldsymbol{\theta}}$ which maximizes $l(\boldsymbol{\theta})$ is,

$$\hat{\boldsymbol{\theta}} = \max_{\theta} l\,(\boldsymbol{\theta}) = \max_{\theta} \ln p(D/\boldsymbol{\theta}) \qquad \text{...(6.4)}$$

The necessary conditions for finding out the solution of this optimization problem, we must consider the gradient of log-likelihood function, $\Delta_{\theta} l(\boldsymbol{\theta})$ and equate it to zero (for finding out the stationary point) such that,

$$\Delta_\theta l(\theta) = 0 \qquad ...(6.5)$$

The solution of the equation may give a global maximum, a local maximum or a saddle point. We must be careful to check the resulting extremum is the true maximum value.

A related class of estimators – "maximum a posteriori estimators or MAP estimator maximizes $l(\theta)p(\theta)$, where $p(\theta)$ indicates the prior. ML estimator can be considered as a special case of MAP estimator for the uniform prior.

Examples

1. **The Gaussian Case – Unknown *μ***

   Assume that the samples $\mathbf{x}_i$ are drawn from a multivariate Gaussian data with mean $\boldsymbol{\mu}$ and covariance matrix Σ and mean is the only unknown parameter to be estimated. Then, the log-likelihood function for sample point $\mathbf{x}_k$ is

$$\ln p(\mathbf{x}_k/\boldsymbol{\mu}) = -\frac{1}{2}\ln[(2\pi)^d |\Sigma|] - \frac{1}{2}(\mathbf{x}_k - \boldsymbol{\mu})^T \Sigma^{-1}(\mathbf{x}_k - \boldsymbol{\mu}) \qquad ...(6.6)$$

   and

$$\Delta_\mu \ln p(\mathbf{x}_k/\boldsymbol{\mu}) = \Sigma^{-1}(\mathbf{x}_k - \boldsymbol{\mu}) \qquad ...(6.7)$$

   Thus, ML estimate of μ must satisfy,

$$\Delta_\mu \ln p(\mathbf{x}_k/\boldsymbol{\mu}) = \Sigma^{-1}(\mathbf{x}_k - \hat{\boldsymbol{\mu}}) = 0 \qquad ...(6.8)$$

   On rearranging the above equation, we can deduce that the ML estimate of $\boldsymbol{\mu}$ is

$$\hat{\mu} = \frac{1}{n}\sum_{i=1}^{n} \mathbf{x}_i \qquad ...(6.9)$$

   Thus, the ML estimate of the unknown mean for multivariate Gaussian distribution is the *sample mean* of the training samples.

2. **The Gaussian Case – Unknown μ and Σ**

   It is the case of general multivariate Gaussian population, neither the mean $\boldsymbol{\mu}$ nor the covariance matrix Σ are known. The parameter vector θ consists of two parameters, such as $\boldsymbol{\mu}$ and Σ. For simplicity, consider the univariate case with parameters $\theta_1 = \mu$ and $\theta_2 = \sigma^2$. The corresponding log-likelihood function for the sample $\mathbf{x}_k$ is

$$\ln p(x_k/\theta) = \frac{1}{2}\ln 2\pi\sigma^2 - \frac{1}{2\sigma^2}(x_k - \mu)^2 \qquad ...(6.10)$$

   and

$$\Delta_\theta \ln p(x_k/\mu) = \begin{bmatrix} \dfrac{1}{\sigma^2(x_k - \mu)} \\ -\dfrac{1}{2\sigma^2} + \dfrac{(x_k - \mu)^2}{2\sigma^4} \end{bmatrix} \qquad ...(6.11)$$

The log-likelihood estimators lead the conditions

$$\frac{1}{\hat{\sigma}^2(x_k - \hat{\mu})} = 0 \qquad ...(6.12)$$

and

$$-\frac{1}{2\widehat{\sigma^2}} + \frac{(x_k - \hat{\mu})^2}{2\widehat{\sigma^4}} = 0 \qquad ...(6.13)$$

On rearranging the log-likelihood estimators for mean and variance are

$$\hat{\mu} = \frac{1}{n}\sum_{i=1}^{n} x_i \qquad ...(6.14)$$

and

$$\widehat{\sigma^2} = \frac{1}{n}\sum_{i=1}^{n} (x_k - \hat{\mu})^2 \qquad ...(6.15)$$

Thus, the generalized estimators for the multivariate Normal distribution case can be formulated as

$$\hat{\boldsymbol{\mu}} = \frac{1}{n}\sum_{i=1}^{n} \mathbf{x}_i \qquad ...(6.16)$$

and

$$\hat{\Sigma} = \frac{1}{n}\sum_{i=1}^{n} (\mathbf{x}_k - \hat{\boldsymbol{\mu}})\,(\mathbf{x}_k - \hat{\boldsymbol{\mu}})^T \qquad ...(6.17)$$

Thus, the ML estimate of the mean vector is the sample mean and ML estimate for the covariance matrix is the arithmetic average of the n matrices $(\mathbf{x}_k - \hat{\boldsymbol{\mu}})\,(\mathbf{x}_k - \hat{\boldsymbol{\mu}})^T$.

6.1.2 Bayesian Estimation

Even if ML estimator and Bayesian estimator give almost identical results, conceptually both of them are different. In Bayesian estimation, we assume that the parameter vector $\boldsymbol{\theta}$ possesses a random variable. Our training data converts the distribution of the random variable to a posterior probability density. We assume that it has a known parametric form and the only unknown quantity is the values of the parameters.

Let $p(\boldsymbol{\theta})$ be the known prior for the parameter vector, $\boldsymbol{\theta}$ and $p(\mathbf{x})$ be the desired unknown probability density which makes the density $p(\mathbf{x}/\boldsymbol{\theta})$ is completely known. Again let D denotes the set of samples and our aim is to find our $p(\mathbf{x}/D)$ which as close as the unknown $p(\mathbf{x})$. We can represent $p(\mathbf{x}/D)$ in terms of the joint density $p(\mathbf{x}, \boldsymbol{\theta}/D)$ as follows.

$$p(\mathbf{x}/D) = \int_\theta p(\mathbf{x}, \boldsymbol{\theta}/D)d\boldsymbol{\theta} = \int_\theta p(\mathbf{x}/\boldsymbol{\theta})p(\boldsymbol{\theta}/D)d\boldsymbol{\theta} \qquad ...(6.18)$$

This equation relates $p(\mathbf{x}/D)$ and $p(\boldsymbol{\theta}/D)$ for the unknown parameter $\boldsymbol{\theta}$. Using Bayes rule, we can expand $p(\boldsymbol{\theta}/D)$ as

$$p(\boldsymbol{\theta}/D) = \frac{p(D/\boldsymbol{\theta})p(\boldsymbol{\theta})}{\int p(D/\boldsymbol{\theta})p(\boldsymbol{\theta})d\boldsymbol{\theta}} \qquad ...(6.19)$$

Moreover, we assume that each sample in the set, D is i.i.d. random variables. Hence, the expanded form of $p(D/\boldsymbol{\theta})$ is

$$p(D/\boldsymbol{\theta}) = \prod_{i=1}^{n} p(\mathbf{x}_i/\boldsymbol{\theta}) \quad ...(6.20)$$

Now the idea is to find out $\hat{\boldsymbol{\theta}}$ such that the $p(\boldsymbol{\theta}/D)$ peaks sharply at $\hat{\boldsymbol{\theta}}$ which makes estimate $\hat{\boldsymbol{\theta}}$ as the true parameter vector. As given in Eq. 6.19, when $p(D/\boldsymbol{\theta})$ peaks, $p(\boldsymbol{\theta}/D)$. Hence using Eq. 6.20, we can find out the $\hat{\boldsymbol{\theta}}$ as the true parameter vector.

Example

1. The Multivariate Case: Unknown $\boldsymbol{\mu}$:

   In this case, we assume that Σ is known, but mean vector $\boldsymbol{\mu}$ is not. Also, we assume that $p(\mathbf{x}/\boldsymbol{\theta})$ and $p(\boldsymbol{\theta})$ follow normal distribution such that $p(\mathbf{x}/\boldsymbol{\theta}) \sim N(\boldsymbol{\mu}, \Sigma)$ and $p(\boldsymbol{\theta}) \sim N(\boldsymbol{\mu}_0, \Sigma_0)$. Our chief assumption is that the parameters $\boldsymbol{\mu}_0$, Σ and Σ_0 are known. Using Eqs. 6.19 and 6.20, we can deduce that

   $$p(\boldsymbol{\mu}/D) = K\prod_{i=1}^{n} p(\mathbf{x}_k/\boldsymbol{\mu})p(\boldsymbol{\mu}) \quad ...(6.21)$$

   where K denotes all other terms which are independent of the parameter $\boldsymbol{\mu}$. By substituting the equations for normal distribution, we can further formulate it as,

   $$p(\boldsymbol{\mu}/D) = K' \exp\left[-\frac{1}{2}\left((\boldsymbol{\mu}^T(n\Sigma^{-1} + \Sigma_0^{-1})\boldsymbol{\mu} - (2\boldsymbol{\mu}^T)\left(\Sigma^{-1}\sum_{i=1}^{n}\mathbf{x}_i + \Sigma_0^{-1}\boldsymbol{\mu}_0\right)\right)\right] \quad ...(6.22)$$

   We can represent this equation in the generalized format of Gaussian distribution $p(\boldsymbol{\mu}/D) \sim N(\boldsymbol{\mu}^*, \Sigma^*)$ as follows.

   $$p(\boldsymbol{\mu}/D) = K'' \exp\left[-\frac{1}{2}(\boldsymbol{\mu} - \boldsymbol{\mu}^*)^T \Sigma^{*-1}(\boldsymbol{\mu} - \boldsymbol{\mu}^*)\right] \quad ...(6.23)$$

   Comparing the corresponding terms in Eqs. 6.22 and 6.23, we get

   $$\Sigma^{*-1} = n\Sigma^{-1} + \Sigma_0^{-1} \quad ...(6.24)$$

   $$\Sigma^{*-1} = n\Sigma^{-1}\sum_{i=1}^{n}\mathbf{x}_i + \Sigma_0^{-1}\boldsymbol{\mu}_0 \quad ...(6.25)$$

   On solving these two equations, we can deduce the following equations. (The derivation is left to the readers of this book.)

   $$\boldsymbol{\mu}^* = \Sigma_0\left(\Sigma_0 + \frac{1}{n}\Sigma\right)^{-1}\frac{1}{n}\sum_{i=1}^{n}\mathbf{x}_i + \frac{1}{n}\Sigma\left(\Sigma_0 + \frac{1}{n}\Sigma\right)^{-1}\boldsymbol{\mu}_0 \quad ...(6.26)$$

   $$\Sigma^* = \frac{1}{n}\Sigma\left(\Sigma_0 + \frac{1}{n}\Sigma\right)^{-1}\Sigma_0 \quad ...(6.27)$$

Hence $p(\mathbf{x}/D)$ is also normally distributed in the form

$$p(\mathbf{x}/D) = N(\boldsymbol{\mu}^*, \Sigma^* + \Sigma) \quad ...(6.28)$$

Even if the ML and Bayesian estimation techniques estimate the parameters of a underlying density functions, the knowledge about the actual density functions may not be known in majority of pattern classification applications. Hence, the following section discusses about the non-parametric techniques which can be applied to any arbitrary density functions.

6.2 NON-PARAMETRIC ESTIMATION TECHNIQUES

Previously, we assumed that the forms of underlying density functions are known of some particular known parametric form. However, in most of the practical scenarios, this assumption is incorrect and most of the real-world entities have multi-modal distributions, whereas classical parametric densities are generally unimodal. In this section, we will examine non-parametric techniques that can be applied to any forms of distributions without the assumption that the underlying density forms are not known previously.

6.2.1 Histogram Density Representation

Consider a single continuous variable $\mathbf{x}$ and let's say we have a set D of n of them $\{\mathbf{x}_1, \mathbf{x}_2, \ldots, \mathbf{x}_n\}$. Our goal is to model $p(\mathbf{x})$ from D. Standard *histograms* simply partition $\mathbf{x}$ into distinct bins of width Δ_i and then count the number n_i of observations $\mathbf{x}$ falling into bin i as shown in Fig. 6.1. To turn this count into a normalized probability density, we simply divide by the total number of observations N and by the width Δ_i of the bins. This gives us,

$$p_i = \frac{n_i}{N\Delta_i} \quad ...(6.29)$$

Generally, the model for the density $p(\mathbf{x})$ is constant over the width of each bin. In Fig. 6.1, the continuous line indicates the true density which is a mixture of two Gaussians. When Δ is very small (RHS - top), the resulting density is quite spiky and hallucinates a lot of structure not present in $p(\mathbf{x})$. When Δ is very big (RHS - bottom), the resulting density is quite smooth and consequently fails to capture the bimodality of $p(\mathbf{x})$. It appears that the best results are obtained for some intermediate value of Δ (RHS-middle). Thus, the histogram density model is dependent on the choice of the edge location of each bin.

The histogram density estimation is simple to evaluate and use. Also, we can throw away D once the histogram is computed and can be computed sequentially if data continues to come in. However, the estimated density has discontinuities due to the bin edges rather than any property of the underlying density. In addition to that we need M^d bins if we divide each variable in a d-dimensional space into M bins.

To estimate the probability density at a particular location, we should consider the data points that lie within some local neighbourhood of that point. Moreover, the value of the smoothing parameter should neither be too large nor too small in order to obtain good results. With these two lessons in mind, we proceed to kernel density estimation techniques.

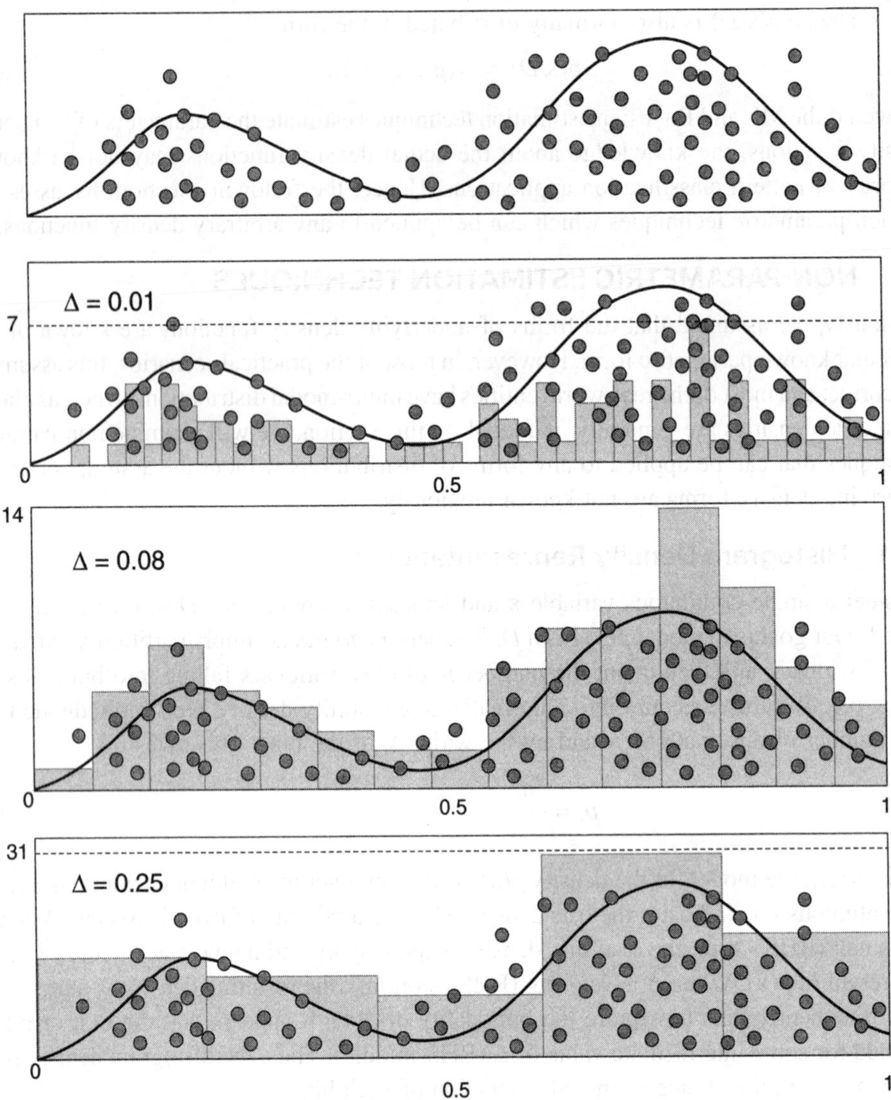

Fig. 6.1 Histogram density as a function of bin width

6.2.2 Kernel Estimation Techniques

Suppose we have n samples $\mathbf{x} \in D$, where D denotes the set of samples with underlying density $p(\mathbf{x})$. Let R be a small region containing $\mathbf{x}$ and the probability P of each sample falling into R is,

$$P = \int_R p(\mathbf{x}')dx' \qquad ...(6.30)$$

The chance of falling k samples in R is binomial distributed and is

$$P_k = \binom{n}{k} P^k (1 - P)^{(n-k)} \quad ...(6.31)$$

Then, the expected value for k is

$$E(k) = np \quad ...(6.32)$$

Thus, the binomial for k peaks very sharply about the mean. So, we expect k/n to be a very good estimate for the probability P. As n increases, this estimation will become more accurate. Suppose the volume enclosed by the region R is V, $p(\mathbf{x})$ is continuous and R is too small. Then, $p(\mathbf{x})$ does not appreciably vary within this region and we can approximate

$$\int_R p(\mathbf{x}')dx' \approx p(\mathbf{x})V \quad ...(6.33)$$

By combining the previous equations, we can deduce the estimate of $p(\mathbf{x})$ as

$$p(\mathbf{x}) \approx \frac{k}{nV} \quad (6.34)$$

The validity of this estimation depends on two contradicting conditions.

1. The region R must be sufficiently small that the density is approximately constant over the region.
2. The region R must be sufficiently large that the number k of points falling inside it is sufficient to yield a sharply peaked distribution.

As per the first condition, we want $p(\mathbf{x})$, so we need to let V approaches to 0. However, R will become so small, that no points will fall into it for fixed n and our estimate would be useless: $p(\mathbf{x}) \approx 0$. To address the second condition, we can fix the volume V and increase the number of training samples. Then, the ratio k/n will converge as desired. However, this will only yield an estimate of the space-averaged density (P/V).

Now a significant question arises. How can we skirt these limitations when an unlimited number of samples if available?

The solution of this question is given below.

- To estimate the density at $\mathbf{x}$, form a sequence of regions R_1, R_2, . . . containing $\mathbf{x}$ with R_1 having 1 sample ($n_1 = 1$), R_2 having 2 samples ($n_2 = 2$) and so on.
- Let V_n be the volume of R_n, k_n be the number of samples falling in R_n, and $p_n(\mathbf{x})$ be the nth estimate for $p(\mathbf{x})$:

$$p_n(\mathbf{x}) = \frac{k_n}{nV_n} \quad ...(6.35)$$

- If $p_n(\mathbf{x})$ is to converge to $p(\mathbf{x})$ we need the following three conditions

$$\lim_{n\to\infty} V_n = 0$$

$$\lim_{n\to\infty} k_n = \infty$$

$$\lim_{n\to\infty} k_n/n = 0$$

- $\lim_{n\to\infty} V_n = 0$ ensures that our space-averaged density will converge to $p(\mathbf{x})$.
- $\lim_{n\to\infty} k_n = \infty$ basically, ensures that the frequency ratio will converge to the probability P (the distribution will be sufficiently peaked).
- $\lim_{n\to\infty} k_m/n = 0$ is required for $p_m(\mathbf{x})$ to converge at all. It also says that although a huge number of samples will fall within the region R_n, they will form a negligibly small fraction of the total number of samples.

There are two common ways of obtaining regions that satisfy these conditions:

- Shrink an initial region by specifying the volume V_n as some function of n such as $V_n = \frac{1}{\sqrt{n}}$. Then, we need to show that $p_m(\mathbf{x})$ converges to $p(\mathbf{x})$. (This is like the *Parzen window* we'll talk about next.)
- Specify k_n as some function of n such as $k_n = \sqrt{n}$. Then, we grow the volume V_n until it encloses k_n neighbours of $\mathbf{x}$. (This is the *k-nearest-neighbour*).

6.2.2.1 Parzen Windows

Let us assume that the region R is a d-dimensional hypercube with l_n being the length of an edge. The volume of this hypercube is given by

$$V_n = l_n^d \quad \text{...(6.36)}$$

Now, our aim is to derive an expression for k_n, we define a *windowing function* as a unit hypercube centred at the origin as follows;

$$\phi(\mathbf{u}) = \begin{cases} 1, & |u_j| \le 1/2 \\ 0, & \text{otherwise} \end{cases}$$

From this equation, we can understand that $\phi\left(\frac{(\mathbf{x} - \mathbf{x}_i)}{l_n}\right)$ is equal to unity if $\mathbf{x}_i$ falls within the hypercube of volume V_n centred at $\mathbf{x}$, and is zero otherwise. Thus, the number of samples in this hypercube is given by

$$k_n = \sum_{i=1}^{n} \phi\left(\frac{(\mathbf{x} - \mathbf{x}_i)}{l_n}\right) \quad \text{...(6.37)}$$

By recollecting the equation for n^{th} estimate of $p(\mathbf{x})$ as, $p_n(\mathbf{x}) = \frac{k_n}{nV_n}$ we can deduce $p_n(\mathbf{x})$ as,

$$p_n(\mathbf{x}) = \frac{1}{n} \sum_{i=1}^{n} \frac{1}{V_n} \phi\left(\frac{(\mathbf{x} - \mathbf{x}_i)}{l_n}\right) \quad \text{...(6.38)}$$

Hence, the windowing function ϕ, in this context called a *Parzen window*, tells us how to weight all of the samples in D to determine $p(\mathbf{x})$ at a particular $\mathbf{x}$.

In Fig. 6.2, comparison between histogram density estimation and Parzen window based estimation techniques is given. The Parzen window density estimate may consist of discontinuities and depends on the bandwidth.

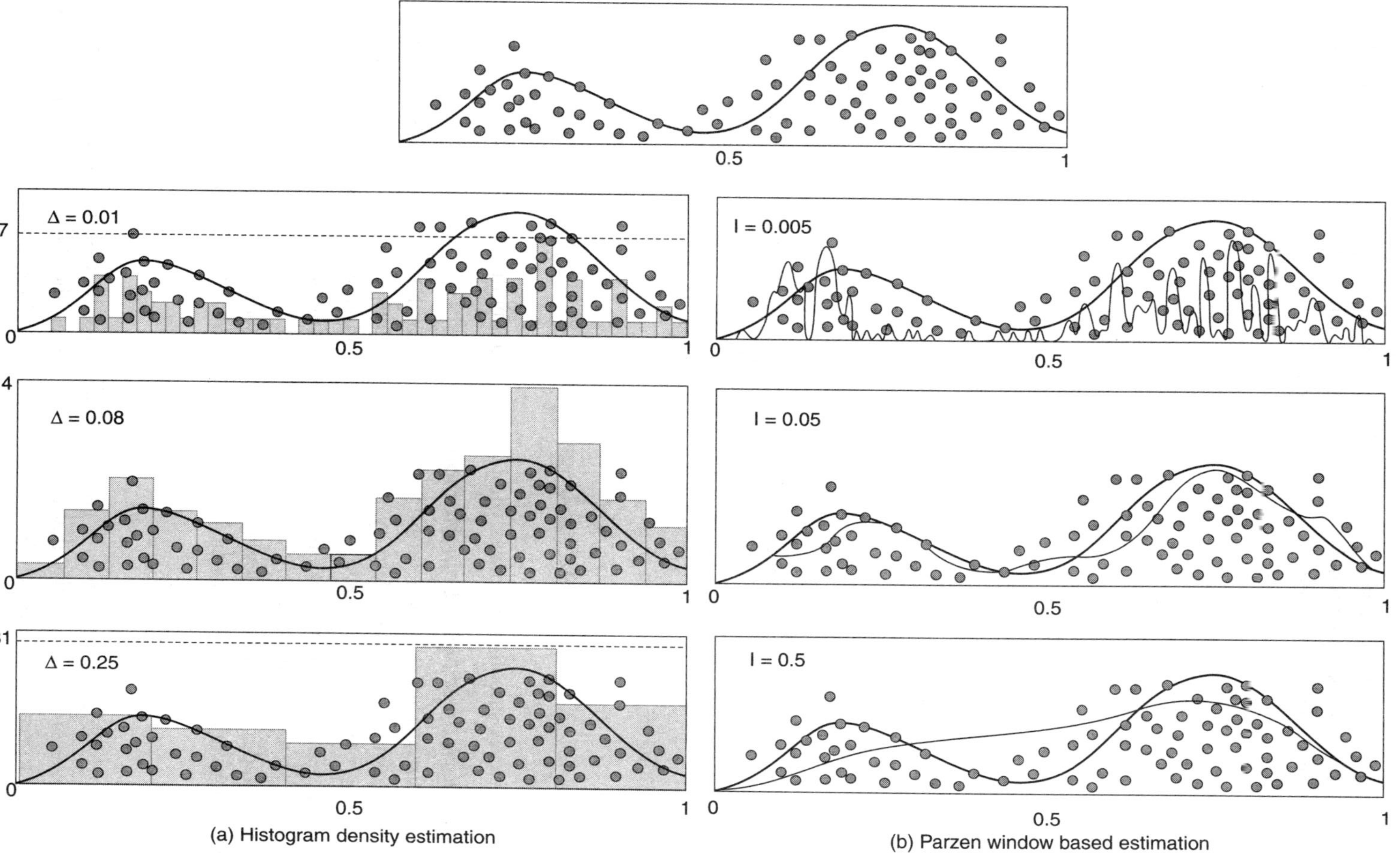

(a) Histogram density estimation

(b) Parzen window based estimation

Fig. 6.2 Comparison between histogram density estimation and Parzen window based estimation

Now, what if we allow a more general class of windowing functions rather than the hypercube? If we think of the windowing function as an interpolator, rather than considering the window function about **x** only, we can visualize it as a *kernel* sitting on each data sample $\mathbf{x}_i$ in D. There are two necessary conditions on the kernel function to make the estimate is proper.

$$\Phi(\mathbf{x}) \geq 0 \quad \text{non-negative} \qquad \text{...(6.39)}$$

$$\int \phi(\mathbf{u})d\mathbf{u} = 1 \quad \text{integrate to 1} \qquad \text{...(6.40)}$$

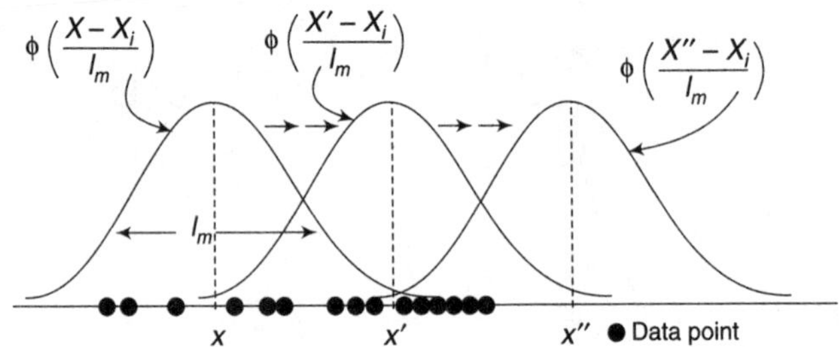

Fig. 6.3 Gaussian kernel

A popular choice of the kernel is the *Gaussian kernel* as illustrated in Fig. 6.3.

$$\phi_i(u) = \frac{1}{\sqrt{2\pi}} \exp\left[-\frac{1}{2}u^2\right] \qquad \text{...(6.41)}$$

The resulting density is given by:

$$p(\mathbf{x}) = \frac{1}{n}\sum_{i=1}^{n} \frac{1}{l_n\sqrt{2\pi}} \exp\left[-\frac{1}{2l_n^2}(\mathbf{x} - \mathbf{x}_i)^2\right] \qquad \text{...(6.42)}$$

It will give us smoother estimates without the discontinuities from the hypercube kernel.

6.2.2.2 k-Nearest Neighbour Methods

Selecting the best window is a severe limiting factor for Parzen window estimators. *k*-NN methods circumvent this problem by making the window size as a function of the actual training data. The basic idea here is to centre our window round **x** and let it grow until it captures k_n samples, where k_n is a function of n. These samples are the k_n nearest neighbours of **x**. If the density is high near **x** then the window will be relatively small leading to good resolution and if the density is low near **x**, the window will grow large, but it will stop soon after it enters regions of higher density. In both cases, we estimate $p_n(\mathbf{x})$ as

$$p_n(\mathbf{x}) = \frac{k_n}{nV_n} \qquad \text{...(6.43)}$$

We want k_n to go to infinity as n goes to infinity thereby assuring us that k_n/n will be a good estimate of the probability that a point will fall in the window of volume V_n which makes k_n/n to zero. This ensures that $p_n(\mathbf{x})$ converges to $p(\mathbf{x})$ as n approaches infinity.

Conclusion

In this chapter, the mathematical formulation for the maximum likelihood estimator that was used in Chapter 3 and the nearest neighbourhood technique of Chapter 4 have been discussed. Understanding the math behind ML algorithms will be an additional strength for designers of ML systems.

Questions

1. Compare parametric and non-parametric methods for probability density function estimation.
2. Suppose the weights of randomly selected American female college students are normally distributed with unknown mean μ and standard deviation σ. A random sample of 10 American female college students yielded the following weights (in pounds): 115 122 130 127 149 160 152 138 149 180

   Based on the definitions given above, identify the likelihood function and the maximum likelihood estimator of μ, the mean weight of all American female college students.
3. What are the basic issues in density estimation?
4. What are the requirements for a general window in the Parzen window method? Give a popular choice of such a window function.
5. Briefly discuss the effect of widow width in Parzen window method.
6. What are the advantages and disadvantages of Parzen window method?
7. How does the k-NN algorithm make the predictions on the unseen dataset?
8. How to choose the k value in k-NN method?
9. Why is k-NN a non-parametric algorithm?
10. Does the k-NN algorithm work for multimodal distributions?

Exercise

1. Suppose that X is a discrete random variable with the following probability mass function: where $0 \le \theta \le 1$ is a parameter.

X	0	1	2	3
P(X)	$\frac{2\theta}{3}$	$\frac{\theta}{3}$	$\frac{2(1-\theta)}{3}$	$\frac{(1-\theta)}{3}$

   The following 10 independent observations were taken from such a distribution: (3, 0, 2, 1, 3, 2, 1, 0, 2, 1). What is the maximum likelihood estimate of θ.
2. A factory produces widgets which can be either good or defective. Let p be the proportion of the entire population of widgets that are defective. We believe that the proportion of defective widgets is at most 0.5. We use a Bayesian approach and take the prior distribution of p to be the uniform distribution on [0, 0.5].

In a sample of n widgets, all of them are defective.

(a) Find the posterior distribution of p for this particular sample.

(b) If we use squared error loss, what is the Bayesian estimator for p?

Hint: Uniform distribution is given as: $\begin{cases} \frac{1}{(b-a)}, & x \in [a, b] \\ 0, & \text{otherwise} \end{cases}$

3. Consider the following data based on which customers are classified into two classes, namely, high purchasing power (HPP) and low purchasing power (LPP) depending on their age, relative income, and number of credit cards.

Customer	*Age*	*Relative Income*	*Number of Credit Cards*	*Class*
C1	25	20	0	LPP
C2	30	55	2	HPP
C3	42	40	1	LPP
C4	64	25	1	LPP
C5	36	63	3	HPP

Using K-NN algorithm, predict the class to which the customer C6 (Age = 44, Relative income = 37, No. of credit cards = 2) belongs to, for K = 3.

4. Given a set of five data points $x_1 = 4$, $x_2 = 4.5$, $x_3 = 5$, $x_4 = 3$, and $x_5 = 8$. Find Parzen probability density estimate at $x = 5$, using the Gaussian function with $\sigma = 1$ as window function.

5. Apply K-NN algorithm and predict the type of food type to which tomato (sweet = 6, crunch = 4) belongs:

Item	*Sweet*	*Food*	*Crunch type*
Grape	8	5	Fruit
Green bean	3	7	Vegetable
Nuts	3	6	Protein
Orange	7	3	Fruit

CHAPTER

7

Unsupervised Learning & Clustering

In this chapter you will

- learn the basics of unsupervised learning techniques,
- understand the theory behind the k-mean clustering,
- formulate Gaussian mixture model (GMM) mathematically, and
- understand the mathematical principles of expectation maximization (EM) rule for GMMs.

7.0 INTRODUCTION

In this chapter, we discuss some important concepts behind the establishment of unsupervised or clustering techniques. We will understand how the unsupervised learning techniques differ from supervised learning techniques. In addition to that, we study the mathematical description of some popular clustering techniques. Throughout this chapter, the terms unsupervised learning and clustering are interchangeably used.

Until now, we've assumed our training samples are "labelled" by their category membership. Methods that use labelled samples are said to be supervised; otherwise, they're said to be unsupervised. We need to address the following two questions to further proceed.

- Why would one even be interested in learning with unlabelled samples?
- Is it even possible in principle to learn anything of value from unlabelled samples?

The answers to these questions are briefed below.

- Collecting and labelling a large set of sample patterns can be surprisingly costly. One example for such an issue is videos are virtually free, but accurately labelling the video pixels is expensive and time consuming.
- Extending to a larger training set by using semi-supervised learning. It can be done either by training a classifier on a small set of samples, then tuning it up to make it run without supervision on a large, unlabelled set or letting a large set of unlabelled data group automatically, then labelling the groupings found.
- Detecting the gradual change of pattern over time.
- Finding the features that will then be useful for categorization.
- Gaining insight into the nature or structure of the data during the early stages of an investigation.

We can achieve the above-mentioned objectives if proper unsupervised or clustering techniques are devised and utilized.

Data clustering is the process of grouping the objects into meaningful categories. For a given representation of N objects, it is an act of finding k clusters based on a measure of similarity. The major goals of clustering are (i) natural classification by exploiting the degree of similarity among forms, (ii) data exploration by discovering the underlying structure, generating hypotheses and detecting the anomalies, (iii) compression for organizing data and (iv) useful in any scientific field that collects data.

Formal Definition of Data Clustering

Consider the set of samples, say $\{\mathbf{x}_1, \mathbf{x}_2, ..., \mathbf{x}_N\}$ in the d-dimensional feature space which belongs to the dataset D and D is partitioned into k disjoint sets based on some similarity. Mathematically, it is

$$D = \bigcup_{i=1}^{k} D_i \qquad \text{such that} \qquad D_i \cap D_j = \varnothing; \qquad i \neq j \qquad ...(7.1)$$

where the points in each subset D_i are similar to each other according to a given criterion J. Now, the data partition is given as

$$\pi = (D_1, D_2, \ldots, D_k) \qquad ...(7.2)$$

and the problem of data clustering is thus formulated as

$$\pi^* \min_{\pi} f(\pi) \qquad ...(7.3)$$

where $f(.)$ is formulated according to given criterion J.

7.1 *k*-MEANS CLUSTERING

k-means clustering is the most simple and popular clustering algorithm. The objective of k-means clustering is to group similar data points together and discover underlying patterns based on this similarity. To attain this objective, the k-means algorithm tries to find out a fixed number, k of clusters in an unlabelled dataset. We will define the number k, which refers to the number of centroids you need in the dataset. A centroid is defined as the location representing the centre of the cluster. The basic idea of k-means clustering is to allot each data point to a particular cluster by finding out the nearest centroid. Thus, the k-means algorithm identifies k number of centroids corresponding to k clusters, and then allocates every data point to the nearest cluster, while keeping the centroids as small as possible. The *'means'* in the k-means clustering refers to finding out sample means (centroids) corresponding the number k.

The k-means algorithm starts with a first group of randomly selected k centroids, which are used as the initial points for every cluster, and then performs iterative calculations to optimize the positions of the centroids. This iterative procedure stops when

- there is no change in the values of centroids.
- the defined number of iterations is achieved.

7.1.1 Algorithm Description of *k*-Means Clustering

Suppose there are k clusters and $\boldsymbol{\mu}_i$ represents the mean of ith cluster. Then, the steps involved in k-means algorithm can be summarized as follows.

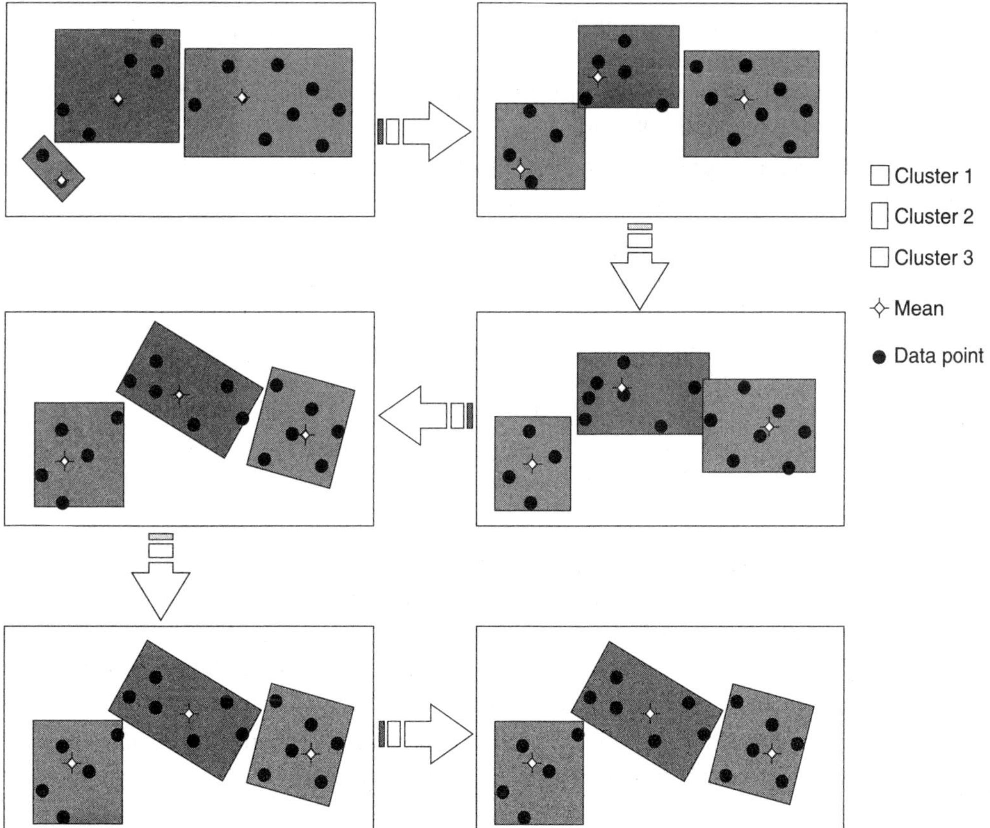

Fig. 7.1 Illustration of k-means algorithm

- Randomly initialize $\boldsymbol{\mu}_1, \boldsymbol{\mu}_2, ..., \boldsymbol{\mu}_k$.
- Repeat until no change in $\boldsymbol{\mu}_i$.
    - Classify N samples according to nearest $\boldsymbol{\mu}_i$.
    - Recompute $\boldsymbol{\mu}_i$

The illustration of *k*-means clustering is shown in Fig. 7.1.

7.2 GAUSSIAN MIXTURE MODEL (GMM)

In the previous section, we have seen that k-means clustering is a "hard" clustering approach where each data point is assigned to a unique cluster depending on how close it is to a particular cluster centre $\boldsymbol{\mu}_i$. But, in certain cases, some of the data points may lie mid-way between different cluster centres. In such cases, a "hard" clustering approach won't be appropriate. This problem can be dealt with in by investigating the level of uncertainty associated with the most appropriate assignment using a probabilistic approach. Gaussian mixture model is such a "soft" clustering approach that gives insight on the probability of a data point belonging to a particular cluster.

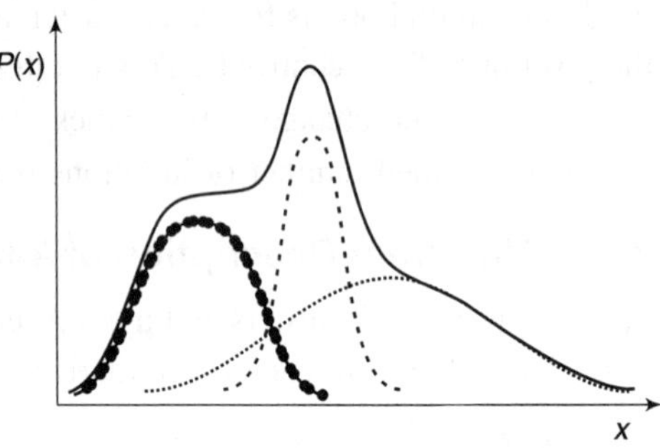

Fig. 7.2 Illustration of GMM

In GMM, the unknown probability density function $p(\mathbf{x})$ is modelled as a linear combination of multiple Gaussian components as shown in Fig. 7.2. This can be expressed as

$$p(\mathbf{x}) = \sum_{k=1}^{K} \pi_k \, N(\mathbf{x}/\boldsymbol{\mu}_k, \Sigma_k) \quad ...(7.4)$$

where the mixing coefficients should satisfy the conditions

$$0 \leq \pi_k \leq 1 \quad ...(7.5)$$

and

$$\sum_{k=1}^{K} \pi_k = 1 \quad ...(7.6)$$

In order to study the formulation of Gaussian mixtures, we introduce a *K*-dimensional latent variable $\mathbf{z}$ in order to represent the Gaussian to which $\mathbf{x}$ belongs to. The latent variable $\mathbf{z}$ follows a one-hot representation scheme such that only one among the z_k is equal to 1 and the remaining are 0. Thus, the elements $z_k \in \{0, 1\}$ and $\Sigma_k z_k = 1$. Depending on which among the z_k takes a value on 1, we can have K different states for the latent variable $\mathbf{z}$.

If we know the joint distribution $p(\mathbf{x}, \mathbf{z})$, then the marginal distribution of $\mathbf{x}$ can be obtained by summing the joint distribution over all possible states of $\mathbf{z}$ as

$$p(\mathbf{x}) = \Sigma_{\mathbf{z}} \, p(\mathbf{x}, \mathbf{z}) \quad ...(7.7)$$

The joint distribution $p(\mathbf{x}, \mathbf{z})$ can be conveniently represented in terms of the marginal distribution $p(\mathbf{z})$ and the conditional distribution $p(\mathbf{x}/\mathbf{z})$ as follows.

$$p(\mathbf{x}, \mathbf{z}) = p(\mathbf{z})\, p(\mathbf{x}/\mathbf{z}) \qquad ...(7.8)$$

In terms of the mixing coefficients, the marginal distribution of $\mathbf{z}$ can be represented as

$$p(z_k = 1) = \pi_k \qquad ...(7.9)$$

Due to the one-hot nature of $\mathbf{z}$, the above distribution can be written as

$$p(\mathbf{z}) = \prod_{k=1}^{K} \pi_k^{z_k} \qquad ...(7.10)$$

The conditional distribution of $\mathbf{x}$ given $\mathbf{z}$ is a Gaussian and it can be represented in the form

$$p(\mathbf{x}/z_k = 1) = N(\mathbf{x}/\boldsymbol{\mu}_k, \Sigma_k) \qquad ...(7.11)$$

This can be modified to be represented in the form given below.

$$p(\mathbf{x}/\mathbf{z}) = \prod_{k=1}^{K} N(\mathbf{x}/\boldsymbol{\mu}_k, \Sigma_k)^{z_k} \qquad ...(7.12)$$

Using Eqs. (7.7), (7.8), (7.10), and (7.12), the marginal density of $\mathbf{x}$ can be written in the form

$$p(\mathbf{x}) = \sum_{\mathbf{z}} \prod_{k=1}^{K} \pi_k^{z_k} N(\mathbf{x}/\boldsymbol{\mu}_k, \Sigma_k)^{z_k} = \sum_{k=1}^{K} \pi_k\, N(\mathbf{x}/\boldsymbol{\mu}_k, \Sigma_k) \qquad ...(7.13)$$

which is of the form given in Eq. (7.4). By representing the marginal distribution $p(\mathbf{x})$ in terms of the joint distribution $p(\mathbf{x}, \mathbf{z})$ as given in Eq. (7.13), we can achieve significant simplifications while dealing with the estimation of parameters.

We can also define the conditional probability of $\mathbf{z}$ given $\mathbf{x}$ from the inferences obtained so far. Using Bayes theorem, $p(z_k = 1/\mathbf{x})$ is given by,

$$g(z_k) = p(z_k = 1/\mathbf{x}) = \frac{p(z_k = 1)\, p(\mathbf{x}/z_k = 1)}{\sum_{j=i}^{K} p(z_j = 1)\, p(\mathbf{x}/z_j = 1)} = \frac{\pi_k N(\mathbf{x}/\boldsymbol{\mu}_k, \Sigma_k)}{\sum_{j=i}^{K} \pi_j N(\mathbf{x}/\boldsymbol{\mu}_j, \Sigma_j)} \qquad ...(7.14)$$

In the above equation, the mixture coefficient π_k is nothing but the prior probability of z_k being 1, and the quantity $\gamma(z_k)$ is the posterior probability obtained after observing $\mathbf{x}$, which is otherwise called the *responsibility* that component k takes for explaining the observation $\mathbf{x}$.

7.2.1 Learning the GMM

For modelling a given set of observations in terms of mixture of Gaussians, we need to estimate the parameter values that give the observed data the highest likelihood. Consider a set of observations $D = \{\mathbf{x}_1, \mathbf{x}_2, \ldots, \mathbf{x}_N\}$. Assuming that the data points are drawn independently from the distribution, the model likelihood can be expresses as

$$L(\boldsymbol{\pi}, \boldsymbol{\mu}, \Sigma) = \prod_{n=1}^{N} p(\mathbf{x}_n) = \prod_{n=1}^{N} \sum_{k=1}^{K} \pi_k N(\mathbf{x}_n/\boldsymbol{\mu}_k, \Sigma_k) \tag{7.15}$$

By taking the log of Eq. (7.15), the objective function can be written in the form

$$\ln L\ (\boldsymbol{\pi}, \boldsymbol{\mu}, \Sigma) = \sum_{k=1}^{K} \ln\left(\sum_{k=1}^{K} \pi_k N(\mathbf{x}_n/\boldsymbol{\mu}_k, \Sigma_k)\right) \quad \text{...(7.16)}$$

The log term present in Eq. (7.16) cannot be pushed inside the sum. Thus, the exponential terms remain in the objective function and the derivative of the same remains cumbersome. So we cannot find a closed-form expression for the maximum likelihood estimator for GMM. Some of the other common issues associated with the maximum likelihood solution are enlisted below.

- **Identifiability:** If we are aiming to model the set of observations in terms of mixtures of K-Gaussians, then we can have $K!$ equivalent solutions for a particular point corresponding to the $K!$ ways of assigning K sets of parameters to K components.
- **Singularities:** Suppose we have a component of the GMM, for which the mean $\boldsymbol{\mu}_j$ is exactly same as one of the data points $\mathbf{x}_n$ as shown in Fig. (7.3). By considering the covariance of this component as $\sigma_j^2\mathbf{I}$, where $\mathbf{I}$ is a unit matrix, then the aforementioned data point contributes a term in the likelihood given by

$$N(\mathbf{x}_n/\mathbf{x}_n, \sigma_j^2 \mathrm{I}) = \frac{1}{(2\pi)^{(1/2)}\ \sigma_j} \quad \text{...(7.17)}$$

When the Gaussian under consideration becomes thinner and thinner, $\sigma_j \rightarrow 0$. This results in the term given in Eq. (7.17) approaching infinity and thereby the likelihood function as a whole goes to infinity. There will always be such singularities whenever a Gaussian collapses to a specific data point. Thus, the maximization of the log likelihood function cannot be treated as a well posed problem.

One of the commonly employed methods to overcome the challenges posed by log-likelihood maximization of GMM is to use the Expectation Maximization (EM) algorithm.

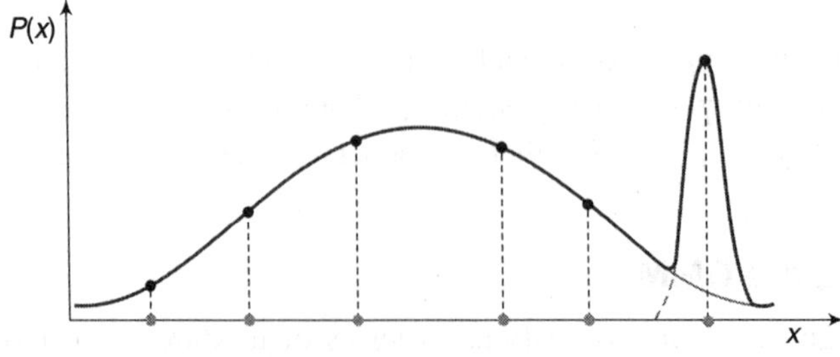

Fig. 7.3 Effect of singularities in the likelihood function of GMM

7.2.2 Expectation Maximization for GMMs

Expectation maximization is a generic algorithm, used to find the parameters of a probabilistic model. Using the iterative EM algorithm, the parameters of the GMM can be found out. We will initially have a discussion on the EM algorithm in the context of GMM, followed by a generalization of the same. The parameters that need to be found in case of a GMM are $\boldsymbol{\pi}$, $\boldsymbol{\mu}$, and Σ.

By setting the derivative of the log-likelihood function given in Eq. (7.16) with respect to the mean $\boldsymbol{\mu}_k$ to zero, we get

$$0 = -\sum_{n=1}^{N} \frac{\pi_k N(\mathbf{x}_n/\boldsymbol{\mu}_k,\Sigma_k)}{(\Sigma_j \pi_j N(\mathbf{x}_n/\boldsymbol{\mu}_j,\Sigma_j)} \Sigma_k(\mathbf{x}_n - \boldsymbol{\mu}_k) = -\sum_{n=1}^{N} \gamma(z_{nk})\Sigma_k(\mathbf{x}_n - \boldsymbol{\mu}_k) \qquad ...(7.18)$$

where $\gamma(z_{nk})$ is the posterior probability that the component k was responsible for generating $\mathbf{x}_n$. Note the natural appearance of the responsibility terms in Eq. (7.18). Multiplying the above equation with Σ_k^{-1} (assuming to be non-singular) and rearranging, we get

$$\boldsymbol{\mu}_k = \frac{1}{N_k} \sum_{n=1}^{N} \gamma(z_{nk})\, \mathbf{x}_n \qquad ...(7.19)$$

where N_k is the effective number of points assigned to a point and is given by

$$N_k = \sum_{n=1}^{N} \gamma(z_{nk}) \qquad ...(7.20)$$

From Eq. (7.19), it can be seen that the mean $\boldsymbol{\mu}_k$ for the kth Gaussian component is obtained by taking a weighted mean of all of the points in the dataset. The weighing factor here is the responsibilities $\gamma(z_{nk})$.

If the derivative of *ln* $L(\boldsymbol{\pi}, \boldsymbol{\mu}, \Sigma)$ given in Eq. (7.16) with respect to Σ_k is set to zero, the ML estimate of the covariance matrix of a single Gaussian can be found out as

$$\Sigma_k = \frac{1}{N_k} \sum_{n=1}^{N} \gamma(z_{nk})\, (\mathbf{x}_n - \boldsymbol{\mu}_k)\, (\mathbf{x}_n - \boldsymbol{\mu}_k)^T \qquad ...(7.21)$$

The covariance matrix so obtained is similar to that of a single Gaussian fitted to a dataset. But here, each data point is weighted with $\gamma(z_{nk})$ and we have the effective number of points associated with the corresponding component in the denominator.

Now, we will find the ML estimate of π_k by maximizing *ln* $L(\boldsymbol{\pi}, \boldsymbol{\mu}, \Sigma)$ with respect to the mixing coefficients. In order to enforce the constraint given by Eq. (7.6), we introduce a Lagrangian multiplier and obtain the following quantity

$$\ln L(\boldsymbol{\pi}, \boldsymbol{\mu}, \Sigma) + \lambda\left(\sum_{k=1}^{K} \pi_k - 1\right) \qquad ...(7.22)$$

By equating the derivative of Eq. (7.22) to zero with respect to π_k, we obtain

$$0 = -\sum_{n=1}^{N} \frac{N(\mathbf{x}_n/\boldsymbol{\mu}_k, \Sigma_k)}{(\Sigma_j \pi_j N(\mathbf{x}_n/\boldsymbol{\mu}_j, \Sigma_j)} + \lambda \qquad ...(7.23)$$

which can be written as

$$0 = \frac{1}{N_k} \sum_{n=1}^{N} \gamma(z_{nk}) + \lambda \qquad ...(7.24)$$

Multiplying both sides of the above equation by π_k and sum over k by using the constraint given in Eq. (7.6), we find that $\lambda = -N$. Thus, we obtain

$$\pi_k = \frac{N_k}{N} \qquad ...(7.25)$$

This tells us that the mixing coefficient for the kth component is given by the average responsibility which that component takes for explaining the data points.

The solutions that we have found in Eq. (7.19), (7.21), and (7.25) are not guaranteed to be closed-form solutions. This is due to the fact that the responsibility terms $\gamma(z_{nk})$ depends on these parameters in a intricate way as given in Eq. (7.14). But, the results obtained do suggest an iterative scheme for finding a solution to the ML problem. The steps involved in the iterative scheme is outlined below.

1. Initialize the means $\boldsymbol{\mu}_k$, covariances Σ_k and mixing coefficients π_k, and evaluate the initial value of the log likelihood. It is common to run the K-means algorithm in order to find a suitable initialization for a Gaussian mixture model.
2. **E step:** Evaluate the responsibilities using the current parameter values

$$\gamma(z_n k) = \frac{\pi_k N(\mathbf{x}_n/\boldsymbol{\mu}_k, \Sigma_k)}{(\Sigma_{j=1}^{K} \pi_j N(\mathbf{x}_n/\boldsymbol{\mu}_j, \Sigma_j)} \qquad ...(7.26)$$

3. **M step:** Re-estimate the parameters using the current responsibilities

$$\boldsymbol{\mu}_k^{\text{new}} = \frac{1}{N_k} \sum_{n=1}^{N} \gamma(z_{nk})\, \mathbf{x}_n \qquad ...(7.27)$$

$$\Sigma_k^{\text{new}} = \frac{1}{N_k} \sum_{n=1}^{N} \gamma(z_{nk})\, (\mathbf{x}_n - \boldsymbol{\mu}_k^{\text{new}})\, (\mathbf{x}_n - \boldsymbol{\mu}_k^{\text{new}})^T \qquad ...(7.28)$$

$$\pi_k^{\text{new}} = \frac{N_k}{N} \qquad ...(7.29)$$

   where N_k is as given in Eq. (7.20)
4. Evaluate the log likelihood given in Eq. (7.16).
5. Check for convergence of either the parameters or the log likelihood. If the convergence criterion is not satisfied, return to step 2 after setting the parameters $\boldsymbol{\mu} = \boldsymbol{\mu}^{\text{new}}$, $\Sigma = \Sigma^{\text{new}}$ and $\pi = \pi^{\text{new}}$.

7.3 SUBSPACE CLUSTERING

Every day, a large amount of data with high dimensional properties is created as a result of technological advancement in various sectors such as commerce, business, information technology, medicine, and other scientific disciplines. Even though these datasets contain a lot of information, dealing with the high dimensionality is a major challenge. One significant challenge is that high dimensional data is highly unstructured. Similarly, data points appeared to be equidistant from each other in a high-dimensional space, potentially masking the available clusters. Another significant issue that clustering algorithms face when dealing with high dimensional data is the *curse of dimensionality*, i.e., distance measures become irrelevant as the number of dimensions in a dataset increases. Clustering algorithms that employ the dimensionality reduction techniques can effectively handle the higher dimensionality of the data. These techniques aim at grouping the data points into respective clusters using a reduced number of features without much loss of information.

Despite of being evenly distributed across the ambient space, high dimensional data is often found in a union of low dimensional structures in many problems. Hence, data in a class can be represented by a low dimensional subspace of the high dimensional ambient space. Among the dimensionality reduction based clustering algorithms, subspace clustering is a prominent clustering as well as dimensionality reduction technique that maps data points from a high dimensional space to a number of low dimensional spaces then clusters them based on their inherent similarity. The underlying idea behind the subspace clustering technique can be well explained with the Union of Subspaces (UoS) model. UoS model relies on the fact that a large collection of data points may not lie on a single higher dimensional space but lie near a union of subspaces. Then subspace modelling is intended to find a multi-subspace representation that fits the data points taken from a high dimensional space. A subspace can be treated as a subset of a large dimensional space. It can be modeled as,

$$S = \bigcup_{i=1}^{N} S_i \qquad ...(7.30)$$

$S \in R^M$ represents the large dimensional space, $s_i \in R^{mi}$ represents the individual subspaces with $m_1 + m_2 + m_3 + ... + m_N = M$ and N is the total number of subspaces. UoS model is pictorially represented in Fig. 7.4. The diagram contains three lines S_2, S_3 and S_4 and one plane S_1 onto which whole data points are mapped individually, based on their distinctive features.

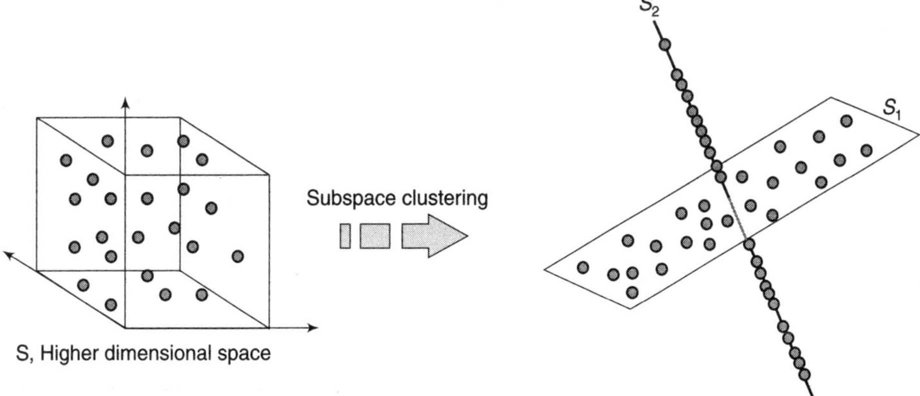

Fig. 7.4 Union of subspaces (UoS) model. Data points in the high dimensional space are mapped on to S_1, S_2, S_3 and S_4 based on their features.

The self-expressive representation of the data is the key idea behind the subspace clustering methodology. According to the self-expressive representation of the data, each data point in a union of subspace can be represented as the linear combination other points in a dataset. Let, $\{S_1\}_{l=1}^{n}$ represent n linear subspaces and assume a group of N data points, $\{\mathbf{x}_i\}_{i=1}^{n}$ are considered to be lying in the union of n subspaces. Then, each datapoint, $\mathbf{x}_i \in \cup_{l=1}^{n} S_1$ can be represented as

$$\mathbf{x}_i = \mathbf{X}\mathbf{z}_i, \quad z_{ii} = 0, \qquad \text{...(7.31)}$$

where, $\boldsymbol{c}_i = [c_{i1}, c_{i2}, ..., c_{iN}]$ and the constraint, $c_{ii} = 0$ eliminates the chance of getting trivial solution of data points. According to sparsity theory, for a matrix $\mathbf{X} \in R^{M \times N}$ there exists a sparse solution $\mathbf{Z} \in R^{N \times N}$ such that the non-zero entries of $\mathbf{Z}$ corresponds to data points belong to the same subspace. It can be represented as $\mathbf{X} = \mathbf{XZ}$, diag($\mathbf{Z}$) = 0, where, diag($\mathbf{Z}$) = 0 eliminates the chance of getting trivial solution of data points. In above expression, the matrix $\mathbf{X} \in R^{M \times N}$ itself acts as the dictionary of data points. Under this scenario, $\mathbf{Z} \in R^{N \times N}$ can be recovered with a sparsest structure such that entries of $\mathbf{Z}$ has fewest non-zero components. Then, the problem can be formulated as

$$\min_{\mathbf{Z} \in R^{N \times N}} \|\mathbf{Z}\|_0 \quad \text{s.t.} \quad \mathbf{X} = \mathbf{XZ} \qquad \text{...(7.32)}$$

where, $\|\cdot\|_0$ is called l_0 norm and it counts the number of non-zero components of the sparse coefficient matrix $\mathbf{Z}$. But, finding l_0 norm is NP-hard such that l_0 norm is replaced by its strong convex surrogate l_1 norm. Thus, minimization using l_1 norm becomes a convex optimization problem such that solution of Eq; (7.32) can be efficiently obtained. Hence, the convex optimization problem can be formulated as

$$\min_{\mathbf{Z} \in R^{N \times N}} \|\mathbf{Z}\|_1 \quad \text{s.t.} \quad \mathbf{X} = \mathbf{XZ} \qquad \text{...(7.33)}$$

In the past decades, a lot of clustering algorithms have been proposed by making the use of subspace clustering techniques. They have been classified into different categories based on their mode of operation, such as iterative methods, algebraic approaches, statistical methods, spectral clustering based methods, and so on. Subsequently, in another track, a set of techniques has been proposed for finding the low dimensional representation of high dimensional data using the principles of sparsity and/or low rankness, and the solution is found out by a global optimization program. The solution of the optimization program obtained is then fed into a spectral clustering framework to infer the final clustered configuration of the data points. On the basis of exploring the information underlying in different perspectives of the data, subspace clustering methods can be divided into two categories, namely,

1. Single-view subspace clustering
2. Multi-view subspace clustering

In single-view based subspace clustering techniques, the information from a single perspective of a datapoint or object is taken into account. In contrast, with the introduction of new forefront technologies in recent days, an information about a single object or a data are described from various perspectives or views. Multi-view subspace clustering techniques are premised on the assumption that incorporating diverse information from multiple views of the data might improve their clustering performance. With the recent advancements in multimedia technology, data with multiple perspectives has been generated, and learning from multi-view data has got substantial attention in various disciplines.

Potential applications for subspace clustering have been found in the fields of image processing and computer vision. Subspace clustering algorithms can be effectively used to cluster imaging data from real-world scenarios. Also, it can be applied in other significant areas such as segmentation of images, motion segmentation and temporal video segmentation. Another potential use of subspace clustering principles is the clustering of hyperspectral data. Subspace clustering method can address the hyperspectral band selection problem by identifying predominant spectral bands and thereby reducing spectral band redundancy. Another area of interest where subspace clustering methodologies have been successful is hyperspectral unmixing. Human action analysis by employing subspace clustering algorithms is an active field of research. Another dynamic area is DNA sequence analysis, which has already been hit and produced notable results using subspace clustering techniques. Information integration systems, which determine and create the best subset of information sources for a given query, are also a powerful platform for subspace clustering techniques to effectively work with.

Conclusion

With this, we conclude our elaborate discussion of the mathematics of unsupervised learning. In Chapter 4, one of these techniques has been discussed as an application. This chapter is very important as unsupervised learning is actually a less explored domain of ML and more applications of this are in the beginning stages. More research into unsupervised learning techniques is the trend as of now.

Questions

1. Differentiate between supervised learning and unsupervised learning.
2. Differentiate between clustering and classification.
3. Discuss the important features of k-means clustering. Give the algorithm for k-means clustering.
4. How can you find the centroid in k-means algorithm?
5. What are the possible stopping conditions in k-means algorithm?
6. How mixture models are created using Gaussian densities?
7. Why GMM is better than k-means?
8. In the EM algorithm, what do the E step and M step represent?
9. EM is better at capturing clusters of different sizes and orientations. Say whether this sentence is true or false.
10. Is GMM parametric?

Exercise

1. Consider the set of two-dimensional data points, x_1 = [1, 1], x_2 = [1, 2], x_3 = [2, 2], x_4 = [2, 3], x_5 = [−4, 5], x_6 = [−3, 5], x_7 = [−4, 4], x_8 = [−3, 4], x_9 = [−7, 8]. Cluster the data points into 2 classes by means of *k*-means algorithm.
2. Consider three data points, $(x_1, x_2, x_3) = (2,4,7)$. Assume two Gaussians and the given data points are generated from one of these Gaussians. The standard deviations of the Gaussians are given as $\sigma_1 = 1/\sqrt{2}$ and $\sigma_2 = 1/\sqrt{2}$. The prior for the Gaussians are given as $\lambda_1 = 0.5$ and $\lambda_2 = 0.5$. With single iteration of the Expectation Maximization algorithm, find the values of the means μ_1 and μ_2 that maximizes the likelihood of the given data.
   Hint: With *m* as the index for data points and *n* as the index for the Gaussians, the latent variable $z_{m,n} = 1$ if Gaussian *n* generates x_m, and 0 otherwise.
3. Consider the following dataset: A = (0, 2), B = (0, 1) and C = (1, 0). The *k*-means algorithm is initialized with centres at *A* and *B*. Find the cluster centres upon convergence.
4. Assume, you want to cluster 7 observations into 3 clusters using k-means clustering algorithm. After first iteration, clusters Q1, Q2, and Q3 has following observations:
   Q1: {(2,2), (4,4), (6,6)}
   Q2: {(0,4), (4,0)}
   Q3: {(5,5), (9,9)}
   What will be the cluster centroids if you want to proceed for the second iteration?

CHAPTER

8

Dimensionality Reduction Techniques

In this chapter you will

- be introduced to the basics of dimensionality reduction techniques,
- formulate principle component analysis (PCA) mathematically,
- understand the mathematical principles of linear discriminant analysis (LDA).
- analyze multiple discriminant analysis (MDA),
- learn the essential concepts of singular value decomposition (SVD), and
- perform numerical calculations based on the above methods.

8.0 INTRODUCTION

In this chapter, we will discuss some of the widespread dimensionality reduction (DR) techniques that are very significant in the field of artificial intelligence (AI) and machine learning (ML). We also do the mathematical formulation of these techniques. The role of DR techniques is very significant because the amount of acquisition, collection, storage, and processing of different kinds of data has grown significantly in recent years. Processing and storing data in this raw form is complicated. DR techniques aim to reduce the dimensionality of this original data without much loss of the relevant information contained in it. Reduction in computational complexity, ease of processing, and storage requirements are the positive outcomes of dimensionality reduction. As we go deeper into the applications of AI and ML, we will be able to appreciate the necessity of such a crucial step of data pre-processing. The mathematical formulations of the forthcoming sections have been explained in an effortless style and need the reader to have only a basic knowledge of vectors and matrices.

8.1 OVERVIEW OF DR TECHNIQUES

Recent developments in data acquisition tools, processing techniques, and storage facilities have resulted in the ease of generating and storing bulk amounts of data in many forms like text, audio, image, video, etc. But, over the years, the size, dimensionality, and complexity of this data have expanded exponentially. Obviously, the higher the dimensionality, the longer the training of AI/ML models will be. This necessitates efficient DR techniques for all AI applications in areas such as business, marketing, computer vision, biomedical, web, education, remote sensing, military, social media and many others.

Most of the existing AI and ML models experience difficulty in processing high-dimensional data. The significant issues are that of *time complexity* and *space complexity*. The reduction of both of them directly translates to improved efficiency of algorithms. The term "*curse of dimensionality*" was derived by Bellman in 1961 to address this scenario which is also closely related to the problem of 'overfitting'.

DR techniques have been developed based on the fundamental principle that even if the original data is high dimensional, it can be confined to an efficient low-dimensional representation in almost all real-world problems. There are two major objectives for DR techniques: (i) remove or reduce the irrelevant features that would otherwise affect the model adversely and (ii) identify a subset of relevant features. DR can be achieved in two ways, one of which is 'feature transformation (extraction)' and the second is 'feature selection'.

Feature transformation is transforming high dimensional data into a reduced dimensional representation by ignoring the irrelevant and redundant features in it. The first challenge associated with this process is the selection of relevant and required features. The second concern is representing the available features in a linear/nonlinear manner and thereby getting a reduced dimensional feature vector. Throughout the process, it is required to ensure that the essential information contained in the original data is not lost because this will adversely affect the efficacy of the model.

Feature selection is selecting the most relevant features from the original data by forming a subset of the original dataset. However, manually selecting the relevant features for an application is laborious. How to handle this difficult task is what we will see as we go ahead.

Generally, DR techniques are performed as a pre-processing step for data before applying them to our AI/ML models. These methods reduce the computational complexity of our models, leading to better performance in resource-constrained environments. However, the selection of DR techniques is application dependent. The method which is very efficient for one application may not be suitable for another. This is because the essential features of different applications may be various for the same set of data. Thus, it is not possible to design a generalized DR technique that is independent of the application. Researchers choose the appropriate DR technique as per their application, considering different factors like accuracy, computational complexity, speed of operation, availability of data, storage requirement, etc.

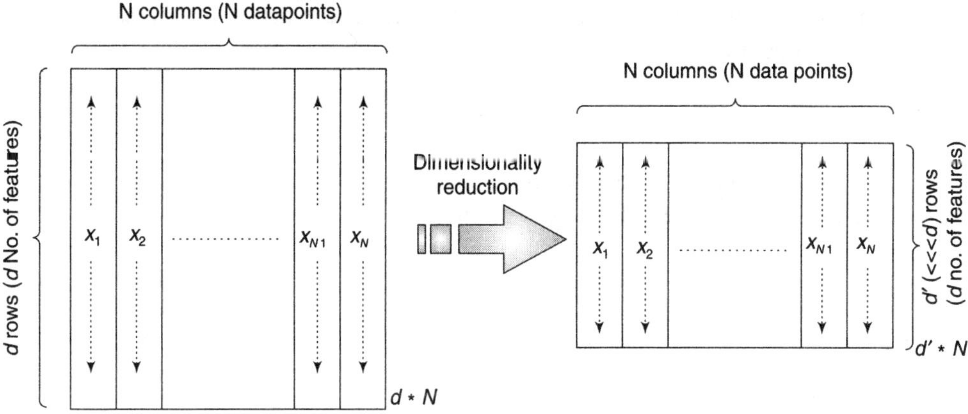

Fig. 8.1 Basic principle of dimensionality reduction techniques

8.1.1 Mathematical Formulation

Let X be a high dimensional data such that $\mathbf{X} = \{\mathbf{x}_1, \mathbf{x}_2, ..., \mathbf{x}_N\} \in R_{n\times N}$, where $\mathbf{x}_i$ represents the ith feature/data vector (observation) in the nth dimensional feature/data space, and N represents the total number of observations. The aim of a DR technique is to transform $\mathbf{X}$ into another data $\mathbf{Y} = \{\mathbf{y}_1, \mathbf{y}_2, ..., \mathbf{y}_N\} \in R_{p\times N}$, where $p << n$ in ideal case. The generalized block diagram of the concept is given in Fig. 8.1.

In the following sections, the mathematical formulations of some of the most popular DR techniques are introduced.

8.2 PRINCIPAL COMPONENT ANALYSIS

Principal Component Analysis (PCA) is one of the popular linear DR techniques in which some simple linear functions are used to transform the higher dimensional data to a lower dimension. Even though multiple strategies are available for PCA, all techniques target preserving the maximum variability present in the data. It is an unsupervised technique based on the concept of eigenvector search. The major application areas of PCA include image and video processing, speech and audio processing, computer vision, robotics, and pattern recognition. The main aim of PCA is to extract the essential uncorrelated features of data known as *principal components* (PCs). The first principal component indicates the almost significant variance of the data, the second one holds the following highest variance, and so on. If we choose only first 'p' relevant principal components (where $p < n$), the dimensionality of the data is reduced from 'n' to 'p'.

8.2.1 Mathematical Formulation of PCA

PCA seeks the best linear transformation making the best lower dimensional projection of data in a least square sense. We start with the problem of representing a set of d-dimensional vectors, say, $\{\mathbf{x}_1, \mathbf{x}_2, ..., \mathbf{x}_n\}$ to a single vector $\mathbf{x}$ (zero-dimensional representation). The basic idea is to find out a vector $\mathbf{x}$ so that the sum of squared distance (squared error) between $\mathbf{x}$

and all other vectors must be as minimum as possible. The function for the squared error criterion is given below.

$$J(x) = \sum_{i=1}^{n} \|\mathbf{x}_i - \mathbf{x}\|^2 \qquad ...(8.1)$$

Thus, we need to find out **x** that minimizes the sum of squared error criterion, $J(\mathbf{x})$. The sample mean of the available samples $\bar{\mathbf{x}}$ is given as

$$\bar{\mathbf{x}} = \frac{1}{n}\sum_{i=1}^{n} \mathbf{x}_\mathbf{i} \qquad ...(8.2)$$

It is possible to prove that $\mathbf{x} = \bar{x}$ gives the representation of $\{\mathbf{x}_1, \mathbf{x}_2, ..., \mathbf{x}_n\}$ to a single vector **x** with minimum $J(\mathbf{x})$. This can be proved in the following manner.

$$J(x) = \sum_{i=1}^{n} \|\mathbf{x}_i - \mathbf{x}\|^2$$

$$= \sum_{i=1}^{n} \|(\mathbf{x} - \bar{\mathbf{x}}) - (\mathbf{x}_i - \bar{\mathbf{x}})\|^2$$

$$= \sum_{i=1}^{n} \|(\mathbf{x} - \bar{\mathbf{x}}) - (\mathbf{x}_i - \bar{\mathbf{x}})\|^2$$

$$= \sum_{i=1}^{n} \|(\mathbf{x} - \bar{\mathbf{x}})\|^2 - 2\sum_{i=1}^{n} (\mathbf{x}_i - \bar{\mathbf{x}})^T (\mathbf{x}_i - \bar{\mathbf{x}}) + \sum_{i=1}^{n} \|\mathbf{x}_i - \mathbf{x}\|^2 \qquad ...(8.3)$$

$$= \sum_{i=1}^{n} \|(\mathbf{x} - \bar{\mathbf{x}})\|^2 - 2(\mathbf{x} - \bar{\mathbf{x}})^T \sum_{i=1}^{n} (\mathbf{x}_i - \bar{\mathbf{x}}) + \sum_{i=1}^{n} \|\mathbf{x}_i - \mathbf{x}\|^2$$

$$= \sum_{i=1}^{n} \|(\mathbf{x} - \bar{\mathbf{x}})\|^2 - \sum_{i=1}^{n} \|\mathbf{x}_i - \mathbf{x}\|^2$$

The second term in the last equation of Eq. 8.3 is independent of **x**; the function $J(\mathbf{x})$ is minimized by selecting $\mathbf{x} = \bar{\mathbf{x}}$. Thus, it is concluded that the sample mean is the zero-dimensional representation of any dataset. However, the zero-dimensional representation of the dataset does not show any variability among the samples which may adversely affect the performance of further processing units. Hence, zero-dimensional model is not advisable for most practical applications.

The next main objective is to preserve the variability among the data in addition to dimensionality reduction. The one-dimensional representation is the simplest solution of this objective by projecting the samples into a line passing through the sample mean, which means ensuring a significant data variability among the samples. Let **e** be the unit vector in the direction of the line passing through the sample mean, $\bar{\mathbf{x}}$. Then, the equation for the line is given as

$$\mathbf{x}' = c\mathbf{e} + \bar{\mathbf{x}} \qquad ...(8.4)$$

where c represents the coefficient that corresponds the distance of any arbitrary sample $\mathbf{x}'$ from the sample mean $\bar{\mathbf{x}}$. Thus, the kth sample $\mathbf{x}_k$ can be described as

$$\mathbf{x}_k = c_k\mathbf{e} + \overline{\mathbf{x}} \qquad ...(8.5)$$

Now, the task is to find out the "optimal" value of the coefficient c_k for all such samples which can minimize the error in the one-dimensional representation. Moreover, it is required to find the optimal direction of the line indicating the optimal unit vector, **e**. Thus, for the one-dimensional representation of samples, it is required to find two sets of values: the optimal coefficients (c_k) and the unit vector, **e**. We can find out such optimal coefficients by minimizing the sum of the squared-error criterion function, which is given below.

$$\begin{aligned} J_1(c_1, c_2, \ldots, c_n, \mathbf{e}) &= \sum_{i=1}^{n} \|(\overline{\mathbf{x}} + c_i\mathbf{e}) - \mathbf{x}_i\|^2 \\ &= - \sum_{i=1}^{n} \|c_i\mathbf{e} - (\mathbf{x}_i - \overline{\mathbf{x}})\|^2 \qquad ...(8.6) \\ &= \sum_{i=1}^{n} c_i^2\|\mathbf{e}\|^2 - 2\sum_{i=1}^{n} c_i\mathbf{e}^T(\mathbf{x}_i - \overline{\mathbf{x}}) + \sum_{i=1}^{n} \|\mathbf{x}_i - \overline{\mathbf{x}}\|^2 \end{aligned}$$

The optimal coefficients (c_i) can be found by finding out the stationary points of the function, $J_1(c_1, c_2, ..., c_n, \mathbf{e})$ by differentiating it with c_i and setting it into zero. While applying this procedure, we obtain the coefficients as (derivation is not given)

$$c_i = \mathbf{e}^T(\mathbf{x}_i - \overline{\mathbf{x}}) \qquad ...(8.7)$$

The next task is to find out the best direction (**e**) for the line (one-dimensional representation). The concept of *scatter matrix* is introduced here, which is useful in finding out the best direction with maximum variance. The scatter matrix (**S**) can be defined as follows. Let us substitute the value of c_k given in Eq. 8.7 in Eq. 8.6. Then,

$$\begin{aligned} J_1(c_1, c_2, \ldots, c_n, \mathbf{e}) &= \sum_{i=1}^{n} c_i^2 - 2\sum_{i=1}^{n} c_i^2 + \sum_{i=1}^{n} \|\mathbf{x}_i - \overline{\mathbf{x}}\|^2 \\ &= - \sum_{i=1}^{n} [\mathbf{e}^T(\mathbf{x}_i - \overline{\mathbf{x}})]^2 + \sum_{i=1}^{n} \|\mathbf{x}_i - \overline{\mathbf{x}}\|^2 \\ &= \sum_{i=1}^{n} \mathbf{e}^T[(\mathbf{x}_i - \overline{\mathbf{x}})(\mathbf{x}_i - \overline{\mathbf{x}})^T]\mathbf{e} + \sum_{i=1}^{n} \|\mathbf{x}_i - \overline{\mathbf{x}}\|^2 \qquad ...(8.8) \\ &= \sum_{i=1}^{n} \mathbf{e}^T[(\mathbf{x}_i - \overline{\mathbf{x}})(\mathbf{x}_i - \overline{\mathbf{x}})^T]\mathbf{e} + \sum_{i=1}^{n} \|\mathbf{x}_i - \overline{\mathbf{x}}\|^2 \\ &= -\mathbf{e}^T\mathbf{S}\mathbf{e} + \sum_{i=1}^{n} \|\mathbf{x}_i - \overline{\mathbf{x}}\|^2 \end{aligned}$$

where, the scatter matrix (**S**) is defined as

$$\mathbf{S} = \sum_{i=1}^{n} [(\mathbf{x}_i - \overline{\mathbf{x}})(\mathbf{x}_i - \overline{\mathbf{x}})^T] \qquad ...(8.9)$$

which indicates (n – 1) times the sample covariance matrix.

From Eq. 8.8, it is clear that the unit vector (**e**) minimizes the squared error criterion function, $J_1(c_1, c_2, \ldots, c_n, \mathbf{e})$ maximizes $\mathbf{e}^T\mathbf{S}\mathbf{e}$. It can be considered a nonlinear programming problem (NLPP) with an equality constraint.

$$\max_{\mathbf{e}} \quad \mathbf{e}^T\mathbf{S}\mathbf{e} \qquad \text{s.t.} \quad \|\mathbf{e}\| = 1 \qquad \ldots(8.10)$$

Clearly, the well-known Lagrangian method can be used for solving this optimization problem. The Lagrangian function of the optimization problem given in Eq. 8.10 can be represented as

$$L(\mathbf{e}, \lambda) = \mathbf{e}^T\,\mathbf{S}\mathbf{e} - \lambda(\mathbf{e}^T\,\mathbf{e} - 1) \qquad \ldots(8.11)$$

where, λ is the Lagrange multiplier. To get the stationary point, it is necessary to differentiate the Lagrangian function, $L(\mathbf{e}, \lambda)$ with respect to **e**.

$$\frac{\partial L(\mathbf{e}, \lambda)}{\partial \mathbf{e}} = \mathbf{e}^T\,\mathbf{S}\mathbf{e} - \lambda(\mathbf{e}T\,\mathbf{e} - 1) \qquad \ldots(8.12)$$

Setting this gradient vector to zero, we get **e** as eigenvector of the scatter matrix, **S**. It can be represented as

$$\mathbf{S}\mathbf{e} = \lambda\mathbf{e} \qquad \ldots(8.13)$$

Equation 8.13 can be rewritten as

$$\mathbf{e}^T\,\mathbf{S}\mathbf{e} = \lambda\mathbf{e}^T\mathbf{e} = \lambda \qquad \ldots(8.14)$$

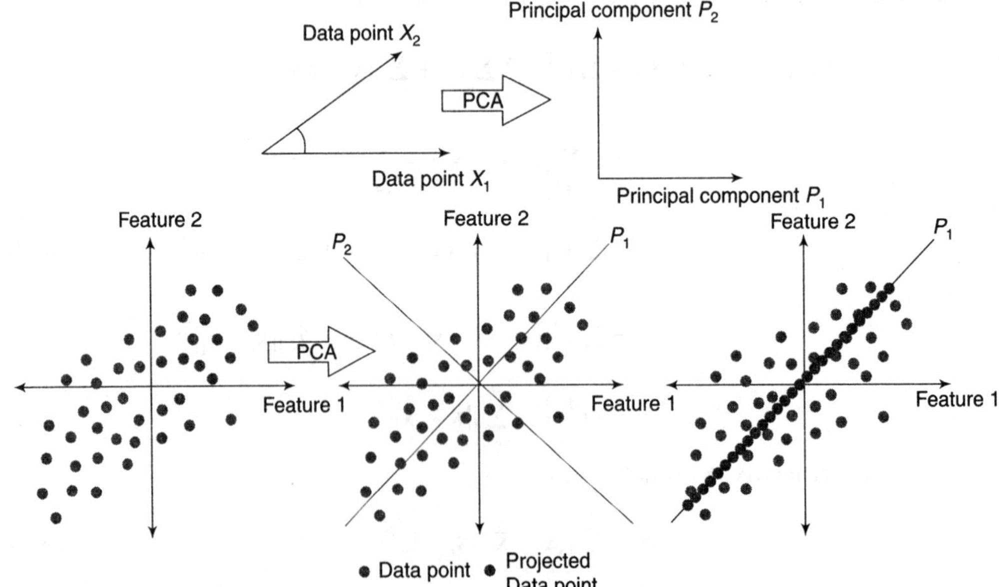

Fig. 8.2 A simple geometrical illustration for PCA

Thus, to maximize $\mathbf{e}^T\mathbf{S}\mathbf{e}$, we need to select the eigenvector corresponding to the largest eigenvalue of the scatter matrix, **S**.

Finally, it can be concluded that the best one-dimensional representation of the data (in the least sum of squared error sense) can be obtained by projecting the samples onto a line passing through the sample mean and in the direction of eigenvector of the scatter matrix corresponding to the largest eigenvalue. A simple geometrical illustration for PCA is shown in Fig. 8.2. This concept can be extended to d' dimensional representation (where $d' \leq d$) by simply extending Eq. 8.4 in the following manner.

$$\mathbf{x}' = \bar{\mathbf{x}} + \sum_{k=1}^{d'} c_k \mathbf{e}_k \quad \text{...(8.15)}$$

The sum of squared error criterion function, in this case, is defined as

$$J'_d = \bar{\mathbf{x}} + \sum_{i=1}^{n} \left\| \left(\bar{\mathbf{x}} + \sum_{k=1}^{d'} c_k \mathbf{e}_k \right) - x_i \right\|^2 \quad \text{...(8.16)}$$

It is easy to prove that this error function can be minimized when the vectors $\mathbf{e}_1$, $\mathbf{e}_2$, ..., $\mathbf{e}_d$, are the eigenvectors of the scatter matrix corresponding to the first d' highest eigenvalues. Since the scatter matrix is real and symmetric, these eigenvectors are orthogonal and they form a natural basis for representing the samples. The coefficients (c_k) are known as the principal components and are the projections of $\mathbf{x}'$ in this basis. Geometrically, the eigenvectors of the scatter matrix are the principal axes of a hyperellipsoid represented by the d-dimensional data points which reduce the dimensionality of the data by concentrating the focus on the directions with maximum variability among the data.

A large number of variants of PCA were developed in terms of the improved performance and the application. Some examples are Generalized PCA, Robust PCA, Multi-linear PCA, Multivariate Functional PCA, Sparse PCA, Random Permutation PCA, etc.

8.2.2 Example

The matrix below represents four samples in $\mathbf{R}^2$.

$$\mathbf{X} = \begin{bmatrix} 6 & -4 \\ -3 & 5 \\ -2 & 6 \\ 7 & -3 \end{bmatrix}$$

(a) We want to project these samples into one-dimensional representation using PCA. What is the one-dimensional subspace which we are projecting onto?

(b) For each sample in **X**, write the coordinates that the point is projected.

Solution: The given data matrix is

$$\mathbf{X} = \begin{bmatrix} 6 & -4 \\ -3 & 5 \\ -2 & 6 \\ 7 & -3 \end{bmatrix}$$

a. The sample mean of X is given as

$$\overline{\mathbf{X}} = [2 \quad 1]$$

Then, $$\mathbf{X} - \overline{\mathbf{X}} = \begin{bmatrix} 4 & -5 \\ -5 & 4 \\ -4 & 5 \\ 5 & -4 \end{bmatrix}$$

and the scatter matrix is given as

$$S = (\mathbf{X} - \overline{\mathbf{X}})^T (\mathbf{X} - \overline{\mathbf{X}}) = \begin{bmatrix} 82 & -80 \\ -80 & 82 \end{bmatrix}$$

The eigenvalues of S are 162, and 2 and the respective eigenvectors are

$$\begin{bmatrix} \frac{1}{\sqrt{2}} \\ -\frac{1}{\sqrt{2}} \end{bmatrix} \text{ and } \begin{bmatrix} \frac{1}{\sqrt{2}} \\ \frac{1}{\sqrt{2}} \end{bmatrix}$$

We are projecting the subspace spanned by $\begin{bmatrix} \frac{1}{\sqrt{2}} \\ -\frac{1}{\sqrt{2}} \end{bmatrix}$ corresponding the highest eigen-value (first principal component).

b. The coordinates of the projected points are

$$\begin{bmatrix} 4 & -5 \\ -5 & 4 \\ -4 & 5 \\ 5 & -4 \end{bmatrix} \times \begin{bmatrix} \frac{1}{\sqrt{2}} \\ -\frac{1}{\sqrt{2}} \end{bmatrix} = \begin{bmatrix} \frac{10}{\sqrt{2}} \\ \frac{-8}{-\sqrt{2}} \\ \frac{-8}{-\sqrt{2}} \\ \frac{10}{\sqrt{2}} \end{bmatrix}$$

8.3 FISHER LINEAR DISCRIMINANT ANALYSIS

Even though PCA provides an efficient low dimensional representation of the data samples, it cannot exploit any discriminability among the data points. The aim of the Fisher Linear Discriminant (FLD) analysis is to provide low dimensional representation and discrimination/

classification of data samples in different classes as a combined action. Consider the case of projecting the d-dimensional samples to a line (one-dimensional representation) as seen in PCA. However, FLD arranges these projections of samples into the line so that the samples belonging to the same class are clustered in a region that is well separated from the other classes. This is the basic objective of conventional discriminant analysis. The basic principle of FLD is illustrated in Fig. 8.3.

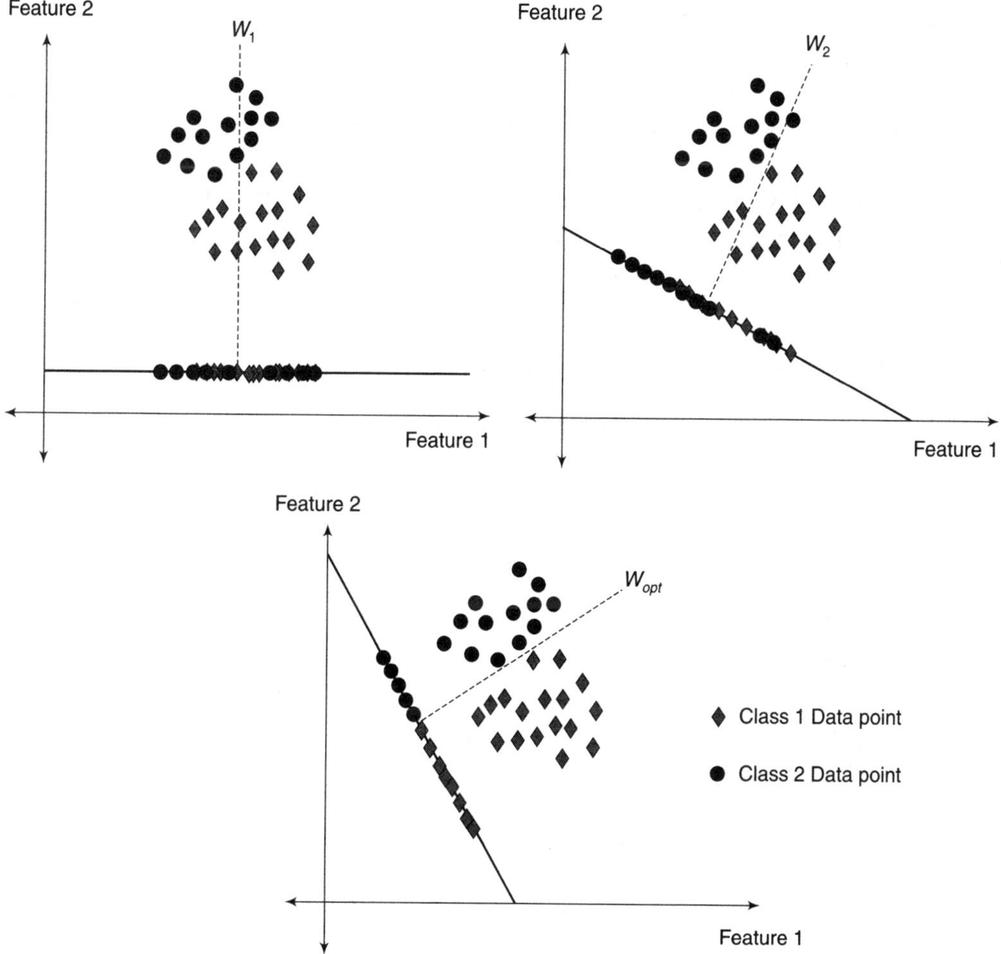

Fig. 8.3 The basic principle of FLD analysis

8.3.1 Mathematical Formulation of FLD

Let us assume that a set of n d-dimensional samples say, $\{\mathbf{x}_1, \mathbf{x}_2, ..., \mathbf{x}_n\}$ belongs to two classes, C_1 and C_2. Suppose n_1 samples belong to C_1 and n_1 samples belong to C_2. If we consider the linear combination of the components of any arbitrary sample $\mathbf{x}$, we get a scalar as given below.

$$z = \mathbf{w}^T\mathbf{x} \qquad ...(8.17)$$

Then, there will be a one-to-one mapping between $\mathbf{x}$ to z in the following manner.

$$\{\mathbf{x}_1, \mathbf{x}_2, ..., \mathbf{x}_n\} \longrightarrow \{z_1, z_2, ..., z_n\} \qquad ...(8.18)$$

The set of such scalars can be decomposed into two subsets corresponding to the classes $C1$ and C_2 say, Z_1 and Z_2 with number of samples n_1 and n_2 respectively. If $\|\mathbf{w}\| = 1$, z_i represents the projection of components of $\mathbf{x}_i$ onto a line in the direction of $\mathbf{w}$. Certainly there is no significance for the magnitude of $\mathbf{w}$. But, the direction of $\mathbf{w}$ is very significant because it decides the least error in the reduced dimensional representation and maximum accuracy for the classification operation. Now, the task is to find the best direction for $\mathbf{w}$, which must measure the classification accuracy and the best low dimensional representation. To improve the accuracy of classification, the separation between the centroids of the subsets C_1 and C_2 must be maximized. Consequently, the distance between Z_1 and Z_2 must be maximized.

The centroid or sample mean of ith class C_i can be found by

$$\bar{\mathbf{x}}_i = \frac{1}{n_i} \sum_{\mathbf{x} \in C_i} \mathbf{x} \qquad ...(8.19)$$

Similarly, the sample mean of projected samples is given by

$$\bar{z}_i = \frac{1}{n_i} \sum_{x \in z_i} z$$

$$\bar{z}_i = \frac{1}{n_i} \sum_{\mathbf{x} \in z_i} \mathbf{w}^T\mathbf{x} \qquad ...(8.20)$$

$$= \mathbf{w}^T\bar{\mathbf{x}}_i$$

From Eq. 8.20, it is clear that the sample mean of projected samples is simply the projection of the sample mean of samples.

As mentioned earlier, for better discrimination, the distance between the means must be maximized. Thus, for the two-class classification problem, the distance between the projected samples means is given as

$$\bar{z}_i = \frac{1}{n_i} \sum_{\mathbf{x} \in z_i} z$$

$$\bar{z}_i = \frac{1}{n_i} \sum_{\mathbf{x} \in C_i} \mathbf{w}^T\mathbf{x} \qquad ...(8.21)$$

$$= \mathbf{w}^T\bar{\mathbf{x}}_i$$

8.3.2 Scatter Matrices

It is beneficial to maximize this distance in terms of variance of a certain class instead of scaling, $\mathbf{w}$. We define another quantity known as the scatter for the projected samples of each class for accomplishing this.

For i^{th} class, the scatter is defined as

$$|\bar{z}_1 - \bar{z}_2| = |\mathbf{w}^T (\bar{\mathbf{x}}_1 - \bar{\mathbf{x}}_2)| \quad ...(8.22)$$

We describe the estimate of the variance of projected samples as, $\frac{1}{n}(\bar{s}_1^2 + \bar{s}_2^2)$, where $(\bar{s}_1^2 + \bar{s}_2^2)$ is called the *total within-class scatter* of the projected samples. The scatter matrices are defined as

$$\mathbf{S}_i = \sum_{\mathbf{x} \in C_i} (\mathbf{x} - \bar{\mathbf{x}})(\mathbf{x} - \bar{\mathbf{x}})^T \quad ...(8.23)$$

the sum of scatter matrices is known as *within-class scatter matrix* and is given as

$$\mathbf{S_w} = \mathbf{S_1} + \mathbf{S_2} \quad ...(8.24)$$

It is proportional to the sample covariance matrix and hence it is symmetric and positive semidefinite.

Now, Eq. 8.22 can be rewritten as

$$\begin{aligned} \bar{s}_i^2 &= \sum_{x \in C_i} (\mathbf{w}^T\mathbf{x} - \mathbf{w}^T\bar{\mathbf{x}})^2 \\ &= \sum_{x \in C_i} (\mathbf{w}^T (\mathbf{x} - \bar{\mathbf{x}})(\mathbf{x} - \bar{\mathbf{x}})^T\mathbf{w})^2 \quad ...(8.25) \\ &= \mathbf{w}^T\mathbf{S}_i\mathbf{w} \end{aligned}$$

Then, the total within-class scatter of projected samples (sum of scatters), $(\bar{s}_1^2 + \bar{s}_2^2)$ can be represented as

$$(\bar{s}_1^2 + \bar{s}_2^2) = \sum_{i=1}^{2} \mathbf{w}^T \mathbf{S}_i\mathbf{w} - \mathbf{w}^T\mathbf{S}_w\mathbf{w} \quad ...(8.26)$$

Now, it is possible to calculate the distance between the projected sample means as

$$\begin{aligned} (\bar{z}_1 - \bar{z}_2)^2 &= (\mathbf{w}^T (\bar{\mathbf{x}}_1 - \bar{\mathbf{x}}_2)^2 \\ &= \mathbf{w}^T (\bar{\mathbf{x}}_1 - \bar{\mathbf{x}}_2)(\bar{\mathbf{x}}_1 - \bar{\mathbf{x}}_2)^T \mathbf{w} \quad ...(8.27) \end{aligned}$$

Now the quantity $(\bar{\mathbf{x}}_1 - \bar{\mathbf{x}}_2)(\bar{\mathbf{x}}_1 - \bar{\mathbf{x}}_2)^T$ is known as the *between-class scatter matrix*, $\mathbf{S_B}$. Then, Eq. 8.27 can be rewritten in terms of $\mathbf{S_B}$ as follows.

$$(\bar{z}_1 - \bar{z}_2)^2 = \mathbf{w}^T \mathbf{S}_B \mathbf{w} \quad ...(8.28)$$

Like the within-class scatter matrix, the between-class scatter matrix is also symmetric and semidefinite. Also, it can be understood that $\mathbf{S_B w}$ is in the same direction of $(\bar{\mathbf{x}}_1 - \bar{\mathbf{x}}_2)$ for any $\mathbf{w}$.

8.3.3 Criterion Function for FLD Analysis

FLD follows a linear function as $\mathbf{w}^T \mathbf{x}$ and the criterion function $J(\mathbf{w})$ is defined as follows.

$$J(\mathbf{w}) = \frac{|\bar{z}_1 - \bar{z}_2|^2}{(\bar{s}_1^2 + \bar{s}_2^2)} \qquad ...(8.29)$$

From Eq. 8.29, it is understood that $J(\mathbf{w})$ must be maximized to ensure that the separation between the two classes is maximized. The numerator of this term is maximized so that the different classes are being well separated from each other. Meanwhile, the denominator of this function should be minimized such that the samples belonging to the same class can be closely clustered together in terms of its centroid. Please note that $J(\mathbf{w})$ is only dependent on the direction of **w** and independent of $\|\mathbf{w}\|$. By substituting Eq. 8.26 and 8.28 in Eq. 8.29, $J(\mathbf{w})$ can be represented as the function of **w**, $\mathbf{S_B}$ and $\mathbf{S_w}$.

$$J(\mathbf{w}) = \frac{(\mathbf{w}^T \mathbf{S}_B \mathbf{w})}{(\mathbf{w}^T \mathbf{S}_w \mathbf{w})} \qquad ...(8.30)$$

Eq. 8.30 follows the generalized Rayleigh quotient, and we can find the maximum of $J(\mathbf{w})$ by following the following relation.

$$\mathbf{S_B w} = \lambda \mathbf{S_w w} \qquad ...(8.31)$$

where, λ is a scalar. Eq. 8.31 can be represented as the generalized eigenvalue problem in the following manner.

$$\mathbf{S}_w^{-1} \mathbf{S}_B w = \lambda \mathbf{w} \qquad ...(8.32)$$

Since $\mathbf{S_B w}$ is in the same direction of $(\bar{\mathbf{x}}_1 - \bar{\mathbf{x}}_2)$ and the magnitude of **w** is immaterial, we can directly find out the value of **w** without calculating the eigenvalues and eigenvectors of Eq. 8.32.

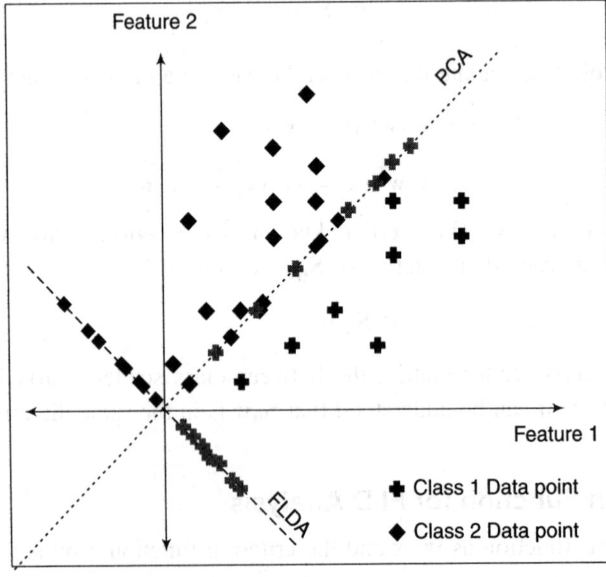

Fig. 8.4 The comparison between PCA and FLD

Thus, the solution for **w** that maximizes $J(\mathbf{w})$ is given as

$$\mathbf{w} = \mathbf{S}_w^{-1} (\bar{\mathbf{x}}_1 - \bar{\mathbf{x}}_2) \quad \text{...(8.33)}$$

Eq. 8.33 represents the solution for maximizing the ratio of between scatter to within-class scatter in FLD analysis. Since this mapping is many to one, the desired accuracy can be achieved only if the training set is sufficiently large. The comparison between PCA and FLD is illustrated in Fig. 8.4.

8.3.4 Example

For the two-dimensional data samples given below, find the optimal LDA projection.

- Class 1: {(1, 2), (2, 3), (3, 3), (4, 5), (5, 5)}
- Class 2: {(1, 0), (2, 1), (3, 1), (3, 2), (5, 3), (6, 5)}

Solution: The given data samples are:

- Class 1, C_1: $\mathbf{X}_1$ = {(1,2), (2,3), (3,3), (4,5), (5,5)}
- Class 2, C_2: $\mathbf{X}_2$ = {(1,0), (2,1), (3,1), (3,2), (5,3), (6,5)}

The within-class scatter matrices are given as

$$\mathbf{S}_i = \sum_{\mathbf{x}\in C_i} (\mathbf{x} - \bar{\mathbf{x}}_i)(\mathbf{x} - \bar{\mathbf{x}}_i)^T$$

$$\mathbf{S}_1 = \sum_{\mathbf{x}\in C_1} (\mathbf{x} - \overline{\mathbf{x}_1})(\mathbf{x} - \overline{\mathbf{x}_1})^T$$

$$\mathbf{S}_1 = \begin{bmatrix} 10 & 8 \\ 8 & 7.2 \end{bmatrix}$$

$$\mathbf{S}_2 = \sum_{\mathbf{x}\in C_2} (\mathbf{x} - \overline{\mathbf{x}_2})(\mathbf{x} - \overline{\mathbf{x}_2})^T$$

$$\mathbf{S}_2 = \begin{bmatrix} 17.33 & 14 \\ 16 & 16 \end{bmatrix}$$

The total within-class scatter matrix is given as

$$\mathbf{S}_w = \mathbf{S}_1 + \mathbf{S}_2 = \begin{bmatrix} 17.33 & 24 \\ 24 & 23.2 \end{bmatrix}$$

The between-class scatter matrix is

$$\mathbf{S}_B = (\bar{\mathbf{x}}_1 - \bar{\mathbf{x}}_2)(\bar{\mathbf{x}}_1 - \bar{\mathbf{x}}_2)^T = \begin{bmatrix} 0.1089 & -0.528 \\ -0.528 & 2.56 \end{bmatrix}$$

The optimal FLD projection is

$$\mathbf{w} = \mathbf{S}_w^{-1} (\bar{\mathbf{x}}_1 - \bar{\mathbf{x}}_2) = \begin{bmatrix} -0.792 \\ 0.888 \end{bmatrix}$$

8.4 MULTIPLE DISCRIMINANT ANALYSIS

As discussed earlier, FLD analysis is defined only for two category/class problems. However, most of the practical applications are multi-class problems. We can generally mention it as c-category/class problems (generally, $c > 2$), where $C_1, C_2, ..., C_c$ represents the subset of pooled data C corresponding to different classes and the set; $n_1, n_2, ..., n_c$ indicates the number of samples in each subset respectively. Multiple discriminant analysis (MDA) is a generalized extension of FLD analysis for multi-class problems. As we know, for a c-category problem, $(c - 1)$ discriminant functions are required to define it properly. Generally, it is assumed that $d \geq c$, where the samples belong to a d-dimensional space. The geometric illustration of MDA for a 3-class classification problem is given in Fig. 8.5.

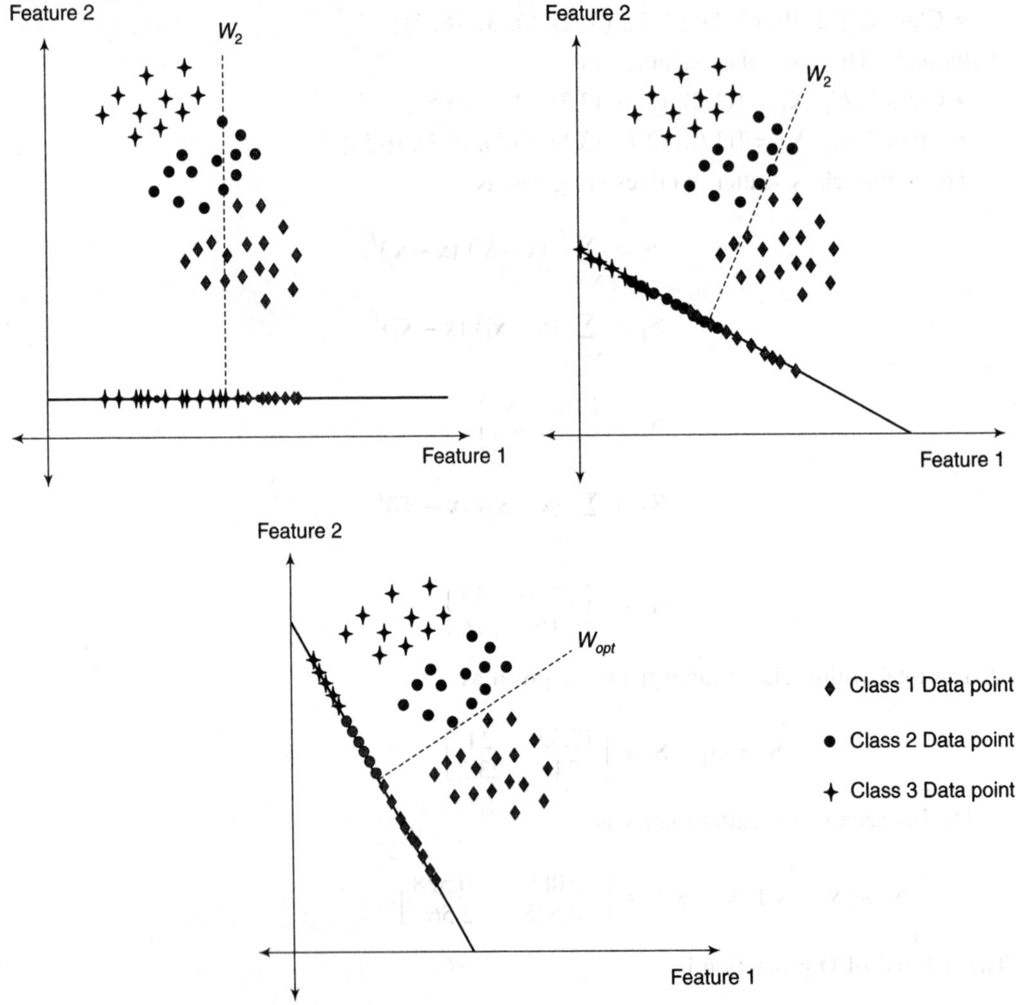

Fig. 8.5 The geometric illustration of MDA for a 3-class classification problem

8.4.1 Mathematical Formulation of MDA

Like FLD analysis, it is required to define the between scatter and within-class scatter matrices in MDA for multi-class problems. The definition of within-class scatter matrix is straightforward, and the extension for the c-class case is sufficient. However, a little more understanding/analysis is required to properly define between-class scatter matrix for c-class problems.

8.4.2 Scatter Matrices in MDA

The within-class scatter matrix for a c-category problem is defined as

$$\mathbf{S}_w = \sum_{j=1}^{c} \mathbf{S}_j \qquad \text{...(8.34)}$$

where,

$$\mathbf{S}_j = \sum_{\mathbf{x} \in C_j} (\mathbf{x} - \overline{\mathbf{x}}_j)(\mathbf{x} - \overline{\mathbf{x}}_j)^T \qquad \text{...(8.35)}$$

and

$$\overline{\mathbf{x}}_J = \frac{1}{n_j} \sum_{\mathbf{x} \in C_j} \mathbf{x} \qquad \text{...(8.36)}$$

Let the total sample mean be $\overline{\mathbf{x}}$ and the total scatter matrix is $\mathbf{S}_T$. Mathematically, these two quantities can be defined as follows.

$$\overline{\mathbf{x}} = \frac{1}{n} \sum_{\mathbf{x}} \mathbf{x} = \frac{1}{n} \sum_{j=1}^{c} n_j \overline{\mathbf{x}}_j \qquad \text{...(8.37)}$$

and

$$\mathbf{S}_T = \sum_{\mathbf{x}} (\mathbf{x} - \overline{\mathbf{x}}_l)(\mathbf{x} - \overline{\mathbf{x}}_l)^T \qquad \text{...(8.38)}$$

Equation 8.38 can be expanded as follows.

$$\begin{aligned} \mathbf{S}_T &= \sum_{j=1}^{c} \sum_{x \in C_j} (\mathbf{x} - \overline{\mathbf{x}}_\mathbf{j} + \overline{\mathbf{x}}_\mathbf{j} - \overline{\mathbf{x}})(\mathbf{x} - \overline{\mathbf{x}}_\mathbf{j} + \overline{\mathbf{x}}_\mathbf{j} - \overline{\mathbf{x}})^T \\ &= \sum_{j=1}^{c} \sum_{x \in C_j} (\mathbf{x} - \overline{\mathbf{x}}_j)(\mathbf{x} - \overline{\mathbf{x}}_j)^T + \sum_{j=1}^{c} \sum_{x \in C_j} (\overline{\mathbf{x}}_j - \overline{\mathbf{x}})(\overline{\mathbf{x}}_j - \overline{\mathbf{x}})^T \qquad \text{...(8.39)} \\ &= \mathbf{S}_w + \sum_{j=1}^{c} n_j (\overline{\mathbf{x}}_j - \overline{\mathbf{x}})(\overline{\mathbf{x}}_j - \overline{\mathbf{x}})^T \end{aligned}$$

The second term in Eq. 8.39 represents the generalized between-class scatter matrix. Thus, the total scatter matrix is the sum of between-class and within-class scatter matrices.

$$\mathbf{S}_B = \sum_{j=1}^{c} n_j (\overline{\mathbf{x}}_j - \overline{\mathbf{x}})(\overline{\mathbf{x}}_j - \overline{\mathbf{x}})^T \qquad \text{...(8.40)}$$

and

$$\mathbf{S_T} = \mathbf{S_w} + \mathbf{S_B} \qquad \text{...(8.41)}$$

For a c-class classification problem, $(c - 1)$ linear discriminant functions are required. It can be mathematically represented as

$$z_i = \mathbf{w}^T{}_i\, \mathbf{x},\ i = 1, 2, ..., (c-1) \qquad ...(8.42)$$

It simply represents the projection of d-dimensional samples to a $(c - 1)$-dimensional vector space. The projection vector can be represented in the single matrix equation as

$$\mathbf{z} = \mathbf{W}^T\mathbf{x} \qquad ...(8.43)$$

where, $\mathbf{z}$ represents the $(c - 1)$ dimensional components vector, the weight matrix $\mathbf{W}$ indicates $d \times (c - 1)$ matrix with columns are the weight vectors $\mathbf{w}_i$. Thus, the d-dimensional samples $\{\mathbf{x}_1, \mathbf{x}_2, ..., \mathbf{x}_n\}$ project to $(c - 1)$ dimensional samples as $\{\mathbf{z}_1, \mathbf{z}_2, ..., \mathbf{z}_n\}$.

$$\{\mathbf{x}_1, \mathbf{x}_2, ..., \mathbf{x}_n\} \longrightarrow \{\mathbf{z}_1, \mathbf{z}_2, ..., \mathbf{z}_n\}$$

Thus, the subsets of samples corresponding to c-classes are also mapped to the corresponding $(c - 1)$ projected space as given below.

$$\{C_1, C_2, ..., C_c\} \longrightarrow \{Z_1, Z_2, ..., Z_c\}$$

The sample mean of samples in the projected space given as

$$\bar{\mathbf{z}}_l = \frac{1}{n_i} \sum_{x \in Z_j} \mathbf{y} \qquad ...(8.44)$$

and

$$\bar{\mathbf{z}} = \frac{1}{n} \sum_{i=1}^{n} n_i\, \bar{\mathbf{z}}_i \qquad ...(8.45)$$

Based on these sample means, we can formulate the mathematical equations for the within-class, and between-class scatter matrices in the projected space as follows.

The within-class scatter matrix is

$$\bar{\mathbf{S}}_w = \sum_{i-1}^{c} \sum_{z \in z_i} (\mathbf{z} - \bar{\mathbf{z}}_i)\, (\mathbf{z} - \bar{\mathbf{z}}_i)^T \qquad ...(8.46)$$

Similarly, the between-class scatter matrix is

$$\bar{\mathbf{S}}_B = \sum_{i=1}^{c} n_i\, (\bar{\mathbf{z}}_i - \bar{\mathbf{z}})\, (\bar{\mathbf{z}}_i - \bar{\mathbf{z}})^T \qquad ...(8.47)$$

We can easily find out the relationship between the scatter matrices of original space and projected space of the c-class problem using the weight matrix $\mathbf{W}$ in the following manner.

$$\bar{\mathbf{S}}_w = \mathbf{W}^T\mathbf{S}_\mathbf{w}\mathbf{W} \qquad ...(8.48)$$

and

$$\bar{\mathbf{S}}_B = \mathbf{W}^T\mathbf{S}_\mathbf{B}\mathbf{W} \qquad ...(8.49)$$

Eqs. 8.48 and 8.49 give the corresponding transformations where the within-class and between class scatter matrices are transformed to a low dimensional space.

8.4.3 Criterion Function for MDA

As mentioned in FLD analysis, MDA aims to maximize the separation between the classes. It can be achieved by maximizing the ratio of between-scatter matrix and within-class matrix in the projected space by finding out the suitable **W** With this concept, a criterion function is formulated as

$$J(\mathbf{W}) = \frac{|\bar{\mathbf{S}}_B|}{|\bar{\mathbf{S}}_W|} = \frac{|W^T \mathbf{S}_B W|}{|W^T S_W \mathbf{W}|} \qquad ...(8.50)$$

In this equation, the determinants of scatter matrices are considered because the simple scalar measure of scatter is the determinant of the scatter. Since finding out the rectangular matrix **W** is difficult, we find out the columns of **W** by considering that $\mathbf{w}_i$ are the eigenvectors corresponding to the largest eigenvalues of the relation given below.

$$\mathbf{S_B w}_i = \lambda_i \mathbf{S_w w}_i \qquad ...(8.51)$$

There are two conditions for finding out the solutions of Eq. 8.51. Firstly, if $\mathbf{S_w}$ is an invertible matrix, we can treat it as a conventional eigenvalue problem. Otherwise, we must ensure that the rank of **SB** is at most $(c - 1)$ so that some algebraic techniques can be used for getting the solution. Even if the solution for **W** is not unique (scaled and rotated), it does not affect the classification performance.

8.5 SINGULAR VALUE DECOMPOSITION

The singular value decomposition (SVD) is another matrix analysis-based dimensionality reduction technique used for a high dimensional data matrix. It is closely related to PCA. Suppose the generalized representation of a data matrix **M** with order $(m \times n)$. The SVD makes the exact representation of this rectangular matrix and eliminates the less significant part from the data which approximates the original data matrix in terms of reduced dimensionality.

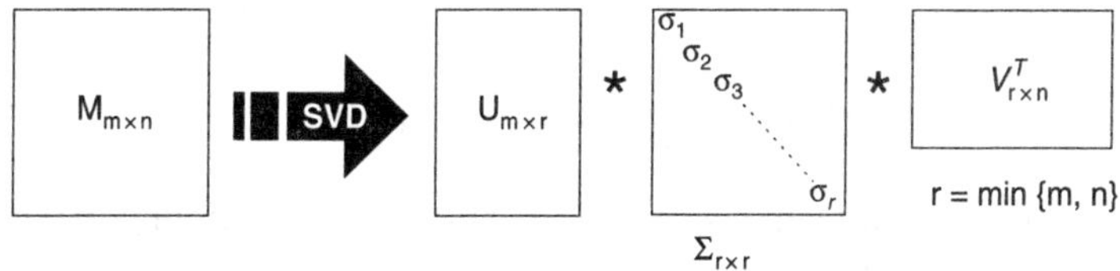

Fig. 8.6 Illustration of singular value decomposition, $\mathbf{M} = \mathbf{U\Sigma V}^T$

8.5.1 Basic Definition of SVD

Suppose **M** is an $(m \times n)$ matrix and let r be the rank of the matrix. Then, according to SVD, **M** can be decomposed into three matrices such as **U**, Σ, and **V** and can be represented in the form $\mathbf{M} = \mathbf{U\Sigma V}^T$. Such a decomposition is possible for any real-valued matrix, **M**. The decomposition is illustrated in Fig. 8.6. The critical properties of SVD are listed below.

1. **U** is an orthonormal matrix of order $m \times r$ such that the columns of **U** are orthonormal vectors.

$$\langle \mathbf{u}_i, \mathbf{u}_j \rangle = 0, \quad \text{if } i \neq j \quad \text{and} \quad \|\mathbf{u}_i\| = 1, \forall i \qquad ...(8.52)$$

where $\mathbf{u}_i$ represents the column vector of **U**.

2. **V** is an orthonormal matrix of order $n \times r$ such that the columns of **V** are orthonormal vectors;

$$\langle \mathbf{v}_i, \mathbf{v}_j \rangle = 0, \quad \text{if } i \neq j \quad \text{and} \quad \|\mathbf{v}_i\| = 1, \forall i \qquad ...(8.53)$$

where $\mathbf{v}_i$ represents the column vector of **V**. Since **V** is used as $\mathbf{V}^T$, its row vectors are orthonormal.

3. Σ is a diagonal matrix of order r such that except the diagonal entries, all elements of Σ are zeros. The diagonal elements of Σ are known as the singular values of **M**, termed as σ_i. The singular value vector of **M** is represented as

$$\sigma = (\sigma_1, \sigma_2, ..., \sigma_r)^T \qquad ...(8.54)$$

In general, the matrices **U** and **V** are not sparse matrices, which means the number of zeros in these matrices is less. If the number of columns of **U**, Σ, and **V** is r and equal to the actual rank of the matrix, **M**, the exact decomposition of **M** is possible. However, when the rank of **M** is higher than the number of columns of these matrices we want, the decomposition of **M** is not exact and it merely represents an approximation. In such a scenario, we need to eliminate that many numbers of the columns of **U** and **V** corresponding to the lower singular values of **M** so that the best approximation is possible.

8.5.2 How to Calculate the SVD of a Matrix?

The calculation of SVD of matrix **M** is closely related to the computation of eigenvalues and eigenvectors of the symmetric matrices $\mathbf{M}^T\mathbf{M}$ and $\mathbf{M}\mathbf{M}^T$. Remember that the SVD of **M** is, $\mathbf{M} = \mathbf{U}\Sigma\mathbf{V}^T$. Then

$$\mathbf{M}^T = (\mathbf{U}\Sigma\mathbf{V}^T)T = (\mathbf{V}^T)^T\Sigma^T\mathbf{U}^T = \mathbf{V}\Sigma\mathbf{U}^T \qquad ...(8.55)$$

Now

$$\mathbf{M}^T\mathbf{M} = (\mathbf{V}\Sigma\mathbf{U}^T)(\mathbf{U}\Sigma\mathbf{V}^T) = \mathbf{V}\Sigma^2\mathbf{V}^T \qquad ...(8.56)$$

Since **U** is an orthonormal matrix, $\mathbf{U}^T\mathbf{U} = \mathbf{I}$, identity matrix. Multiply on both sides of Eq. 8.56 on the left sides by **V**, we get

$$\mathbf{M}^T\mathbf{M}\mathbf{V} = \mathbf{V}\Sigma^2\mathbf{V}^T\mathbf{V} = \mathbf{V}\Sigma^2 \qquad ...(8.57)$$

Since Σ is a diagonal matrix, Σ^2 is also a diagonal matrix and the diagonal entries of Σ^2 are the square of the corresponding entries of Σ. Eq. 8.57 is in the generalized form of an eigenvalue eigenvector problem, and it says that **V** represents the matrix of eigenvectors of $\mathbf{M}^T\mathbf{M}$ and Σ^2 is the diagonal matrix whose diagonal entries are the corresponding eigenvalues of Σ^2. Thus, Eq. 8.57 gives the orthonormal matrix **V** and the singular values of **M**, square roots of eigenvalues of $\mathbf{M}^T\mathbf{M}$.

Now, the remaining task is the calculation of **U**. It can be calculated similarly to that of the calculation of **V** as follows.

$$\mathbf{MM}^T = (\mathbf{U\Sigma V}^T)(\mathbf{V\Sigma U}^T) = \mathbf{U\Sigma}^2\mathbf{U}^T \quad \text{...(8.58)}$$

Similarly,

$$\mathbf{M}^T\mathbf{MU} = \mathbf{U\Sigma}^2\mathbf{U}^T\mathbf{U} = \mathbf{U\Sigma}^2 \quad \text{...(8.59)}$$

Thus, **U** is the matrix of eigenvectors of $\mathbf{MM}^T$.

As defined earlier, the orthonormal matrices **U** and **V** have *r* columns. However, $\mathbf{M}^T\mathbf{M}$ is an $n \times n$ matrix, and $\mathbf{MM}^T$ is an $m \times m$ matrix, where *m* and *n* are at least as large as *r*. Hence, there are additional $(n - r)$ and $(m - r)$ respective eigen pairs present for $\mathbf{M}^T\mathbf{M}$ and $\mathbf{MM}^T$ matrices. Since the rank of **M** is assumed as, *r*, these additional eigen pairs are irrelevant and need not be considered in the decomposition. These eigen pairs are treated as zero and are not helpful in SVD.

8.5.3 Dimensionality Reduction using SVD

Consider a huge matrix **M**, which we want to represent using the SVD components **U**, Σ, and **V**. Since **M** is a large matrix; its decomposition also results in large-sized components, which will not reduce the storage requirements sufficiently. The best method to reduce the dimensionality is to reduce the value of *r* such that the smaller and insignificant singular values in the decomposition can be avoided. This principle significantly reduces the number of columns of SVD components **U**, Σ, and **V**. This is achieved by making the smaller singular values beyond a threshold as zero. However, we must ensure that the best approximation in the decomposition by suitably choosing the value of *r*. The concept is illustrated with a simple example in Fig. 8.7.

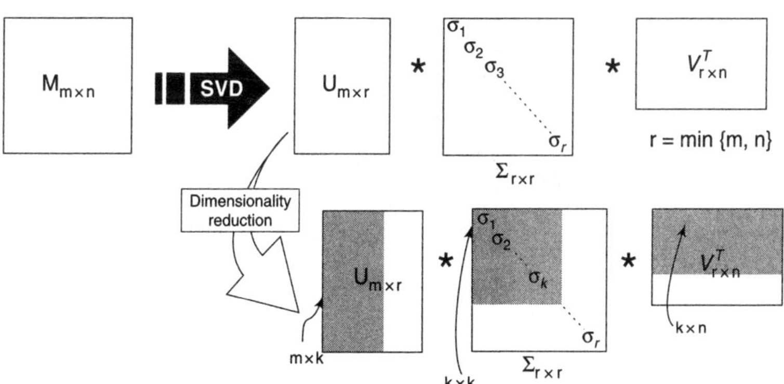

Fig. 8.7 The concept of dimensionality reduction using SVD with a simple example

8.5.4 How Many Singular Values must be retained?

The thumb rule for such a question is to retain the required number of singular values to keep at least 90% of the energy in Σ. Luckily, in almost all practical situations, this required energy is maintained in the first few singular values, and the remaining singular values can be easily neglected without creating significant problems in the approximation.

It can be decided by minimizing the root mean square error (RMSE) between the original matrix and its approximation. The Frobenius norm of the matrices can be used for finding the error in the approximation by comparing the Frobenius norm of the matrices involved. Recall that the Frobenius norm of a matrix is defined as the square root of the sum of squares of the elements of the matrix and is denoted as ||**M**|| for matrix, **M**. Note that if **D** represents the difference between one matrix and its approximation, then the Frobenius norm of **D**, ||**D**|| is proportional to the RMSE between the matrices.

Suppose the SVD of M is $\mathbf{M} = \mathbf{U\Sigma V}^T$ Let σ_i be the ith singular value of Σ. Suppose we want to preserve the first k highest singular values out of r and discard the $(r - k)$ smallest singular values. Then, the resulting approximated matrix $\mathbf{M}'$ can be represented as

$$\mathbf{M}' = \mathbf{U\Sigma' V}^T \quad ...(8.60)$$

where, Σ' is the resulting diagonal matrix after setting the $(r - k)$ smallest singular values to zero. Then the difference matrix, $\mathbf{D} = \mathbf{M} - \mathbf{M}'$ gives the error in the proposed approximation. Thus, to calculate the error, $\| \mathbf{M} - \mathbf{M}' \|^2$, it is required to calculate the sum of the squares of the diagonal elements of $\Sigma - \Sigma'$. However, $\Sigma - \Sigma'$ has zero only for the first k diagonal elements. That is, $\| \mathbf{D} \|^2$ is the sum of the squares of the elements of Σ that are set to 0. Hence in order to minimize $\| \mathbf{D} \|^2$, it is required to select those elements to be the smallest in the singular value vector, σ. So doing gives the least possible value of $\| \mathbf{D} \|^2$ under the constraint that we preserve k of the highest singular values, and it minimizes the RMSE under the same constraint.

8.5.5 Example

Suppose the following matrix represents the data samples in **R**5.

$$M = \begin{bmatrix} 1 & 1 & 1 & 0 & 0 \\ 2 & 2 & 2 & 0 & 0 \\ 3 & 3 & 3 & 0 & 0 \\ 4 & 4 & 4 & 0 & 0 \\ 5 & 5 & 5 & 0 & 0 \\ 0 & 2 & 0 & 4 & 4 \\ 0 & 0 & 0 & 5 & 5 \\ 0 & 1 & 0 & 2 & 2 \end{bmatrix}$$

a. Find out the SVD of **M**.

b. Reduce the dimensionality of SVD to 2.

Solution:

a. Since the first, sixth, and seventh rows the matrix **M** are independent, the rank of the matrix **M** is $r = 3$. We have used three columns for **U**, Σ, and **V** because they decompose the given matrix of rank three. The decomposition is given as below.

$$\begin{bmatrix} 1 & 1 & 1 & 0 & 0 \\ 2 & 2 & 2 & 0 & 0 \\ 3 & 3 & 3 & 0 & 0 \\ 4 & 4 & 4 & 0 & 0 \\ 5 & 5 & 5 & 0 & 0 \\ 0 & 2 & 0 & 4 & 4 \\ 0 & 0 & 0 & 5 & 5 \\ 0 & 1 & 0 & 2 & 2 \end{bmatrix} = \begin{bmatrix} .13 & .02 & -0.01 \\ .41 & .07 & -.03 \\ .55 & .09 & -.04 \\ .68 & .11 & -.05 \\ .15 & .59 & .65 \\ 0.07 & -.73 & -.67 \\ .07 & -.29 & .32 \end{bmatrix} \begin{bmatrix} 12.4 & 0 & 0 \\ 0 & 9.5 & 0 \\ 0 & 0 & 1.3 \end{bmatrix} \begin{bmatrix} .56 & .59 & .56 & .09 & .09 \\ .12 & -.02 & .12 & -.69 & -.69 \\ 40 & -.80 & .40 & .09 & .09 \end{bmatrix}$$

b. This decomposition has three singular values. To reduce the number of dimensions to two, we must set the smallest of the singular values, which is 1.3, to zero. The resulting decomposition and the approximated matrix are given below.

$$\begin{bmatrix} .13 & .02 \\ .41 & .07 \\ .55 & .09 \\ .68 & .11 \\ .15 & -.59 \\ .07 & -.73 \\ .07 & -.29 \end{bmatrix} \begin{bmatrix} 12.4 & 0 \\ 0 & 9.5 \end{bmatrix} \begin{bmatrix} .56 & .59 & .56 & .09 & .09 \\ .12 & -.02 & .12 & -.69 & -.69 \end{bmatrix} = \begin{bmatrix} .93 & .95 & .93 & .14 & .14 \\ 2.93 & 2.99 & 2.93 & .000 & .000 \\ 3.92 & 4.01 & 3.92 & .026 & .026 \\ 4.84 & 4.96 & 4.84 & .040 & .040 \\ 0.37 & 1.21 & 0.37 & 4.04 & 4.04 \\ 0.35 & 0.65 & 0.35 & 4.87 & 4.87 \\ 0.16 & 0.57 & 0.16 & 1.98 & 1.98 \end{bmatrix}$$

The resulting matrix is quite close to the matrix **M**.

Conclusion

In the initial section of this chapter, the significance and the fundamentals of dimensionality reduction techniques in AI and ML applications are discussed. It is followed by the mathematical formulation of the popular linear dimensionality reduction technique, PCA. The combined action of dimensionality reduction and classification for two-class classification problems using FLD analysis is explained in the next section. The extension of FLD, known as MDA, is portrayed in the following section. The basic principle of SVD and how it works for dimensionality reduction are explained in the last section of this chapter.

Questions

1. Explain curse of dimensionality. State the significance in pattern recognition problems.
2. How principal component analysis (PCA) is used for dimension reduction of features.
3. What will happen if eigenvalues are equal in PCA?
4. What are the properties of principal components in PCA?

5. Can we use PCA for feature selection?
6. Briefly explain the principles of LDA. Also explain how to learn the model and predict using LDA.
7. Discuss the terms within class variance and between class variance associated with LDA.
8. Explain the steps in constructing a lower dimensional space for projecting examples using Fisher's criterion.
9. Suppose $u_1, u_2, \ldots\ldots u_n$ and $v_1, v_2, \ldots\ldots v_n$ are orthonormal bases for R^n. $A = U\Sigma V^T$ is the matrix which transforms each v_j in to u_j. If $Av_1 = u_1, Av_2 = u_2, \ldots\ldots Av_n = u_n$, what is Σ?
10. Suppose A is a 2 × 2 symmetric matrix with eigenvalues $\lambda_1 = 3, \lambda_2, = 2$, what are the matrices U, Σ, V^T in SVD?

Exercise

1. Consider the data points $x_1 = (-1, -1)$, $x_2 = (0, 0)$ and $x_3 = (1, 1)$.
   (a) Project the data onto the one-dimensional space using PCA, and identify the approximations x_1, x_2 and x_3 corresponding to the given data points.
   (b) What is the variance of the projected data?
   (c) For the projected data you just obtained above, now if we represent them in the original 2-D space and consider them as the reconstruction of the original data points, what is the reconstruction error.
2. Consider performing linear discriminant analysis (LDA) with two classes. Class C has the class-conditional distribution $N(\mu_C, \Sigma)$, and class D has the class-conditional distribution $N(\mu_D, \Sigma)$.
   We define a quadratic function $Q_C(x) = ((\sqrt{2\pi})^d f_C(x)\pi_C))$
   where $f_C(x)$ is the PDF for class C and π_C is the prior probability for class C. For class D, we define $Q_D(x)$ likewise. For simplicity, assume $\pi_C = \pi_D = \frac{1}{2}$.
   (a) Write down the LDA decision boundary as an equation in terms of $Q_C(x)$ and $Q_D(x)$. Then substitute the definition above and show that the decision boundary has the form $\{x: \omega. x + \alpha = 0)$ for some $\omega \in R^D$ and $\alpha \in R$.
   (b) What is the value of ω?
3. For a two-dimensional dataset consisting $X_1 = (4,1), (2,4), (2,3), (3,6), (4,4)$ and $X_2 = (9,10), (6,8), (9,5), (8,7), (10,8)$, find the within-class scatter matrix and the between-class scatter matrix.
4. For the two-dimensional dataset given in Question 3, find the optimal linear discriminant projection.
5. Given 3 data points in a 2-dimensional space (1, 1), (2, 2), and (3, 3). What is the variance of the data if the original data points are projected into 1-dimensional space using the optimal principal component?

CHAPTER

9

Search Algorithms in AI

In this chapter you will

- learn state representation for search problems in AI.
- evaluate uninformed search algorithms: breadth first search, depth first search, and Uniform cost search.
- analyze informed search algorithms: Greedy search and A* search.

9.0 INTRODUCTION

Consider the following problem of going from A, the initial state, to M, the final or goal state in the shortest possible time, as shown in Fig. 9.1. This could be, for example, an agent trying to start in city A and reach city M in the shortest possible time, where the road distance between the cities are mentioned along the edges of the graph.

Such problems arise commonly in:

- Delivery scheduling: Optimize the series of routes taken by a delivery agent for delivering all goods in the shortest possible time.
- Scheduling such that workers are available through the 24-hour period for continuous manufacturing in factories, and emergencies in hospitals.
- Database retrieval: Retrieve a record, matching the requirement, from a database starting from the initial record.

The objective of such an AI agent is to take a series of actions that transform the initial state towards the goal state. In this chapter we will assume that given a state, and an action taken by the agent, the agent moves to the next state following a deterministic function. This will be relaxed in Part 4, which deals with reinforcement learning, where the next state is a stochastic function of the current state and action. The problem of determining a sequence of actions that lead towards the goal is referred to as a search problem.

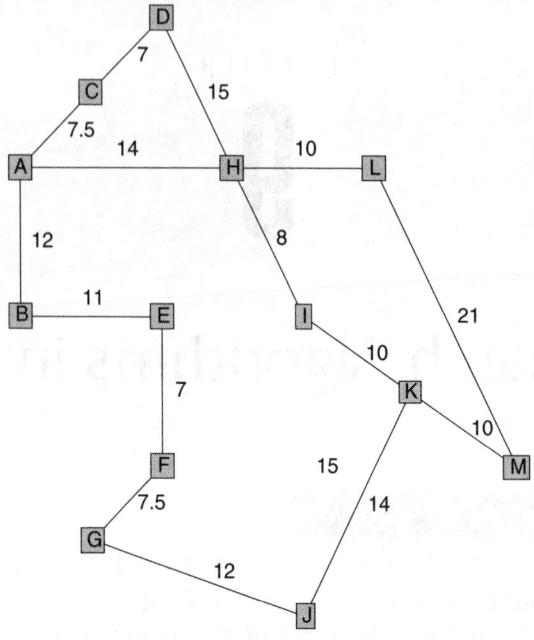

Fig. 9.1 An example of a network with costs between the nodes. The agent starts in node A and the goal is to reach M. Figure adapted from *Artificial Intelligence,* Russel and Norvig

9.1 STATE REPRESENTATION

Before discussing the various search algorithms, let us first formalize the search problem through the state representation.

1	Initial state	State in which the agent starts.
2	State space	The set of all states reachable from the initial state.
3	Action set	Given a particular state, *s*, *Actions(s)* gives the set of actions that can be executed in a particular state.
4	Transition model	*Result (s,a)* returns the state, that results from doing action *a* in state *s*, where $a \in Actions(s)$.
5	Goal test	A function, *GoalTest*(*s*) that determines if the goal state is reached or not.
6	Path cost	$C(s, a, s')$ is the cost of taking action *a* in state *s* and reaching *s′*.

As an Example, consider Figure 9.1.

1	Initial state	A
2	State space	All cities in the road network since they are reachable from A
3	Action set	For example, the action set at A is Go (B), Go (C), and Go (H).

4	Transition model	For example, Result (A, Go (B)) = B
5	Goal test	Here the Goal test function checks if the state is M or not. For example, *GoalTest* (*A*) = 0.
6	Path cost	The path cost is given along the edges *C*(*A*, Go (B), B) = 12

9.2 DATA STRUCTURE FOR SEARCH PROBLEMS

A data structure that is useful for search problems is a tree data structure. A tree data structure consists of a node and branches connecting these nodes, referred to as edges. In addition, the tree data structure also encodes a hierarchy, as shown in Fig. 9.2.

At the top most hierarchical layer, we have a root node. Nodes that are connected via edges to the root node are referred to as the children or neighbours of root node. In general, nodes of the 'lower' hierarchical layer that are connected via edges to the nodes of a 'higher' hierarchical layer are referred to as children nodes. Leaf nodes are nodes without any children. The depth of a node is its distance from the root node. The height of a tree is the maximal distance from the root node to any of the leaf nodes.

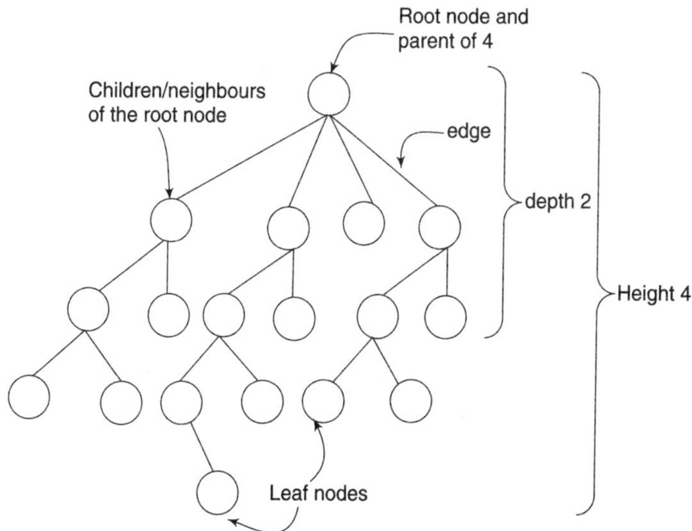

Fig. 9.2 A tree data structure

9.2.1 Tree for Search Problems

How to encode the search problem into the tree data structure? We start with the initial state of the agent as the root node. The edges from the root correspond to actions that can be taken at the root node. The children node of the root node, corresponding to each edge, are the states that results from taking the action along the edge. In order to simplify notation, we assume that at each node, we have access to an *EXPAND*(.) function. The *EXPAND*(.) function takes the state corresponding to a particular node, iterates over all actions possible, and creates edges and children nodes corresponding to an action and the result of taking the action. For example, Fig. 9.3a show the initial tree with just the root node at A. Expanding the root node at A, using the *EXPAND*(.) function gives Fig. 9.3b. Suppose the agent decides to take the action Go (H) at root node, then calling *EXPAND*(.) function at H gives Fig. 9.3c and so on.

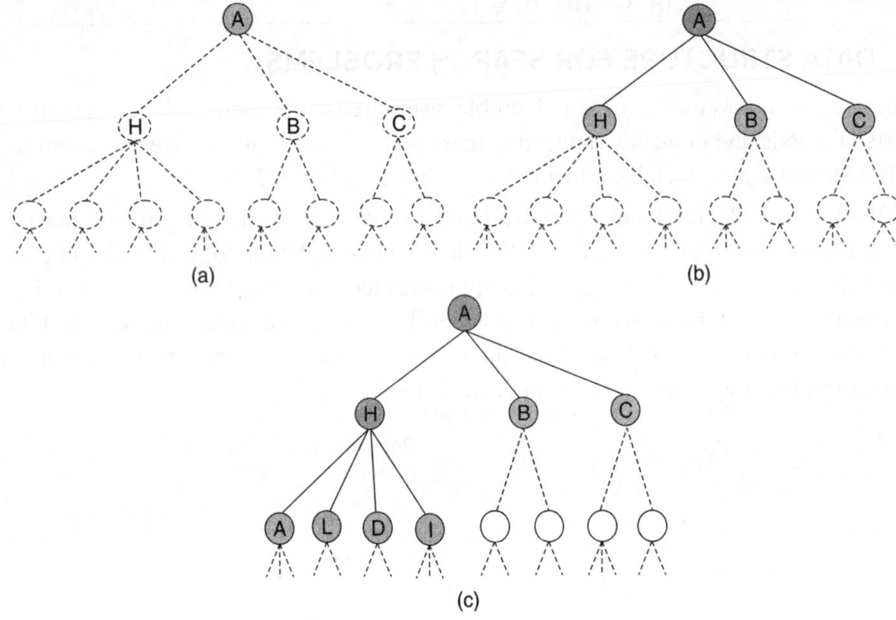

Fig. 9.3 Initial tree with only the root node as A in (a). Tree obtained by expanding A in (b), tree obtained subsequently by expanding H in (c)

9.2.2 General Tree Search Algorithm

Given the tree data structure, how to 'search' for the goal state starting from the initial root node? Algorithm 1 provides a general pseudocode for how to accomplish this. The key idea is that we keep expanding the tree until we get to a goal state.

```
function Tree Search (Initial State, Goal state)
    Initialize frontier with Initial state
    While frontier is not Empty()
            state=frontier.Remove()
            If Goal Test(state)
                    return SUCCESS
            EXPAND(state)
            For neighbour in state.Neighbours ().
                    frontier.add(neighbour)
    return FAILURE
```

Algorithm 1: Pseudocode for a general tree search algorithm

In the pseudocode in Algorithm 1, we see a new concept called *'frontier'*. Frontier captures the set of leaf nodes that are available for expansion at any time. For example, suppose we start with the initial state of A, we initialize the frontier with A. Since the frontier is not empty, and the goal state has not been reached, we apply the *EXPAND* function on A which gives us H, B, and C as neighbours of A, as shown in Fig. 9.3b. The neighbours are added into the frontier. Repeating the loop, we find that the frontier is still not empty. Let us remove state H from the frontier. Since H is not the goal state, we call *EXPAND* on H and the result is shown in Fig. 9.3c. Notice from Fig. 9.3c that A also appears as a child node of H, as it is possible to visit A starting from H. Having such 'repeated' nodes could result in an infinite tree. In Step 3 of Algorithm 1, we arbitrarily remove one state from the frontier. The process of selecting which state to remove from the frontier is part of the search strategy, which will be discussed later.

In order to fix the problem of repeated nodes in the frontier, we augment the tree search algorithm with the 'explored' set; as the name suggests this set keeps track of already expanded nodes. The modified algorithm is referred to as Graph search and is shown in Algorithm 2. In comparison to the tree search algorithm in Algorithm 1, in step 10 of Algorithm 2, we check if the nodes are present in either explored or not already present in frontier before adding it to the frontier to be expanded.

```
function Graph Search (Initial State, Goal state)
1.   Initialize frontier with Initial state
2.   explored = null
3.   While frontier is not Empty()
4.           state=frontier.Remove()
5.           explored.add(state)
6.           If Goal Test (state)
7.               return SUCCESS
8.           EXPAND(state)
9.           For neighbour in state.Neighbours ().
10.              If neighbour ∉ (frontier ∪ explored)
11.                  frontier.add(neighbour)
12.  return FAILURE
```

Algorithm 2: Pseudocode for a general tree search

9.2.3 Performance Measures

In the tree search algorithm (Algorithm 1) and the graph search algorithm (Algorithm 2), we arbitrarily remove one state from the frontier for expansion. The order in which nodes are selected for expansion in part of the search strategy. The performance of a search algorithm depends on the search strategy that we adopt. We will characterize the performance of the search strategy based on the following four criteria:

1. Completeness: Does the search strategy always find a solution if one exists?
2. Time complexity: How long does the search strategy take to find the solution?
3. Space complexity: How much memory is needed to perform the search?
4. Optimality: Does the search strategy find the optimal solution?

The performance measures of various search strategies are summarized using the following characteristics on the tree generated.

- b: Maximum number of successor nodes of any node.
- d: Depth of the shallowest goal node.
- m: Maximum length of any path in the state space.

For example, in Fig. 9.4, $b = 3$, $d = 1$ and $m = 3$. b depends on the actions that could be taken at any state.

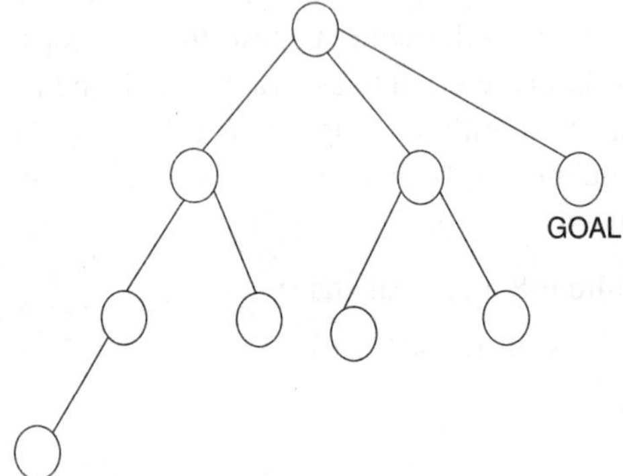

Fig. 9.4 Sample tree generated by a search strategy. Here, $b = 3$, $d = 1$, and $m = 3$

In Sections 9.3 and 9.4, we discuss the two broad classes of search strategy.

9.3 UNINFORMED SEARCH

Uninformed or blind search strategies are those which use only the state representation given in the problem definition. This is in contrast to informed search, where in addition to the state representation, additional information is provided.

9.3.1 Breadth First Search (BFS)

As the name suggests in the breadth first search we will explore every node at a given depth before the next depth of nodes. Of course, in order to do that we need to keep track of the depth of the node as well in the frontier set. For example, in Fig. 9.5a, A is the initial state, on expanding A, we get nodes B and C in the frontier set. On expanding B in Fig. 9.5b, we get nodes D and E. Now looking at the frontier set, it consists of nodes C, D, E. But C has a depth of 1, in comparison to nodes D, E which are at a depth of 2. Hence, we will next choose to expand node C, then we will get F and G, as in Fig. 9.5c.

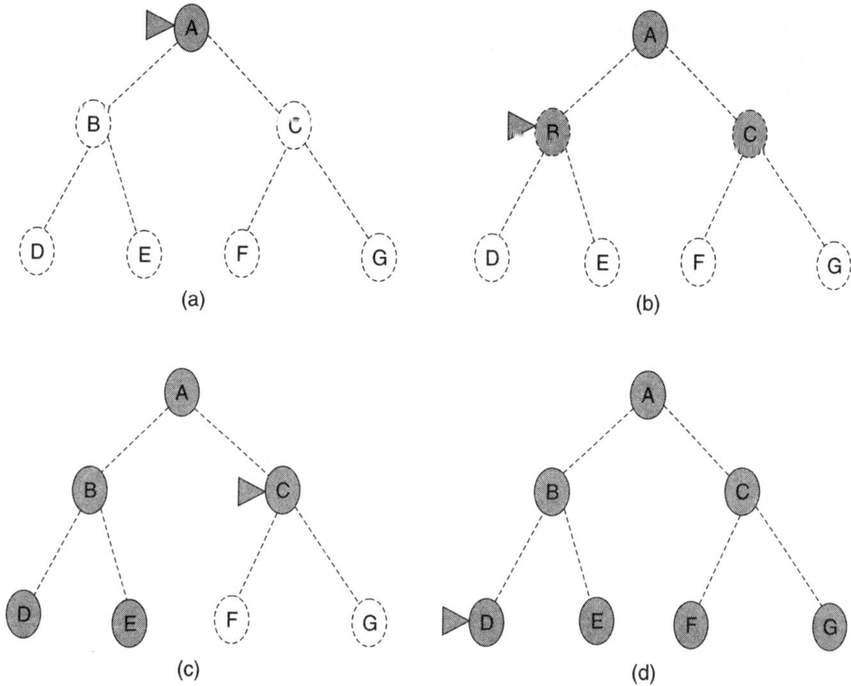

Fig. 9.5 Breadth first search

9.3.1.1 Breadth First Search: Performance Measures

BFS is complete, assuming b is finite, since regardless of the depth of the solution we will find the solution.

Time complexity: The time complexity can be calculated as follows. Assume the solution is at a depth d and search node have at most b children node. At a depth of 1, we have at most b children node and at a depth of 2, we have at most b^2 children node and so on. Hence, the time complexity is $b + b^2 + ... + b^d = O(b^d)$.

Space complexity: Assume we are at a depth $d - 1$. All the nodes in this level and above (at a depth $d - 2$ ..., 1) are in explored set and all the nodes at a depth d (at most b^d) nodes are in the frontier. Hence, space complexity is $O(b^{d-1})$ in the explored set and $O(b^d)$ in the frontier set. Hence, space complexity is $O(b^d)$. Because of the exponential nature of both time and space complexity, BFS is rarely used in practice.

9.3.1.2 Breadth First Search: Pseudocode

As we mentioned before, in order to implement BFS, we need to keep track of the depth of the nodes. This can be easily achieved by a FIFO structure. The pseudocode is as shown below.

```
function BFS (Initial State, Goal state)
    frontier = Queue.New (Initial State)
    explored = null
    While not frontier.isEmpty()
            state=frontier.dequeue ()
            explored.add(state)
            If Goal Test (state)
                return SUCCESS
            EXPAND(state)
            For neighbour in state.Neighbours ().
                If neighbour ∉ (frontier ∪ explored)
                    frontier.enqueue (neighbour)
    return FAILURE
```

Algorithm 3: Pseudocode for breadth first search (BFS)

Algorithm 3 is similar to the general graph search algorithm in Algorithm 2, except that the frontier is implemented using a FIFO. The enqueue and dequeue operations in the FIFO ensure that all the nodes at a given depth are explored before going to a higher depth.

9.3.2 Depth First Search (DFS)

As the name suggests in depth first search (DFS), we explore nodes at a higher depth compared to other nodes at a lower depth. Consider the sequence of nodes in Fig. 9.6. The initial state in A. Expanding A gives nodes B and C. Expanding nodes B gives D and E. Now the frontier set contains C at a depth of 1 and D and E at depth of 2. DFS prefers to expand a higher depth node and hence, expands D and so on.

9.3.2.1 Depth First Search: Pseudocode

DFS is implemented using a Last In First Out (LIFO) data structure, as shown in Algorithm 4. LIFO has two operations, push() and pop (). Push(), 'pushes' nodes into the LIFO data structure and pop(), 'pops out' the latest node that has been pushed in, implementing the LIFO architecture.

```
function DFS (Initial State, Goal state)
    frontier = stack.New (Initial State)
    explored = null
    While not frontier.isEmpty()
            state=frontier.pop ()
            explored.add(state)
            If Goal Test (state)
                return SUCCESS
            EXPAND(state)
            For neighbour in state.Neighbours ().
                If neighbour ∉ (frontier ∪ explored)
                    frontier.push (neighbour)
    return FAILURE
```

Algorithm 4: Pseudocode for depth first search (DFS)

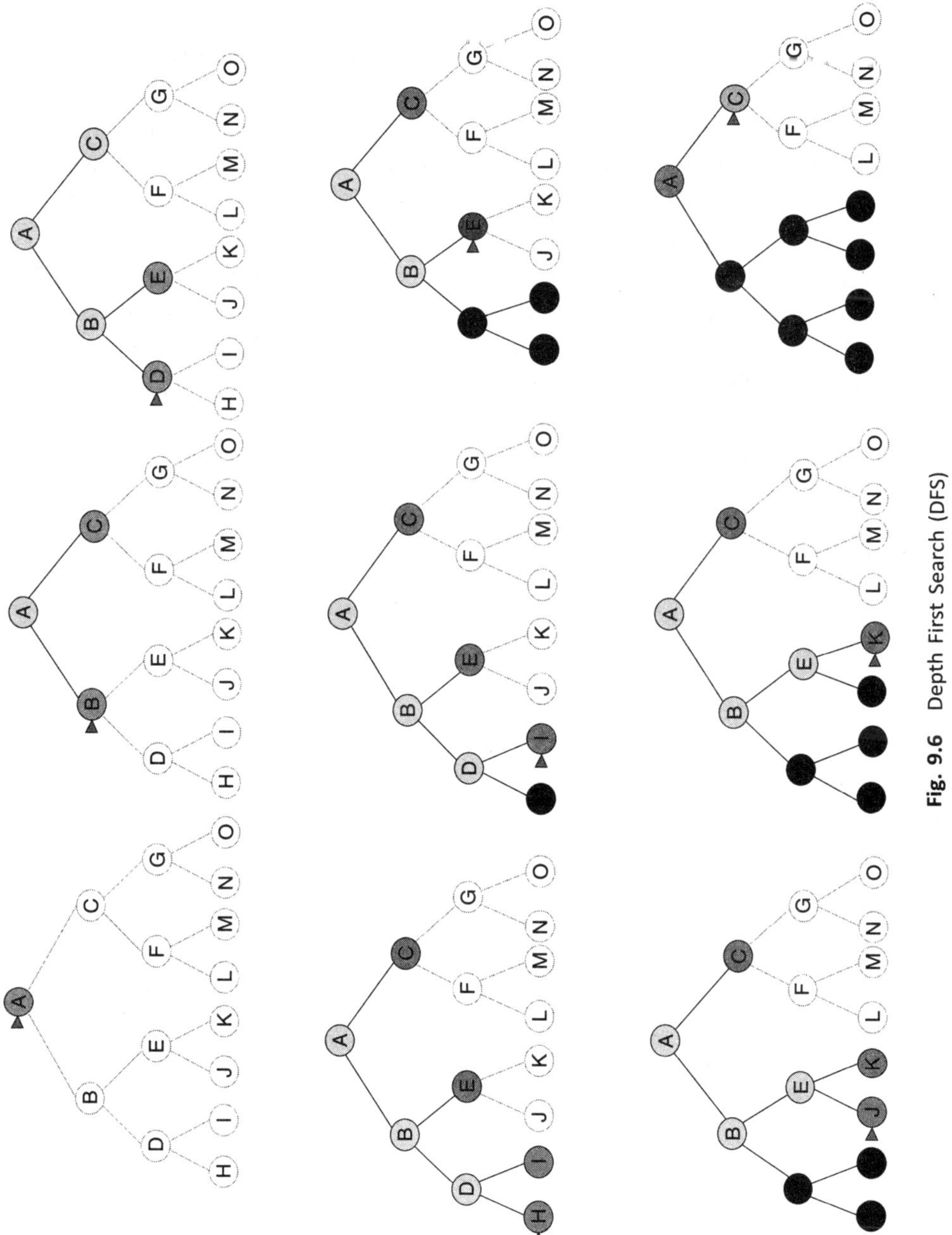

Fig. 9.6 Depth First Search (DFS)

9.3.2.2 Depth First Search: Performance Measures

Complete: DFS is complete, for finite state space and finite set of actions.

Time complexity: In a DFS, the time complexity is similar to BFS. Let b be the maximum depth possible for a tree. Then in the worst case, we would generate all possible nodes up to the depth of b. Hence, time complexity $b + b^2 + b3 + ... + b^m = O(b^m)$.

Notice than in comparison to BFS, the exponent in DFS is the maximum depth b, compared to the depth of the goal state d. In general, we would let the maximum depth of tree expansion be greater than d and hence the time complexity of DFS is bad compared to BFS.

Space complexity: The biggest advantage of DFS is space complexity of $O(bm)$ which is linear in b. To explain the space complexity, consider Fig. 9.7, in which A is the initial state and O is the goal state. Assume $m = 3$. Suppose we expand A to get B and C then we expand B to get D and E. Expand D to obtain H and I, since H and I are at the maximum depth of 3. We apply the goal test and both H and I fails, so we can remove H and I from frontier, since we don't plan to expand H and I. Since D has been already expanded and all children nodes of D (H and I) also fail the goal test, we can also remove D from frontier. Hence, we can prune the paths of the search tree. So, in the worst case the frontier contains the maximum depth path (of size m) with each node along the path having b branches. Hence, the frontier in the worst case contains only $O(bm)$ nodes.

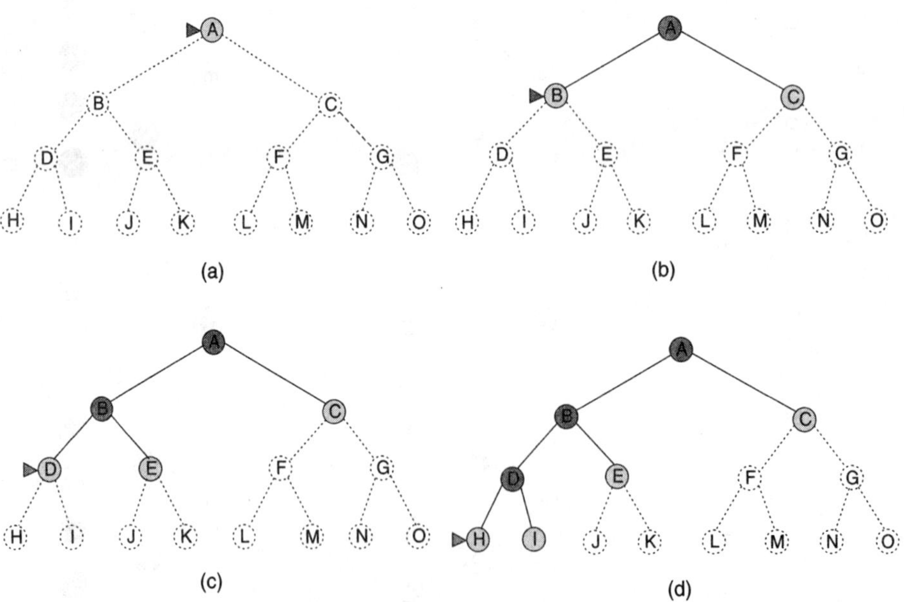

Fig. Contd.

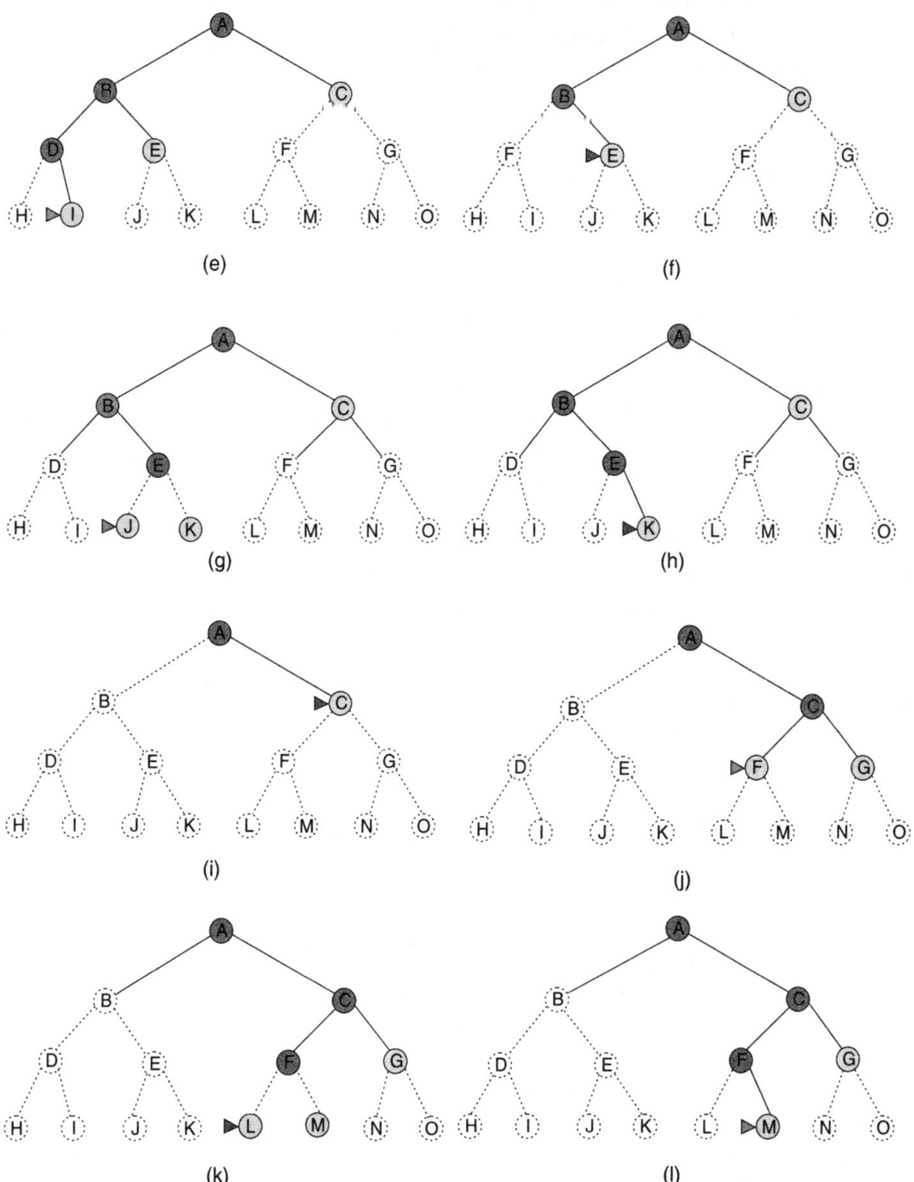

Fig. 9.7 Space complexity of DFS is linear in both *b* and *m*

9.3.3 Uniform Cost Search (UCS)

So far in the discussion of BFS or DFS, we have not looked at the path cost. For example, in Fig. 9.1, where we had a road network, the distances between the various cities were provided along the edge of the graph. In this section, we will modify the BFS algorithm to consider the 'path cost'. The key idea is to prioritize expanding the frontier by the path cost.

For example, consider the following network in Fig. 9.8 (a subset of Fig. 9.1). The start or initial state is A, and the goal state is G. After expanding A, we get nodes B and D. *Pathcost* (*B*) = 8, *Pathcost* (*D*) = 10. Since B has a smaller path cost we will choose to expand B. B has one leaf node C, the path cost of C is the sum of path cost of B and path cost of going from B to C. Hence *Pathcost* (*C*) = 8 + 10 = 18. Since now C and D are in the frontier and path cost of D is lower than the path cost of C, we expand D and we get G with a *Pathcost* (*G*) = 30. Since C is still in the frontier, we expand C and the leaf node is G, with *path cost* (*G*) = 28. So now we have a smaller path cost to reach our goal G. Hence the path cost of G is updated as 28 and since no nodes are remaining in the frontier, we have found the lowest cost path from A to G.

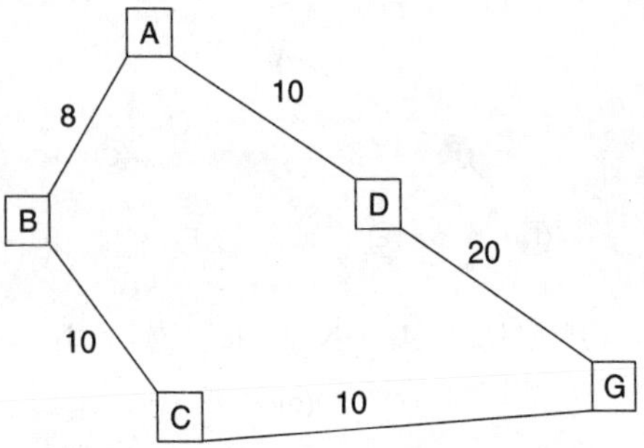

Fig. 9.8 Subset of the road network in Fig. 9.1, for illustration of uniform cost search

9.3.3.1 Uniform Cost Search: Pseudocode

The pseudocode of uniform cost search is similar to the BFS. However, we cannot stop once the goal state is reached, since there may be another path with a lower path cost. This is taken care by Steps 12-13 in Algorithm 5.

```
function UCS (Initial State, Goal state)
1.  | Frontier = Heap.New (Initial State)
2.  | explored = null
3.  | While not frontier.isEmpty()
4.  |         state=frontier.deleteMin () // Prioritize by the path cost
5.  |         explored.add(state)
6.  |         If Goal Test (state)
7.  |             | return SUCCESS
8.  |         EXPAND(state)
9.  |         For neighbour in state.Neighbours().
10. |             | If neighbour ∉ (frontier ∪ explored)
11. |             |         | frontier.insert(neighbour)
12. |             | Else If neighbour ∈ frontier
13. |             |         | frontier.decreaseKey(neighbour)
14. | return FAILURE
```

Algorithm 5: Pseudocode for the uniform cost search (UCS)

The step frontier.deleteMin() is where we prioritize by the path cost. The last else if statement looks if an explored state can be reached by more than one path and update the explored state by the minimum path cost. The uniform cost search is very similar to Dijkstra's algorithm for a single source single sink case.

9.3.3.2 Uniform Cost Search: Performance Measures

The UCS algorithm is both *complete and optimal.*

Time and Space complexity: Assume that each edge cost is at least $\in$ and assume that the optimal path cost is C^*. Then the depth of the tree is at most $\frac{C^*}{\in}$. Then, the UCS is a breadth first search with effective depth of $\frac{C^*}{\in}$ and hence the time complexity is $O(b^{\frac{C^*}{\in}})$. Again, a similar argument gives a space complexity of $O(b^{\frac{C^*}{\in}})$.

9.4 INFORMED SEARCH

So far, we have dealt with uninformed search where we are given a state description, the path cost and the initial and final goal states. The strategy was to explore the state space and find a sequence of states to reach from initial state to final goal state. Often, additional domain specific information is available. For example, in Fig. 9.1, it might be possible to obtain the straight-line distance (as crow flies) from various states to the goal state. This additional information is often referred to as a heuristic. A formal definition of a heuristic function is as follows.

Heuristic function ($h(s)$): A heuristic function is an estimate of how close we are to a goal, based on domain-specific information, that is computable from current state description.

9.4.1 Greedy Search

In the greedy search methodology, the nodes that "appear" closest to the goal state as given by the heuristic is expanded and explored. The pseudocode of greedy search is given in Algorithm 6. The pseudocode is exactly as the uniform cost search, except that we use the heuristic function to prioritize the frontier.

```
function GreedySearch (Initial State, Goal state)
    Frontier = Heap.New (Initial State)
    explored = null
    While not frontier.isEmpty()
        state=frontier.deleteMin () // Use the heuristic function h(s)
        explored.add(state)
        If Goal Test (state)
            return SUCCESS
        EXPAND(state)
        For neighbour in state.Neighbours().
            If neighbour ∉ (frontier ∪ explored)
                frontier.insert(neighbour)
            Else If neighbour ∈ frontier
                frontier.decreaseKey(neighbour)
    return FAILURE
```

Algorithm 6: Pseudocode for the greedy search algorithm

For example, suppose for the problem in Fig. 9.1, let the heuristic be as shown in Table 9.1. This shows the straight-line distance between A (initial state) and M (goal state). We start from A, where the straight-line distance of 40, the neighbours of A and their straight-line distances are given below: H (25), B (33) and C (37). In this case H has much lower heuristic cost and hence we expand H. Continuing this, we expand L. Expanding L leads to the final goal state of M.

Table 9.1 Heuristic for the graph in Fig. 9.1.

State(s)	*Heuristic h(s)*	*State (s)*	*Heuristic h(s)*
A	40	H	25
B	33	I	19
C	37	J	16
D	38	K	10
E	33	L	17.5
F	24.5	M	0
G	24		

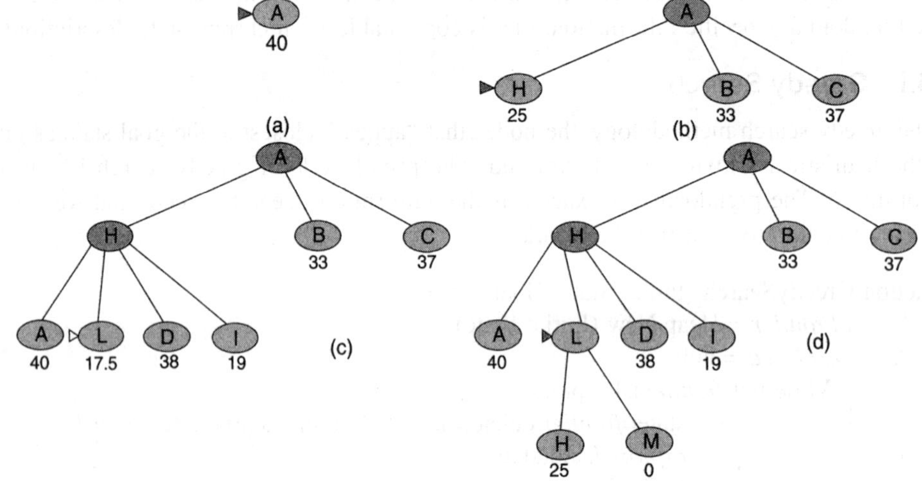

Fig. 9.9 Illustration of the greedy search algorithm

However, just relying on heuristics is not ideal. For example, consider the following problem in Fig. 9.10. Assuming all edge costs are 1 (the heuristic value is given next to the node), we see that using the greedy search we find a goal of g, with a path cost of 5 in comparison to the goal j with a path cost of 3. This raises the question of what is a 'good' heuristic. We will answer this question in the context of *A** search in the next section. What are the performance measures of greedy search? The greedy search is simply a UCS with heuristic used for prioritizing nodes and UCS, in turn, is a BFS search strategy. Hence, time and space complexity are $O(b^m)$.

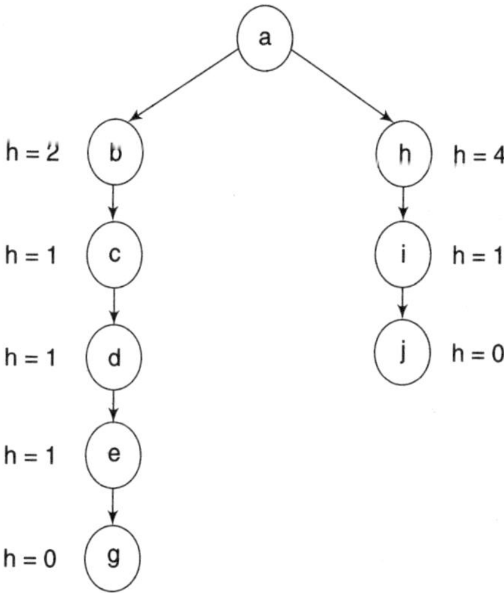

Fig. 9.10 A bad heuristic leads to a sub-optimal goal

9.4.2 A* Search

As we saw in greedy search, relying on just the heuristic to guide the search strategy, can lead to sub-optimal goals. In A^* search, the algorithm uses the following metric to guide the search policy

$$f(s) = g(s) + h(s),$$

where $g(s)$: actual path cost from start to node s.
$h(s)$: heuristic function at node s.

The implementation of A^* is similar to the UCS algorithm, where $f(s)$ would be used instead to guide the search policy.

Consider the heuristic in Table 9.1, where the heuristic is the straight-line distance from the node to the goal state. Expanding the initial state of A, we get H, B and C.

$$f(H) = g(H) + h(H) = 14 + 25 = 39$$

$$f(B) = g(B) + h(B) = 12 + 33 = 45$$

$$f(C) = g(C) + h(C) = 7.5 + 37 = 44.5$$

Here H has the lowest $f(\cdot)$ value. Expanding H, we get A, L, D and I.

$$f(L) = g(L) + h(L) = 24 + 17.5 = 41.5$$

$$f(D) = g(D) + h(D) = 29 + 38 = 67$$

$$f(I) = g(I) + h(I) = 22 + 19 = 41$$

The process goes on, as shown in Fig. 9.11.

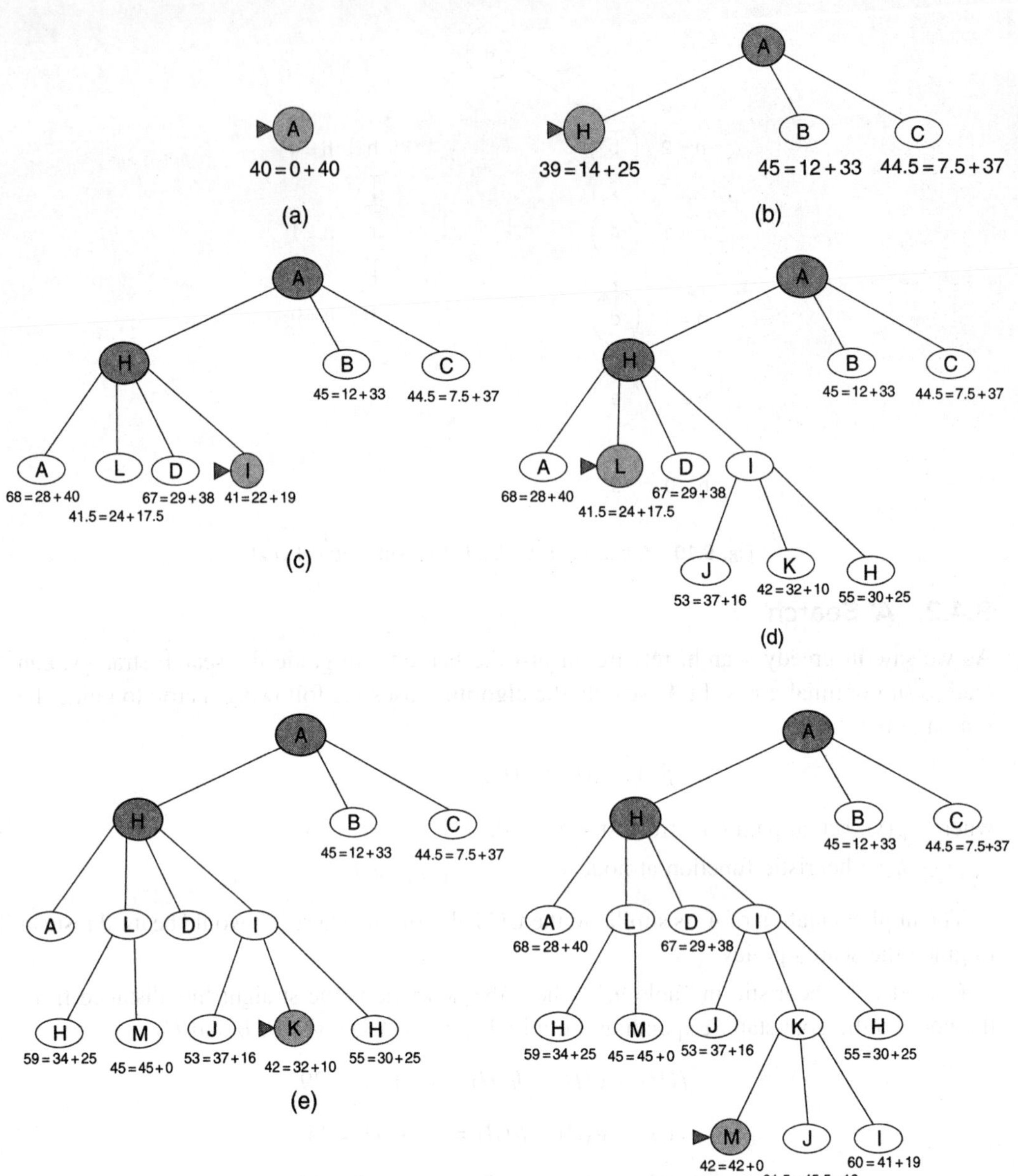

Fig. 9.11 *A** algorithm

The time and space complexity would be similar to UCS or Greedy Search algorithm. However as before, the convergence to the optimal solution depends on the heuristic. So, what is a good heuristic?

9.4.2.1 Admissible and Consistent Heuristic

One good property that a heuristic should satisfy is that it should never over-estimate the actual cost to reach the goal, i.e., it should be optimistic. Hence $h(n) \leq h^*(n)$, where $h^*(n)$ is the true cost of reaching the goal from node n. Such a heuristic is called admissible heuristic.

A slightly stronger condition is called a consistent heuristic.

Consistent heuristic: A heuristic is consistent if for every node n and every neighbouring node n' if $h(n) \leq c(n, n') + h(n')$.

It is easy to see that a consistent heuristic is also admissible.

9.4.2.2 Optimality of A* under Consistent Heuristic

In order to show the proof of optimality of A^* with a consistent heuristic, we proceed as follows:

1. If $h(n)$ is consistent, then the value of $f(n)$ along any path is non-decreasing.

   The proof is directly obtained by the definition of consistency. Suppose we start at node n, and move to n' then, $f(n) = g(n') + h(n') = g(n) + c(n, n') + h(n') \geq g(n) + h(n) = f(n)$.
2. Whenever A^* selects a node n for expansion, the optimal path to the node has been found.

   The proof follows by contradiction. Assume that g is an optimal goal state with a path cost of $f(g)$, and s is a sub-optimal goal that with a path cost of $g(s) \geq f(g)$ that n is a node on an optimal path to g. we are assuming that A^* select s instead of n. since h is admissible, $f(g) \geq f(n)$ if n is not chosen over s for expansion by A^*, $f(n) \geq f(s)$ then the $f(g) \geq f(s)$. Since s is a goal state, $h(s) = 0$, so $f(s) = g(s)$. Thus, $f(g) \geq g(s)$. This contradicts the statement that s is sub-optimal so it must be true that A^* never chooses a suboptimal path.

Conclusion

In this chapter, we discussed the importance of search algorithms in Al. We began with classical breadth first search and depth first search approaches. The depth first search has the advantage of low memory complexity compared to breadth first search. These approaches do not use domain-specific information. In many situations, additional heuristic information is available. To utilize the heuristic information, we discussed the greedy search and the A* search. In addition, under certain restrictions on the heuristic, we showed that A* search is optimal.

Questions

1. Find the state representation of the following problem, given the start state and the end state as shown below.

(empty)	0	6
7	1	2
5	3	4

Start state

(empty)	0	1
2	3	4
5	6	7

Goal state

Fig. 9.12

The checked square is empty and any number may be moved to the space. Assume that the checkered square can be moved left, right, top or bottom.

2. Find the optimal path of going from the start point a to the goal state (house) using the A^* algorithm. The heuristic for each node is provided next to the node.

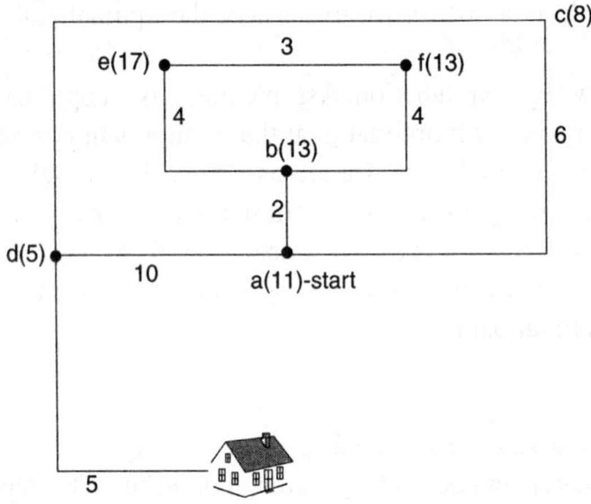

Fig. 9.13

3. (Adapted from Russel and Norvig): Suppose two friends live in different cities on a map, such as the one shown in Fig. 9.1. On every turn, each of the friends can simultaneously move to a neighbouring city. The amount of time needed to move from city i to neighbour j is equal to the road distance $d(i, j)$ between the cities, but on each turn the friend that arrives first must wait until the other one arrives (and calls the first on his/her cell phone) before the next turn can begin. The two friends to meet as quickly as possible. **(a)** Write a detailed formulation for this search problem. (b) Let $D(i,j)$ be the straight-line distance between cities i and j. Which of the following heuristic functions are admissible? (i) $D(i,j)$; (ii) $2 \cdot D(i,j)$; (iii) $D(i,j)/2$.
4. (Adapted from Russel and Norvig): The missionaries and cannibals' problem is usually stated as follows. Three missionaries and three cannibals are on one side of a river, along with a boat that can hold one or two people. Find a way to get everyone to the

other side without ever leaving a group of missionaries in one place outnumbered by the cannibals in that place.

(a) Formulate the problem precisely, making only those distinctions necessary to ensure a valid solution. Draw a diagram of the complete state space.

(b) Implement and solve the problem optimally using an appropriate search algorithm. Is it a good idea to check for repeated states?

5. (a) Figure 9.14 shows some important cities in the map of India. The distances between the connected cities via road are measured as the Cost function and the straight line aerial distance is used as the heuristic function.

(i) Draw the **BFS and DFS** trees to reach Kozhikode from New Delhi.
[Note: Use 'alphabetic ' order to enter the nodes in the tree.]
List the order of nodes visited for each case (BFS and DFS)

(ii) Use the UCS algorithm to find the shortest distance from New Delhi to Kozhikode Show the order of nodes visited.

(iii) List the path obtained and the distance from the source to destination for each algorithm (BFS, DFS and UCS).

(iv) Given the straight line distance (heuristic) to New Delhi from each city, find the path obtained using A^* and the greedy best fit search algorithm.

India
Major Cities

CITY	HEURISTIC
Agra	180
Ahmedabed	775
Bangalore	1740
Bhopal	600
Chennai	1760
Coimbatore	1960
Guwahati	1460
Hyderabad	1250
Jaipur	240
Kolkata	1900
Kozhikode	1300
Lucknow	410
Ludhiana	280
Mumbai	1150
Nagpur	850
New Delhi	0
Patna	1050
Pune	1170

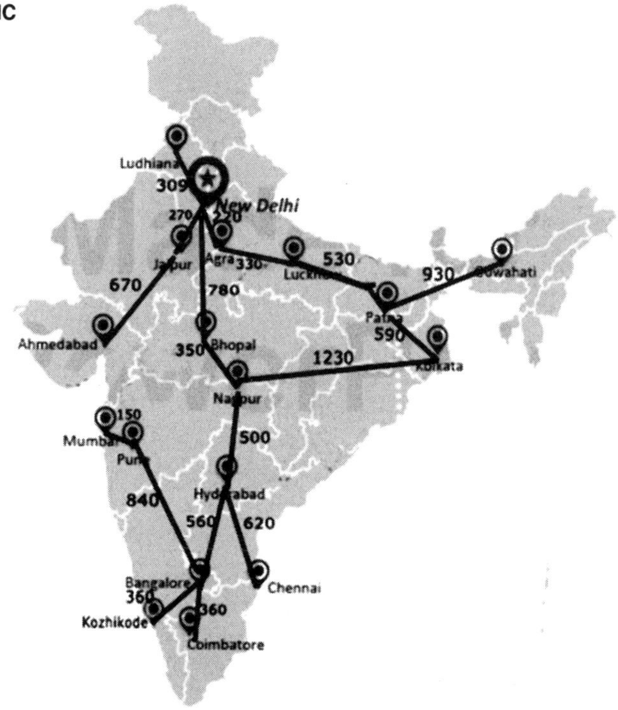

Fig. 9.14 Road distance and aerial distances

Part II

Deep Learning

CHAPTER

10

Deep Learning Basics: Artificial Neural Networks, Backpropagation and Further Optimizations

In this chapter you will

- understand the need for deep learning,
- learn the concept of neurons and neural networks,
- analyze the working of a perceptron and MLP,
- study backpropagation through calculations and analysis,
- evaluate optimization of gradient descent,
- discuss advanced optimization techniques used in deep learning, and
- compare new activation functions that are popular.

10.0 INTRODUCTION

Deep learning is a subset of machine learning and is relatively new. The word 'deep' simply means that this approach is based on multiple layers of Artificial Neural Networks (ANNs). The concept of ANN was inspired by the network of neurons in the human brain. Deep learning algorithms process data, do learning in many layers of artificial neural networks and create abstractions from the data, thus trying to mimic the way humans process data. The concept of deep learning was considered to be first introduced by Walter Pitts and Warren McCulloch in 1943 when they tried to make a computer model to mimic the neural networks in the human brain.

In the 1990s, Artificial Neural Networks (ANNs) became a very hot topic of research and applications. The key algorithm of neural networks, namely, 'backpropagation', was propounded then and a lot of research was done both in the industry and academia. But in a short while, this field lost its sheen – the reason was the non-availability of high speed computational hardware required to run the thousands of iterations proposed by the theory. But now, in the last ten years, the concept of neural nets has returned with its new designation of 'deep learning' The only reason for the new found enthusiasm is that the computational capability of computers has multiplied hundredfold and it is now easy to run the cumbersome computations involved. The point is that current computers have powerful, high speed, multi core CPUs as well as parallel GPUs and the implementation issues of ANN algorithms have been taken care of.

Note: CPU stands for Central Processing Unit, GPU for Graphical Processing Unit.

10.1 DEEP LEARNING: THE NEED

The basic idea behind traditional machine learning algorithms is to extract the features of the input data and do classification based on a trained model. For example, if we want to predict the chances of rainfall from weather information, we will have a set of predefined features that will help to do the prediction. These features can be wind speed, intensity of sunlight, season, humidity and temperature. So when the user gives these features as input to a trained machine learning system, it predicts the output, which in this case is the prediction of Rain/ No Rain. Giving a set of inputs and taking an output is the basic principle of any machine learning system. The problem may be a classification, regression, or clustering as discussed in the previous chapters.

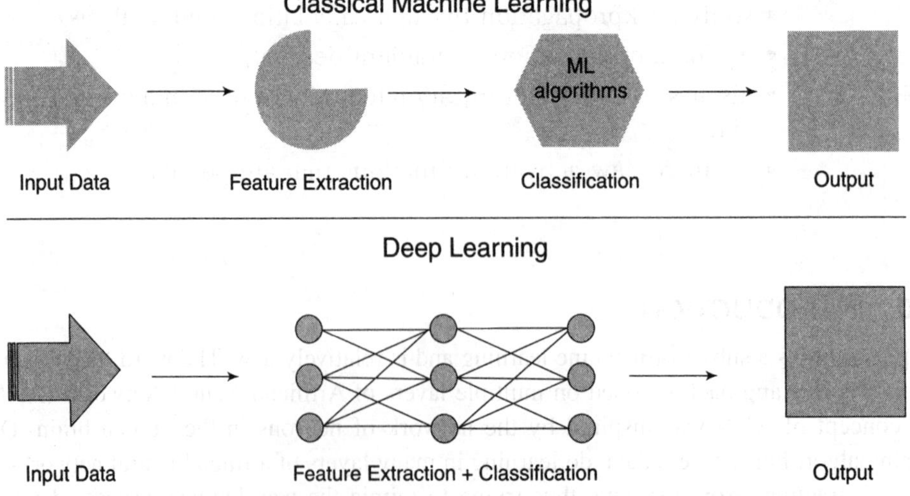

Fig. 10.1 Machine learning vs deep learning

During the training of such a classical machine learning system, (for supervised learning, say) we will have a dataset with values for all the weather parameters of different days and seasons, and the corresponding labels of Rain/No Rain. The machine learning algorithm learns from this dataset and creates a model using which it can do prediction of Rain/No Rain when a test input is given.

Classical machine learning has limitations when the feature extraction step is not easy. In many complex applications like Natural Language Processing (NLP), Speech Recognition, Image Processing, etc., defining the set of features that will help in training the system can be tiresome or impossible even for a domain expert. These applications might require analyzing different sets of features at different levels of abstraction and combining the levels to create the final output. This is how the human brain seems to do data processing. This has motivated the development of deep learning algorithms where the learning is similar to the neural networks in the human brain. Then the step of feature extraction is included in the deep learning system and there is no need for an additional 'feature extraction' stage. See Fig. 10.1 which shows this aspect for classical ML and deep learning.

In addition, the performance and accuracy of deep learning models is much higher than that of classical machine learning algorithms but has dependence on the size of the training dataset. Figure 10.2 illustrates this point. Note that when more data is used, deep learning system performance improves proportionally, while classical ML algorithms remain saturated with respect to performance. The computational complexity of training a deep learning model is much more than that of classical machine learning algorithms and thus high power computational devices are needed. In addition, due to the necessity of having to do feature extraction within its stages, deep learning models take more time to train. But all these are simple because of the high speed and powerful computing hardware available currently. Because of all these encouraging trends, deep learning (DL) has become very important and its use is spreading to every aspect of artificial intelligence.

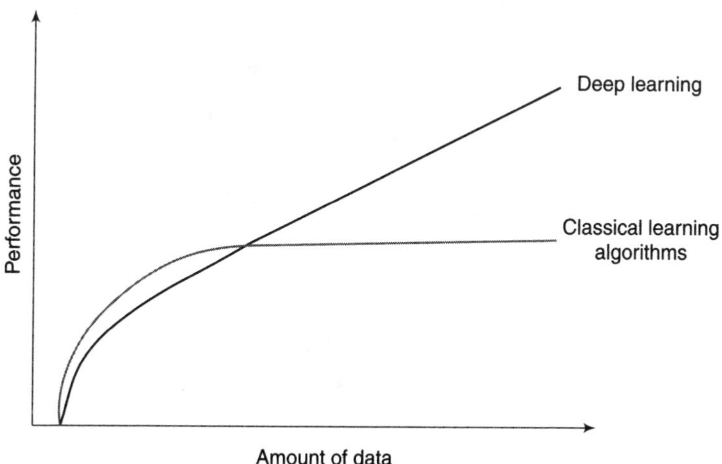

Fig. 10.2 Performance of Deep Learning vs. Classical ML algorithms

10.1.1 Artificial Neural Networks

'Artificial neural networks' constitute the basic units of a deep learning system. According to Dr. Robert Hecht Nielsen, the inventor of one of the first neurocomputers, a neural network is defined as "*a computing system made up of a number of simple, highly interconnected processing elements, which process information by their dynamic state response to external inputs*". This is similar to how the human brain is thought to perform.

The concept of neural networks is motivated from the biological concept of neurons in the human brain. A neuron is the basic computational unit in the human brain. There are around 85 billion neurons in the human brain and they are interconnected. Figures 10.3a and b show that the brain is a structure containing interconnected neurons. Figure 10.4 shows the mathematical model of a simple network of artificial neurons. In this, a node represents a neuron of the brain.

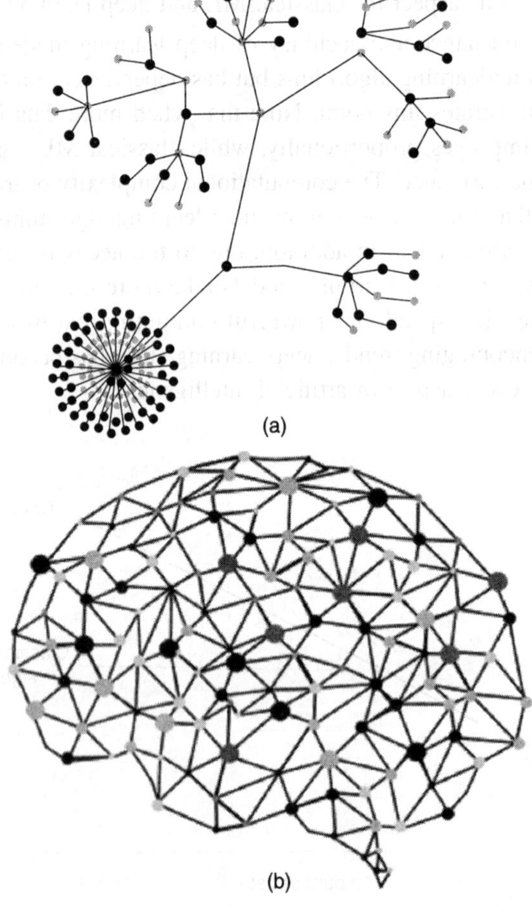

Fig 10.3 (a) and (b) The neural networks in the brain

The neurons or nodes are the basic units in the neural network. They receive inputs from other nodes or from external sources. Each input connection is associated with a weight W. The weights define the importance of an input with respect to the other inputs. The function to compute the output uses the weighted sum of all inputs. During the training or learning phase, the neural network adjusts the weights in each iteration in such a way that the difference between the expected output and the actual output is reduced (in many iterations). In the ideal case, this difference should become zero. This concept will be elaborated further.

10.1.2 The Perceptron

The development of the 'perceptron' was a major step in the history of deep leaning. It was in 1949 that Donal Hebb sought to revolutionize the way of looking at artificial neurons. His book *The Organization of Behaviour* proposed the concept of 'weighted inputs'. Frank Rosenblatt added weights to the original McCulloch-Pitts neuron and thus the first perceptron came into being.

We consider a perceptron to be the smallest unit of a large neural network. See Fig. 10.4 which shows such a perceptron which is a small ANN with one input layer and one output layer. There are a number of neurons at the input to which signals are fed. The output layer has only one neuron. The input is a vector **x** which has d features.

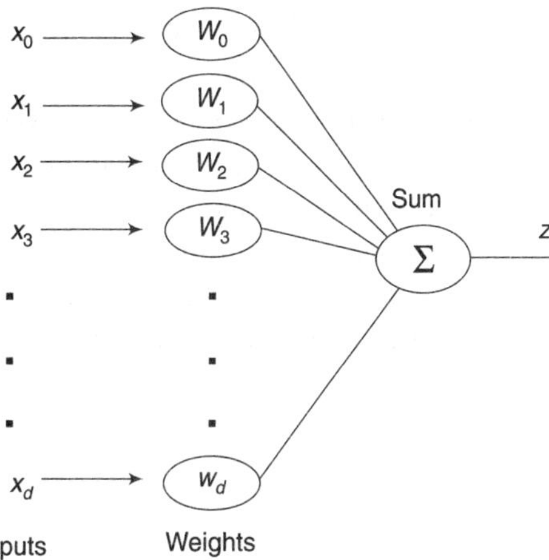

Fig. 10.4 Mathematical representation of a neural network

$$\mathbf{x} = [x_0, x_1, x_2 \ldots \ldots \ldots . x_d]^T \quad ...(10.1)$$

For each feature x_i there is a level of importance attached, which we call a 'weight'. The weighted sum of the inputs is

$$z = w_0x_0 + w_1x_1 + \ldots. + w_dx_d \quad ...(10.2)$$

Computing the weighted sum of these inputs is the fundamental task of the perceptron. This is obviously a linear operation from **x** to z.

Now how do we use this as a supervised machine learning unit? The first step in this process is training. For each vector **x** we have a label which is the value expected at z. Let us call that value as the target. Training means that the weights of the network should be the right values which will give us the 'target' value at z. Let us now list out the steps in the training process:

1. Initialize the weights w_i with random values.
2. Calculate z which we call the actual output.
3. Compare z with the target and find the error between the two which is

$$E = \frac{1}{2}\,(\text{Output} - \text{Target})^2 \qquad \text{...(10.3)}$$

This is the squared error.

4. If the error is greater than a minimum predefined value, use the magnitude of the error as a reference quantity to modify the weight vector **w**.
5. Continue the process of recalculating the value of z and updating the values of **w** until the error goes below the minimum value.
6. We then say that convergence has occurred. The process is then stopped.

   Note: E is also referred to as the Cost function when the error is averaged over all the samples of the input. The operation of the network is to iteratively reduce the cost until it goes below a minimum value.

In the above setup, the perceptron seems to be used for linear regression where we get z as a real number. In practice, the perceptron is used for classification which means that a non-linear activation is required for z to be converted into a categorical label. The simplest case is binary classification and what we need is to convert z into one of two probabilities, which we may designate as Positive/Negative, 0/1, –1/+1, High/Low, etc. The simplest activation function for that is a step/threshold function. When this signal is applied to z, we get y. What the step function does is obvious, when $z \geq T$, $y = 1$, otherwise it is 0.

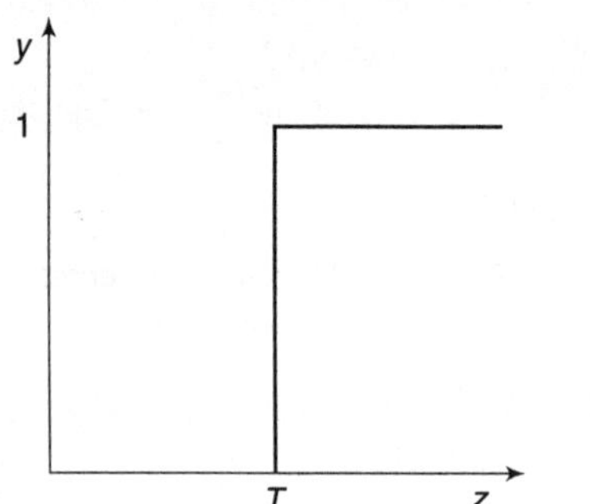

Fig. 10.5 (a) An abrupt 'Threshold function'

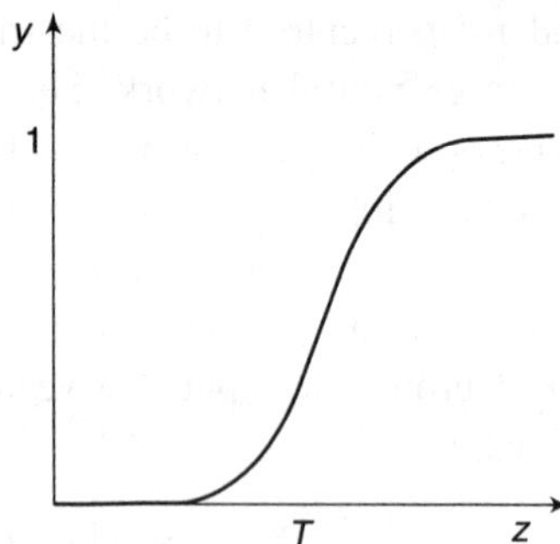

Fig 10.5 (b) A smooth 'Threshold function'

Thus there is a threshold T at which the decision steps abruptly from $y = 0$ to $y = 1$. This may be represented by a step function as shown in Fig. 10.5a. This is a case of a hard threshold where a small change in z will change the decision from $y = 0$ to $y = 1$ abruptly. This is not a good function practically as well as mathematically (because of not being differentiable, the necessity for which we will see in further discussions). Thus, a practical decision making model prefers a smoother curve which is shown in Fig. 10.5b.

Let us now make a few minor changes to Eq. 10.1 which is copied here.

$$z = w_0\,x_0 + w_1\,x_1 + \ldots. + w_d\,x_d$$

The $w_0 x_0$ term is usually separated out and named as bias 'b'. This is to have a term which is independent of the input values and which may be used as an offset/intercept and can be used to move the activation function left or right of the origin. This means that the threshold value may be kept within our control by the use of the bias term.

Now Eq. 10.1 is rewritten as

$$z = \sum_{i=1}^{d} w_i * x_i + b \qquad ...(10.4)$$

This can be expressed as a dot product.

$$z = \mathbf{w} \cdot \mathbf{x} + b \qquad ...(10.5)$$

In Eq. 10.5, **w** is the weight vector and **x** the input vector.

Now let us formally state that the operation of the practical perceptron is to calculate the weighted sum of the inputs and then apply a signal so as to realize a soft threshold. The chosen signal is a Sigmoid $\sigma(z)$ which is described by Eq. 10.6 and has the form as shown in Fig. 10.6. The complete diagram for a perceptron acting as a binary classifier is given in Fig. 10.7. Note that the output of a perceptron is given by Eq. 10.7

$$\sigma(z) = \frac{1}{1 + e^{-z}} \qquad ...(10.6)$$

$$y = \sigma(z) \qquad ...(10.7)$$

10.1.3 The Sigmoid Function

What does this function do?

It squashes the value of output to lie between 0 and 1. So it converts any value to a binary probability if a threshold is fixed. This was discussed in the context of logistic regression (Section 3.3.1)

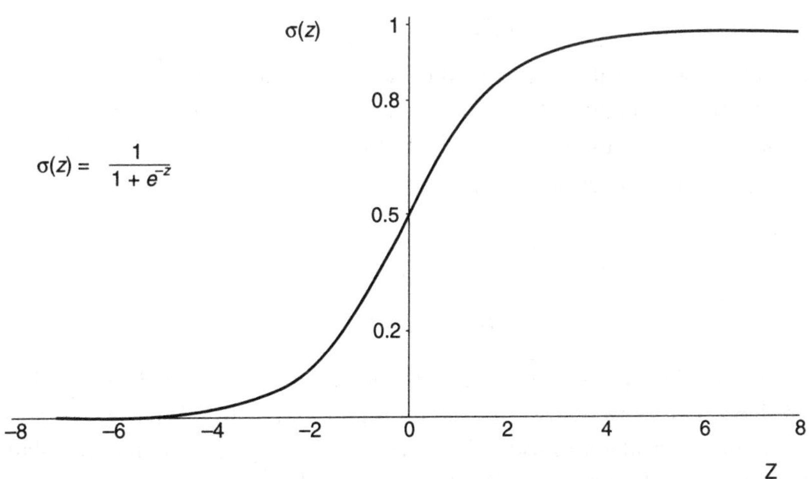

Fig. 10.6 The Sigmoid function

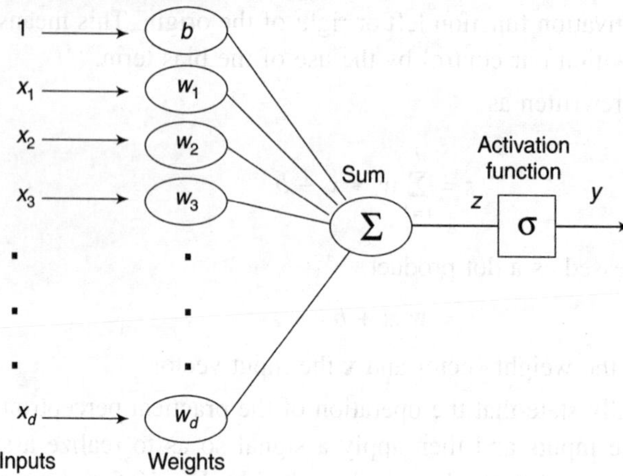

Fig. 10.7 The complete perceptron used for classification

Example 10.1 Let us do a calculation to understand the perceptron.

$$\mathbf{w} = \begin{bmatrix} 0.1 \\ 0.4 \\ 0.5 \end{bmatrix} \quad x = \begin{bmatrix} 0.1 \\ 0.3 \\ 0.2 \end{bmatrix}$$

$b = 0.35$

Solution: Using Eq. 10.4,

$$\begin{aligned} z &= 0.1 \times 0.1 + 0.4 \times 0.3 + 0.5 \times 0.2 + 0.35 \\ &= 0.01 + 0.12 + 0.10 + 0.35 \\ &= 0.58 \end{aligned}$$

Thus, we get the output value corresponding to a weighted sum of inputs. This is obviously a linear system. To get an application of the perceptron as a binary classifier, we must apply a nonlinear activation function to its output and then fix a threshold for the classification.

Applying the sigmoid function to z, we get

$$\begin{aligned} y = \sigma(z) &= \frac{1}{1 + e^{-0.58}} \\ &= 0.641 \end{aligned}$$

As mentioned earlier, we avoid using a step function but to make a decision, we still need to fix a threshold. Let's say that we fix the threshold as $T = 0.5$. What we mean is that, if $y \geq 0.5$ the output is considered 'Positive', otherwise it is 'Negative'. In this calculation, since $y > 0.5$, the output is categorised as "Positive'.

10.1.4 Linear Separability

Now let us take a practical example of binary classification using the perceptron in which we try to separate two kinds of items which have two features (plotted on the X and Y axes). A typical problem is to classify a set of fruits as papaya or mango. The features are the length and width of the fruits. In Fig. 10.8, the length is plotted on the X axis and weight on the Y axis. Plus signs are for papaya and minus signs for mango. Many iterations (only four are shown in the figure) may be required until the separating boundary in the X-Y plane is clearly obtained. Finally, we get a linear boundary that separates the two fruits based on these two features.

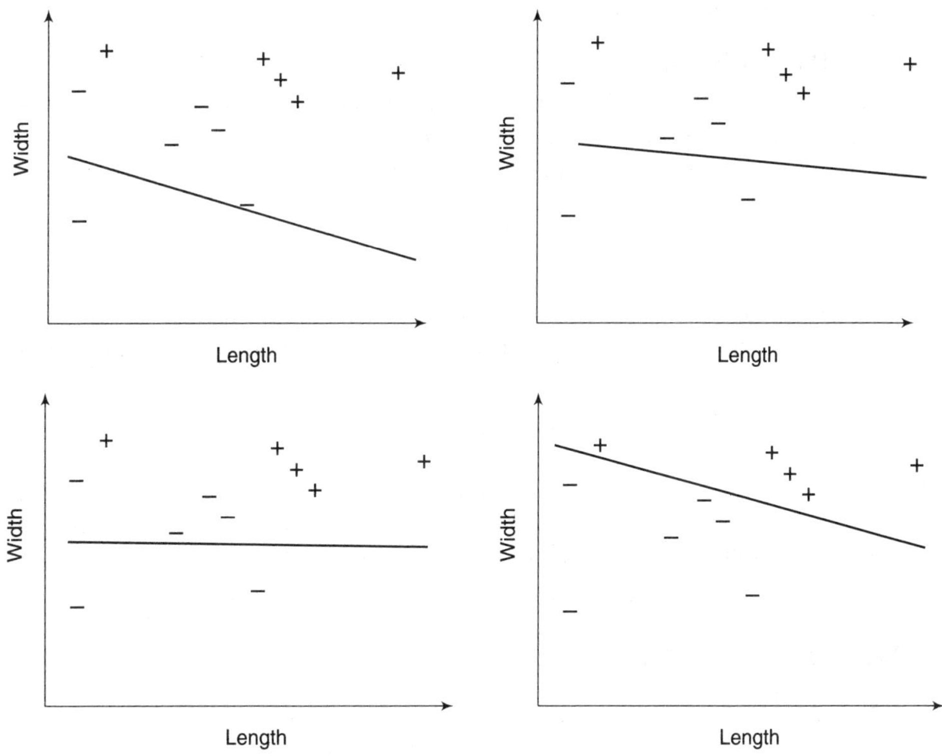

Fig. 10.8 Convergence using many iterations of the perceptron algorithm

This example is for a case where the data is linearly separable which means that a single straight line/plane can separate the data. In fact, the perceptron is a perfect classifier only for linearly separable data. Figure 10.8 shows the case of two features only, in which the separation is done by a line. For more number of features, the separation boundary is a hyperplane.

Why does the perceptron cater only to linearly separable data?

Let us try to make sense of it for the simplest case of just two features, where we can plot the points in a two-dimensional plane.

$$w_1 x_1 + w_2 x_2 + b = 0 \quad ...(10.8)$$

This equation is the equation for a line. We can express it in the form $y = mx + c$ by rewriting it as

$$x_1 = -\frac{w_2}{w_1}x_2 - \frac{b}{w_1} \quad ...(10.9)$$

This line acts as the decision boundary such that, for one set of input features, the output is 'Positive' and the corresponding points lie on one side of the line. For another set of input features, the output is 'Negative' and the points lie on the other side of the line. Let us try to understand this for the case of the simple AND, OR and XOR gates. We try to implement these logic gates using the perceptron.

10.1.4.1 AND and OR Logic

Let us avoid the bias term of Eq. 10.4, and concentrate on the logic alone. The first two columns of Table 10.1 are the two inputs for an AND gate realized with a perceptron. We use the values of the weights of the network as: $w_1 = 0.75$, $w_2 = 0.75$. The threshold is selected as $T = 1$. Use the equation:

$$z = w_1 x_1 + w_2 x_2 \quad (10.10)$$

The values of x_1 and x_2 can be taken from columns 1 and 2 of the table to get the value of z (third column). We find that for the first three cases, the value of z is below the threshold T.

For $x_1 = 1$ and $x_2 = 1$, $z = 0.75x_1 + 0.75x_2 = 1.5$

This is above the value of T. The last column of the table shows the value of y which is the output after applying the threshold. We note that the value of y for the four cases of x_1 and x_2 indicates an AND logic. Now see Fig. 10.9 showing the line which separates the two classes of the output y. We can conclude that AND logic is linearly separable.

Table 10.1 AND Logic

x_1	x_2	z	y
0	0	0	0
0	1	0.75	0
1	0	0.75	0
1	1	1.5	1

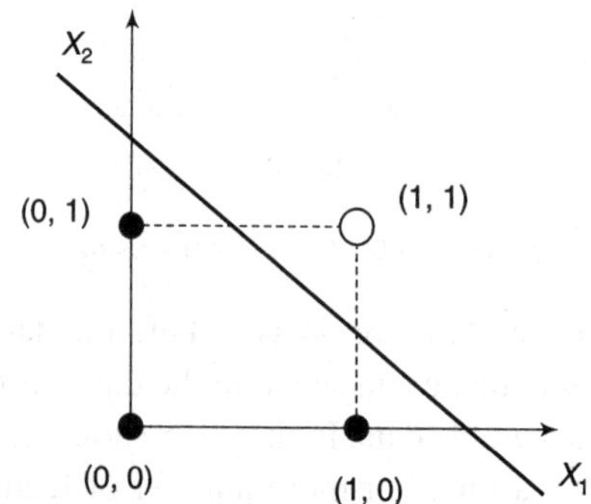

Fig. 10.9 Transfer function for AND logic

Table 10.2 shows a similar case for OR logic. The weights and threshold are chosen as $w_1 = 1$, $w_2 = 1$, $T = 0.5$. Column four of the table indicates that OR logic is obtained by these values. Figure 10.10 shows the line of separation between the two classes.

Table 10.2 OR Logic

x_1	x_2	z	y
0	0	0	0
0	1	1	1
1	0	1	1
1	1	2	1

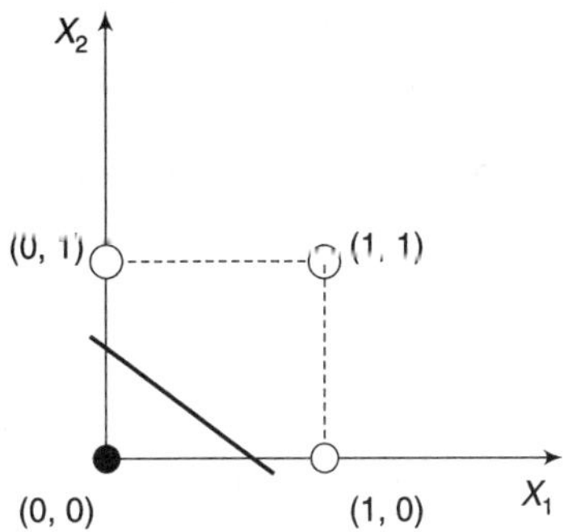

Fig. 10.10 Transfer function for OR logic

Note: There are many other choices for the values of the weights, inputs and threshold which can give the same result.

10.1.4.2 XOR

Table 10.3 XOR Logic

X_1	X_2	y
0	0	0
0	1	1
1	0	1
1	1	0

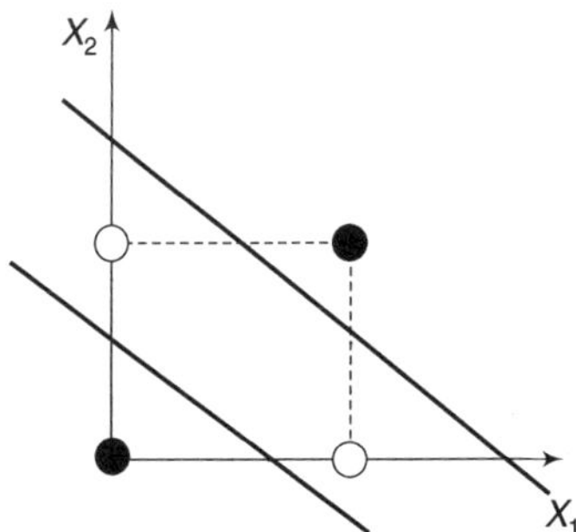

Fig. 10.11 Transfer function for XOR logic

The XOR logic is shown in Table 10.3. Figure 10.11 shows that two lines or a curve is needed for separating the output into two separate classes. Thus, the XOR logic is not a case of 'linearly separable' data. Whatever values we give to the parameters of the perceptron and the inputs, it is impossible to separate the data using a single straight line. This is called the XOR problem and solutions are there for it using neural networks, but not with the simple perceptron configuration. We will have to use an additional hidden layer to get XOR logic using ANNs.

We conclude that the perceptron is not suitable when data is not linearly separable. This is a major limitation as non-linearity is the characteristic of most data. A perceptron is a simple ANN with one input layer and one output layer. The necessity of having to deal with 'non-linearly separable' data is why more layers are added to the basic perceptron to make it a 'multi-layer' perceptron.

10.2 MULTI-LAYER PERCEPTRON

The next big idea that followed the perceptron and was able to overcome the limitation of the perceptron was the multi-layer perceptron (MLP) in which additional layers are introduced between the input and output layers (See Figs. 10.12 a and b). These additional layers are named 'hidden layers' as these additional layers are not visible at the input or output side.

10.2.1 Feedforward Neural Networks

The MLP network is designed as a 'feedforward network ' as information flows in one direction only–from the input to the output. There is no feedback from output to input–in terms of graphs, we can say that there are no cycles.

The whole network can be stacked into layers and there are connections from one layer to the next. All the neurons of one layer are connected to all the neurons of the next layer and this forms a 'fully connected' network. Over the period of time, the number of hidden layers gradually increased and that led to the terminology 'deep learning' for the algorithms associated with such networks. Figures 10.12a and b show two cases – one with just one hidden layer and another with four hidden layers.

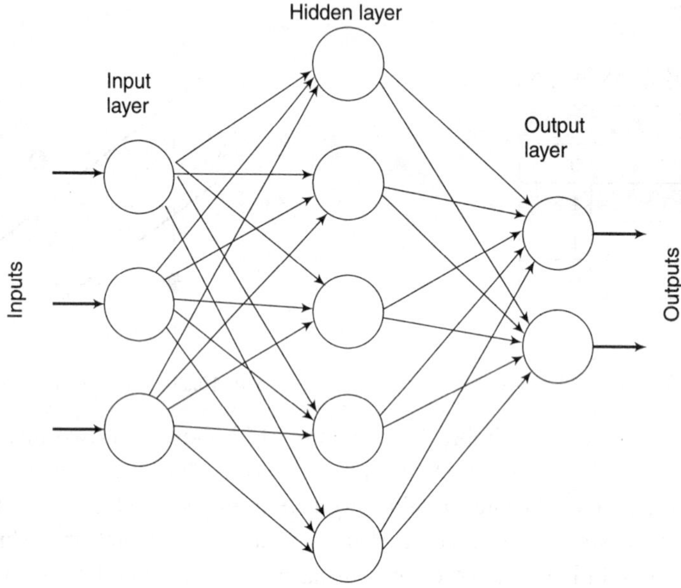

Fig. 10.12 (a) A multi-layer perceptron with one hidden layer

How do we use an MLP for supervised learning?

Supervised learning has a label associated with each input sample. During training, for input data x, the model creates a function $f(x)$ by which it tries to approximate the mapping of the input x to its label y. Thus, function $f(x)$ is the model created by this network. For any training sample x, the network must be able to give an output label which closely matches the actual label. If there is a difference between the 'obtained label' and 'expected label', an error is said to have occurred. The whole point of the network operation is to reduce this error and that can be done only iteratively.

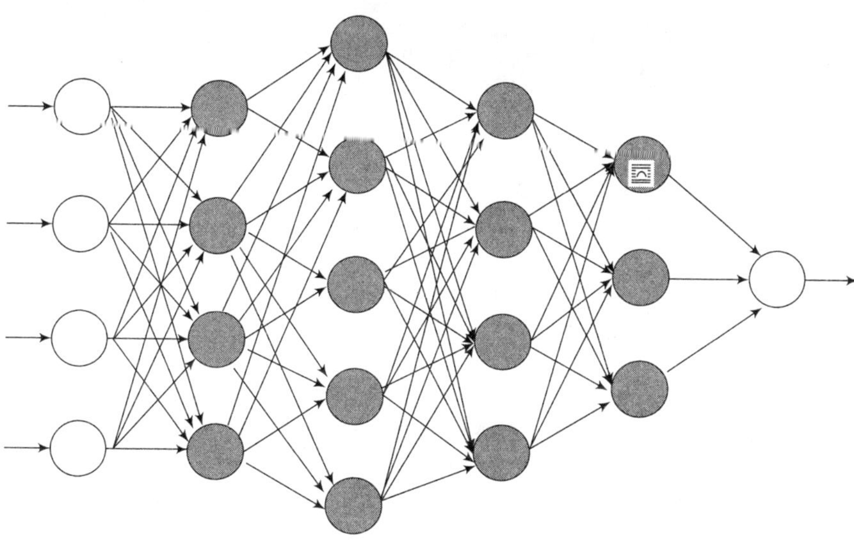

Fig. 10.12 (b) A multi-layer perceptron with four hidden layers

Note: Terms like 'ground truth', 'gold label' and 'target' are terms frequently used for the expected output.

10.2.2 The Feedforward Learning Algorithm

We have seen that a perceptron is the basic unit of a neural network. In it, there is a linear computation which is a weighted summation of the input variables. Following this, a non-linear activation function is applied. In a multi-layered network, this whole process of 'a weighted summation followed by a non-linear activation' is repeated for every layer. For now, we use the activation function that we are already familiar with, which is the Sigmoid.

Next, let us do some calculations based on a simple MLP, so as to become clear about how one training sample is processed by the network. This will give us the basic understanding of a multi-layered neural network. The Cost function we use is the mean squared error and the objective of the algorithm is to minimise this error. There are many other types of Cost functions used in ANNs, but we start with the simplest one first.

Example 10.2 Consider the network of Fig. 10.13 with just one hidden layer.

The input vector is $\mathbf{x} = \begin{bmatrix} x_1 \\ x_2 \end{bmatrix}$. The output layer has just one neuron. The target value (label) at the output is 1 for the values of $\mathbf{x} = \begin{bmatrix} 3 \\ 2 \end{bmatrix}$. Find the mean squared error at the output neuron for the given parameters.

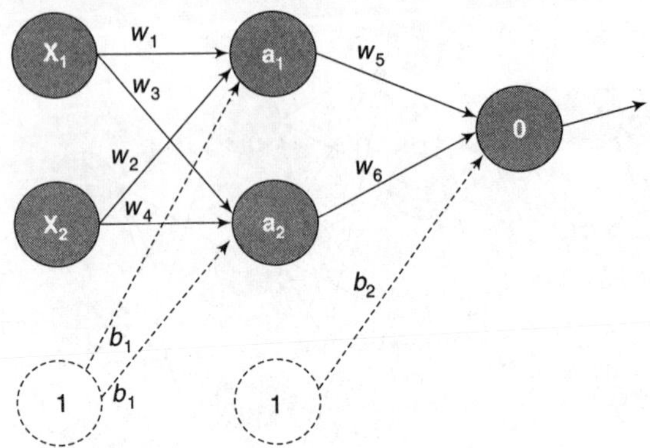

Fig. 10.13 An MLP with one hidden layer

Parameter values

w_1	w_2	w_3	w_4	w_5	w_6	b_1	b_2
0.21	0.11	0.08	0.12	0.04	0.15	0.3	0.4

Solution: Let us redraw the diagram of Fig. 10.13 showing the functions at each neuron. At the hidden neurons and output neuron, first a summation is done followed by an activation. The Sigmoid is used as the activation function. To calculate the error for the chosen values of the parameters, we will first do the forward pass.

Forward Pass 1 Figure 10.13 is redrawn as Fig. 10.14a for calculations to be clear.

From Fig. 10.14a, it should be clear that 'Net_{a1}' is the name given to the sum of weighted inputs at the hidden neuron a_1. 'Out_{a1}' is obtained after applying a Sigmoid activation to Net_{a1}. Similar notations are used for the computations involving hidden neuron a_2 and the output neuron 'o'.

$$\text{Net}_{a_1} = w_1 * x_1 + w_2 * x_2 + b_1 * 1 = \mathbf{1.15} \quad \text{...(10P.1)}$$

$$\text{Out}_{a_1} = \frac{1}{1 + e^{-\text{Net}_{a_1}}} = \mathbf{0.7595} \quad \text{...(10P.2)}$$

$$\text{Net}_{a_2} = w_3 * x_1 + w_4 * x_2 + b_1 * 1 = \mathbf{0.78} \quad \text{...(10P.3)}$$

$$\text{Out}_{a_2} = \frac{1}{1 + e^{-\text{Net}_{a_2}}} = \mathbf{0.6857} \quad \text{...(10P.4)}$$

$$\text{Net}_o = w_5 * \text{Out}a_1 + w_6 * \text{Out}a_2 + b_2 * 1 \quad \text{...(10P.5)}$$

$$= 0.7595 * 0.04 + 0.6857 * 0.15 + 0.4 * 1$$

$$= \mathbf{0.533235}$$

$$\text{Out}_o = \frac{1}{1 + e^{-\text{Net}_o}} \quad \text{...(10P.6)}$$

$$= \mathbf{0.63023}$$

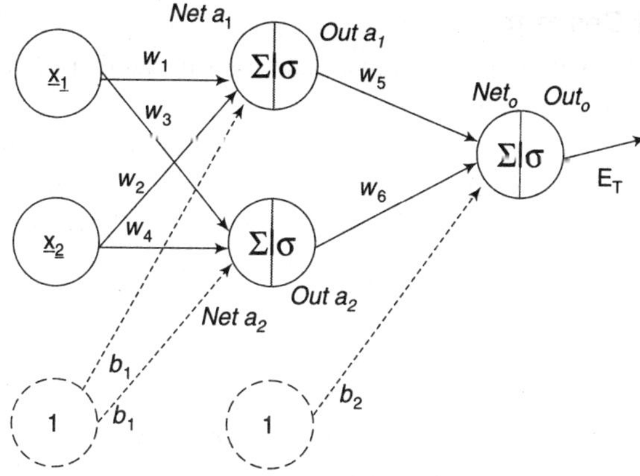

Fig. 10.14 (a) Redrawn Figure 10.13 for calculations

This is the output obtained from this network with the parameters chosen. Since the target value is 1, there is an error. The mean squared error is calculated as:

$$E_T = \frac{1}{2}(\text{Target}_o - \text{Out}_o)^2 = \mathbf{0.068365} \qquad ...(10P.7)$$

Since there is an error, it is clear that the weights and biases have to be changed iteratively. We should find a way to bring the output value as close as possible to the target.

10.2.3 The Backpropagation Algorithm

In this small sample MLP network, we see that when starting with random weights, we did not obtain the expected output value for the given training sample. For the simple perceptron, it was made clear that updating the weights based on the error value is the method for generating the right label.

For a multilayer perceptron, the method is the same. But it needs to be realized that there are weights at all layers. Figure 10.13 has only one hidden layer, but in general, there are multiple hidden layers used for 'deep learning'. In Fig. 10.13, the weights at the output layer are w_5 and w_6. Obviously, they need to be changed to change the output value. Also the weights between the hidden and input layers, which are w_1, w_2, w_3 and w_4 also contribute to the error. The method is to find the contribution of each weight to the output error. The chain rule of calculus is employed to get the contribution to the error, of each of the weights. The error is sensed only at the output of the network but this error value is used at the hidden layers and thence sent to the input side for the purpose mentioned. Since the effect of the error at the output is sent backwards, this is called the 'backpropagation' algorithm.

Backpropagation is the algorithm that is used to calculate the 'gradient' of the error at the output with respect to the parameters of the network. This algorithm is the basic building block of deep learning. This concept was introduced in the 1960s but became popular only after 1989 and that was due to the paper "Learning representations by back propagating errors" by Rumelhart, Hinton and Williams.

10.2.3.1 Gradient Descent

The concept of 'gradient descent' has been described in detail in Section 3.1.2 and so its analysis is not repeated here. But as a recap, let us note that it is an optimization algorithm meant to find the parameters of the network which minimize the output error. For a single data sample, the term 'loss/loss function' is used for this error. For all the samples of the input dataset, the accumulation of the loss/error is given the name 'Cost function'. Many types of Cost functions representing the error are possible but our first analysis will be based on the mean squared error, as in Example 10.2.

In Example 10.3, we do a sample calculation to get a good understanding of the steps of backpropagation. This is a continuation of Example 10.2 in which one forward pass is made to calculate the error. Then backpropagation is done to get the gradient of error E_T with respect to each weight and bias. Using these gradients, all weights are updated. The concept of using the gradient of the Error is based on the gradient descent optimization algorithm (Section 3.1.2)

Example 10.3 In this, the gradient of the error E_T (obtained from Example 10.2) is calculated with respect to each weight and bias. This is a numerical example of the backpropagation algorithm.

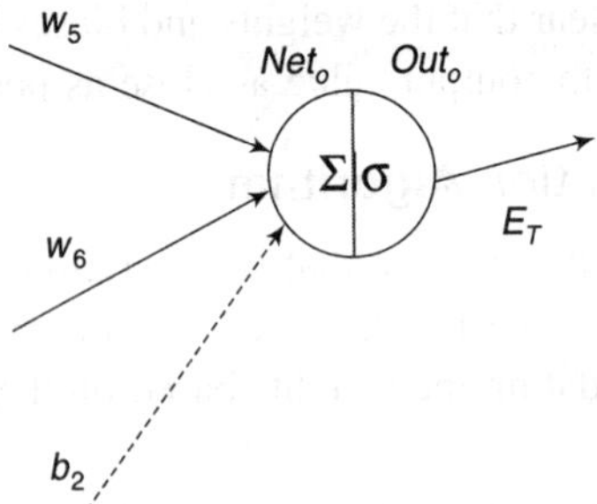

Fig. 10.14 (b) The connections at the output of the network of Fig. 10.13

Solution: We have to find the contribution of each weight to the error, E_T. Let us start with w_5. See Fig. 10.14b which shows the output neuron 'o' and the weights and biases associated with it. The error E_T is observed at the output.

Using the chain rule of calculus, we get

$$\frac{\partial E_T}{\partial w_5} = \frac{\partial E_T}{\partial \text{Out}_o} * \frac{\partial \text{Out}_o}{\partial \text{Net}_o} * \frac{\partial \text{Net}_o}{\partial w_5} \quad \text{...(10P.8)}$$

From (10P.7)

$$\frac{\partial E_T}{\partial \text{Out}_o} = \frac{1}{2} * 2 * (\text{Target}_o - \text{Out}_o) * -1 \quad \text{...(10P.9)}$$

$$= \mathbf{-\ 0.36977}$$

$$\text{Out}_0 = \frac{1}{1 + e^{-\text{Net}_o}} \quad \text{...(10P.10)}$$

So $$\frac{\partial \text{Out}_o}{\partial \text{Net}_o} = \text{Out}_o\,(1 - \text{Out}_o) \quad \text{...(10P.11)}$$

$$= 0.63023 * 0.36978 = \mathbf{0.23304} \quad \text{...(10P.12)}$$

From (10P.5) $$\frac{\partial \text{Net}_o}{\partial w_5} = \text{Out}_{a1} = \mathbf{0.7595}$$

Using (10P.8) $$\frac{\partial E_T}{\partial w_5} = -\,\mathbf{0.36977 * 0.23304 * 0.7595}$$

$$= -\,\mathbf{0.065447}$$

From (10P.5) $$\frac{\partial \text{Net}_o}{\partial w_6} = \text{Out}_{a2} \quad \text{...(10P.13)}$$

$$= \mathbf{0.6857}$$

From (10P.5) $$\frac{\partial\,\text{Net}_o}{\partial b_2} = \mathbf{1} \quad \text{...(10P.14)}$$

Similarly,

$$\frac{\partial E_T}{\partial w_6} = \frac{\partial E_T}{\partial \text{Out}_o} * \frac{\partial \text{Out}_o}{\partial \text{Net}_o} * \frac{\partial \text{Net}_o}{\partial w_6} \quad \text{...(10P.15)}$$

$$= \mathbf{-0.059088}$$

$$\frac{\partial E_T}{\partial b_2} = \frac{\partial E_T}{\partial \text{Out}_o} * \frac{\partial \text{Out}o}{\partial \text{Net}o} * \frac{\partial \text{Net}_o}{\partial b_2} \quad \text{...(10P.16)}$$

$$= \mathbf{-0.086171}$$

So, we have calculated gradients with respect to w_5, w_6 and b_2 which are at the output side of the network.

Going to the input side, we have w_1, w_2, w_3, w_4 and b_1. Refer to Fig. 10.14a.

$$\frac{\partial E_T}{\partial w_1} = \frac{\partial E_T}{\partial \text{Out}_{a1}} * \frac{\partial \text{Out}_{a1}}{\partial \text{Net}_{a1}} * \frac{\partial \text{Net}_{a1}}{\partial w_1} \quad \text{...(10P.17)}$$

$$\frac{\partial E_T}{\partial \text{Out}_{a1}} = \frac{\partial E_T}{\partial \text{Out}_o} * \frac{\partial \text{Out}_o}{\partial \text{Net}_o} * \frac{\partial \text{Net}_o}{\partial \text{Out}_{a1}} \quad \text{...(10P.18)}$$

$$= -\,0.36977 * 0.23304 * 0.04$$

$$= \mathbf{-\,0.00345}$$

$$\frac{\partial \text{Out}_{a1}}{\partial \text{Net}a1} = \text{Out}_{a1}\,(1 - \text{Out}_{a1}) \quad \text{...(10P.19)}$$

$$= 0.7595 * 0.2405$$

$$= \mathbf{0.1827}$$

$$\frac{\partial \text{Net}_{a1}}{\partial w_1} = x_1 \quad \text{...(10P.20)}$$

$$= 3$$

$$\frac{\partial E_T}{\partial w_1} = -0.00345 * 0.1827 * 3$$

$$= \mathbf{-0.00189}$$

Similar calculations will give us

$$\frac{\partial E_T}{\partial w_2} = -0.001261$$

$$\frac{\partial E_T}{\partial b_1} = -0.000630315$$

$$\frac{\partial E_T}{\partial w_3} = \frac{\partial E_T}{\partial \text{Out}_{a2}} * \frac{\partial \text{Out}_{a2}}{\partial \text{Net}_{a2}} * \frac{\partial \text{Net}_{a2}}{\partial w_3} \quad \text{...(10P.21)}$$

$$= -0.01293 * 0.21552 * 3$$

$$= \mathbf{-0.008359}$$

Similar calculations will give us

$$\frac{\partial E_T}{\partial w_4} = -0.0055732$$

$$\frac{\partial E_T}{\partial b_1} = -0.0027866$$

Now that all the required gradients are obtained, we can get the updated values of weights and biases.

Let the learning factor $\eta = 0.5$. The updated weight w_1 is obtained as:

$$w_1^{\text{new}} = w_1 - \eta * \frac{\partial E_T}{\partial w_1} \quad \text{...(10P.22)}$$

$$= 0.21 - 0.5 * -0.00189$$

$$= \mathbf{0.210945}$$

With similar calculation, we get

$$w_2^{\text{new}} = 0.110063$$

$$w_3^{\text{new}} = 0.0841795$$

$$w_4^{\text{new}} = 0.122787$$

$$w_5^{\text{new}} = 0.07272$$

$$w_6^{\text{new}} = 0.179544$$

$$b_1^{\text{new}} = 0.300854$$

$$b_2^{\text{new}} = 0.443086$$

Now, let us do a second forward pass to find the new error with the new parameters.

Forward pass 2

$$\text{Net}_{a_1} = w_1 * x_1 + w_2 * x_2 + b_1 * 1 = \mathbf{1.153815} \quad ...(10P.23)$$

$$\text{Out}_{a_1} = \frac{1}{1 + e^{-\text{Net}_{a_1}}} = \mathbf{0.76020} \quad ...(10P.24)$$

$$\text{Net}_{a_2} = w_3 * x_1 + w_4 * x_2 + b_1 * 1 = \mathbf{0.7989665} \quad ...(10P.25)$$

$$\text{Out}_{a_2} = \frac{1}{1 + e^{-\text{Net}_{a_2}}} = \mathbf{0.68975} \quad ...(10P.26)$$

$$\text{Net}_o = w_5 * \text{Out } a_1 + w_6 * \text{Out } a_2 + b_2 * 1 \quad ...(10P.27)$$

$$= \mathbf{0.622208218}$$

$$\text{Out}_o = \frac{1}{1 + e^{-\text{Net}_o}} \quad ...(10P.28)$$

$$= \mathbf{0.65072}$$

$$\text{Error, } E_T = \frac{1}{2}(\text{Target}_o - \text{Out}_o)^2 = \mathbf{0.0609982592} \quad ...(10P.29)$$

We note that the error has decreased by a small amount. The output value has changed from **0.63023 to 0.65072.** To reach the target value of 1, many more iterations are required. The whole process should be repeated until the error falls below a predefined threshold. We then say that convergence has been obtained.

Note: (i) If a smaller value of η had been chosen, the change in value of the output would have been smaller.

(ii) In each step, 'all' the gradients are calculated and then all weights and biases are updated 'simultaneously'.

The network of Fig. 10.13 is tested for convergence using Python code (not shown here) for η = 0.2. The same code is also used with η = 0.6. The number of iterations needed for convergence is observed for each value of η.

Results:

With η = 0.2, convergence is obtained after 12,56,574 iterations, and with η = 0.6, convergence is obtained after 4,18,846 iterations.

10.3 OBJECTIVE FUNCTIONS USED FOR DEEP LEARNING

So far, we did not use the term 'objective function' in this chapter. We have however discussed 'optimization'. The word 'objective function' is related to optimization. In the process of 'training', a function has to be 'optimized', which means it has to be maximized or minimized. There are objective functions which are meant to be maximized. An example is 'Maximum Likelihood Estimation' (MLE). A 'Cost function' is an objective function which is to be minimized.

In different literature, you may find words such as 'loss' and 'error'. These terms are supposed to mean the error corresponding to just one data sample. The term 'Cost function' is the loss corresponding to the full dataset. But many people tend to use these three terms synonymously.

Until now, the Cost function we used in all our discussions, is the Mean Squared Error (MSE) over all the input samples. The square of the error between the 'expected' output (target) and the obtained/actual output is the basis of this Cost function. If you refer back, we see that we take the difference between two real numbers as the error value. Recollect that real numbers as the output are applicable only in the case of 'regression'. For regression problems, it is invariably the MSE that can be used as the objective function.

On the other hand, when the problem at hand is classification, there is the option to use another Cost function. This is found to be the best fit for classification. Binary classification can be done using logistic regression which was discussed in Section 3.3.7.1.

This Cost function discussed is the 'Log Loss' function which is the objective function used in doing gradient descent and backpropagation in neural networks as well. Why it is highly preferred is made clear in Section 3.3.7.1. Note that the property of the 'Log loss function' when used as the Cost function is:

(i) When the prediction is correct ($y = \hat{y}$), Cost = 0.

(ii) When the prediction is wrong (($y != \hat{y}$), the Cost function is large and tends to infinity.

This means that the prediction is 'highly penalised' when it is wrong. This is a very desirable property for a Cost function and that is why this is a highly preferred Cost function for most classification problems.

10.3.1 Comparing the Log-Loss and MSE Loss for a Single Input Sample

Let's consider Example 10.2 Assume that we are going to use the ANN in Fig. 10.13 for classifications. Then there are two possibilities for calculating the error. These two possibilities shown at the output side of a multi-layered neural network. One possibility is to use the log-loss function as in Fig. 10.15a. The other is to use the mean squared error as in Fig. 10.15b.

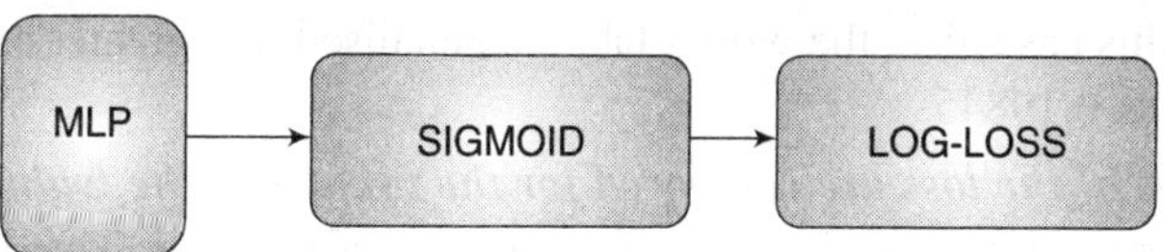

Fig. 10.15 (a) Log-loss used as Cost function

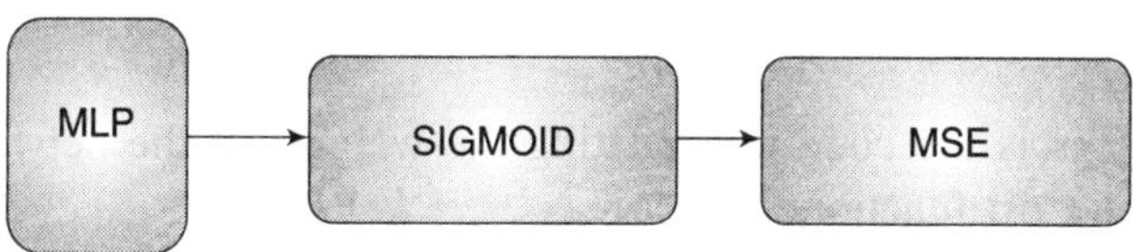

Fig. 10.15 (b) MSE used as Cost function

Example 10.4 We use the error value obtained in the calculation done in Example 10.2. For the given input sample, the label is to be '1' in value.

Case 1: Using the Log-Loss error

The predicted output is the value we get after the Sigmoid. In Example 10.2, for the initial values of the parameters, we got the output as $\text{Out}_o = 0.63$. The target label is $y = 1$.

This means that for the *target* $y = 1$, we get the *predicted output,* $\hat{y} = 0.63$.

If the target y had been 0, the predicted output $\hat{y}$ is much more farther way from it.

From Fig. 3.20a, we copy the Cost function equations and number them as 10.11 and 10.12.

$$\text{Cost}(\hat{y}, y) = -\log_e(\hat{y}) \text{ if } y = 1 \qquad ...(10.11)$$

$$= -\log_e(1 - \hat{y}) \text{ if } y = 0 \qquad ...(10.12)$$

From Eqs. 10.11 and 10.12, we get:

For $y = 1$ the loss is calculated to be $= -[\log_e 0.63] = 0.462$

For $y = 0$, the loss is calculated to be $= -[\log_e 0.37] = 0.99$

We find that for the prediction which is further from the target, we get a bigger value for the Cost function. The prediction further away from the target may be called the 'wrong output' and so we can state that the Cost function penalises this case 'more'.

Case 2: Using the Mean Squared Error

Figure 10.15b will be the case then. In Example 10.2, when the target output is to be 1, we calculated the squared error value as 0.068365.

If the target value is taken as 0, the squared error value is

$$\frac{1}{2}(0 - 0.63)^2 = 0.19845$$

We see that, in this case also, the wrong label is penalised to a greater extent than the right label, and the loss is 0.19845

But if the values of the loss are compared for the two cases, the 'values' are greater for the log-loss function. Getting a higher magnitude of loss is better. That is why the log-loss error is preferred and widely used in deep learning where classification is required.

It can also be proved that the gradient of the Cost function is greater is the case of log loss.

Example 10.5 This is the code for updating the weights of the network of Fig. 10.13, using log-loss as the Cost function.

The updated weights will be different from what is calculated in the Example 10.3. The number of iterations for reaching convergence is also different.

```
import numpy as np
import math
def sig(x):
  return 1 / (1 + np.exp(-x))

weights = [0.21, 0.11, 0.08, 0.12, 0.04, 0.15]
bias = [0.3, 0.4]
inputs = [3, 2]
threshold = 0.001
iter = 1000000
neta = 0.2

for i in range(iter):
   net_a1 = weights[1] * inputs[1] + weights[0] * inputs[0] + bias[0]
   net_a2 = weights[2] * inputs[0] + weights[3] * inputs[1] + bias[0]
   out_a2 = sig(net_a2)
   out_a1 = sig(net_a1)
   net_out = weights[4] * out_a1 + weights[5] * out_a2 + bias[1]
   output = sig(net_out)
   convergence =0
   #print(output)
   #print(( 1-output))
   if ((1-output) < threshold):
  print(i)
  break
```

```
### Error Calculation
error = 0.5 * pow((1 - output), 2)
de_outo=-1/(output)
douto_neto=output*(1-output)
dneto_outa1=weights[4]
douta1_neta1=out_a1*(1-out_a1)
dneta1_w1=inputs[0]
dneta1_w2=inputs[1]
dneto_outa2=weights[5]
douta2_neta2=out_a2*(1-out_a2)
dneta2_w3=inputs[0]
dneta2_w4=inputs[1]
dneta1_b1=1
dneto_w5=out_a1
dneto_w6=out_a2
dneto_b1=1
### Change in Weights
#delw1 = (output - 1) * output * (1 - output) * weights[4] * out_a1 *
(1 - out_a1) * inputs[0]
#delw2 = (output - 1) * output * (1 - output) * weights[4] * out_a1 *
(1 - out_a1) * inputs[1]
#delw3 = (output - 1) * output * (1 - output) * weights[5] * out_a2 *
(1 - out_a2) * inputs[0]
#delw4 = (output - 1) * output * (1 - output) * weights[5] * out_a2 *
(1 - out_a2) * inputs[1]
#delw5 = (output - 1) * output * (1 - output) * out_a1
#delw6 = (output - 1) * output * (1 - output) * out_a2

delw1=de_outo*douto_neto*dneto_outa1*douta1_neta1*dneta1_w1
delw2=de_outo*douto_neto*dneto_outa1*douta1_neta1*dneta1_w2
delw3=de_outo*douto_neto*dneto_outa2*douta2_neta2*dneta2_w3
delw4=de_outo*douto_neto*dneto_outa2*douta2_neta2*dneta2_w4
delb1=de_outo*douto_neto*dneto_outa1*douta1_neta1*dneta1_b1
delw5=de_outo*douto_neto*dneto_w5
delw6=de_outo*douto_neto*dneto_w6
delb2=de_outo*douto_neto*dneto_b1

### Updation in weights
weights[0] = weights[0] - (neta * delw1)
weights[1] = weights[1] - (neta * delw2)
```

```
    weights[2] = weights[2] - (neta * delw3)
    weights[3] = weights[3] - (neta * delw4)
    weights[4] = weights[4] - (neta * delw5)
    weights[5] = weights[5] - (neta * delw6)
print("convergence occurs at the step at 0.2:", convergence)
print(i)
weights = [0.21, 0.11, 0.08, 0.12, 0.04, 0.15]
bias = [0.3, 0.4]
inputs = [3, 2]
threshold = 0.001
```

Result

Learning Rate (η)	Number of Iterations Required Case: MSE	Number of Iterations Required Case: Log Loss
0.2	1256574	2520
0.6	418846	838

We note that 'log loss' reaches the desired output with lesser number of iterations as compared with MSE.

Note: This Cost function has names such as : "*log loss*", "*cross-entropy*" and "*negative log-likelihood*". There are slight differences in the connotations in the use of these terms, but for our purpose here, they mean the same.

10.4 ANALYTICAL EXPLANATION OF BACKPROPAGATION

This numerical Examples 10.2 and 10.3 are meant to get an easy understanding of the backpropagation algorithm. Now let us look at backpropagation analytically. *Those who have already gained a good understanding of the backpropagation method and do not want to do a generalized analysis may skip this portion.*

Figure 10.16 shows a general deep learning network. The input is a vector of d elements. The network in the figure is said to have 4 layers –3 hidden and one output layer. The input layer is not usually 'counted' as a layer in deep networks, though we may still use the term 'input layer'.

The weight vector between one layer and the next layer now becomes a matrix **W**. The following is the activity between one layer and the next. First there is a linear summation and then a non-linear activation. Let us write the equations using the matrix notation, Note that **W** is a matrix and **x** and **b** are vectors.

$$z = \mathbf{Wx} + \mathbf{b} \qquad //z \text{ is the pre-activation value} \qquad ...(10.13)$$

$$\alpha = \sigma(z) \qquad // \text{ is the post-activation value} \qquad ...(10.14)$$

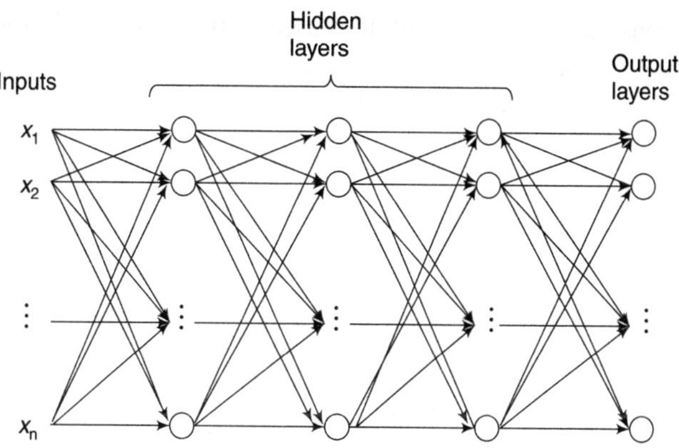

Fig. 10.16 A general diagram for a deep learning network

To understand how to notate weights and biases with reference to layers, refer to Fig. 10.17. w^l_{jk} is notated as the weight from the kth neuron in the $(l - 1)$ (layer to the jth neuron in the lth layer. In a general case with L layers, each layer is notated as 'l', where ($l = 1$ to L). We use the index j for the input side and k for the output side of each weight from one layer to the next one. The superscripts in Eqs. 10.15 to 10.18 notate the 'index' of the layer. Examples of how weights are notated are shown in Fig. 10.17.

The notation for biases and activations are also needed. b^l_j is used to indicate the bias of the jth neuron in the lth layer. For activations, a^l_j is the activation for the jth neuron in the lth layer.

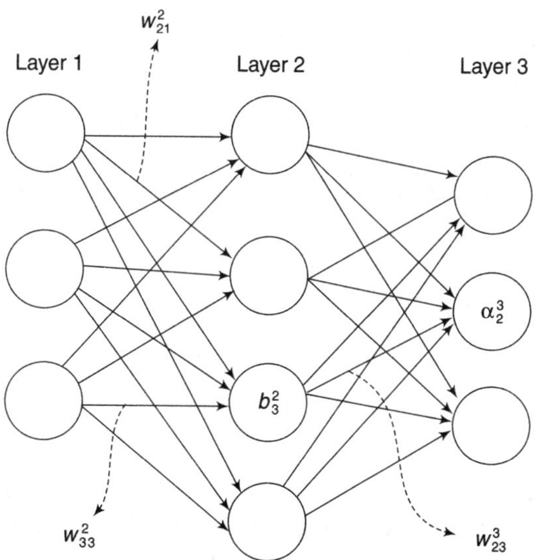

Fig. 10.17 Notation for weights, biases and activations in the network

Note: These notations are consistent with that used in the book, *Neural Networks and Deep Learning* by Michael Nielson.

For each layer l, these equations hold:

$$z^{(l)} = W^{(l)} a^{(l-1)} + b^{(l)} \quad ...(10.15)$$

$$a^{(l)} = \sigma(z^{(l)}) \quad ...(10.16)$$

$$a^{(1)} = x \quad ...(10.17)$$

x is the input vector.

$$a_j^l = \sigma\left(\sum_k w_{jk}^l a_k^{l-1} + b_j^l\right) \quad ...(10.18)$$

This is the activation a_j^l of the jth neuron of layer l with respect to the activations in the $(l-1)^{th}$ layer. The summation is for all the k neurons in the $(l-1)^{th}$ layer.

10.4.1 Cost Function

If we use the Mean Squared Error as the loss function, the Cost function, which is a function of the weights and biases of the whole network is defined as:

$$C(W, b) = \frac{1}{2n} \sum_{x \in X} \|y(x) - a^{(L)}(x)\|^2 \quad ...(10.19)$$

In this equation $y(x)$ is the target value (expected output) and $\alpha^{(L)}(x)$ is the obtained output (which is the post activation value at the output layer) and the Cost function is computed for all training samples ($x \varepsilon X$). The output layer may have a number of neurons and therefore the output will be a vector.

For deep learning which is popularly used for classification, the Cost function is the log-loss function as discussed in Section 3.3.7.1

We have discussed two types of Cost functions in Section 10.3.1. Both are convex functions, having only one minimum (global) The whole process involved in the backpropagation algorithm is to get the parameters of the network corresponding to this minimum point of the Cost function.

$$w_{jk}^{(l)} := w_{jk}^{(l)} - \eta \frac{\partial C}{\partial w_{jk}^{(l)}} \quad ...(10.20)$$

$$b_j^{(l)} := b_j^{(l)} - \eta \frac{\partial C}{\partial b_j^{(l)}} \quad ...(10.21)$$

This means that, we have to apply the update Eqs. (10.20 and 10.21) for each weight and bias. These equations show that every weight and every bias are to be updated by taking the partial differential of the Cost function with respect to that weight and that bias. This was the calculation done in Example 10.3. The learning rate η is a hyperparameter using which the rate of update is adjusted. The importance of using an optimum value for η was discussed in Section 3.1.3.

Gradient Descent vs Backpropagation

Are they the same?

The answer is 'No'. The backpropagation algorithm calculates the gradient of the Cost function with respect to each of the parameters of the network. Gradient descent is the optimization algorithm using which, calculations are done to find the network parameters that minimise the Cost function. In other words, we follow the direction of the slope of the surface created by the Cost function downhill until we reach the lowest point. The learning rate η determines the size of the steps we take to reach the minimum. It is a hyperparameter to be specified by the programmer who does coding for this problem.

10.5 OPTIMIZATIONS

Now we will see that the gradient descent algorithm has three variants in implementations, which are named as Batch, Stochastic and Mini Batch.

In Example 10.3, calculation for parameter updates of the network was done based on one data sample only. The error was calculated for this input sample, gradients corresponding to this error were computed and the weights and parameters were updated. The whole point of the calculations done in Example 10.3 was to get a good understanding of backpropagation and gradient descent.

10.5.1 Batch Gradient Descent (BGD)

But in a practical case, the input dataset will have many samples. The method will then be to do the forward pass for every sample, find the error for each, and take the average of the errors. This Cost function is used as a reference to do backpropagation and the weights and biases are updated. Once round of this is called an 'epoch'. An epoch consists of

(i) Forward pass (for all the samples)

(ii) Calculation of the Cost function

(iii) Backpropagation for gradient computation

Based on the computed gradients, the weights and biases are updated. This method of gradient descent wherein all the samples of the input data are used to calculate the Cost function, is called 'Batch Gradient Descent (BGD)'. The whole batch of the input dataset (training data) is used at one go. It should be noted that many epochs are needed to reach the minimum point of the Cost function, but with each epoch, the cost reduces. Figure 10.18 shows the gradual reduction of the cost as a function of the number of epochs. Figures 10.19 illustrates that in the case of 'batch gradient descent', the path to the central minimum point of the Cost function, is smooth.

BGD is also referred to as Vanilla Gradient Descent. The word 'vanilla' usually implies 'standard'. Batch gradient descent has the problem of being compute-intensive as in practical cases, the number of input samples is large and each sample will have a large number of parameters. Consider the case of a dataset with 100,000 samples and 15 features for each sample. One update can occur only after training with all these samples.

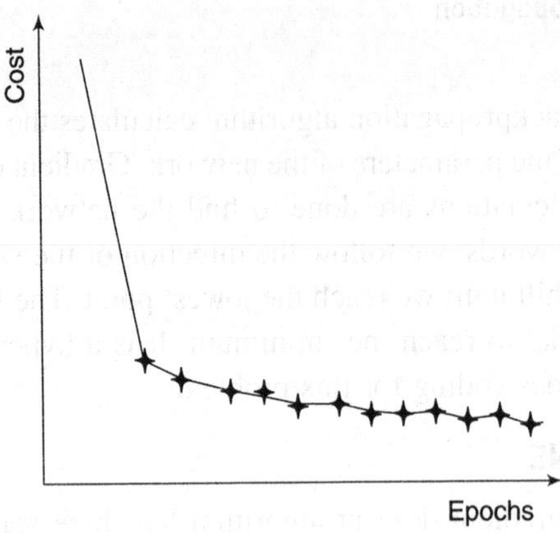

Fig. 10.18 Cost function reduction as a function of the number of epochs

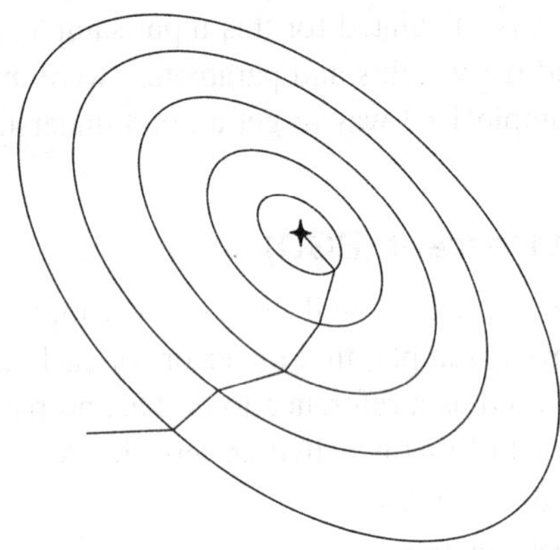

Fig. 10.19 Batch gradient descent-smooth path to the minimum of the Cost function

10.5.2 Stochastic Gradient Descent (SGD)

In contrast to the BGD, we can do loss computation and parameter update using just one sample of the training data (like in Example 10.3). This sample is chosen randomly. The word 'stochastic' implies the randomness of this choice. When we update the network, after one iteration (one forward and one backward pass), and then apply a second sample of the input, we may find that the cost is greater/lesser than in the previous case. We do an update of the network parameters using this second cost. We repeat this process for many samples. It is obvious that the Cost function keeps fluctuating continuously – it may increase or decrease for each iteration. It has been proved that in spite of the fluctuations of the Cost function, ultimately the minimum point will be reached, but it won't be a smooth reduction as in the case of BGD. See the corresponding Fig. 10.20. Figure 10.21 shows the difference in pattern in reaching the minimum for both these cases, plotted for a single parameter.

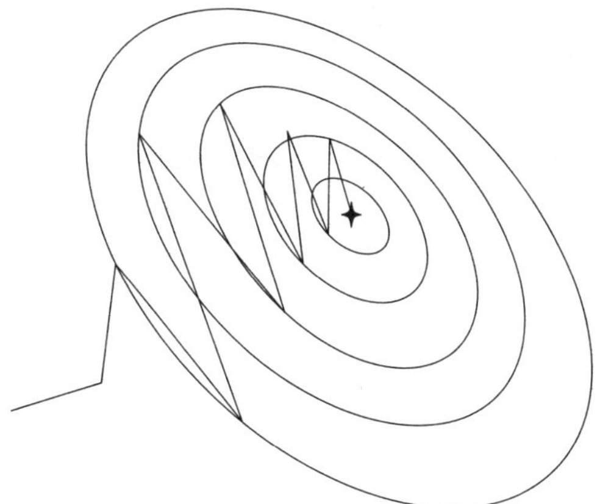

Fig. 10.20 Stochastic gradient descent non-smooth path to the minimum of the Cost function

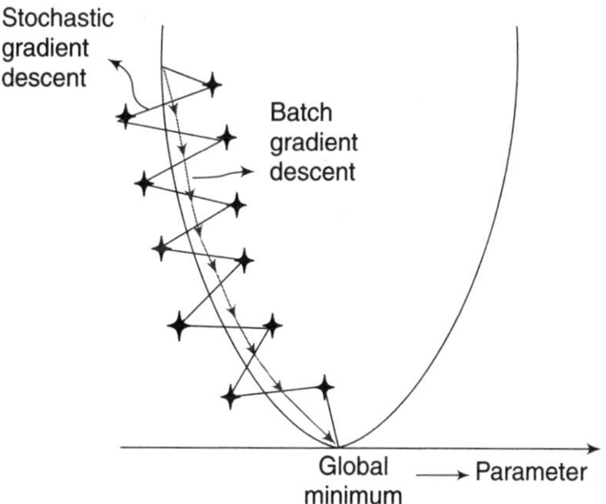

Fig. 10.21 Path to the minimum path for 'Batch' and 'Stochastic' gradient descent

10.5.3 Mini Batch Gradient Descent

SGD is time consuming, obviously. This is because we do updates after each sample. When the dataset size is large, the time involved to complete the update is very large. A combination of SGD and BGD is obtained by using a mini-batch of the input samples. This means that we choose a random set of the input samples, calculate the Cost function corresponding to this set, and update the parameters of the network. We then repeat this for many mini-batches until all the training data is used. The traversal to the minimum point will still have fluctuations, but will be less in the case of SGD. But the computation time will be less than for SGD, and computation complexity less than for BGD. Many references use the word 'stochastic' for the mini-batch GD also – it is made stochastic by choosing the mini-batches randomly. The size of the mini-batch is a hyperparameter. It is usually based on memory constraints (if any), or set to some value, e.g., 32, 64 or 128. Powers of 2 are used as in practice because many vectorized operation implementations work faster when their inputs are sized in powers of 2.

10.6 EXPLODING AND VANISHING GRADIENTS

The backpropagation algorithm which is central to the working of ANNs is based on calculating the gradient of the Cost function with respect to the network parameters. As the loss is propagated from the output side backward to the input side, the gradient computation becomes a multiplication of a number of derivatives. If most of them have values <1, the resultant product will tend to become smaller and smaller until it becomes too small to be of any use. This is the case of the 'vanishing gradients problem'.

On the other hand, if each gradient has large values, the resultant problem is the 'exploding gradients problem'. When gradients explode, the calculated weights become too large. This makes the network unstable.

There are techniques adopted and corrections done to tackle both these problems. We will see some of them as we proceed.

10.7 ADVANCED TOPICS: FURTHER OPTIMIZATIONS

Now that we have covered the basic ideas of deep learning, let us take up some advanced techniques. *This section is intended only for those who are interested in dealing with the practical issues that come up during implementation.* Note that basic theoretical aspects have already been covered.

Over the period of time, new techniques have come up which have capabilities to improve gradient descent. To achieve the aim of getting the best results in the shortest time with the minimum amount of effort, many optimization techniques have come into play. Some of them have made a lot of difference to the practical aspects of deep learning. These topics are to be considered 'further optimizations' meant to be used to improve performance in deep learning networks. Good knowledge of these techniques is useful for better performance in practical applications. Let us have a brief discussion of some of these popular techniques.

10.7.1 Dropout

This is a technique that came into popularity around the year 2012 and brought about a big change in the performance of deep learning practices. Overfitting (Section 2.5.1) had always been a serious problem in large neural networks. Large datasets coupled with large networks imply complicated relationships between the training data and the network. It is found that as training proceeds, some of the connections between some of the neurons become more capable of prediction than others. As iterations progress, these connections become stronger than the others. This means that these connections have more role in predicting the labels of the training set. The role of the other connections then become minimal. This phenomenon is named 'co-adaptation' and when the test data is applied, the performance is seen to be poor. This is a problem of 'overfitting'—we say that the network is incapable of 'generalization'. Using ensemble methods may be a cure for this problem.

The concept of ensemble methods (Section 4.4) is to train many networks with the same data and average their predictions. This is a good solution, but it is computationally expensive to train on many different networks each of which may be quite large.

The computational complexity (for getting an ensemble average) may be reduced by using thinned networks, which are different configurations of the same network. Each 'thinned' network is obtained by dropping some of the connections of the original network. This means that some neurons and the incoming and outgoing connections to/from them are switched off. This is done randomly. This concept is named 'Dropout'. The probability of dropout p, is usually taken between $p = 0.5$ and $p = 0.8$. Dropout is done during the time of training. During the test phase, the effect of averaging these predictions done on the thinned networks is obtained by using the original unthinned network but which has smaller weights (each weight is multiplied by p). See Fig. 10.22(b) which shows a 'thinned' network obtained from the original network in Fig. 10.22(a).

Dropout has proved to be a very robust regularisation technique and all deep learning libraries in Python have the provision to implement it.

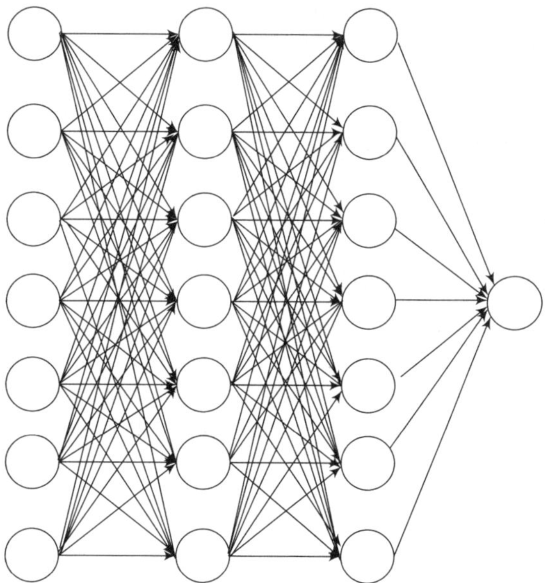

Fig. 10.22 (a) Original network

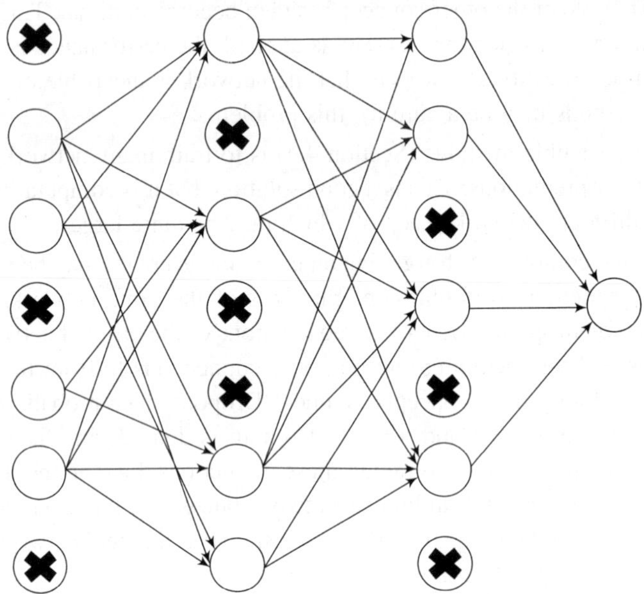

Fig. 10.22 (b) Network 'thinned' using 'dropout'

Is Dropout the same as Bagging?

This is a frequently asked question. Bagging (Section 4.4.4) is an ensemble method in which the input data is sampled. From one dataset, many sets of training data are generated. Each time, some input data samples are not applied to the network.

Dropout is different. From one network, many networks (albeit, thinned) are generated. Because some parts of the network are dropped out each time, the effect is that some features of the input data are not presented to the network. We say that dropout is operative in the feature space, while bagging is affected in the input sample space.

10.7.2 The Momentum Method

See Figure 10.23 in which the Cost function is seen to be decreasing with time but not smoothly, because there are oscillations. We want the oscillations (vertical axis) to be as small as possible. Along with that, we would like a fast convergence which means that on the horizontal axis, the cost should reduce to zero for small values of t, so that 'fast convergence' occurs.

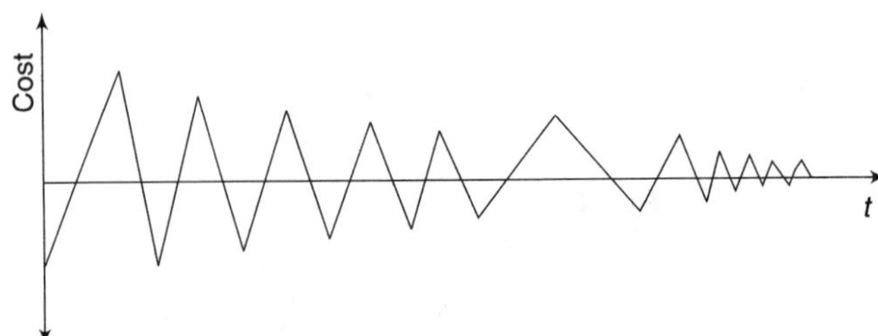

Fig. 10.23 Cost function as a function of time

One of the optimizing techniques for handling these issues is called 'gradient descent with momentum'. The word 'momentum' is based on a concept in physics. When a ball is kicked down a slope, it gathers momentum and so has more capability to bounce over small hills and valleys and reach the destination faster.

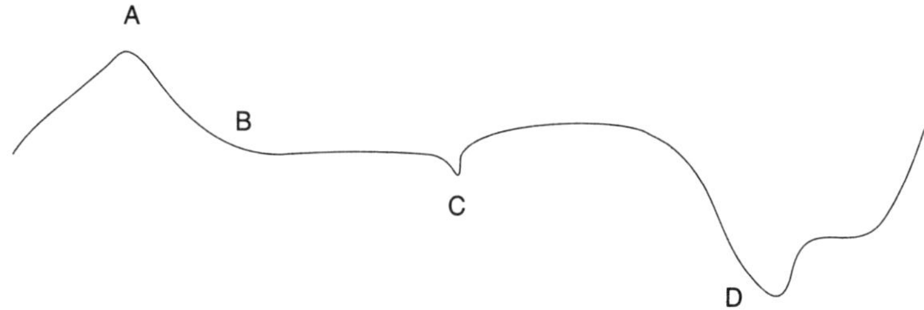

Fig. 10.24 An example scenario

See Fig. 10.24 which shows a typical pattern of the Cost function as it changes with respect to time. From A to B, the gradient is good enough, but at the flat area from B to C, the gradient gradually reduces and may even go down to zero which means there is no further progress to reach the global minimum point D. But with a very small gradient at B, if it does reach point C sluggishly – it may have the tendency to get trapped in local minimum C (even though the Cost function is convex, local minima may still occur due to various instabilities in the network).

To overcome these problems, if a momentum is built up during the time it was in AB, it will overcome the 'slowness' in area B, will reach C, overstep that local minimum and reach D. Thus, the convergence towards point D in Fig. 10.24 is reached faster and the oscillations are reduced.

How do we explain that the oscillations get reduced?

When the sign of the gradient changes (like in the upward movement when in C) the effective momentum decreases and the size of the update reduces. To summarize, remember that the space of the loss function is multidimensional. In dimensions in which the gradients have the same sign, the momentum term increases and in dimensions in which there is a change of sign (change in direction of movement), the momentum decreases and so the updates (oscillations) reduce. That is, how we get both faster convergence and reduction in oscillations.

How do we include momentum in the update equations?

We add a factor of the past update into the current update equation. If the current update done at time t is to get the weights for time $t + 1$, the previous update is of time $t - 1$. The update equation for a weight w is

$$w_{t+1} = w_t - \eta \frac{dC}{dw_t} + \gamma \frac{dC}{dw_{t-1}} \qquad \text{...(10.22)}$$

In Eq. 10.22, we show that a fraction of one previous update is added to the current update. γ is the proportion of the previous update which is included in the current update equation. It is a hyperparameter less than 1. $\gamma = 0.9$ is a typically used value. In practice, the momentum term is used in a way such that it accumulates an exponentially decaying moving average of past gradients. Contribution of many previous updates may be used in this equation but the most recent update contributes more to the equation than earlier ones.

10.7.3 AdaGrad (Adaptive Gradient)

In Example 10.3, only two input features (x_1, x_2) were used. But in practice, any data will have multiple features and then the space in which we are operating is multidimensional. The gradient descent algorithm finds the minimum point in that space. To reach that point, a learning rate (η) is chosen which decides the rate of the update. The point to note is that the learning rate is the same for each dimension, which means it is the same for each input feature.

It is found that a better performance is possible if the learning rate is different for each feature. This is the optimization done in the AdaGrad technique. In dimensions where the gradient is steep, a small learning rate (step size) is chosen, so that there is no overshoot. A larger step size is chosen in dimensions with small gradients. This speeds up the updates. Such an adaptation is observed to give better performance in the case of data with sparse gradients, like infrequent words in word embeddings (Section 17.1) and some applications in computer vision.

AdaDelta, AdaMax, RMSprop (Root Mean Square propagation), ADAM (Adaptive Moment Estimation) Nesterov accelerated gradient (NAG), etc., are optimizations based on the same principle but with minor variations in their implementation equations.

10.7.4 Batch Normalization

Next we will discuss the idea of Batch Normalization or 'Batchnorm' as it is usually referred to. This was first suggested in by Sergey Ioffe and Christian Szegedy in their paper titled '*Batch Normalization: Accelerating Deep Network Training by Reducing Internal Covariate Shift*'. Batch Normalization is seen to give a faster and more stable training of deep networks, though the reason for its effectiveness is still not well understood.

A deep learning network is a complicated mass of computations because of many layers and varying distribution of input values at each layer. After one backward pass, the values of the weights change. Because the inputs to each layer are affected by the weight and bias changes of the previous layers, the model requires careful handling by using low learning rates. This, in turn, makes training to be a slow process. Also, if the non-linear activation is done by a function like the Sigmoid, there is the tendency for the values to go to the saturation regions of the function, which causes the gradient to reduce to almost zero and cause the 'Vanishing gradients' problem.

The authors of the paper have referred to this problem as 'internal covariate shift', and sort to address it by normalizing the inputs at each layer. This means that at each layer, just after the summation and before the application of the activation function, the input is 'normalized' (Section 3.4.2.1). Since minibatch Gradient Descent is the usually used method, the word 'Batch Normalization' is given to this method.

The use of BatchNorm makes training faster – less number of steps are needed for convergence to occur. According to the authors, "Batch Normalization allows us to use much higher learning rates and be less careful about initialization, and in some cases eliminates the need for Dropout".

Previous results by LeCun et al., in 1998b and Wiesler & Ney in 2011, proved that convergence of networks occurs faster if the inputs are decorrelated and linearly transformed to have zero mean and unit variance. This 'whitening' if done at each layer will effectively be a step towards the goal of obtaining a fixed distribution of inputs. This is the suggested method to remove the bad effects of internal covariate shift.

The steps are as follows:

For a minibatch named B with input $x_1 \ldots x_m$, the following operations are done on the input data at each neuron *after the summation unit and before the application of the activation function.*

$$\mu_B := \frac{1}{m}\sum_{i=1}^{m} x_i \qquad \text{//mini-batch mean} \qquad \ldots(10.23)$$

$$\sigma_B^2 := \frac{1}{m}\sum_{i=1}^{m} (x_i - \mu_B) \qquad \text{//mini-batch variance} \qquad \ldots(10.24)$$

Equation 10.24 calculates the variance of the mini-batch, using Eq. 10.23. The next step is normalization.

$$\hat{x}_i := \frac{x_i - \mu_B}{\sqrt{\sigma_B^2 + \varepsilon}} \qquad \text{//normalize} \qquad \ldots(10.25)$$

The normalization step is that, from each input value, the mean of the mini batch is subtracted and then this is divided by the standard deviation. Now each input has zero mean and unit variance. The value of ε seen in Eq. 10.19 is very small. This is used just to ensure that the denominator never goes to 0.

When $\mu = 0$, it means that for an input, its swing is equal in the positive and negative sides. Hence, when activation is done by a function like the Sigmoid, the tendency to go to its saturation region is reduced. (In the saturation region, the gradient vanishes because the Sigmoid is in the 1 or 0 state.)

$$y_i := \gamma\hat{x}_i + \beta \equiv BN_{\gamma,\beta}(x_i) \qquad \text{//scale and shift} \qquad \ldots(10.26)$$

The last step (Eq. 10.26) does a scaling by γ and shifting by β which are parameters learnt in the course of training. An attempt to explain this step has been given by Good fellow in the book *'Deep Learning'*. The explanation is that the operations of normalization (making mean = 0 and standard deviation = 1) done (on any unit) tend to decrease the 'expressive power' of that unit. To recapture that, scaling and shifting operations are done. The γ and β parameters are 'learnt' during training, and the dynamics of these new scaling and shifting parameters are different from that of the original data. They introduce a new mean and deviation. These ideas will be better understood by experience gained by the practice of training deep networks.

10.7.5 Data Augmentation

This is an optimization technique which is used in image based applications and is meant to avoid overfitting. The training set is made bigger as more data which is 'synthetically' created, is added to it. The original data is modified by geometric transformations and colour, illumination and size transformations and the modified image data is considered to be 'more data'. Some geometric techniques employed are:

(i) Vertical and horizontal flipping
(ii) Translation
(iii) Scaling
(iv) Cropping
(v) Rotating

All this is possible because the ANNs used for images are invariant to such geometric transformations plus size, illumination and angle. Data augmentation is found to be very useful because the training set may not contain the range of variations that may be found in the application scenario.

10.7.6 Early Stopping

When training is 'too much', there is the tendency for overfitting. This necessitates the stopping of training after a certain number of epochs. What we want is to be able to stop training just before overfitting starts. To get the 'right number of epochs', the method is to run a validation set after each training epoch. As we repeatedly do this, at some epoch number we will find the lowest loss point of error for the validation set. (See Fig. 10.25.) This is the point at which the error starts increasing for the Validation set. This is the epoch number at which training should be stopped.

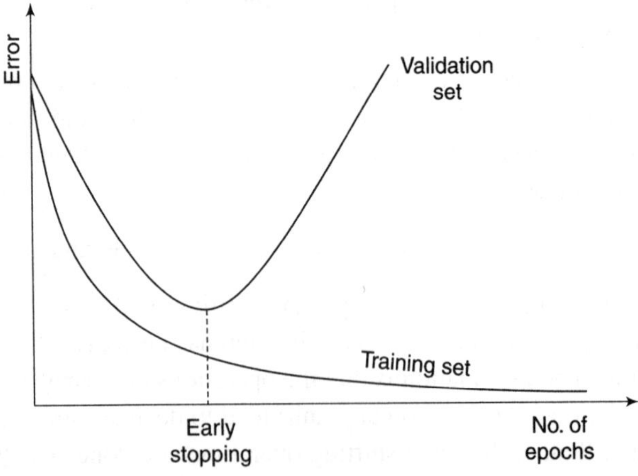

Fig. 10.25 The lowest loss point using the validation set

Figure 10.25 also shows that if we continue training beyond this, it will show lower training errors, but that should not be our motivation to continue training. If we continue training, we will find ultimately that the test error will be high. The parameters corresponding to the lowest loss point of the validation set should be stored and used as our network parameters. The 'Early Stopping callback' in Keras can be used to monitor this. Early stopping is a very good regularisation technique which can be easily incorporated into deep learning programs.

10.7.7 Gradient Clipping

This is a direct solution to the Exploding Gradient Problem. The method is to clip the gradient by setting a ceiling on it. There are two methods:

(i) Clip by value: A defined ceiling – maximum value – is defined for the gradient and when the gradient goes above this, it is clipped to remain at this maximum value.

(ii) Clip by norm: A threshold is defined for the norm of the gradient and the action is the same as the clip by value method.

With this we conclude the part of the chapter in which many heuristics are used to improve the performance of deep learning networks.

10.8 NON-LINEAR ACTIVATION FUNCTIONS

Now let's go back to one of the basic ideas involved in ANNs. Why do we need non-linear activation functions? To understand that, we should re-examine the basic precept regarding machine learning.

What exactly does supervised machine learning do?

When there is a system which has inputs and corresponding outputs, it means that there is a function that maps the inputs to the output. $y = f(x)$ is this mapping. A Supervised machine learning algorithm has knowledge only of the input x and the output y. From this, the algorithm has to find the function $f(x)$–in effect, it models the system. The ML system can only find an approximation to $f(x)$. If (the real mapping) is linear, the approximation should also be a linear function.

But most mappings are not linear. They may be polynomials of high degrees. The ML algorithm should be able to extract this mapping from the input data and its labels. An artificial neural network (ANN) is also a machine learning algorithm. To extract a nonlinear mapping, it should have non-linearities within it. This accounts the necessity for nonlinear activation functions in each of its layers. Complex patterns in the data can be extracted only through the use of nonlinear functions.

The only other computation in an ANN is a linear summation of weighted inputs at each layer. That is just a linear regression. With this alone, even if many, many layers are used, the network will still be a linear regression model. The use of ANN for many kinds of non-linear mappings comes about only because the dynamics of the network changes with the inclusion of nonlinear activation functions. We see that these non-linear activation functions are present at each layer of the ANN – without this, there will not be the gradient needed for backpropagation, which is the basic action of the ANN. The fact that a gradient is involved also indicates that the activation function should be differentiable.

Now let's take a look at the various activation functions that are popularly used.

10.8.1 Sigmoid

This function has already been discussed in Section 10.1.3. It is a smooth approximation to a step function and it is useful when we need binary classification. It has the name logistic function as it is used in logistic regression (Section 3.3.1) In Examples 10.2 and 10.3, it is the Sigmoid that is used for activation at each layer. It squashes any input to a value between 0 and 1 which corresponds to a binary probability. This is a very important reason for its popularity in binary classification.

The Sigmoid is a reasonably popular function for activation, but it has a few problems associated with it. The first problem of using the Sigmoid function is that more computation is involved in it, than the currently more popular *ReLU* function.

Another point is as follows: When the signal applied to it is very high or very low, it saturates to its upper or lower level. Then the derivative becomes zero and so backpropagation cannot occur. This is called the 'vanishing gradient' problem. See Fig. 10.26 which shows the differential going to zero. As the network gets deeper, the vanishing gradient problem becomes more acute and the error does not propagate properly to the input side.

One solution to this is to use batch normalization (Section 10.7.4). In this, since the mean of the input at each layer is made 0, the signal has equal swings in both directions. Therefore, it does not cause the output of the activation stage to saturate.

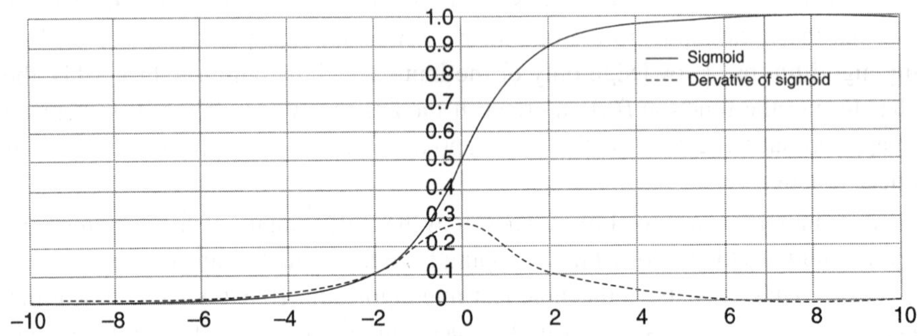

Fig. 10.26 The Sigmoid and its derivative

10.8.2 Hyperbolic Tangent (*Tanh*)

This is essentially a modified Sigmoid, the difference being that the output is squashed to lie between –1 and +1. The function along with its differential is shown in Fig. 10.27. It is preferred over Sigmoid because the data gets centred around 0 (in contrast with the Sigmoid which gets centred around 0.5). There is also an opinion that the preference is because the derivative of *Tanh* is higher than that of Sigmoid. (Compare Fig. 10.27 with Fig. 10.26)

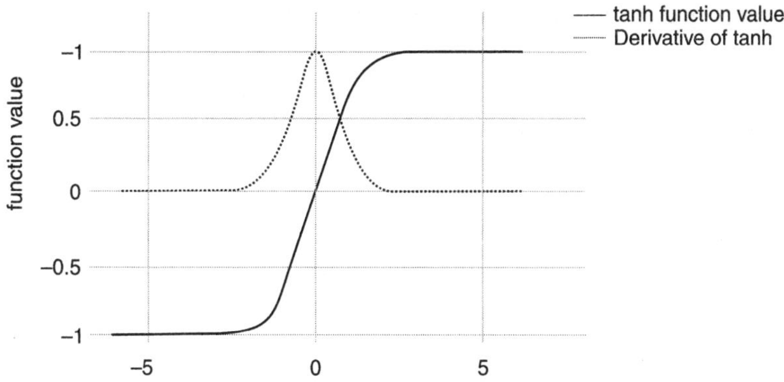

Fig 10.27 The Tanh Function and its derivative

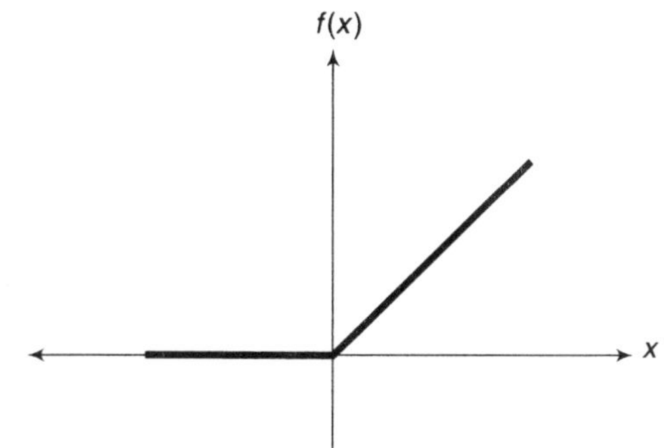

Fig. 10.28 The ReLU function

10.8.3 ReLU (Rectified Linear Unit)

The current most popular activation function is the Rectified Linear Unit (ReLU) shown in Fig. 10.28. It was around the year 2010 that that this function started to become popular. Let us spend more space and time in understanding why this is the activation function of choice in many applications. Equation 10.27 defines the ReLU function.

$$f(x) = \begin{cases} 0, & \text{if } x < 0 \\ x, & \text{if } x \geq 0 \end{cases} \quad ...(10.27)$$

where x is an input value.

Salient points regarding ReLU are:

(i) ReLU is used only in the hidden layers.

(ii) If the input value is positive, the ReLU function returns that value itself; if it is negative, it returns 0. Thus, all negative inputs are squashed to 0.

(iii) It has a linear region and does not saturate. In the linear region, the derivative is 1. Recall that the vanishing gradient problem is caused by multiplying many small derivatives. But for ReLU, the derivative is 1 in the linear region. So it does not cause the vanishing gradient problem and as such it can easily be used in networks which are very deep.

(iv) The function returns 0 if it receives any negative input, but for any positive value x, it returns that value itself. Since it gives an output that has a range from 0 to infinity, ReLU may cause the output to explode. To avoid this, it is advised to start training using very small values for the weights.

(v) The most important property of ReLU is that it introduces what is called 'sparsity'. Neuroscience has explained that in biological neurons, all neurons are not ON all the time. This is the concept of sparsity which is applicable here. In an ANN, this can be achieved using by ReLU because all negative inputs cause the activation to become zero and thus many neurons are switched OFF. See Fig. 10.29 in which the shaded blocks correspond to the ON neurons and the white ones to the OFF neurons.

This introduces 'sparsity' into the network and this is one of the important features of ReLU which none of the other activation functions possess.

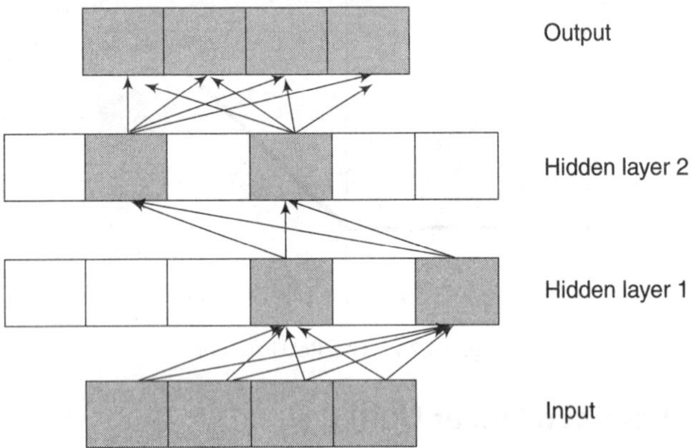

Fig 10.29 Sparse connection of nodes

Why are sparse representations considered good?

(a) They are less entangled. Dense representations have the chance of data becoming strongly correlated during the training phase which causes 'overtraining'. This means that the abstract features which are encoded in the hidden units become entangled.

(b) It will be seen that most deep learning networks have a Softmax layer or even an SVM layer at the output. Sparse representations have a greater chance of bringing in 'linear separability' which is useful for easy classification using these output functions.

(c) The last point in favour of sparsity is that, because of lesser interactions, we get a distributed representation which is one of the goals of a neural network representation.

All this is made possible by ReLU which is a simple method of turning neurons ON and OFF leading to sparsity.

To conclude, let us list out the prominent features of ReLU which are:

(i) Because there is no complicated computation, training using it, is fast.
(ii) Its range is from 0 to infinity.
(iii) All negative inputs are squashed to 0.
(iv) It is piecewise linear.
(v) It can be used only in hidden layers. This is to say that it can't be used at the output layer.

10.8.4 Leaky ReLU

The sparsity that is good to a certain extent may not be beneficial if too many neurons remain inactive or dead. In that case, the network finds it difficult to recover from this state. This is called the 'dying ReLU' problem. To solve this problem, the 'leaky ReLU' is available which outputs a small negative value for negative inputs. (See Fig. 10.30).

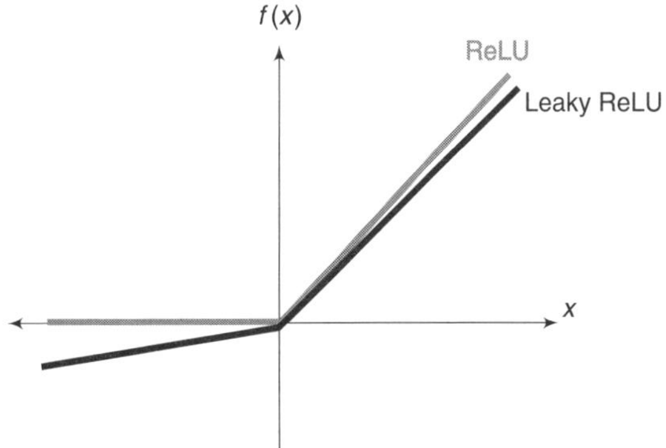

Fig. 10.30 The leaky ReLU function

10.8.5 The Softmax Function

Finally, we come to a very important activation function which is used at the output when an ANN acts as a multiclass classifier. Recollect that the Sigmoid is used for binary classification. It converts any value to a probability between 0 and 1. The Softmax does the same – only it is non-binary and it can handle any number of classes where the probability of each class is spelt out by this function. The sum of the probabilities of all the classes is 1. The Sigmoid is only a special case of the Softmax function

The equation for Softmax for n classes with values $x_1, x_2 \ldots \ldots \ldots .. x_n$ is given by

$$S(x_i) = \frac{e^{x_i}}{\sum_{j=1}^{n} e^{x_j}} \qquad \ldots(10.28)$$

What this means is that any value of x_i is converted to a probability. Let's use an example.

Example 10.6 Convert the values of **x** to probabilities, using Softmax.

Let
$$\mathbf{x} = \begin{bmatrix} 1.2 \\ 0.9 \\ 0.4 \end{bmatrix}$$

Solution: Using these values of **x** in Eq. 10.22, the denominator is:

$$e^{1.2} + e^{0.9} + e^{0.4} = 3.320 + 2.46 + 1.49 = 7.27$$

Using Eq. 10.22, we get $S(x_i)$ for all $i = 1$ to 3

Table 10.4 Softmax calculations

x_i	e^{x_i}	$S(x_i)$
1.2	3.32	0.46
0.9	2.46	0.34
0.4	1.49	0.20

We find that the $S(x_i)$ sums up to 1 and each x_i is converted to an equivalent probability. We will see later that many deep learning networks use Softmax at the output layer for multi-class classification.

Conclusion

In this chapter, many fundamental concepts of deep learning have been discussed. Knowing these basic principles is absolutely necessary for doing quality work in this field. Besides that, advanced optimizations have also been covered. Knowing all these will be a good basis for dealing with the complex deep learning networks which are in popular use.

Questions

1. In what way does deep learning differ from classical machine learning in method as well as performance?
2. What is the role of the Sigmoid in the working of a perceptron?
3. What is meant by the term 'linear separability' in the context of a perceptron?
4. Discuss the meaning and relevance of the terms 'Feed forward network'and 'Back-propagation'.
5. Why is 'Mini-batch gradient descent' preferred as the method to find the parameters of a deep learning network?
6. Explain why the log-loss Cost function is preferred over MSE?
7. How are the weights and biases notated in a deep learning network? Explain using examples.
8. How does 'momentum' make a positive difference to training of deep learning networks?

9. What is the principle of use of the Batch Normalization technique?
10. Give a brief explanation of why the ReLU function is the choice for many DL networks.

Exercise

1. In Examples 10.2 and 10.3, the updating of weights has been done using the quadratic Cost function (MSE).

   Do a re-calculation of the weights using 'log loss' as the Cost function.
2. MNIST is a data base of handwritten digits. Write and test a program to do handwriting recognition. Find the metrics of classification.
3. With examples, discuss the use of constants, variables and place holders as used in Tensor Flow.
4. (a) What is meant by the word 'Tensor'?
   (b) Write simple programs (two each) in TensorFlow using constants, variables and placeholders
   (c) Using TensorFlow, do backpropagation. You may use any standard data base or your own data.

CHAPTER

11

Convolutional Neural Network (CNN)

In this chapter you will

- learn the basics of image representation,
- practise Image filtering techniques,
- understand how to handle colour images,
- discover the different layers of a CNN,
- be introduced to standard CNNs,
- analyze advanced techniques used in the latest networks,
- assess the importance of Transfer learning,
- discuss the different types of object detection methods, and
- do a detailed study of Yolo for object detection.

11.0 INTRODUCTION

The Convolutional Neural Network (CNN), also known as ConvNet is a well known deep learning model which is focused on the applications of Computer Vision. The term 'Computer Vision' indicates that human vision is complemented, enhanced and augmented using the principles of image processing and machine learning. It also implies that machines are made to emulate human capabilities in vision. In general, it is easy for humans to recognise objects, classify them, process this data, extract information from them and interpret the results. Using machine learning techniques and image processing algorithms, computers should also be able to recognise patterns from still and moving images. The CNN is a specialized type of neural network which can be used for this and there are applications for CNNs even in fields not strictly within the domain of computer vision.

The CNN has many layers, some of which do image processing and some of which are just the fully connected layers or MLPs that we discussed in Chapter 10. Also, CNNs may also be used for applications which do not involve images. For the case of Natural Language Processing (NLP), there are more appropriate types (Chapter 12) of deep learning networks, but CNNs are not entirely ruled out for it.

11.1 IMAGE PROCESSING BASICS

Understanding CNNs requires a basic knowledge of how to handle images, so let us start with that. Readers who are already thorough with image processing principles may also read this part because calculations relevant for understanding CNNs start in this section. The discussion on image processing basics will be limited to image representation and image filtering.

11.1.1 Image Representation

An image is a space which is divided into a number of very small areas called 'picture elements' or pixels. Thus, an image is a two-dimensional array of pixels. For an M × N digital image, there are M pixels along the width and N pixels along the height. See Fig. 11.1 in which there are M columns and N rows.

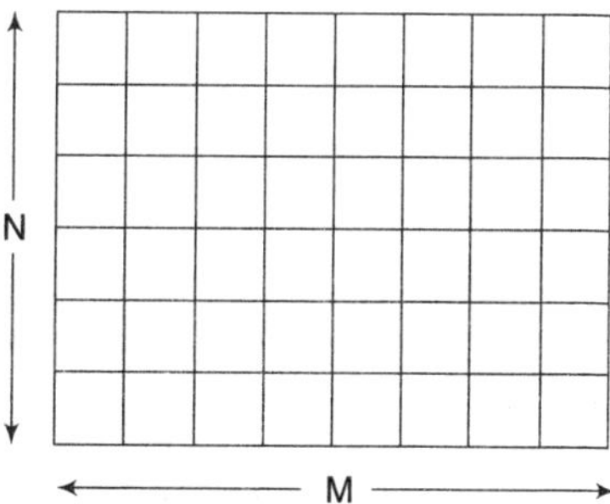

Fig. 11.1 An 8 × 6 image matrix

Images are represented digitally as a two-dimensional array (matrix) of numbers. Let us first think of a black and white image which is also referred to as 'grey scale image'. This is because the only information that is represented are the intensity values which are just different shades of grey. Figure 11.1 is an 8 × 6 image. Each square in the image is named a 'pixel'.

The only information that we need about a pixel is its intensity value and its position in the M × N grid. We call it 'spatial information'. In digital representation, each pixel value is represented using 8 bits. Thus, intensity values range from 0 to 255. The highest intensity value is 255 which represents a pixel of maximum whiteness. The lowest intensity value 0 will appear on the image as a black pixel. Any intensity value in between these two numbers results in shades of grey.

Intensity values are represented as elements of an image matrix. For the 8 × 8 grid of Fig. 11.2 which has alternate values of the highest and lowest intensity, we get a chessboard pattern as the displayed image. See the values in the image matrix and the corresponding image. In general, the resolution of an image is expressed in terms of M and N. The 8 × 6 image of Fig. 11.1 has 48 pixels in it. An image of size 1280 × 1024 has 1,310,720 pixels which we denote as a resolution of 1.3 megapixels. Another value of resolution is 2048 × 1536 = 3,145,728 pixels or 3.1 megapixels. But we can acquire images in other ranges and then re-size them using any of the many software tools available.

$$\begin{bmatrix} 255 & 0 & 255 & 0 & 255 & 0 & 255 & 0 \\ 0 & 255 & 0 & 255 & 0 & 255 & 0 & 255 \\ 255 & 0 & 255 & 0 & 255 & 0 & 255 & 0 \\ 0 & 255 & 0 & 255 & 0 & 255 & 0 & 255 \\ 255 & 0 & 255 & 0 & 255 & 0 & 255 & 0 \\ 0 & 255 & 0 & 255 & 0 & 255 & 0 & 255 \\ 255 & 0 & 255 & 0 & 255 & 0 & 255 & 0 \\ 0 & 255 & 0 & 255 & 0 & 255 & 0 & 255 \end{bmatrix}$$

Fig. 11.2 A chessboard pattern and its corresponding matrix of intensity values

$$f(x, y) = \begin{bmatrix} f(0, 0) & f(0, 1) & f(0, 2) & \cdots & f(0, M-1) \\ f(1, 0) & f(1, 1) & f(1, 2) & \ldots & f(1, M-1) \\ \vdots & \vdots & \vdots & & \vdots \\ f(N-1,0) & f(N-1,1) & f(N-1,2) & \ldots & f(N-1,M-1) \end{bmatrix}$$

Fig. 11.3 Notation for a M x N image

Figure 11.3 shows the notation used for an image matrix named $f(x, y)$. There are M columns and N rows. Each matrix element is an intensity value of the pixel at that location.

Figure 11.4 shows an image and its digital representation. In the top left hand corner, we have the maximum intensity. The intensity reduces from left to right as well as from top to bottom. The pixel values indicate this.

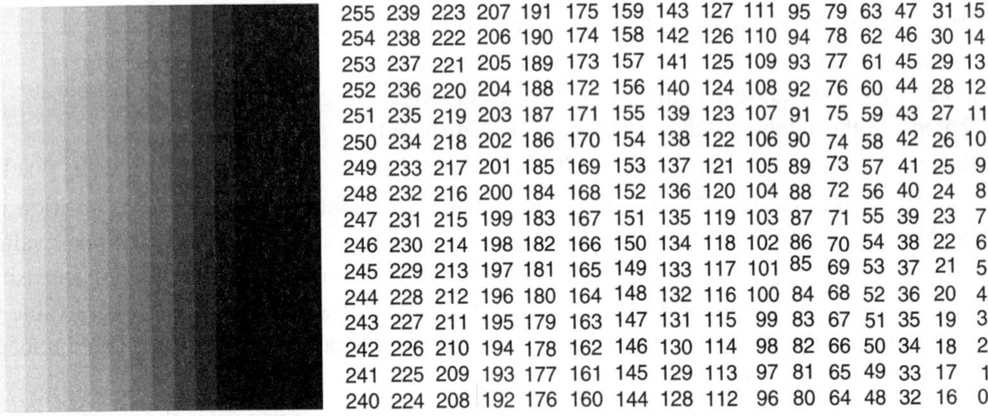

255	239	223	207	191	175	159	143	127	111	95	79	63	47	31	15
254	238	222	206	190	174	158	142	126	110	94	78	62	46	30	14
253	237	221	205	189	173	157	141	125	109	93	77	61	45	29	13
252	236	220	204	188	172	156	140	124	108	92	76	60	44	28	12
251	235	219	203	187	171	155	139	123	107	91	75	59	43	27	11
250	234	218	202	186	170	154	138	122	106	90	74	58	42	26	10
249	233	217	201	185	169	153	137	121	105	89	73	57	41	25	9
248	232	216	200	184	168	152	136	120	104	88	72	56	40	24	8
247	231	215	199	183	167	151	135	119	103	87	71	55	39	23	7
246	230	214	198	182	166	150	134	118	102	86	70	54	38	22	6
245	229	213	197	181	165	149	133	117	101	85	69	53	37	21	5
244	228	212	196	180	164	148	132	116	100	84	68	52	36	20	4
243	227	211	195	179	163	147	131	115	99	83	67	51	35	19	3
242	226	210	194	178	162	146	130	114	98	82	66	50	34	18	2
241	225	209	193	177	161	145	129	113	97	81	65	49	33	17	1
240	224	208	192	176	160	144	128	112	96	80	64	48	32	16	0

Fig. 11.4 A digital image and its matrix representation

The digital representation of an image in the space domain is called a 'spatial representation'. A number of operations can be done on this spatial representation–enhancement, de-noising and filtering are some of them. Since our aim is only to understand the aspects of image processing which are necessary for understanding CNNs, we will limit ourselves to discussing only filtering. For that, we start with the concept of 'frequency' for digital images.

11.1.2 Frequencies in an Image

Usually, frequency is defined as the rate of change with respect to time. For a still image, there is no dimension of time, instead we have the dimension of space. Frequency corresponds to the change of intensity in the dimension of interest. In Fig. 11.2, there is a sharp change of intensity along both the X and Y coordinates. The 'sharp' change is because the intensity changes from the maximum value to the minimum value. If we have a sensor for detecting the intensity along one horizontal line, we get a square wave (Fig. 11.5) which shows an abrupt change of intensity from full black to full white. If each square of the image corresponds to one pixel, this is the maximum rate of change possible. A similar waveform will be obtained along a line in the vertical direction as well.

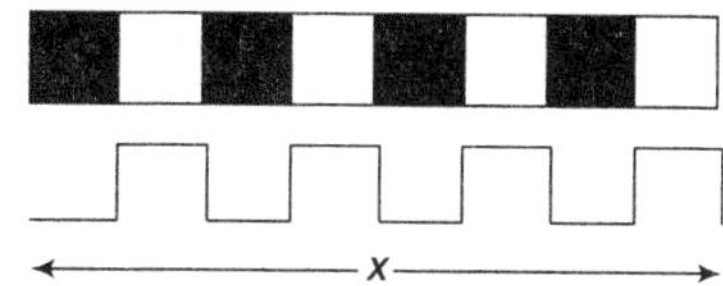

Fig. 11.5 The rate of change of intensity in the X/Y coordinate of Fig 11.2 (conceptualized as a square wave)

This change of intensity is what we denote as 'spatial frequency' in the image. Thus, the image of Fig. 11.2 shows the maximum rate of change of intensity in both the horizontal and vertical dimensions. If we analyze this square wave, it is composed of a number of sine wave frequencies. The repetition rate of the square wave is the lowest frequency, and the other frequency components are its harmonics.

A monochrome image with very little intensity changes within its space is a low frequency image. An image which is completely white or black or grey has no intensity changes within its space, but it has its level of average intensity. A pure white image has a high average intensity of value 255, a grey one has less of it and a black image has an average intensity of 0. It is customary to use the term 'DC value' to mean 'average intensity'.

(a) Source image

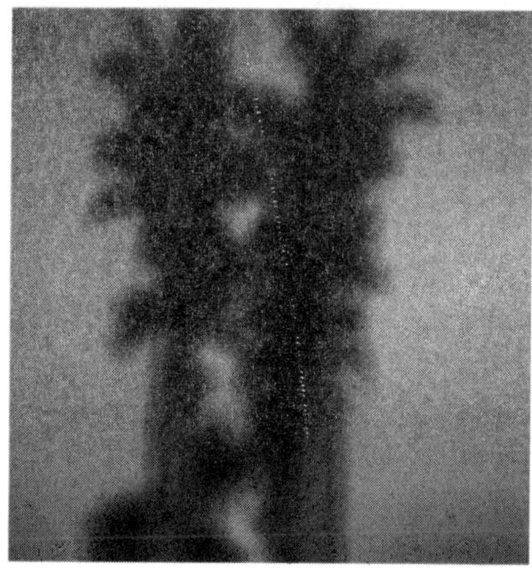

(b) Low-pass filtered (blurred) image

Fig. 11.6

A monochrome image is composed of many different intensity values. The patterns in it are characterized by intensity changes. Filtering is the process by which some of the frequencies are blocked or removed. Low-pass filtering is when only low frequencies are passed – higher frequencies are blocked. High-pass filtering is when only frequencies above a specific value are passed.

Take a look at Fig. 11.6a. This shows a reasonably good image in which there are multiple frequencies. Many different intensity values are present in it.

What happens when low-pass filtering is done on this image?

The answer is that the high frequencies are blocked out – this means that the sharp intensity changes will no longer appear in the image. This leads to a blurred image as in Fig. 11.6b. A low-pass filter which does this can be realized as a spatial filter or a frequency domain filter.

(a) Source image

(b) High-pass filtered image

Fig. 11.7

Now observe Fig. 11.7b. For the source image (11.7a), high-pass filtering is applied to get 11.7b. This means that the low frequency components have been blocked out. Note that the image has lost its 'average intensity' which is the DC value (lowest frequency) and so the background is black. Also, the pattern of sharp variations of intensity which correspond to high frequencies, has been clearly outlined.

11.1.3 Edges in an Image

When there is a change in intensity, we have an 'edge'. In Fig. 11.8 where there is a sharp change from full black to full white, we have an abrupt edge. In fact, that image is a binary image of just two intensity values. But in general, most images have many intensity values, as in Fig. 11.8 where a gradual edge (change of intensity) is also shown.

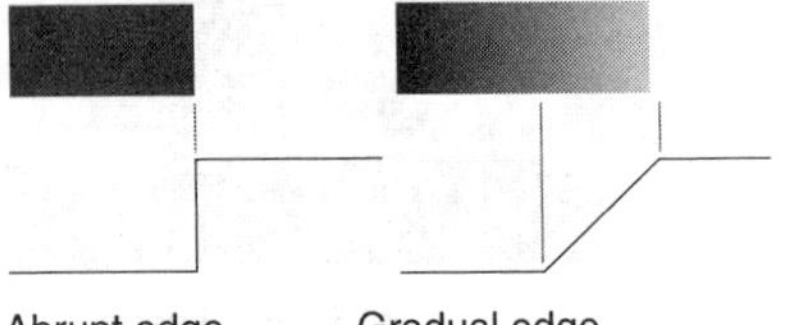

Fig. 11.8 Gradual and abrupt intensity changes acting as edges

How do we identify objects in an image?

The method is to detect the edges of the image which indicates the 'form/outline' of the object in it. The concept of 'edge detection' is a fundamental operation for most kinds of image applications. If the edges of an object in an image are obtained, the object may be identified. Edge detection is a very important method in object detection and classification.

See Figs. 11.9a and b which show two edge detected images. The first one has only its horizontal edges highlighted and the second one has the vertical edges identified . The source image is the same 'coconut tree' image that was shown in Figure 11.7a. In essence, it should be obvious that edge detection is the first step in object detection.

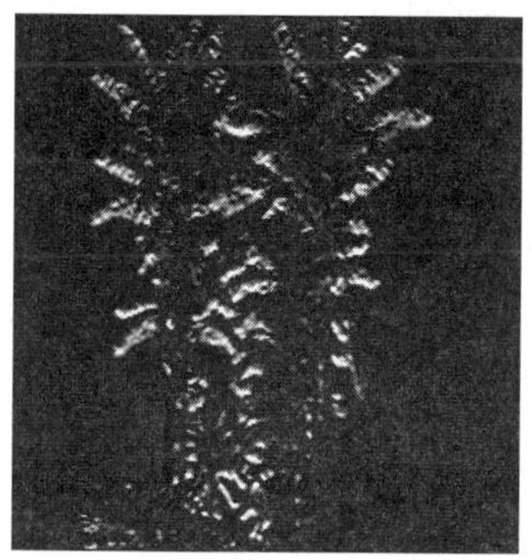

(a) Horizontal edge detected image

(b) Vertical edge detected image

Fig. 11.9

How are all these operations realized?

There are 'filters' for each of these operations. In fact, there are different kinds of filters with different design parameters and design goals. In this, we will make a review of only 'spatial filters' which means that filters are defined and implemented in the space domain. All the images and operations we have seen in this section so far have been only in the space domain where the operation is done directly on the pixel values of the image.

Note: There are frequency domain filters also, but we omit discussions of such filters.

11.1.4 Spatial Filters

A spatial filter is also given names such as mask or kernel. In our discussions here, the word kernel/mask is given to the matrix of numbers meant to realize a type of filter. They are matrices with numbers used according to the type of the 'filtering' operation we need. The operation by which filtering is done is named 'convolution', though it is not exactly identical to the 1D convolution operation done in the context of signal processing. The operation of convolution applied to an image involves multiplication, addition and shifting. The mask is applied to a small neighbourhood of the image and as the operation progresses, the neighbourhood changes because of the shifting operation. We say that the 'receptive field' of the convolution operation is small. The word 'sparse convolution' is used in the field of machine learning when using the operation in this way.

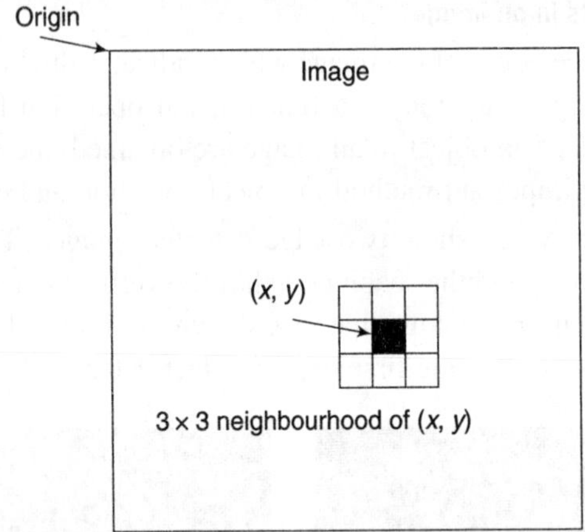

Fig. 11.10 A small neighbourhood in an image

Figure 11.10 shows a 3 × 3 neighbourhood of a pixel in an image. A neighbourhood is just the pixels surrounding the reference pixel. The smallest neighbourhood is 3 × 3. Figure 11.11 shows a 3 × 3 mask/filter. It is actually a 3 × 3 image with pixel values $w_1, w_2 .... w_9$. Filters may be 5 × 5 or 7 × 7 or of larger sizes. The quality of the filtered image is affected by the size of the filter. But we will not go deep into those aspects as our interest is only in understanding the process of filtering done on images.

W_1	W_2	W_3
W_4	W_5	W_6
W_7	W_8	W_9

(a) A 3 x 3 mask/filter

1/9 x

1	1	1
1	1	1
1	1	1

(b) An averaging filter

Fig. 11.11

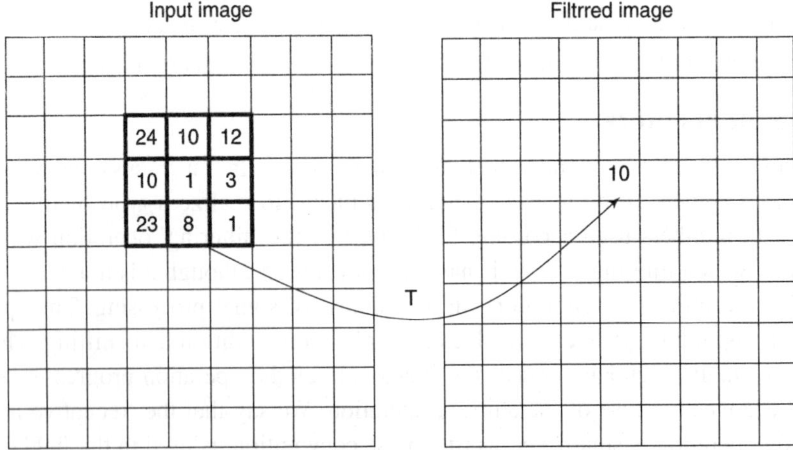

Fig. 11.12 The spatial filtering process (sparse convolution)

The operation of filtering is as follows. The mask (filter) is placed over the neighbourhood in the image and the corresponding pixels are multiplied and the product is summed. The centre pixel of the neighbourhood of the image is replaced with the value obtained by the operation. The filter is best understood with an averaging filter as shown in Fig. 11.11b. This is a local averaging operation in which the centre pixel is replaced by the average of the pixel values of the neighbourhood.

If the centre pixel of the neighbourhood is $f(m, n)$, the filtering operation using the filter in Figure (11.12) is as given in Eq. 11.1. $g(m, n)$ is the value with which the centre pixel in the image is replaced.

$$\begin{aligned} g(m, n) = \frac{1}{9} &((f(m-1, n-1)) + (f(m-1, n)) + (f(m-1, n+1)) \\ &+ (f(m, n-1)) + (f(m, n)) + (f(m, n+1)) + (f(m+1, n-1)) \\ &+ (f(m+1, n)) + (f(m+1, n+1))) \end{aligned} \quad \text{...(11.1)}$$

Let us do the calculation for getting the filtered result of one pixel of the image corresponding to Fig 11.12.

$$\begin{aligned} g(m, n) &= 1/9\ [24 \times 1 + 10 \times 1 + 12 \times 1 + 10 \times 1 + 1 \times 1 + 3 \times 1 + 23 \times 1 \\ &\quad + 8 \times 1 + 1 \times 1] \\ &= 1/9[92] = 10.2 \end{aligned}$$

After this operation, the centre pixel of the neighbourhood is replaced by the value 10 as shown in Fig. 11.12. The next step is to move the filter one step to the right and do the same operation. The process is repeated for all the pixels of the given image. Note that the replacement of pixel values is done only after all the 'new pixel values' are obtained.

In practice, this operation will start at the top left hand corner of the image, move to the right till the last pixel in that row. Then the filter is shifted one step down to the next row (from the left edge) and this will be continued until all the pixels in the image are replaced by the result of the filtering operation. Note that after one such 'convolution' operation, the filter in the example is moved 'one step/pixel' to the right or downward. This step size is called 'stride'. The stride can be made more than one. If stride = 2, the filter is shifted by two pixels horizontally/vertically.

11.1.4.1 Handling Pixels at the Sides of the Image

In this filter movement, there is a hitch when the centre of the filter is on the pixels at the borders of the image. When the centre pixel of the filter is at the horizontal and vertical edges of the source image, there are no image pixels (under some parts of the filter) with which to multiply the filter elements, because one/more rows and columns of the filter is outside the 'space' of the image. See Fig. 11.13.

This can be handled in two ways.

(i) Pad with zeros

Zeros may be added to the borders of the image as in Fig. 11.14. Then the border pixels do not lose their roles in the output image. When we add zeros to the borders of the image,

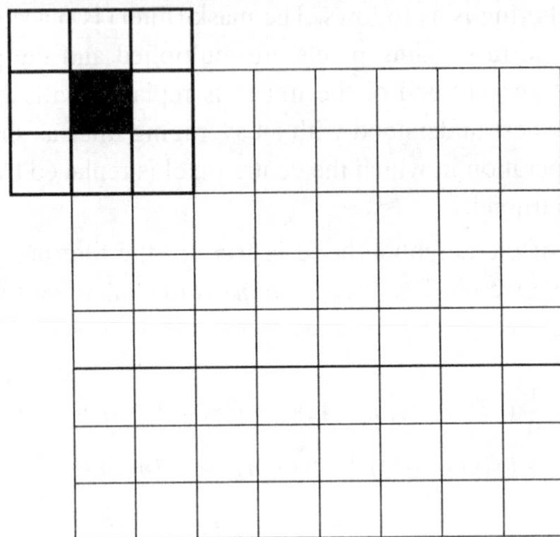

Fig. 11.13 Placing the mask at the side of the image

the size of the image increases to (W + 2P × H + 2P), where 2P is the number of rows or columns of zeros added to the image. Such 'zero padding' when used is also called 'same padding'. The word 'same' implies that the filtered output will have the same size as the input image. In Fig. 11.14 $P = 1$.

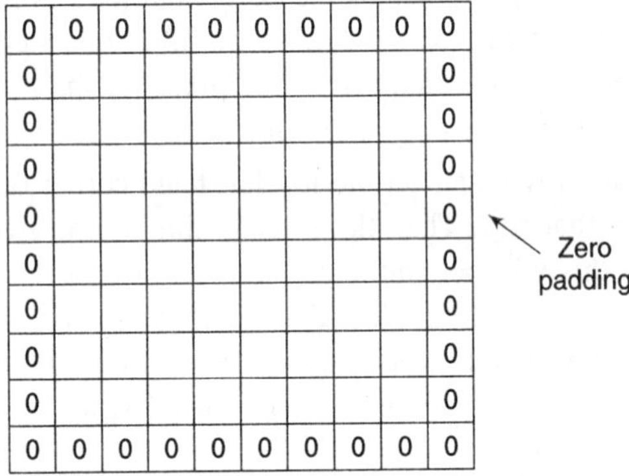

Fig 11.14 Zero adding of the image

(ii) No Padding

If the image is not padded with zeros, the filter centre will not be placed on the border pixels. So the output image has the size excluding the border pixels. So, if padding is not done, that is, if $P = 0$, the filtered image becomes smaller than the input image. This method is called 'valid' padding.

11.1.5 Dimensions of Image after Filtering

If the input image has a size $W \times H$, and the filter has size $F \times F$, the output image dimensions $W_o \times H_o$ is given by the formula:

$$W_o = W - F + 1,\ H_o = H - F + 1 \qquad \text{...(11.2)}$$

For same padding, when we want the output activation to be the same size as the input image,

$$P = \frac{(F-1)}{2} \qquad \text{...(11.3)}$$

So far, we considered stride = 1, which means, that the filter is moved only one pixel step when moving to the right or downwards. But strides greater than 1 may be used. The formula for calculating the output image size when stride is included is:

$$W_o = \left(\frac{W + 2P - F}{S}\right) + 1 \qquad H_o = \left(\frac{H + 2P - F}{S}\right) + 1 \qquad \text{...(11.4)}$$

Strides are chosen in such a way that the output image size is an integer, rather than fractions.

Formulas

Input image size: $W \times H$, Filter size: $F \times F$, Padding: P, Stride: S

Output image size: $W_o = \left(\frac{W + 2P - F}{S}\right) + 1 \quad H_o = \left(\frac{H + 2P - F}{S}\right) + 1$

With stride $S = 1$, $W_O = W - F + 1$, $H_O = H - F + 1$.

For same padding, $P = \frac{(F-1)}{2}$

Fig. 11.15 Formulas for filtering

Example 11.1 Calculate the output image size when convolution is done with valid padding and the following specifications:

Solution: Image size, $W \times H = 8 \times 6$

Filter size, $F = 3 \times 3$

Padding = 0 (valid padding)

Solution: Output image size: $(W - F + 1) \times (H - F + 1)$

$$= (8 - 3 + 1) \times (6 - 3 + 1)$$

$$= 6 \times 4$$

Example 11.2 Calculate the padding needed for an input image of size 32×32 for filters of size (i) 3×3 (ii) 5×5 (iii) What is the padding needed for an input of size 64×64 and filters of size 7×7?

Solution: $P = (F - 1)/2$.

Padding depends only on the size of the filter.

For $F = 3$, $P = 1$, For $F = 5$, $P = 2$, For $F = 7$, $P = 3$

Filters may be of different sizes: 3 × 3, 5 × 5 and 7 × 7 are commonly used sizes – but they can be bigger. If the filter size is 5 × 5, it is obvious that two rows and columns of zeros (on each edge) will be needed for padding. For any filtering, the size of the filter, padding and stride are to be specified. The size of the filters does have an effect on the quality of the filtered image. But more discussion on image processing principles is beyond the scope of this chapter.

Example 11.3 For an image of size 5 × 4, in Fig. 11.15a, find the filtered image using the weighted average filter of Fig. 11.15b, for the case: 'with zero padding'

100	110	200	220	20
90	50	120	250	40
200	190	210	50	30
110	100	100	202	120

$$\frac{1}{16} \times \begin{bmatrix} 1 & 2 & 1 \\ 2 & 4 & 2 \\ 1 & 2 & 1 \end{bmatrix}$$

Fig. 11.15 (a) Image to be filtered 11.5 (b) A 3 × 3 filter

Solution: With padding, the output image size is the same as the input figure. Figure 11.15c shows the result of filtering.

53	84	125	123	53
85	120	154	145	64
108	143	147	122	62
76	100	104	94	62

Fig. 11.15 (c) The result of filtering.

11.1.6 Edge Detection

In Section 11.1.3, we discussed that edge detection is an important action to detect objects in images. In fact, edge detection stages are the first layers in a CNN. Let's now take a look at one of the many standard edge detection filters. See Eqs. 11.5.a and b, which shows H_x and H_y, which are horizontal and vertical Prewitt edge detection filters.

$$H_x = \frac{1}{3}\begin{bmatrix} -1 & -1 & -1 \\ 0 & 0 & 0 \\ 1 & 1 & 1 \end{bmatrix} \quad ...(11.5a)$$

$$H_y = \frac{1}{3}\begin{bmatrix} -1 & 0 & 1 \\ -1 & 0 & 1 \\ -1 & 0 & 1 \end{bmatrix} \quad ...(11.5b)$$

Example 11.4

200	200	200	10	10
220	201	210	8	10
202	200	201	10	9
205	200	201	9	10
201	199	202	10	10

Fig. 11.16 (a) An image matrix

The matrix of Fig. 11.16a is an image with high intensity pixels on one side and low intensity pixels on the other. Filter it with the vertical edge detection filter (Eq. 11.5b). Use $P = 0$. Display the output image using the OpenCV library in Python.

Solution:

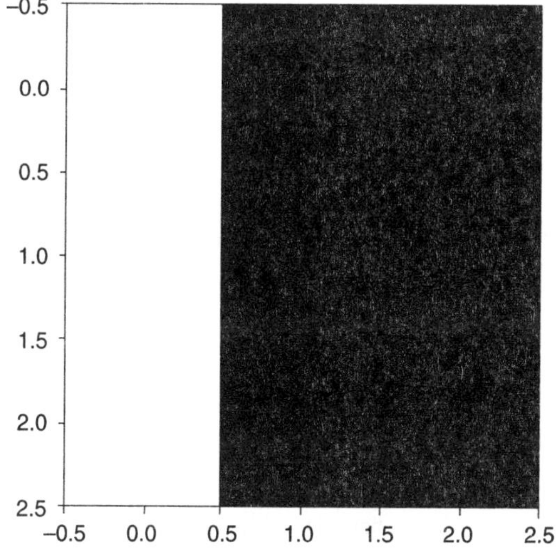

Fig. 11.16 (b) Vertical edge detected by filtering

Figure 11.16b shows the vertical edge identified by the vertical edge detection filter. The output, also called 'feature map', has the size of 3 × 3 which is a very small size image. That is why the black and white portions are seen to be broad. For a normal, bigger sized image, the edges will be seen as fine white lines on a black background as in Figs. 11.9 a and b.

11.1.7 Colour Images

All the processing that we discussed so far is based on black and white images. But most images that we use currently are colour images. So we should know how to deal with colour.

The colour standard used in computers is based on the additive mixing of colours. In this, three primary colours, red, green and blue, are defined and any other colour may be obtained by mixing these primary colours in the right proportions. Thus any colour picture frame has three colour components and three matrices corresponding to the red, blue and green components of the colour image. Colour images are therefore three dimensional. Figure 11.17 shows three matrices stacked together to form a 'volume'. There is a red channel, green channel and a blue channel. So we consider a colour image to be a 3D volume. For instance, If $W = 32$, and $H = 32$ for the three colour matrices, the colour image is specified to be of size 32 × 32 × 3. The depth of the image is 3, as there are three channels denoted by 'C'.

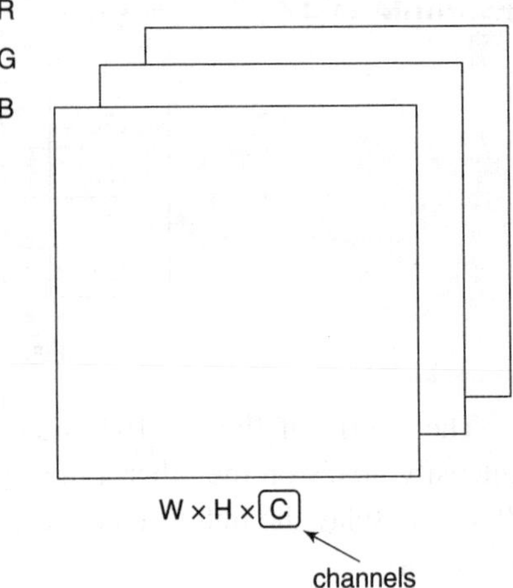

Fig. 11.17 Three channels of a colour image

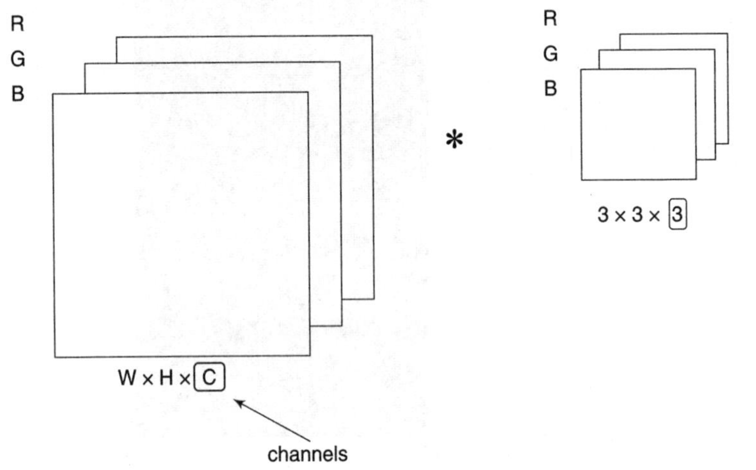

Fig. 11.18 A 3-channel image and a 3-channel filter

11.1.7.1 3D Convolution

How do we do 3D convolution?

For the type of 'sparse' filtering that we discussed in earlier sections, we need to do 3D convolution when colour images are involved. Suppose the application is edge detection. This means that we are interested in detecting edges in the red, green and blue channels. It should be obvious that the filter should be a set of three kernels/masks – one each for each channel. The kernel operations for each channel may be the same or different. For example, it may be that the red and blue channels may use kernels for detecting horizontal edges while the green channel can have a kernel for detecting vertical edges. Note that the filter is also three dimensional. A 3-dimensional filter with three different kernels is shown in Fig. 11.19.

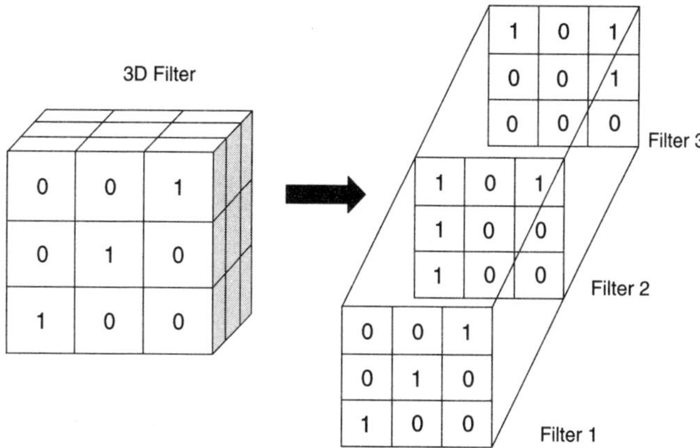

Fig. 11.19 A three-dimensional filter with three different kernels for each channel

Now let's do convolution of a 5 × 5 × 3 image with 3 × 3 × 3 filter. The steps are:

(i) Place the respective filter over a neighbourhood of each channel of the image.

(ii) Convolve the red channel image matrix with the red kernel – 9 multiplications

(iii) Convolve the green channel image matrix with the green kernel – 9 multiplications

(iv) Convolve the blue channel image matrix with the blue kernel– 9 multiplications

(v) Add all the products and get one number.

(vi) This is the value of the centre pixel of the corresponding neighbourhood of the output image.

(vii) The filters are then shifted to the next neighbourhood and the operation is repeated.

(viii) With padding = 1 and stride = 1, the output image will have a dimension of 5 × 5 × 1, that is, it will have only one channel.

Example 11.5 Find the output matrix for the R, G and B image matrices given in Fig 11.20 and the corresponding R, G and B filters shown in Fig. 11.21. Use (i) padding = 1 and stride = 1 (ii) padding = 0 and stride = 1.

R

100	100	110	1	2
100	110	120	1	1
100	120	100	1	1
80	90	100	2	1
90	80	100	1	1

G

10	20	5	10	20
10	1	12	11	10
10	12	10	10	11
15	12	10	20	10
9	8	10	1	1

B

200	220	210	110	2
230	110	120	100	10
210	120	100	1	1
250	60	10	2	1
70	10	100	10	1

Fig. 11.20 Three image matrices of a colour image

Red	Green	Blue
1 0 −1	1 0 −1	1 1 1
1 0 −1	1 0 −1	0 0 0
1 0 −1	1 0 −1	−1 −1 −1

Fig. 11.21 Three kernels of a 3D filter

Solution: The resulting matrices are shown in Fig. 11.22.

−571	−397	−122	227	2
−273	263	648	326	3
−315	103	558	317	4
−290	−30	286	297	4
−170	−30	167	198	3

263	648	532
103	558	535
224	388	296

Fig. 11.22 Output matrices after filtering (a) with padding and (b) without padding

Interpretation of the result of filtering:

(i) What is the size of the image in each case?

(ii) What do the negative numbers in the output matrix mean?

(iii) How are values greater than 255 handled? What do they mean in ML processes?

The answers to these questions are:

(i) With padding ($P = 1$), the output image size is 5 × 5 × 1. Without padding ($P = 0$), it is 3 × 3 × 1. In both cases, the output image is a single channel one.

(ii) For display (if necessary), the maximum value in the output matrix is mapped to 255, and the minimum (some of which may be negative) is mapped to 0. The other values are mapped proportionally. This can be done using OpenCV commands.

(iii) When the feature maps are obtained as part of the many stages of convolutional layers in an ML process, these values are acted upon by ReLU (Section 10.8.3) and the negative values are squashed to 0. Further on, before going to the next stage of filtering, batch normalization (Section 10.7.4) ensures that the values of pixels are normalized.

11.1.7.2 Filtering with more than One Filter

For a three-dimensional image, the filter used has to be of three dimensions. That is, since the image has 3 channels, the filter also should have three channels. We noted that with a single three-dimensional filter of size 3 × 3 × 3, an image of size 5 × 5 × 3 becomes an image of 5 × 5 × 1, that is, it becomes a single channel 'output activation'. There can be many filters applied on the same input image. If two filters are simultaneously applied, the output image will be of size 5 × 5 × 2. Thus, the number of channels of the output is 2, that is, C = 2. With 10 such filters, the volume of the output increases much more and its dimension is now 5 × 5 × 10. We say that the output image has 10 channels. (C = 10) Each of these ten filters can have different kernels, each meant for detecting some specific feature of the image.

11.2 CONVNET /CNN

Now that we have a grip of the image processing steps which are necessary for understanding a Convolutional Neural Network (CNN, also known as ConvNet), let us dive deep into its computing stages. Even though the CNN may initially seem complicated to understand, it is actually not so. If you have understood the filtering process and its parameters, then the operations of the CNN are quite simple to comprehend.

11.2.1 Architecture of CNN

The initial stages of a CNN perform detection of features such as edges and curves. Let us assume that our application is one that involves object detection for colour images. To detect objects in an image, we must be able to identify the edges of the objects – there will be vertical, horizontal and diagonal edges. These lines/edges are the desired features. We use appropriate filters for this and get the output matrix, also known as 'feature map/output activation' (in the CNN literature).

The output activation from the first stage of filtering is applied to more filter stages. What is the logic of this? The initial layers extract lines – vertical, horizontal, diagonal – using appropriate filters. These are features detected at a low level of abstraction. The feature maps obtained from this are subject to more filtering at the next stages. In these stages, a combination of the previously detected features is obtained. For example, at the final stage we can detect the complete paw of an animal or the face of a person, while in the first stage it is just the outline of these that are identified. In short, the features are detected hierarchically from the lowest level of abstraction to the highest.

An important point to note is that in any deep learning network, the parameters of the networks (most of them) are meant to be 'learnt', that is, their values are not hard coded, rather, they are decided by the iterative procedure involving backpropagation and gradient descent. The parameters of the convolutional filters of the CNN – that is, the weights corresponding to the filter kernels, are also to be 'learnt' through the process of 'training' using training data.

A typical CNN has the following components:

(i) Convolution layers
(ii) Fully connected layers
(iii) Output layer

We will analyze each layer separately and then put them all together.

11.2.2 Convolutional Layers

These are the stages which perform the convolutional operation on the input image. There can be many convolutional layers. A convolutional layer consists of (i) convolutional filtering, (ii) ReLU activation, and (iii) pooling. For the beginning we restrict ourselves to a discussion of the process of convolutional filtering alone. We know that this is the part which detects features from input images. We can have many filters because each filter can detect a particular kind of feature. To achieve this, different kernels are used.

11.2.2.1 One Convolutional Layer

We now perform an analysis of the steps associated with the convolutional layers. For the purpose of understanding, let us assume a very small colour image of size of 8 × 6, that is, W = 8, H = 6. So the input image size is 8 × 6 × 3. Let us use two feature detection filters, each of size 3 × 3 × 3, same padding (P = 1) and stride = 1. Note that each filter is to be three dimensional, just as the image is.

As Fig. 11.23 shows, convolution with each three-dimensional filter gives an output image of size 8 × 6 × 1. Since padding is applied, the input and output image sizes are the same. After this stage, biases b1 and b2 are added to each output matrix. This amounts to just adding the bias to each of the elements of the matrix. Then the ReLU activation is applied and then we get two output matrices of size 8 × 6 × 1,which can now be considered a volume of dimension 8 × 6 × 2. For this to be a complete convolution layer, a pooling layer is also necessary. Since pooling is yet to be introduced, we will conclude at this point saying that this is 'one convolution layer' (without the pooling).

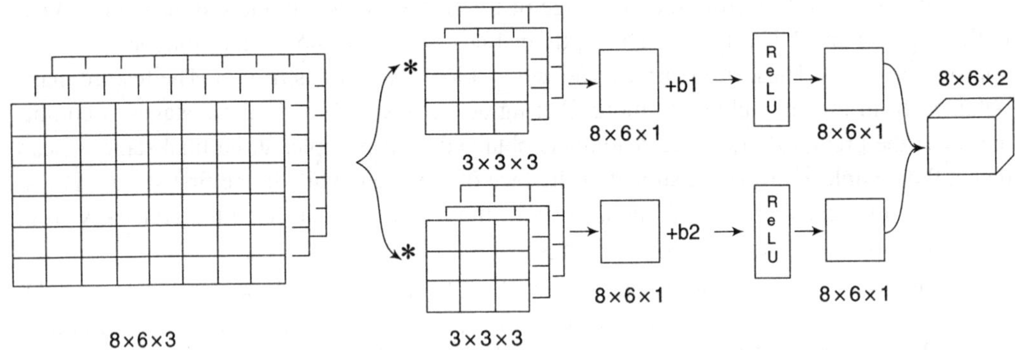

Fig. 11.23 Details of one convolutional filtering stage

How many 'learned/learnable' parameters are there for this stage?

We already know that the filters are not hard coded, Their 'values' are to be 'learnt'. In a neural network, the filter parameters are essentially the weights of the network. How many are they? There are two sets of 3 channel filters, each of which has 3 × 3 × 3 elements. This works out to be 27 × 2 = 54 parameters. Two biases *b*1 and *b*2 are also to be added. Thus, the total learnable parameters are 56 in number. Even if the input image is bigger in size, say 32 × 32 or 64 × 64 or 128 × 128, if the filter size is the same, the number of parameters to be learnt does not change.

Why is sparse convolution preferred?

Sparse convolution is the process of doing convolution with a 'filter of size much smaller than the input image'. Note that filter sizes of 3 × 3, 5 × 5, 7 × 7, etc., are much smaller than sizes of images used. In contrast, if feature detection is done by filters of the same size as an input image of size, say 8 × 6 × 3, the number of parameters is calculated as (8 × 6 × 3 × 2) + 2 = 290. Note that with sparse filtering, the number of parameters is only 56. For large size images the number of parameters would become prohibitively large. This is how 'sparse convolution' leads to a great saving in computations.

This calculation shows the great savings we get in using filtering on a small neighbourhood of an image and then shifting the kernel throughout the image. This operation is equivalent to 'sharing the weights' of the neural network.

11.2.2.2 CNN with more Layers

Now let us consider a CNN with more than one convolutional layer. Our interest is to understand how the dimensions of the image change with each stage of convolution. We will observe that with each stage, the width and height of the output of each stage diminishes while the volume increases. This happens because the filtering stages do not use padding (P = 0), but many channels (C) of filters are employed in each stage. This is typical of most CNNs. See Table 11.1 and Fig. 11.24 which help us get a grip on the size of the stages of convolutional filtering. Equation 11.4 has been used to calculate the size of the filtered output at each layer.

11.2.3 Pooling Layer

The pooling layer comes just after the ReLU activation for each convolutional layer. Pooling has the function of reducing the size of the representation at each stage which directly leads to a reduction in computations. It also makes the detected feature more prominent and robust

Table 11.1 Calculation of the size of output activations at convolutional layers

Layers of filtering	*Input image size*	*Filter size, F*	*No of filter channels, C*	*Stride*	*Output size (Feature maps after each stage of filtering)*
Layer 1	47 × 47 × 3	5 × 5	6	S = 1	43 × 43 × 6
Layer 2	43 × 43 × 6	3 × 3	20	S = 2	21 × 21 × 20
Layer 3	21 × 21 × 20	7 × 7	40	S = 1	15 × 15 × 40

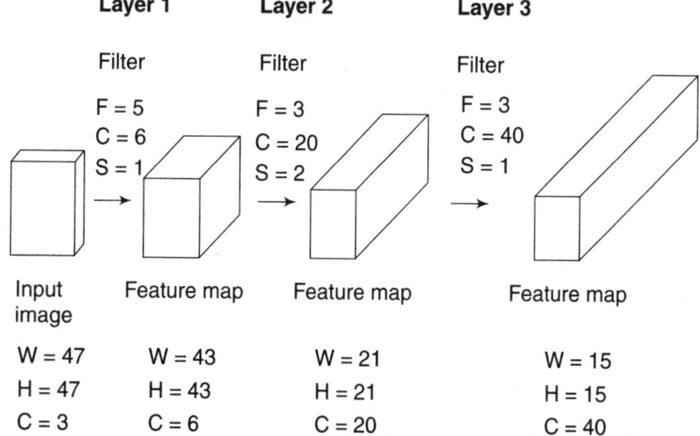

Fig. 11.24 Dimensional changes in feature maps after each stage of convolutional filters

and reduces overfitting. Two types of pooling are available (i) max pooling, and (ii) average pooling

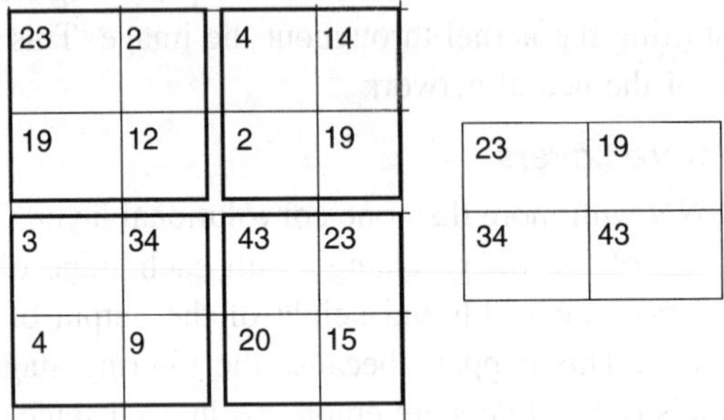

Fig 11.25 Max pooling—source matrix and pooled output matrix

11.2.3.1 Max Pooling

See Fig. 11.25 in which a 4 × 4 matrix is shown. This is part of the output activation at a convolutional layer. The logic behind max pooling is that when we need to choose the best number out of the four (in this case), choose the highest number. All the numbers represent some feature and the strongest and most prominent feature is chosen. Probably we would like to keep the remaining features as well, but since we also have the requirement of wanting less data, we choose the best value.

In Fig. 11.25, the dimensions of the pooling filter are taken as F = 2, S = 2. This means that we extract the maximum value from a 2 × 2 portion of the image. Stride S = 2 implies the step size to be equal to 2. For such a specification, pooling reduces the height and width by 2. For a 4 × 4 matrix, we get a pooled output of size 2 × 2. Note that the formulas in Fig. 11.15 are applicable to pooling as well. For instance, a 128 × 128 image, after pooling becomes a 64 × 64 image. The number of channels (C) remains the same.

11.2.3.2 Average Pooling

Instead of taking the maximum of the numbers in a pool, the average may also be used. This has proved to be less effective than max pooling and is rarely used nowadays.

Note: None of the parameters of pooling are to be 'learnt'. The stride and filter size of the pooling filters are hyperparameters.

11.2.3.3 Overlapped Pooling

There is a type of pooling in which there is overlap of the image data used in the steps of pooling. Then the value of stride will be less than the size of the pooling filter. Let us see an example of such a case.

Example 11.6 Given in Fig. 11.26a is an input matrix of shape 7 × 7. What will be the output on applying a max pooling of size 3 × 3 with a stride of 2?

Solution: Using Eq. 11.4, the output should be of size 3 × 3. For max pooling, each 3 × 3 portion of this matrix should be identified and the maximum value of that should be chosen. After that, the next neighbourhood should be chosen after a step of two pixels. In Fig. 11.26

b, steps with stride = 2 in the horizontal direction are shown. Step 3 would again be a stride of 2 in the horizontal direction. Step 4 is a downward movement of two pixels and is shown in Fig. 11.26c. From each of the chosen parts of the matrix, the maximum value is chosen and inserted in the output image of size 3 × 3. Figure 11.26 d is the final pooled output.

6	8	13	2	4	5	21
12	23	2	4	14	34	45
29	19	12	2	19	45	56
76	3	34	43	23	34	38
2	4	9	20	15	34	19
9	5	6	17	23	10	13
2	16	28	32	12	1	0

Fig. 11.26 (a) A 7 × 7 matrix to be pooled

Step 1

6	8	13	2	4	5	21
12	23	2	4	14	34	45
29	19	12	2	19	45	56
76	3	34	43	23	34	38
2	4	9	20	15	34	19
9	5	6	17	23	10	13
2	16	28	32	12	1	0

Step 2

6	8	13	2	4	5	21
12	23	2	4	14	34	45
29	19	12	2	19	45	56
76	3	34	43	23	34	38
2	4	9	20	15	34	19
9	5	6	17	23	10	13
2	16	28	32	12	1	0

Fig. 11.26 (b) Steps 1 and 2 of overlapped pooling

6	8	13	2	4	5	21
12	23	2	4	14	34	45
29	19	12	2	19	45	56
76	3	34	43	23	34	38
2	4	9	20	15	34	19
9	5	6	17	23	10	13
2	16	28	32	12	1	0

Fig. 11.26 (c) Step 4 of pooling

29	19	56
76	43	56
28	32	34

Fig. 11.26 (d) Final pooled output

11.2.4 Fully Connected Layers

Up to the pooling layer, the image's spatial information is retained. Note that the pixel positions haven't changed even though the dimensions of the image has changed. A feature in the top left corner of the image is still retained in the top left corner.. After many convolutional layers, it is assumed that all possible features of the input image have been detected. The next stage is a regular neural network, which in this case, is called a fully connected (FC) layer (in contrast to the convolutional layer, which is sparsely connected). The input to a fully connected layer should be a vector. So The output of the last pooling layer is 'flattened' into a vector and applied to the FC network. There can any number of FC layers. The activation function after each FC layer is ReLU.

11.2.5 Output Layer

Now let us look at the output of the CNN for classification tasks. If it is 'binary' classification that we need, the activation function at the output will be the Sigmoid function which performs logistic regression (Section 10.8.1). When it is multiclass classification, it is the Softmax function that is used. This function has been discussed in Section 10.8.5. Let us now see how it becomes useful in the output layer.

Assume that the application is image classification with 4 classes. Multiple images have to be classified as animal, bird, aeroplane and boat. Figure 11.27 shows the output stage for such an application. The last fully connected layer will have 4 neurons at its output side. These neurons will give a value which is named as the class score (Table 11.2). These scores are given to the Softmax layer which computes the Softmax values for each score. The Softmax values sum to 1 and are the probabilities corresponding to each class. In this example, the highest probability is for the image to be classified as 'animal'. After the Softmax layer, we can optionally add a one-hot layer which then gives an output of 1 for the class with the highest probability. All other outputs are zero.

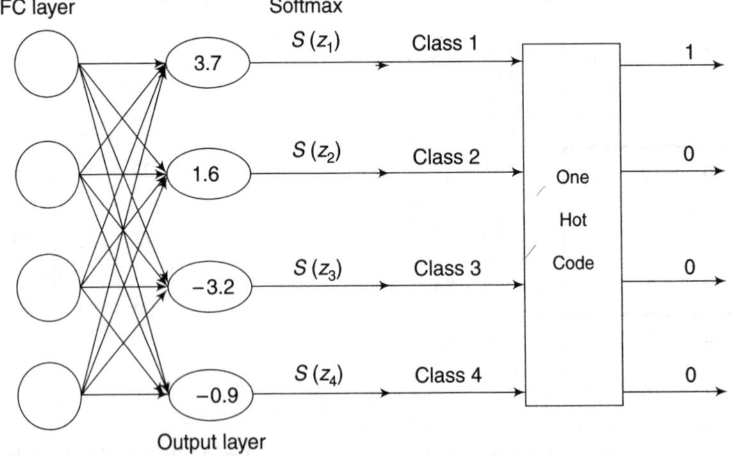

Fig. 11.27 The Softmax layer

Table 11.2 Class score converted to probability values using Softmax

	Class score at FC layer	$S(Z_i)$
Animal	3.7	0.889
Bird	1.6	0.108
Aeroplane	−3.2	0.889×10^{-3}
Boat	−0.9	8.867×10^{-3}

11.2.6 A Complete CNN

Now it is time to see a complete CNN with all the different layers arranged logically. Note that a CNN should have:

(i) Many convolution layers each of which is comprised of convolutional filters, ReLU activations and pooling
(ii) Many fully connected layers
(iii) An output layer

We have discussed in detail, the dimensional changes of the feature map as it goes through a number of stages of the convolution and pooling layers. A convolution layer is defined as consisting of a set of convolution filters, ReLU activation followed by a pooling layer. There will usually be many convolutional layers in a typical CNN. Figure 11.28 is a sample CNN with convolutional layers (only one is shown), FC layers, and an output Softmax layer.

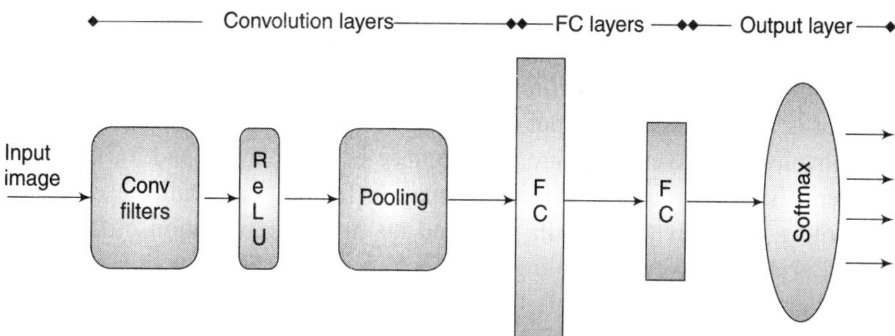

Fig. 11.28 A typical CNN showing convolution layers, fully connected layers and Softmax layer

When using a CNN for an application, we should be aware of what parameters we need. There are two types of parameters. One type is called 'learnable/learnt' parameters and the other set is called 'hyperparameters'. Let us list out both these for a CNN. As mentioned earlier, 'learnt' parameters are obtained by training the network. Hyperparameters are to be specified by the user.

11.2.7 Parameters and Hyperparameters of a CNN

Parameters:

(i) Elements of the convolutional filters (they are equivalent to the weights of a neural network).

(ii) Bias added to each element of the feature map
(iii) Weights and biases of the fully connected (FC) network

Hyper parameters:
(i) Size of filters
(ii) Number of channels for the filters
(iii) Stride and padding for the filtering operations (convolutional and pooling filters)
(iv) Learning rate for gradient descent

11.3 STANDARD CNNs

Many deep learning research teams are very active the world over. A lot of work has been done in the field of CNNs and over the period of time, many networks have proved their capabilities in the field of image classification, object detection and similar applications. So now let's take a look at some of these standard configurations of CNNs.

11.3.1 LeNet

We start with the architecture of 'LeNet', which was introduced in the research paper "Gradient-Based Learning Applied to Document Recognition" in the year 1998 by Yann LeCun, Leon Bottou, Yoshua Bengio, and Patrick Haffner. The latest version of this network named 'LeNet 5' is introduced here. The earlier versions had used Tanh and Sigmoid for activation but anyone who uses LeNet architecture now will use the ReLU function instead. Figures 11.29(a) and (b) show its architecture. Figure 11.29(a) shows LeNet as filters and feature maps. Figure 11.29(b) shows the outputs as volumes.

LeNet was first used for the recognition of handwritten digits, which are grey scale images. Thus the input is a single channel input of size 32 × 32. Five layers are shown in the figure – two are convolutional layers, two are fully connected (FC) layers and the last one is the Softmax layer. The dimensions of the output images (feature maps) after each convolution and each pooling are shown in the diagram and no further explanation of that is needed. Incidentally, LeNet used average pooling.

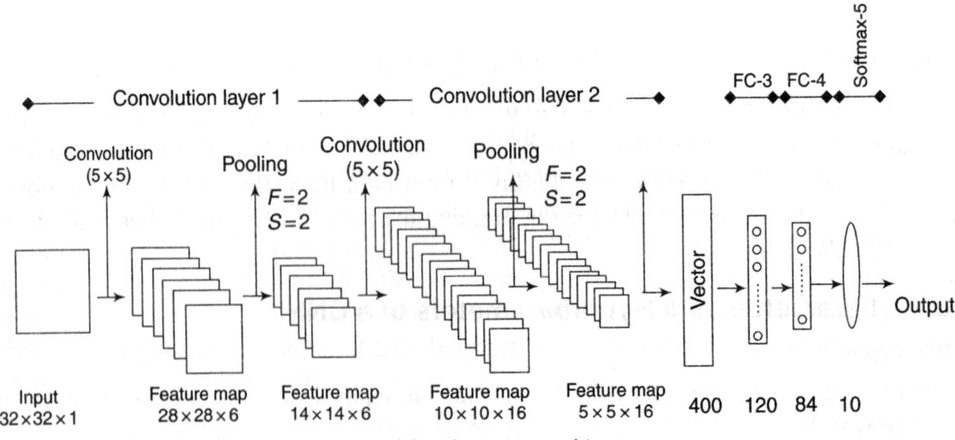

Fig. 11.29 (a) The LeNet architecture

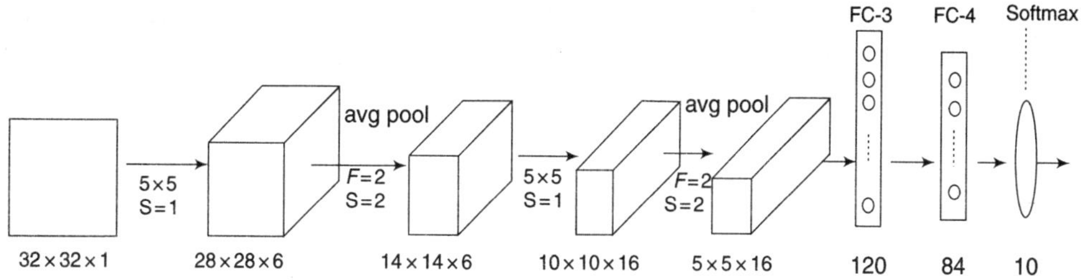

Fig. 11.29 (b) The LeNet feature maps shown as image volumes

Note that the output dimension after the last pooling layer is 5 × 5 × 16. This, when flattened, becomes a vector of size 400. This is connected to 120 neurons. For the FC layers, we say that 400 input numbers are fed into 120 neurons. So there is a full set of connections between 400 input neurons and 120 hidden neurons. Following this, there is another FC layer of size 84. After this, there is a Softmax layer with 10 outputs. which gives the highest probability to the correct digit. This is coded as a one hot output.

Salient features of LeNet

- It has five layers, two convolutional layers, two fully connected layers and one output layer.
- The parameters of these layers have to be learnt.
- The input is a grey scale image – shown as a single channel one.
- It uses average pooling.
- The output layer uses Softmax activation.
- The parameters which are obtained by training is around 60,000. The calculation is shown in Table 11.3.

For LeNet, how many parameters have to be learnt during the training phase? We see from Table 11.3 that the number of parameters to be learnt is in the order of 60K.

Table 11.3 Calculation of parameters of LeNet

	Size of filter/connections	*Number of parameters*
Conv1	5 × 5 × 6	(5 × 5 × 6) + 6 (bias) = 156
Conv2	5 × 5 × 16	(5 × 5 × 16) + 16 (bias) = 416
FC3	400 × 120	(400 × 120) + 1 (bias) = 48001
FC4	120 × 84	(120 × 84) + 1 (bias) = 10081
FC5 (Softmax)	84 × 10	(84 × 10) + 1 (bias) = 841
Total number of parameters	59,495	

11.3.2 AlexNet

This CNN was introduced in 2012 in the paper 'Image Net Classification with Deep Convolutional Neural Networks'. The authors are Alex Krizhevsky, Ilya Sutskever and Geoffery Hinton. They trained their network on the standard 'ImageNet' data. 'ImageNet' is a dataset of over 15 million labelled high-resolution images belonging to approximately 22,000 classes.

AlexNet was the winner of the competition titled 'ImageNet Large Scale Visual Recognition Challenge (ILSVRC 2012)', This CNN obtained an error rate of 15.3% for an image recognition application, while the second place went to a team whose work gave an error rate of 26.3%. In subsequent years, the winners of this competition were networks which followed the precedent set up by AlexNet. That is why AlexNet was a big step that started a revolution leading to deep networks for computer vision applications.

Now let us find out how and why this CNN brought about a great change in the field of deep learning for images. The previous important network was 'LeNet'. It was trained on handwritten images (monochrome) of the MNIST database. Till AlexNet came up, there was no standard CNN to handle other kinds of images. There was also the problem of not having a good data base for images. The extensive dataset named 'ImageNet' made a great difference to this. ImageNet is a large database of colour and monochrome images designed for applications such as image classification and object detection. AlexNet used this database to prove its efficacy.

What innovations were introduced in AlexNet?

(i) It was trained on the ImageNet dataset.

(ii) There were 5 convolutional layers and three fully connected layers.

(iii) It used two GPUs (Graphical Processing Units) which proved to be the reason that the training on a large dataset was possible.

(iv) It used ReLU as the activation function and so the network operation became fast. Recall that the earlier versions of LeNet used Tanh activation.

(v) It used optimization techniques such as Local Response Normalization (LRN), which is a variant of Batch Normalization (Section 10.7.4), Dropout (Section 10.7.1), SGD with momentum (Section 10.7.2) and Data Augmentation (Section 10.7.5).

(vi) It used overlapping pooling (Section 11.2.3.3) with claims that it is better in avoiding overfitting.

(vii) AlexNet had 60 million parameters, a major issue in terms of overfitting. But because of the many optimization techniques adopted, overfitting did not happen.

AlexNet architecture: Fig. 11.30 shows the architectural details which are also listed in Table 11.4. The input image is of size 224 × 224 which is the size used in ImageNet.

Table 11.4 Stages in AlexNet

Layers	*Specifications*
Convolutional Layer 1	F = 11 × 11, C = 96, ReLU activation, Max pooling 3 × 3
Convolutional Layer 2	F = 5 × 5, C = 256, ReLU activation, Max pooling 3 × 3
Convolutional Layer 3	F = 3 × 3, C = 384, ReLU activation, No pooling
Convolutional Layer 4	F = 3 × 3, C = 384, ReLU activation, No pooling
Convolutional Layer 5	F = 3 × 3, C = 256, ReLU activation, Max pooling 3 × 3
Fully Connected Layer (FC-6)	4096 nodes with ReLU activation
Fully Connected Layer (FC-7)	4096 nodes with ReLU activation
Fully Connected Layer (FC-8)	1000 nodes with Softmax activation

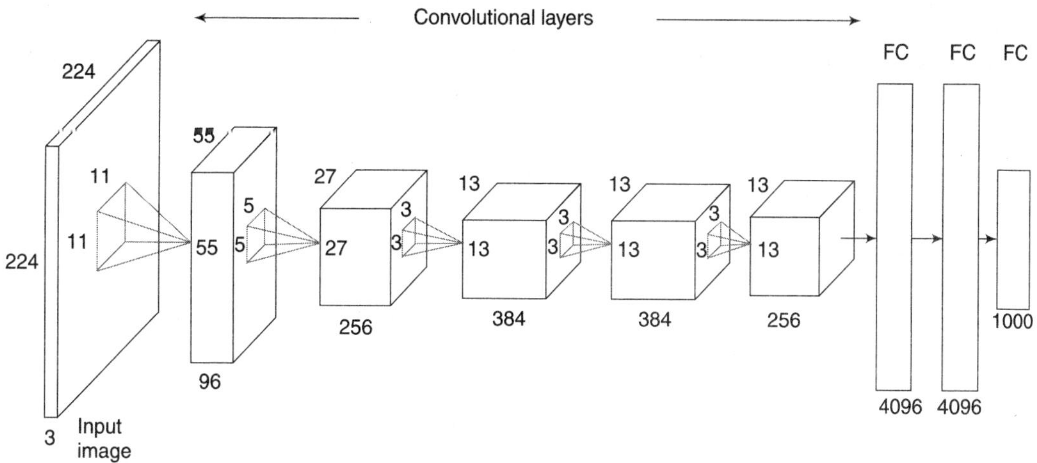

Fig. 11.30 The stages of AlexNet

11.3.3 Recent CNNs

Over the period of time, many more ConvNets came to be realized by various research groups. Some of them presented new concepts into the basic architecture. We now look into some of these new ideas.

11.3.3.1 1 × 1 Convolution

Before we try to understand some of the more recent CNNs, it is important to be clear about the concept of 1 × 1 convolution which also has names such as 'network in network' and 'microconv'. The concept of 1 × 1 convolution was proposed in the paper 'Network in Network', by Min Lin, Qiang Chen and Shuicheng Yan in the year 2014.

To understand this, it is necessary to recollect the steps of 3D convolution as listed in Section 11.1.7.1. In that, we used a 3 × 3 window. 1 × 1 convolution means convolving all the pixels in the source image with a single pixel filter. Figure 11.31 shows a single channel image being convolved by a single pixel of value 6. Obviously, this involves just doing a multiplication of all the pixels of the source image (of size 5 × 5), with the single pixel value of value 6. The operation only performs a weighting of the source image. We can say it does

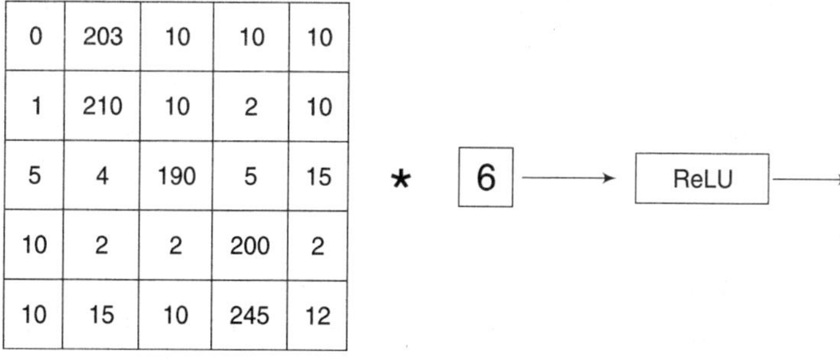

Fig. 11.31 1 × 1 Convolution

a linear projection of the image. Thus, a 1 × 1 convolution is called a projection layer. Like any convolution process, there is an activation done, usually by ReLU. The output image size remains as 5 × 5.

How does such an operation become useful?

It is used for dimensionality scaling of feature maps in a CNN. Actually, it changes the value of C, the number of channels of the output image (feature map). The values of W and H of the image remain the same. The volume of the feature maps can be scaled up and down.

To understand how we get such a result, let us recollect the process of convolution on a W × H × 3 image with a 3-channel filter (Section 11.1.7.1). From this, the output is W × H × 1 (assuming same padding). If we use 10 filters of the same dimensions, we get a feature map of volume W × H × 10. Now, instead of using a 3 × 3 × 3 filter, if we use a 1 × 1 × 3 filter, we still get a W × H × 1 output image. If we use 16 such filters, we get a W × H × 16 feature map.

Now we can look at it in another way. An image of dimension W × H × C may be convolved with N numbers of 1 × 1 filters. The dimension of the image now becomes W × H × N. Thus, we have a result in which only the depth of the image changes.

In newer CNNs like the VGG Net and GoogLeNet (Inception net) which are much more deep, such 1 × 1 convolution is used in many stages. It is left to the interested reader to find out more about the reasons for using it and how it reduces dimensionality of feature maps. Since we have done a thorough study of the basic concepts of CNN, only brief references to these networks are taken up here.

11.3.4 VGGNet

One of the winners for the ILSVRC competition in 2014. was the Visual Geometry Group (VGG) Department of Engineering Science, University of Oxford. They named their network as VGG Net. This network got the first prize for image localization and second prize for classification. The paper, 'Very Deep Convolutional Networks for Large Scale Image Recognition', by Karen Simonyan & Andrew Zisserman gives the details of their work. VGGNet follows the principles elucidated in AlexNet – however, the developers introduced new concepts to bring down the error rate. The convolutional filters used here are of size 3 × 3 only. They also used 1 × 1 convolution. VGGNet is very deep. (VGG-16 has 16 layers and VGG-19 has 19 layers), but all the convolutional filters have sizes 3 × 3. This reduces the receptive field and shows better capability at capturing the features of images. Even though the depth of the network increased, the number of learnable parameters did not increase as much, because the size of the filters is small. We will not go into greater details of this network. Note that it has many similarities with AlexNet while being simpler and better in performance.

11.3.5 GoogLeNet

GoogLeNet was the winner at ILSVRC 2014 getting the 1st place in both classification and detection tasks. In classification tasks, it recorded an error of 6.67%. This network, attributed to a team at Google, is also a deep network and uses the name Inception Net which is borrowed from the famous movie dialogue 'We need to go deeper' of the movie 'Inception'. The name GoogLeNet includes the name 'LeNet' which is the name of the first standard CNN. One very interesting idea adopted in this network is the use of a 1 × 1 convolution layer between two other layers. The result of this was a reduction in the number of learnable parameters. More details of this network are left to the interested student to search and find.

11.3.6 ResNet

The last of the standard networks we discuss is the ResNet where 'Res' stands for 'Residual'. This CNN was developed in 2015 by Kaiming He, Xiangyu Zhang, Shaoqing Ren and Jian Sun and published in their paper "Deep Residual Learning for Image Recognition". This paper introduced the concept of skip connections to reduce the effect of the degradation caused by the increase of depth.

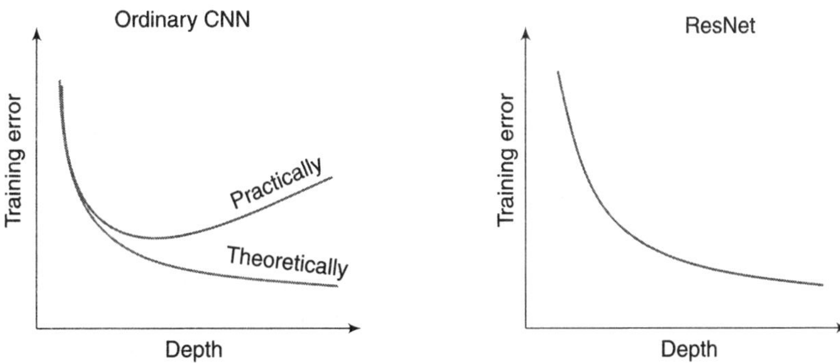

Fig. 11.32 (a) Theoretical and practical cases of Depth vs Error

Fig. 11.32 (b) The Depth vs Error graph for ResNet

Theoretically, as depth increases, the training error should keep reducing, but in practice, the error keeps going down up to a certain depth beyond which error is found to increase. This is considered to be a degradation (See Fig. 11.32a). The explanation for this is the issue of 'vanishing gradients'. To ensure that there is sufficient value for the gradient, such that the error vs depth follows the curve in Fig. 11.32b, some modifications are made. These modifications form the basis of ResNet.

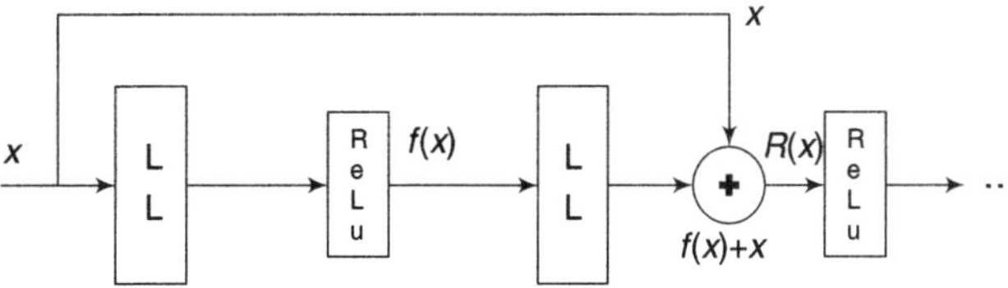

Fig. 11.33 The logic of a residual connection

See Fig. 11.33. We find a direct connection (called identity connection) which does not pass though the linear layer (LL) and its non-linear activation. This direct connection is called the 'residual connection'. The reason for the word 'residual' may be explained from the following equations:

In Fig. 11.33, if $$\boldsymbol{R}(x) = f(x) + x \quad ...(11.6)$$

then $$f(x) = \boldsymbol{R}(x) - x \quad ...(11.7)$$

Each layer is asked to train to perform fitting for $f(x)$ which is defined from equation 11.7 to be a 'residue' (what is left after subtraction). A number of such residual blocks are what ResNet consists of, as can be seen in Fig. 11.34. Such a set of many residual layers is able to give the advantages of a deep network while avoiding the degradation shown in Fig. 11.32a. There are many explanations given for this improved performance. One logic is that during 'backpropagation', there are two paths for the gradient to be propagated backwards. One path is a direct connection which is not affected by the multiplication of gradients and hence the degradation due to 'loss of gradients' is avoided.

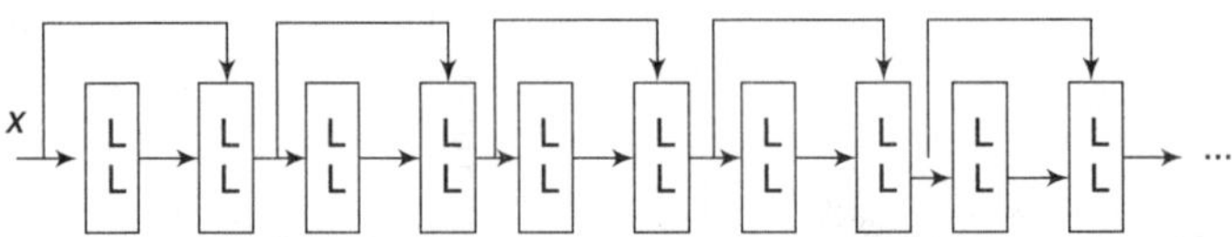

Fig. 11.34 A set of residual blocks for a typical ResNet

ResNet won the ILSVRC prize for image recognition in 2015. It used a 34 layer plain network to which skip connections are incorporated as in Fig. 11.34. The term 'skip connections' is because one block is skipped when a direct connection is made.

11.4 TRANSFER LEARNING

In this chapter, a number of ConvNets and their principles have been discussed. As more and more people are interested in the field of deep learning, an important question is whether each and every application entails the development of new models. Do developers have to start from scratch and use their data on their own customized model? The answer is: 'not necessarily'. The point is that currently many standard and proven networks are available which have been developed by the hard work of many teams over many years. These teams have proved the efficacy of their networks for many kinds of training data. Why not use the same network for our work with our own dataset?

This idea is named 'Transfer learning' which is employed in many fields of deep learning but is an accepted norm in areas such as Computer vision and Natural Language Processing where well proven and efficient networks are available and can be used by new developers for their specific data. Such proven networks have already been trained using very large datasets. So 'reuse' of such models for smaller datasets is likely to give good results.

Many research institutions have released their proven networks to be used by new developers. The user should select the best out of the many such models available. Transfer learning is a method wherein a network model which was developed and tested for one application is used as the starting point to develop a model for a new application. Some points are to be kept in mind when such pre-trained models are used. Let's conceive the use of some standard CNN as the source and another application which has a smaller dataset as the destination of 'transfer learning'.

The basic idea on which transfer learning is based is this: We take a model which was trained on a large dataset and transfer its knowledge to a dataset which is smaller. Conceive the idea of an application of object detection using VGGNet or AlexNet which are networks for classifications and have been trained on ImageNet data. For any application involving images, what the initial layers do is the detection of low level features such as edges, lines and curves.

When using transfer learning, the weights of the first layers of the source network may be freezed. This forms the pre-trained network. The last layers may then be customized for the user's new application and be trained on the data of the new application. For example, for object detection, the final layers need to do classification and regression. So this part alone has to be customized for this. But the initial layers may be 'borrowed' from a standard pre-trained network.

The steps are:

(i) Get a pre-trained network which has already been trained on a large dataset.
(ii) Its weights are 'freezed' – that means they should not be 'learnable' further.
(iii) Append this network with the custom network for the application at hand.
(iv) Train the custom network with the data of the required application.
(v) After this, as an optional step, unfreezing all or part of the weights of the complete network may be done and this complete network may be trained with a small learning rate. This step is called 'fine tuning'.

Figure 11.35 elucidates the concept of transfer learning.

11.4.1 Applications of CNN

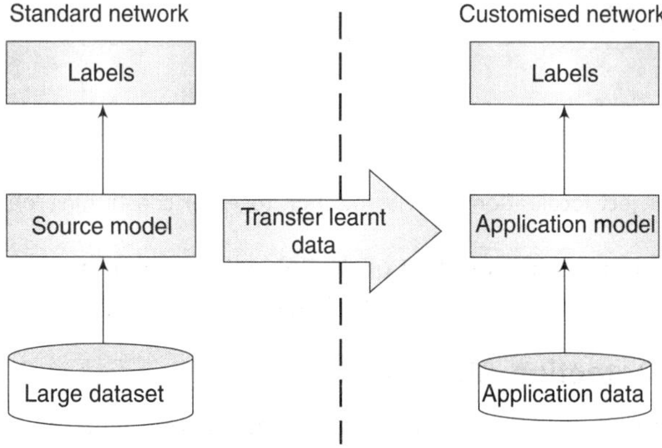

Fig 11.35 The concept of transfer learning

CNNs are widely used in many applications some of which are listed below:

(i) Optical character recognition
(ii) Image recognition and classification
(iii) Image analysis in the field of healthcare
(iv) Object detection in self-driving vehicles
(v) Image captioning

Now let us go into some detail of a very important application which is object detection.

11.5 OBJECT DETECTION

One of the important applications of CNNs are object detection and classification. There are many uses for it, but one is to find the objects surrounding an autonomous car (Section 1.4) while it is moving. Object detection must be possible for still images as well as videos. In this section, we discuss the principles behind this application and see how it is implemented.

11.5.1 Methodology

In an image frame, there may be one or many objects. It also may be that there are no objects in the image. We say it has only the background. Thus, the first step is to 'detect' the presence or absence of objects. If objects are detected, the location of each object is to be found out. This part is called 'object localization' and this indicates that the 'position' of the object in the image is to be obtained. Then the class of the object should be identified. This is 'object classification'. These two together constitute the task of object detection as shown in Fig. 11.36 which shows classification alone, localization alone and then 'Object detection' which is a combination of the two. When the class of the object in the bounding box is indicated (as cat), then object detection is said to have bene performed.

Fig. 11.36 Object localization and classification together constituting 'object detection'

Let us try to build up the perspective of the 'object detection' problem so that we can be clear about the way the solution has been formulated.

11.5.2 Object Detection Algorithms

The most important part of the problem is that of localization wherein the coordinates of the bounding box for the object have to be obtained. Over the years, many algorithms have been used. Let's make a brief reference to some of them.

11.5.2.1 Sliding Windows Technique

One of the first methods of getting bounding boxes for objects is by generating sliding windows. Using various image processing concepts, boxes are created throughout the image, these bounding boxes or windows are made to slide across the image and it is checked whether one of the prospective objects is found within these windows. The sliding of these windows (with progressively bigger sizes) is computationally heavy and this is no longer a preferred method.

11.5.2.2 Region Proposals (R-CNN)

This is a better method than the sliding windows approach. In this, regions are created and named as 'Region Proposals'. Similar pixels form a region. Using the technique of image segmentation, patches of areas in the image are identified and they grow into regions and then become bounding boxes in which objects are found and then the class of the object is identified. See Fig. 11.37 in which we see a lot of separate regions. Then bounding boxes can be fitted over these regions and the object encapsulated in the boxes may be identified.

Fig. 11.37 Regions defined for an image

All region proposals that we obtain by this method may not be useful because they may be noisy and may not encapsulate the object correctly. But there may be some which are appropriate to be looked upon as a good fit for some objects. We identify these by using probability scores.

These region based methods have been improved and there are versions named as R-CNN, Fast R-CNN and Faster R-CNN. This algorithm runs in two steps. The first step is the generation of 'Region proposals' and this uses the 'Selective Search' algorithm. In the next step, the classification of the object within each region is done. This algorithm performs well, but its speed is not sufficient for real-time object detection.

11.5.3 Yolo

In 2016, the paper "You Only Look Once: Unified, Real-Time Object Detection" by Joseph Redmon, Santosh Divvala, Ross Girshick and Ali Farhadi made a big change in this field. Object detection by YOLO proved to be fast enough for real-time applications because of its speed. The speed was achieved because the Yolo algorithm does not operate in two stages as R-CNN does. It does the object localization and classification in one single step. We have seen that once an object is detected to be present, we need to find its class and location, which entails the need for doing classification and regression. In YOLO, both these tasks are done together – that is why the name given to this method is YOLO which stands for 'You look only once'. Previous object detection algorithms (like R-CNN) did classification and localization in separate steps which entailed 'looking' at the image more than once. Very soon, YOLO became the de facto standard for fast object detection. Its negative aspect is that detection of small objects is not as good as in the versions of R-CNN.

We now take a deep dive into the methodology of YOLO. One of the well performing standard CNNs is generally used as a pre-trained network. To find the class of the object, the CNN has a 'classification' output. But when numbers such as height and width of the bounding boxes are also to be outputted by the CNN, it is obvious that a regression output is also needed. That means that the output layer of the CNN used for this cannot be just a classifier, it should have regression outputs as well. That is why YOLO is frequently referred to as a regression network.

11.5.3.1 Training

The first step is that of training. In this phase, we need a large set of images in which objects have been detected, localized and labelled. During training, for each image the objects in it are enclosed in bounding boxes and the class of each image is labelled. Labelling has to be done manually with the help of software tools. See Fig. 11.38 (a) and (b) in which objects are shown enclosed in bounding boxes. When the image is part of the training set, such bounding boxes are called the 'ground truth' bounding box, because it is the 'right' bounding box for the object which has been labelled correctly.

Fig. 11.38 (a) Object detection with two non-overlapped bounding boxes

Fig. 11.38 (b) Object detection showing three overlapped bounding boxes

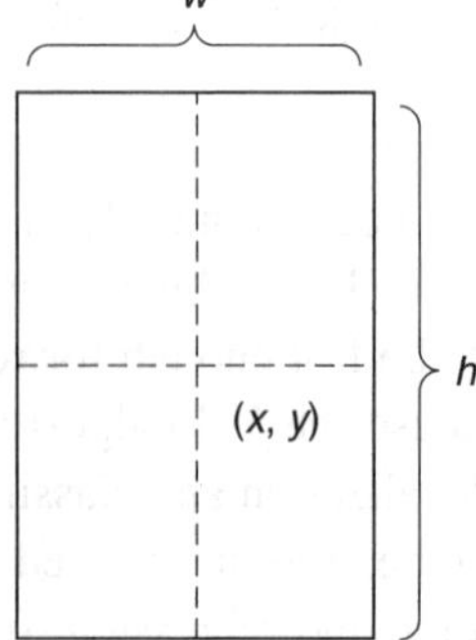

Fig. 11.39 Definition of a bounding box

Now see Fig. 11.39 in which a bounding box is defined. The coordinates (x, y) of its centre, its width b and height h are coded as a vector (Fig. 11.40a). For any image, the relevance of bounding boxes comes only when there is an object in it. For any image, we denote the probability of finding objects as P_c. P_c is appended to the vector of Fig. 11.40a, to get Fig. 11.40b. If $P_c = 1$, it means objects are present and only then there is the necessity of defining bounding boxes for each object. Some images have no objects as in Fig. 11.41a and we say they contain only the background. Then $P_c = 0$, as no objects are present. The vector when no objects are present uses don't care for a box definition. The vector is then written as $[0\ X\ X\ X\ X]^T$. For Fig. 11.41b, the corresponding vector is $[1\ x\ y\ w\ h]^T$.

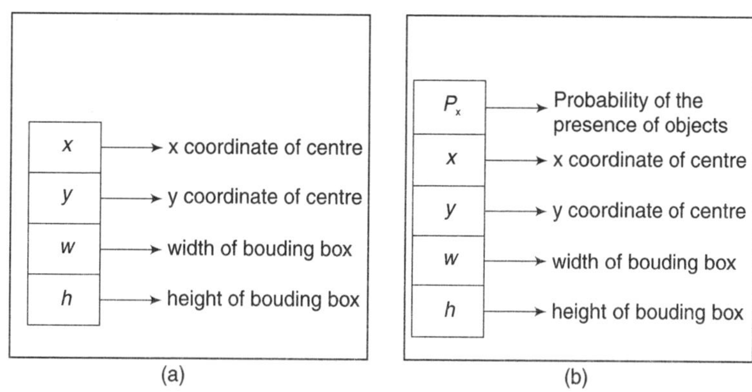

Fig. 11.40 (a) Vector for a bounding box (b) Vector with PC included

Fig. 11.41 (a) An image with no objects (b) An image with one object

The dimensions of a bounding box are calibrated in terms of the image in which it is located. In Fig. 11.42, note that the image coordinates are normalized and defined as (0, 0) for the top left hand corner of the image. The lowest point on the right corner of the image has the coordinates (1, 1). The dimensions and the location of each bounding box must be defined with respect to these coordinates. We write the vector as $[P_C, x, y, w, h]^T$. The bounding box shown in Fig. 11.42 has the approximate values $[1, 0.8, 0.3, 0.25, 0.45]^T$. Note that (x, y) is the co-ordinate of the centre of the bounding box.

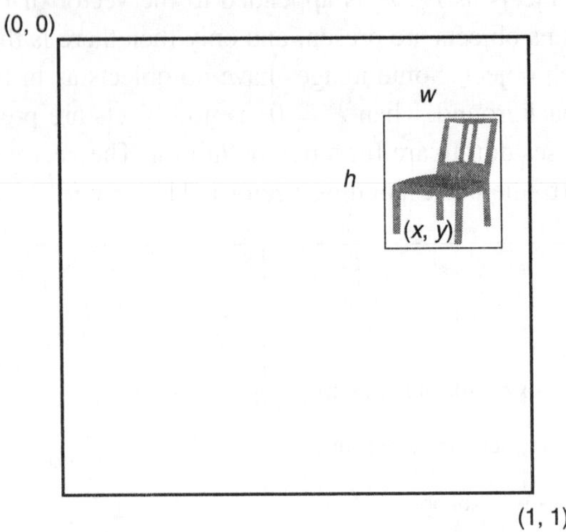

Fig. 11.42 Calibration of a bounding box

There can be many objects in an image and for each of them, bounding boxes have to be defined (See Fig. 11.43). In this, there are four objects and they are enclosed in respective bounding boxes. Along with the bounding box, the class of each label should also be included in the vector associated with each box. The class label is a one hot vector with size equal to the number of classes in the training set. If there are six classes, $[C_1, C_2, C_3, C_4, C_5, C_6]^T$ will be the vector for the class. As an example, let's say the classes, $C_1, C_2, C_3, C_4, C_5, C_6$ are: person, animal, car, ship, bird, building. Then the training vector for the bounding box of an image which has one object of class 3, is $[1\ x\ y\ w\ h\ 0\ 0\ 1\ 0\ 0\ 0]^T$.

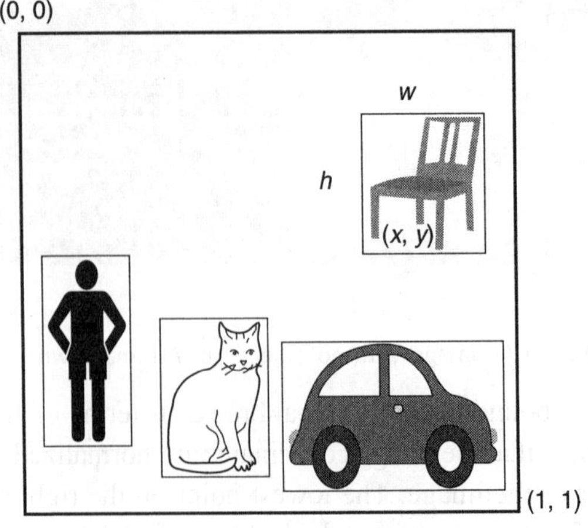

Fig. 11.43 An image with four bounding boxes

Thus in general, the tensor for the objects in an image has B * (5 + C) elements where B is the number of bounding boxes in the image (same as the number of objects in the image), the number '5' corresponds to the vector of Fig. 11.40b plus the number of classes (C) in the training set. For the image of Fig. 11.43, B = 4, C = 6, so the size is: 4 × (5 + 6) = 44.

During training, the loss function will be calculated differently for each part of the output vector. P_c has two possibilities, so logistic regression is used. The next four elements are real numbers, so the loss function is 'Mean Squared Error (MSE), as is used for linear regression. For classification, the multi-class log loss function is used. The output stage of the CNN should be modified to get all this as the Yolo output.

11.5.3.2 YOLO Output

Now let's see how YOLO does prediction of the position and class of the objects in an image. We already know that in the training phase, for every image in the training set, objects are labelled and localized by bounding boxes which are called 'ground truth' bounding boxes.

In YOLO, the image is divided into cells as shown in Fig. 11.44. If the centre of an object falls in a cell, that cell is responsible for that object. (The centre of an object indicates the centre of the bounding box corresponding to that object.) In Fig. 11.44, since the centre of the object is in the tenth cell, it is that cell whose bounding box will identify that object. In practice, it is possible that more than one object's centre is in the same grid cell. So that cell needs to output more than one prediction – it needs to specify more than one box for the objects in it. The name 'anchor box' is used during the test phase of YOLO.

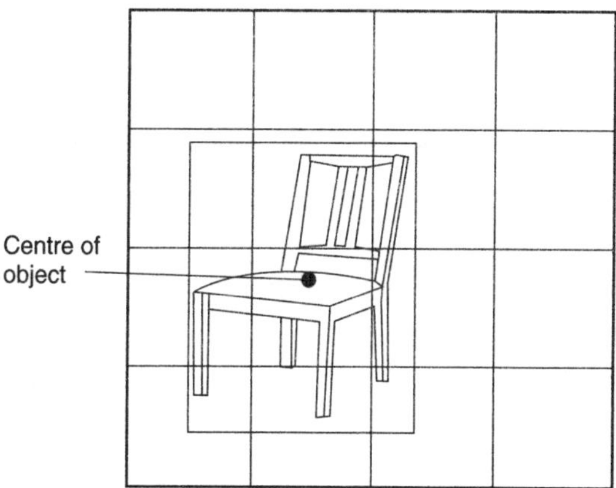

Fig. 11.44 YOLO grid cells – centre of an object seen in the 10th cell

What is an anchor box?

In the testing phase, when objects have to be detected, a number of boxes are generated in each cell. They are given the names 'anchor boxes' and they are fed into the network before prediction, as a list of numbers corresponding to their width and height. Anchor boxes are obtained by a *k*-means clustering method and there are some stipulations about the size and aspect ratio of expected objects. This is based on the ground truth bounding boxes defined according to objects in the training set. Look back at Fig. 11.38(b) which shows a person and a horse. For a person, it has to be a vertical box, while for the horse, it seems to need a square box. In Fig. 11.38(a) where a bus and a person are to be detected, the size and aspect ratios of the two boxes are entirely different.

Anchor boxes can be thought of as 'predictions' of bounding boxes. For any object, ground truth bounding boxes are already available. At the time of testing, if an anchor box and its ground truth bound box for an object overlap fully and the predicted label matches fully with the ground truth label, then we get the full information of the object's location and label as being that of the ground truth box itself. But in practice, anchor boxes may not overlap fully with any ground truth box. So we need to define a minimum level of overlap, based on which we can accept the predicted anchor box as being equivalent to a ground truth box. This overlap is defined by a term called 'IOU' between the two boxes.

11.5.3.3 Intersection Over Union (IOU)

This is used as an evaluation metric in object detection. It relates to the bounding boxes drawn over an object. The right box based on the actual label (ground truth) and the one predicted by the model may not be the same. We need to evaluate how good our model is, in comparison to the ground truth. For that we compare the 'right' bounding box with the predicted one. If the model is perfect, both of them overlap fully and IOU (Intersection Over Union) = 1. Otherwise, IOU is less than one. See Fig. 11.45 which shows the right one and the predicted boxes. They don't overlap completely. To ascertain the mismatch between them, IOU is defined as

$$IOU = \frac{\text{Area of intersection (overlap)}}{\text{Area of union}} \qquad ...(11.8)$$

Fig. 11.45 Image with a actual and predicted bounding boxes

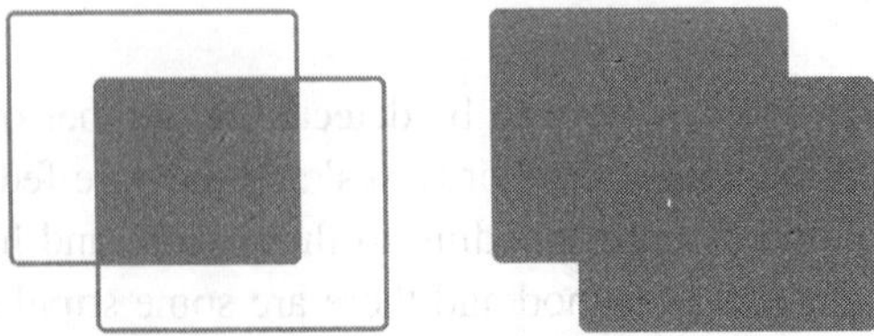

Fig. 11.46 (a) Overlap (intersection) (b) Union

See Fig. 11.46 to relate to the terms ' intersection' and 'union', in this context. When doing the evaluation, an IOU of 0.5 or greater is considered acceptable. Many programmers take this threshold to be even 0.7.

11.5.3.4 Confidence Score

Now for each predicted box, there is a 'Confidence' which indicates how sure the system is 'that the anchor box contains an object'.

Box Confidence $$C = P_C * IOU \qquad ...(11.9)$$

Since $P_C = 1$ if there is an object, this confidence score is simply equal to the IOU.

Besides the box confidence score, 'class confidence' is also needed. For any classification, the classifier will give a conditional probability which is: *P(Class/Object)*, which means that 'given that there is an object, what is the probability that this object is of a specified class'. This conditional probability indicates how confident the classifier is about its class prediction. If the classifier predicts that the object is a car with 70% confidence, it means: : *P(Car/Object)* = 0.70.

Based on both these levels of confidence, we can define the confidence of the system to localize and classify an object as:

$$\text{Confidence score} = \text{Box confidence} \times \text{Conditional class probabilty} \qquad ...(11.10)$$

11.5.3.5 Non-Maximal Suppression (NMS)

But for each object, many anchor boxes will be present as in Fig. 11.47(a). Which one to select? Of course, the one with the highest IOU. That means that the others have to be removed. The steps in removing the unwanted ones is called Non-Maximal Suppression.

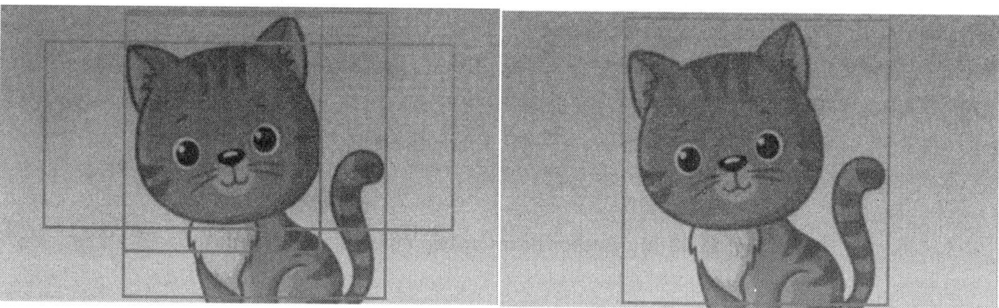

Fig. 11.47 (a) Many anchor boxes for an object

Fig. 11.47 (b) One anchor box remaining after non-maximal suppression

To do that, these steps are to be followed:

(i) Each of these boxes has a confidence score. Let's use a threshold of say, 0.5. Remove the boxes with lower scores because they will not be the ones competing with our predicted box. (They may even be the bounding boxes corresponding to other objects.)

(ii) Out of the remaining, choose the one with the highest confidence score. This is named as the current 'predicted' one.

(iii) Find the IOU of the remaining boxes with this predicted one.

(iv) If the overlap between this and any remaining box is greater than a threshold, remove that box. *This indicates that we don't need that box, because we already have a box which is as good.*

(v) Repeat this whole process until only one box is left.

(vi) This will give the predicted box for one object.

(vii) There will be other boxes in the image for other objects. Do the same procedure for those boxes.

11.5.3.6 YOLO Output Vector

Anchor boxes hold the idea that objects of different shapes need anchor boxes of different aspect ratios. If two objects have their centres in the same cell of YOLO and have different orientations, then the anchor boxes for each may be as shown in Fig. 11.48(a). Also, if two objects are to be detected in the same cell, the ouput vector of YOLO becomes double its normal size. This is because the vector corresponding to the two anchor boxes (Fig. 11.48b) is simply concatenated.

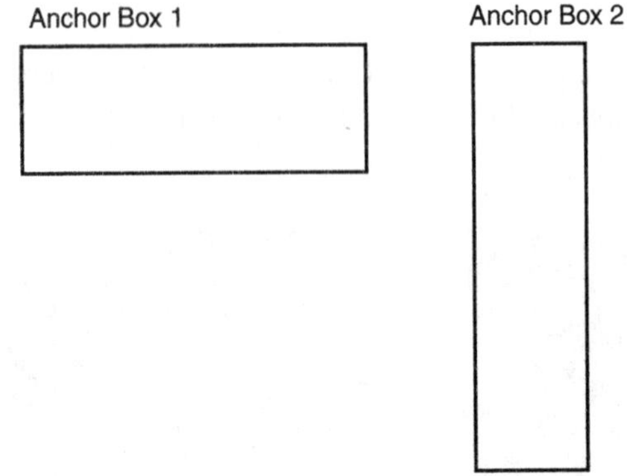

Fig. 11.48 (a) Anchor boxes of two different aspect ratios

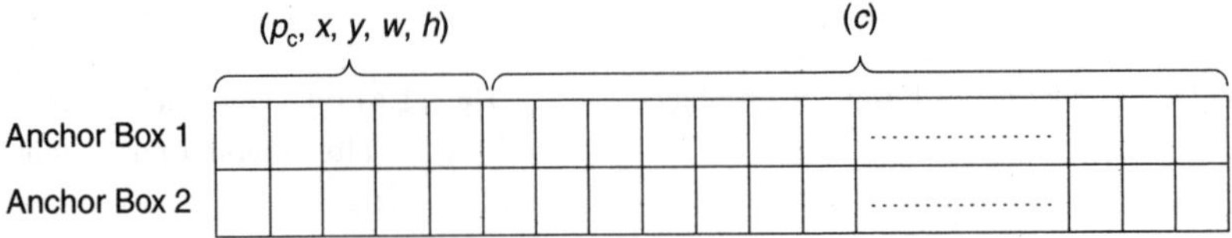

Fig. 11.48 (b) Coding for two anchor boxes

11.5.3.7 YOLO : History and Current State

It was in 2015 that Joseph Redmon et al., published the paper titled 'You Look Only Once: Unified, Real Time Object Detection". The speed at which this model worked overtook the R-CNN models available then and proved itself to be capable of 'real time' object detection. In subsequent years, newer versions of YOLO were released. Yolo v3 is the last version released by Joseph Redmon. His 'Darknet' is the framework on which it works. It is an open source framework which is written in C and CUDA and can be run on GPU for getting high speed. The original Darknet had 53 layers with filter sizes 3 × 3 and 1 × 1 and has a ResNet (Section 11.3.6) like architecture.

YOLOv4 and YOLOv5 are later versions but they are not from Joseph Redmon. Anyhow, many new augmentations have come up for object detection and standard codes are available for this. The recommended dataset for object detection is the COCO (Microsoft Common Objects in Context) dataset which has 382K images in 80 object categories.

Conclusion

We now come to the end of our discussion on ConvNets. Only one application has been discussed, but many other applications can be easily done once you get familiar with the general CNN framework.

Questions

1. What is the effect of high-pass and low-pass filtering on images?
2. Why does high-pass filtering on a monochrome image produce an image with a black background?
3. Explain what happens to the size of an image when it is filtered with (i) zero padding, and (ii) no padding?
4. What is the depth of the image obtained when a 3D image is filtered with a 3D filter?
5. Does pooling involve 'learning'? Why or why not?
6. What input was used in (i) LeNet (ii) AlexNet?
7. Does 1 × 1 convolution change the image dimensions? Explain.
8. What is the effect of the skip connection of ResNet?
9. What are anchor boxes? How many anchor boxes are possible in each grid cell of Yolo?
10. Why is YOLO called a 'regression network'?

Exercise

1. (a) Convert into probabilities using the Softmax function. Fill in the last column of (Table 11.5).

Table 11.5

	Class score	*Probability*
X_1	−2.2	
X_2	1.6	
X_3	2.1	
X_4	−0.9	

2. Calculate the output image size when convolution is done with valid padding and the following specifications:
   Image size: 43 × 43, F = 3 × 3, Stride = 2
3. Calculate the 'learnable 'parameters for this network. Fill in the third column and also find the total number of parameters in the last row (Table 11.6).

Table 11.6

	Size of filter/connections	*Number of parameters*
Conv1	3 × 3 × 4	
Conv2	5 × 5 × 10	
Conv3	3 × 3 × 20	
FC4–output neurons	400	
FC5-output neurons	100	
FC6 (Softmax)	30	
Total number of parameters		

4. Find the resultant matrix after applying max pooling with F = 3 and Stride = 2, of Fig. 11.49.

85	13	2	5	21
23	22	97	34	45
190	112	2	45	24
3	34	87	34	38
42	9	20	34	109

Fig. 11.49

5. Make a customized (your own design of number of layers and filters, etc). CNN using Keras/TensorFlow. Find a way to indicate how good it is, by using a simple application.
6. Use any standard CNN for an application.

7. Perform object detection using
   (a) YOLO
   (b) Use your own images
   (c) Answer the following questions:
      (i) How is YOLO used as transfer learning?
      (ii) Which is the pretrained network used?
      (iii) How is it trained?
      (iv) Are you using GPU?
      (v) Write the code with explanation.
      (vi) Show output with just one object.
      (vii) Show output with two objects.
      (viii) Show multiple objects.

CHAPTER

12

Sequence Modeling: RNN, LSTM, GRU

In this chapter you will

- learn the basic RNN cell, its theory and applications,
- identify the problems of RNN, and
- understand LSTM, GRU and their gates.

12.0 INTRODUCTION

The basic concepts of deep learning have been covered in detail in chapter 10. In chapter 11, we discussed the use of these concepts for the cases when the input is a grid in space. Such a network is found to have applications in the field of image and video processing.

In this chapter, we come to a slightly different scenario. The first point is that we deal with data which may be of variable length. The aspect of 'time' and events occurring in a sequence of time steps is the second point. In that case, the CNN of Chapter 11 is not the network of choice.

12.1 SEQUENCE MODELING

In the case of Natural Language Processing (NLP), the above two points hold good. Many sentences are applied to the network and each of these sentences will be of different lengths. In a sentence, the second word can come only after the first word. The second word has relevance only because of the first word. Thus, the event of the second word occurring is dependent on the occurrence of the first word. These concepts have been discussed in depth in Part III, which covers most aspects of NLP. The core aspect of such a scenario is that any current event has dependencies on the past. This simply means that a network that deals with such cases should have something which seems to be like a kind of 'memory'. The concept of 'time' as a sequence of steps becomes relevant. We use the term 'sequence modelling' for applications of this type.

So a sequential network is the choice for applications of Natural Language Processing (NLP). In NLP, words form sentences but sentences are intelligible only due to the order of the words. This 'order' is what is implied as time. If the application is to predict the last word of a given sentence, the rest of the words must have a specific order. Thus, there is a first word, second word and so on. If the words are jumbled, no intelligible result is possible.

This chapter focuses on the types of deep learning networks which are used for applications such as these. As such, most of the applications of sequence models are for NLP, though there are other applications like music generation and time series predictions also. In this book, there is an entire section devoted to the principles of NLP. For applications directly involving NLP, Part III should be referred to. But here in this chapter, we do the necessary analysis to ensure a thorough understanding of the working of sequence modeling using deep learning.

12.1.1 Recurrent Neural Network (RNN)

An RNN illustrates the basic concept involved in all the sequence models that we are out to discover. It involves a serial connection between a number of cells, each passing information to its successor.

The whole idea of 'recurrence' is to feed the current output back to the input, such that the next output is a function of the present input as well as the past input. But don't visualize this to be a direct feedback mechanism, because here 'recurrence' is elaborated in terms of 'time steps'.

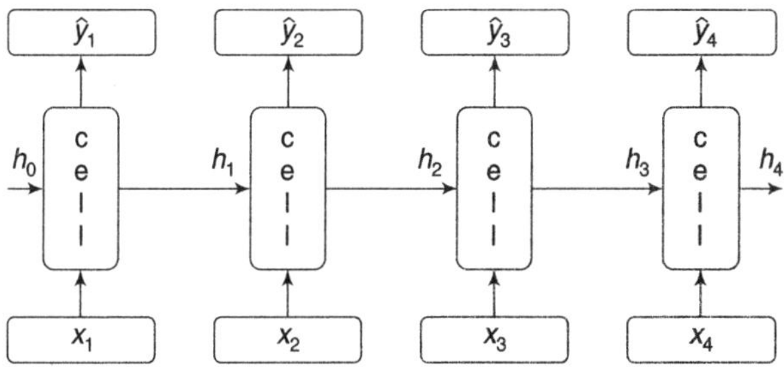

Fig. 12.1 A recurrent neural network (RNN)

A recurrent neural network (RNN) is made up of a number of cells as shown in Fig. 12.1. One cell is connected to the next one in a serial fashion. Each cell has also a specific input x, and 'may have' an output $\hat{y}$ (we notate the output as $\hat{y}$ instead of y, because the output for an application is usually a 'predicted' output, not the ground truth value). Having an 'output' is not mandatory for each cell. It depends on the application and we will see many different possibilities of using/not using $\hat{y}$. But for now, let us consider an RNN with many cells, each having an input x_t and a corresponding output $\hat{y}_t$. Right now we discuss a case in which 'the number of inputs x = number of outputs $\hat{y}$. Note that 't' stands for time where $t = 1 \ldots n$.

Let's start with trying to understand a 'single cell' as in Fig. 12.2. We see that for each cell, there are two incoming and two outgoing connections. We see that x_t is the input at the current instant. h_{t-1} is the 'hidden state' of a previous time step. This comes from a previous cell. 'h' denotes the 'hidden state' of the cell. This hidden state for each cell is obtained by the manipulation of the current input with the state of a previous cell. In Fig. 12.2, we see that when x_t and h_{t-1} are applied to a cell, we get its 'updated' hidden state h_t.

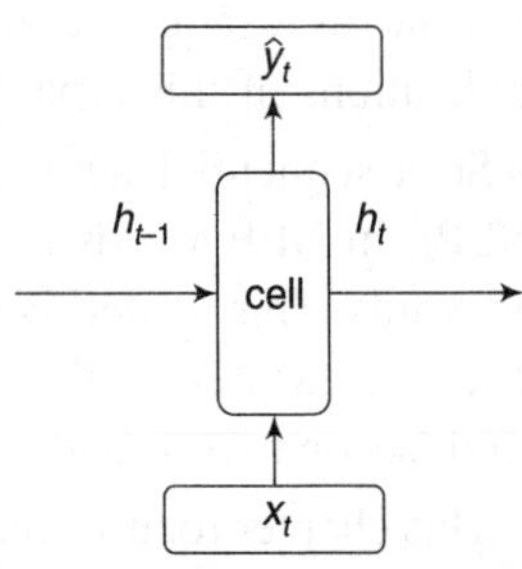

Fig. 12.2 A single RNN cell

Thus, the 'h' values turns out to be the memory of the recent past that is retained in each cell. $\hat{y}_t$ is the predicted output which depends on the application. It may be a classification or may be part of a sequence generation and it could also be that there need not be an output taken from each cell (Section 12.1.1.4).

Depending on the application, we should make ourselves clear about what exactly is the 'past' that we mean. In language applications, any word has a dependence on the previous words. Consider an NLP application such as 'prediction of the next word'. We train the network with a number of sentences. For instance, if one training input sentence is of the four words: 'I have a plan', the words can be visualized to appear sequentially. Then the first word is '*I*'. The second word is 'have' and so on. Then $x_1 = I$, $x_2 = have$, $x_3 = a$, $x_4 = plan$. See Fig. 12.3.

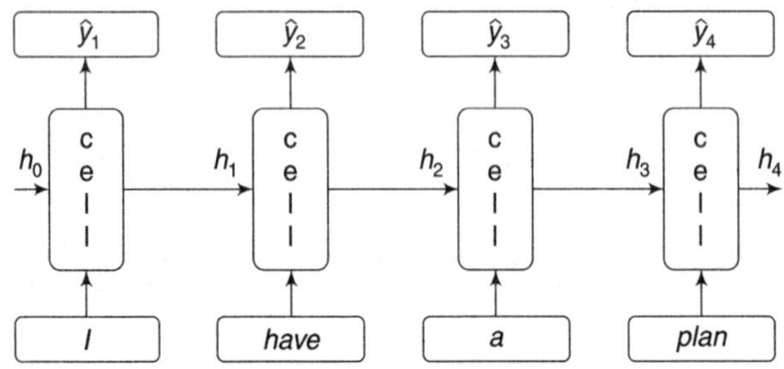

Fig. 12.3 A sentence as input to an RNN

The points to note at this point are:

(i) Each cell is concerned with time t, which is the 'present'.

(ii) Each cell is concerned with time $t - 1$, which is the previous time step.

(iii) At each time step, the hidden state of the cell is updated to include the hidden state of the previous time step.

(iv) The 'recent past' is obtained from the previous cell which has remnant information from many cells of the past.

(v) The current hidden state is obtained as a function of the 'present' and the 'recent past' notated as x_t and h_{t-1}.

(vi) For the first cell, the hidden state h_{t-1} can be a zero vector.

There are weights associated with the present input x_t, recent past h_{t-1} and output $\hat{y}_t$.

We shall denote them as W_{hx}, W_{hh} and W_{yh} respectively. One important point about RNNs is that, for one network, there is only one W_{hx}, one W_{hh} and one W_{yh}. We say that 'weight sharing' is done between the different cells. That is why it is possible to draw an RNN as a single 'rolled' network as in Fig. 12.4a. To understand it properly, we unroll it and get it as in Fig. 12.4b.

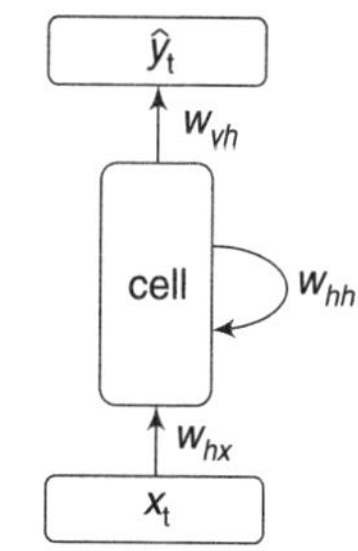

Fig. 12.4 (a) A rolled RNN

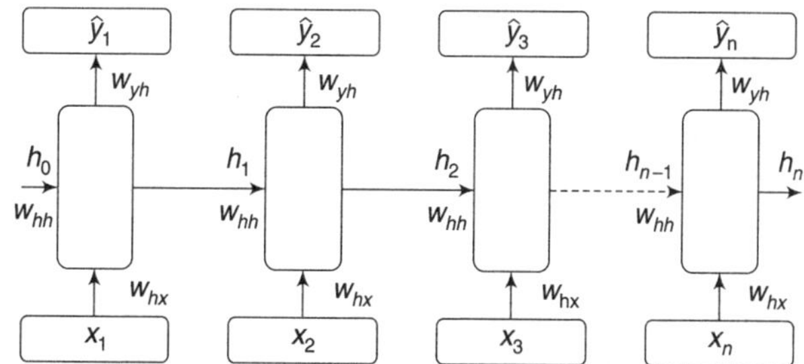

Fig. 12.4 (b) The unrolled network of Fig. 12.4a comprising of *n* cells

12.1.1.1 Mathematical Expressions

If you have familiarized yourself with the backpropagation algorithm in Section 10.2.3, the mathematical expressions of RNN will be very simple to follow. From each cell, there are two outgoing connections. One is the output $\hat{y}_t$ and the other is h_t which feeds into the next cell. The activation function at each stage of the network may be a *ReLU* or *Tanh*, but currently *Tanh* is more commonly used. *ReLU* if used, may cause large outputs. Of course, as discussed in Section 10.8.2 the *Tanh* function may cause the problem of vanishing gradients, but there are other ways to tackle that (Section 12.1.2).

$$h_t = f(W_{hh}\, h_t - 1 + W_{hx}\, x_t + b_h) \qquad ...(12.1)$$

This is the multiplication of the inputs of each cell with the corresponding weights and adding them along with a bias term. The function '*f*' is *Tanh*

For the output $\hat{y}_t$, the activation may be a Softmax or Sigmoid function depending on the application. We write:

$$\hat{y}_t = g(W_{yh}\, h_t + b_y) \qquad ...(12.2)$$

where *g* is the activation function corresponding to the output required. So $\hat{y}_t$, is obtained by the multiplication of the hidden cell state with the corresponding weight, adding a bias term and then applying the necessary activation function.

One simplification that will be done (and will be useful later on) is to stack (side by side) the weight matrices W_{hh} and W_{hx} and give it the name, W_h. Then the vectors x_t and h_{t-1} are concatenated (stacked one on top of the other) and the operations are shown in Eqs. 12.3 and 12.4.

$$[W_{hh}\ W_{hx}] = W_h \quad ...(12.3)$$

$$[W_{hh}\ W_{hx}]\begin{bmatrix} h_{t-1} \\ x_t \end{bmatrix} = W_{hh}\, h_{t-1} + W_{hx}\, x_t \quad ...(12.4)$$

Thus, 12.1 may re-written using 12.3 and 12.4. We get

$$h_t = f(W_h\ [h_{t-1}, x_t] + b_h) \quad ...(12.5)$$

Equation 12.5 indicates that the input data along with the memory of the recent past (x_t and h_{t-1}) is encoded (multiplied by weights and a bias added), and is acted upon by a *Tanh* function which squashes it to lie between −1 and +1. This is shown in Fig. 12.5. We say that we get a 'normalized encoding of data' with these operations. This is the operation that happens in a 'cell'. The hidden cell state (h_t) is the result of this operation.

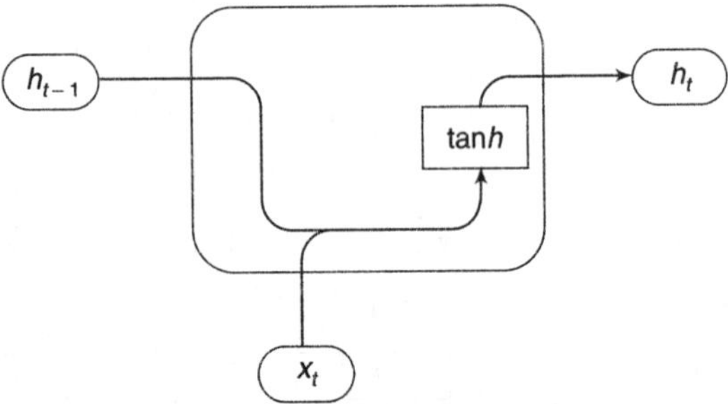

Fig. 12.5 Visualisation of equation 12.5

12.1.1.2 Backpropagation through Time

The RNN also follows the same concept of loss and backpropagation as discussed in Section 10.2.3. Since a factor related to time is involved, we call it 'Backpropagation through time'. But the algorithm will run into trouble when the input sequence is very long. For instance, if we are dealing with a sequence which is 1000 words long, we should ideally do back propagation after the full sequence is presented to an RNN with 1000 cells. Then the loss corresponding to the 1000 outputs should be considered the total loss. The problem that arise then is that during backpropagation, the derivatives corresponding to these 1000 cells will be multiplied and the product will become a very small number. This will lead rapidly to the 'vanishing' of gradients, so that there is no useful 'backpropagation' beyond a few backward steps.

The solution to this is called 'truncated' BPTT. After *k* forwards steps, the loss is calculated and backpropagated and weight updates are done. Thus, the possibility of the 'vanishing' of gradients is reduced. This is done regularly every *k* time steps. For each input x_t, the output from the cell is $\hat{y}_t$. The ground truth value at the output is y_t. The error(log loss) between y_t and $\hat{y}_t$ is summed for all values of *k* and becomes the total loss of the RNN. This loss is backpropagated using gradient descent as was discussed in Section 10.2.3.1. The weight matrices W_{hx}, W_{hh} and W_{yh} are updated accordingly.

In an NLP application, say, the truncation may give rise to a problem as this. The dependence of the 1000th word on the first word is not being taken into account. For instance, if $k = 20$, only the dependence of the 20 words backward is taken into consideration. Thus, the 'memory' of the system gets limited. To get a longer range for memory, new ways have been sought and we will discuss those methods soon (Section 12.1.2.2).

12.1.1.3 Bidirectional RNN

In our discussion so far, we have considered the flow of information to be unidirectional with respect to time. When the first word is given to the RNN, the network has knowledge of only that word. The corresponding $\hat{y}$ is based on that one word (there is no previous cell state as well).

Let us consider the dependence of the predicted output on the input sequence. As the words are applied one after the other, more information and more sense appears. So the first output $\hat{y}_1$ has dependence on only the current input, x_1. Output $\hat{y}_2$ depends on x_1 and x_2, $\hat{y}_3$ depends on x_1, x_2 and x_3 and so on. But this is essentially a unidirectional dependence. The first output $\hat{y}_1$ has absolutely no dependency on x_1, x_2.... For some applications this is a serious drawback.

Consider the following two sentences used for training.

(i) Ramanath Kovind is the President of India.

(ii) Ramanath is the name of my friend.

For the same first word, two 'senses' are inbuilt. This difference will be clear only when the full sentence has appeared. Thus, it should be clear that unidirectional RNNs cannot capture the sense associated with the future. This is why bidirectional RNNs are necessary. (See Fig. 12.6).

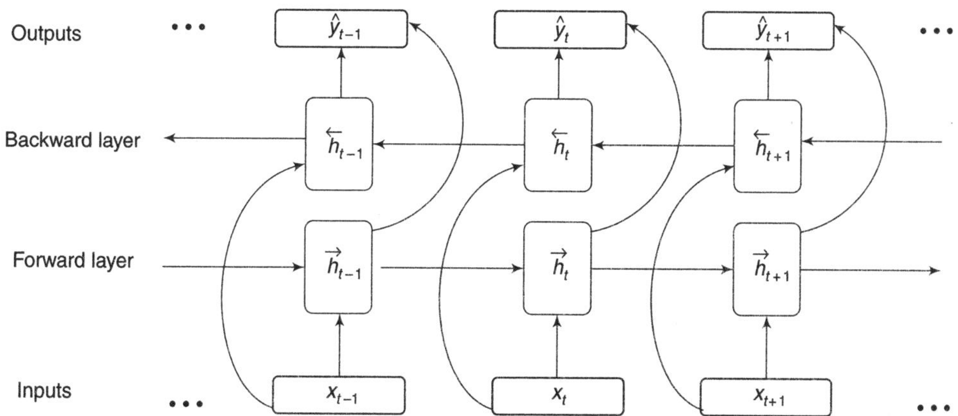

Fig. 12.6 Bidirectional RNN

For the sentence: "Ramanath Kovind is the President of India", the forward layer would feed the sequence as such and the backward layer does the same in the reverse order. The same words are fed to each cell. For instance, note that x_t is fed to the forward cell as well as the backward cell. Weights are generated by concatenating the forward and reverse h_t as $\left[\overrightarrow{h_t}\,\overleftarrow{h_t}\right]$ and using the same Eq. 12.5 as for the unidirectional RNN.

- The hidden state for each time step is obtained by using simultaneously the data before and after the current time step.
- The output $\hat{y}$ is obtained by using the forward and backward hidden states h_t. See Fig. 12.6.

If this network is used for speech recognition, then only after the full speech is over can the backward RNN start its work. So it is not suitable for a real-time speech application. But for NLP applications where text data is available, there is no such problem and it is used widely. In practice, it is either LSTMs or GRUs that are actually used. They are the 'practical' models of the conceptual RNN. We will go into that from Section 12.1.2.

12.1.1.4 Types of RNNs

Now that the basic idea of an RNN has become clear, let us see the configurations used in popular applications. In the previous sections, the RNN configuration discussed was one in which the number of inputs and the number of outputs are shown to be the same, that is, $i = 1$ to n for both and x and $\hat{y}$. But there are applications in which this does not hold. Let's examine some such cases.

(i) Many to one RNN.

An application could be one of 'sentiment classification'. One or more sentences are the input which is fed in sequentially. But the output required is just the sentiment, 'Positive or Negative'. This is aptly named as a 'many to one' network. (See Fig. 12.7).

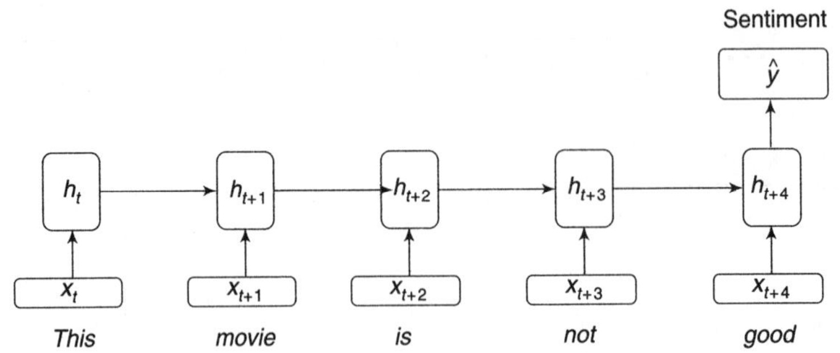

Fig. 12.7 Many to one RNN—An application of sentiment analysis

(ii) One to many RNN

If music is to be generated, there is only one input. The output from each cell is fed as input to the next cell. This is shown in Fig. 12.8.

(iii) Many to many

This is similar to the case we started with, (Fig. 12.1) but there are cases when the number of inputs is not the same as the number of outputs. One example is machine translation. If we translate from a source language (say English) to a destination

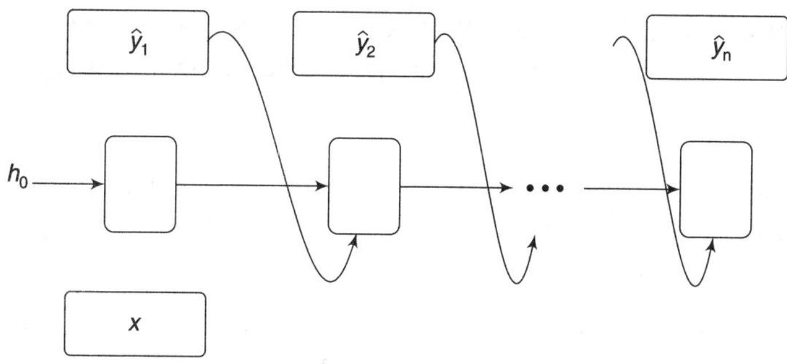

Fig. 12.8 An application of a 'One to many RNN'

language (say Hindi), the number of words of the source and destination need not be the same.

12.1.1.5 Stacked RNNs

In the case of MLPs, we found that having many layers imparted flexibility to the system. In the case of CNN for example, multiple layers are used – the initial layers captured the fine features while the final layers would take care of high level patterns.

Can the concept of 'depth' be applied to RNNs also?

The answer is 'yes'. We get deep RNNs by stacking cells in the form of layers as in Fig. 12.9.

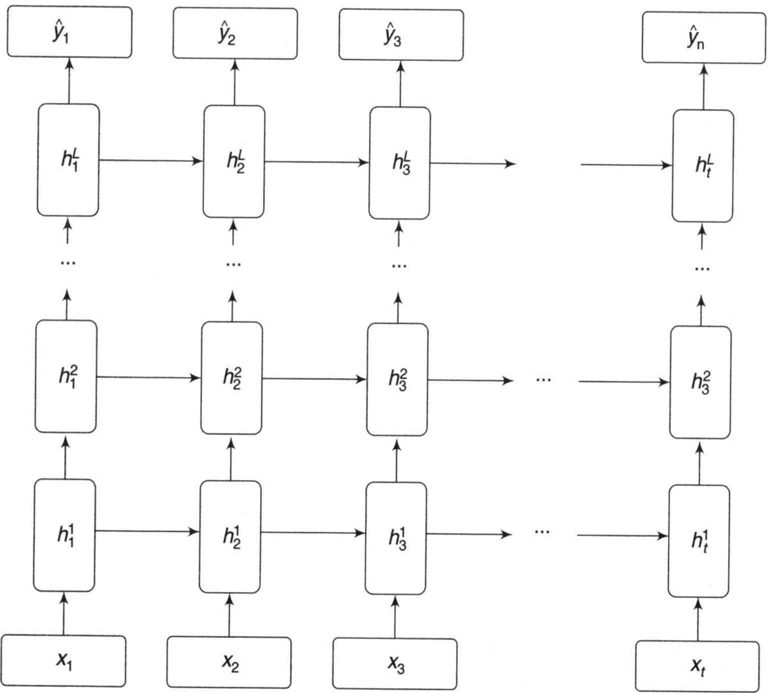

Fig. 12.9 Stacked RNN

Figure 12.10 shows such a stacked RNN with L layers. The hidden state h_t of one cell is passed on to the cell above it. Thus at any layer (except the lowest layer), there are two inputs to a cell. One in the hidden state of the cell in the next lower layer and the other is the hidden state of the cell in the previous time step of the same layer. In a practical implementation, the number of layers may be in the range of single digit numbers and this number may be specified as a hyperparameter. Such deep RNNs are the norm in sequence to sequence networks which is covered in Section 18.1.

12.1.1.6 Problems with RNN

Now that we have seen the configuration of the RNN and the applications it is generally used for, let us try to understand its main shortcoming. For applications with a small set of words, this basic RNN is reasonably good. But as the number of words of the input sequence increases, its efficacy reduces because of the vanishing/exploding gradient problem (Section 10.6). Keep in mind that the weights are the same throughout the network. Backpropagation is a product of many differentials. If the differentials are small, then the product will become very small, while if the differentials are large, the product will be a larger number. These two cases lead to either a vanishing or exploding gradient problem. The exploding gradient problem can be solved by using gradient clipping (Section 10.7.7), but the vanishing gradient problem becomes acute. In short, the basic RNN is not a choice for such applications.

This problem then manifests as a case in which the network has difficulty in 'remembering' words far back in the sequence and makes predictions based only on the recent ones. We know that in every time step, the hidden state h_t is updated with new information. As the length of the network becomes long, there is no guarantee that the oldest information is retained in the current hidden state h_t. That means that the hidden state does not encode any information of the past beyond the most recent. In short, we conclude that RNNs have limited memory because no special effort is made here to ensure the retention of the states of all the earlier cells.

Consider the following paragraph which contains many sentences:

I studied in Delhi in my school days. That was because my dad was an army officer and we lived in many places in North India. My friends and I used to talk in Hindi then ....

....

....

....

....

....

Later we returned to South India and I have been here in Kerala for the last twenty years. I have got back to talking in Malayalam. However because of my exposure to Delhi I can still converse fluently in ____.

If we read through this full paragraph, it is quite clear that the word to fill in is 'Hindi'. But can the RNN remember all the information back to the first two sentences? The answer is 'Unlikely'. Each RNN cell has a proportion of the information from the recent past but that constitutes only a sort of 'short-term memory'. This is the major problem of the basic RNN configuration.

Also, when word sequences are fed in for an application, it is necessary that there is a mechanism to extract the required features from the sequences. Some parts of the text data may be irrelevant and other parts may be very important for the application. There should be a method to retain what is important and remove what is not. If this is done, the RNN will be able to store and carry forward the necessary information as a 'memory' which is maintained for 'long term'.

Using the basic RNN as a concept, better cells have been created which incorporates the features mentioned above. The first of these 'better cells' uses the 'short-term memory block' (of RNN) as the basic structure but manages to get a 'long-term memory'. That is why the name 'Long Short Term Memory (LSTM)' has been given to this improved structure. The LSTM was developed in 1997 by Sepp Hochreiter and Jürgen Schmidhube. Later, a simplified version of it was developed and given the name GRU (Gated Recurrent Unit). Currently in all applications, even where the term RNN is mentioned, it is either the LSTM or GRU cells that are actually used.

Note: There may be difficulties encountered in getting to understand LSTM and GRU completely in one reading. So try first to grasp the concept only. Once that is clear, you can try to understand the math involved. If only conceptual information is required for coding, the math behind it can be left out.

12.1.2 The LSTM: What is Different?

The LSTM is a modified RNN which can take care of remembering long sequences. This RNN model involves a number of gates. As we know, gates are structures that can be opened and closed. To allow a particular word or sequence to be prevented from going forward into the 'Cell State', the gate is 'closed', otherwise it is kept open.

Recollect that the basic RNN cell overwrites (updates) the 'hidden cell state' at each time step. The LSTM however, can decide the features it wants to carry over a long distance (sequence length) which is equivalent to capturing and retaining long-term dependencies. That is the reason for its usefulness in NLP applications.

To get 'long-term memory retention', many enhancements are made on the basic RNN cell to make it an LSTM. It is used as a chain of cells just as an RNN. The basic RNN cell is as seen in Fig. 12.1. A basic LSTM cell is as in Fig. 12.10. This figure looks pretty complicated in comparison to Fig. 12.1. But as we find the use of each of the parts of this cell, the LSTM will be demystified and we will be able to appreciate its simplicity. Figure 12.11 is a concise 'block diagram' which shows the inputs to the cell from a previous cell, which is used in this cell to get the updated values of h_t, the hidden state, and C_t, the cell state. Figure 12.12 indicates the meanings of the symbols used in the LSTM and GRU diagrams. Figure 12.13 is a conceptual representation of an LSTM as a series of gates

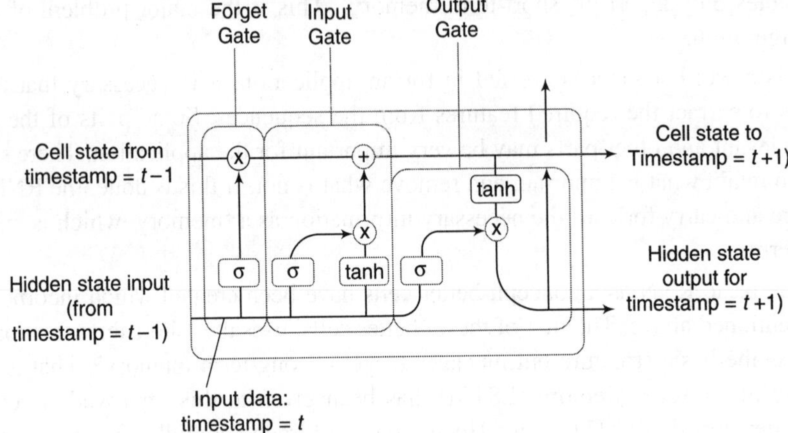

Fig. 12.10 The detailed structure of the LSTM cell

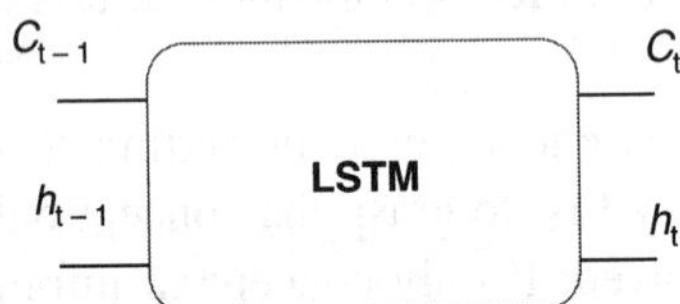

Fig. 12.11 LSTM – A block diagram

Symbol	Meaning
	Copy
	Concatenate
●	Elementwise operator

Fig. 12.12 The symbols used (in figures) and their meanings

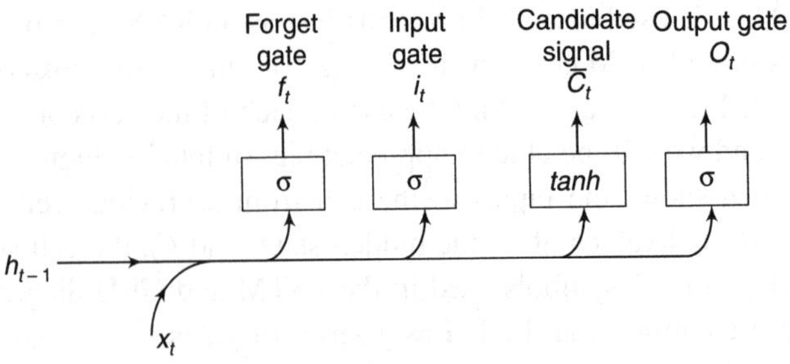

Fig. 12.13 The LSTM represented with gates

12.1.2.1 Cell State

The most important component the LSTM has is called its 'cell state' (this is not present in an RNN). This 'cell state'carries the information from the beginning of any sequence and thus serves as the aggregrate of the information applied to the LSTM chain. It is the global memory of the system. See Fig. 12.14 which shows C_{t-1}, the previous cell state and C_t, the updated cell state from a cell. This will be carried to the next cell in the chain.

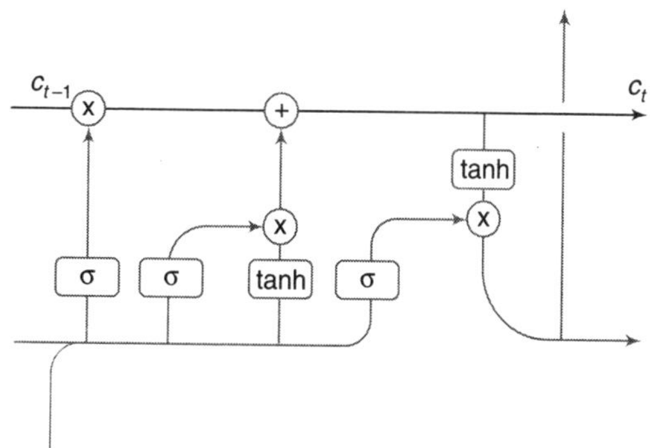

Fig. 12.14 The cell state of an LSTM

In Fig. 12.14, the straight line on the top of the digram shows the cell state from a previous time stamp $t-1$, getting updated to the current time stamp to become C_t, the current cell state. This line goes on to the next cell and is frequenctly compared to a 'conveyor belt' which carries bagagge from a source to a destination. However, the cell state (unlike a conveyor belt) gets updated as it traverses along the path to the last cell. A number of 'gates' work on it to create the updated cell state. The '⊗' and '⊕' symbols in the path of the 'conveyor belt' indicate the action of the gates that we will talk about.

12.1.2.2 Gates

Gates actually select and enter into the 'cell state', certain fetaures of the input. Some features which are unnecessary are removed or 'forgotten', others are retained. There are weights for each of the gates which select the proportion of the features to be entered into the cell state.

12.1.2.2.1 Forget Gate

The forget gate selectively prevents some parts of the given input from entering into the cell state. An example of where it can be useful is given below. Note the following three sentences:

My mother and her sisters used to play badminton. Their brother, however, loved to play cricket. These days he spends a lot of time and money for his favourite game.

After the first sentence, the context changes from badminton to cricket. As such, it is best that the first sentence is forgotten or blocked. This is what the forget gate accomplishes.

12.1.2.2.2 Input Gate

My background is South Indian. My food habits are such that I am fond of sāmbhar, idli and uppuma.

See the above two sentences. These two sentences are allowed as 'input' as they are in the same context. An input gate can ensure this.

12.1.2.2.3 Output Gate

I remember my friend Harish was very good in all courses related to science and maths. When competitions based on maths and science were conducted, it was natural that prizes went to intelligent__.

In the above case, to get the correct word, we need to output the word 'Harish' from a previous context. The output gate ensures this.

12.1.2.3 LSTM Mathematics

Now let's get into the mathematics of these functions. If you have assimilated the mathematical concepts of RNN (Eq. 12.5), then, it will be quite easy to appreciate similar equations for the LSTM.

In Fig. 12.14, two activation functions *Tanh* and Sigmoid are seen. What are their roles?

Fundamentally, the LSTM is like an RNN in that it is a repeating sequence of cells. The RNN cell is simpler, however. From a previous hidden state, a current hidden state is obtained by concatenating it with the current input and applying a *Tanh* nonlinear activation. This was what Eq. 12.5 indicated. It is the same thing here when we see a Tanh activation in the LSTM.

The Sigmoid, however, has a specific function of being the 'controller' of the gates. Recollect that a Sigmoid squashes any input to lie between 0 and 1. If we want to remove any information, it must be small enough such that it appears close to the 0 part of the Sigmoid. If we want to retain any data, it must be high enough to appear at the '1' part of the Sigmoid such that it passes unhindered. This is the logic of how and why a Sigmoid comes in handy.

12.1.2.3.1 Forget Gate Equations

$$f_t = \sigma(W_f \cdot [h_{t-1}, x_t] + b_f) \quad \text{...(12.6)}$$

Figure 12.15 shows the action of a forget gate in tune with Eq. 12.5. Remember that $[h_{t-1}, x_t]$ is the concatenated value of the previous hidden state and current input. W_f and b_f are the weight and bias for this gate (Eq. 12.6). Using the right weights makes the signal to the gate to be small or big such that the Sigmoid can cause it to be forgotten or retained. In the example sentence pertaining to this gate (Section 12.1.1.6), the signal corresponding to the first sentence must be small, so that the Sigmoid squashes it to 0. After that, the forget gate output f_t is entered into the cell state using 'element wise' multiplication (Hadamard product). These steps are made clear in Fig. 12.15. In effect, we observe that the forget gate selectively enters information into the cell.

Note: The element wise multiplication is faster than matrix multiplication and is preferred in situations where the exact value of the product is not critical. The symbol for it is $\otimes$.

12.1.2.3.2 Input Gate Equations

Figure 12.16 is the diagram of the Input gate. The corresponding equation is

$$i_t = \sigma(W_i [h_{t-1}, x_t] + b_i) \qquad ...(12.7)$$

The operation is similar to the forget gate, only the weights and bias are different.

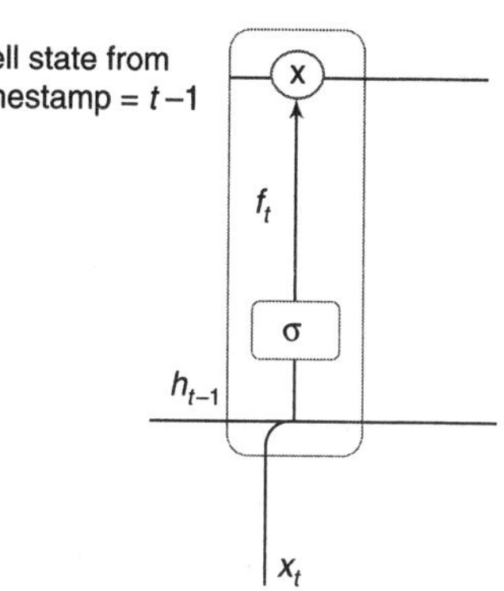

Fig. 12.15 The action of the forget gate

In addition, another operation also is done. The same input is also subjected to a *Tanh* activation as in Eq. 12.8 giving $\tilde{C}_t$ which is referred to as a 'Candidate signal' as this *Tanh* gate has the name Candidate gate. It has also the name 'Intermediate cell state'.The outputs of the Sigmoid and *Tanh* gates are subjected to a element wise multiplication and added to the cell state as In Fig. 12.16.

$$\tilde{C}_t = Tanh\ (W_c \cdot [h_{t-1}, x_t] + b_c) \qquad ...(12.8)$$

It is a bit difficult to be convinced of the exact logic of these operations. But remember that a *Tanh* function acting on $[h_{t-1}, x_t]$ was mentioned to be an encoded feature extraction (Section 12.1.1.1). When multiplied by the Sigmoid, only the parts of the input which are worthy to be retained are chosen. Together, these two operations do a feature extraction of the 'relevant' data $[h_{t-1}, x_t]$. Only the 'necessary' features get added to the cell state, C_t.

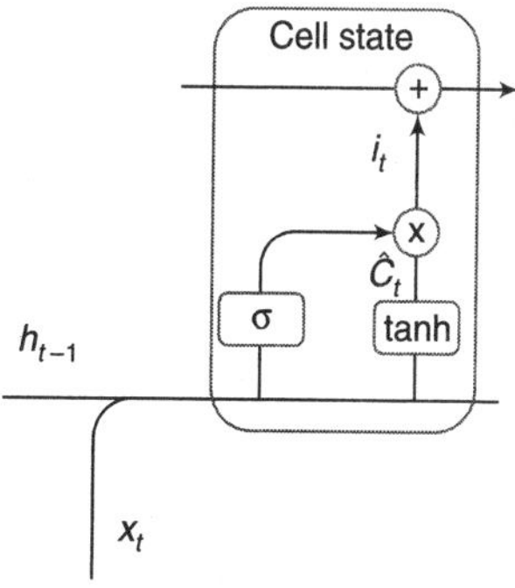

Fig. 12.16 The action of the Input gate

12.1.2.3.3 Output Gate Equations

The final step is related to the output gate (Fig. 12.17). First a Sigmoid is used which decides which information from the input needs to be considered useful to be denoted as O_t (Eq. 12.9). Then Eq.12.10 shows that the cell state C_t is subject to a *Tanh* activation and multiplied (elementwise) with O_t to get the updated hidden state h_t of the cell.

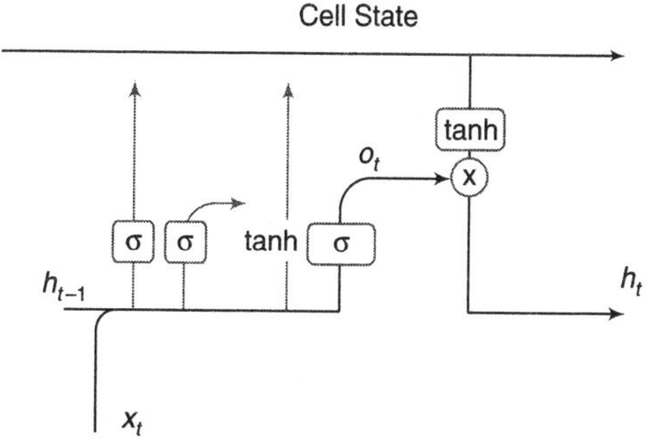

Fig. 12.17 Action of the output gate

$$O_t = \tanh (W_o [h_{t-1}, x_t] + b_o) \quad ...(12.9)$$

$$h_t = O_t * \tanh (C_t) \quad ...(12.10)$$

Note that for a cell, it is the hidden state h_t that actually constitutes the value that can be taken from a cell and given to the next cell. This h_t is seen to be taken as an encoded value of the cell state C_t and we should realize that now the global information carried by C_t, is also available in h_t. This is seen in Eq. 12.10 pertaining to the output gate.

To conclude, let us list out some salient points regarding LSTM.

(i) A basic RNN rewrites the hidden state with a new value, while an LSTM retains all the relevant information of the past in the cell state C_t and then, an encoded value of this cell state becomes the new hidden state h_t of the cell.
(ii) The 'relevant 'information is chosen by the use of 4 gates.
(iii) There are other configurations of realizing LSTMs which can be obtained from various research papers.
(iv) Many remarkable results for NLP came about after the LSTM came into the picture.

12.1.3 The Gated Recurrent Unit

Now that we have gained an understanding of the LSTM, let us take a look at the Gated Recurrent Unit (GRU) which was developed in 2014 and is considered to be simpler and faster than an LSTM though not as good in performance.

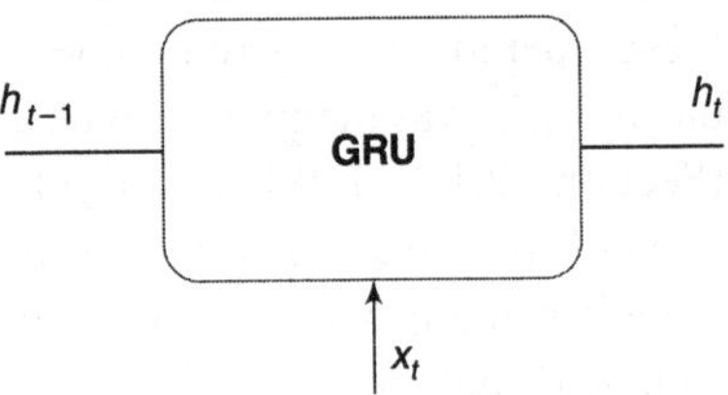

Fig. 12.18 The block diagram of a GRU

The GRU differs from the LSTM on two points:

(i) It does not have a 'cell state'. See Fig. 12.18.
(ii) It has only two gates.

12.1.3.1 The Gates of the GRU

The Relevance Gate: This is used to decide how relevant the information that comes to it is. A Sigmoid is used to remove irrelevant information. Equation 12.11 introduces the gate r_t, the Relevance gate.

$$r_t = \sigma(W_r [h_{t-1}, x_t + b_r) \quad ...(12.11)$$

My mother and her sisters used to play badminton. Their brother however loved to play cricket. These days he spends a lot of time and money for his favourite game.

In this case, the first sentence becomes irrelevant when the second sentence appears. The weights of the equation should be such that value of r_t becomes small for the information which corresponds to the first sentence.

The Update Gate: This is meant to retain the required state as long as it is needed. The 'update' implies that when new information comes, it should be retained and not forgotten. This is carried forward to the future. z_t as described in Eq. 12.12 indicates this.

$$z_t = \sigma(W_z \cdot [h_{t-1}, x_t] + b_z) \qquad ...(12.12)$$

My background is South Indian. My food habits are such that I am fond of sambhar, idli and uppuma.

In the above case, when the second sentence comes, the first sentence should still be retained.

The next operation is an intermediate state called the candidate value $\bar{h}$.

$$\bar{h}_t = tanh\ (W \cdot [r_t * h_{t-1}, x_t] \qquad ...(12.13)$$

Here, there is an element wise multiplication between r_t and h_{t-1}.

Finally, the resultant hidden state of the cell h_t is obtained in terms of the update gate as Eq. 12.14 shows.

$$h_t = (1 - z_t) * h_{t-1} + z_t * \bar{h}_t \qquad ...(12.14)$$

From this equation, the role of z_t is obvious. When z_t is close to 1, there is no update, h_t is the same as h_{t-1}. When z_t is close to 0, there is an update. The role of the update gate z_t in this context is to calculate the current hidden state h_t, which in turn, also decides the proportion of the previous hidden state, which gets included in the current h_t. In short, the update gate is the reason that the GRU has 'long-term memory. Figure 12.19 shows a complete GRU.

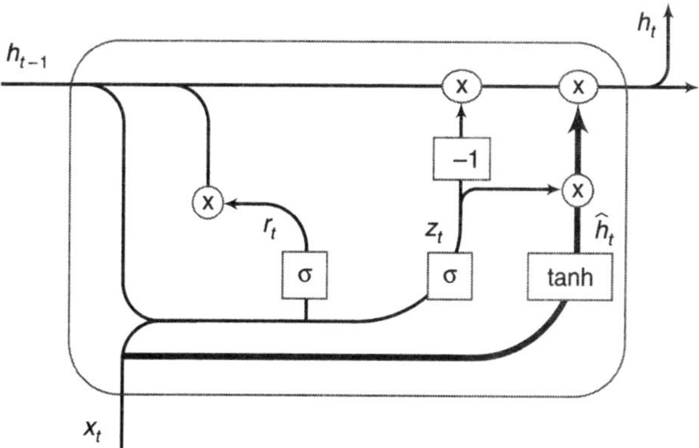

Fig. 12.19 Figure showing the internal details of a GRU

Applications of RNNs

Many applications of RNNs have been highlighted and discussed in this chapter. We started with a basic RNN and moved on to LSTM and GRU. It is to be noted that the RNN is a concept and LSTMs and GRUs are the practical implementations of a well performing sequential network. For all applications in which we use the term RNN, the practical implementation would be either LSTM/GRU.

Conclusion

This chapter is meant to give a basic introduction to the theoretical aspects of sequential deep learning networks. The applications of such networks for NLP tasks is well known. The advanced models of the use of such networks have been taken up in Chapter 18. There you will also see that a new model named transformers has come which has done away with 'sequential' processing. Thus many applications of NLP have shifted to transformers. However, there are still many applications in which sequential processing is mandatory. In such cases, RNNs and their practical models such as LSTMs and GRUs will continue to be useful. Also for small applications, the simplicity of these networks makes them important.

Questions

1. What is the principle of RNN?
2. How is h_t obtained from h_{t-1} and x_t?
3. Why do we say that every RNN cell need not have an output y?
4. What is meant by 'unrolling' an RNN network?
5. What is the use of the Sigmoid function in LSTM?
6. Why are basic RNN cells not used in applications?
7. How does the gates help in obtaining 'long-term memory' in LSTMs?
8. Compare LSTM and GRU in performance.

Exercise

1. Write codes to realize the following:
   (i) A basic RNN
   (ii) An LSTM network
   (iii) A GRU network

CHAPTER

13

Generative Adversarial Network (GAN)

In this chapter you will

- take a look at unsupervised learning,
- understand the concept of latent spaces,
- study the principle of autoencoders,
- get an exposure to variational encoders, and
- discover the principles of GANs and their working.

13.0 INTRODUCTION

In all our discussion on deep learning, the focus has been only on supervised learning, where labels are to be present in training data. But 'labelling' data is an expensive process which involves a huge amount of manual work. Once labels are given for a data (image, for example), we use that data for purposes such as classification, recognition, object detection etc. The supervised form of deep learning has been widely researched and many applications have been found for it.

13.1 UNSUPERVISED LEARNING

The unsupervised form of deep learning is a relatively unexplored area, but many new applications are coming up for it recently. The important aspect of having 'unlabelled data' is that hidden patterns in the dataset can be identified and brought to use. New ways of thinking (different from the view of labelled data) are needed to do this. Consider a case of having lots of photographs taken over a period of say, two years. If I want to arrange it and store it in different folders, how is to be done? If I want to do it manually, I could do it based on many criteria that I have chosen. But if automation is preferred, the ML algorithm should find a way out by finding patterns and clustering 'similar' photographs so that they are stored in one folder. Many such folders will have to come out as the output of the algorithm.

The point is that we need an algorithm that identifies some aspects (patterns) in the images and segregates them accordingly. That requires a clustering mechanism. This means that 'patterns' in the data have to be detected by the algorithm. This is likely to be more difficult than in the case of supervised learning and is a relatively unexplored area as far as deep learning is concerned. Applications such as dimensionality reduction and feature learning are the natural outcomes of this way of thinking.

In this chapter, we will discuss a few terms which have association with a relatively new and upcoming application of deep learning which is considered an upsupervised approach. This will lead us to the currently most exciting application arena of deep learning which is 'Generative Adversarial Learning' or GAN as it is called.

13.1.1 Latent Space

We know that a vector space (Section 2.1) is defined as a n-dimensional space where each point may be represented by an n-dimensional vector. If words are represented by 512 length vectors, the space in which words lie has 512 dimensions. In this context, a relevant question is whether it is possible to represent words with lesser dimensions, or shorter vectors? In Section 17.1, we could see that it is possible. The same word was seen to be represented by a 10-element vector as well as 100-element vector. Definitely, the smaller vector is a lossy compressed form of the 100 element vector. But if a 10-element vector can represent the most relevant information regarding the word and may be sufficient for many practical purposes, we would prefer to depend on that smaller dimensional space.

This idea implies that the most 'relevant' information of words is hidden and if we could extract that alone, we could have a lower dimensional representation. This applies to other kinds of data like images also. If an image is represented as pixels, a 100 × 100 image is a vector in a 10,000 dimension space. If a meaningful representation of this data is possible in a lower dimensional space, that space is called a 'latent space'.

A latent space may be defined to be an abstract space which is multidimensional and has embedded in it vectors, which are a coded and lower dimensional representation of the original data. We should note that this latent space should hold 'meaningful information' of the data. This 'meaningful' information may not be directly observable in the original higher dimensional space. The most important point about 'latent space' is that similar samples of the data are found to be positioned close together. This is the key intuition behind the concept of latent space.

In Section 17.1, we will see that in the latent space in which words are represented, similar words are found close together. Words like *joy* and *happiness* are found close together and separated far away from words like *sadness* and *depression*. This is because the 'features' of these words, that is, word semantics(meanings), have been captured by the characteristics of this latent space. Refer to Figure 17.1a.

For images, if we can take an image of size 10 × 10 and represent it as a vector of size 3 × 1, it means that we have done a mapping from the original 100 dimensional space into a three-dimensional latent space. In CNNs (Chapter 11), when we extract features of images, we are actually taking the image data in pixel space ($M \times N$ pixels) and mapping it into a latent space, which we notate as 'feature space'. We have captured the 'hidden information' of each image and compressed it into a set of features. This is sufficient to identify any image. If images of dogs and cats are the original data, classification is possible only because of observing that there are structural differences between the images of dogs and cats. In the latent space of features, these structural differences are observable. But in the original pixel space, these differences may not be extractable/observable. Figure 13.1 shows that in deep learning, we extract features, project them into latent space and use it for applications which may be classification, regression, representation, etc.

If the classification problem is to differentiate animal images from that of vehicles and mountains, animal data would be close together and separated in space from that of the other objects (See Fig. 13.2). We find similar items clustered together but distant from dissimilar items, in n-dimensional latent space (though the figure is drawn in two dimensions).

Since latent space contains a representation of data, interpolation may be done. This concept has been used in the Word2Vec model of text representation. In Fig. 17.1(b), the algebraic

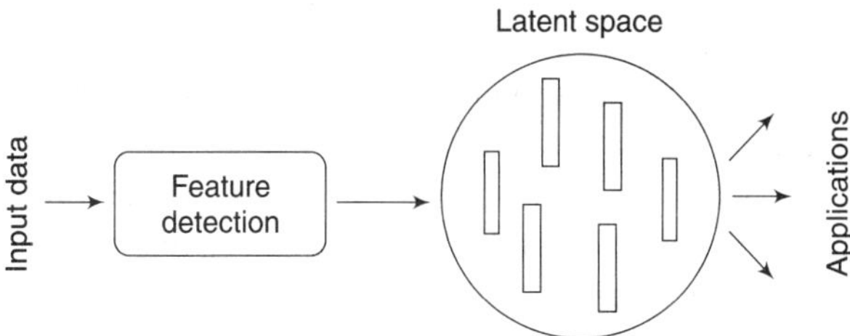

Fig. 13.1 Features of the input data in latent space

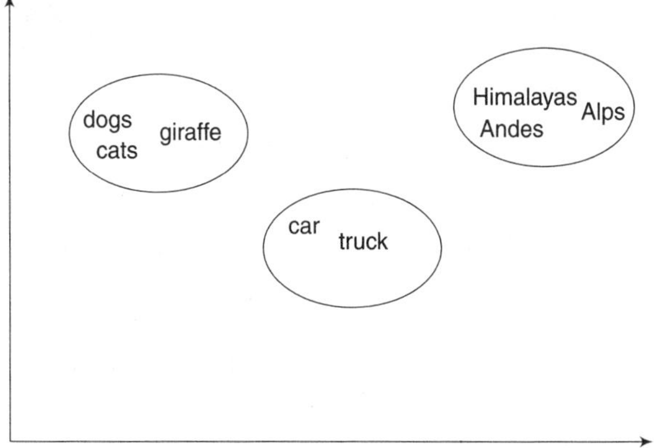

Fig. 13.2 Similar items close together in latent space

operation of hero – boy = heroine – girl is highlighted. This could be rewritten as hero = boy + heroine – girl. Similar interpolations can be done for other data as well.

Let's see how this idea is useful for image data. An application in image processing which we call 'representation' is envisaged as follows. In latent space, Eq. 13.1 holds meaning from which we get Eq. 13.2. Figure 13.3 highlights this.

Laughing man – Neutral man = Laughing woman – Neutral woman ...(13.1)

Laughing man = Neutral man + Laughing woman – Neutral man ...(13.2)

Fig. 13.3 Interpolation of vectors in latent space

So we see that we get a new image by interpolating other images. This seems to be a direct application of the use of latent space.

Other ways of using latent spaces are possible because arithmetic can be done on the latent vectors. If a point in the space corresponds to a woman's face, it is possible to add another vector to this and get the image of the woman with glasses. In another application, a linear path between the points corresponding to two faces was found to represent a set of faces transitioning from one to the next smoothly. In Fig. 13.4, between the image on the left, to the image on the right, there are a number of points each representing a face, which transitions slowly with slight differences between one and the next one. These are applications which are seen in papers discussing GANs (Section 13.3)

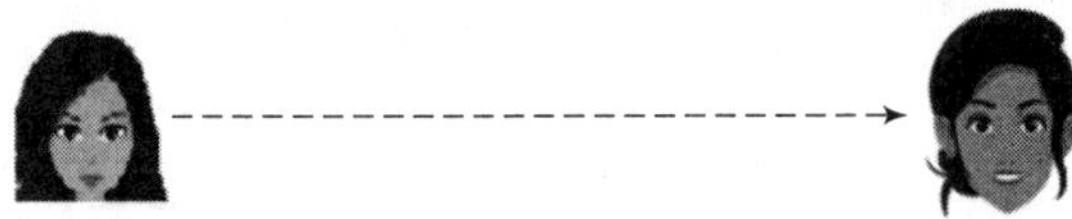

Fig. 13.4 interpolation of image points in latent space

Why do we need latent space encoding of raw data?

One answer is 'compression'. If raw data is high dimensional, it takes space for storage. Also, in cases where we need to analyze data for some applications, it may be impossible to extract relevant information directly from raw data. Deep learning networks may be directly used for encoding high dimensional raw data into a low dimensional latent space representation. We will now see such a network named 'Autoencoder'.

13.2 AUTOENCODER

An autoencoder is a network which does only this, that is, it takes an input data and produces a lower dimensional form of it, which essentially amounts to data compression.

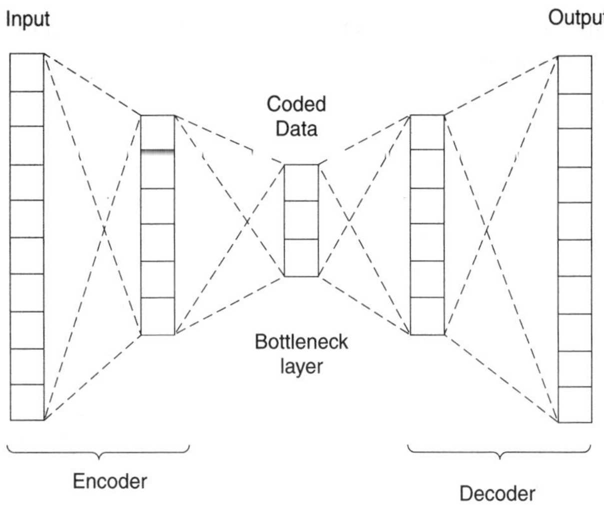

Fig. 13.5 The conceptual form of an autoencoder

Figure 13.5 shows the encoder and decoder of the network, both of which are 'a number of layers' of MLPs. They may be fully connected (FC)/convolution networks (CNN). The figure shows the 'coded data' to be a compressed/lower dimensional version of the input data. The layer containing the coded data is named 'bottleneck' layer because the physical appearance (as is seen in the figure) represents a bottleneck (smaller size compared to the layers behind and ahead of it).

The concept behind the autoencoder is very simple. The encoder takes the input data x and converts it to a lower dimensional representation, z. The decoder attempts to use this coded data to do a reconstruction. If the coded data (z) contains all the relevant information of x, the output ($\hat{x}$) should be equal to x. If not, there is an error. Being a neural network, backpropagation, which is an iterative optimization process, is used to bring the error down to zero. The Cost function may be the log loss or MSE and may be chosen according to the type of data. Applications of autoencoders include data compression and denoising. Figure 13.5 shows the operation of an autoencoder.

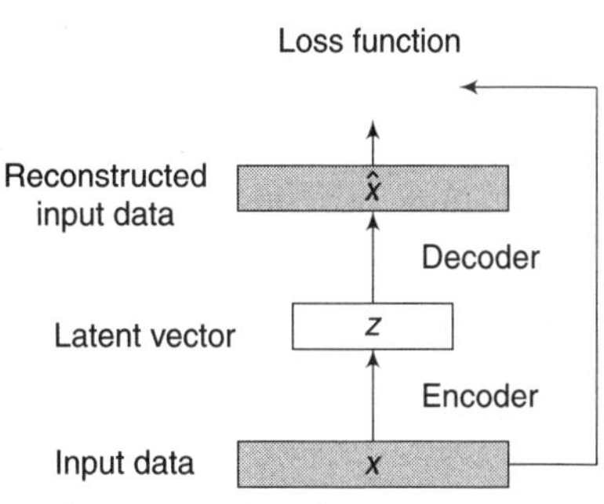

Fig. 13.6 Operation of an auto-encoder

Note that the data at the output side of the autoencoder is not needed and therefore it is called a fake task (Section 17.2.1). We need the 'coded data' alone from the autoencoder. The autoencoder is an unsupervised technique but is also referred to a 'self supervised' because a loss is used like in the case of supervised learning, but there are no labels for the data.

One point to note is that the purpose of the autoencoder is to reduce the dimensions while ensuring that the structural information of the original data is retained in its reduced form.

The two hyperparameters to be careful about to ensure this, are the depth of the network and the dimension of the latent space.

13.3 GENERATIVE MODELS

Our next endeavour is to learn more about generative models and their capabilities. In Section 4.2, we touched upon the difference between discriminative and generative models used for binary classification. The discriminative model has the duty of getting $P(y/x)$ by which a decision boundary is modelled. A generative model does not do this. Given a new input data, x_{new}, it predicts its most likely label (outcome of classification).

This is the same principle by which generative models 'generate' data. We are already aware that given a sequence of input samples, x, they can predict the most likely outcome. For example, if a series of video frames are given, a new frame can be generated. Search engines predict a word based on the previous words inputted by the user. We can say formally that : *given training data, they can generate new samples from the 'same distribution'*. This is the simple statement that illustrates the principle used by generative models in machine learning.

Generative modelling does not require labels and hence it is an unsupervised learning task. It generates new data samples using the probability distribution of the given training data which are sets of observations without labels. The method is to obtain a model for the underlying probability distribution of this training data, such that we can generate samples similar to this data. Given a data distribution, it is not possible to learn its distribution exactly – only an approximation is possible. Since neural networks are function approximators, the power of deep learning networks may be leveraged to perform this function of getting an approximate distribution using a true distribution.

Currently, generative models are the next great thing in machine learning and many new applications of artificial intelligence have generative models at their core. Two methods are available and are used for getting 'synthetic data' — one is the 'Variational Autoencoder' and the other is 'Generative Adversarial Networks (GANs)'. The latter method has produced much better results for image data and we will discuss it in some depth, while making only a brief reference to the former.

13.3.1 Variational Autoencoder (VAE)

We have just seen that generating synthetic data is what generative networks are to be used for. Data may be text, audio or video. Let us say we have a set of images. From this set, we want to generate images which are slightly different. For example, if we have many images of gardens, we want to obtain images with different settings for lawns and flower beds, trees, etc. If we have with us images of human faces, we would like images in other angles, poses, expressions, etc. What is the method to do this?

The concept of latent space should give us the knowledge that data is available in this space in a form in which the structure of the data is recognizable. That is what we get with autoencoders. If we plot the latent space of some images in a set, it may be visualized as points. If we take one point, it will correspond to the latent representation of some image. What about the point close to it? It is likely to be of an image similar to the first one. Thus, clustered around one point we have the latent representation of similar images. If we could pick the right one for our 'synthetic' image generation, we have realized our objective. This principle is behind VAEs. But we need the latent space to be continuous so as to allow easy interpolation.

The VAE is an encoder-decoder setup like the autoencoder but more mathematical principles are inculcated into it to 'regularize' the organization of latent space. The aim in this is to ensure that the distribution obtained from the encoder follows a standard normal (Gaussian) distribution. The 'regularity' implied here has two aspects:

(i) Continuity – this means that two points close together in latent space, should not give representations which are widely different.

(ii) Completeness – this means that for a chosen data distribution, meaningful content should be obtained from the points sampled from its latent space.

To understand VAEs in depth, we need to know about variational inference (from statistics) and KL divergence (from information theory), which are beyond the scope of this chapter. We will conclude by saying that VAEs have produced good results in the domains of text and audio but in the image domain, their performance is lacking.

13.3.2 Generative Adversarial Network (GAN)

A generative adversarial network (GAN) is a generative model introduced by Ian J. Goodfellow in the year 2014. The purpose of GANs is to get synthetic data which can be passed off as real. Applications of GAN include image generation, text to image translation, image to image translation and image quality enhancement.

As the name indicates, GANs are meant to 'generate'. We already know the concept of 'generative modeling'. The next word 'adversarial' means 'characterized by conflict or opposition'. Instead of viewing it as conflict it would be best to view the working of a GAN as a competition/game played by 'adversaries', each trying to win. In AI game theory, we have the 'minimax' setting for a two player game. There is only one score for the game, one player tries to maximize the score and the other attempts to minimize it. This same principle is used in GANs. But before we go to the score/Cost function involved, let us look at it intuitively.

GANs are explained as a set of two entities, say, two people: one, a counterfeiter making counterfeit goods that may be currency, paintings, sculpture, etc., and a detective/buyer trying to assess whether the goods offered are genuine or not. In the beginning, the counterfeiter is not successful in fooling the buyer, but with time, the counterfeiter improves his trade so much that the buyer is fooled into mistaking fake goods as real. For instance, consider that the counterfeiter tries to make paintings similar to paintings of a famous painter like Raja Ravi Varma. The buyer tries to assess it on the basis of the real paintings that he has knowledge of. At the end of the story, we find the counterfeiter to have become successful in making a counterfeit painting look exactly the same as the original.

Thus, the ultimate aim of GANs is to produce fake data that looks as good as the original. The adversaries in this game are named appropriately as 'generator' and 'discriminator'. The aim of the game is to generate synthetic data, for example, images, referenced on some "real data". The generator G is fed random data, that is, noise, and its goal is to produce data that is similar to data from the set of real images.

Figure 13.7 shows the generator with 'z' as input, using which it generates images. Obviously, these images are not real. Figure 13.8 shows the second part of GAN–a discriminator to which the generator output and real images from a training set are given as input. The discriminator has to say whether the data from the generator to it is real or fake. The set of genuine images is the reference and the generator tries to mimic this.

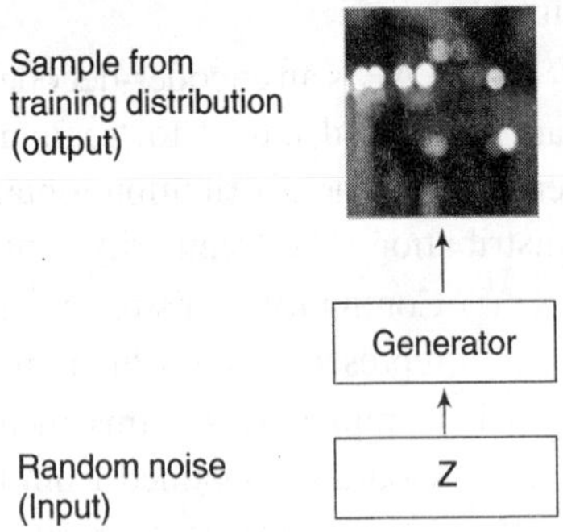

Fig. 13.7 The generation of data using random noise as input

In the beginning of the action phase, the discriminator is very clear about what is real and what is fake. The discriminator's response is used by the generator to improve itself. It tries to improve the images it generates. With time, the generator becomes better at its job and then the discriminator finds it more and more difficult to distinguish between real and fake images. When the discriminator fails completely, that is, when it loses the capability to discriminate between real and fake, then the aim of GANs is realized. The system has become capable of generating synthetic data which can be passed off as real.

The concept of GAN is based on unlabelled data which means that there are no labels for the training data. However, during the working the system, fake data is given the label 0 and real data the label 1. This is necessary for defining a Cost function. The discriminator and generator are MLPs and a Cost function is used to perform backpropagation to update the weights of both these entities.

The salient points are:

- The generator tries to fool the discriminator by generating real looking images. It starts with random noise as input and tries to imitate the data from a training set.
- For every sample from the noise z, we want a sample from the training distribution x (Fig. 13.9) to go to the discriminator which makes an evaluation. Essentially, the discriminator tries to discriminate between real and fake images.

  What we need is:

  - To have a discriminator which is very good at discriminating between real and fake images
  - To have a generator which is very good at generating fake images

13.3.2.1 Cost Function

In the paper that introduced the concept of GAN, a minimax Cost function is the objective function. (Eq. 13.3)

$$C = E_x[\log(D(x))] + E_z[\log(1 - D(G(z)))] \qquad ...(13.3)$$

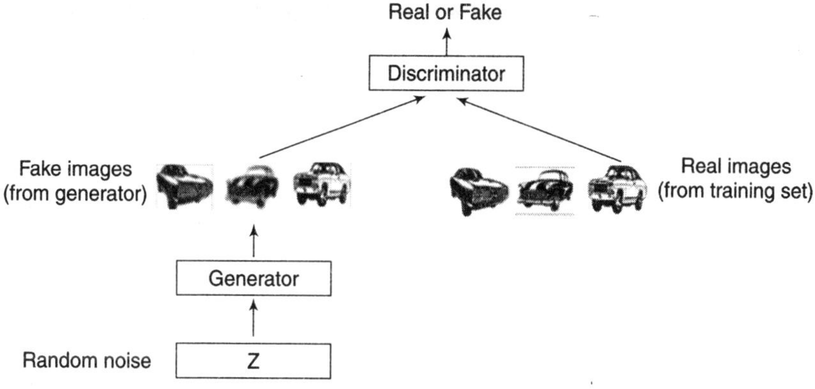

Fig. 13.8 The discriminator in action

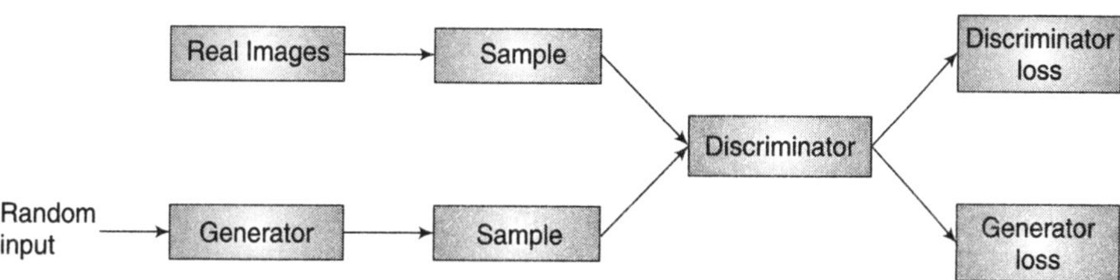

Fig. 13.9 Loss obtained from the discriminator

The generator tries to minimize this Cost function C while the discriminator tries to maximize it. Let us try to understand each term in this Cost function.

- $D(x)$ is the discriminator's output for real data, which is the probability that the data from the training set x, is real.
- $G(z)$ is the output of the generator for the input noise, z.
- $D(G(z))$ is the discriminator's output for fake data – this is the probability that a fake instance is considered to be real.
- E_x is the expected value (mean) over all real data instances and E_z is the mean over all the fake instances $G(z)$.

This formula is basically our log loss/cross entropy loss (Eq. 3.55) between the generated and real data distributions.

So what do the generator and discriminator want?

- Note from Fig. 13.9, that both generator loss and discriminator loss are obtained from the discriminator.
- The **discriminator** wants to **maximize the Cost function** so that $D(x)$ is close to 1 for real data and $D(G(z))$ is close to 0 for fake data. The discriminator is penalized when it misclassifies (Fig. 13.9).

- The **generator** wants to **minimize the Cost function** so that $D(G(z))$ is close to 1. (the generator wants to fool the discriminator). The discriminator's classification is what constitutes generator loss (Fig. 13.9). If the discriminator is fooled, the loss is reduced. If not, the generator is penalized as its loss increases.

13.3.2.2 Training

Theoretically, the training of the discriminator and generator are to be done jointly. But in practice, this is not possible. Hence, the generator and discriminator are trained alternatively.

The training processes for the generator and discriminator are different. GAN training takes place in two phases: For one or more epochs, the generator is trained and then for one or more epochs, the discriminator is trained. This repeats until the GAN network converges. During the generator training phase, we maintain the discriminator constant. Otherwise, the discriminator would be attempting to strike a moving target and would be unlikely to ever converge. Similarly, during the discriminator training phase, we keep the generator constant.

13.3.2.3 The Rationale behind GANs

How is it that a network such as this becomes capable of generating data?

The concept employed is that of learning the mapping from a latent distribution $p(z)$ to a real data distribution $p(x)$. For example, assume we want to generate images. Think of the abstract space of images represented by $M \times N$ pixels. These images reside in a very high dimensional space (Section 13.1.1). Suppose we want to get similar or slightly modified images from this high dimensional space. It is quite difficult to sample from this high dimensional space. The easy method is to draw from a simpler distribution $p(z)$ which is from a latent space and map it towards the image distribution that we want. This is what GANs do. They do it through 'adversarial' training rather than by 'matching'.

The generator formulation is this $g: Z \rightarrow X$, where $Z \varepsilon R^d$ is the d-dimensional latent space with a Gaussian distribution. X stands for the image space, and in this space, each sample possesses certain semantic information. For example, for a face there is the information of age, gender, etc. That constitutes a sematic space. The action done by GAN is of bridging the gap between the latent space Z and semantic space.

We have seen (Section 13.1.1) some properties of latent space. By manipulating/disentangling the entangled vectors in latent space, many amazing results are possible. For instance, for face synthesis, we need to have a good understanding of how latent vectors can be disentangled to produce the features that we want. In the latent space corresponding to faces, it is possible to associate a certain direction with gender and another direction for the presence of eye glasses and another for pose, etc. A lot of results of GAN have been obtained by exploring the concept of decoupling the semantics associated with latent vectors.

13.3.2.4 Applications of GAN

GAN finds various applications some of which are listed here.

(a) Super resolution GAN (SRGAN) was proposed by Twitter researchers. The goal of this design is to recover finer textures from the image when it is up-scaled, ensuring that the image's quality is preserved.

(b) CycleGAN: Image-to-image translation involves creating a new synthetic version of an existing image with a specific change such as as changing a winter scene to a summer one. A large collection of matched examples is often required to train a model for image-to-image translation. CycleGAN is a GAN architecture extension that involves training two generator models and two discriminator models at the same time. The models are trained with a set of photos from the source and target domains that are not connected in any way. The first generator receives photos from the first domain and creates images for the second domain, while the second generator takes photographs from the second domain and generates images for the first domain.

Cycle consistency is a significant extension to the architecture used by the CycleGAN. This is the concept of using an image generated by the first generator as input to the second generator, with the second generator's output matching the original image. The cycle GAN for image-to-image translation uses two generators and two discriminators. Generator 1 and discriminator 1 are used for image translation from domain 1 to domain 2. The generated images are translated back to domain 1 from domain 2 using generator 2 and discriminator 2. CycleGAN is used in season translation images, photograph generation from paintings, etc.

(c) StyleGAN: StyleGAN was introduced by NVIDIA researchers. StyleGAN generates the artificial image in stages, beginning with a low resolution and progressing to a high resolution. It controls the visual features, both coarse and finer in one level, without impacting other levels, by adjusting the input of each level separately.

Conclusion

GAN is a hot area of research and many more awe inspiring results are coming up every now and then.

Questions

1. Give some examples of applications of unsupervised learning.
2. What information we get from latent space representations?
3. Why do we say that autoencoders work on the principle of self supervised learning?
4. How are VAEs different from autoencoders?
5. What is the principle of working of GANs?
6. Can generation be done without the 'adversarial' approach? Elaborate.
7. Why is training of GANs difficult?

Exercise

1. Refer a few research papers on GANs and write about new developments and new applications for GANs
2. Write code to do image generation using a GAN.

Part III

Natural Language Processing (NLP)

CHAPTER

14

Introduction to Natural Language Processing and Text Pre-processing

In this chapter you will

- learn the basic concepts and applications of NLP,
- understand the basic principles of text pre-processing,
- get an exposure to 'regular expressions',
- discover the NLTK and SpaCy libraries for NLP, and
- implement coding examples for pre-processing.

14.0 INTRODUCTION

This is our first chapter on Natural Language Processing which we will henceforth refer to with the acronym NLP. A language is the mode of communication between human beings and also from "man to machine". To communicate with a machine, a 'programming' language is necessary–something that has been taught and learnt formally. But human communication is done by a language that comes 'naturally' to humans. This is why we use the word 'Natural' in this context. NLP principles may be applied to any such natural language–be it English, Hindi, Spanish, Japanese or any of the hundreds of languages available in this world. Each language has its own peculiarities and special features. In that case, 'language specific' processing may be needed. But still, most of the general principles of NLP apply to all languages. In this book, we use the English language as the basis of our theory and practice.

NLP techniques use the semantic and syntactic analysis of data using the methods of computer science and artificial intelligence. By extracting meaningful information from raw data, many real world problems may be automated. Examples are text summarization/simplification, caption generation, speech recognition, machine translation, chatbots, etc.

14.1 SYNTAX AND SEMANTICS

Let us start by saying that applying machine learning principles in the field of NLP is more challenging than other arenas. What seems 'natural' for human beings is typically difficult for machines and vice versa. Handling and understanding natural language is easy for humans but not for machines. This is because of the ambiguities associated with natural language. Contrast it with the field of image and video processing. Images are well defined in terms of intensity and colour values and the process of applying machine language algorithms is very direct. But this is not so in the case of NLP. The use of 'words' which are the features here, is pretty ambiguous in terms of syntax and semantics. We will see some examples of this.

'Syntax' indicates the arrangement of words to form a meaningful sentence. There are a variety of ways for arranging the many possible words to convey some specific information and this itself is a matter of concern for ML algorithms. The 'right syntax' leads to a grammatically correct sentence for a specific language.

Consider the following two sentences:

She was hit by a tennis ball.

A tennis ball hit her.

They convey the same meaning, don't they? The NLP algorithm should be able to identify this point and that is not so easy. In addition, the rules of grammar for one language will be totally different for another language and that will necessitate methods which are 'language specific'.

'Semantics' is another issue. How do we get the meaning of sentences? First there is 'logical semantics' which is associated with the 'sense' of the word. Then comes 'lexical semantics' which deals with word meanings and the relations between words. Some examples will help to clarify this concept. Observe the following sentence:

The market crashed.

The sentence is syntactically correct, but what would you infer from this? It depends on the 'sense' in which 'market' is referred to. It also needs the 'knowledge' of the person involved. It could refer to the stock market. It could refer to the building in which a market is housed. The sense of the sentence is related to the context in which the words are used – this is *logical semantics*.

Lexical semantics is about the exact 'meaning' of the word. See how the word 'point' is used in these three sentences

(i) Your point is clear.
(ii) This pencil has a sharp point.
(iii) She pointed to that window.

In two cases, the word is a noun and in one case, a verb. This difference should be identified by NLP algorithms and the associated meaning of the sentences as well. Getting an NLP algorithm to analyze the different usages of the same word necessitates a lot of background work.

Another problem of asking machines to handle natural language is that, in contrast to humans, they don't have common sense or common knowledge. See these two sentences:

I am working on my computer. Later I will go for a walk.

These two sentences give a lot of information which humans can relate to. Two simple things are that the person is indoors, maybe in the office or at home. The second sentence implies that he will leave his office/home and go outdoors. But the computer does not have the basic 'sense' to understand these kinds of implications. It needs to be told directly or made part of some data base or algorithm to get the machine to make these inferences.

What has been briefly discussed are just a few of the many different kinds of ambiguities that language tasks pose. The whole field of NLP is complicated by additional aspects like dialects, slangs, abbreviations, language mixing and so on.

14.2 APPLICATIONS OF NLP

Natural language processing has become a very important segment of AI. In fact, it is a booming business sector as well. It promises automation in many fields where human effort and intervention was/is mandatory. Let's take a brief tour of its many applications.

14.2.1 Email Applications

All of us have experienced the use of NLP applications in this field though we may not have given a second thought as to how it is done. We see spam filtering, mail classification, priority inbox, extraction of calendar events, auto complete and so on. Recently, we find gmail ready to reply to our emails also (this may seem a bit unnerving, though it is very useful sometimes).

14.2.2 Search Engines

We have all taken for granted, the ways of search engines like Google and Bing. This means that we are unlikely to have given a thought as to how they work and the intelligent algorithms that power them. Search engines are based on the concept of 'Information Retrieval'. Give a word or combination of words and very many documents related to that comes up in view in a short time! It is wonderful and it seems to be improving day by day. Powerful NLP algorithms coupled by deep learning networks are the clue to this. Question answering is a sub-task to this application.

14.2.3 Chatbots

Voice based and text based conversational agents are named Chatbots. Siri, Alexa and, Cortana are some of the well known chatbots of Apple, Amazon and Microsoft respectively. They are general-purpose chatbots. In addition, there are chatbots for specialized fields like library/factory assistants. Such chatbots need to understand language, sort out its inherent ambiguities and give answers. Developing more powerful voice based bots is one of the hot areas of NLP applications and all the big software companies are in competition for this.

14.2.4 Machine Translation

This is again an application area which is wide open for greater accuracies and better results. Already translators are available for many source and destination languages. The task ahead is only to make them better and smarter.

14.2.5 Text to Speech and Speech to Text Conversion

This application involves speech recognition as well as speech synthesis. Currently, the accuracies of such systems are not good enough and the scope for better implementations is wide open.

14.2.6 Sentiment/Text Classification

This application refers to automatically identifying product reviews, mining opinions from text and classifying text based on the topics it deals with. These are important applications which are in use already but which can definitely be improved.

In addition to the applications listed above, many language tasks are getting automated– summarising text, grading essays and answering questions are some of them.

14.3 PYTHON LIBRARIES FOR NLP

NLTK and SpaCy are the two Python libraries of NLP which have the necessary tools for NLP applications. Both have their plusses and minuses–but for a student who is just learning NLP, either of them will suffice. SpaCy is a relatively new library and is continually being updated and thus developers prefer it. In addition it has an 'object oriented approach' which is better than the 'string based' approach of NLTK. In our discussions and resources of the book, both libraries will be used.

14.4 STEPS IN THE NLP PROCESS

Let us get started on using NLP algorithms for the tasks we have just listed. What are these steps?

The first step is data acquisition. This is the task of taking the text data from the source and ensuring that it is in the right format for the software to handle it. Remember that text comes in different forms and formats such as pdf, doc, html, scans, etc. These have to be converted into pure 'text'. For pdf, there are converters, for scanned documents, OCR systems are available, and for HTML documents, removal of HTML scripts is necessary. These steps are not part of the NLP process, but they are 'necessary' before NLP algorithms step in.

'Corpus' is the name given to the collection of documents we use as input to an NLP process (the plural is Corpora). A corpus will contain a number of documents. The 'training' of our application will be done on this corpus. So the corpus that we use should be based on the 'domain' of our application. That means that if we want to classify documents about Indian politics, we cannot train the system on a corpus of ancient Indian epics. There are other implications as well on corpora. Various dialects, age group of the writers/speakers, demographical differences, mixing up of different languages in the same documents – all these factors have to be considered while choosing a corpus for an application. Remember that the performance of supervised ML algorithms depend on the training data and for NLP, it is the corpus on which we do training.

14.4.1 Vocabulary

This word means the list of words in a language. But for NLP applications, we don't use the vocabulary of the entire language–we use the words which belong to our corpus. This set of unique words becomes the vocabulary for our application. In many applications, 'stop words' (Section 14.4.7) are not part of the vocabulary. The remaining unique words are the ones which cater to our application.

14.4.2 Text Pre-Processing

NLP steps start with the splitting up of a corpus into documents.

The corpus has to be made in the form that it is 'machine readable' by the algorithm. It has to be cleaned of unnecessary characters and we should finally get it in the form of words/ sentences which we designate as tokens. To that end, all or some of the following listed steps will have to be done. We call these steps as Text Cleanup /Pre-processing. The steps are:

- Remove spelling mistakes
- Remove scripts like in html, java scripts, tags, etc.
- Remove special characters
- Remove punctuations
- Remove numeric characters
- Remove stop words
- Normalization
    - Convert units to uniform/standard form
    - Take out contractions like isn't, aren't, etc.
    - Case Folding/Lower casing
    - Stemming/Lemmatization
    - Sentence Segmentation
    - Word tokenization

Some of these listed steps are direct and obvious, but some others need explanation.

14.4.3 Normalization

The words that are in the corpus should be in a standard form. One aspect is that the same words should be used for the same thing.

For example, we may be processing data that pertains to dynamics in physics. In the documents, we may find different notations for the same quantity. Speed, for example, may be expressed as miles per hour, kilometres per hour, metres per second, etc. All these are to be normalized to be in the same unit. And again, some quantities are expressed in different ways. In this case itself, 'second' may be written as sec, s, etc. These again have to be brought to the same notation. Such situations arise in different ways for different corpora and sometimes manual intervention may be necessary to sort out the matter.

14.4.4 Take Out Contractions

This is very obvious. Words like aren't, isn't, etc., are to be converted to its uncontracted form of 'are not', 'is not', etc.

14.4.5 Case Folding

Case folding is the step to convert all capital letters to lower case characters. This is not a mandatory step but in many cases it is necessary. Suppose we are talking about cars. The beginning of a sentence may start with 'Car' but in other parts of the text, the word is 'car'. We don't want our NLP algorithm to take both of them as different words, so lower casing is done.

14.4.6 Sentence Segmentation/Tokenization

Sentence Segmentation/Tokenization is the step in which the text is divided into separate sentences. Word tokenization lists out the words in the text.

14.4.7 Stop Word Removal

This is a relevant step for many applications, especially in frequency based methods (Chapter 16). In English sentences, words like 'the, a, is, of', etc., are words that do not add meaning to the text. As such, in many applications, it will be good to remove them as they simply cause the dataset to become large while not adding any additional benefit. In the NLTK and SpaCy libraries, there are a list of words defined as 'stop words'. It may be that sometimes, some of our useful words also seem to be listed as stop words. In that case, we should edit that list or make our own custom list of stop words.

As an example, note this sentence:

Don't buy this product.

Typically 'don't is a stop word. But if the application is one of sentiment analysis (Section 16.5) removing the word converts a negative sentiment to one of positive sentiment. Thus, we should take a look at the standard list of stop words and make alterations to our NLP process accordingly.

14.4.8 Stemming/Lemmatization

These are two ways of getting the root of a word. The root of the words 'better' and 'best' is 'good'.

The words seen, saw, etc., have the root 'see'. 'Standing' and 'stood' are inflected forms of 'stand'. Plurals have to converted to the singular which we take as the 'base' word. Buses, fruits, ships, etc., become bus, fruit, ship, etc. In all these, the inflected/derived word is reduced to its base word.

How is it done?

The simplest way of doing this is named stemming. In this, the end of words are chopped off in the expectation of getting the root word. The method is obviously a bit crude, but the advantage is that it is fast. In this, cars and beds will easily be stemmed to 'car' and 'bed'. But all words don't do well. A word such as 'leaves' is stemmed to 'leave' and 'trembling' to 'trembl'. One stemmer available in NLTK is the Porter Stemmer.

Lemmatization gives better results, but it is a bit more involved and takes more time. This is because it refers to a vocabulary and does morphological analysis of words.to get the dictionary form or 'lemma' of the word. For example, the word 'better' when lemmatized gives 'good' as the result and 'leaves' give 'leaf' as the output of lemmatization.

Let us now see a few examples on the results of text pre-processing.

Example 14.1 Show the results of text pre-processing steps applied to the poem titled as the Original Text.

The original Text

Who has seen the wind?
Neither I nor you:
But when the leaves hang trembling,
The wind is passing through.
Who has seen the wind?
Neither you nor I:
But when the trees bow down their heads,
The wind is passing by.

Results of various pre-processing steps on this poem is shown step by step.

After lower casing:

who has seen the wind?
neither i nor you:
but when the leaves hang trembling,
the wind is passing through.
who has seen the wind?
neither you nor i:
but when the trees bow down their heads,
the wind is passing by.

Removing punctuations and converting to word tokens:

['who', 'has', 'seen', 'the', 'wind', 'neither', 'i', 'nor', 'you', 'but', 'when', 'the', 'leaves', 'hang', 'trembling', 'the', 'wind', 'is', 'passing', 'through', 'who', 'has', 'seen', 'the', 'wind', 'neither', 'you', 'nor', 'i', 'but', 'when', 'the', 'trees', 'bow', 'down', 'their', 'heads', 'the', 'wind', 'is', 'passing', 'by']

After removing stop words :

['seen', 'wind', 'neither', 'leaves', 'hang', 'trembling', 'wind', 'passing', 'seen', 'wind', 'neither', 'trees', 'bow', 'heads', 'wind', 'passing']

After stemming :

['seen', 'wind', 'neither', 'leav', 'hang', 'trembl', 'wind', 'pass', 'seen', 'wind', 'neither', 'tree', 'bow', 'head', 'wind', 'pass']

After lemmatization:

['seen', 'wind', 'neither', 'leaf', 'hang', 'trembling', 'wind', 'passing', 'seen', 'wind', 'neither', 'tree', 'bow', 'head', 'wind', 'passing']

Note: For an application, we use either Stemming or Lemmatizing—not both. Here, both are done just to show the differences. The results are different in the case of a few words only. See Table 14.1 (below)

Original word	*Stemmed word*	*Lemmatized word*
leaves	leav	leaf
trembling	trembl	trembling
passing	pass	passing

Example 14.2 Show the results of text pre-processing on this document which contains numerics, upper case sentences and special characters.

Original Text

STEP 1: FIND A BASE PRICE BY GETTING TO KNOW COMMON PRICING STRATEGIES IN YOUR INDUSTRY

Thousands of entrepreneurs and decades of learning have paved the way for new businesses to craft a strategy that utilizes the most innovative pricing options available.

Knowing which pricing models work best in your industry can simplify how you price a product, and give you confidence knowing that you're not simply guessing.

COST-BASED PRICING

One of the most simple ways to price your product is called cost-based pricing.

Cost-based pricing involves calculating the total costs it takes to make your product, then adding a percentage markup to determine the final price.

For example, let's say you've designed a product with the following costs:

- Material cost = ₹2000
- Labour cost = ₹1000
- Overhead = ₹800
- Total cost = ₹3800

You then add your markup percentage, let's say 50% (retail industry standard), to the total costs to give you a final product price of ₹57.00 (₹38 × 1.50). If you remember our "Charm Pricing" tactic from the beginning, you might mark this product at ₹57.99.

This method is simple, fast, and lets you quickly add a profit margin to any product you intend to sell.

Solution: Note that the original text has upper case characters, numbers, punctuations, special characters, stop words, etc.

Suppose you want the tokens alone after 'lower casing' and removing all the above, we get the final tokens as below, after Lemmatizing.

['step', 'find', 'base', 'price', 'getting', 'know', 'common', 'pricing', 'strategies', 'industry', 'thousands', 'entrepreneurs', 'decades', 'learning', 'paved', 'way', 'new', 'businesses', 'craft', 'strategy', 'utilizes', 'innovative', 'pricing', 'options', 'available', 'knowing', 'pricing', 'models', 'work', 'best', 'industry', 'simplify', 'price', 'product', 'give', 'confidence', 'knowing', 'simply', 'guessing', 'cost', 'based', 'pricing', 'one', 'simple', 'ways', 'price', 'product', 'called', 'cost', 'plus', 'pricing', 'cost', 'based', 'pricing', 'involves', 'calculating', 'total', 'costs', 'takes', 'make', 'product', 'adding', 'percentage', 'markup', 'determine', 'final', 'price', 'example', 'let', 'say', 'designed', 'product', 'following', 'costs', 'material', 'costs', 'rs', 'labour', 'costs', 'rs', 'overhead', 'rs', 'total', 'costs', 'rs', 'add', 'markup', 'percentage', 'let', 'say', 'retail', 'industry', 'standard', 'total', 'costs', 'give', 'final', 'product', 'price', 'x', 'remember', 'charm', 'pricing', 'tactic', 'beginning', 'might', 'mark', 'product', 'method', 'simple', 'fast', 'lets', 'quickly', 'add', 'profit', 'margin', 'product', 'intend', 'sell']

With these steps, we get the list of all the useful words (tokens) and these tokens are the ones that we will use for our NLP algorithms.

14.5 REGULAR EXPRESSIONS

This is part of all programming languages but is very useful in NLP and is included in NLP libraries. Regular Expressions (Regex) is a tool to search a string and find out if a substring is present therein. We can use it to extract email ids, telephone numbers, hashtags, special characters, etc., from a large text. It is, in essence, a pattern extractor and its fundamental method is pattern matching. It checks the bigger string for the pattern corresponding to the substring. It cannot only find the substrings, but can also replace/delete these substrings. There are many more operations that are possible with Regex. In Python, there is a built-in module named 're' to use Regular Expressions.

A few examples of its use are shown in Example 14.3

Example 14.3 This example lists the use of a few cases of Regex as used in the NLTK library.

```
1. Find a word in text
import re
alljobs = re.findall('ashwin','ashwin was looking for the other ashwin.')
for i in alljobs:
  print(i)
```

Output:

ashwin

ashwin

::

```
2. Getting the starting and ending index of a string
import re
alljobs = 'jobs was looking for jobs.'
for i in re.finditer('jobs',alljobs):
 loctup = i.span() #tuple with starting and ending index of the matched string
 print(loctup)
```

Output:

(0, 4)

(21, 25)

::

```
3. Replace a string
import re
str = 'name,fame,shame,lame,tame'
regex = re.compile("[l]ame")
str = regex.sub("blame",str) # replace'lame' by 'blame'
print(str)
```

Output:

name, fame, shame, blame, tame

matches: 4

::

```
4. backslash prob
import re
str = "my name is \\saurabh"
print(re.search(r'\\saurabh',str))
```

Output:

<re.Match object; span=(11, 19), match='\\saurabh'

::

Note: Use the NLTK/SpaCy manuals to get all the Regex features embedded in them.

Conclusion

This chapter is meant to be a very gentle introduction to the first steps in NLP. Advanced techniques will be gradually introduced in the forthcoming chapters.

Questions

1. Differentiate between the terms 'syntax' and semantics for natural language.
2. Mention some of the ambiguities that 'natural language ' poses that makes it difficult for computers to handle it.
3. Visualize and list out some of the problems that have to be tackled in speech-to-text conversion.
4. What is meant by saying that the 'corpus must be domain specific'?
5. For an NLP application, what is considered as the vocabulary?
6. How is Lemmatization different from stemming?
7. What is meant by 'Regex'? Give two examples which are not covered in the chapter.

Exercise

1. Show the results of text pre-processing on:
   (a) A popular song/poetry of at least 8 lines
   (b) A paragraph which contains alphanumeric characters
   (c) An html document

   Show the code used and the results of each stage of pre-processing.
2. Try pre-processing on this text and show the results. Remember that you cannot afford to lose the information in the text.

   A 5.4 kg bird is ready to fly. It starts from rest and after one step is airborne. After 3.0 s of flying horizontally, it reaches a height of 5.0 m. Can its velocity in m/sec be calculated with this data?

   (i) Did you have to use manual intervention?
   (ii) What are the text processing steps that you used?

   Find out how numerical quantities are retained and taken care of in text pre-processing.

CHAPTER

15

Statistical Language Models

In this chapter you will

- learn the *N* gram statistical model,
- understand language modeling,
- evaluate Language models using perplexity,
- decide how to handle words out of the vocabulary,
- identify Parts of Speech in English,
- implement POS tagging and NER,
- study the use of hidden Markov models, and
- analyze the Viterbi algorithm for POS tagging.

15.0 INTRODUCTION

Building Language models is a very important task in NLP. A language model is one that predicts the next word or phrase in an application. In Chapter 14, we discussed why NLP is challenging. The main point is the ambiguity involved. What are the words that will complete a sentence? It is not possible to know this with certainty. We can only make some probabilistic assumptions. This is the basis of the task of building language models. Language models predict the probability of a word or sequence of words. All models ultimately depend on the corpus on which the system has been trained with. The right set of words can only be obtained from the corpus of the right domain. That is to say that we can't expect to use a corpus of documents which discusses movies, to obtain words for a language model for use in medical transcription.

15.1 APPLICATIONS

Let's list out some applications of Language models—some of which we are familiar with.

(i) Auto completion and Spelling Correction

This is a very familiar case. How does the system know the word that can complete the sentences we start typing? The system does a probabilistic analysis of the possible words. Spelling correction is also done this way.

(ii) Smart Compose/Reply

This is something that we have seen in Gmail and it is a language model that handles this.

(iii) Speech Recognition and Speech to Text converters

In a Speech to Text converter when there is lack of clarity of the speech, a language model has to do some 'guesses' to fill in these words. So also in the case of chatbots which have to recognise the instructions/questions asked of it. Voice based assistants like Siri, Alexa, Cortana, etc., have language models built into them.

(iv) Machine Translation: When a sentence in one language is translated into another, the system has to refer to a language model to make sure of the output sentences. The language model simply chooses the sequence of words which have the highest probability of being correct.

For example, there is an ambiguity between these two translated sequence of words:

I. this is my right hand

II. right hand my this is

The language model must be able to confirm that the probability of the first sequence is higher than that of the second. That is, it has to confirm the following probability:

P(this is my right hand)>P(right hand my this is)

15.1.1 Types of Language Models

A basic subdivision may be as follows.

(i) Statistical Language Models

These are based on well known probabilistic techniques of statistics. This is the language model that we cover in this chapter. N grams and Parts of Speech Tagging based on Hidden Markov models are covered here.

(ii) Neural Language Models

Deep learning techniques are used widely in all AI applications and NLP is no exception. It has been demonstrated that better language models may be built by deep learning. More flexibility and better detection of long-term dependencies are the features of such models. Such deep learning networks are covered in Chapter 18.

15.2 THE N GRAM MODEL

Let us start with the *n* gram model. This is probably one of the simplest cases of language modeling. A probability distribution for a sequence of length '*n*' is the basis of this method.

An 'n gram' is just a set of n words/characters. Here, let us focus on '**word**' n grams alone. A word n-gram is a sequence of n words.

- Andhra Pradesh (is a 2-gram)
- The three idiots (is a 3-gram)
- She looked up sadly (is a 4-gram)

15.2.1 The Unigram

If $n = 1$, we get a Unigram. With $n = 2$, 3, and 4, we get the Bigram, Trigram and 4-gram respectively.

First we take up the use of a Unigram.

Example 15.1 *Betty Botter bought some butter,*
But she said the butter is bitter

What is the unigram probability of the sentence?

Solution: Since it is based on Unigrams, we don't need to mark the start and end of the sentence as in the case of other n grams (Section 15.2.3), since each word is independent and does not depend on the order of the words. We notice that it contains 12 words in it with the word butter occurring twice. So, the unigram probability for the word butter is $\frac{2}{12}$ and for each of the other words is $\frac{1}{12}$. So, the probability of the sentence would be

$P = P(Betty) * P(Botter) * P(bought) * P(some) * P(butter) * P(but) * P(she) * P(said) * P(the) * P(is) * P(bitter)$

$$= \frac{1}{12} * \frac{1}{12} * \frac{1}{12} * \frac{1}{12} * \frac{2}{12} * \frac{1}{12} * \frac{1}{12} * \frac{1}{12} * \frac{1}{12} * \frac{1}{12} * \frac{1}{12}$$

$$= 2.6917\text{e-}12$$

In speech recognition, it is quite possible that some words are inaudible or not clear. In that case, the 'language model' should fill in the words based on some criteria. The method is to fill the blank space with the word which has the highest probability as obtained from the corpus.

For this corpus, the probability of every word except 'butter', is $\frac{1}{12}$. The word 'butter' occurs twice and as such, has a probability of $\frac{2}{12}$. So if there is any necessity to fill in a blank space, the highest probability word of the corpus will be chosen and that is 'butter'.

For example, if the test sentence is

She bought some ___.

This will be filled up as

She bought some ***butter.***

But this sort of a choice seems quite illogical because the ordering of the words is not taken into consideration. It is obvious that the word 'butter' is correct in the case shown above, but will be a wrong choice in many other instances. Unigrams consider each word to be independent which means that the spatial ordering is not taken into consideration in the target sentence of the application. Obviously, this is not a good language model. We will now check the cases of n grams with $n > 1$.

We know intuitively that the choice of a next word always depends on the previous word/words. With the above examples, a basic idea of the concept of n gram models has been presented. Before we consider the use of the n gram model, it will be logical to introduce the laws of conditional probability. Let's put it all into a mathematical framework based on the chain rule of probability.

15.2.2 The Chain Rule of Probability

Recall the rule of conditional probabilities which is as follows, for two variables.

$$P(AB) = P(A)P(B/A) = P(B)P(A/B) \quad ...(15.1)$$

The chain rule for n variables is

$$P(X_1 \ldots\ldots X_n) = P(X_1)P(X_2/X_1)P(X_3/X_{1:2}) \ldots\ldots P(X_n/X_{1:n-1}) \quad ...(15.2)$$

$$= \prod_{k=1}^{n} P(X_k/X_{1:k-1}) \quad ...(15.3)$$

How does this rule help us?

Since the n gram word model is one based on the conditional probability of one or a set of previous words occurring, this rule may be directly applied as:

$$P(w_{1:n}) = P(w_1)P(w_2/w_1)P(w_3/w_{1:2}) \ldots \ldots \ldots P(w_n/w_{1:n-1}) \quad ...(15.4)$$

$$= \prod_{k=1}^{n} P(w_k/w_{1:k-1}) \quad ...(15.5)$$

where w_1 is the first word and w_n the last word of the sentence we are dealing with. $w_{1:n}$ means the first n words. Similarly, $w_{1:n-1}$ indicates the first $n-1$ words.

Directly applying the chain rule on the sentence 'I am waiting for my bus', we get:

P(I am waiting for my bus) =

$$P(I)P(am/I) * P(waiting/I\ am) * P(for/(I\ am\ waiting) *$$

$$P(my/(I\ am\ waiting\ for) * P(bus/(I\ am\ waiting\ for\ my)$$

In this equation, the probability of a sentence depends on Unigrams, Bigrams, Trigrams, Four grams and Five grams. But in general, applications of the n gram model chooses a fixed value of N. As we go ahead, this will be clear.

Example 15.2 See this paragraph:

"Life is a game of waiting. All of us have spent time waiting for some or other things. In my younger days, it was the case of waiting for my bus, waiting for my exams, waiting for my results, waiting for my friends and so on. As I grew older, I realized that I am doing just the

same as I have to wait for my boss in office or for my time to go back home after a tiring day. Earlier it was the case of waiting for my wife. Now I spend time waiting for my son when I have to pick him up from school. Waiting for my results–which is of the sales work I do is also stressful. Also, my type of work is travel based, and so I have to spend time waiting for my bus, waiting for my flight and waiting for my train. Life is such a game and I have no other option. But I think that waiting for my bus is my most regular activity these days."

Using the above paragraph as the corpus, let us try completing the following incomplete sentence.

I am waiting for my _____.

The single word that will complete this sentence is based on the above corpus and has many possibilities, some of which are friends, exams, wife, son, daughter, results, bus, train, flight, etc. So how does the language model choose the apt word? The choice is made on the basis of which word has the highest probability to fit in properly here, and that is obtained by analysing the corpus used for training.

The *n* gram language model checks the combination of the '*n*' previous words. The sentence that needs to be completed is '*I am waiting for my* ___'. Let's take the three previous words which are '*waiting for my*'. We see that there are many such word combinations in the corpus.

The question to ask is – What is the probability of a word in the corpus given that the previous three words are '*waiting for my*'. To answer this, we simply look at the corpus and find the 'count' of the joint occurrences of the words specified. For example, to consider whether 'wife' is the right word, compute the following probability.

$$P(wife/\ waiting\ for\ my) = Count\ (\ waiting\ for\ my\ wife\ /waiting\ for\ my) = \frac{1}{12}$$

This may be explained thus: Find how many times the word combination "*waiting for my wife*" occurs. Also count the occurrence of the word combination "*waiting for my*". Divide the first count by the second, This is the required probability. The same computation is to be done for other probable words. Some other probabilities are:

$$P(son/waiting\ for\ my) = Count\ (waiting\ for\ my\ son/waiting\ for\ my) = \frac{1}{12}$$

$$P(bus/waiting\ for\ my) = Count\ (waiting\ for\ my\ bus/waiting\ for\ my) = \frac{3}{12}$$

$$P\ (results/waiting\ for\ my) = Count\ (waiting\ for\ my\ results/waiting\ for\ my) = \frac{2}{12}$$

Similar calculations are done for all other possible words like train, flight, exams and friends. Which of these conditional probabilities is the highest? The word corresponding to that is our chosen word to fill the blank space in the sentence. This is a 'Maximum Likelihood Estimation (MLE)' method. Referring to our corpus, the highest probability corresponds to the word 'bus' and so our test sentence is completed as:

I am waiting for my ***bus***.

In this example, one 'next' word and three previous words are involved in the decision making process. Since totally 4 words are involved, this is called a 4-gram model. If only the previous two words are used (totally three words), then it is a Trigram model. With just one previous word, it is the Bigram model as totally two words are used to make a decision.

In general, we use the term 'n gram model' when we refer to the case of using the previous $n - 1$ words. That means we truncate the history (that we use) to the previous $n - 1$ words.

The conditional probability '$P(w_n/w_{1:n-1}$' is the conditional probability of the nth word, given the joint probability of the previous $n - 1$ words. For trigrams and bigrams, this reduces to:

$$P(w_n/w_{n-1}) \quad \text{//just the previous word for bigram} \qquad ...(15.6)$$

$$P(w_n/w_{n-2}, w_{n-1}) \quad \text{//two previous words for trigram} \qquad ...(15.7)$$

How are these probabilities obtained? Taking counts of word sequences, as in Example 15.2 is the method.

$$P(w_3/w_1, w_2) = \frac{C(w_{1;2}, w_3)}{C(w_{1;2})} \qquad ...(15.8a)$$

$$= \frac{C(w_1, w_2, w_3)}{C(w_1, w_2)} \qquad ...(15.8b)$$

For a trigram, Eq. 15.8 makes it clear where C stands for 'count of occurrence'. The numerator and denominators indicate 'joint occurrence' of three and two words respectively.

For the general case of a Maximum Likelihood Estimate (MLE) n gram model,

$$P(w_n/w_{n-N+1:n-1}) = \frac{C(w_{n-N+1:n-1}, w_n)}{C(w_{n-N+1:n-1})} \qquad ...(15.9)$$

In Example 15.2, if we decide to use the trigram model (instead of the 4 gram model), we need to compute some of the following probabilities. The count in the denominator is only for the two-word sequence 'for my'.

P(wife/ for my) = Count (for my wife / for my)

P(bus/ for my) = Count (for my bus / for my)

P(time / for my) = Count (for my time / for my) and so on.

This may be better, because the counts of the combinations of the two words "*for my*" may be higher than '*waiting for my*' (as used in Example 15.2).

Things are much easier when using bigrams because only one previous word is involved. For predicting 'wife' as the next word, we can use *P(wife/my) = Count (my wife/my)*.

Similar counts will be computed for other target words.

Now let us go onto more details of the concept of the n gram model. Higher and lower order n gram models have strengths and weaknesses. High order n grams have more sensitivity to the context and will give better results, but the counts obtained will be sparse. For lower order n grams, the counts are more, but they consider only a limited context and hence their performance is not as good. We can definitely say that trigrams are better than bigrams, Four grams are better than trigrams and so on. But beyond four grams, it is very difficult to get a sufficient count of the required 'combination of words'.

15.2.3 Bigrams

In Section 15.2, we concluded that unigrams is not a logical option for language models. Let us consider the next best option–that is, a bigram model in which only one previous word is taken into account. The idea that looking far into the past is unnecessary is named the Markov assumption (Section 15.3.3)

$$P(w_n / w_{n-1}) = \frac{C(w_{n-1}, w_n)}{C(w_{n-1})} \quad ...(15.10)$$

If $n = 2$

$$P(w_2 / w_1) = \frac{C(w_1, w_2)}{C(w_1)} \quad ...(15.11)$$

Let's do the bigram analysis of the following three sentences.

Corpus 2

- *I am a teacher.*
- *Any teacher loves to teach.*
- *A teacher has also to learn before he can teach.*

As part of pre-processing, let's do the lower casing of these sentences. We also insert the start of document symbol <s> and the end of document symbol </s>. We get:

<s>i am a teacher</s>

<s>any teacher loves to teach</s>

<s> a teacher has also to learn before he can teach</s>

To extract the **bigrams, we should visualize a window that covers two words each time and moves along the text.** We get, for the first sentence:

<s> i

i am

am a

a teacher

teacher </s>

A similar bigram extraction must be done for the other sentences also. Calculating, some bigram probabilities,

- *P(i/<s>) =C(<s>,i)/C(<s>)=1/3*

In this, the denominator indicates the number of times <s>occurs in the corpus. The numerator expresses the number of times 'i' occurs after <s>. The rest of the probabilities are calculated in a similar manner.

- *P(am/i)=1/1*
- *P(a/am)=1*
- *P(teacher/a)=2/2*
- *P(</s>/teacher)=1/3*
- *P(any/<s>) =1/3*
- *P (teach/to)=1/2*

In many cases, when the test sentence/sentences has words which are not in the order of the words of the bigrams of the training set, the probability of some bigrams becomes zero causing the complete calculation to become zero. To get around this problem, Laplace smoothing is done using the formula (Section 4.2.2.1)

$$P\left(\frac{N_r}{N_d}\right) = \frac{(N_r + 1)}{N_d + V} \qquad ...(15.12)$$

This simply means that for each computation of the probability, add 1 to the numerator (N_r), and V to the denominator (N_d). V is the size of the vocabulary, that is, the number of unique terms in the training set. Let us use this methodology for our next example.

Example 15.3 Using Corpus 2 as the training set, calculate the probability of the following sentence.

Any teacher has to learn to teach.

Solution: Pre-processing gives us:

<s> any teacher has to learn to teach </s>

The calculation of the probability is:

P(any/<s>) × P(teacher/any) × P (has/teacher) × P(to/has) × P(learn/to) × P(to/learn) × P(teach/to) × P(</s>/teach)

Calculating the probabilities directly gives us:

- *P(any/<s>) =1/3 = 0.333*
- *P(teacher/any) = 1/1 = 1*
- *P(has/teacher) =1/3*
- ***P(to/has) = 0***
- *P(learn/to)=1/2 = 0.5*
- ***P(to/learn) = 0***
- *P (teach/to)=1/2 =0.5*
- *P(</s>/teach)=2/2 = 1*

Two of the probabilities are 0. We will use the Laplace smoothing technique.

The unique words and their frequency is listed in Table 15.1.

Table 15.1 Word frequencies of Corpus 2

WORD	FREQUENCY
<S>	3
</S>	3
i	1
am	1
a	2
teacher	3
any	1
loves	1
to	2
teach	2
has	1
also	1
learn	1
before	1
he	1
can	1

The number of unique words is 16 as in Table 15.1, but since the end of sentence symbol </s> never comes in the denominator of a bigram calculation, we will not take it as a unique word. Thus, the size of the vocabulary is taken as 15 and the probability calculations are as shown below.

$$P(any/<s>) = \frac{1 + 1}{3 + 15} = \frac{2}{18} = 0.11$$

$$P(teacher/any) = \frac{1 + 1}{1 + 15} = \frac{2}{16} = 0.125$$

$$P(has/teacher) = \frac{1 + 1}{3 + 15} = \frac{1}{18} = 0.12$$

$$P(to/has) = \frac{0 + 1}{1 + 15} = \frac{1}{16} = 0.0625$$

$$P(learn/to) = \frac{1 + 1}{2 + 15} = \frac{2}{17} = 0.117$$

$$P(to/learn) = \frac{0 + 1}{1 + 15} = \frac{1}{6} = 0.0625$$

$$P(teach\ to) = \frac{1 + 1}{2 + 15} = \frac{2}{17} = 0.117$$

$$P(</s>teach) = \frac{2 + 1}{2 + 15} = \frac{3}{17} = 0.176$$

Hence, P(sentence) = 0.11 × 0.125 × 0.12 × 0.0625 × 0.117 × 0.625 × 0.117 × 0.176

$= 14.23 \times 10^{-9}$

In calculations involving the product of probabilities, the final product becomes quite small leading to an underflow error. To avoid this, converting to logarithms is the method adopted. This will be discussed in Section 16.5.1.

Note: For this example, the zero probabilities are not because there are 'unknown' words. The case of unknown words is discussed in Section 15.2.4.2.

15.2.4 Evaluation of a Language Model

There should a quantitative measure to evaluate language models. One method is called extrinsic evaluation. This is done on the application for which the model is used. For example, if the model has 'machine translation' as the application, the model is evaluated after the application is developed. This sort of an evaluation is fraught with risks because it may become too late to correct the model if its performance is not up to the mark. Also, one has to wait until the application is developed.

Having an evaluation done at an early stage, based on just the developed language model is a better alternative. This method is called intrinsic evaluation. In this, a measure called perplexity is defined. As the word indicates, perplexity measures how 'puzzled/confused' the model is. If the model is very sure of its correctness, its perplexity is low. So let us now take a look at the concept of 'perplexity'.

What are the characteristics of a good language model?

- The model should attribute high probabilities in the case of sentences with the right syntax while assigning low probabilities to those sentences which are grammatically wrong. Semantically wrong and infrequent sentences (as based on the corpus)should also have low probabilities. For example:

  "I am on my way to school" should be a better model than **"I is way to school."**

  "The cat plays on the mat" should be a more probable outcome of the language modeling than "**the mat and cat plays**."
- A test set which has high probability simply means that the model is not puzzled or confused. The perplexity is low for this case and that is because of its good understanding of the working of the language.
- In order to have a metric that is not dependent of the size of the dataset, the probability of the test data is divided by the total number of words. This leads to a per word measure.

For a unigram model, The probability of the test set is

$$P(W) = P(w_1, w_2, \ldots, w_N) = P(w_1)P(w_2) \ldots P(w_N) = \prod_{i=1}^{N} P(w_i) \qquad \ldots(15.13)$$

Taking the natural logarithm of both sides gives

$$\ln(P(W)) = \ln\left(\prod_{i=1}^{N} P(w_i)\right) = \sum_{i=1}^{N} \ln P(w_i) \quad ...(15.14)$$

To obtain the **per-word log probability,** we can now normalize this by dividing by N, and then remove the log by exponentiating: (N is the number of tokens in the test set).

$$\frac{\ln(P(W))}{N} = \frac{\sum_{i=1}^{N} \ln P(w_i)}{N} \quad ...(15.15)$$

$$e^{\frac{\ln P(W)}{N}} = e^{\frac{\sum_{i=1}^{N} \ln P(w_i)}{N}} \quad ...(15.16)$$

$$\left(e^{\ln(P(W))}\right)^{\frac{1}{N}} = \left(e^{\sum_{i=1}^{N} \ln P(w_i)}\right)^{\frac{1}{N}} \quad ...(15.17)$$

$$P(W)^{\frac{1}{N}} = \left(\prod_{i=1}^{N} P(w_i)\right)^{\frac{1}{N}} \quad ...(15.18)$$

The inverse probability of the test set is now defined as its **Perplexity**

$$PP(W) = \frac{1}{P(w_1, w_2, \ldots, w_N)^{\frac{1}{N}}} \quad ...(15.19)$$

$$= \sqrt[N]{\frac{1}{P(w_1, w_2, \ldots, w_N)}} \quad ...(15.20)$$

We obtained normalization by taking the Nth root (N is the number of tokens in the set). Since we take the inverse probability, a lower perplexity indicates a better model.

For an '*n*' gram model, the perplexity would be as follows (by using the chain rule)

$$PP(W) = \sqrt[N]{\prod_{i=1}^{N} \frac{1}{P(w_i \mid w_1, \ldots, w_{i=1})}} \quad ...(15.21)$$

For a bigram, where only one previous word is considered,

$$PP(W) = \sqrt[N]{\prod_{i=1}^{N} \frac{1}{P(w_i \mid w_{i-1})}} \quad ...(15.22)$$

N is the count of all tokens in our test set, including SOS/ EOS and punctuation. SOS stands for 'Start of Sentence' and EOS for 'End of Sentence'. In Example 15.3, $N = 16$. To calculate the perplexity of a single sentence, W would simply be considered that one sentence.

Example 15.4 Calculation of perplexity using Corpus 2.

Take:

(i) Unigram, and (ii) bigram assumptions.

Test sentence:

Any teacher has to learn to teach.

Solution: For a unigram, all the tokens in the training set have to be considered. There are 25 tokens including <s.> and </s>.

Unigram:

<s> any teacher has to learn to teach </s>

Unigram probability = P_u

$$= \text{P(<s>).P(any).P(teacher).P(has).P(to).P(learn).P(to).P(teach).P(</s>)}$$

$$= \frac{3}{25} \times \frac{1}{25} \times \frac{3}{25} \times \frac{1}{25} \times \frac{2}{25} \times \frac{1}{25} \times \frac{2}{25} \times \frac{2}{25} \times \frac{3}{25}$$

$$= \frac{216}{3814697265625} = 5.66 \times 10^{-11}$$

$$\text{Perplexity} = \sqrt[9]{\frac{1}{P_u}} = \sqrt[9]{\frac{1}{5.66 \times 10^{-11}}} = 13.7362$$

Bigrams:

The probability of the test sentence was calculated in Example 15.3

The perplexity is calculated as follows:

Bigram:

Bigram probability = *P(sentence)* = 14.23×10^{-9}

N = 8 as there are 8 bigrams.

$$\text{Perplexity} = \sqrt[8]{\frac{1}{P_{sen}}} = \sqrt[8]{\frac{1}{14.23 \times 10^{-9}}} = \mathbf{9.5868}$$

The perplexity of higher gram models is less, but to make better sense of it, large corpora should be used. Our corpus is only three sentences. For the WSJ (Wall Street Journal) corpus, with a training set of 38 million words and test set of 1.5 million test words, the perplexity for different N grams are as in Table 15.2.

Table 15.2 Perplexity for the WSJ corpus

N-gram order	*Perplexity*
Unigram	962
Bigram	170
Trigram	109

15.2.4.1 Perplexity and Branching Factor

How do we say that a language model is perplexed? The model tries to guess (logically and using quantitative measures), the next word in a sentence. If there are many possibilities for this next word, the model will have to do more hard work to get the correct word. We use the word 'branching factor' for the options. When the branching factor is higher, the perplexity is more. Consider the following incomplete sentence:

My name is ____.

If the problem is to fill the blank space in the sentence given above, and there are hundreds of words in the corpus which may be the possible word, naturally the model is highly perplexed.

Another case is to complete the phrase '*Bangalore* ___'. The corpus gives options of '*city, suburbs, days, mayor*'. The branching factor is lower and the perplexity is lower.

15.2.4.2 Out-of-vocabulary Words

For applications like Speech Recognition and Machine language, the words in the vocabulary are usually fixed –so there is no question of having to deal with what are called 'Out of Vocabulary (OOV) words'. Such systems are examples of closed vocabulary systems.

But there can be open vocabulary systems in which we expect 'never before seen' words which are called unknown words. This can happen when the test sentence contains a word which is not in the training corpus. In the case of applications like 'search', a user is likely to enter some word which is not in the vocabulary defined by the search algorithm. In both these cases, the 'zero probability' of this word hinders the working of the model.

One way to deal with this is to convert the system into a closed vocabulary system by notating these words with an 'UNK' symbol. By adding such a symbol, what will we have in our defined closed vocabulary? We will then have a number of known words and also a set of UNK symbols. In many cases, words with low frequencies of occurrence in the corpus are also designated as UNK. This ensures that the probability assigned to the UNK symbol is not too low.

Example 15.5 Consider the training set to be:

Jack and Jill went up the hill

To fetch a pail of water.

Jack fell down and broke his crown

And Jill came tumbling after.

How is the unknown word handled in the following test sentence?

Jack and Jim went to fetch a pail of water.

Solution: Since 'Jim' is a hitherto unseen word, normally its probability is rated as zero and thus the probability of the whole sentence becomes zero. If instead, there is the UNK notation for any unknown word, there will be a non-zero probability for the UNK symbol and hence for the whole sentence.

The test sentence is rewritten as:

Jack and <UNK> went to fetch a pail of water.

Example 15.6 Training set:

- *I went home.*
- *Daddy and grandpa also went home.*
- *Mummy, daddy, grandpa, maid and I are home.*

Solution: Let us take the decision that words with counts less than 2 are to be replaced by the UNK symbol. Then the vocabulary and training data is changed as follows:

Training Set:

I went home.

Daddy and grandpa went home.

<UNK>,daddy, grandpa,<UNK> and I <UNK>home

Vocabulary : *I, went, home, Daddy, grandpa, and, <UNK>*

A test sentence:

Avantika went home.

This is modified as:

<UNK> went home.

The above example is meant just to show the way OOV words may be coded in a vocabulary. In practice, it is necessary that the number of UNK symbols be kept low to avoid degeneration of the efficiency of the language model.

We have covered a lot of space regarding 'Language models'. We will now move on to the next important topic.

15.3 PARTS OF SPEECH TAGGING

Now let us move to a new but related topic named 'Part of Speech'. In any language, each word will be one of the many 'Parts of Speech", to give the exact meaning of the sentence in which it is used. In man-to-man communication, this is not a difficult task because of the implicit knowledge of language possessed by us. But making machines understand this involves a bit of effort.

But let us first understand what is meant by the term "Parts of Speech". In a sentence, each word has a particular role to play. One word acts as a noun, another as a verb, another as a preposition and so on. In many cases, the same word may have different roles to play in different contexts. In the following two sentences, the word 'point' is used as a noun in the first, and as a 'verb' in the second.

*I note your **point**.*

*Please **point** to the correct answer.*

In each of these two sentences, there are other words too which have parts of speech (POS) 'tags' such as verb, proposition, etc.

In many NLP applications, it may be necessary to know and identify the role and function of each word within the structure of the sentence. The methods for doing that involves some knowledge of the linguistic properties of the language. When computers do this, probabilistic algorithms are involved. But some basic knowledge of the linguistics of the language is required and let us start on that note.

15.3.1 'Parts of Speech' in English

In English, the fundamental parts of speech are nine in number. They are listed as:

- Noun
- Pronoun
- Verb
- Adjective
- Adverb
- Article/Determiner
- Preposition
- Conjunction
- Interjection

Let us understand each of them in some detail.

Noun: As we all know, a noun is used to name a person, place, name, thing or concept. A noun may be classified as a proper noun or common noun. A proper noun is a unique identifier. Common nouns are general names and they can again be subdivided as concrete nouns, abstract nouns and collective nouns. Table 15.3 makes all this clear.

Table 15.3 Examples of different kinds of nouns

Proper nouns	*Common Nouns*		
	Abstract Nouns	*Concrete Nouns*	*Collective Nouns*
India	courage	book	heap (of books)
Deepak	love	pen	pack (of lions)
Ganga	ability	table	swarm (of ants)

Pronoun: This is a word used in place of a noun when the listener (or reader) knows who or what the pronoun refers to. For example,

Anusha is my friend. She is a very intelligent girl.

The word 'she' is a pronoun used in place of the proper noun 'Anusha'.

Other pronouns are he, it, they, I, me, her, him and so on.

Verb: A verb expresses an action which may be in the present, past or future.

She runs. He walked. I will bring.

These are sentences with verbs in the present, past and future tenses.

Adjective: An adjective qualifies or describes a noun.

Examples are: **beautiful** dress, **black** car, **deep** knowledge, **intense** longing, etc.

Adverb: An adverb describes an action. Examples are:

He runs **fast**.

She is sitting **quietly**.

Article/Determiner

Words such as 'a, the, an' are called articles/determiners.

Preposition: They are used to connect and thus specify the relationship between words.

I kept the book on the table.

She is in a bad mood.

The words 'on' and 'in' are prepositions.

Conjunction: They 'join' multiple words or phrases or sentences.

Examples: 'and', 'but'

I like bread **and** butter, **but** dosha **and** chutney are my favourite breakfast items.

Interjection: It is a word used to express a strong emotion and is usually followed by an exclamation mark.

Wow! Oh! Alas! Ah!

Parts of Speech (POS) may be classified as closed or open. Functional words like prepositions and conjunctions are unlikely to be added newly and they are said to be 'closed class'. An open class is one in which new words may be added. For example, new nouns and verbs may be added to the language – examples are hard disk, pen drive, Lol, Instagram, etc. Adjectives, adverbs and interjections are also open class.

15.3.2 POS Tagging

What we have covered is just the fundamental concepts of what 'POS' means to us. If we go deeper, we will find subclasses for each POS. In NLP applications, where machines are made to identify parts of speech, there should be a library of well defined names for each 'part of speech'. These names are called 'tags'. The method of associating a word to its part of speech is called POS tagging. Figure 15.1 defines 'POS tagging' as a mapping of the words $w_1 \ldots\ldots\ldots w_5$ to its corresponding POS tags T1 to T5.

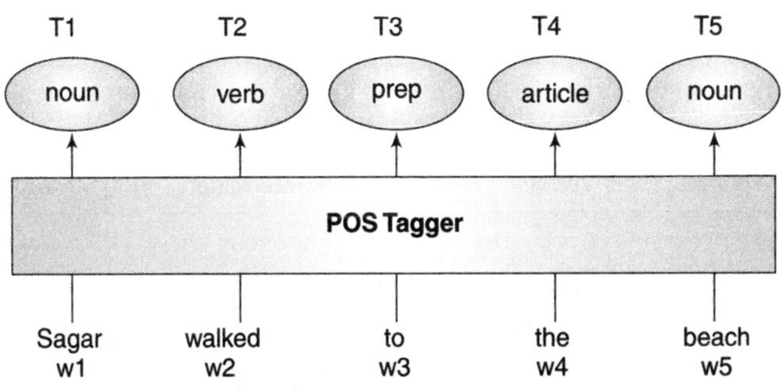

Fig. 15.1 POS tagger sample

For many applications of NLP, we use the POS tags trained on the 'Penn Tree Bank (PTB) Corpus' in which tags have been defined as in Table 15.4. PTB is one of the corpora used by NLTK. Let us take a look at the PTB tagset by using a few examples.

In this, there are four ways of tagging a noun. A noun may be classed as being singular or mass (NN), plural (NNS), singular proper noun (NNP) or plural proper noun (NNPS). Articles used in English such as 'the, a, an' are referred to as determiner (DT). Adverbs are of three kinds—adverb (RB), adverb comparative (RBR) and adverb superlative (RBS). Good, better and best are examples of these three. It is necessary for us to make a thorough study of this table before we start the process of using POS tagging. Now we will do some coding to extract POS tags.

Table 15.4 Penn Treebank POS tagset

Penn Treebank tagset 1/2			*Penn Treebank tagset 2/2*		
Tag	*Description*	*Example*	*Tag*	*Description*	*Example*
CC	Coordinating conjunction	and	PRP	Personal pronoun	I, he, it
CD	Cardinal number	1	PRPS	Possessive pronoun	My, his
DT	Determiner	the	RB	Adverb,	However, usually
EX	Existential there	There is	RBR	Adverb, comparative	better
FW	Foreign word	d'oeuvre	RBS	Adverb, superlative	best
IN	Preposition/ subordinating conjunction	In, of, like	RP	particle	Give up
JJ	Adjective	Green	TO	to	To go, to him
JJR	Adjective comparative	greener	UH	interjection	uhhuhhuhh
JJS	Adjective superlative	greenest	VB	Verb, base form	take
LS	List marker	1)	VBD	Verb, past form	took
MD	Modal	Could, will	VBG	Verb, gerund present participle	taking
NN	Noun, singular noun	Table	VBN	Verb, past participle	taken
NNS	Noun-plural	tables	VBP	Verb, sing, present, non-3rd person singular present	take
NNP	Proper noun singular	John	VBZ	Verb, 3rd person singular present	takes
NNPS	Proper noun- plurals	Vikings	WDT	Wh-determiner	which
PDT	Pre-determiner	Both the eyes	WP	Wh-pronoun	Who, what
POS	Possessive ending	Friend's	WPS	Possessive wh-pronoun	whose
			WRB	Wh-adverb	Where, when

Example 15.7 Do POS tagging using the NLTK library for the following sentence:

Ashwin and Varun arrived at the station before noon, and so I could not meet them.

Solution:

```
import nltk
from nltk.tokenize import word_tokenize
from nltk.tag import pos_tag
ex1 = "Ashwin and Varun arrived at the station before noon, and so I could not meet them."
defpreprocess(sent):
  sent = nltk.word_tokenize(sent)
  sent = nltk.pos_tag(sent)
return sent
sent = preprocess(ex1)
sent
pattern = 'NP: {<DT>?<JJ>*<NN>}'
cp = nltk.RegexpParser(pattern)
cs = cp.parse(sent)
cs.draw()
```

Result displayed as two columns:

Table 15.5 Result of POS tagging for Example 15.7

[('Ashwin', 'NNP'),	(',', ','),
('and', 'CC'),	('and', 'CC'),
('Varun', 'NNP'),	('so', 'RB'),
('arrived', 'VBD'),	('I', 'PRP'),
('at', 'IN'),	('could', 'MD'),
('the', 'DT'),	('not', 'RB'),
('station', 'NN'),	('meet', 'VB'),
('before', 'IN'),	('them', 'PRP'),
('noon', 'NN'),	('.', '.')]

Example 15.8 Do POS tagging using the Spacy library for the sentence:

She sells sea shells on the seashore.

Solution:

```
import spacy
nlp=spacy.load('en_core_web_sm')
test1=("She sells sea shells on the sea shore").lower()
doc1=nlp(test1)
```

```
for token in doc1:
  print(token.text,token.pos_)
```

Result:

she PRON

sells VERB

sea NOUN

shells NOUN

on ADP

the DET

sea NOUN

shore NOUN

Note: The POS tags used in SpaCy are not based on the Penn Tree Bank and therefore are named differently.

15.3.3 Named Entity Recognition

In the Penn Tree Bank, we saw that proper nouns have two kinds of tags–singular and plural. But there is no differentiation as to whether the proper noun refers to a person or a place or product. In many applications, this identification is of utmost importance. Such an identification is done by a process called NER or Named Entity Recognition.

A lot of ambiguity is possible when a named entity is identified. Narmada, Ganga, Yamuna are rivers but there can be organizations like 'Ganga Travels', 'Narmada Bank' and so on. It is necessary that the NER algorithm is able to concatenate words into a string and identify what type of entity it refers to. For any such identification, the type of corpus used for training is of utmost importance. If the training is done on a corpus based on the geographical locations of America, it will not recognize the named entities in a document discussing the heritage monuments of India. NER is part of the NLTK and SpaCy libraries.

The type of named entities that NER identifies are name of person, location, organization and so on. Now let's see the results of a typical NER process.

Example 15.9 Identify the named entities in the following paragraph using the NLTK and SpaCy libraries:

Mahabharata and Ramayana are the epics of India based on true stories of ancient times. Mahabharata tells us about the very famous battle of Kurukshetra. The Bhagwat Gita is part of this great epic. Arjuna and Krishna are two among the many heroes of this epic. Ramayana contains the reasons behind celebrating festivals like Dussehra and Diwali. Ramayana talks about Rama, Sita, Ravana, Hanuman and their battle of Lanka.

Solution:

Table 15.6 Result of NER using NLTK and SpaCy libraries

SpaCy	*NLTK*
mahabharata PERSON india GPE mahabharata PERSON kurukshetra LOC bhagwatgita PERSON krishnaPERSON two CARDINAL ramayanaPERSON dussehra LOC diwaliPERSON sita PERSON ravana GPE hanuman ORG lanka GPE	Mahabharata : GPE Ramayana : GPE India : GPE Mahabharata : GPE Kurukshetra : GPE Bhagwat Gita : ORGANIZATION Arjuna : GPE Krishna : PERSON Ramayana : GPE Dussehra : ORGANIZATION Diwali : GPE Ramayana : GPE Rama : PERSON Sita : PERSON Ravana : PERSON Hanuman : PERSON Lanka : GPE

Example 15.10 Use the SpaCy library to identify named Entities in the following document.

Panasonic Corporation, the Japan-based electronics company, plans to set up a new plant at Jhajjar in Haryana, which will manufacture refrigerators for the Indian market, along with setting up a research and development (R&D) centre for appliances consisting of two technical divisions to strengthen the product development in the country. Samsung India Electronics Ltd has signed a deal to lease 100,000 square feet (sqft) of space at Oberoi Realty Ltd's commercial property Commerz II in Goregaon suburb of Mumbai, for setting up its new corporate office.

Result:

panasoniccorporation ORG

japan GPE

jhajjar GPE

haryana GPE

indianNORP

two CARDINAL

samsungindia electronics ltd ORG

100,000 square feet QUANTITY

oberoi realty ltd's ORG

mumbai GPE

Table 15.7 shows the different entities referred in the SpaCy library but it is possible to use entities other than these by making another dictionary with other training sets.

Table 15.7 NER definition in SpaCy library

Type and description – Set 1/2		*Type and description – Set 2/2*	
PERSON	People, including fictional.	NORP	Nationalities or religious or political groups.
FAC	Buildings, airports, highways, bridges, etc.	ORG	Companies, agencies, institutions, etc.
GPE	Countries, cities, states.	LOC	Non-GPE locations, mountain ranges, bodies of water.
PRODUCT	Objects, vehicles, foods, etc. (Not services.)	WORK_OF_ART	Titles of books, songs, etc.
EVENT	Named hurricanes, battles, wars, sports events, etc.	LAW	Named documents made into laws.
LANGUAGE	Any named language.	DATE	Absolute or relative dates or periods.
TIME	Times smaller than a day.	PERCENT	Percentage, including "%".
MONEY	Monetary values, including unit.	QUANTITY	Measurements, as of weight or distance.
ORDINAL	"first", "second", etc	CARDINAL	Numerals that do not fall under another type.

Now that we have seen what POS tagging is, we should find out the methods adopted for POS tagging. The first method is based on linguistics. It is a rule based system.

15.3.4 Rule Based Tagger

In this, the rules of the language are used to frame a set of rules to determine the POS tags. Because of the complexities of natural language, the set of rules are large and it tends to grow disproportionately to the problem. A typical rule could be like –'if the first word is an article, the next word will be a noun'. Then there will be the necessity and other rules to verify what kind of noun it is. The development of such a set of rules depends on linguistic knowledge and there are systems which work this way. However, probabilistic methods have proved to be more effective and we will discuss such methods which are named 'stochastic methods'.

15.3.5 Stochastic Tagger – The Markov Model

The stochastic tagger that we discuss here is the one based on the hidden Markov model. A Markov model is a probabilistic model. It is a state based model which models changing patterns. Weather patterns is one example. The model is represented with N states and connections between the states. See a typical state transition diagram in Fig. 15.8. Transitions occur from one state to the other with a specified probability, and this probability is referred to as the state transition probability a_{ij} which notates the probability of transitioning from state i to state j. The sum of all the transition probabilities will be 1, that is,

$$\Sigma a_{ij} = 1 \quad \text{...(15.23)}$$

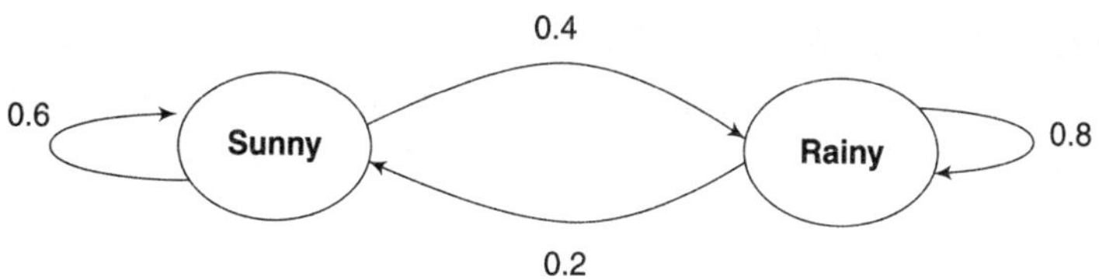

Fig. 15.2 A Markov model

Figure 15.2 is a two-state model. There are only two states, Sunny and Rainy. The transition probabilities *P(Sunny/Rainy)* indicates the probability of transitioning to state 'Sunny' given that the current state is 'Rainy'. *P(Rainy/Sunny)* is the probability of transitioning to state 'Rainy' given that the current state is 'Sunny'. There is also *P(Sunny/Sunny)* and *P(Rainy/Rainy)*,which are the probabilities of remaining in the same state. Note that:

$$P(Rainy/Sunny) + P(Sunny/Sunny) = 1, \text{ that is, } 0.4 + 0.6 = 1$$

$$P(Sunny/Rainy) + P(Rainy/Rainy) = 1, \text{ that is, } 0.2 + 0.8 = 1$$

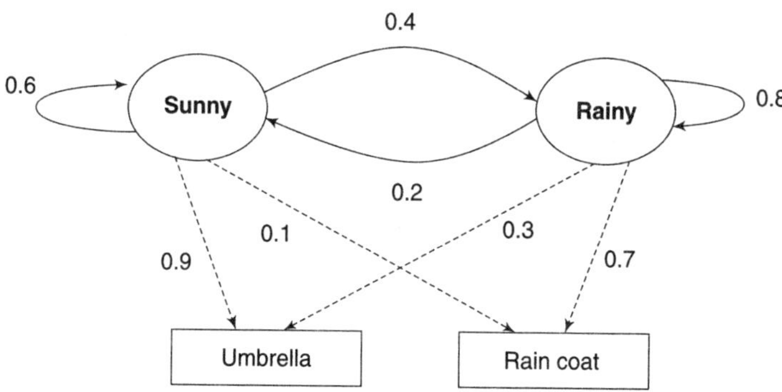

Fig. 15.3 A hidden Markov model

For such a Markov process, there will be an initial state. The current state will depend on previous states. For a first order Markov process, the current state is dependent only on one previous state. This is similar to a bigram (Section 15.2.3) where the probability of a word is dependent only on one previous word. We have a transition matrix (Table 15.8) corresponding to this state diagram. The rows correspond to the next state and the columns to the current state. We see that the sum of the rows is 1.

Table 15.8 Transition matrix for Fig. 15.2

Current State	*Next State*	
	Sunny	*Rainy*
Sunny	0.6	0.4
Rainy	0.2	0.8

15.3.5.1 Hidden Markov Model (HMM)

Observe Fig. 15.3. Assume I have a friend who comes to work daily from a place far away. I don't know the state of the weather in his home town, but I am able to guess whether it is sunny or rainy there, based on whether he is carrying an umbrella or a rain coat. When he has a raincoat with him, I guess that it is raining in his place, and when he has an umbrella, it is probably because it is sunny when he left home. But these observations are not very deterministic as the figure shows. There is a probability associated with them which depends on the state. For example, *P(Umbrella/Rainy)* = 0.3 and *P(Raincoat/Rainy)* = 0.7. Also, *P(Raincoat/Sunny)* = 0.1, *P(Umbrella/Sunny)* = 0.9. One point is that – when it is sunny, there is a 90% probability that he will carry an umbrella. The other way of looking at it is that, when I observe him carrying an umbrella, there is a 90% probability that it was sunny when he left home.

These probabilities are called emission/observation probabilities and we can draw a corresponding observation probability matrix (see Table 15.9). Note that the sum of the rows is 1. This model is called the hidden Markov model because the states that correspond to the observations are hidden. We see only the 'emission/observation' corresponding to each state and not the actual state. The actual states are hidden.

Table 15.9 The observation/emission matrix

State	*Observation*	
	Umbrella	*Raincoat*
Sunny	0.9	0.1
Rainy	0.3	0.7

Now let's bring in the hidden Markov model to the case of POS tagging. The probability of the occurrence of a POS tag can be modelled on such a state transition diagram as in Fig. 15.4. Consider this state transition diagram in which the two states are the POS tags Noun and Verb. Say, the initial state is noun (corresponding to the first word of a sentence).The second word may be a verb or a noun itself

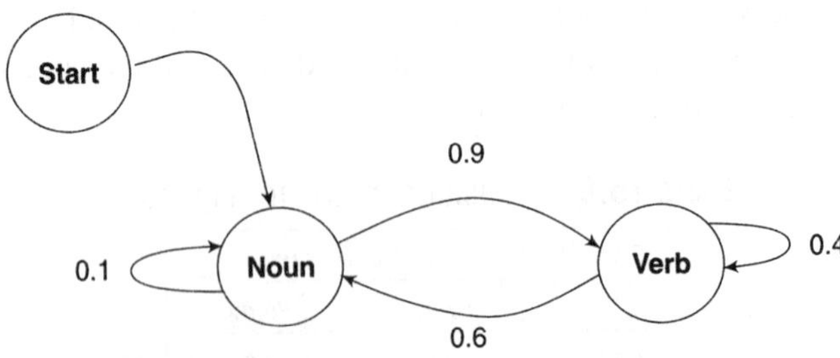

Fig. 15.4 HMM for POS tagging –an example

The transition probability P(Verb/Noun) means the probability that the next tag is a verb given that the current tag is a noun. From Fig. 15.4, we get the transition probabilities to be *P(Verb/Noun)* = 0.9, *P(Noun/Noun)* = 0.1, *P(Noun/Verb)* == 0.6, *P(Verb/Verb)* = 0.4. For the above state diagram, we find that if a sentence starts with a noun, the highest probability for the next tag is a verb. This conclusion is based on just the transition probability matrix. But we will now see that this matrix alone is not sufficient for decision making.

To make it a hidden Markov model, there should be an observation corresponding to each state. A general model of such a hidden Markov model for POS tags is as shown in Fig. 15.5. From an initial tag state T_0, the system transitions to tags T_1, T_2, etc., and at each new state, there is an observation, namely, w_1, w_2 ...respectively which are the words of a sentence. The probability for an observation (also called emission/observation probability) is $P(w_i/T_i)$ for $i = 1, 2, \ldots n$. This HMM can model the tags of the words of a sentence. The initial state is the starting symbol <s> of the sentence.

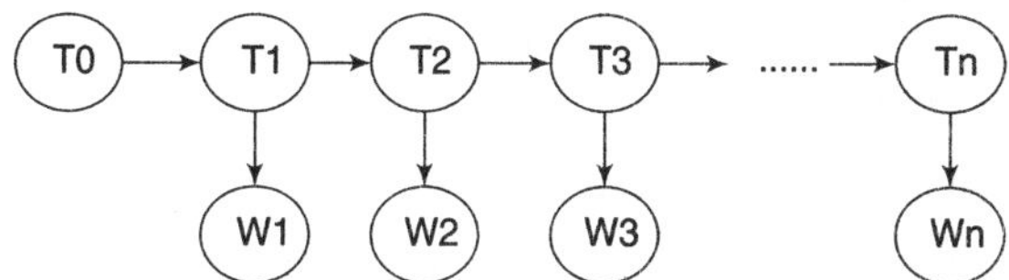

Fig. 15.5 The emission/observations (words) for each tag

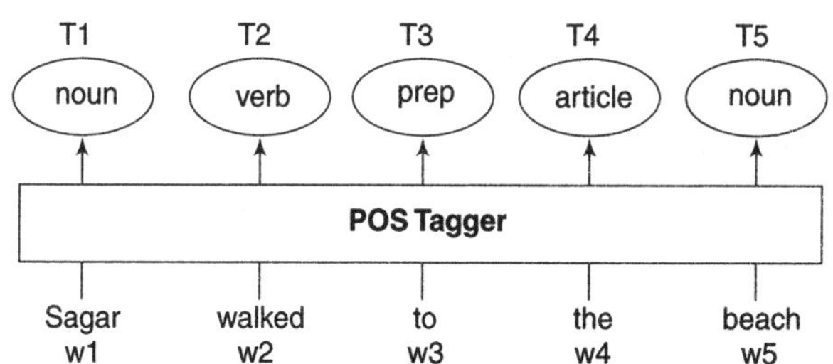

Fig. 15.6 A POS tagger for an example sentence

When we use language, the POS tag of the observations (words) is hidden – we observe only the words, one after the other. In Fig. 15.6, we see that as tags change, words w_1, w_2 ... are observed. Then the function of the stochastic POS tagger, is to determine probabilistically the best POS tag of the observed word using the transition matrix as well as the observation probability matrix.

The HMM model for POS tagging is defined as in Table 15.10.

Table 15.10 Definition of the HMM model for POS tagging

$T_1, T_2 \ldots .. T_n$	A set of *N* states which are the probable POS tags.
The *T* matrix	The *T x T* transition matrix, T_{ij} is the probability of transitioning from state *i* to state *j*. $\Sigma T_{ij} = 1$
$W = w_1, w_2 \ldots$	The observations (emissions) from each state, which are words.
The O matrix	The matrix of observation likelihoods and emission probabilities is a *T x V* matrix where *V* corresponds to the size of the vocabulary.

Let us connect our discussion of HMM with the POS tagging of the sentence given below:

He will end the race.

The observations, which are the words of the sentences are the only things we see. They are:

<s> ->he ->will ->end->the->race-></s>

The hidden part is the sequence of POS tags for the sentence. For any word, there can be more than one POS tag possible, so a certain amount of ambiguity is involved. The task of 'POS Tagging' is one that does disambiguation, which means that it clears the ambiguity and discovers the tag of each word based on the context in which it is used in the sentence. In our sentence, the words 'end' and 'race' may each be a noun or verb. The correct tag is to be finalized based on the T and O matrices.

How do we formulate this problem and find a solution?

The method is a Maximum Likelihood Estimation problem in which the joint probability as given in Eq. 15.24 is to be maximized. Here 'i' corresponds to the number of words of the sentence. For each value of i, t is the probable tag and w is the observed word.

$$P(t, w) = \prod_i P(t_i | t_{i-1})\, P(w_i | t_i) \qquad ...(15.24)$$

The probable (predicted) tag sequence ($\hat{t}_{1:n}$) for the sentence of n words is obtained as

$$\hat{t}_{1:n} = \text{argmax}_{t_1......t_n} P((t_1......t_n/w_1 \;..... \; w_n)(t_1 \ldots t_n | w_1 \ldots w_n) \qquad ...(15.25)$$

$$\approx \text{argmax}_{t_1......t_n} \prod_{i=1}^{n} P(w_i | t_i)\, P(t_i | t_{i-1}) \qquad ...(15.26)$$

where,

$P(w_i | t_i)$ is the emission probabiliy

$P(t_i | t_{i-1})$ is the transition probability

The two assumptions made for HMM taggers are:

(i) One POS tag is dependent only on the previous tag (bigram assumption).

(ii) Each observation (word) depends only on the tag which produces it.

We will define an HMM tagger with two matrices – a T matrix which contains the tag transition probabilities and an O matrix of observations with respect to tags.

Note: In our discussions, we will use the tag notations as in the case of the Penn Treebank of Table 15.4.

P(NN/VB) means the probability of a tag NN occurring given that the tag of the previous word is VB. How do we estimate this? These probabilities are obtained from the corpus on which the system has been trained. This is done similar to getting bigram probabilities (Section 15.2.3).

$$P(t_i/t_{i-1}) = \frac{\text{Count }(t_i, t_{i-1})}{\text{Count }(t_{i-1})} \quad ...(15.27)$$

The numerator is the maximum count of the case of the 'joint occurrence' of two tags t_i and t_{i-1}. The denominator is the count of the occurrences of the tag t_{i-1} alone. Suppose tag $t_{i-1} = NNP$, $t_i = VB$. Then

$$P(VB/NNP) = \frac{\text{(Count of the number of times NNP and VB occur one after the other in the corpus)}}{\text{(Count of the number of times NNP occurs alone)}} \quad ...(15.28)$$

The second matrix is named as the 'O' matrix which corresponds to the Observation/ Emission probabilities. For example, *P(Raj/NNP)* means the probability that the observed word is 'Raj' given that the tag is a proper noun. *P(work/VB)* means the probability of the word 'work' being the observation, for the tag *VB*. The observation probabilities are also obtained from the corpus and is based on counts similar to Eq. 15.27.

For each word and probable tag, the transition probabilities and observation probabilities are multiplied as in Eq. 15.25. All the probable tag sequences are evaluated and the sequence with the highest product (Eq. 15.26) is the chosen one. All these points will be made clear in the following example.

Example 15.11 Consider the following sentence.

The people back the move.

A human evaluator who has good knowledge of English will evaluate the POS tags as DT->NN->VB->DT->NN. But the computer algorithm for doing this will have to evaluate many possibilities and choose the best case. The words 'people', 'back' and 'move' may each be a noun or a verb (NN or VB). With five words in the sentence, and three words having the possibility of two tags each, there are 8 possible tag sequences. Table 15.11. lists the probable tags for each word.

Table 15.11 Tags for each word (T matrix)

Words	*Probable Tags*
the	DT
people	VB, NN
back	VB, NN
the	DT
move	NN, VB

These tags have been drawn as circles in Fig. 15.7 and in the explanation, we will denote these circles as nodes as they have incoming and outgoing paths.

After pre-processing and adding the start and end symbols, we get the sentence to be:

<s>the people back the move </s>

The first symbol in the sentence is the start symbol '<s>'. The tag of the first word is DT, the only possibility (Table 15.11). P(DT/<S>) is taken from the T matrix. This is obviously the probability of the tag of the first word being 'DT'.

In the first step, the product corresponding to Eq. (15.24) is evaluated as

$$\underbrace{P(DT/<S>)}_{\text{From T Matrix}} * \underbrace{P(the/DT)}_{\text{From O Matrix}} \quad ...(15.29)$$

In the next step, for the word 'people', there are two probable tags. Thus there arise two paths as shown by Eqs. 15.30 and 15.31.

$$P(DT/<s>) \times P(the/DT) \times P(NN/DT) \times P(people/NN) \quad ...(15.30)$$

$$P(DT/<s>) \times P(the/DT) \times P(VB/DT) \times P(people/VB) \quad ...(15.31)$$

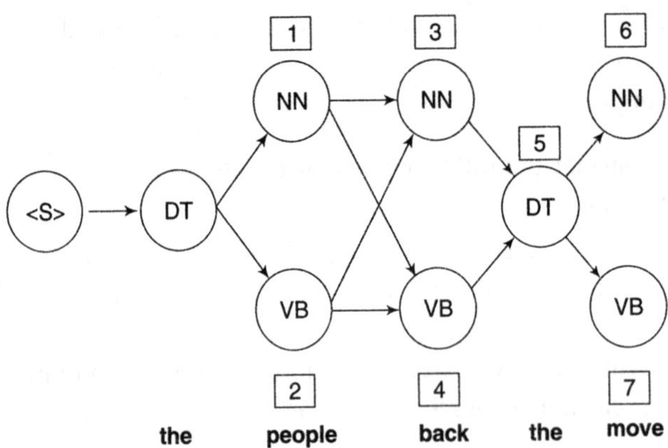

Fig. 15.7 Probable tag sequence

These equations are a continuous multiplication of the tag and observation probabilities of the words. Equations 15.30 and 15.31 give the 'evaluation metric' for the probable 'tag sequences' for the sentence upto 'the people'.

This process will continue for the rest of the words and by the end of the sentence, there are eight paths (See Figure 15.7) to be computed and compared. This is obviously a brute force method in which the metric of each and every path is to be computed. For long sentences and many tag possibilities for each word, the computation will become prohibitively large. Consider a general case in which each word in a sentence of 5 words, has four possible tags. Thus, the total number of paths will be $4^5 = 1024$. What about a similar case for a sentence of word length 10? This will be 4^{10}. The exponential growth of computations makes the direct method of HMM impractical. An improved version of this which involves dynamic programming is called the Viterbi algorithm and we will now discuss that.

15.3.6 The Viterbi Algorithm for POS Tagging

The best path gives the optimum tag sequence, and is based on Maximum Likelihood Estimation (MLE) where this path has the highest path metric. The intuition behind this dynamic programming method is that he best path ending in state i will include the best path of length $i - 1$. Each step which leads to a state, chooses the best possible path (out of the many incoming paths). This means that the others are truncated and discarded. At this current state, the best path is then extended by 1 and the process continues till the 'end of sentence' symbol (</s>) is encountered.

Example 15.12 Given the T and O matrices (obtained from the corpus), find the optimum tag sequence for the sentence *'The people back the move'*. Use the Viterbi algorithm.

Table 15.12 The transition matrix

Current State	*Next State*		
	DT	*NN*	*VB*
START	0.82	0.18	0
DT	0	0.85	0.15
NN	0	0.5	0.5
VB	0.5	0.5	0

Table 15.13 The observation matrix

P(POS/w)	*The*	*people*	*back*	*move*
DT	0.2	0	0	0
NN	0	0.1	0.25	0.15
VB	0	0.2	0.1	0.3

Calculations:

<s>the people back the move </s>

The first symbol is the start symbol and we assign it the tag <s>. The tag of the word of the sentence 'the' is DT. There is no ambiguity for this word.

Up to the word 'the', the path metric is given by:

$$P(DT/<s>) \times P(the/DT) = 0.8 \times 0.2 = 0.164$$

The next word 'people' has two options – it may be NN or VB.

For the case of it being NN, the path calculations are:

$$0.164 \times P(NN/DT) \times P(people/NN)$$

$$= 0.164 \times 0.85 \times 0.1 = 0.01394 \text{ at Node '1'}$$

For the case of it being VB, the path calculations are:

$$0.164 \times P(VB/DT) \times P(people/VB)$$

$$= 0.164 \times 0.15 \times 0.2 = 0.00492 \text{ at Node '2'}$$

Two possible paths are seen here, but there is only one incoming path to each of the nodes 1 and 2 (as shown in Fig. 15.7). So we retain both these paths. At the next step, for the word 'back', there are the options of NN and VB. At the node 3 marked NN, there are two incoming paths for which the path probabilities are:

This path comes from Node 1 : *0.01394 × P(NN/NN) × P(back/NN)*

$$= 0.01394 \times 0.5 \times 0.25 = \mathbf{0.0017425}$$

This path comes from Node 2: *0.00492 × P(NN/VB) × P(back/NN)*

$$= 0.00492 \times 0.5 \times 0.25 = 0.000615$$

Of these two incoming paths, the one with the lower path probability is removed, as it is unlikely to be part of the optimum path. We remove the path from node 2.

Note: We delete/remove a path only if there is more than one incoming path to a node.

The same exercise is done for the two incoming paths at node 4,

The path probabilities are i):

$$0.01394 \times P(VB/NN) \times P(back/VB)$$
$$= 0.01394 \times 0.5 \times 0.1 = \mathbf{0.000697}$$

This comes from Node 1

The path probabilities are (ii):

$$0.00492 \times P(VB/VB) \times P(back/VB)$$
$$= 0.00492 \times 0 \times 0.1 = 0$$

This comes from Node 2

The path with the lower metric (0) is removed.

We are now left with the two probable tag sequences (see Fig. 15.8)

DT-NN-NN (at Node 3) and

DT-NN-VB (at node 4).

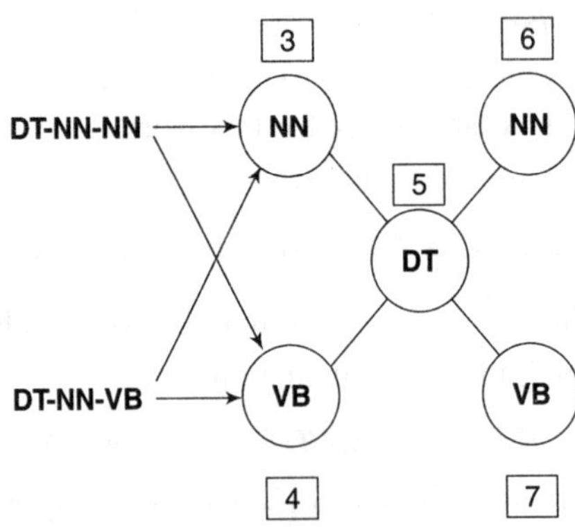

Fig. 15.8 Part of the Viterbi tree

So, at nodes 3 and 4, we have two paths with path metrics:

(i) 0.0017425 for the tag sequence *DT-NN-NN*

(ii) 0.000697 for the tag sequence *DT-NN-VB*

The process is continued for the next word 'the' which has an unambiguous tag of DT.

The incoming path probabilities at node 5 are:

(i) 0.0017425 × P(DT/NN) × P(the/DT) = 0.0017425 × 0 × 0.2 = 0

(ii) 0.000697 × P(DT/VB) × P(the/DT) = 0.000697 × 0.5 × 0.2 = 0.0000697

Here also, we remove the path of lower probability, which comes from node 3 and the resultant path metric is now 0.0000697 with the tag sequence *DT-NN-VB-DT*.

There is one more word for the sentence which is 'move' which may *VB or NN*.

The path probabilities are:

(i) *0.0000697 × P(NN/DT) × P(move/NN)*

= 0.0000697 × 0.85 × 0.15 = **0.00000889**

(ii) *0.0000697 × P(VB/DT) × P(move/VB)*

= 0.0000697 × 0.15 × 0.3 = 0.00000314

We choose the path with the higher probability, which has the path metric of 0.00000889 which is the node numbered 6 (Fig. 15.9). The corresponding tag sequence is *DT-NN-VB-DT-NN*, which is correct as per the evaluation of a human observer.

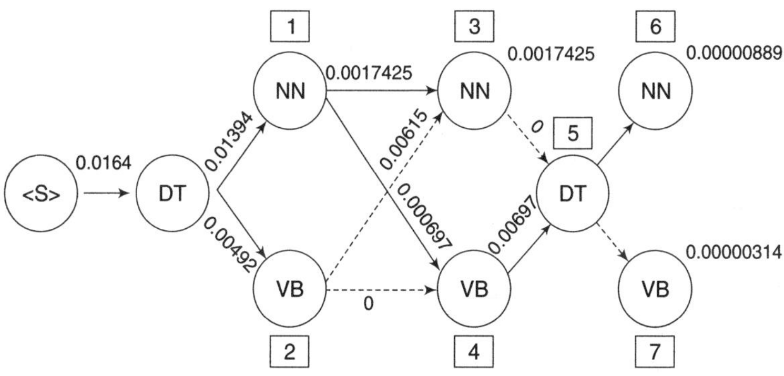

Fig. 15.9 The final tag sequence on the tree

The conclusion is that the Viterbi algorithm has been able to obtain the correct tag sequence *DT->NN->VB->DT->NN* without having to compute all the 8 paths that the simple HMM had to.

Note: Just as in the case with Sentiment analysis and N gram models we find that the numbers corresponding to path probabilities become progressively small, which will lead to the underflow problem. To circumvent this, the negative log of the probabilities is used in practice. In that case, the 'minimum' is chosen, rather than the 'maximum' path metric.

What is the advantage of the Viterbi algorithm?

At each level, when there is more than one incoming path to a node, the path with the highest metric is chosen, removing all the others. Thus, the exponential growth of computation which was the problem in the case of the direct HMM mode, is eradicated.

There is another POS tagger named Conditional Random Fields (CRF) but we will not go to the details of that.

15.4 MINIMUM EDIT DISTANCE

This is one more concept that is needed to be understood when dealing with NLP. When comparing two strings, say character strings, we may need to know how similar they are. One application of this is a spell checker. Say, we have the word 'appropriate'. But a document contains the word 'apropriate'. This may be a spelling mistake. To correct it, some editing must be done. In this example, the only necessity is to insert another 'p' after the first p. The operation is 'insertion'. There can be cases when the operation is deletion or substitution. To convert appolo to apple, the first o must be deleted and the last 'o' must be replaced by 'e'.

Thus, there are three basic operations involved in converting one string to another. They are:

(i) Insertion
(ii) Deletion
(iii) Substitution

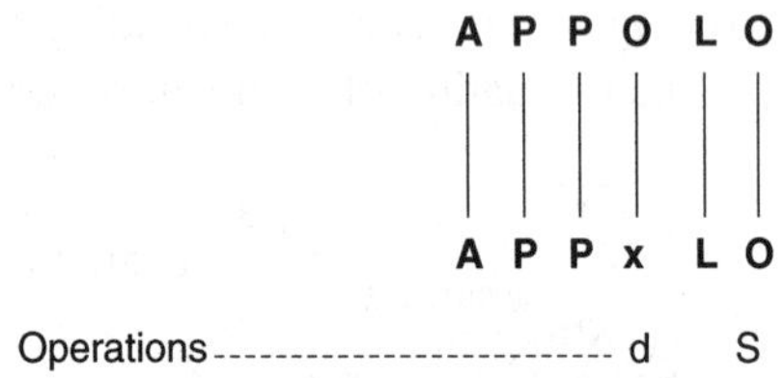

Fig. 15.10 The delete and substitute operations

If each operation is associated with a 'distance', then the 'edit distance' between the two words in Fig. 15.10 is 2.

This is a simple and direct case. But in many cases, it may be that there are different ways to convert one string to another. In such cases, it is necessary to do it with the minimum number of operations. That is the requirement for finding the 'minimum edit distance' between two strings.

The strings need not be character strings – they may be strings of words. In machine translation, speech recognition and NER, it may be that there are strings of words obtained as output. It will be necessary to ascertain if what is meant by one string is the same as the other string.

String 1: *The Government spokesman admitted that a mistake had been made.*

String 2: *The Government representative confirmed that a mistake had been made.*

These two sentences mean actually the same and one may be converted to another. The trick is to do some or all of the three operations mentioned above so that string 1 is converted to string 2 or vice versa.

If done randomly, converting one string to another may turn to be a very inefficient process. This is because the problem becomes a tree search with infinite possibilities. Thus there is the requirement to do the conversion with 'minimum edit distance'.

The problem is formulated as below:

Initial State: The source string

Goal state: The destination string

Operations: Insert, Delete, Substitute

Path: The sequence of edits

Path costs: If each operation is given a cost of 1, then the sum of the costs is to be minimised.

The problem of finding the minimum edit distance is usually solved by a dynamic programming method, the details of which are left to the interested reader to search and find out.

Conclusion

This chapter has taken up many important statistical methods which are needed to be clear to get a good understanding of the basic principles of Natural Language Processing.

Questions

1. What is meant by language modelling?
2. Why are unigrams not suitable for creating language models?
3. Compare (in terms of merits and demerits), the use of trigrams vs bigrams for use in language modeling.
4. Distinguish between 'intrinsic and extrinsic' testing of language models.
5. What is the logic of the definition of perplexity?
6. What do you know about the WSJ corpus? List out its important features.
7. What is meant by the term 'branching factor'? Give two examples to make this clear.
8. How are 'out of vocabulary' words taken care of?
9. What is the necessity of POS tagging and NER for NLP applications?
10. What is the relevance of the word 'hidden' in the hidden Markov model?
11. How does the Viterbi algorithm reduce calculations in POS tagging?
12. Using an example, show the concept of 'minimum edit distance'.

Exercise

1. (a)What is the unigram probability of the words in the following corpus? What is the probability of the last line? Show the calculations.
   But I have promises to keep,
   And miles to go before I sleep,
   And miles to go before I sleep.
2. I see a boat on the river
   It is sailing to the sea
   And on the river is a ship too
   Sailing to the sea

Use this corpus to find the bigram probability of the following sentence:

I see a boat and a ship sailing to the sea.

Note:

(i) Laplace smoothing may be used if necessary.
(ii) Make a table of the unique words in the test sentence and their frequencies.
(iii) List the conditional probabilities of every word in the test sentence.
(iv) Calculations must be shown.

3. For the corpus and Test sentence in Exercise 2, calculate the unigram and trigram probabilities. Show the calculations.
4. This is a corpus of five sentences:

   Manju has a cat.

   The cat sleeps on the mat.

   The cat spills milk on the mat.

   The cat and Manju play on the mat.

   Manju also likes to sleep on the mat.

   List the unique words in the corpus and their counts

   Using bigrams,

   (i) find the probability of the third and fifth sentences.
   (ii) Find the probability of occurrence of the following test sentences
      (a) *The cat and Manju sleep on the mat.*
      (b) *Manju spills milk on the mat.*

   Note: If probability becomes 0, use Laplace smoothing.
5. Using Python code, do POS tagging for the following sentences:
   (i) While playing football, the ball thrown by my friend hit the boy crossing the street.
   (ii) Lalitha is very sick today and we will take her to the hospital now, before she gets worse.
6. Using Python code, do NER on the following paragraph

   The best semiconductor companies are Intel, AMD, ARM, Samsung and Apple. All of them have their offices in USA in Seattle and San Francisco. They have outsourced their work to countries such as India, China and Taiwan. Steve Jobs was the best known leader of Apple even though Tim Cooks is now the CEO. India's Prime Minister Narendra Modi wants more investment from these companies to come to India. Bangalore is the hub of electronics in South India and the chief minister of Karnataka, Yedurappa, has invited these companies to set up their production houses in Bangalore.
7. Do POS tagging using Viterbi algorithm (manually or using coding) on the sentence:

   The race to the end.
8. What is meant by the word 'chunking' in NLP?

CHAPTER

16

Frequency Based Methods

In this chapter you will

- learn text representation as vectors,
- observe text representation as one hot vectors,
- study the count vector model,
- analyze the TF-IDF model,
- understand the concept of word and document similarity,
- calculate cosine similarity,
- deduce the co-occurrence matrix,
- perform sentiment analysis and text classification, and
- test concepts using Python code.

16.0 INTRODUCTION

In the previous chapters, we discussed some basic aspects of Natural Language Processing including its major applications. We also had an exposure to the task of text pre-processing which should be done before any application can be taken up for coding. Thus in this and later chapters, we should remember that any algorithm will start with a basic text pre-processing/cleaning up step. In this chapter, we take up many of the fundamental tasks involved in NLP.

Here we start with the concept of how text may be represented. Since algorithms can deal only with numbers, it is obvious that 'text' has to be represented in terms of numbers. Text vectorization is the name given to this technique in which text is converted to vectors. There are many different vectorization methods and the best representation gives the best results for the application in hand. In this chapter, we discuss 'frequency based' methods to convert text to numbers. The frequency is the 'count' of words in documents. This is the classical method of text vectorization. More effective methods based on prediction have evolved, but frequency based methods have not lost their relevance.

Information retrieval is something that we do on an everyday basis while we do web searching and querying. When we need to locate any document, we search for it using a relevant term or a set of terms. The basic activity in this is to compute the similarity between the query words and web documents. In this chapter, we consider the basics of computing the similarity between words and between documents.

Another very popular and interesting application of NLP is the automation of reviews. This application is generally referred to as sentiment analysis. A popular method for identifying whether a review is to be taken as positive, negative or neutral is based on the classical machine learning algorithm named as the Naïve Bayes classifier (Chapter 4). Logistic regression and SVM are other supervised learning methods, the theory and practice of which were already covered in Chapter 3. In this chapter, we will look into the concepts of sentiment analysis as well as text classification based on these algorithms.

There are many languages in use the world over and NLP principles may be applied to each and every one of them. But there are special attributes for each language due to which processing techniques tend to differ. In this book, we deal with English alone.

16.1 TEXT REPRESENTATION

How do we start with text processing? As discussed in the previous chapters, we have a set of documents named corpus. In a corpus, there are many documents each of which contains a number of 'terms'. In NLP, we tend to use the nomenclature 'term' in place of 'word'.

Is there a difference between 'term' and 'word'?

A 'term' could be a single word or a combination of words. It should convey a meaning specific to the context. For example, 'misunderstanding' is a term, but suppose you are searching for something more specific and want to know how often the term 'cultural misunderstanding' occurs in a document. Then you will consider this two-word combination as a term and you may want to know how many times this term occurs in a document. 'Back pain' and 'full stop' are terms – but 'back', 'pain', 'full', and 'stop' are also terms. In short, we should refer to text data as a collection of 'terms'.

Note: In NLP, we are permitted to use 'word' and 'term' interchangeably – they mean the same. In this book, we follow this convention.

16.1.1 One Hot Vector Representation

The simplest and most obvious vector representation of a word is by a one hot vector. Such a vector has only a single '1' in it – the rest are zeros. If there are 10,000 words to be represented, we need 10,000 vectors. Each vector will be 10,000 elements long in which only one element is non-zero.

Example 16.1 Take this sentence which has been converted to lower case and derive its one-hot vector representation:

my garden is lovely

Solution: There are four words in it, and each word may be converted to a vector as in Table 16.1.

Table 16.1 One hot representation of each word in the sentence

my	1000
garden	0100
is	0010
lovely	0001

If you run a Python program to print the one hot vectors for this sentence, you will get the following matrix.

[[1 0 0 0]
[0 1 0 0]
[0 0 1 0]
[0 0 0 1]]

The drawbacks of such a representation are obvious – for a large vocabulary, the vector is too long and takes up a lot of space. It seems a waste to expend such a lot of space for just zeros. But the most important drawback is that many applications envisaged for NLP cannot be supported by this representation. For example, how can the similarity of two words be computed? The standard method of computing similarity between vectors is to take their dot product. This method will fail here, as the dot product of any two terms will always be zero. There is also no way to encode a meaning or 'semantics' into any word. Hence, this is not a preferred way to represent text. Let us check the other methods available.

16.1.2 The Bag of Words (BOW) Concept

This is the model which is easy to visualize. Imagine picking up all the words in a document and dropping them into a bag. Obviously, the order of the words is lost which leads to a loss of meaning for the entire document. The spatial relationship between the words in a document is lost. In this model, it is the number of times a word appears in the corpus that matters. In general, a count or frequency is denoted as histogram. Thus, the BOW model words on the histogram of the words in a document. There are two ways in which this is used. One is a simple direct 'count vector' model. The second is a weighted model.

Fig. 16.1 A conceptual view of the Bag of Words (BOW) model

16.1.2.1 The Count Vector Model

In this, a matrix is created with documents and the terms contained in each document. A number of terms in the corpus are picked and their raw count is found. This information is listed as a matrix. Each document is now looked up as a vector containing the raw counts of the words in the vocabulary corresponding to the corpus. The whole process is made clear in Example 16.2.

Example 16.2 Consider a corpus of these three documents, each of which is a sentence as shown below. As part of text pre-processing, they have been converted to lower case.

1. today is a happy day for me
2. it is a sunny day
3. any sunny day is a happy day for me

Develop the 'Count Vector' model for this corpus.

Solution: The number of unique words and their counts is listed in Table 16.2, after removing the stopwords.

Table 16.2 Count of the words in the corpus

Words	*Count*
today	1
happy	2
day	4
me	2
sunny	2
any	1

Now see how each document in the corpus is represented in the BOW matrix.

Table 16.3 The count vector matrix for the given corpus

	today	*happy*	*day*	*me*	*sunny*	*any*
Doc1	1	1	1	1	0	0
Doc 2	0	0	1	0	1	0
Doc3	0	1	2	1	1	1

In essence, the vectors of each document are as below. Each document is a five-element vector in a five-dimensional space.

Document 1: [1 1 1 1 0 0]

Document 1: [0 0 1 0 1 0]

Document 3; [0 1 2 1 1 1]

This is a very simple and basic model meant to understand the concepts of NLP. It is not used in practical situations because it has a fundamental problem in that more frequent words have greater weights (bigger numbers corresponding to the higher frequency of occurrence of a word). We will see that such a quality does not lead to a discriminative judgment regarding a document.

This 'count vector' model is also a sparse matrix, usually. Consider a corpus with a vocabulary size of 50,000 words. Only some of these words are likely to appear in each document leading to many zeros in each row of the matrix.

Note: We can also have a binary model in which the count of each term is not listed – instead only the presence or absence of a term is listed as a '1' or '0' respectively.

16.1.2.2 The TF-IDF Model

This is also a 'Bag of words' model but it is a weighted BOW model. The weights correspond to a quantity named TF-IDF which we will understand now. TF–IDF is the product of the term frequency and the 'Inverse document frequency'.

Term Frequency

Term frequency is a count of how many times a term occurs in a document. Documents are of varying lengths and longer documents may have more occurrences of terms.

So there is the need to normalize the term count with respect to the total count of terms in the document. Hence, term frequency is defined as the normalized count of a term in a document as in Eq. 16.1.

TF is defined (for a term '*t*' in a document '*d*') as

$$\text{TF}(t, d) = \frac{\text{(Number of times term } t \text{ appears in a document)}}{\text{(Total number of terms in the document)}} \qquad ...(16.1)$$

For large documents, TF may become quite small leading to an underflow problem during computations. For such cases, it is recommended that the logarithm (to the base 10) be used to define term frequency. This compresses the number and also makes more sense as a word occurring 10 times in a document does not necessarily have 10 times importance. Additionally, some terms may have a count of 0, but log 0 is undefined. So the definition TF (*t*, *d*) is modified by adding 1 to the logarithm of the count as in Eq. 16.2

$$tf_{t,d} = \log_{10}(\text{count}(t, d) + 1) \qquad ...(16.2)$$

Note: In many cases, this log based definition is not used and TF is used as in Eq. 16.1. In our examples, we will use the definition of Eq. 16.1. Many software packages use the definition as given in Eq. 16.2. Some use the natural log instead of log to the base 10.

Inverse Document Frequency (IDF)

In documents, some terms are very distinctive and will be present only in a few documents of the corpus. The concept of IDF helps to identify such distinctive terms which help in discriminating between documents. The practice of using the 'inverse' document frequency is to get a measure of how important a term is. If the term occurs in all documents, the IDF is 1 which means the discriminating property of the term is low. But if it is much more than 1, it implies that it is present only in a few documents.

As a matter of practice, the IDF is also defined using logarithms. This again, is to compress its value to a smaller number, because usually the documents used in NLP applications are very large in number (millions of documents are normal in the web). See the definition of IDF for a term t as in Eq. 16.3.

$$idf_t = \log_{10}\left(\frac{N}{df_t}\right) \quad ...(16.3)$$

Let's use a few examples to get a clear understanding of these concepts.

Example 16.3 A corpus has three documents. (each document is just a sentence). Find the TF-IDF weighted matrix of the corpus and identify the most distinctive words.

Document 1: The sea is rough.

Document 2: A storm is expected over the sea.

Document 3: Boats are not expected on rough seas.

Solution: After lower casing, removing punctuations, removing stopwords and tokenizing, the documents have words as given below.

Document 1: "sea", "rough"

Document 2: "storm", "expect", "sea"

Document 3: "boat" " expect" "rough" "sea"

The term–document frequency matrix is as shown in Table 16.4. The number of terms in the three documents are 1, 2 and 3 respectively.

Table 16.4 The term-document frequency

	sea	*rough*	*storm*	*expect*	*boat*
Doc1	1/2	1/2	0	0	0
Doc2	1/3	0	1/3	1/3	0
Doc3	1/4	1/4	0	1/4	1/4

Now let's calculate the IDF of each of these terms. $N = 3$, the number of documents.

Table 16.5 The calculation of IDF

	N/df_t	*IDF = Log (N//df_t)*
sea	3/3	0
rough	3/2	0.176
storm	3/1	0.4771
expect	3/2	0.176
boat	3/1	0.4771

Table 16.6 The TF-IDF matrix

	sea	*rough*	*storm*	*expect*	*boat*
Doc1	0	0.088	0	0	0
Doc2	0	0	0.159	0.05866	0
Doc3	0	0.044	0	0.044	0.1192

What is the information we get from the TF-IDF Table 16.6? We can make the following conclusions.

(i) The term 'sea' which is present in all the three documents has a weight of 0. This implies that it is not a term that serves to distinguish between the three documents.

(ii) The highest TF-IDF is for the term storm. It is present in only one (second) document and is therefore distinctive.

(iii) The next highest TF-IDF weight is for 'boat'. This is also present in only one (third) document. However, its 'term frequency' is less than that of 'storm' because this document has more terms than the second one.

Using the concept of TF-IDF weighting, the three documents referred here are represented as vectors as given by the rows of Table 16.6.

Does the TF-IDF model follow the concept of 'Bag of Words'?

Yes, this is also a bag of words model in the sense that the terms do not retain their spatial information. They are picked and dropped into a bag just as we saw in Section 16.1.2. However, we are able to extract some relevant information from this model because of the way the weights have been chosen.

This model also leads to a sparse matrix where the vector length will be the size of the vocabulary. Thus, a vocabulary of 100000 terms will lead to vectors of that size with a lot of the vector elements being zero.

Example 16.4 Consider the descriptive reviews of five English movies: Cleopatra, Lawrence of Arabia, Titanic, My Fair Lady and The Sound of Music. The term-document matrix and the size of each document, are given in Tables 16.7 and 16.8. Find the TF-IDF matrix.

Note: Those who have seen these movies will be able to relate well with these word occurrences!!!

Table 16.7 The term-document matrix

	Cleopatra	*Titanic*	*My Fair Lady*	*The Sound of Music*	*Lawrence of Arabia*
jack	0	20	0	0	0
opera	0	0	10	15	0
sea	8	20	0	5	9
iceberg	0	4	0	0	0
rome	15	0	0	0	0
women	12	14	20	20	6

Table 16.8 Size of each document

Document	*No. of terms*
Cleopatra	1020
Titanic	1000
My Fair Lady	930
The Sound of Music	780
Lawrence of Arabia	1002

Solution: The steps of calculations should be clear from the Tables 16.8 to 16.11.

Table 16.9 Calculations of term frequencies (the term-document matrix)

	Cleopatra	*Titanic*	*My Fair Lady*	*The Sound of Music*	*Lawrence of Arabia*
jack	0	20/1000	0	0	0
opera	0	0	10/930	15/780	0
sea	8/1020	20/1000	0	5/780	9/1002
iceberg	0	4/1000	0	0	0
rome	15/1020	0	0	0	0
women	12/1020	14/1000	20/930	20/780	6/1002

Table 16.10 Calculations of IDF

	N/Dft	$Log_{10}\left(\frac{N}{df_t}\right)$
jack	5/1	0.698
opera	5/2	0.398
sea	5/4	0.097
iceberg	5/1	0.698
rome	5/1	0.698
women	5/5	0

Table 16.11 The TF-IDF matrix

	jack	*opera*	*sea*	*iceberg*	*rome*	*women*
Cleopatra	0	0	0.00076	0	0.01026	0
Titanic	0.01396	0	0.00194	0.00279	0	0
My Fair Lady	0	0.00428	0	0	0	0
The Sound of Music	0	0.00765	0.00062	0	0	0
Lawrence of Arabia	0	0	0.00087	0	0	0

Each document is represented by 6 words only – thus we can visualize a six-dimensional space for each document. The document vectors for each document are the rows of Table 16.11 weighted by the TF-IDF.

TF-IDF relates to the importance of a term that makes it distinctive and thus important (refer once again to Table 16.11). The word 'women' occurs in all the five documents. So that word does not give much information about how one document is different from another. Its TF-IDF is 0. The highest TF-IDF weighting is given to the word 'jack'. It occurs only in the document named Titanic and is very distinctive of that document. The next higher weighted word is 'opera'. It is less distinctive as it is present in two documents. The word 'iceberg' occurs only in the document Titanic. However, its count in that document is very low and this low TF causes it to have a low TF-IDF. If it had a higher term frequency, it would have been a very important term.

Applications of the TF-IDF model

One very obvious application is information retrieval. If we are using a query term (like Jack in example), the search algorithm will identify and rank documents in which the TF-IDF of that term is high. Another related application is 'keyword extraction'. From any document, the words with high weights may be extracted from the TF-IDF matrix. They will be the most distinctive terms of the document and be considered the keywords of the document.

Now let's go ahead to more aspects of words as vectors in a 'V dimensional vector space. Let us look into the concept of document similarity.

16.2 DOCUMENT SIMILARITY

How do we know if two or more documents have similar contents? They are likely to have some common terms. The more the frequency of the common words, the greater is the similarity. A mathematical framework can be derived for this based on the concept of term counts. This is the basis of information retrieval based on queries. Example 16.5 gives some insights into the logic of the process.

Example 16.5 Consider again the descriptive reviews of five English movies: Cleopatra, Lawrence of Arabia, Titanic, My Fair Lady, The Sound of Music. Let us use another set of words now. Five words and the histogram (frequency of occurrence) of this set of words in each document are listed in Table 16.12.

Table 16.12 Term frequency matrix of the corpus

	Cleopatra	*Titanic*	*My Fair Lady*	*The Sound of Music*	*Lawrence of Arabia*
war	9	0	0	0	12
love	10	15	5	12	1
music	2	5	15	20	0
battle	12	0	0	0	20
actor	10	15	14	20	8

Table 16.12 is a matrix in which the rows represent the terms we are using and the columns carry the names of the documents. We use this toy example to show the concept of how a document may be represented as a vector. Here only five words have been used. So each

document is represented in terms of a five-dimensional vector. For example, the column vector for the document Cleopatra is as shown in Table 16.13.

Table 16.13 Vector representation of 'Cleopatra'

$$\begin{bmatrix} 9 \\ 10 \\ 2 \\ 12 \\ 10 \end{bmatrix}$$

Now we would like to know which of these five movies have similar themes. To do this, we can compare their document vectors. Check Table 16.12 again. The document vectors of the documents 'Cleopatra'(first column) and 'Lawrence of Arabia' (fifth column) seem to have numbers which are in close ranges, except for one entry. This is explicitly shown in Table 16.14. Shall we conclude that these documents refer to movies with some similarity?

But if we take a look at the first and third colums of Table 16.12, we find that only one row has similar numbers. Thus, they are document vectors of relatively dissimilar documents. (They are of the movies Cleopatra and My Fair Lady).

Table 16.14 Document vectors of Cleopatra and Lawrence of Arabia

$$\begin{bmatrix} 9 \\ 10 \\ 2 \\ 12 \\ 10 \end{bmatrix} \begin{bmatrix} 12 \\ 1 \\ 0 \\ 20 \\ 8 \end{bmatrix}$$

This information, derived from Table 16.12, is that the document named Cleopatra is a point in a five-dimensional vector space. Similar is the case for the other five documents. A five-dimensional space is very difficult to visualize. So let us try to relate to something that is easy – a two-dimensional space. Suppose we consider that each document can be identified and represented by just two words, then we can easily make sense of some basic concepts of document similarity. Let's use a part of Table 16.12 for this purpose.

Consider four movies and their two-dimensional vectors as listed in Table 16.15. Thus, each document is represented by a two-element vector as marked in the table. Each document is now a point in a two-dimensional vector space having coordinates as listed here:

Cleopatra (10, 2), Titanic (15, 5), My Fair Lady (5, 15), The Sound of Music (12, 20).

Let's plot each vector in an X-Y coordinate system. The count of the term 'love' is plotted on the X-axis and music on the Y-axis. This is shown in Fig. 16.2.

Table 16. 15 Documents represented by 'two-element' vectors

	Cleopatra	Titanic	My Fair Lady	The Sound of Music
love	10	15	5	12
music	2	5	15	20

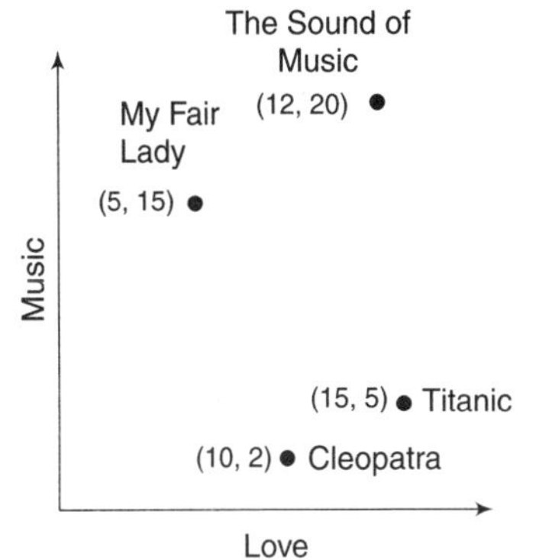

Fig. 16.2 (a) The document points

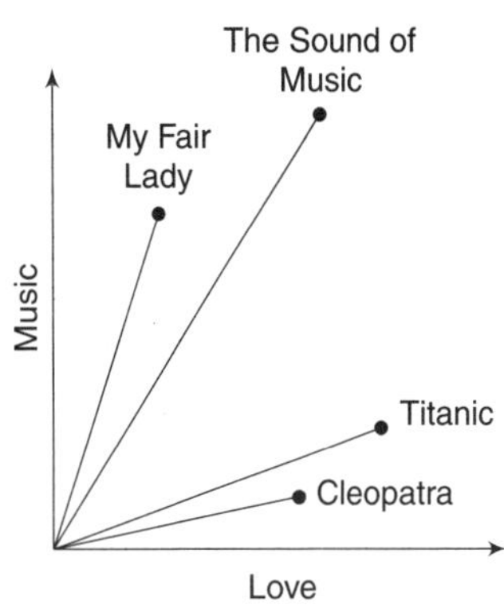

Fig. 16.2 (b) The angle between the documents

On examining Fig. 16.2a, we find that the points corresponding to the document 'Sound of Music (SM)' and 'My Fair Lady (MFL)' are huddled close together. The points corresponding to documents Titanic and Cleopatra are similarly close together but far away from the other two. One conclusion from this figure may that the documents SM and MFL have similar content. The same is the case for the documents Titanic and Cleopatra.

On drawing a line from the origin to these points (Fig. 16.2b), we can find the angular separation between these four vectors. The concept of similarity is related to the angle between the vectors and from this, we can develop a mathematical framework for similarity measures.

It is well known from linear algebra concepts that two vectors which have the same orientation are similar. Having the same orientation means that the angle between them is zero. For documents in a vector space, the smaller the angular difference, the greater is the similarity. The cosine function has the property to give a measure of similarity. When cos 0 is 1, it is maximum similarity as the vectors are along the same line. When the angle between the vectors is 90, the vectors are orthogonal, meaning that they are dissimilar. Figure 16.3 shows the angular separation between two vectors A and B, which is mathematically calculated in terms of a cosine distance as in Eq. 16.4.

The similarity is expressed in terms of the cosine distance between two vectors A and B (Fig. 16.3) and is defined as in Eq. 16.4.

$$\text{Similarity} = \cos(\theta) = \frac{\mathbf{A}.\boldsymbol{B}}{\|\boldsymbol{A}\|\|\boldsymbol{B}\|} = \frac{\sum_{i=1}^{n} A_i B_i}{\sqrt{\sum_{i=1}^{n} A_i^2}\sqrt{\sum_{i=1}^{n} B_i^2}} \qquad ...(16.4)$$

The numerator is the dot product of the vectors, The denominator is the product of the magnitude of the two and is meant to normalize the product. Normalization is necessary because otherwise, vectors with bigger numbers will give a bigger dot product. So, we divide the dot product by the product of the length of the vectors.

Let's do the computation of cosine distance between the vectors of the documents of Table 16.15.

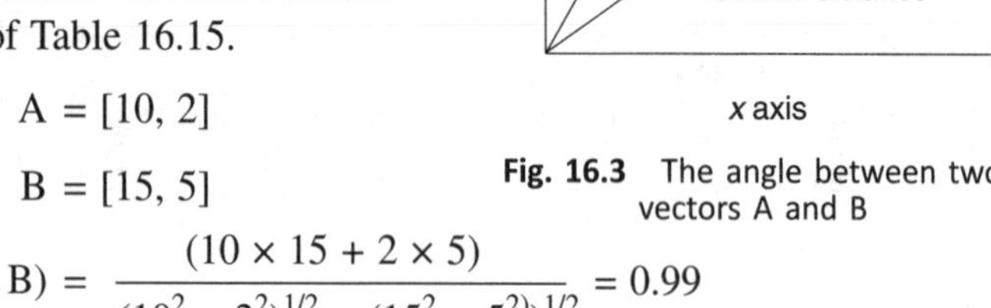

Fig. 16.3 The angle between two vectors A and B

$$A = [10, 2]$$

$$B = [15, 5]$$

$$\text{Cosine distance} \quad (A, B) = \frac{(10 \times 15 + 2 \times 5)}{(10^2 + 2^2)^{1/2} \times (15^2 + 5^{2)})^{1/2}} = 0.99$$

Table 16.16 gives the results of cosine distance calculation for the case of the two element vectors of Table 16.15.

Table 16.16 Cosine distance between vectors A and B

Vector A	*Vector B*	*Cosine distance*
Cleopatra (10,2)	Titanic (15,5)	0.99
My Fair Lady (5,15)	The Sound of Music (12,20)	0.97
Cleopatra (10,2)	My Fair Lady (5,15)	0.49

It seems that Cleopatra and My Fair Lady show the greatest dissimilarity because the cosine distance between the two is the lowest in the list.

Let us repeat the calculation based on the five element vectors of Table 16.12. We find the similarity measures between 'Cleopatra' and the other four documents as in Table 16.17. Obviously, Cleopatra has the greatest similarity with Lawrence of Arabia. Those who have seen all these movies can vouch for the similarity considerations that we have derived.

Table 16.17 Cosine distance of Cleopatra with the other four documents

Titanic	0.6867
My Fair Lady	0.5029
The Sound of Music	0.5657
Lawrence of Arabia	0.8569

16.2.1 Practical Considerations

In practical applications, the vectors for most documents correspond to hundreds and thousands and even millions of terms. To use this method for information retrieval using a query vector, the cosine distance of the query vector is computed with respect to each of the documents and the documents with the highest similarity are ranked and selected.

Another application could be recommendation systems. A simple example is like this—say, two books are to be compared. The features used are these two attributes of the content—say, romance and war.

Book 1: Love in the time of cholera—Its binary vector corresponding to [romance, war] = [1,0]

Book 2: Guns of Navarone with its feature vector = [0,1]

Obviously, the cosine distance is zero between the two vectors. The vectors are orthogonal to each other and a recommendation for one book excludes the other and vice versa.

Note: Cosine distance is the most popular method of ascertaining similarity for text vectors. Other methods like Euclidean distance, Manhattan distance and Jacquard distance exist but are less popular.

16.3 WORDS AS VECTORS

So far we were talking about documents being represented by terms/words. Can words be represented similarly by the documents in which they are present? Yes, it is logical, because the meaning of a word is related to the context in which it is used. This implies that it can be represented in terms of the documents in which it is present. The rows of Table 16.18 show that words may be represented by documents. Two words have been highlighted – love and war. In terms of the five documents, the words war and love have the following representations:

$$\text{war} = [9\ 0\ 0\ 0\ 12]$$

$$\text{love} = [10\ 15\ 5\ 12\ 1]$$

Table 16.18 Words as vectors of documents

	Cleopatra	*Titanic*	*My Fair Lady*	*The Sound of Music*	*Lawence of Arabia*
war	9	0	0	0	12
love	10	15	5	12	1
music	2	5	15	20	0
battle	12	0	0	0	20
actor	10	15	14	20	8

16.3.1 Similarity of Words/Terms

Now let's discuss an aspect of word 'similarity'. Is it possible to detect synonyms from their presence and count in documents? (Refer Table 16.19).

In the documents of this table, the words war and battle have been used. But since, they are two different words, NLP algorithms have no clue to the fact that they have similar meanings. Suppose we list the count of these words as in our table and observe the contents of the rows of the two words. Don't we find a similar pattern in the word vectors (which is taken horizontally across the table)? We note that the count of both the words is high for the movies 'Cleopatra' and 'Lawrence of Arabia'. We have already found out that the corresponding documents have similarity in their themes. The possibility we want to consider is whether words used in similar contexts can have similar meanings.

Table 16.19

	Cleopatra	*Titanic*	*My Fair Lady*	*The Sound of Music*	*Lawence of Arabia*
war	9	0	0	0	12
love	10	15	5	12	1
music	2	5	15	20	0
battle	12	0	0	0	20
actor	10	15	14	20	8

Let's try to delve deeper into the matter of word similarity? How do we find word similarity? For example, consider the words 'love' and 'attachment' – are they related? It depends on the context in which they are used. If 'attachment' refers to a file used as an attachment, obviously it is not related to love. So the way to check the semantic similarity of words is by referring to the words used 'along' with the theme words. A famous quote by J.R. Firth, a noted linguist, expresses this as "you shall know a word by the company it keeps".

Words like terminal, baggage and check-in, etc., are likely to be used in documents talking about flights and airports. They are obviously related words or have similar contexts. If there is a baking recipe, word like flour, sugar and stir are likely to be found in it.

This is what is presented in Table 16.20.

Table 16.20 Terms used in similar/dissimilar contexts

	cake	*biscuit*	*flight*	*airport*
sugar	20	12	1	3
flour	15	13	0	0
stir	5	6	0	0
terminal	0	0	10	15
baggage	0	0	15	8
check-in	0	0	13	9

What do we deduce from the table? Words like terminal, baggage and check-in are used heavily in contexts which are applicable for words like flight and airport. So they are all related words.

Compare the first and fourth rows of Table 16.20. We easily get the notion that 'sugar' and 'terminal' are unrelated words.

16.4 CONTEXT WORDS

From the previous section, we should have developed the notion that the 'semantics' of terms has a relationship to the context in which they are used. One of the biggest leaps in the field of NLP has been the recognition that for any word, it is the 'surrounding words'(aka 'context words') that give it meaning. For any word, its context words are the ones that can highlight its semantics. This is the idea behind 'dense vector embeddings' which will be dealt with in Chapter 17.

In any portion of text, every word has 'context words' which are the words within a defined context window. If the context window is of size '1', the context is the one word left of, and one word right of, our theme word. The context window will usually be more than 1 – it may go up to 10 in practical situations.

How does context relate to the semantics (meaning) of a word?

Let's use an example to get this clear.

Example 16.6 See the five short sentences listed below.

I love cars.

I love bikes.

I enjoy mountaineering.

I love driving.

I enjoy travelling.

Take a look at the words in these sentences and note the 'context words' in a window of size 1. Focus on the context of the words 'love' and 'enjoy'.

For 'love', the context words are:

I, cars

I, bikes

I, driving

What conclusions can be drawn from this?

It is highly probable that the context words of love are related – One context word 'I' is common. The other words – cars, bikes, driving – are similar or related words. Similarly, the context words of enjoy are I, mountaineering and travelling. We should also conclude that mountaineering and travelling are related words.

In a multi-dimensional space of words, we are likely to find related words to exist in close proximity. If we visually reduce our word space to just two dimensions we will find our conclusions picturised as in Fig. 16.4. We see the set of words 'bikes, cars, travelling' in close proximity. So also is the case for the words 'travelling, mountaineering'.

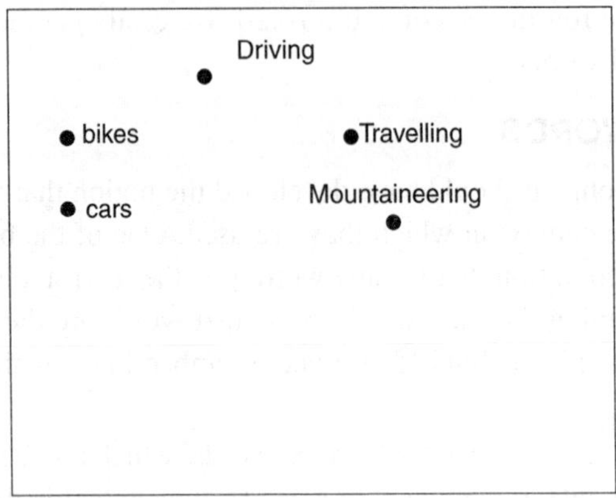

Fig. 16.4 Two-dimensional visualization of a multidimensional word space

16.4.1 Co-occurrence Matrix

Now let us take up the idea of a co-occurrence matrix. We use the same five sentences of Example 16.5 (after case folding and removing punctuations) as continuous text for building this matrix. The unique words are listed in the rows and columns. A context window of 1 is used. How do we make this matrix? Take the first row word 'i'. In its context are the words 'love' and 'enjoy' only. (There is no context on its left because it is a separate sentence.) So in the column corresponding to 'love', enter the number 3 as there are three cases where i and love co-occur in the context window. Similarly, in the column corresponding to 'enjoy', enter the number 2. In the first cell, the entry is '0', because 'I' does not co-occur with 'I'. The whole matrix is in Table 16.21.

Text:

i love bikes i love cars i enjoy mountaineering i love driving i enjoy travelling

Table 16.21 The co-occurrence matrix

	i	*love*	*cars*	*bikes*	*enjoy*	*mountaineering*	*driving*	*travelling*
i	0	3	0	0	2	0	0	0
love	3	0	1	1	0	0	1	0
cars	0	1	0	0	0	0	0	0
bikes	0	1	0	0	0	0	0	0
enjoy	2	0	0	0	0	1	0	1
mountaineering	0	0	0	0	1	0	0	0
driving	0	1	0	0	0	0	0	0
Travelling	0	0	0	0	1	0	0	0

This co-occurrence matrix in Table 16.21 is a very small space of a very small set of words. Imagine a practical scenario in which the size of the vocabulary is in the order of tens of thousands. The co-occurrence matrix (with a bigger size context window, usually) will be a sparse matrix of very high dimensions. Extracting the required information from such a matrix will be very cumbersome given that each word will exist in that high dimensional space. To reduce the dimensionality of this matrix, the technique of dimensionality reduction using Singular Value Decomposition(SVD) may be used.

But the computation needed will still be very high. Co-occurrence matrix with SVD was one of the popular methods of NLP, but it has been superseded with newer and better techniques of dense vector embeddings like Word2Vec and GloVe. This will be discussed in Chapter 17.

16.5 SENTIMENT ANALYSIS/OPINION MINING

This topic is included in this chapter itself because classification of sentiments/opinions is done in terms of the frequency of word occurrences. In Chapter 4, the Naïve Bayes classifier was discussed as one of the fundamental algorithms in the list of classical machine learning algorithms, This classifier has its most important application in NLP. Even though the presumptions and assumptions made for deriving the method are not completely realistic, the classifier performs very well in NLP tasks such as sentiment analysis, spam detection and text classification. We will start with the concept of sentiment analysis. The same logic is applicable to spam detection and text classification.

Sentiment analysis is a very important task in NLP. It can also be designated as opinion mining, emotion detection, etc., depending on the context of the application for which it is used. From written text, we need the system to tell us the opinion or sentiment behind a document, paragraph or just a few sentences. As a simple example, consider a seller site like Amazon which has reviews from many buyers. We need an algorithm to classify each review as positive or negative. This is the case of binary sentiment analysis. There can be more classes such as positive, negative and neutral. In the case of emotions having to be distinguished, the number of classes will be much more. The problem that needs to be resolved is how a sentiment /opinion may be extracted from the given text.

Is this a difficult problem? It is, for sure. This is because human communication using natural language is based on nuances. The word nuance means 'a subtle difference in or shade of meaning, expression, sound'. Sentiments are not clear from pure text – facial expressions and sound play a part in it. But these are not matters of our concern here. Our only objective is to extract opinions from written text. But that itself is difficult because of the variations in the way different people talk and write. The context in which an opinion is expressed has a role–besides that, humour, sarcasms, metaphors, irony, slang, dialect, etc., make the whole scene extremely difficult.

In spite of all these issues, a lot of headway has been made in this field and automation of sentiment analysis has above 80% accuracy for most cases. If the words used to express opinion are direct, the problem becomes very simple. For example, words like good and bad are directly attributed to positive and negative sentiments respectively. But the computer needs to know how to link the term 'not good' to negative sentiment. There can be cases when in the same sentence, both sentiments are included–for example: "The food was good but the ambience was terrible", is such a sentence. Additional problems can come when both positive and negative opinions are expressed in a big document. Should the document be classified as supportive of a specific opinion or not? These are unresolved questions and a final conclusion is based on the context as well as on what is the intent for which the sentiment analysis is being done.

Examples of reviews

"Ha! I really liked this product! It is a seventeenth-century version of a twenty-first century computer."

Any one reading this can make out that a negative sentiment is embedded in it. But a computer algorithm may see the positive words in it and classify it as a positive review.

Take a look at these three sentences:

The dress is simply perfect.

It is okay for the price.

Can't think of a worse product.

These three sentences are directly translatable to positive, neutral and negative opinions. If we want to restrict to two sentiments, the first two would be positive and the last will be negative.

Now that we know the issues to be taken care of, let us discuss a simple example. In this example, we define a vocabulary from a set of training sentences which have already been labelled as positive or negative. Then we apply a 'test' sentence and the algorithm is to classify it as an expression of either a positive or negative sentiment.

16.5.1 Naïve Bayes Classifier

In Section 4.2.2, this classifier was discussed as being a 'generative' type of classifier. In tune with our conventions, y is the label and $\boldsymbol{x}$ is the input where $\boldsymbol{x}$ is a vector containing the features of the input.

The Naïve Bayes formula gives the label y_{new} of the test sentence, based on whether the probability of y being a positive sentiment or negative, is higher. This means that we should calculate both probabilities, $P(y_{Positive}/x)$ and $P(y_{Negative}/x)$. Equation 16.5 is to be used for the label y_{new} (Refer Section 4.2.2). y_{new} is the product of the probability of $P(y)$, and a set of conditional probabilities. The latter corresponds to the probability of a feature occurring in the corresponding class. Here the features are the words of the test sentence.

$$y_{\text{new}} = argmax_{y \varepsilon Y} P(y) \prod_j \underbrace{P(x_j/y)} \quad ...(16.5)$$

In this equation, the second term is a conditional probability. The conditional probability $P(x_j/y)$ is to be estimated for each token (word) of both the classes (positive and negative). j is the number of words of the vocabulary which are in the test sentence. We just have to take the counts of how many times each word (in the test sentence) appears in each class. Since some of the conditional probabilities may be 0 and cause Eq. 16.5 to become 0, these conditional probabilities are smoothed using the +1 Laplace smoothing formula. In this method, 1 is added to the numerator and the size of the vocabulary is added to the denominator.

The Laplace smoothing formula is:

$$P(x_j/y) = \frac{N_C + 1}{N_Y + V} \quad ...(16.6)$$

where

- N_C is the count of that particular word in the specified class
- N_Y is the number of words of the vocabulary, that is in the specified class
- V is the size of the chosen vocabulary

When test sentences are long, the product of probabilities (Eq. 16.5) will tend to be very small numbers and lead to the underflow problem. The remedy is to convert each of the probabilities to logarithms. Then the computation is reduced to simple addition.

Example 16.6 will make clear the method of using the Naïve Bayes classifier for a simple sentiment classification problem.

Example16.7 Identify the sentiment in each of the test sentences, given the training data with labels..

The test sentences are:

1. Good quality and comfortable material but useless fitting and high price.
2. Bad buy for the price
3. Beautiful and quality material

Training data is as given in Table 16.22.

Table 16.22 The training data with labels

Positive (+) Category	*Negative (–) Category*
Material is very good and comfortable	Very poor quality of the material
Beautiful colour and nice fitting	Sad and disappointed
Price is appropriate	Don't buy, this is useless.
	Bad material and high price

Solution: We choose the vocabulary after removing the stop words.

Vocabulary: material, very, good, comfortable, beautiful, fitting, price, poor, appropriate, quality, sad, disappointed, high, useless, don't, bad, colour, nice, buy

The size of the vocabulary, $V = 19$.

The number of words of the vocabulary, which is in the positive class is 10 (N_y)

The number of words of the vocabulary, which is in the negative class is 13 (N_y)

Case 1: Test sentence: **Good quality and comfortable material but useless fitting and high price.**

The words in the test sentences which are in the vocabulary are listed in column 1 of Table 16.23. The calculations of conditional probabilities of these test words using Eq. 16.7 is done for both the classes and is shown in Table 16.23.

Table 16.23 Calculations of conditional probabilities for both classes

	Positive Class			*Negative Class*		
Test words	N_Y	N_C	$\frac{N_C + 1}{N_Y + V}$	N_Y	N_C	$\frac{N_C + 1}{N_Y + V}$
good	10	1	$\frac{2}{10 + 19} = \frac{2}{29}$	13	0	$\frac{1}{13 + 19} = \frac{1}{32}$
quality	10	0	$\frac{1}{29}$	13	1	$\frac{2}{32}$
comfortable	10	1	$\frac{2}{29}$	13	0	$\frac{1}{32}$
material	10	1	$\frac{2}{29}$	13	2	$\frac{3}{32}$
useless	10	0	$\frac{1}{29}$	13	1	$\frac{2}{32}$
fitting	10	1	$\frac{2}{29}$	13	0	$\frac{1}{32}$
high	10	0	$\frac{1}{29}$	13	1	$\frac{2}{32}$
price	10	1	$\frac{2}{29}$	13	1	$\frac{2}{32}$
Product of Conditional Probabilities			6.39×10^{-11}			4.36×10^{-11}

(i) Calculation based on probability

C_N and C_P stand for class Negative and Positive respectively

Three of the 7 training sentences belong to the class Positive (C_P) and 4 of them belong to the Negative class (C_N). So

$$P(C_P) = 3/7$$
$$P(C_N) = 4/7$$

Probability (sentence to be in Positive class) $= P(C_P) \times \prod P(x_j/C_P)$

$$= 3/7 \times 6.39 \times 10^{-11}$$
$$\mathbf{= 2.7385 \times 10^{-11}}$$

Probability (sentence to be in Negative class) $= P(C_N) \times \prod P(x_j/C_N)$

$$= 4/7 \times 4.36 \times 10^{-11}$$
$$\mathbf{= 2.4914 \times 10^{-11}}$$

Since ***P*** (sentence to be in Positive class) **>** ***P*** (sentence to be in Negative class), **the test sentence belongs to the Positive class.**

It is observed from Table 16.23 that the product of the conditional probabilities is a very small number. We should convert the individual conditional probabilities to $\log_{10}$ and add them.

$$\prod_j P(x_j/y) = \sum_j \log P(x_j/y) \quad \text{...(16.7)}$$

The calculation is repeated for the same test sentence using Eq. 16.7.

C_P and C_N are notations for class Positive and class Negative. The log of the conditional probabilities of each word (*j* is the number of words) of the test sentence is calculated and added, for both the Positive and Negative categories.

Test sentence: **Good quality and comfortable material but useless fitting and high price**

Positive Category

$P(C_p) = \log \frac{3}{7}$

$\log P(\text{good}/C_p) = \log \frac{2}{29}$

$\log P(\text{quality}/C_p) = \log \frac{1}{29}$

$\log P(\text{comfortable}/C_p) = \log \frac{2}{29}$

$\log P(\text{material}/C_p) = \log \frac{2}{29}$

$\log P(\text{useless}/C_p) = \log \frac{1}{29}$

$\log P(\text{fitting}/C_p) = \log \frac{2}{29}$

$\log P(\text{high}/C_p) = \log \frac{1}{29}$

$\log P(\text{price}/C_p) = \log \frac{2}{29}$

P(Positive Category)

$= \log P(C_p) + \log P(\text{good}/C_p) + \log P(\text{quality}/C_p) + \log P(\text{comfortable}/C_p) + \log P(\text{material}/C_p) + \log P(\text{useless}\ /C_p) + \log P(\text{fitting}\ /C_p) + \log P(\text{high}\ /C_p) + \log P(\text{price}/C_p)$

$= \log\frac{3}{7} + \log\frac{2}{29} + \log\frac{1}{29} + \log\frac{2}{29} + \log\frac{2}{29} + \log\frac{1}{29} + \log\frac{2}{29} + \log\frac{1}{29} + \log\frac{2}{29} = \mathbf{-\ 10.56}$

Negative Category

$\log P(C_n) = \log \frac{4}{7}$

$\log P(\text{good}/C_N) = \log \frac{1}{32}$

$\log P(\text{quality } /C_N) = \log \frac{2}{32}$

$\log P(\text{comfortable } /C_N) = \log \frac{1}{32}$

$\log P(\text{material } /C_N) = \log \frac{3}{32}$

$\log P(\text{useless } /C_N) = \log \frac{2}{32}$

$\log P(\text{fitting } /C_N) = \log \frac{1}{32}$

$\log P(\text{high } /C_N) = \log \frac{2}{32}$

$\log P(\text{price}/C_N) = \log \frac{2}{32}$

$P(\text{Negative Category}) = \log P(C_N) + \log P(\text{good}/C_N) + \log P(\text{quality } /C_N) + \log P(\text{comfortable}/C_N) + \log P(\text{material } /C_N) + \log P(\text{useless } /C_N) + \log P(\text{fitting } /C_N) + \log P(\text{high } /C_N + \log P(\text{price}/C_N)$

$= \log\frac{4}{7} + \log\frac{1}{32} + \log\frac{2}{32} + \log\frac{1}{32} + \log\frac{3}{32} + \log\frac{2}{32} + \log\frac{1}{32} + \log\frac{2}{32} + \log\frac{2}{32} = \mathbf{-10.602}$

$= \mathbf{-10.602}$

Max (P(Positive Category), P(Negative Category))

=Max (–10.56, –10.602) = –10.56

The class is Positive

Similar calculations are done for the next two sentences. The result is:

1. *Bad buy for the price* –Class is Negative
2. *Beautiful and quality material* –Class is Negative

Conclusions drawn

We have done an elaborate calculation for the first test sentence. The result says that the first sentence belongs to the Positive category while the remaining two are classified as sentences expressing Negative sentiments. The second test sentence is obviously negative, but why is the third sentence also showing a Negative sentiment? The sentence is 'Beautiful and quality material'. This has to be a Positive sentiment in the view of the reviewer. But our algorithm has classified it to be Negative. This is because, out of the three words of the sentence which are in the vocabulary, two have greater counts in the Negative class.

This example shows that it is the count (frequency) and presence of the words that determine the final result. Sentiment analysis is also a bag of words model. The semantics and order of the words do not matter. We have just picked up the relevant words and dropped it into a bag as mentioned in Section 16.1.2.

16.5.2 Text Classification

This is a problem exactly similar to sentiment classification. Based on the BOW concept and the count of the relevant words in the chosen vocabulary, it may be needed to classify documents under labels such as Sports, Education, Home, Politics, Health, etc.

In Example 16.8 a training set and two test sentences are shown. Calculations are not shown as the method is exactly the same as in Example 16.7. But coding using Python has been done and is shown as Example 16.8a.

Example 16.8

Doc 1: of class POLITICS: India is a constitutional democracy with a parliamentary system of government, and at the heart of the system is a commitment to hold regular, free and fair elections.

DOC 2 of class SPORTS: Cricket is the most popular sport in India and is played almost everywhere – in villages and cities, it is a regular scene to see teams hold free and fair games.

Test Sentences

- *The democracy of India is tested at regular periods with free and fair elections held to uphold the constitutional system.*
- *Cricket as a game is fun only if it is free and fair and played regularly.*

Result: Test sentence no. 1 is of class Politics and sentence no. 2 is of class Sports. This has been arrived at using Python code and is shown in Example 16.8a.

16.5.3 Algorithms other than Naïve Bayes

For these classification problems, SVM (Section 3.5) and Logistic Regression (Section 3.3) also give good results and may be employed. However, the Naïve Bayes algorithm is a very popular NLP method, because it performs very well and is less complex than the other two algorithms.

16.6 PYTHON CODE WITH NLTK LIBRARY

The code corresponding to Example 16.8 is listed below. The TF-IDF model has been used for text vectorization.

The code used the Naïve Bayes, SVM and logistic regression algorithms and the same result was obtained in all the cases.

Example 16.8a

```
import nltk
import re
from sklearn.datasets import load_files
nltk.download('stopwords')
from sklearn.feature_extraction.text import TfidfVectorizer
from sklearn.naive_bayes import MultinomialNB
```

```
from sklearn.pipeline import make_pipeline
from nltk.corpus import stopwords
from nltk.stem import WordNetLemmatizer
from sklearn.linear_model import LogisticRegression
from sklearn.naive_bayes import GaussianNB
from sklearn.svm import SVC

train_data = load_files(r"D:\NIT_PhD\Class\AI\Assignment4_NLP\Dataset") #
path of training set
test_data1 = load_files(r"D:\NIT_PhD\Class\AI\Assignment4_NLP\test1") #
path of test set 1
test_data2 = load_files(r"D:\NIT_PhD\Class\AI\Assignment4_NLP\test2") #
path of test set 1

print('\nTrain data:', train_data.data)
print('\nTarger Classes:', train_data.target)
print('\nTest data1:', test_data1.data)
print('\nTest data2:', test_data2.data)
stopwords1 = stopwords.words('english')

def remove_stopwords(text):
  clean_text=' '.join([word for word in text.split() if word not in stopwords1])
  return clean_text

#Text Preprocessing
def text_preprocessing(X):
  documents = []
  stemmer = WordNetLemmatizer()

  for sen in range(0, len(X)):
  # Remove all the special characters
  document = re.sub(r'\W', ' ', str(X[sen]))

  #document = re.sub(r'-\s+', ' ', document)
  #Remove stop words
  document = remove_stopwords(document.lower())

  # remove all single characters
  document = re.sub(r'\s+[a-zA-Z]\s+', ' ', document)

  # Remove single characters from the start
  document = re.sub(r'\^[a-zA-Z]\s+', ' ', document)
```

```
    # Substituting multiple spaces with single space
    document = re.sub(r'\s+', ' ', document, flags=re.I)

    # Removing prefixed 'b'
    document = re.sub(r'^b\s+', '', document)

    # Converting to Lowercase
    document = document.lower()

    # Lemmatization
    document = document.split()
    document = [stemmer.lemmatize(word) for word in document]
    document = ' '.join(document)
    documents.append(document)
    return documents

print('\nAfter test preprocessing:')
train_doc = text_preprocessing(train_data.data)
print('\nTrain doc:',train_doc)
test_doc1 = text_preprocessing(test_data1.data)
print('\nTest doc1:',test_doc1)
test_doc2 = text_preprocessing(test_data2.data)
print('\nTest doc2:',test_doc2)

#Convert text to numbers using TF-IDF vector
import pandas as pd
vectorizer = TfidfVectorizer(smooth_idf=True,norm='l1')
X = vectorizer.fit_transform(train_doc).toarray()
df = pd.DataFrame(X.tolist(), columns = vectorizer.get_feature_names() )
print('\nBag Of Words:', vectorizer.get_feature_names())

import pandas as pd
df_idf = pd.DataFrame(vectorizer.idf_, index=vectorizer.get_feature_
names(),columns=["idf_weights"])
#print(vectorizer.vocabulary_)
print('\nIDF:\n', df_idf)
print('\nTF-IDF Vector:\n', df)
print('\nTF-IDF Vector:\n', X)

# sort ascending
df_idf.sort_values(by=['idf_weights'])
```

```
# Build the model using NB
model = make_pipeline(TfidfVectorizer(), MultinomialNB())
model.fit(train_doc, train_data.target)

# Build the model using logistic Regression
model1 = make_pipeline(TfidfVectorizer(), LogisticRegression())
model1.fit(train_doc, train_data.target)

# Build the model using linear SVM
model2 = make_pipeline(TfidfVectorizer(), SVC(kernel='linear'))
model2.fit(train_doc, train_data.target)

# Predict the categories of the test data
print('\nClassification:')
print('\nUsing Naive Bayes:\n')
predicted_categories = model.predict(test_doc1)
print('predicted_category for test_data1:',predicted_categories)
predicted_categories = model.predict(test_doc2)
print('predicted_category for test_data2:',predicted_categories)

# Predict the categories of the test data
print('\nUsing Logistic Regression:\n')
predicted_categories = model1.predict(test_data1.data)
print('predicted_category for test_data1:',predicted_categories)
predicted_categories = model1.predict(test_data2.data)
print('predicted_category for test_data2:',predicted_categories)

# Predict the categories of the test data
print('\nUsing linear SVM:\n')
predicted_categories = model2.predict(test_data1.data)
print('predicted_category for test_data1:',predicted_categories)
predicted_categories = model2.predict(test_data2.data)
print('predicted_category for test_data2:',predicted_categories)
```

Conclusion

With this, we come to the end of the topic of frequency based text applications. Understanding the theory and logic of the methods of this chapter is a fundamental necessity and prerequisite for grasping the aspects of more complex methods of text vectorization and their applications which will be taken up in the next chapters.

Questions

1. Which are the BOW models used in text representations?
2. Why do BOW models like count vector and TF-IDF lead to sparse matrics?
3. How is IDF defined?
4. What is meant by document similarity?
5. How is cosine similarity defined?
6. For a word, what is meant by its 'context'?
7. What is the information available in the co-occurrence matrix?
8. Why is sentiment analysis and text classification seen to be difficult tasks?

Exercise

1. Write the one hot representation of each word in the following sentence.
   Also write a python code for it and get the output.
   This world is beautiful.
2. Find the list of stopwords as used in NLTK
3. (coding not required)
   A corpus has three documents. (each document is just a sentence). Find the (i) count vector model (ii) TF-IDF weighted matrix of the corpus and identify the most distinctive words.
   Document 1: *The trees here are evergreen.*
   Document 2: *Evergreen trees have green leaves always.*
   Document 3: *Coniferous trees have green leaves always. They are evergreen.*
   Note: Do pre-processing including stop word removal.
   The TF matrix, IDF, etc., should be shown. No steps are to be missed.
4. Find the TF–IDF vector of the data in Tables 16.24 and 16.25. Also find the most distinctive term.

Table 16.24 Count of terms

Document	No. of terms
Electronic circuits	1120
Embedded systems	3400
Electrical networks	1300
Electrical machines	1970
Power electronics	1700

Table 16.25 Count of words in each document

	Electronic circuits	*Embedded systems*	*Electrical networks*	*Electrical machines*	*Power electronics*
Reset	0	32	0	0	0
op-Amp	60	0	10	15	0
resistor	50	20	10	5	12
transistor	100	20	120	10	106
motor	0	15	0	200	0

5. Using cosine similarity, calculate the similarity between the document 'Electronic circuits' and the other documents shown in Tables 16.24 and 16.25. Show the steps and tabulate the results.
6. Using calculations and coding, do sentiment analysis for the following data using Naïve Bayes algorithm.

Positive category	*Negative category*
Great phone at a great price	Regret buying this phone
The phone looks awesome	Poor in performance
Awesome price and looks	Not great for the price

Test sentence: *Great phone in price but not in performance.*

7. Find sentiment analysis problems using a large dataset available online.

Do coding to define the sentiment. Use (i) Naïve Bayes (ii) SVM (iii) Logistic Regression

The text should be vectorized using

(i) Count vector

(ii) TF-IDF

Do coding for both cases.

CHAPTER

17

Prediction Based Methods for Word Embeddings: Word2Vec

In this chapter you will

- learn the concept of dense vector embeddings,
- understand the features of Word2Vec,
- compare CBOW and Skipgram,
- analyze the creation of a typical word embedding,
- discover the use of hierarchial Softmax,
- analyze the use of negative sampling, and
- implement vector embeddings for words.

17.0 INTRODUCTION

Let us first be clear about the term 'word embedding'. This simply means that we embed words as vectors of numbers. In the last chapter, this was done using simple counts and weighted (by TF-IDF) counts. This is a frequency based method because the frequency of word occurrence in a document is what produces the vectors. The resultant vectors of any document would have the size of the vocabulary of the system. Since vocabulary sizes for practical applications have sizes ranging to millions, the size of each vector is very large and these vectors also have many zeros in them. Such embeddings are referred to as 'sparse vector embeddings'. One aspect of these embeddings is that the semantic and syntactic relationships between words are not explicitly observed. Such sparse embeddings of very high dimensions had been the method for 'text representation' until a new method was proposed and implemented in 2013.

The concept of 'dense vector embeddings' of smaller dimensions was proposed by Tomas Mikolov and implemented by his team in Google. His implementation named Word2Vec was published in 2013 in a paper titled "Efficient Estimation of Word Representations in Vector Space". Over time, it has been improved and now there is also another standard named GloVe (Global Vectors for Word Representation). This was made by Stanford University. FastText developed by Facebook is an improvement on Word2Vec because it can cater to parts of words denoted as 'subwords'. In this, smaller datasets are possible to be used and unknown words are handled better.

Dense vector embeddings for words discussed in this chapter is a 'prediction' based method because the vectors are obtained by the principle of 'target words being predicted by context words' or 'context words being predicted by target words'. We will get into details of this now.

17.1 WORD2VEC

In Word2Vec, each word is represented as a dense vector of numbers between -1 and +1. Below, we see the word 'computer' being represented as a 10 element vector.

[0.04252458 0.01968815 –0.00370141 0.02047303 –0.00246323 –0.01602578
 0.0271402 –0.04732982 0.02253118 0.02593592]

This looks very odd, doesn't it? How does the word 'computer' become such a set of numbers? What is the logic behind such a representation? What do these numbers indicate? What is the method to get this representation? What information do we get from such a representation? What is the validity of such a representation? These are the questions to which we seek answers. In Section 16.4, we discussed the co-occurrence matrix and the concept of context words. The importance of context words for any 'centre word' is based on the concept of statistical semantics. J.R. Firth, an English linguist had made the remark that "a word is characterized by the company it keeps". This simply means that the meaning of a word can be gauged by the words surrounding it, which are called its context words.

When words are projected onto a high dimensional vector space, similar words tend to cluster together. Similarity need not mean that these words are synonyms. It could be topical similarity – for example, the words related to automobiles are likely to be seen together–gear, clutch, accelerator, engine, car, truck, spark plug, etc., may be seen to lie close together in such a space. Similar emotions will be clustered in one area–joy, happiness, love, euphoria, etc., will be in one area and sadness, disgust, anger, hate, despair, etc., will be in another distant area in the multidimensional space. These characteristics of words are simply due to their context.

Counts of word occurrences, cosine similarity and context windows covered in Chapter 16 are also ideas related to 'distributional semantic modeling in vector spaces' that will lead to the dense vector embeddings of the Word2Vec model. On the final note, it is important to note that any representation is dependent on the corpus on which the training has been done.

So there is nothing 'binding or permanent' on the elements of the 10 element vector which was shown to represent the word 'computer'. That vector is in a 10-dimensional space. We can generate a 300 element vector for the same word because the dimension of the embedding vector is a hyperparameter to be specified in the Python program. Google's Word2Vec is trained on around 100 billion words from a Google News dataset. Each word is represented by a 300-500 element vector.

17.1.1 Features of Word2Vec

One of its many features is that semantic relationship between words is seen to be very clearly retained. In the specified multidimensional vector space, related words are seen to be placed close together. In Fig. 17.1, we find that words which are related to similar topics are crowded together/related by similar distances. This is shown in two- and three-dimensional space — actually the whole thing is in a multidimensional space which is difficult to visualize, but it will be worthwhile to imagine related words as clusters of points where each point is a word.

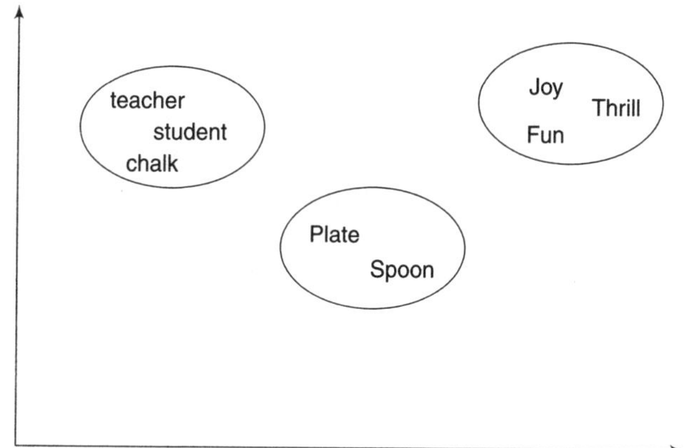

Fig. 17.1 (a) Words with 'topical' similarity clustered together

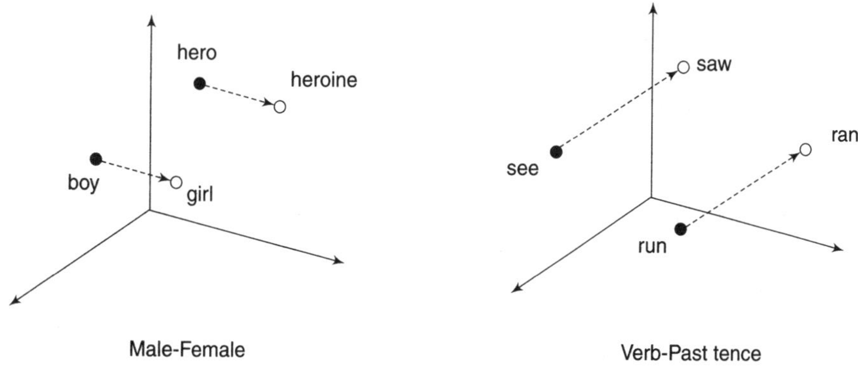

Fig. 17.1 (b) Relationship between related words shown in three-dimensional space

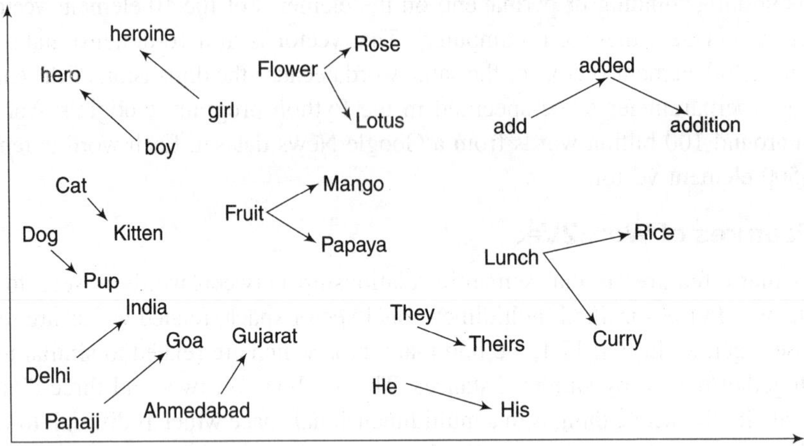

Fig. 17.1 (c) Semantic relations of related words

All these features are possible because any word is embedded based on its context. Figures 17.1a,b and c show that in vector space, the positions of vectors are related based on their meanings and relations as used in the training corpus. Figure 17.1a shows words with 'topical' similarity to be crowded together. Figure 17.1b shows gender related words and verbs related to their different inflections—in short, distances are shown to be similar. Fig 17.1c shows more instances of 'related' words being together. Interestingly, the paper by Mikolov mentions that it could be shown that by using algebraic operations on their vectors, King – man + woman = Queen, or King – man = Queen – woman. This is the same as what we see in Fig, 17b, it seems that hero – boy = heroine – girl.

Note: Now we will start our discussion on the methods used in Word2Vec to produce the vectors for each word in the training corpus. This is not a topic that you will be able to grasp in one single reading unless you have a very good understanding of the aspects of neural networks such as dimensionality of weight vectors, and the use of activation functions such as Softmax and Sigmoid. However, by a patient perusal of the chapter again, along with cross-checking exact details of neural network functioning, things will start getting simpler until a clear picture will emerge.

17.2 CBOW VS SKIPGRAM

There are two models in the Word2Vec prediction method. One is the 'CBOW' (Continuous Bag of Words) and the other is called the Continuous Skipgram or simply 'Skipgram'. Let us try to understand how these methods differ. Keep in mind that our entire focus is on getting a vector representation of a target word based on its context words. The vector dimensionality is decided by the parameters of the network. The word 'continuous' in this context indicates that the words are continuous in the *d*-dimensional space of their representation, in contrast to the discrete representation done by one hot vectors.

Take this particular sentence:

*He Likes Maths **Physics** Chemistry Programming and Biology.*

Let us mark 'Physics' as the centre word and also name it as the 'target word'. The 'context words' are the words on the right and left of the target word. If the 'context window' is of size 2, the context words are the words 'Likes, Maths' on the left of the target word and 'Chemistry, Programming' which are on the right.

The words, 'Maths' and 'Chemistry' are the context words if the context window is of size 1. Now observe Figs. 17.2a and 17.2b. In the CBOW method, the context words (Maths, Chemistry) are used to predict the target word 'Physics'. In the Skipgram, it is just the reverse, the target word 'Physics' is used to predict the context words 'Maths' and 'Chemistry'.

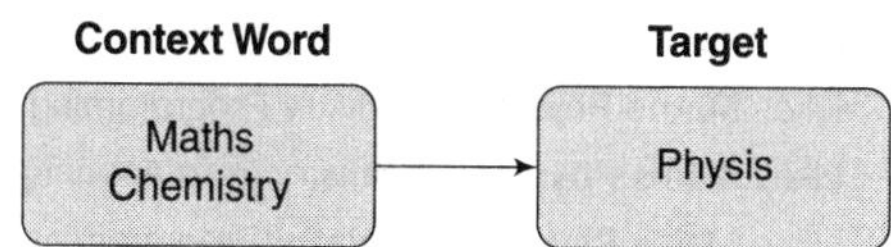

Fig. 17.2 (a) CBOW prediction-context words predict the target

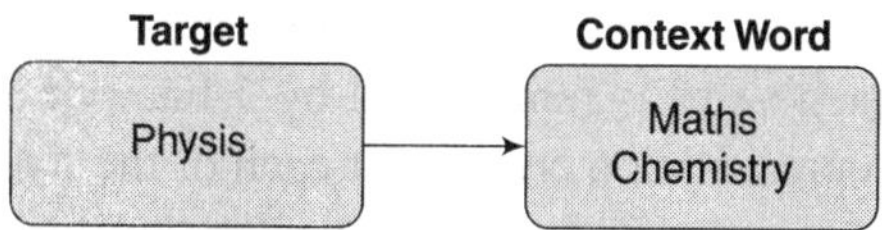

Fig. 17.2 (b) Skipgram-prediction of context words from the target word

17.2.1 Neural Word Embeddings

To perform the operation of prediction, a shallow neural network is used–one with an input layer, a hidden layer and an output layer. We know that in a neural network, when an input is given, the output is expected to match the 'ground truth'. This simply means that when we give an input to a neural network, we have an expectation of what the output should be. If the output does not match our expectation, the weights of the network are updated until the expected values are obtained at the output. In mathematical terms, a 'Cost function' is minimized and the gradient descent algorithm is used to update the weights of the network. In Word2Vec, the 'final updated weights at the hidden layer' are chosen as the vector embedding of a word. We will discuss more to make this point clear.

17.2.2 The CBOW Model

Let's start with the CBOW model. The name stands for 'Continuous Bag of Words'. To understand the basic concepts, we will now use a very small vocabulary of five words and relate these words to the working of the model.

Let us stick to the sentence that we started with, but use only the set of words.

'Likes Maths Physics Chemistry Programming' as our reference set. There are only five words in our vocabulary.

In Figs. 17.2a and b, we saw only one instance of the context window of size 1. In practice, the context window is continuously moved over the text as the training proceeds. Let us discuss the simplest possible case of:

(i) the context window being of size just 1, and

(ii) only the context word on the right side of the target word being used.

Figure 17.3 shows the context window being moved over the text and as it does so, we get different target and context words at each training instant. The words in bold in the square box are the target words at each instant.

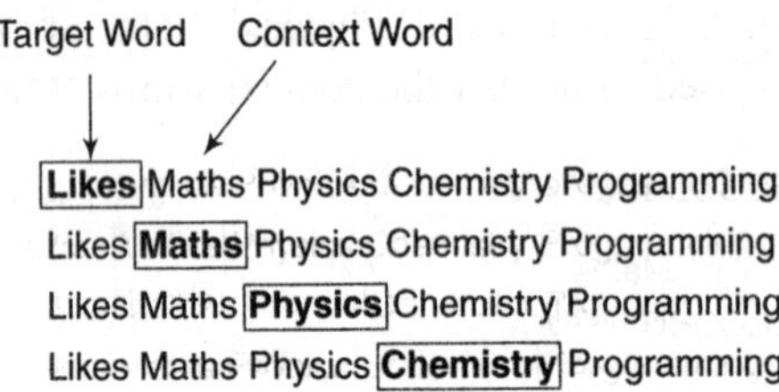

Fig. 17.3 The target words and context word for 4 training instances

In the beginning, the target and context words are represented as one hot vectors. Since the vocabulary size is 5, each word is represented by 5 bits out of which only one bit is a '1'. Table 17.1 shows the representation chosen for each of the five words. Table 17.2 shows the context word–target word pairs. This table indicates that for a particular context word applied at the input, a specific target word is expected at the output. For example, when the context word is 'maths' represented by the vector [01000], the target vector at the output layer should be 'likes' with the vector [10000].

Table 17.1 One hot vectors of all the words in the example

Words	*One hot representation*
Likes	10000
Maths	01000
Physics	00100
Chemistry	00010
Programming	00001

Table 17.2 Context word vs target word for the example

Training instant	*Context word at the input layer*	*Target word at the output layer*
1	Maths [01000]	Likes [10000]
2	Physics [00100]	Maths [01000]
3	Chemistry [00010]	Physics [00100]
4	Programming [00001]	Chemistry [00010]

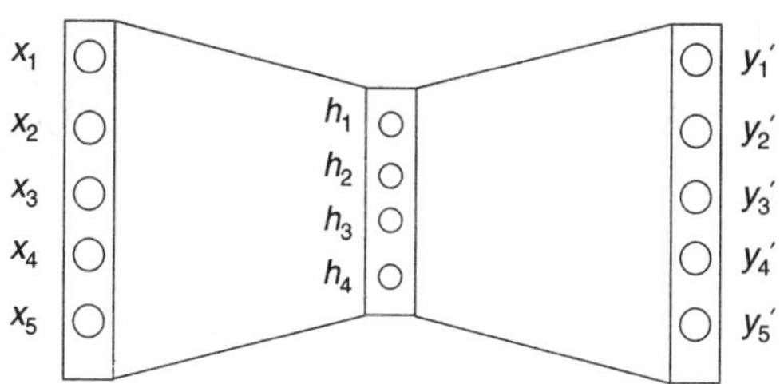

Fig. 17.4 The CBOW network for our example

For CBOW, the context word is fed in at the input layer, and the target word is expected at the output layer. The objective function should maximize the probability $P(w_T/C)$ for each training sample. (w_T = *Target Word*, C = *Context*). Now let's focus our attention on the dimensions at the different layers for our example (Figure 17.4). The input and output layer neurons are five in number. We have chosen a hidden layer of 4 neurons, as we want our embedding vector space to be of dimensionality 4. Each word will then be embedded as a 4 element vector.

Length of the input vector $\mathbf{x}$ = 5, the input vector is $[x_1\ x_2\ x_3\ x_4\ x_5]$

Length of the output vector $\mathbf{y}'$ = 5, the output vector is $[y'_1\ y'_2\ y'_3\ y'_4\ y'_5]$

Length of the hidden layer vector $\mathbf{h}$ = 4, $[h_1\ h_2\ h_3\ h_4]$

The dimension of the weight matrix between the input and hidden layers = 5 × 4

The dimensions of the weight matrix between the hidden and output layers = 4 × 5.

Figure 17.5 shows the dimensions of the h vector and elements of the weight matrices.

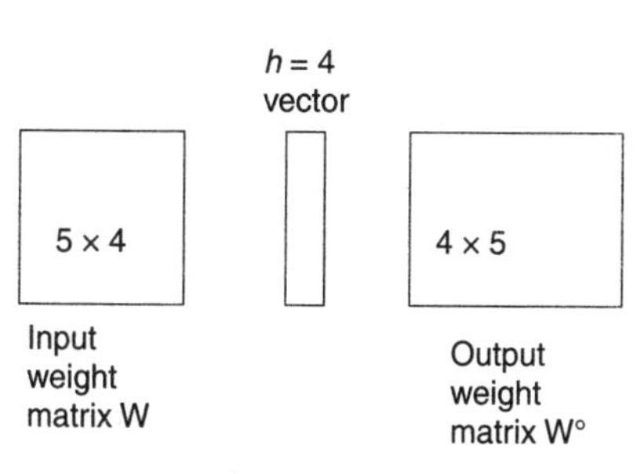

Fig. 17.5 (a) Dimensions of the weight matrices and the h vector of our example

w_{11}	w_{12}	w_{13}	w_{14}
w_{21}	w_{22}	w_{23}	w_{24}
w_{31}	w_{32}	w_{33}	w_{34}
w_{41}	w_{42}	w_{43}	w_{44}
w_{51}	w_{52}	w_{53}	w_{54}

Fig. 17.5 (b) The input weight matrix (5 × 4) of our example

w^o_{11}	w^o_{12}	w^o_{13}	w^o_{14}	w^o_{15}
w^o_{21}	w^o_{22}	w^o_{23}	w^o_{24}	w^o_{25}
w^o_{31}	w^o_{32}	w^o_{33}	w^o_{34}	w^o_{35}
w^o_{41}	w^o_{42}	w^o_{43}	w^o_{44}	w^o_{45}

Fig. 17.5 (c) The output weight matrix (4 × 5) of our example

$$\mathbf{h} = \boldsymbol{W}^T\boldsymbol{x} \qquad ...(17.1)$$

Equation 17.1 is the computation at the hidden layer as shown in Fig. 17.6. But since context words have only one non-zero element, we simply copy the kth row of the W matrix (Fig. 17.5b) to h (k^{th} column of $\mathbf{W}^T$). $k = 2$.

$$\mathbf{W}^T \cdot x = \mathbf{h}$$

w11	w11	w31	w41	w51
w12	w22	w32	w42	w52
w13	w23	w33	w43	w53
w14	w24	w34	w44	w54

$$W^T x = h$$

$$* \begin{bmatrix} 0 \\ 1 \\ 0 \\ 0 \end{bmatrix} = \begin{bmatrix} w21 \\ w22 \\ w23 \\ w24 \end{bmatrix} = h$$

Fig. 17.6 Computation at the input side for our example

Context word is maths = [01000]. Figure 17.6 shows the resultant **h** vector. Thus, one of the rows of the input weight matrix becomes the hidden layer weights. One important point to note about this network is that there is no non-linear activation (as is the case in usual neural networks) after the hidden layer. The hidden layer weights are directly projected to the output layer and that is why this is frequently referred to as the 'projection layer'.

$$y' = \mathbf{W}^{o^T}\boldsymbol{h} \qquad ...(17.2)$$

w^o_{11}	w^o_{21}	w^o_{31}	w^o_{41}
w^o_{12}	w^o_{22}	w^o_{32}	w^o_{42}
w^o_{13}	w^o_{23}	w^o_{33}	w^o_{43}
w^o_{14}	w^o_{24}	w^o_{34}	w^o_{44}
w^o_{15}	w^o_{25}	w^o_{35}	w^o_{45}

$$* \begin{bmatrix} h_1 \\ h_2 \\ h_3 \\ h_4 \end{bmatrix} = \begin{bmatrix} y_1' \\ y_2' \\ y_3' \\ y_4' \\ y_5' \end{bmatrix}$$

Fig. 17.7 (a) Computation at the output side (for our example)

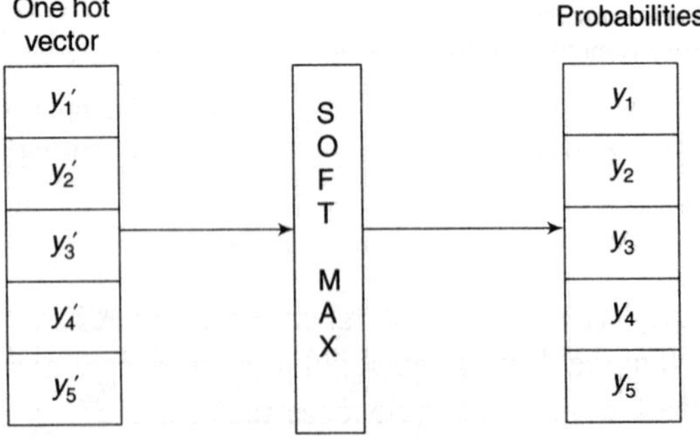

Fig. 17.7 (b) The Softmax computation at the output

Equation 17.2 is the computation at the output side. See Fig. 17.7a. After that $\mathbf{y}'$ is multiplied by the Softmax function to get a list of probabilities corresponding to each of the 5 words of the Vocabulary. (See Fig. 17.7b). The word with the highest probability is the correct target word when convergence occurs. Note that each output line of y corresponds to one word in the vocabulary.

Figure 17.8 shows the fully connected network for the dimensions we have selected for our example.

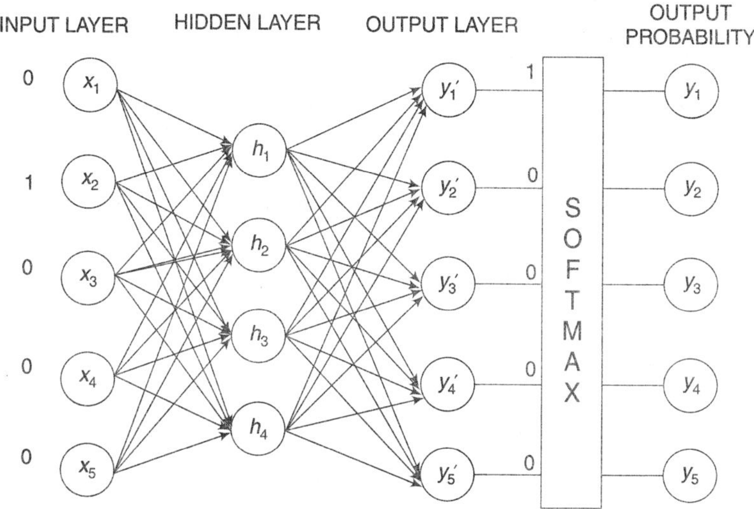

Fig. 17.8 The fully connected network corresponding to our example

Now that we have seen the mathematical operations from the input side to the output, let us list out the steps and dimensions of the different sections of a general network.

- The input vector $\boldsymbol{x}$ is of length V and is one hot encoded. In our example, $V = 5$.
- The multiplication of the binary vector $\boldsymbol{x}$ and the input weight matrix W of size $V \times N$ gives us the embedding vector which is the kth row of the weight matrix W. In our example, $N = 4$.
- This vector of dimension N forms the hidden layer vector $\boldsymbol{h}$.
- The multiplication of the hidden layer and the output layer weight matrix W° of size $N \times V$ produces the output vector $\boldsymbol{y}'$ of size V. This is a one hot vector.
- The vector $\boldsymbol{y}'$ vector is multiplied by a Softmax function to get $\boldsymbol{y}$. This is a set of probabilities for each of the words of the vocabulary.
- The vector $\boldsymbol{h}$ at the hidden layer is the vector embedding of the target word.

At the beginning of training for each input, the $\boldsymbol{h}$ vector will be random. At the end of the training with that specific context word, this vector would have been updated such that the output will give a high probability for the expected output, which should be the exact target word corresponding to the input context word.

The training objective (for one training sample) is to maximize the conditional probability of observing the right target word at the output given the context word as the input, $P(w_T/C)$. This is the logic of using this $\boldsymbol{h}$ vector as the vector embedding for the target word.

17.2.2.1 CBOW with more than One Context Word

What we have just done is an evaluation of the case of a target word with just one context word. This was discussed only for understanding the process. In a real situation, even with a context window of just one, there will be two context words–one on the left and the other on the right, of the target word. Then the average of the two context words will be the input. Take a look at Table 17.2 once again. Let's use Physics as the target word. Then the context words are 'Maths' and 'Chemistry' with vectors as in Table 17.1. At the input of the network, the sum of the vectors of Maths and Chemistry will be used which is [01010]. This sum vector when applied to the W matrix, will choose two rows (the second and fourth rows). These two rows are added and the sum is divided by the number of context words to get the average.

Let's use a numerical example. The W matrix (5 × 4) is shown in Fig. 17.9.

0.10	0.13	0.12	0.3
0.2	0.2	0.11	0.23
0.23	0.32	0.15	0.17
0.32	0.10	0.8	0.6
0.2	0.23	0.8	0.21

Fig. 17.9 A sample W matrix

This is multiplied by the sum of the context words which is [01010]. Note that only two bits (2nd and 4th) of this is '1'. The computation here is as given in Eq. 17.1. The 2nd and 4th rows of the $\boldsymbol{W}$ matrix (Fig. 17.9) alone contribute to form the **h** vector. These rows are added. After that, this vector is divided by C where C is the number of context words. This is necessary because in a practical scenario, the context window will be greater than 1. Here $C = 2$. In the calculation $\boldsymbol{h} = [0.26\ 0.15\ 0.455\ 0.415]^T$ (see Fig. 17.10). This is the initial value of the **h** vector and is the vector projected to the output matrix.

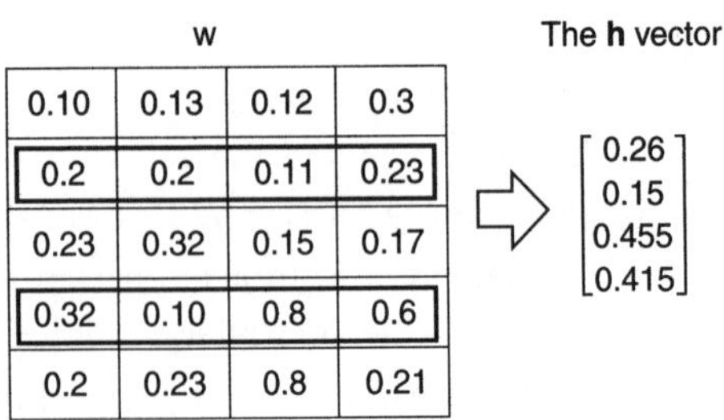

Fig. 17.10 The computation of the initial **h** vector for two context words

After the computations and training, the right target word will be chosen from the set of V words. Figure 17.11 shows a general CBOW configuration. The context window shown here is 2 and thus are four context words. w_t is the target word. The context words on its left and right are notated as w_{t-1}, w_{t-2}, w_{t+1} and w_{t+2}. In practice, larger context windows are used and our choice depends on the application.

In short, we can conclude that the CBOW is an architecture for creating word embeddings which uses the past '*n*' words and future '*n*' words with respect to a target word.

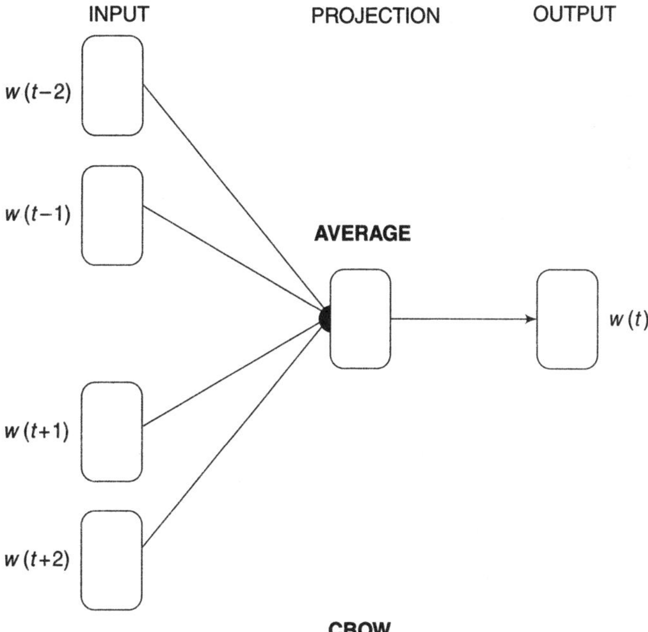

Fig. 17.11 The CBOW network showing two context words each on each side of the target

17.2.2.2 The Softmax Layer

The final output layer is a Softmax layer whose function is to convert the y' vector into a set of probabilities (Refer Section 10.8.5). At the output, there are V neurons and when the value of V is very large as in practical cases, the computation of the Softmax function will be an enormous task. When V = 10,000 (say) the probability calculations have to be done for all the 10,000 words for each training instance. Following each such computation, the weight matrices $\boldsymbol{W}$ and W^O have to be updated. Take V = 10,000 and N = 500. Then the weight matrices $\boldsymbol{W}$ and $\boldsymbol{W}^{\boldsymbol{O}}$ will each have elements numbering 50,00,000. This whole process is to be repeated until the highest probability is obtained at the output for the right target word. This is definitely highly compute-intensive.

The CBOW model has therefore been slightly modified at the output end. This is named 'Hierarchial Softmax' and let's see how it reduces computation.

17.2.2.2.1 The Hierachical Softmax

For CBOW, the output is a Softmax layer which has to give a high probability to the 'right target word'. This implies that the probability calculation for all the V words is to be done repeatedly for each training instance. Hierarchial softmax reduces this by fitting the V words onto a binary tree thus reducing the complexity from $O(V)$ to $O(\log_2 V)$. If $V = 50,00,000$, the complexity reduces to 22. This is a dramatic reduction.

Let's see how the output stage of the CBOW is modified. Figure 17.12 shows the usual functionality of the output part of the original CBOW network. With the Softmax calculation, each word in the vocabulary is attributed a probability to be the target word. Figure 17.12 shows the probability of a target word w_T given a context C, $P(w_T/C)$ as a set of probabilities. There are 8 words in the vocabulary and 'college' is the word with the highest probability (0.28) of being the target word for the given context, C. Note that the probability of each word is obtained from the Softmax computation.

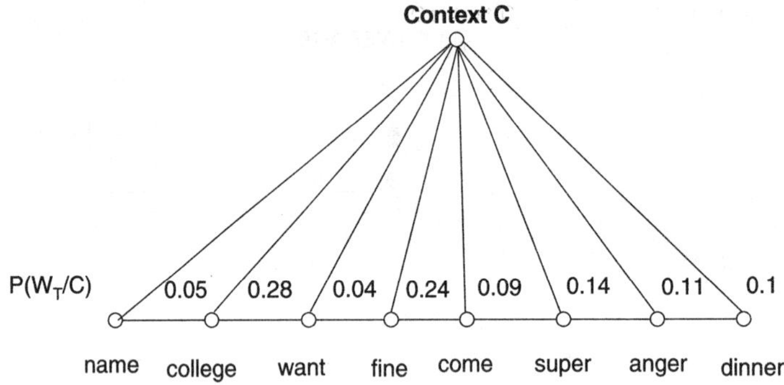

Fig. 17.12 Softmax probabilities for sample vocabulary of 8 words

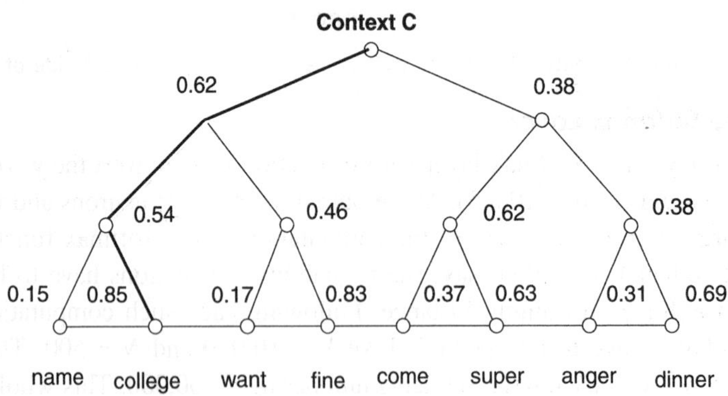

Fig. 17.13 Implementation of Hierarchial Softmax using a tree at the output

In Hierarchial Softmax, this output stage is replaced by a binary tree as shown in Fig. 17.13. The words in the vocabulary are at the leaves of the tree. To reach a particular leaf, a path from the root must be selected. The path with the highest probability is chosen and the word at the corresponding leaf is the chosen target word. This entails finding the product of the probabilities of each edge along the path to the leaf node.

At each node, there are two options – to take a path to the left or to the right. At the root, when one path is chosen, it means that the entire 'other half' is left out and thus the computation is halved there itself. At each of the lower nodes also, similar savings in computation is obtained.

Let's see the calculation of probabilities for two words 'college' and 'super'. The product of the probabilities of the path is:

$$P(college/C) = 0.62 \times 0.54 \times 0.85 = 0.28$$

$$P(super/C) = 0.38 \times 0.62 \times 0.63 = 0.14.$$

The same result is obtained as before and 'college' is chosen.

What is the difference between Fig. 17.12 and 17.13?

In the former, the Softmax function computes the probabilities of all the V words. In the latter, only the probability of the chosen path is computed. This is done by taking a left or right path at each node.

Some insights on looking at these figures are:

(i) This is a binary tree and we need to evaluate only $\log_2 V$ levels.

(ii) Note that each node's probability sums to one.

(iii) As we walk down the tree, the choice of whether to go left or right, is to be made. We use the Sigmoid function to calculate the probability distribution between the left and right nodes.

(iv) The probability of all leaf nodes sum to 1 and thus it is clear that this is a normalized probability distribution over all V words. In terms of this, Fig. 17.13 is equivalent to Fig. 17.12.

In effect, the network structure beyond the hidden layer is modified as a tree and the parameters of the tree are continuously learnt according to the context at the input layer. So, in spite of the changed structure, this is still a neural network. The number of updates to be done in the output side is dramatically reduced and this has contributed to the popularity of CBOW based word embeddings.

There is another intuition behind this tree. For a certain context, if similar items are on the same subtree, the higher is the probability of finding the required target word at the leaf of that subtree (see Fig. 17.14). In this figure, the probability of finding the word 'chess' is higher in the left subtree. To reach the word chess, traverse along the path 0 → 1 → 3 → chess. The tree in Fig. 17.14 is a reasonably good tree as games are found on the left subtree and fruits on the right subtree. If the tree is randomly sorted and haphazard, it won't be possible to get this result. To get such a reasonable tree, there are methods suggested by Morin and Bengio (2005) in their paper "Hierarchical Probabilistic Neural Network Language Model". The hierarchical decomposition they proposed is a "binary hierarchical clustering constrained by the prior knowledge extracted from the WordNet semantic hierarchy".

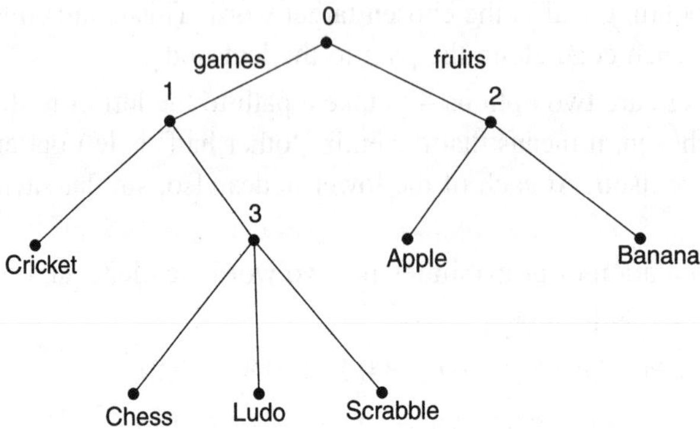

Fig. 17.14 Example of a semantically well ordered tree

The point is that words are clustered based on their meanings which are obtained by referring to 'Wordnet' which is a lexical database widely used for NLP applications. Also note that Fig. 17.14 does not show a balanced tree. In practice, the trees in CBOW are not balanced. A Huffman coding logic is also incorporated into the tree. CBOW builds a Huffman tree, grouping words with low counts (of occurrence in the corpus) into longer root-to-leaf paths. The result of this is that words which occur very frequently end up with the shortest paths. This also contributes to the speed of the algorithm.

Why is CBOW called a 'Self-Supervised, fake' Task ?

(i) The task being done by the neural network here is frequently referred to as a 'fake task' because the output data is not used – the output stage is used only to extract the updated weights of the hidden layer.

(ii) For each context, the target word is the label. But there are no predefined labels. So this is frequently referred to as 'unsupervised'. But for each training instance, the target word chosen from the input text is the label–hence this task is better referred to as 'self-supervised' because labels are generated continuously from the input data.

Note: These points are applicable to the next model as well.

17.2.3 The Skipgram

Now let's take a look at the other Word2Vec model named Skipgram. The methodology in this is similar but the input and outputs are reversed. Here the target word is applied at the input and the corresponding context words are expected at the output. The context words are many in number, depending on the chosen size of the context window.

Figure 17.15 shows that corresponding to the target word w_t, four context words (window size=2) are predicted to appear at the output. How will training be done when four words are expected? Figure 17.16 shows the sequence of training for a sliding context window of size 2.The target word and context words are shown in light and bold boxes respectively. For each training instance, the network is trained with one target word and one context word. It

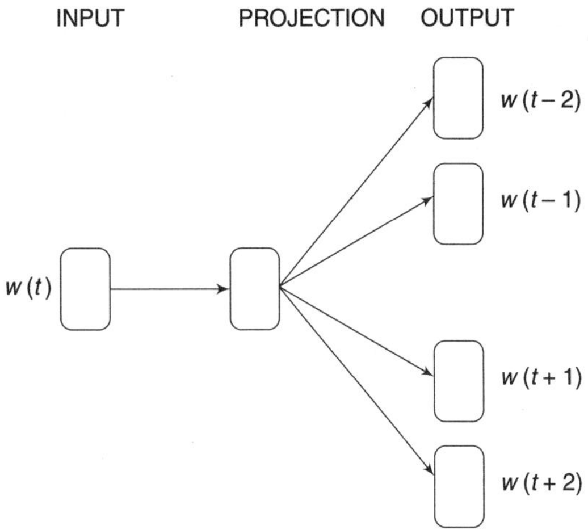

Fig. 17.15 The Skipgram network

is important to note the point that this is a sequential process and takes time unlike the case of CBOW where all the context words are averaged and taken at one go.

The same issue of 'massive amount of calculations' due to the Softmax computation holds good in this model as well. To reduce this, a technique named 'Negative sampling' has been resorted to. This technique has close resemblance to 'Noise Contrastive Estimation'.

Training Instance	Target	Training pairs for each training instances	
		Target	Context
1	He likes Maths Physics Chemistry Programming	**He**	likes
2		**He**	Maths
3	He likes Maths Physics Chemistry Programming	**likes**	He
4		**likes**	Maths
5		**likes**	**Physics**
6	He likes Maths Physics Chemistry Programming	**Maths**	He
7		**Maths**	likes
8		**Maths**	Physics
9		**Maths**	Chemistry
10	He likes Maths Physics Chemistry Programming	**Physics**	likes
11		**Physics**	Maths
12		**Physics**	Chemistry
13		**Physics**	Programming

Fig. 17.16 Skipgram training for context window size=2

17.2.3.1 *Negative Sampling*

Mikolov proposed this method which converts the Softmax calculation into a Sigmoid calculation as in logistic regression. As you know, this corresponds to binary classification. This binary computation itself is performed only for a few number of samples–in that way, computation is brought down drastically.

The method is this: A few words from the vocabulary are chosen. The output of the network has to answer the question of whether or not a given specific word is one of the words in the context window of the input target word. The answer will be a Yes or No, and now the problem reduces to one of binary classifications which can be handled by a Sigmoid. The words are chosen such that one positive sample and $k + 1$ negative samples are used. A negative sample is a word which answers 'No' to the question of being a context word or not. Such negative samples are considered 'noise'. Since the labels are 1 for a positive sample and 0 for negative samples, this now becomes a supervised training problem. Only the weights corresponding to these $k + 1$ words are updated on each iteration. Mikolov has suggested that for small datasets, the value of k is to be 5-20 and for large datasets it is to be 2-5.

Let's take an example with a sample sentence which is:

*she sells **seashells** on the seashore.*

Assume 'seashells' to be the input (target) word. All the other words in the sentence are its context words (w_C). We choose positive and negative samples as in Table 17.3. The idea is that, if the model can develop the capability to distinguish between positive and negative samples, it can generate good vector embeddings for a target word.

Table 17.3 An example of negative and positive samples $P(C/w_T)$

Target word	*Context word*	*Positive/Negative sample ?*	*Probability of being a context word C for a Target word w_T*
seashells	*seashore*	Positive	$P(C/w_T) = 1$
seashells	*computer*	Negative	$P(C/w_T) = 0$
seashells	*book*	Negative	$P(C/w_T) = 0$
seashells	*capital*	Negative	$P(C/w_T) = 0$
seashells	*cat*	Negative	$P(C/w_T) = 0$
seashells	*life*	Negative	$P(C/w_T) = 0$

The output stage of the network has V neurons but each of them is activated by a Sigmoid which needs to make only a 1/0 decision. That itself is a simplification. The second aspect is that out of these V output neurons, only $k + 1$ are chosen each time for iteration. Initially, the probability values at these $k + 1$ output neurons will have random values (see Fig. 17.17). After a number of iterations, the output probabilities converge, with the positive sample getting a high probability and the probability at the other neurons tending to zero. In the course of these iterations, the weights at the output matrix corresponding to these output neurons get updated and along with that, the weights at the hidden layer also get updated. When convergence occurs, the hidden layer weights are chosen as the word embeddings just as in the case of CBOW.

$$\begin{bmatrix} 0.316 \\ 0.224 \\ 0.192 \\ 0.23 \\ 0.013 \\ 0.025 \end{bmatrix} \quad \begin{bmatrix} 0.559 \\ 0.124 \\ 0.101 \\ 0.192 \\ 0.003 \\ 0.21 \end{bmatrix} \quad \cdots\cdots\cdots\cdots \quad \begin{bmatrix} 0.997 \\ 0.000 \\ 0.001 \\ 0.001 \\ 0.000 \\ 0.001 \end{bmatrix}$$

Iteration 1 Iteration 2 .... Iteration n

Fig. 17.17 The convergence of probabilities for $k + 1$ words after n iterations

17.3 GENERAL ASPECTS OF WORD2VEC

Now that we have studied both models of the Word2Vec implementation, let's see two additional techniques for performance optimization which have been adopted in them.

17.3.1 Subsampling

We know that many frequent words don't contribute much information to the application in hand. Thus such words are subsampled. An equation is used in the code which calculates the probability of wanting to retain the word in the vocabulary. If $f(w_i)$ is the unigram probability of a word and $P(w_i)$ is the probability of keeping the word, Mikolov's paper gives this formula.

$$P(w_i) = 1 - \sqrt{\frac{t}{f(w_i)}} \qquad ...(17.3)$$

where $f(w_i)$ is the frequency of word w_i and t is a chosen threshold, typically around 10^{-5}. Mikolov and his team chose this subsampling formula because, according to them, "it aggressively subsamples words whose frequency is greater than t while preserving the ranking of the frequencies". Although this subsampling formula was chosen heuristically, they found it to work well in practice. They found that this formula improved the accuracy of the embedding of rare words.

With this, most frequent words like the, and, in, was, is, etc., are likely to be removed. One direct result of subsampling is that these words don't appear in context windows thus giving better chances for more relevant words to be in the context window. This also indicates that stop word removal as part of pre-processing is not necessary when using Word2Vec.

17.3.2 Context Window Weighting

Another innovation implemented is of assigning different weights to words in the context window based on their closeness to the target word. This is implemented by simply varying the size of the context window. If a size of 5 is specified, it means the window size can vary between 1 and 5 for successive iterations. It should be realized that as words are farther away from the target word, their importance gets reduced.

17.3.3 Comparing Skipgram and CBOW

Mikolov explains from his experience: "Skipgram works well with small amount of the training data, represents well even rare words or phrases. CBOW is several times faster to train than Skipgram and has slightly better accuracy for frequent words". (These sentences are copied from the Word2Vec website.)

Why is Skipgram slower?

There are several context words and each 'context word–target word' combination has to be used for training (Refer Fig. 17.16). This will take more time especially for large context window sizes. CBOW uses context words at the input, and it is the average value of all the context words that is used for training.

Table 17.4 shows which of the two models has been found to give better response for five aspects of NLP. But when comparing Hierarchial Softmax with Negative sampling, it is found that the latter has better performance and therefore compensates for the loss in speed which Skipgram experiences due to its many training pairs.

Table 17.4 Performance comparison

Training speeds	Capturing syntactic similarity	Frequent words	Rare words	Small datasets
CBOW	CBOW	CBOW	Skipgram	Skipgram

17.4 CODING EXAMPLES

17.4.1 Coding Question

- Take a one-page document and convert it to word2Vec using different vector sizes.
- Do text preprocessing and convert to word tokens.
- Display the vectors of all the tokens.
  - Try short vectors – say of size 10
  - Try longer vectors – 100 and more
- Find the context words of some words in the corpus you have used.
- Find similar words of some words in the corpus you have used.

```
import bs4 as bs
import urllib.request
import re
import nltk
from gensim.test.utils import datapath

f = open('C:/Users/Lenovo/Desktop/NITC PHD/Course work/AI/word2vec/
AI.txt','r',encoding='UTF8')
article_text = f.read()

print(article_text)
```

```
# Cleaing the text
processed_article = article_text.lower()
processed_article = re.sub('[^a-zA-Z]', ' ', processed_article)
processed_article = re.sub(r'\s+', ' ', processed_article)

# Preparing the dataset
all_sentences = nltk.sent_tokenize(processed_article)
all_words = [nltk.word_tokenize(sent) for sent in all_sentences]

# Removing Stop Words
from nltk.corpus import stopwords
from gensim.models import Word2Vec

for i in range(len(all_words)):
  all_words[i] = [w for w in all_words[i] if w not in stopwords.words('english')]
  #print(all_words)

word2vec = Word2Vec(all_words, min_count=2,vector_size=10)
words = list(word2vec.wv.index_to_key)

for i in range (len(words)):
  v1 = word2vec.wv[words[i]]
  sim_words = word2vec.wv.most_similar(words[i])

v1 = word2vec.wv[words[0]]
sim_words = word2vec.wv.most_similar(words[0])

corpus=words
length_of_corpus=len(corpus)
context_word_array=[]

for i,word in enumerate(corpus):
  index_target_word = i
  target_word = word
  context_words = []
  window_size = 2
  if i == 0:
  context_words = [corpus[x] for x in range(i + 1, window_size + 1)]

  elif i == len(corpus)-1:
  context_words = [corpus[x] for x in range(length_of_corpus - 2, length_
of_corpus -2 - window_size, -1 )]
  else:
  before_target_word_index = index_target_word - 1
  for x in range(before_target_word_index, before_target_word_index - window_size, -1):
  if x >=0:
```

```
  context_words.extend([corpus[x]])

  after_target_word_index = index_target_word + 1
  for x in range(after_target_word_index, after_target_word_index + window_size):
  if x < len(corpus):
  context_words.extend([corpus[x]])
  context_word_array.append([target_word,context_words])

print("\n sample word2vec with vector size 10")
print(words[0])
print(v1)
print("\n context word to "+ str(words[0]))
print(context_word_array[0])
v2= word2vec.wv[context_word_array[0][1]]
print("\n word2vec of context word "+ str(context_word_array[0][1]))
print(v2)
print("\n similar word to "+ str(words[0]))
print(sim_words)

v1 = word2vec.wv[words[1]]
sim_words = word2vec.wv.most_similar(words[1])
print("\n sample word2vec with vector size 10")
print(words[1])
print(v1)
print("\n context word to "+ str(words[1]))
print(context_word_array[1])
v2= word2vec.wv[context_word_array[1][1]]
print("\n word2vec of context word "+ str(context_word_array[1][1]))
print(v2)
print("\n similar word to "+ str(words[1]))
print(sim_words)

word2vec = Word2Vec(all_words, min_count=2,vector_size=100)
words = list(word2vec.wv.index_to_key)

for i in range (len(words)):
  v1 = word2vec.wv[words[i]]
  sim_words = word2vec.wv.most_similar(words[i])

v1 = word2vec.wv[words[0]]
sim_words = word2vec.wv.most_similar(words[0])
print("\n sample word2vec with vector size 100 ")
print(words[0])
print(v1)
print("\n similar word to "+ str(words[0]))
print(sim_words)
```

RESULT:

sample word2vec with vector size 10
ai
[-0.00385466 -0.00063092 0.06728168 0.09408784 -0.08712614 -0.06983861
0.07828316 0.10125764 -0.05852638 -0.04832929]
context word to ai
['ai', ['intelligence', 'learning']]
word2vec of context word ['intelligence', 'learning']
[[0.0754175 -0.01766019 -0.0314765 0.06890088 -0.0436923 -0.01632185
0.0420523 0.01985823 -0.09027268 -0.10244263]

[0.07842559 0.04925765 0.08082432 0.01023063 0.06849579 -0.03246404
0.00518097 0.06907358 -0.08401724 -0.04711393]]
sample word2vec with vector size 100
ai
[-0.00129489 0.00110027 0.0053308 0.00877506 -0.00943038 -0.00858633
0.00675609 0.01079895 -0.00549438 -0.00416399 0.00794262 -0.00269691 -0.00473239
0.00675221 -0.00490262 -0.00174327 0.00324532 -0.00067513
-0.008757 -0.01138747 0.00697556 0.00543907 0.00714523 0.00036885
0.00567607 -0.0024933 -0.00106717 0.00521218 -0.00796263 -0.00381292
-0.00671906 -0.00064042 0.00997445 -0.00745363 -0.00287949 -0.00073652
0.0087511 -0.00647033 0.00026968 -0.00620347 -0.009682 0.00355204
-0.00937655 -0.00410626 0.00078093 -0.00040647 -0.00794209 0.00909394
0.00517239 0.00993222 -0.00759382 0.00388784 -0.00365371 0.00071648
0.00841421 -0.00401788 0.00489182 -0.00688229 -0.00476735 0.00991029
-0.00168632 0.00083283 -0.00376678 -0.00816569 -0.00241734 0.00303248
-0.00020835 0.00708104 -0.00347739 0.00333619 0.00492084 0.008597
-0.00074042 -0.00930008 0.00536244 0.00106552 0.00742124 -0.00092667
-0.0038141 -0.00828113 -0.00086445 0.00347312 0.00439987 0.00862436
-0.0061003 0.00202696 0.00724719 -0.00383836 -0.00239195 0.00650863
0.00243775 0.0008466 0.00354663 0.00092807 0.01135567 0.00566943
-0.00778746 -0.00784654 0.0010592 0.00632306]
similar word to ai
[('self', 0.3166106641292572), ('uses', 0.30218613147735596), ('virtual', 0.2661040723323822), ('technology', 0.2499459832906723), ('also', 0.24659736454486847), ('publish', 0.23388274013996124), ('ethics', 0.23344343900680542), ('enables', 0.22865745425224304), ('data', 0.22863943874835968), ('process', 0.1979006677865982)]

17.4.2 Coding Question

The following are to be done using the pre-trained network of Google or some Word2Vec embedding you have done with some corpus.

- Take pairs of sentences and check their similarity –what is the result?
- Take words and check their similarity

```
import gensim
import nltk
from gensim.models.doc2vec import TaggedDocument
from nltk.tokenize import word_tokenize
from scipy import spatial
import numpy as np
from gensim.models import KeyedVectors
from gensim.utils import simple_preprocess

model = gensim.models.KeyedVectors.load_word2vec_format('C:/Users/Lenovo/
Desktop/NITC PHD/Course work/AI/word2vec/GoogleNews-vectors-negative300.
bin', binary=True)

print("similarity between two words love and adore ")
print(model.similarity("love", "adore"))

def tidy_sentence(sentence, vocabulary):
  return [word for word in simple_preprocess(sentence) if word in vocabulary]

def compute_sentence_similarity(sentence_1, sentence_2, model):
  vocabulary = set(model.index_to_key)
  tokens_1 = tidy_sentence(sentence_1, vocabulary)
  tokens_2 = tidy_sentence(sentence_2, vocabulary)
  return model.n_similarity(tokens_1, tokens_2)

#wv = KeyedVectors.load('model.wv', mmap='r')
print("similarity between two sentences : this is a sentence & this is
also a sentence")
sim = compute_sentence_similarity('this is a sentence', 'this is also a
sentence', model)
print(sim)
```

RESULT: similarity between two words 'love' and 'adore'

0.68168736

similarity between two sentences : 'this is a sentence' & 'this is also a sentence'

0.95966756

Conclusion

In this chapter, the best and latest method of 'text representation' has been presented. It is to be kept in mind that current implementations of NLP use such dense representations.

Questions

1. What is meant by dense vector embeddings?
2. Why is 'dense vector embedding' better than the other vector embeddings that you have learnt so far?
3. What is the reason for the use of the names 'CBOW' and Skipgram in these models?
4. How do we say that semantic relationships are preserved in Word2Vec. Give examples to prove your point.
5. How do CBOW and Skipgram differ in their basic idea?
6. What is the logic of using the hidden layer weights as the vector of a word?
7. Why is hierarchical Softmax used in the CBOW output stage?
8. What is the logic of negative sampling as used in Skipgram?
9. Compare the performance of CBOW and Skipgram.
10. Why is the task in Word2Vec named as a 'fake task'?

Exercise

1. What do you know about Word2Vec, Glove and FastText?
2. Compare the above in terms of methodology, performance and area of application.
3. Take two pages of text and do Word2Vec embedding using it:
   (i) Find the vector representation of selected words in dimensions: 20, 150
   (ii) Take a few words and find the words most similar to it.
   (iii) Take another two pages of text which has some common words with the previous document and do Word2Vec embedding using it.
   (iv) Find the vector representation of the same words from (i).
   (v) Take the words that you used in (ii) and find similar words.
   (vi) What are the conclusions drawn from these actions?
4. Download the pretrained Word2Vec and do the following:
   (i) Find similarity between words and sentences.

CHAPTER

18

Applications of NLP Using Deep Learning Techniques

In this chapter you will

- discover the encoder-decoder model for NLP,
- learn the concept of teacher forcing for training,
- understand the importance of the context vector,
- analyze the Encoder-Decoder attention mechanism,
- survey the architecture of the 'Transformer',
- list the important applications of NLP, and
- check a sample code for machine translation.

18.0 INTRODUCTION

Now that we have got a clear idea of the basics of NLP from Chapters 14 to 17, and deep learning techniques from Chapters 10 to 12, it is time to take a look at how important NLP applications fare with the use of deep learning.

Most high-end applications are currently being implemented on deep learning networks. In Chapter 12, such networks have been discussed in depth. But things have moved beyond that and a new methodology named 'Transformers' is slowly but surely replacing the LSTMs and GRUs that had made a lot of changes to the NLP field. But before we step into understanding transformers, we should gain an insight of 'Sequence to Sequence Network/Encoder–Decoder Network' which has made great strides in applications such as machine translation, question answering, text summarising, etc. In this chapter, we will talk about encoder-decoder networks, transformers and list some important applications of NLP.

18.1 ENCODER–DECODER NETWORK

The name Sequence to Sequence network abbreviated as 'Seq2seq' network is also a method of using deep learning based on the sequential processing of words which are the basic entities in most NLP applications.

18.1.1 The Architecture of a Seq2Seq Model

We have learnt (Chapter 12) the architectures of LSTMs and GRUs and we also know that one of them is likely to be the choice for implementing sequential networks. They are just the practical versions of the basic RNN. In our discussions ahead, we will continue to use the term 'RNN' and the reader is expected to understand that the actual cell used may be either an LSTM or GRU.

In Section 12.1.1.4, we had talked about RNN applications in which the number of outputs $\hat{y}$ need not be equal to the number of inputs, x. For NLP, this is the case when the number of words obtained as the predicted sequence of words will be different from the number of words given as input. This will be typical of cases such as machine translation, text summarization, question answering, image/video captioning, speech recognition, etc. Such networks have the name 'Sequence to Sequence Network'. The term 'Encoder-Decoder architecture is also used (See Fig. 18.1). The state of the encoder is fed as a 'context vector' to the decoder. Terms such as 'thought vector and 'encoder vector' are also used for the state of the encoder.

The encoder and decoder are a set of RNN cells. They are usually bidirectional (Section. 12.1.1.3) and stacked RNNs (Section 12.1.1.5). Such a setup implies a high level of complexity for the system. *However, in our discussion, we will visualize the system as a single layer, unidirectional cell sequence. This will keep the discussion simple and easy to follow.*

The hidden state from the last cell of the encoder is called the context vector/encoder vector. This 'vector' should contain ideally, the information pertaining to the whole input sequence. This vector feeds into the first cell of the decoder part and produces the output. The point is that the final state of the encoder is the initial state h_0 of the decoder. This means that the decoder is to start generating the output sequence based on the information that the encoder has encoded. This, in general, is the working of the encoder-decoder configuration.

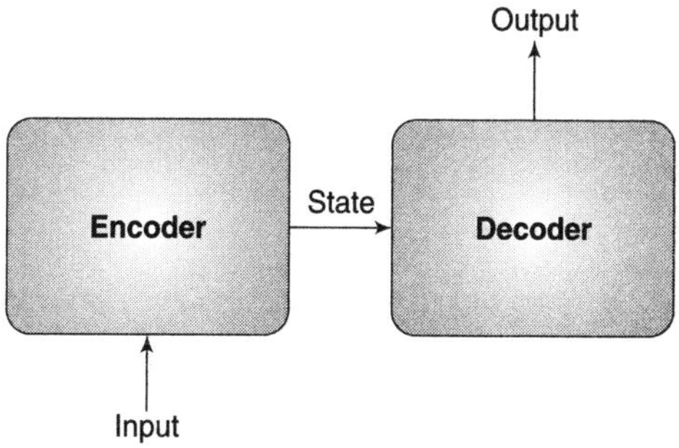

Fig. 18.1 The block diagram of an encoder–decoder network

To go ahead, let us take the setup of a system which uses machine translation as the application, though the same principles apply to other applications as well. Let us do a translation from English to Hindi. The source and destination sentences are as below.

English: *My dog's name is Bingo.*

Hindi: *mere kutte ka naam bingo hai.*

In this case, the input sentence has five words, while the output has 6 words. The encoder is the RNN setup which handles the input English sentence, while the decoder takes care of the translated Hindi sentence.

So the encoder takes in the five English words and also an 'EOS' (End of Sentence) token. The last encoder cell's hidden state is fed into the first cell of the decoder as S_0. The decoder produces the first output token which is the first word 'mere' in Hindi. The decoder has also a 'Start' signal at which point of time, the translation operation starts. The predicted output word of the first cell of the decoder is fed in as the input of the second decoder cell. Each decoder cell also has as input, the 'state' of the previous cell.

A well trained, well set up configuration should produce the remaining words one after the other and also an EOS at the end. This is how a simple Neural Machine Translation works. Each output word will be chosen using a Softmax computation which gives the highest probability to the output word chosen from the vocabulary of Hindi words for which the system has been trained (see Fig. 18.2 a and 18.2b). In the encoder, the hidden states are notated as h_0 ... . h_6 and decoder states as S_0 ... . S_7

Note: The value of h_0 may be taken as 0, because there are no cells before it.

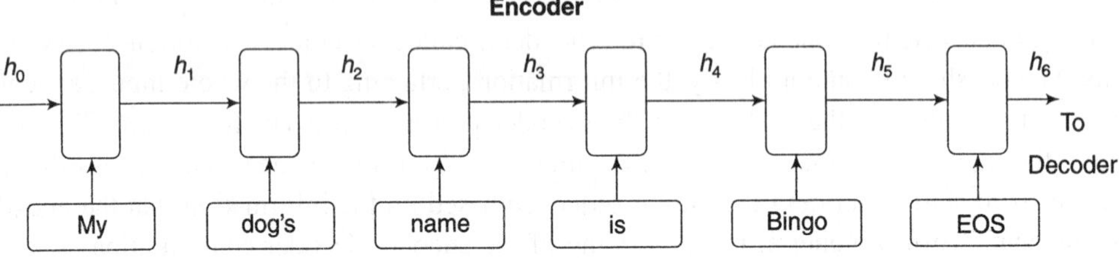

Fig. 18.2 (a) The encoder network for machine translation

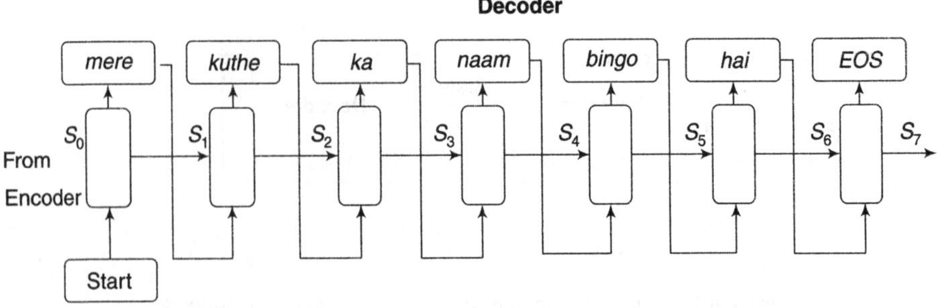

Fig. 18.2 (b) The decoder network for machine translation

18.1.2 Training using Teacher Forcing

A network for machine translation is to be trained for a large dataset of the words and sentences of the source and destination languages. A method known as 'teacher forcing', if used, is seen to give better results. This is done during the training phase. At the decoder side, after the first word is generated, it is to be fed as the input to the second cell. In this method, instead of feeding the predicted word, the 'ground truth' word is the one fed to the next cell.

Let's use an example to make this clear. At the decoder side, the input to the first decoder cell is a Start token. Along with that, the context vector from the encoder is given as h_0 (hidden cell state) to the first cell. The decoder has to start the generation of Hindi words once it obtains the Start signal. The first cell should give the word 'mere' as output and this is to be fed in to the second cell. But assume that the decoder produces the word 'hamara' instead. This is wrong and this wrong word when given to the next cell will cause the generation of further wrong words from the next cells. To prevent this, a correction is made at this cell. The right word 'mere' is taken from the training set and given to the second cell. This is expected to set the tone for correct translations following it. This sort of 'intervention' can be made by using the 'ground truth' label at all points in the decoder.

The logic for teacher forcing is simple. If the first predicted word is wrong and is given to the second cell, the probability of its prediction being wrong is higher still. Continuing with this erroneous output will cause the later words to be completely wrong. By forcing the correct word into the decoder during training, the network gives pretty good results during the inference/testing phase.

18.1.3 The Context Vector

(i) It is the hidden state taken from the last cell of the encoder.

(ii) It is expected that this vector has encapsulated the information from the whole input sentence such that the decoder can give an accurate translation.

If this 'single' vector can really carry all the information for the whole input sequence, it would be a very good system. But in practice, this doesn't work very well, especially when the length of the input sequence is large. For long sentences, this vector carries more information pertaining to the last words of the input and the first words are somewhat 'lost' or forgotten. So depending on this encoder vector alone does not seem to be good enough.

Note: In many cases of machine translation, the input sentence is applied in the reverse order such that the first word appears close to the decoder input. The encoder vector tends to be biased to the words applied last, which are the first words of the sentence, Thus gives a better probability for the first translated words to be correct and therefore a greater chance is there for the whole output to be correct. But this may work only for cases in which the order of words in the sentences of both the languages are the same (as in our example). This may not hold for all languages.

18.1.4 Seq2Seq Network with Attention

It should be clear from our discussion so far that having to depend on just a single encoder vector may not give the results that we want. Some modifications are necessary such that the important words of the input sequence are identified and given greater weightage, or a bigger role in producing the output. This method is named 'Attention'. It is based on how humans perceive information. When observing a picture and then recollecting it later, we realize that we had concentrated on only some parts of the picture. A 'image captioning' system will definitely have to concentrate on some parts of the picture to deduce an appropriate caption for it.

Consider a question answering system asking : "How many pounds are there to a kilogram?" In this sentence, words such as 'are, there, to, a' do not contribute much to the output answer. Our attention will be on the words 'how, many, pounds, kilograms'.

Focussing or concentrating on more relevant information for the current time instant means we are giving it our 'attention' now. This is exactly how an attention based network is to behave. Note that the main problem in the Seq2seq network is that the encoder vector may not have sufficient information because many relevant parts of an input sequence are forgotten or not properly encapsulated in the context vector.

An 'attention based mechanism' is one which can choose the relevant parts of the input 'at each time step' of the decoding process. Such a context vector is dynamic and depends on the 'current time step' of the decoding process. Thus, the context vector for a 'network with attention' is defined in a different way. Let us discuss this using our machine translation example.

Consider the translation of our previous sentence:

Englsh: *My dog's name is Bingo.*

Hindi: *mere kutte ka naam bingo hai.*

In the encoder, there are five RNN cells and an EOS. Thus the hidden states are h_0 ... . h_6. At the decoder side, during the first time step, it should give the output word 'mere'. The second decoder cell should give an output word 'kutte' and so on.

Let's name the decoder states as S_0, S_1 .... S_7 including the *EOS* (Ref. Fig. 18.2.). Let's consider time step t_2 of the decoder when its state is S_2. At this time step, when it should produce the output word '*kutte*', which encoder states are relevant for it? Obviously h_1 and h_2 because these states have direct knowledge of the words '*My*' and '*dog's*'. The relevance of the other encoder states is less, comparatively.

For the decoder state S_5 (when outputting 'Bingo'), the encoder state h_5 will definitely have high relevance. So, on looking from the 'decoder 'side, the relevance of the encoder states keeping changing for each time step of the decoding process. This means that if we can find a relevance score for each decoding step, there will be a better chance to get the right output words. This is what 'Attention' does. It creates a vector C_i by taking a weighted sum of the hidden states of the encoder, for the ith state of the decoder. Higher scores are attributed for the encoder states of higher relevance.

This means that there should be a method to quantify this relevance. How is it done?

How do we get these scores for the ith decoder cell? One of the methods is to use the dot product of the encoder hidden states with the hidden state of the previous decoder cell. Another method is to use a neural network to learn these scores using backpropagation and gradient descent. There are still other methods, but in principle, the score is calculated as a function of all the encoder states and S_{i-1}, which is the decoder state of the previous decoder cell. The formula for the attention score is:

$$\alpha_j = g(h_i, S_{i-1}) \quad ...(18.1)$$

where g is the function we have chosen and α_j is the notation for these attention scores.

This score α_j is computed for all the encoder states h_j, j = 1 to N. This is utilized to tell the decoder state S_i how relevant each encoder state is to the current decoder state. These scores are normalized to lie between 0 and 1, using Softmax.

Let's use an example:

Our scores of the encoder states h_1 to h_6, for the decoder state S_2 could be:

Input	My	dog's	name	is	Bingo	EOS
α_j	0.15	0.6	0.15	0.04	0.04	0.02

Note that these scores sum to 1, because of the application of Softmax (Section 10.8.5).

Finally, the context vector C_i is taken as the weighted sum of the encoder hidden states (h_j) where the weights are the attention scores α_1 to α_6.

In general, the context vector C_i is given as:

$$C_i = \Sigma_j\, a_j\, h_j \quad ...(18.2)$$

For our example,

$$C_i = \alpha 1 * h1 + \alpha 2 * h2 + \alpha 3 * h3 + .\alpha 4 * h4 + \alpha 5 * h5 + \alpha 6 * h6$$

What is done with this context vector C_i?

For each decoder cell, the corresponding context vector is concatenated with the previous decoder state S_{i-1}. Also note that the output from the previous decoder cell is also fed into the current decoder cell (See Fig. 18.3).

Let's list out the salient points.

(i) For the first decoder cell with state S_1, the previous state S_0 is taken from the last cell of the encoder.

(ii) The decoder produces the output sequence one after the other in a series of time steps.

(iii) The decoded output of one cell is fed to the next cell.

(iv) The decoder at the current time t, has the following inputs: the context vector C_i concatenated with S_{i-1} and the decoded output of the previous decoder cell.

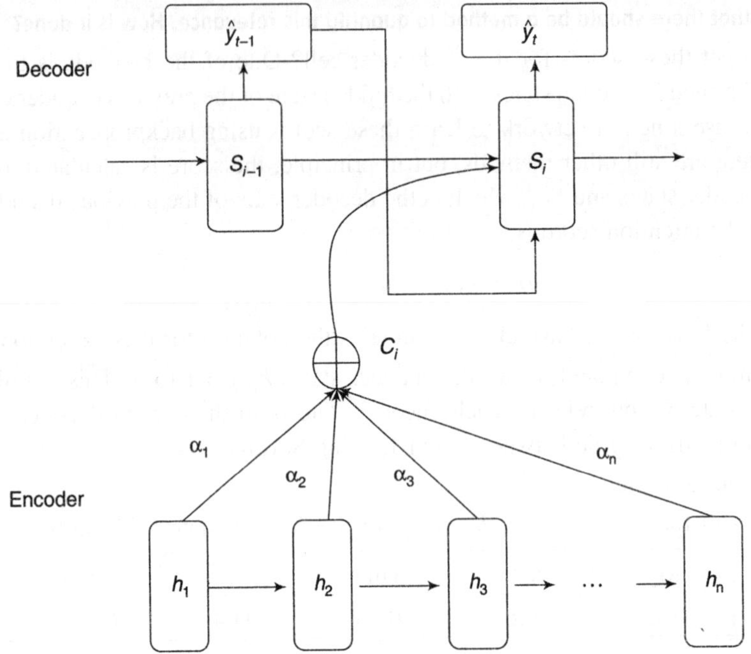

Fig. 18.3 The encoder-decoder attenction mechanism

(v) The decoder then proceeds to generate the next output word from the next cell. **At this time, it gets a new context vector based on a new computation of the scores.**

(vi) Thus the decoding process is assisted dynamically by a new context vector at every time step.

18.1.5 History of Attention and Conclusion

It was in the years 2014-15 that this kind of 'attention' came into being used widely. Many NLP applications became efficient and smart with this. Since the attention is applied to a decoder input and is related to the encoder states, this attention mechanism is given the name 'encoder-decoder attention'. In around 2017, another new development came up with the concept of 'self-attention'. We will go into that now.

18.2 THE TRANSFORMER

Converting 'an input string to an output string' or 'one sequence to another' is what we have discussed in Section 18.1. The word transduction may be applied to that task. It must be for that reason that the name 'Transformers' was given to the new kind of Seq2Seq network developed in 2017 by Ashish Vaswani and his team. Let's get to know more about this.

We have covered a lot of distance in NLP and its applications. With RNNs and its practical versions such as LSTM s and GRUs, many problems in NLP were solved, especially after these units were used in Sequence to sequence networks. Good results were obtained for applications such as language translation, question answering, text summarising and so on. Things seemed to be doing pretty well for NLP applications when in 2017, the paper 'Attention is all you need' by Ashish Vaswani et al., created a sensation that made a great leap for not only NLP but for neural networks in general. The first applications of it were in NLP, but later it began to be used for image applications as well.

The paper which showcased a machine translation application, proposed "a novel, simple network architecture based solely on an attention mechanism, dispensing with recurrence and convolutions entirely". This means that RNNs were completely removed and a new way of handling such tasks was proposed.

This architecture which the authors named as 'transformers' was found to give superior results for many applications. Parallelisation of tasks (which is not possible in RNNs) made it fast and easy to train. With this new development, the importance of LSTMs and GRUs reduced significantly. The new ideas introduced in this new model which did not use RNNs or CNNs, are:

(i) Self-attention

(ii) Parallelisabilty of input data

Let us now look into the internal working of the transformer model.

In the first reading, this will definitely seem confusing, but repeating the sequence of reading and ruminating over the details will lead to a demystification of the concepts involved. Finally, by working on implementations such as BERT or GPT, complete clarity will be obtained.

18.2.1 Self-Attention

This model is also an encoder-decoder network but does not use 'recurrence' or 'convolutions'. The decoder receives its inputs from the encoder and uses it in an 'auto-regressive' fashion which means that it predicts future values based on past values. This simply means that the decoder receives as input, its own predicted output word of its previous time step just as was mentioned in Section 18.1.1.

We have also seen what is meant by the word 'attention', in Section 18.1.4. This process may be designated as 'encoder-decoder' attention as the scores are built based on the relationship between the decoder and encoder words.

Now we come to the concept of 'self-attention'. This has to do with the input sequence alone. For a word sequence, we know that any word is related to the words close to it, in its proximity. We call those words as the context of the source word–that is, the words in close proximity to a specific word are its context, and the context 'gives meaning' to this word. While this is true for many cases, this is not the full story. Words far way from our specific word may also have a role in the semantics of the sentence.

Let us suppose that we want to quantify the importance of a 'specific word' to the other words in the same sentence. Let us name this specific word as a 'query'. We would like to know what is the relevance score of our query word with respect to the other words in the same sentence.

Note the following sentence:

Anju went to meet her teacher, but ***she*** *was not there.*

In this sentence, do we know who is the 'she' that is referred here? Yes, we definitely know that it refers to the teacher. But a computer will have a difficult time trying to decide whether the 'she' refers to Anju or her teacher. Now see this sentence:

Anju went to meet her teacher, but ***she*** *could not meet her.*

Here again, we know that the 'she' refers to Anju, but the computer may need help to come to this conclusion. Thus, we understand that things are not very simple unless some attention mechanism is incorporated in such instances. What the algorithm needs for the first sentence is a method that compares the word 'she' with the other words and gives a high score to the word 'teacher'. This high score will indicate that the 'she' is more similar to the word 'teacher'. It means that when the word 'she' is used, attention should be focussed on the word 'teacher'. For the second sentence, the attention for 'she' should be on 'Anju'. A system which can be trained to do this is necessary to make sense in NLP applications (See Fig. 18.4).

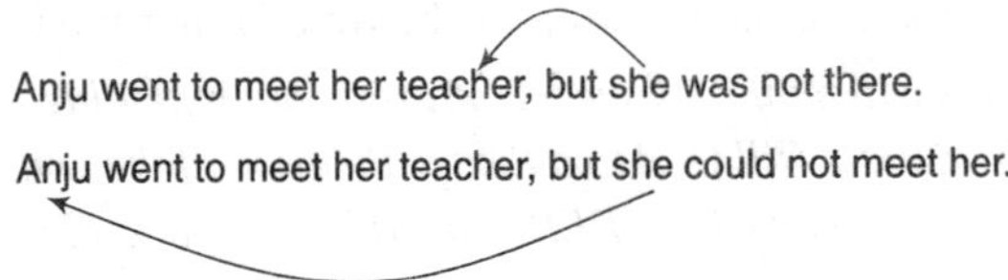

Fig. 18.4 The concept of self-attention with respect to a sentence

This way of using attention is called 'self-attention' – the word 'she' is the query and the other words in the sentence are named 'keys'. The term 'self-attention' is because the query and keys are in the same input sequence. The self-attention mechanism computes the relevance of each word to the other words in the same sentence.

We know that words are represented by 'vector embeddings' as we have seen in Chapter 17. Thus the keys and query are vectors, the dimension of which is within our choice. Each word is represented by a 512 element vector in the paper 'Attention is all you need'. We have already seen (Section 17.2.1) that a word embedding is related to the meaning of a word as well as how it is used in a particular situation.

The dot product between vectors is a measure of similarity and so the operation of self-attention is that of computing the dot product of the query vector with each of the words in the sentence. We refer to each of the words in the sentence as 'keys'.

Anju went to meet her teacher, but she was not there.

Consider the above sentence. This sentence has 11 keys $k_1, k_2 \ldots\ldots\ldots.. k_{11}$. The word 'teacher' is k_6. In practice, each word has a chance to be taken as a query and thus there will be 11 queries $q_1, q_2 \ldots\ldots\ldots.. q_{11}$. The word 'she' is q_8. Let us consider the case of q_8 being the query. When the querying process is done, it should give a high score for the dot product of $q_8 . k_6$ and lesser scores for the dot product of q_8 with the other keys. It is by this that we make sure that 'she' which is q_8 is related more to the word 'teacher' which is k_6. The dot products are scalars, numbers, so as to say. These numbers are normalized to lie within 0 and 1, so that they form a probability distribution. This is easily done using the Softmax function.

18.2.2 Query, Key and Value Matrices

Now that the concept of self-attention is clear, let us discuss the steps of transformer processing, using a very small sentence of 4 words which is:

Music for the soul

Let us name the vector embeddings for these words as e_1, e_2, e_3 and e_4. When we use each of these words for querying, they are notated as q_1, q_2, q_3 and q_4. When querying is done, the input words are named as keys k_1, k_2, k_3 and k_4. Let us use 'soul' as the query word. Thus q_4, the query is compared with all the keys k_1, k_2, k_3 and k_4.

Let's examine Fig. 18.5. The dot product of all the four keys are taken for the query vector q_4. The result is a set of four numbers S_{41}, S_{42}, S_{43} and S_{44}. These numbers are normalized by the Softmax function and are now named W_{41}, W_{42}, W_{43} and W_{44}. These numbers are used as weights to 're-weigh' the embedding vectors of our input sequence (which is the sentence *Music for the soul*) which we now designate as v_1, v_2, v_3 and v_4 as they are called 'values' at this point. Thus, the vectors corresponding to the input words have been 'weighted' by the scores of 'self-attention'. They are then added and the resultant vector is named y_4. Remember this re-weighing has been done with respect to the query vector, q_4. Thus, y_4 has information with respect to the query q_4 (soul) and the sentence.

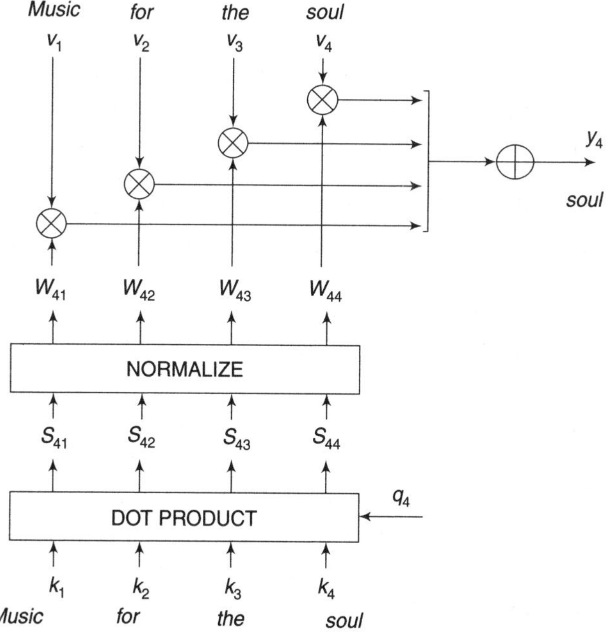

Fig. 18.5 The steps in getting the key, query and values for a sentence

The same operation is done for each of the other words of the sentence which will act as query vectors. We get vector y_1, y_2, y_3 in the same way as we got y_4. These vectors are of the same dimensions as that of the input embeddings, that is, 512. So what we have done using self-attention is that of getting embeddings of each input word which is more meaningful than what we started with. These embeddings y_1, y_2, y_3 and y_4 have captured the inter-relationships between the words in the sequence. Thus they are the required self-attention vectors (see Fig. 18.6).

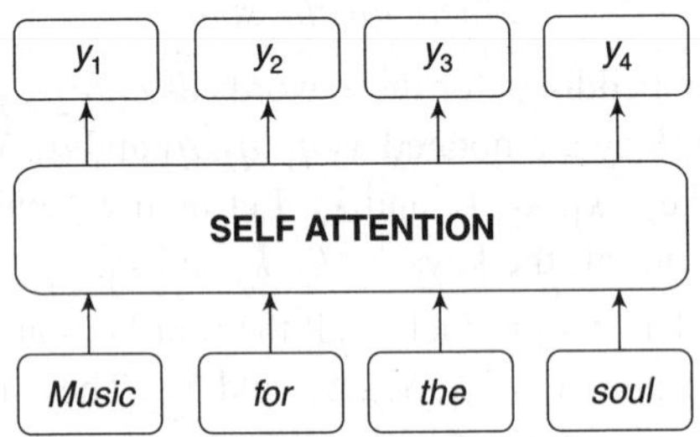

Fig. 18.6 The attention outputs for a sentence

Thus, we see that the three key components of the transformer's self-attention block are named as keys, queries and values. But since there are no weights associated with this setup, this cannot be useful in a neural network environment, because the processes involved in neural networks is that of updating 'weights' by training.

So we will associate three weight matrices with the keys, queries and values. They are named M_q, M_k and M_v. If the dimension of the input vectors is n, the weight matrices will be dimension $n \times n$. Multiplying these matrices with each of the vectors will produce another vector of dimension $1 \times n$. The necessity of using weight matrices is to make the whole system 'trainable' where during training, the weights are learnt through backpropagation.

18.2.3 Implementation in the Reference Paper

Now that the basic concept involved in the idea of transformers is understood, let us discuss how this idea has been implemented in the paper referred. We will discuss the specifications of the system as described in the paper and its component parts. The input sequences are taken from the set of word embeddings with dimension $d_m = 512$. Thus, every word is represented with a vector of 512 elements.

But we will see in Section 18.2.4 that there are 8 self-attention blocks operating in parallel and for this, the 512 element vector is divided into 8 chunks of 64 and the results are concatenated after performing the operations that we now discuss.

Figure 18.7 shows the 'self-attention' block used in transformers. The Q and K vectors are seen to be given to a MATMUL block which stands for 'Matrix Multiplication'. The following operations are included in this block.

(i) Multiplying Q and K with the weight matrices M_q and M_k.

(ii) Taking the dot product between these weighted query and key vectors, as in Section 18.2.2.

After that a 'scaling' is shown. This needs an explanation. Dot products are numbers which may be quite large (positive or negative) values. The dot products are to be normalized using the Softmax functions which involves exponentiation. When such large values are exponentiated, numerical instability may occur. Since backpropagation is also involved, 'losing the gradients due to this instability' cannot be allowed. To avoid these issues, the dot product is scaled by the square root of the dimensions (64) of the embedding vector chunks. The scaling factor is $\sqrt{64}$ which is 8.

This is then subject to a Softmax computation. Then there is Matmul which does the following:

(i) Multiplying v with the weight matrix M_V.

(ii) Taking the sum of the resultant vectors to get the vector $\boldsymbol{Y}$.

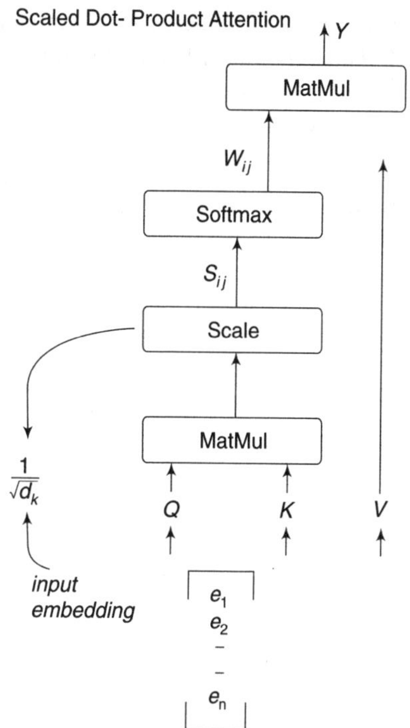

Fig 18.7 The self-attention block

This $\boldsymbol{Y}$ is the attention vector for one query.

This process is done for every query vector. Note that all these processes operate in parallel for all the words of the input sequence. Figure 18.7 is identical to the steps shown in Fig. 18.5. The reference paper says this operation is done simultaneously on a set of queries which are, packed together into a matrix Q. The keys (k) and values (v) are also packed together into matrices K and V. The attention vector is calculated as

$$\text{Attention } (Q, K, V) = \text{Softmax}\left(\frac{QK^T}{\sqrt{d_k}}\right)V \qquad \text{...(18.3)}$$

Note that QK^T corresponds to the dot product between Q and K. This is scaled by $\sqrt{d_K}$ and then Softmaxed. This is the essence of the operations done as in Fig. 18.7. Note that the operations in Figs. 18.7 and 18.5 are the same except that in the former, the weight matrices are also mentioned.

18.2.4 Multi-head Attention Block

In practice, many such self-attention blocks are used. Thus came the name 'multi-head attention block' and they all operate in parallel. The authors of the paper state that they found that "Instead of performing a single attention function with d_{model}-dimensional keys, values and queries, they found it beneficial to have multiple parallel operations by randomly cutting the 512 dimensional vector into 8 vectors with dimensions 64. Thus, $d_k = d_q = d_v = 64$. Thus, the multi-head attention block produces 8 output vectors $Y_i (i = 1 \text{ to } 8)$. Then Y_1 to Y_8 is concatenated into single vector Y (see Fig. 18.8). The outputs of these multiple attention heads are concatenated to become a 512 dimensional vector and then passed through a dense (linear) layer (see Fig. 18.9). In it, 8 attention heads are shown. The word 'linear' implies multiplying by a weight matrix M the weights of which are learnt through the back prop process. There is no bias term. Figure 18.9 shows this.

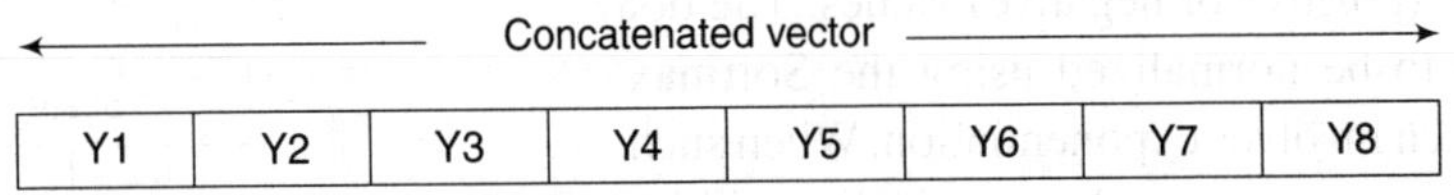

Fig. 18.8 Concatenation of the Y vectors

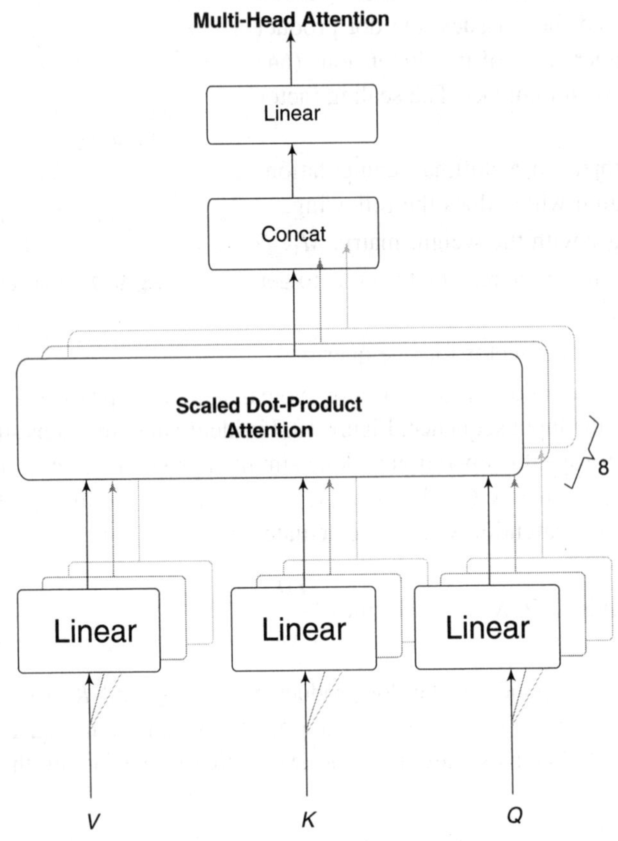

Fig 18.9 The multi-head attention block

18.2.5 The Complete Encoder

Figure 18.10 shows the encoder block as depicted in the reference paper. Let's try to get some explanation regarding two parts of the diagram which haven't been discussed as yet.

18.2.5.1 *Positional Encoding*

Whenever a sequence of words is given as an input, all the words are processed in parallel and there is no relevance or importance for the position of a word in the sequence. Two sentences such as 'The man bit the dog' and 'The dog bit the man' are analyzed as the same sequence. That means that the system is 'invariant' to the position of words. This does not fare well for NLP. To correct this deficiency, the input word embedding is summed with the output of a positional encoder which gives word positions the necessary weightage. Thus the input embedding summed with the position information is applied to the encoder block. Explicit details of the method of positional encoding are not taken up here.

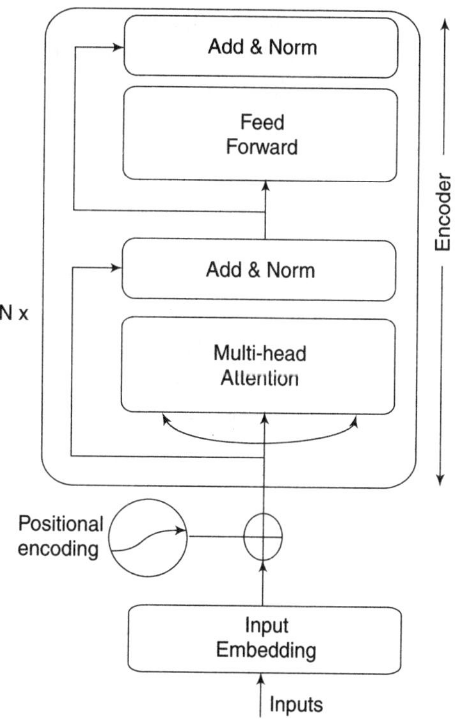

Fig. 18.10 The encoder with positional encoding

Note: In the block diagrams, wherever a block is named 'linear', it simply indicates a multiplication with a matrix. A 'feed forward' layer on the other hand is a fully connected neural network with non-linear activations (ReLU). It can be of multiple layers.

18.2.5.2 *Add and Normalize*

Refer to Fig. 18.10 again. In this, we have the multi-head attention block. After this, there is an 'add and normalize' block which involves a 'skip connection' like a Resnet block (Section 11.3.6). The technique is used to reduce the problem of vanishing/exploding gradients. When the gradients pass backwards to the input side, because of the 'deep' layers with non-linear activation functions, the gradients tend to explode or vanish (depending on the weights). Skip connections allow gradients (in the backward path) to flow through a network directly, without passing through non-linear activation functions. Such an additional path is beneficial for convergence as has been experimentally validated.

The 'normalized' function has the function of making the mean and variance of the signal to zero. This has been discussed in Section 10.7.4 under the title 'Batch Normalization'. Here we use the term 'layer normalization' but it serves the same purpose.

18.2.5.3 *Number of Encoders*

Now that the inner workings of the encoder are clear, we should go ahead and realize that there can be more than one encoder. In Fig. 18.10, N_x denotes this. In the reference paper,

$N_x = 6$ has been chosen. Six encoders are used stacked one on top of the other, with the output of one encoder fed in as the input of the next one. Figure 18.11 shows that six decoders are used in this architecture

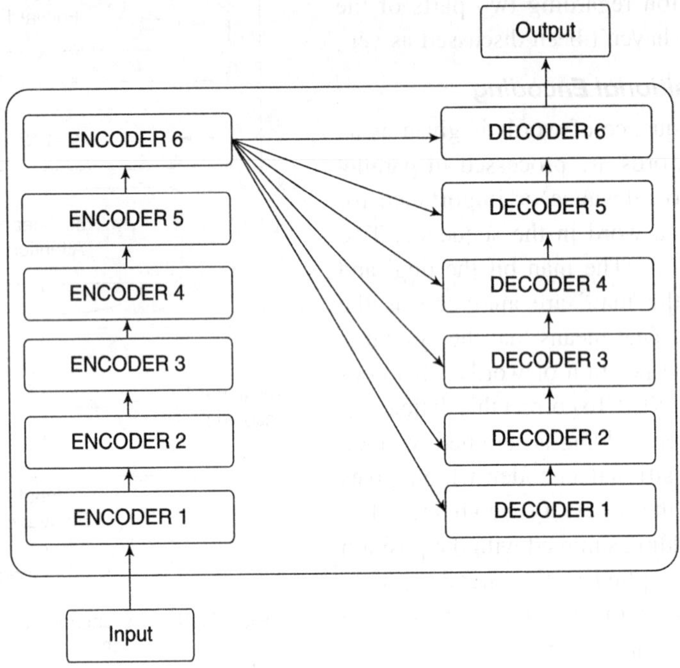

Fig. 18.11 The stacking of encoders and decoders

Each encoder block has the configuration shown in Fig. 18.10. The output of one encoder is fed to the one above it. The final (topmost encoder) one's output is shown as going to all the decoder blocks which are also six in number as in Fig. 18.11.

Figure 18.12 shows a high level view of the encoder block which has three words as its current input sequence. Note that positional encoding is added to the vector embedding of each word and that there is a feed forward layer corresponding to each word.

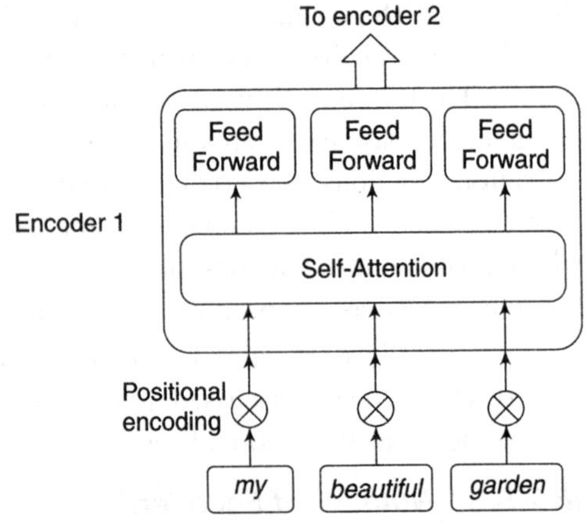

Fig. 18.12 A high level view of an encoder for a sentence

18.2.6 The Decoder

The transformer is also an encoder-decoder network in the sense that the encoder's output is given to the decoder. The input sequence is given to the encoder and the output words come from the decoder. Figure 18.13 shows a high level view of one decoder block.

The decoder has inputs from two sources:

(i) From the encoder, since the decoded output is dependent on the input.

(ii) The output of the decoder from the previous time step is fed into the decoder just as was done in the encoder-decoder network in Section 18.1.1. To this input, positional encoding is added for the same reason as for the encoder (Section 18.2.5.1).

The decoder has two attention mechanisms embedded into it.

(i) Self-attention (with masking, which will be discussed further ahead)

(ii) Encoder decoder attention as was discussed in Section 18.1.4.

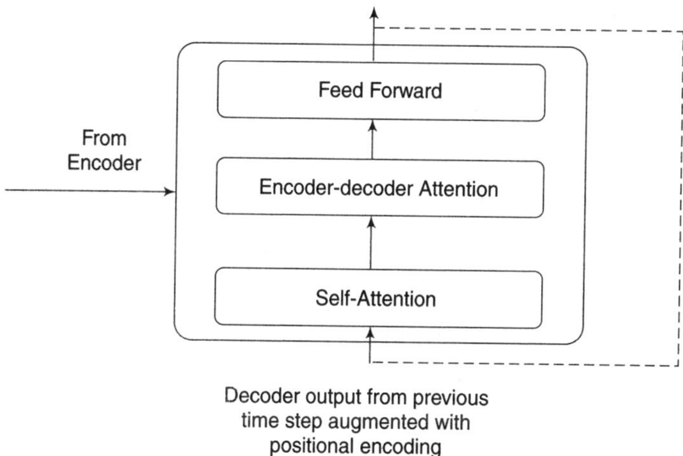

Fig. 18.13 The deecoder – a high level view

The decoder has the same structure as the encoder except that it has two attention blocks But we also see that that the self-attention block is notated as being 'masked' (Fig. 18.14). The logic of this is as follows: When querying is done for the keys of a sequence, it should be done only for the keys before the key that is used as the query. It should not be done for the 'future' keys. What does this mean?

Consider the sentence: *My watch does not give the correct time.*

In this case, when the word 'correct' is used as the query vector, the self-attention calculation with the next word which is 'time' should not be used–it should be masked. This sort of a mechanism may be used (optionally) in the encoder also. But it is mandatory in the decoder. In the decoder, "predictions" are being done and we cannot have attention scores for words that have not yet been predicted.

Figure 18.14 shows a more detailed diagram of the decoder. The decoder is just the same as the encoder except that the last stage is a classifier which gives higher scores for the most probable words. The Softmax computation produces a probability distribution for the words predicted. The correct word is chosen as the one which has the highest probability (out of the words in the vocabulary of the labels in the training set). This is the same as the case with other deep learning network applications such as we have seen in Chapter 11. Figure 18.15 shows the encoder and decoder together.

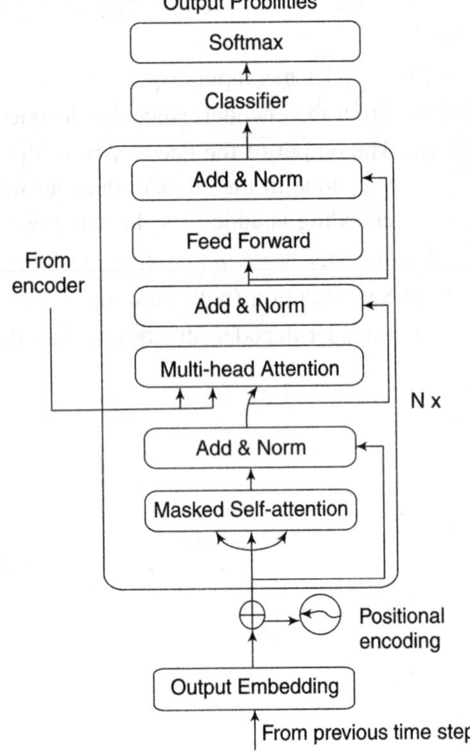

Fig. 18.14 The complete decoder

Now that we have discussed the transformer, let us list out the salient points. Look at Fig. 18.16 which shows the encoder and decoder with $N_x = 2$, that is, the number of encoder and with decoder blocks are 2.

(i) The words in the input sequence can be given in parallel.

(ii) In the encoder side, self-attention is used. Masking is not necessary but it may be done if needed.

(iii) In the decoder side, both self-attention (with masking) and encoder-decoder attention are used.

(iv) At the decoder side, the words generated at the decoder output of one time step are fed into it to act as the decoder input for next step decoding, just as in Section 18.1.1.

(v) In Fig. 18.2 which shows English to Hindi translation, the Hindi words generated at the output of the decoder at one time step are fed as input to the decoder at the next time step.

(vi) Positional information is added to the word embeddings at the input of the encoder as well as the decoder.

18.3 PRE-TRAINED MODELS

The idea of transfer learning was mentioned in Section 11.4. This idea is what is spurring many new applications in computer vision. In NLP, the convenience of using a pre-trained transformer model for one's own specialized dataset has many takers. Two very popular models are BERT and GPT.

BERT stands for Bidirectional Encoder Representations from Transformers. Jacob Devilan and his team at Google created the BERT model in 2018. As the name indicates, it does bidirectional training and has only the encoder part. (Users can add the decoder part.) It has been trained on 2.5 billion words.

Another network named GPT stands for 'Generative Pre-trained Transformer'. The latest version is GPT-3 which has been trained (unidirectionally) on a massive corpus of 175 billion

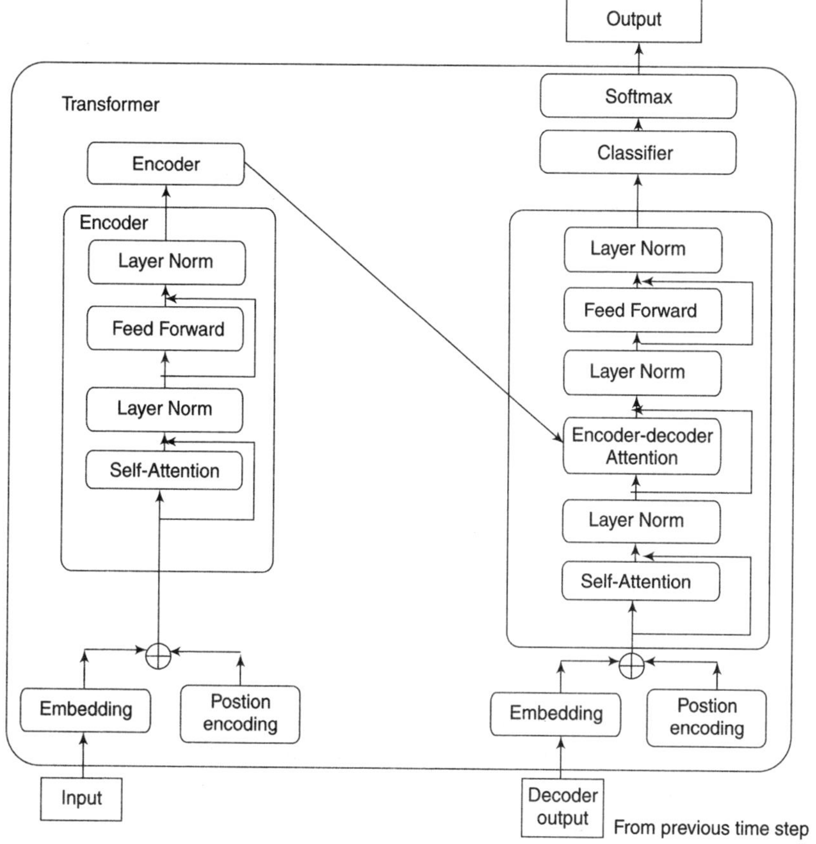

Fig. 18.15 The encoder and decoder

parameters. We will not go into the details of these models as they are just 'transformers' with some customizations.

18.3.1 NLP Applications Using Pre-trained Models

Now let us list out some important applications of NLP.

(i) Information Retrieval
(ii) Document Search
(iii) Machine Translation
(iv) Chatbots
(v) Question Answering
(vi) Text Summarization
(vii) Text Simplification
(viii) Essay Grading
(ix) Sentiment Analysis

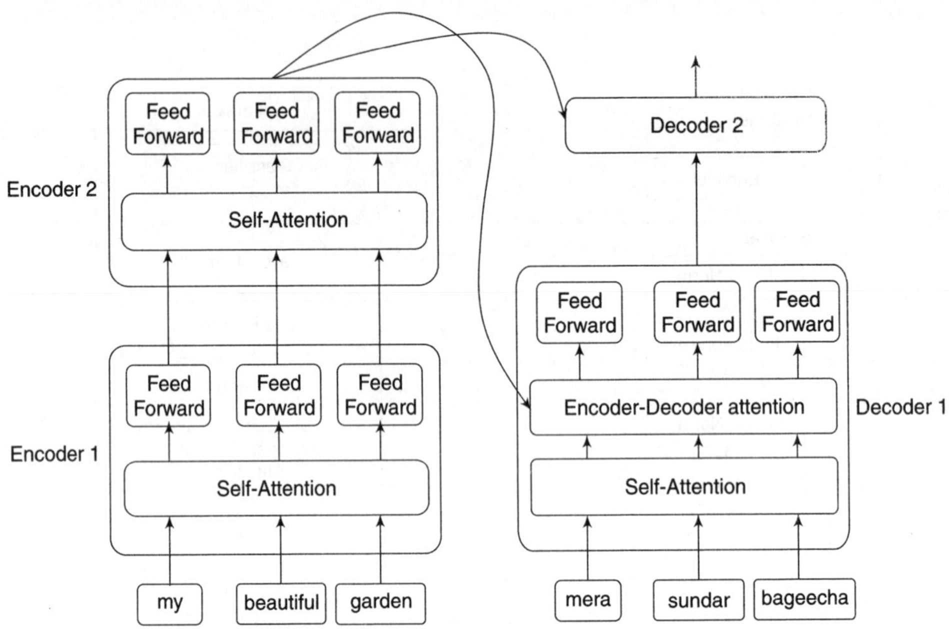

Fig. 18.16 The Encode-Decode mechanism for $N = 2$

We have discussed the principles and models for most of these applications. Currently deep learning techniques are very popular for the solution for these problems, but it is necessary to be familiar with the fundamental concepts of NLP such as pre-processing and text representation as vectors. Seq2Seq models and transformers are increasingly being used as the target network for many applications of NLP. Pre-trained models which have been trained on very large datasets are a boon to the current researchers of NLP.

18.3.2 Machine Translation Example

A code tested for use as a small scale translator for translation from English to three different languages is presented here. The target languages are Hindi, French and Malayalam. The network used is a 'Seq2Seq' model with Attention.

The accuracy of the language translator is observed to depend on the size of data used for training the model. The three datasets which were used here contain around 10,000 English sentences and the corresponding Hindi/French/Malayalam translations. After training the model it is tested for some random sentences. The Source Link is:

https://www.kaggle.com/code/nikhilxavier/english-to-hindi-machine-translation-attention/notebook

Dataset: https://github.com/jackfrost1411/machine-translation-english-to-hindi.

This dataset contains only English and Hindi. The Malayalam and French datasets have been created manually by looking up 'Google translate' for these languages.

Translation Using Seq2Seq Model with Attention

Generate a language translator for converting English language sentences into three different languages – Hindi, French and Malayalam.

```
import os
import string
import numpy as np
import pandas as pd
from string import digits
import matplotlib.pyplot as plt
import re
import logging
import tensorflow as tf
tf.compat.v1.enable_eager_execution(
  config=None, device_policy=None, execution_mode=None)
os.environ['TF_CPP_MIN_LOG_LEVEL'] = '3'
tf.compat.v1.logging.set_verbosity(tf.compat.v1.logging.ERROR)
logging.getLogger('tensorflow').setLevel(logging.FATAL)
import matplotlib.ticker as ticker
from sklearn.model_selection import train_test_split
import unicodedata
import io
import time
import warnings
import sys
import numpy as np
# Download the file

PATH = "/content/Hindi_English_Truncated_Corpus - newjersy.csv"

# Converts the unicode file to ascii
def unicode_to_ascii(s):
  return ''.join(c for c in unicodedata.normalize('NFD', s)
  if unicodedata.category(c) != 'Mn')

def preprocess_sentence(w):
  w = unicode_to_ascii(w.lower().strip())

# creating a space between a word and the punctuation following it

  w = re.sub(r"([?.!,¿])", r" \1 ", w)

# replacing everything with space except (a-z, A-Z, ".", "?", "!", ",")
```

```
  w = re.sub(r'[" "]+', " ", w)
  w = re.sub(r"[^a-zA-Z?.!,¿]+", " ", w)
  w = w.rstrip().strip()
  return w

def hindi_preprocess_sentence(w):
  w = w.rstrip().strip()
  return w

def create_dataset(path=PATH):
  lines=pd.read_csv(path,encoding='utf-8')
  lines=lines.dropna()
  en = []
  hd = []

# adding a start and an end token to the sentence
# so that the model know when to start and stop predicting.

  for i, j in zip(lines['english_sentence'],lines['hindi_sentence']):
    en_1 = [preprocess_sentence(w) for w in i.split(' ')]
    en_1.append('<end>')
    en_1.insert(0, '<start>')
    hd_1 = [hindi_preprocess_sentence(w) for w in j.split(' ')]
    hd_1.append('<end>')
    hd_1.insert(0, '<start>')
    en.append(en_1)
    hd.append(hd_1)
    return hd, en

def max_length(tensor):
  return max(len(t) for t in tensor)

def tokenize(lang):

#tokenisation of sentences
  lang_tokenizer = tf.keras.preprocessing.text.Tokenizer(filters='')
  lang_tokenizer.fit_on_texts(lang)
  tensor = lang_tokenizer.texts_to_sequences(lang)
  tensor = tf.keras.preprocessing.sequence.
    pad_sequences(tensor,padding='post')
  return tensor, lang_tokenizer
```

```
def load_dataset(path=PATH):

# creating cleaned input, output pairs

  targ_lang, inp_lang = create_dataset(path)
  input_tensor, inp_lang_tokenizer = tokenize(inp_lang)
  target_tensor, targ_lang_tokenizer = tokenize(targ_lang)
  return input_tensor, target_tensor, inp_lang_tokenizer, targ_lang_tokenizer

input_tensor, target_tensor, inp_lang, targ_lang = load_dataset(PATH)
max_length_targ, max_length_inp = max_length(target_tensor), max_
length(input_tensor)

# Creating training and validation sets using an 80-20 split

input_tensor_train, input_tensor_val, target_tensor_train, target_tensor_
val = train_test_split(input_tensor, target_tensor, test_size=0.2)

# Show length

print(len(input_tensor_train), len(target_tensor_train), len(input_tensor_
val), len(target_tensor_val))

#index to word mapping

def convert(lang, tensor):
  for t in tensor:
    if t!=0:
      print ("%d ----> %s" % (t, lang.index_word[t]))

print ("Input Language; index to word mapping")
convert(inp_lang, input_tensor_train[0])
print ()
print ("Target Language; index to word mapping")
convert(targ_lang, target_tensor_train[0])

#Create a tf.data dataset

BUFFER_SIZE = len(input_tensor_train)
BATCH_SIZE = 8
steps_per_epoch = len(input_tensor_train)//BATCH_SIZE
embedding_dim = 128
```

```
units = 256
vocab_inp_size = len(inp_lang.word_index)+1
vocab_tar_size = len(targ_lang.word_index)+1

dataset = tf.data.Dataset.from_tensor_slices((input_tensor_train, target_
tensor_train)).shuffle(BUFFER_SIZE)
dataset = dataset.batch(BATCH_SIZE, drop_remainder=True)

# Writing the encoder model

class Encoder(tf.keras.Model):
  def __init__(self, vocab_size, embedding_dim, enc_units, batch_sz):
    super(Encoder, self).__init__()
    self.batch_sz = batch_sz
    self.enc_units = enc_units
    self.embedding = tf.keras.layers.Embedding(vocab_size, embedding_dim)
    self.gru = tf.keras.layers.GRU(self.enc_units,
                                   return_sequences=True,
                                   return_state=True,
                                   recurrent_initializer='glorot_uniform')

  def call(self, x, hidden):
    x = self.embedding(x)
    output, state = self.gru(x, initial_state = hidden)
    return output, state

  def initialize_hidden_state(self):
    return tf.zeros((self.batch_sz, self.enc_units))

encoder = Encoder(vocab_inp_size, embedding_dim, units, BATCH_SIZE)

# Bahdanau Attention mechanism

class BahdanauAttention(tf.keras.layers.Layer):
  def __init__(self, units):
    super(BahdanauAttention, self).__init__()
    self.W1 = tf.keras.layers.Dense(units)
    self.W2 = tf.keras.layers.Dense(units)
    self.V = tf.keras.layers.Dense(1)

  def call(self, query, values):
    hidden_with_time_axis = tf.expand_dims(query, 1)
```

```
    score = self.V(tf.nn.tanh(
      self.W1(values) + self.W2(hidden_with_time_axis)))
      attention_weights = tf.nn.softmax(score, axis=1)
      context_vector = attention_weights * values
      context_vector = tf.reduce_sum(context_vector, axis=1)
      return context_vector, attention_weights

# Writing the decoder model

class Decoder(tf.keras.Model):
  def __init__(self, vocab_size, embedding_dim, dec_units, batch_sz):
    super(Decoder, self).__init__()
    self.batch_sz = batch_sz
    self.dec_units = dec_units
    self.embedding = tf.keras.layers.Embedding(vocab_size, embedding_dim)
    self.gru = tf.keras.layers.GRU(self.dec_units,
                         return_sequences=True,
                         return_state=True,
                         recurrent_initializer='glorot_uniform')
    self.fc = tf.keras.layers.Dense(vocab_size)
    self.attention = BahdanauAttention(self.dec_units)

  def call(self, x, hidden, enc_output):
    context_vector, attention_weights = self.attention(hidden, enc_output)
    x = self.embedding(x)
    x = tf.concat([tf.expand_dims(context_vector, 1), x], axis=-1)
    output, state = self.gru(x)
    output = tf.reshape(output, (-1, output.shape[2]))
    x = self.fc(output)
    return x, state, attention_weights

decoder = Decoder(vocab_tar_size, embedding_dim, units, BATCH_SIZE)

optimizer = tf.keras.optimizers.Adam()
loss_object = tf.keras.losses.SparseCategoricalCrossentropy
  (from_logits=True, reduction='none')

#optimizer and loss function

def loss_function(real, pred):
  mask = tf.math.logical_not(tf.math.equal(real, 0))
  loss_ = loss_object(real, pred)
```

```
  mask = tf.cast(mask, dtype=loss_.dtype)
  loss_ *= mask
  return tf.reduce_mean(loss_)

checkpoint_dir = './training_checkpoints'
checkpoint_prefix = os.path.join(checkpoint_dir, "ckpt")
checkpoint = tf.train.Checkpoint(optimizer=optimizer,
                                 encoder=encoder,
                                 decoder=decoder)

@tf.function

#Training

def train_step(inp, targ, enc_hidden):
  loss = 0
  with tf.GradientTape() as tape:
    enc_output, enc_hidden = encoder(inp, enc_hidden)
    dec_hidden = enc_hidden
    dec_input = tf.expand_dims([targ_lang.word_index['<start>']] * BATCH_SIZE, 1)
    # Teacher forcing
    for t in range(1, targ.shape[1]):
      predictions, dec_hidden, _ = decoder(dec_input, dec_hidden, enc_output)
      loss += loss_function(targ[:, t], predictions)
      dec_input = tf.expand_dims(targ[:, t], 1)

  batch_loss = (loss / int(targ.shape[1]))
  variables = encoder.trainable_variables + decoder.trainable_variables
  gradients = tape.gradient(loss, variables)
  optimizer.apply_gradients(zip(gradients, variables))
  return batch_loss

EPOCHS = 20
for epoch in range(EPOCHS):
  start = time.time()
  enc_hidden = encoder.initialize_hidden_state()
  total_loss = 0
  for (batch, (inp, targ)) in enumerate(dataset.take(steps_per_epoch)):
    batch_loss = train_step(inp, targ, enc_hidden)
    total_loss += batch_loss
    if batch % 100 == 0:
```

```
        print('Epoch {} Batch {} Loss {:.4f}'.format(epoch + 1,
                                          batch,
                                          batch_loss.numpy()))
    if (epoch + 1) % 2 == 0:
      checkpoint.save(file_prefix = checkpoint_prefix)

    print('Epoch {} Loss {:.4f}'.format(epoch + 1,
              total_loss / steps_per_epoch))
    print('Time taken for 1 epoch {} sec\n'.format(time.time() - start))

def evaluate(sentence):
    attention_plot = np.zeros((max_length_targ, max_length_inp))
    sentence = preprocess_sentence(sentence)
    inputs = [inp_lang.word_index[i] for i in sentence.split(' ')]
    inputs = tf.keras.preprocessing.sequence.pad_sequences([inputs],
                                            maxlen=max_length_inp,
                                            padding='post')
    inputs = tf.convert_to_tensor(inputs)
    result = ''
    hidden = [tf.zeros((1, units))]
    enc_out, enc_hidden = encoder(inputs, hidden)
    dec_hidden = enc_hidden
    dec_input = tf.expand_dims([targ_lang.word_index['<start>']], 0)
    for t in range(max_length_targ):
      predictions, dec_hidden, attention_weights = decoder(dec_input, dec_
hidden,enc_out)
      predicted_id = tf.argmax(predictions[0]).numpy()
      result += targ_lang.index_word[predicted_id] + ' '
      if targ_lang.index_word[predicted_id] == '<end>':
        return result, sentence
      dec_input = tf.expand_dims([predicted_id], 0)
    return result, sentence

def translate(sentence):
    result, sentence = evaluate(sentence)
    print('Input: %s' % (sentence))
    print('Predicted translation: {}'.format(result))

checkpoint.restore(tf.train.latest_checkpoint(checkpoint_dir))

translate(u'she likes bananas and grapes.')
```

```
while True:
  strn = input("Enter the sentence in english to convert:")
  print('strn:', strn)
  translate(strn)
  val = input("Do you want to continue Translation(1/0): ")
  if val == '0':
    break
```

A sample of the results:

Input: she likes bananas and grapes.

Predicted translation: उसे केले और अंगूर पसंद हैं। <end>

strn: he dislikes bananas and oranges.

Input: he dislikes bananas and oranges.

Predicted translation: वह केले और संतरे को नापसंद करता है। <end>

strn: india is beautiful during august, but it is never snowy in may.

Input: india is beautiful during august, but it is never snowy in may.

Predicted translation: अगस्त के दौरान भारत सुंदर है, लेकिन यह कभी भी जून में कभी बर्फीला नहीं हो सकता है। <end>

Conclusion

With this chapter, we conclude our discussion of NLP. Most of the important concepts of NLP have been covered in Chapters 14 to 18.

Questions

1. Why is an encoder-decoder network named as 'Sequence to Sequence' network?
2. What are the basic elements of a Seq2Seq network?
3. What is 'teacher forcing' and how is it implemented?
4. What is the inadequacy of a simple 'context vector'?
5. What is the principle of the attention mechanism?
6. How is attention between the encoder and decoder computed?
7. Give an example of 'self-attention' for a sentence.
8. How are the q, k and v vectors obtained ?
9. What is the relevance of the term 'multi-head' in transformers?
10. Name a few applications in which transformers have been used.

Exercise

1. Make a study of the various transformer networks available for NLP applications.
2. Find out how transformers have been used in computer vision.
3. Write a code using BERT for machine translation.
4. Discuss the use with code of a chatbot made using transformers.
5. How is text simplification done using transformers?
6. Automatic essay scoring is an application of NLP. Give details on how it can be implemented.

Part IV

Reinforcement Learning

CHAPTER

19

Reinforcement Learning: Introduction, Motivation and Brief History

In Chapter 9, we looked at search problems, where the objective was to find a sequence of actions such that a "goal" is achieved. The assumption implicit in search problems is that the next state is a deterministic function of the current state and action. In real world, this deterministic assumption is often unrealistic. For example, consider an autonomous driving vehicle, even though the current state might indicate that the current lane is empty and the vehicle can safely accelerate, there is always a possibility that the car in a nearby lane can change lane, or a pedestrian might choose to cross the road. Other examples include in robotics, where there are noise in the sensors and the robot can hit unseen obstacles, or in resource allocation where a manufacturer wants to produce various goods, but is uncertain regarding the consumer preference.

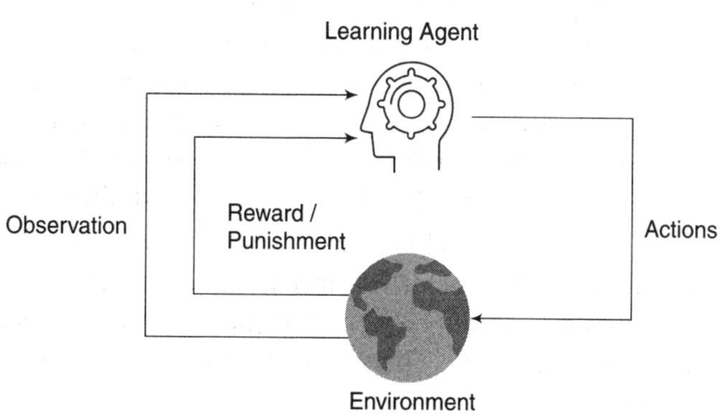

Fig. 19.1 An agent learns by interacting with the environment

In Part 4 of this book, we look at how to model such problems and obtain solutions. In Chapter 20, we consider modeling such problems using the framework of "Markov Decision Processes" (MDP). In the subsequent chapters, Chapter 21, Chapter 22, and Chapter 23, we look at "Reinforcement Learning", the central theme of Part 4. In short, in reinforcement learning we assume that the model parameters of the "Markov Decision Processes" is unknown. The agent "learns" by interacting with the environment as shown in Fig. 19.1. The interaction with the environment happens by the agent taking various possible actions, and based on feedback recieved either as observation or rewards or both, the agent learns "good behaviour" in the uncertain environment.

Learning from interaction is a fundamental and foundational idea underlying all theories of intelligence. Reinforcement is essentially a behavioural concept, based on the fact that responses vary according to their effects.

The history of reinforcement learning has three main threads:

1. **Trial and Error Learning:** This thread originates from the psychology of animal learning. For example, a baby bird learns to associate food by pecking at the parent birds' bill. There are two important aspects of trial and error learning: *selectional*, i.e., trying several alternatives and selecting among them by comparing the consequences, and *associative*, i.e., alternatives found by selection are associated with particular situations. These two aspects embody the essence of reinforcement learning, i.e., trying and selecting the best options among many and remembering the best actions for a particular context.
2. **Optimal Control:** The term optimal control, describing theory and methods to control a dynamical system such that a desired objective is optimized, came into use in the late 1950s. Richard Bellman, extending the theory of Hamilton and Jacobi, developed a class of methods for solving the optimal control problem by solving "Bellman equation", which later came to be known as dynamic programming. Bellman also introduced the discrete stochastic version of the optimal control problem known as Markov Decision Processes (MDP), which form the basis of modern reinforcement learning framework and Ron Howard in 1960 devised the policy iteration method for MDP. Dynamic programming is widely considered the only feasible way of solving general stochastic optimal control problems. It suffers from what Bellman called "the curse of dimensionality", meaning that its computational requirements grow exponentially with the number of state variables.
3. **Temporal Difference Learning:** The third thread to the history of reinforcement learning is temporal difference learning. It is driven by the concept of the difference between temporally successive estimates of the same quantity. The origins of temporal difference learning are in part in animal learning psychology, in particular, in the notion of secondary reinforcers. Arthur Samuel (1959) was the first to propose and implement a learning method that included temporal difference ideas.

Andrew G. Barto and Richard S. Sutton, whose excellent textbook is considered the bible on reinforcement learning, described learning rules driven by changes in temporally successive predictions and developed a psychological model of classical conditioning based on temporal-difference learning. This eventually led to the development of the famous "actor-critic" algorithm.

A principled mathematical framework for reinforcement learning existed in the earlier 21st century. However, the framework lacked scalability and were limited to low dimensional problems. The advent of deep learning had a significant impact on all areas including reinforcement learning, leading to deep reinforcement learning (DRL) The important characteristics of deep learning is its ability to effectively perform *function approximation* and *representation learning*, i.e., deep neural networks can efficiently find low dimensional representation of high dimensional data such as images, text and audio. Perhaps, the two watershed moments of DRL in contemporary history is:

1. DeepMind developing an algorithm that could play a range of Atari 2600 video games at a superhuman level directly from image pixels.
2. A hybrid DRL system called AlphaGo that defeated the human world champion in Go, paralleling the historic achievement of IBM's Deep Blue in chess more than two decades ago and IBM's Watson system that beat the best human Jeopardy! players.

In this part of the book, we will talk about all the principles and algorithm underlying mordern deep reinforcement learning algorithms.

CHAPTER

20

Markov Decision Process

In this chapter you will

- learn a principled framework for sequential decision making, namely, the Markov Decision Process (MDP),
- model real-world sequential decision-making problems using an MDP,
- learn about finite horizon and infinite horizon class of MDP, and
- Bellman optimality equation and it's numerical solution.

20.0 INTRODUCTION

Consider the following classical dice game, where in each round you choose to either (stay and) play the game or quit. If you quit, then you get \$10, and the game ends and if you chose to stay and play the game, then you get \$4 and a dice is rolled. If the dice comes up either as 1 or 2, then the game ends, else the game goes to the next round. There are several important aspects of the game above that merits attention:

1. **Probabilistic transition:** The "state" of the game is not deterministic; it depends on the decision of the player and probabilistically on the outcome of the dice cast.
2. **Cumulative reward:** The player is, obviously, interested in choosing decisions that maximize cumulated payout at the end of the game (or as long as the player can play). It is straightforward to argue that the optimal decision is to choose to play at every round so as to accumulate the \$4 reward.

The above aspects are the intrinsic properties of a *sequential decision-making* problem: A decision maker (or player) is offered a choice at every time instant (or round) where the state of the system is probabilistic and the decision maker chooses decision at each time step to maximize the cumulative reward. Note that the decision choice affects not only the reward at the current time but also future choices as well, and hence the cumulative reward.

The sequential decision-making problem appears in a variety of contexts:

- **Robotics:** Deciding when and where to move, but actuators and sensors can fail and see unknown obstacles.
- **Resource allocation:** Deciding what and how much to produce in a factory, with uncertainty over customer demand for various products.
- **Agriculture:** Deciding what to plant, but don't know the weather condition and hence, the crop yield.

In this chapter, we introduce *Markov Decision Process*, a class of sequential decision-making problem where the probabilistic transitions obey the Markov property. Before we start, Section 20.1 provides an overview of Markov chain. As a prelude to Markov Decision Process in Section 20.3, we discuss Markov Reward Process in Section 20.2. Finally, Section 20.4 presents numerical algorithms for solving the Markov decision process.

20.1 MARKOV CHAIN

Let $X_1, X_2, \ldots, X_N$ be a set of random variables indexed by time. Consider the conditional distribution $P(X_n|X_1, \ldots, X_{n-1})$ at time n, i.e., the conditional distribution of the "current" random variable conditioned on the history $(X_1, \ldots, X_{n-1})$. If the above conditional distribution is same as $P(X_n|X_{n-1})$, i.e., conditioned on the random variable at the previous time instant, the conditional distribution is independent of the history, then we say that the set of random variables satisfies the Markov property.

Markov Property $$P(X_n|X_1, \ldots, X_{n-1}) = P(X_n|X_{n-1}) \qquad \ldots(1)$$

A process that obeys the *Markov property* and takes values in a finite set (S) is called a *Markov chain*. The state of a Markov chain at time n is the value of X_n, and hence, S is referred to as the *state space*. A Markov chain can be characterized by $P(X_n|X_{n-1})$, known as the *one step transition probability* (or simply transition probability). An alternate convenient notation for the transition probability is given below:

$$P^n_{i,j} = P(X_n = j|X_{n-1} = i). \qquad \ldots(2)$$

Note that in the definition in (2), the transition probabilities depend on the time index n. For a Markov chain with *stationary transition probabilities*, $P^n_{i,j}$ is independent of n. In this book, we will only deal with Markov chains with stationary transition probability.

Example 20.1 (Gambling model) Consider a gambler, who at each play of the game, wins \$1 with probability p and loses \$1 with probability $1 - p$. The gambler stops gambling, when either he is broke or when the reaches \$$N$.

The gambler's fortune at each time X_n can be modeled as a Markov chain. $X_n \in \{0, 1, \ldots, N - 1, N\}$, since the gambler stops playing either when he is broke (fortune of 0) or when he reaches a fortune of \$$N$.

The transition probability of the Markov chain is given by:

$$P_{i,j} = \begin{cases} p & j = i+1, \\ 1-p & j = i-1, \quad i = 1, 2, ..., N-1, \\ 0 & \text{else} \end{cases}$$

$$P_{0,0} = P_{N,N} = 1$$

Transition Probability Matrix of a Markov Chain: Sometimes it is convenient to write the transition probability of the Markov chain in matrix form given by $P = [P_{i,j}]$, where the rows are indexed by the previous state and the columns are indexed by the next state. For example, the transition probability matrix of the Markov chain in Example 20.1 for $p = 0.4$ and $N = 4$ is given by

$$P = \begin{bmatrix} 1 & 0 & 0 & 0 & 0 \\ 0.6 & 0.4 & 0 & 0 & 0 \\ 0 & 0.6 & 0.4 & 0 & 0 \\ 0 & 0 & 0.6 & 0.4 & 0 \\ 0 & 0 & 0 & 0 & 1 \end{bmatrix}$$

Transition diagram of a Markov Chain: A transition diagram is another way of visualizing the Markov chain. For example, the transition diagram of the Markov chain in Example 20.1 is given in Fig. 20.1.

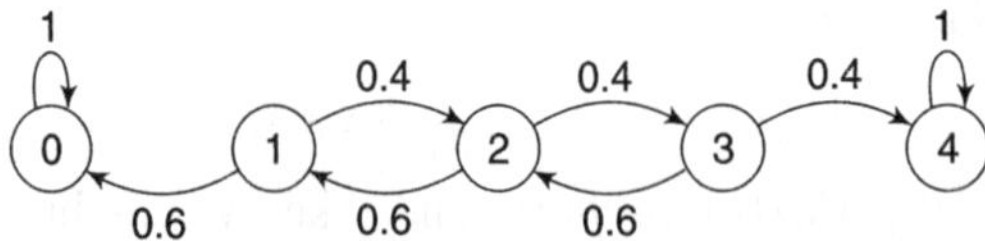

Fig. 20.1 Transition diagram of the Markov chain in Example 20.1 for $N = 4$, and $\rho = 0.4$

Here the circles denote the possible states of the Markov chain and the arrows represent the transitions from one state to other, with the probability of transition indicated besides the arrow.

Properties of Markov Chain: An important property of the Markov chain is given in (3). The property is intuitive: Given the Markov chain is in state i, in the next time step, it transitions to any of the possible states.

$$\sum_j P_{i,j} = 1 \quad ...(3)$$

A consequence of the above property is that the rows of the transition probability matrix sum to 1, i.e., P is a stochastic matrix.

20.2 MARKOV REWARD PROCESS

A Markov reward process is a Markov chain augmented with a reward function. Formally, a Markov reward process is a tuple $\langle S, P, r, \gamma \rangle$,

- S and P are the state space and the transition probability of the Markov chain, respectively.
- $r : S \rightarrow R$, is the reward function which maps the state of the Markov chain to a real value.
- $\gamma \in [0, 1]$ is the discount factor. The role of the discount factor will be discussed later in the section.

The Gambling model in Example 20.1 is an example of Markov reward process. If the reward at time t, corresponds to the wealth of the gambler, then $r(s_t) = s_t$.

As mentioned in the introduction to this chapter, decision makers are interested in maximizing the cumulative reward. Even though decision making is not part of Markov reward process, we can formally define the cumulative reward as follows.

Given sequences of states $\tau_t^T = \{s_t, s_{t+1}, ..., s_T\}$ starting at time t for a time horizon of $T < \infty$, the cumulative reward

$$G_t\,(\tau_t^T) = r_t + r_{t+1} + ... + r_T, \tag{4}$$

where, $r_t = r(s_t)$.

Remark 1: $r_t = r(s_t)$ is the *immediate reward* and the others are *future reward*. Hence, the cumulative reward G_t^T is the sum of the immediate reward and future rewards.

The above formulation for $T < \infty$ is referred to as the *finite horizon* Markov reward process. In contrast, the case $T \rightarrow \infty$ is referred to as the *infinite horizon* Markov reward process.

The cumulative reward for the infinite horizon case is defined as follows.

Infinite horizon: Given sequences of states $\tau_t = \{s_t, s_{t+1}, ...\}$ starting at time t, the cumulative reward

$$G_t\,(\tau_t) = r_t + \gamma r_{t+1} + \gamma^2 r_{t+2} + ... \qquad ...(5)$$

Note that in contrast to the finite horizon definition in (4), the definition for the infinite horizon case in (5) includes the discount factor (γ).

Why discount factor?

1. **Technical requirement:** This is perhaps the most important reason for including the discount factor. As $T \rightarrow \infty$ in (4), the sum G_t^T can grow unbounded (or in engineering terminology could go to infinite). It is easy to see that, when discount factor is included, $G_t < r_{\max} \dfrac{1}{1-\gamma}$ where $r_{\max} = \max_s r(s)$.
2. **Economic interpretation:** This arises out of the preference of *human decision makers*. As humans, we prefer to receive \$1 today, instead of tomorrow. For example, if we were to deposit the \$1 recieved today in a bank, the bank pays a fixed interest and the value of the deposit tomorrow is higher than \$1.

   In addition, this provides a methodology to model the short-term and long-term ambitions of decision makers. As, $\gamma \rightarrow 0$, decision makers are concerned with only the "short term" immediate rewards; and as $\gamma \to 1$, decision makers are concerned with "long term" cumulative reward, where decision makers could sacrifice short term rewards for improving long term cumulative reward.

3. **Game theoretic interpretation:** The interpretation results from thinking about Markov reward process as a game being played with environment and a player. The player obtains reward based on the state of the environment. At each time, with some probability $1 - \gamma$, the environment may decide to stop playing the game, then the expected reward under this setting is same as in the formulation mentioned in (5). For example, the movement of a stock can be interpreted as Markov reward process; there is some small, but finite, probability that a financial crisis could cause the stock to go "under".

Since many of the reasons for including discount factor is also valid for the finite horizon case, we will include a discount factor for finite horizon as well.

Finite horizon with discount factor: Given sequences of states $\tau_t^T = \{s_t, s_{t+1}, ..., s_T\}$ starting at time t for a time horizon of $T < \infty$, the cumulative reward

$$G_t\,(\tau_t^T) = r_t + \gamma r_{t+1} + ... + \gamma^{T-t} r_t, \qquad ...(6)$$

where, $r_t = r(s_t)$.

20.2.1 Value Function and Bellman's Theorem

How do we characterize the various states in a Markov reward process? It might be the case that in some states the immediate reward may be high, but the system "quickly" transitions to states with lower reward, leading to lower cumulative reward. However, in other states, even though the immediate reward might be low, it might transition to higher rewarding states more often, leading to higher cumulative reward. One way to characterize the states in a Markov reward process is to find the expected long-term reward that can be accumulated starting from any state, referred to as the value function. Formally, the value function $V_t(s_t)$ of state s_t at time t is defined as the total *expected* rewards that are accrued from time t.

20.2.1.1 Finite Horizon Markov Reward Process

For the finite horizon reward process, the value function in terms of the cumulative reward is given in (7).

$$V_t(s_t) = E_{\tau_t^T | s_t}\,[G_t]. \qquad ...(7)$$

The expectation in (7) is taken with respect to all the trajectories starting with state s_t at time t, and for a horizon of T.

From (7), it looks like finding the value function is quite complicated. Fortunately, Bellman's theorem provides a method to compute the value functions.

Theorem 1 Bellman's theorem (finite horizon Markov reward process)

The value function for a finite horizon Markov reward process is given by

$$V_t(s) = r(s) + \sum_{s'} P_{s,s'} V_{t+1}(s') \quad ...(8)$$

$$V_T(s) = r(s) \quad ...(9)$$

Proof: It is straightforward to note that $V_T(s) = r(s)$.

$$\begin{aligned}
V_t(s) &= V_t(s_t = s) = \mathbb{E}_{\tau_t^T | s_t = s}[G_t(\tau_t^T)] = \sum_{\tau_t^T | s_t = s} \mathbb{P}[\tau_t^T | s_t = s] G_t(\tau_t^T) \\
&= r(s) + \gamma \sum_{\tau_{t+1}^T | s_t = s} \mathbb{P}[\tau_{t+1}^T | s_t = s] G_t(\tau_{t+1}^T) \\
&= r(s) + \gamma \sum_{\tau_{t+1}^T | s_t - s} \sum_{s'} \mathbb{P}[\tau_{t+1}^T, s_{t+1} = s' | s_t = s] G_{t+1}(\tau_{t+1}^T) \\
&= r(s) + \gamma \sum_{\tau_{t+1}^T | s_t = s} \sum_{s'} \mathbb{P}[s_{t+1} = s' | s_t = s] \mathbb{P}[\tau_{t+1}^T | s_t = s, s_{t+1} = s'] G_{t+1}(\tau_{t+1}^T) \\
&= r(s) + \gamma \sum_{s'} \mathbb{P}[s_{t+1} = s' | s_t = s] \sum_{\tau_{t+1}^T | s_t = s} \mathbb{P}[\tau_{t+1}^T | s_t = s, s_{t+1} = s'] G_{t+1}(\tau_{t+1}^T) \\
&= r(s) + \gamma \sum_{s'} P_{s,s'} V_t(s')
\end{aligned}$$

The third step in the proof above is due to the law of total probability, and the fifth step uses the Markov property.

20.2.1.2 Infinite Horizon Markov Reward Process

Before we proceed to the Bellman theorem for infinite horizon, note that in infinite horizon the following property holds.

Property 1 In infinite horizon Markov reward process, for times t and t',

$$V_t(s) = V_{t'}(s) \ \forall s \in S \quad ...(10)$$

Property 1 states that the value function in an infinite horizon Markov reward process is *stationary*, i.e., it doesn't depend on the time. The proof is straightforward, and the main idea is since there is infinite amount of time left, it doesn't matter when the value function is evaluated. Now we are ready to state Bellman's theorem for infinite horizon Markov reward process.

Theorem 2. Bellman's theorem (infinite horizon discounted Markov reward process). The value function is given by

$$V(s) = r(s) + \gamma \sum_{s'} P_{s,s'} V(s') \quad ...(11)$$

The proof proceeds exactly as in the finite horizon case and hence is omitted.

Remark 2. The value function is the *fixed point* of the set of equations in (11). The existence of the fixed point can be shown by using Banach fixed point theorem and by showing that the right-hand side of (11) is a contraction mapping.

Example 20.2 Consider the two-state Markov chain in Fig. 20.2. The reward function, is mentioned along with the state. Assume infinite horizon discounted Markov reward process. Compute the value function for each of the two states?

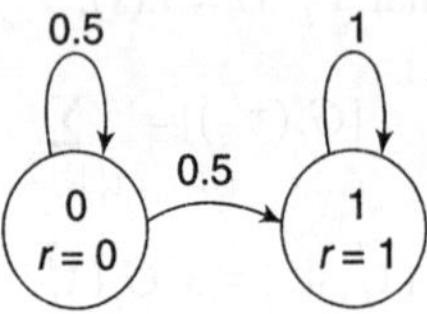

Fig. 20.2 Transition diagram of a 2-state Markov reward process

If the Markov chain starts in state 1, then there is only one sequence of states possible (and that occurs with probability 1) and the cumulative reward is given by

$$G_t|\{S_t = 1\} = 1 + \gamma \times 1 + \gamma^2 \times 1 + \ldots = \frac{1}{(1-\gamma)} \qquad \ldots(12)$$

Hence, $V(s = 1) = E[G_t|\{S_t = 1\}] = \frac{1}{1-\gamma}$.

However, this is not the case when Markov chain starts in state 0. Below, we tabulate the various trajectories, starting in state 0 and their probability of occurrence.

$\mathbb{P}[G_t|\{S_t = 0\}]$	$G_t|\{S_t = 0\}$
0.5	$0 + \gamma \times 1 + \gamma^2 \times 1 + \gamma^3 \times 1 + \ldots = \frac{1}{1-\gamma}$
0.25	$0 + \gamma \times 0 + \gamma^2 \times 1 + \gamma^3 \times 1 + \ldots = \frac{\gamma^2}{1-\gamma}$
0.125	$0 + \gamma \times 0 + \gamma^2 \times 0 + \gamma^3 \times 1 + \ldots = \frac{\gamma^3}{1-\gamma}$
$\vdots$	

Compared to $G_t|\{S_t = 1\}$ in (12), $G_t|\{S_t = 0\}$ is a random variable (this is usually the case). Hence, $V(s = 0) = E(G_t|\{S_t = 0\} = 0.5 \times \frac{\gamma}{1-\gamma} + 0.25 \times \frac{\gamma^2}{1-\gamma} + \ldots = \frac{1}{1-\gamma}\frac{0.5\gamma}{1-0.5\gamma}$.

It is easy to see that $V(s = 0)$ is less than $V(s = 1)$, for all values of γ. This is intuitive since state 1 has a higher reward and there is less uncertainty about the reward.

20.3 MARKOV DECISION PROCESS

Markov decision process is an extension of Markov reward process, where the rewards and state transitions can be influenced by the actions of the decision makers. Formally, a Markov decision process is a tuple $\langle S, P, r, A, \gamma\rangle$.

- S is the state space of the Markov chain.
- A is the action space of the decision maker, i.e., the set of actions available to the decision maker. For example, in the Gambling model in Example 20.1, the action space is either to gamble or not. Hence, $A = \{Gamble, Not\ Gamble\}$.

When the action space is dependent on the state of the Markov chain, it is denoted by $A(s)$.

- $P(\cdot)$ is the transition probability of the Markov chain. However, in contrast, to the Markov reward process, the transition probability also depends on the action of the decision maker. For example, $P_{i,j}(a)$ is the probability of transition from state i to state j when action a is taken.
- $r: S \times A \to R$, is the reward function which maps the state of the Markov chain, and the action taken by a decision maker to a real value. In contrast to Markov reward process, the reward depends not only on the state but also the action of the decision maker.
- As in Markov reward process, $\gamma \in [0, 1]$ is the discount factor.

Remark 3. An equivalent formulation also considers the case where the reward function, in addition to the current state and action of the decision maker, also depends on the next state. The reader is asked to show the equivalence of the two formulations in Exercise 8.

As in the Markov reward process, we proceed by considering the finite horizon and the infinite horizon cases, in turn.

20.3.1 Finite Horizon MDP

In the case of a finite horizon MDP, the decision maker accrues reward for a finite number of time steps. However, in contrast to Markov reward process, the actions of the decision maker also influence the reward of the decision maker.

Policy: The "policy" of the decision maker prescribes an action to the decision maker. Since the objective of the decision maker is to maximize expected cumulative reward, an optimal policy is one that maximizes expected cumulative reward. For a finite horizon MDP, it is sufficient to consider policies that are a *deterministic* function of the current state, i.e.,

$$a_k = \mu_k(s_k), \qquad ...(13)$$

where μ_k is the policy at time k. The policy of the decision maker for a finite horizon MDP is the vector

$$\mu = (\mu_0, \mu_1, \ldots \mu_{N-1}) \qquad ...(14)$$

where μ_k, as defined in (13), is the policy at time k.[#]

An optimal policy μ^* is one that maximizes the expected cumulative reward,

$$\mu^* = \text{argmax}_\mu \mathbb{E}\left[\sum_{k=0}^{N-1} r_k(s_k, \mu_k(s_k)) + r_N(s_N)\right] \qquad ...(15)$$

For notational convenience, define

$$J_\mu(x) = \mathbb{E}\left[\sum_{k=0}^{N-1} r_k(s_k, \mu_k(s_k)) + r_N(s_N) \mid s_0 = x\right] \qquad (16)$$

[#] Notice that for simplicity of notation, we always start from $t = 0$.

$J_{\mu}(x)$ is the expected cumulative reward for a policy μ with the Markov chain starting at state x. Hence, the optimal policy in (15) is simply that policy, among all policies, that maximizes the expected cumulative reward for all possible starting states.

Finding the optimal policy for an N horizon Markov decision problem amounts to finding an optimal mapping from state to action for N time instant. From the optimization problem in (14), finding the optimal policy looks complicated. Fortunately, Bellman dynamic programming theorem provides a recursive solution to compute the optimal policy.

Theorem 3 Bellman's theorem (finite horizon discounted Markov decision process)

$$J_k(s) = \max_{a\in A}\left[r_k(s,a)+\gamma\sum_{s'} P_{s,s'}(a)J_{k+1}(s')\right] \tag{17}$$

$$\mu_k(s) = \text{argmax}_{a\in A}\left[r_k(s,a)+\gamma\sum_{s'} P_{s,s'}(a)J_{k+1}(s')\right]$$

with $J_N(s) = r_N(s)$.

The proof of Theorem 3 is similar to the Theorem 1 - Bellman theorem for Markov reward process. Hence, the proof is omitted. In subsequent chapters, we will extensively use the Q-function notation. The Q-function for the finite horizon discounted MDP, is as below:

$$Q_k(s, a) = r_k(s, a) + \gamma \sum_{s'} P_{s,s'}(a)\, J_{k+1}(s'). \qquad ...(18)$$

Using the Q-function notation, (17) can be written as:

$$J_k(s) = \max_{a\in A} Q_k(s, a), \qquad ...(19)$$

$$\mu_k(s) = \text{argmax}_{a\in A} Q_k(s, a).$$

Example 20.3 Consider the Markov decision-making problem in Fig. 20.3. Two actions a_1 and a_2 are possible in state 1. No actions are possible in state 2 and state 3. The state transitions arrows are marked with the action and the probability of transitions associated with that action. Find the optimal policy for a horizon of $T = 2$, starting from $t = 0$.

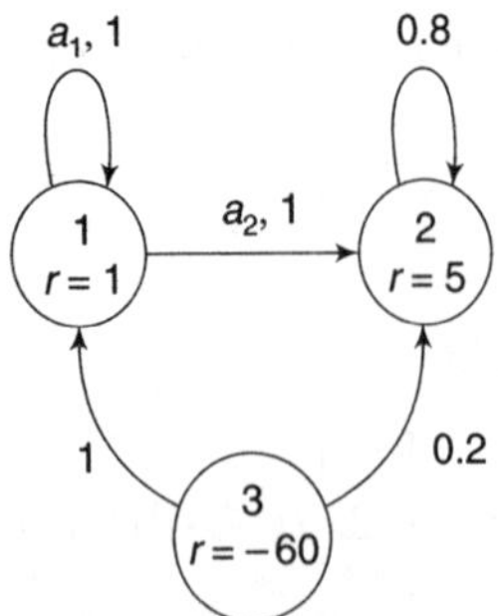

Fig. 20.3 Transition diagram of Markov decision-making problem for Example 20.3

At time, $T = 2$, $J_2(1) = 1$, $J_2(2) = 5$, $J_2(3) = -60$.

For time, $t = 1$, for states 2 and 3,

$$J_1(3) = r(3) + \sum_s P_{3,s}\, J_2(s) = r(3) + 1\, J_2(1) = -60 + 1 = -59$$

$$J_1(2) = r(2) + \sum_s P_{2,s}\, J_2(s) = r(2) + 0.8\, J_2(2) + 0.2\, J_2(3) = 5 + 0.8 \times 5 + 0.2 \times -60 = -3$$

For time $t = 1$ and state is 1, since two actions are possible we consider each of them in turn. If action chosen is a_1:

$$Q_1(1, a_1) = r(1) + \sum_s P_{1,s}\,(a_1)\, J_2(1) = r(1) + 1J_2(1) = 1 + 1 = 2$$

Similarly, if action a_2 is chosen:

$$Q_1(1, a_2) = r(1) + \sum_s P_{1,s}\,(a_2)\, J_2(1) = r(1) + 1J_2(2) = 1 + 5 = 6.$$

$$V_1(1) = \max_a Q_1(1, a) = 6,\ \mu_1\,(1) = \text{argmax}_a\, Q_1\,(1, a) = a_2.$$

Finding the Q-value, the optimal policy at time $t = 0$ is left as an exercise.

20.3.1.1 Forward Recursion Formulation

Consider the following change of notation:

$$V_n(\text{s}) = J_{N-n}(\text{s})\ 0 \le n < N \qquad \text{...(20)}$$

$$V_0(\text{s}) = J_N(s) = r_N(s)$$

The $V_n(\cdot)$ is referred to as the *value function* in Markov decision process. Hence, the Bellman dynamic programming equation using the value function notation is given as:

$$V_n(s) = \max_{a \in A}\left[r_{N-n}(s, a) + \sum_{s'} P_{s,s'}(a)\, V_{n-1}(s') \right] \qquad \text{...(21)}$$

with $V_0(s) = r_N(s)$.

20.3.2 Infinite Horizon MDP

For the infinite horizon MDP, the expected cumulative reward

$$J_\mu(x) = \mathbb{E}_\mu\left[\sum_{k=0}^{\infty} \gamma^k r(s_k, \mu_k(s_k)) \mid s_0 = x \right] \qquad \text{...(22)}$$

As in the finite horizon MDP, the infinite formulation the policy is given by

$$\mu = (\mu_0, \mu_1, \ldots), \qquad \text{...(23)}$$

where, μ_k is the policy at time k is the mapping from the state to action. The optimal infinite horizon policy $\mu^* = (\mu^*_0, \mu^*_1, \ldots)$ is the infinite horizon policy that maximizes $J_\mu(x)$ in (22) for all possible starting states, i.e.,

$$\mu^* = \text{argmax}_\mu \, J_\mu(x). \quad ...(24)$$

From (23), it looks like solving an infinite horizon MDP requires finding infinite policies. However, the following property states that solving an infinite horizon MDP requires finding only a single policy.

Property 2 For an infinite horizon discounted MDP, there exists a *stationary* optimal policy, i.e., $\mu^* = (\mu^*, \mu^*, \cdots)$.

The intuition of Property 2 is similar to the stationarity of the value function in the infinite horizon discounted Markov reward process, in that since there is an infinite amount of time left it doesn't matter when we start the decision making.

Using finite horizon Bellman equation, we have

$$J_k(s) = \max_a \left[\gamma^k r(s,a) + \sum_{s'} P_{s,s'}(a)\, J_{k+1}(s) \right] \quad ...(25)$$

with $J_{N=\infty}(s) = \lim_{k \to \infty} \gamma^k r(s, a) = 0$.

Similar to the finite horizon, we change to the value function notation using $V_n(s) = \gamma^{n-N} J_{N-n}(s)$:

$$V_n(s) = \max_a \left[r(s,a) + \gamma \sum_{s'} P_{s,s'}(a)\, V_{n-1}(s) \right] \quad ...(26)$$

with $V_0(s) = 0$.

With this, we are now ready to state the Bellman equation for infinite horizon MDP.

Bellman's dynamic programming for infinite horizon discounted Markov decision process

Theorem 4 Optimal policy μ^* and the optimal value function V^* is the unique solution of the following set of equations:

$$V^*(s) = \max_a \left[r(s,a) + \gamma \sum_{s'} P_{s,s'}\, V^*(s') \right] \quad ...(27)$$

$$\mu^*(s) = \text{argmax}_a \left[r(s,a) + \gamma \sum_{s'} P_{s,s'}\, V^*(s') \right] \quad ...(28)$$

Similar to the finite horizon formulation, rewriting in Q-notation:

$$Q(s, a) = r(s, a) + \gamma \sum_{s'} P_{s,s'}\; V^*(s') \quad ...(29)$$

$$\mu^*(s) = \text{argmax}_a \, Q(s, a) \quad ...(30)$$

$$V^*(s) = \max_a Q(s, a) \quad ...(31)$$

Example 20.4 This example considers a simplified model of the classical decision-making problem of selling a house. There are B types of buyers. For simplicity, buyer type i bids i for the house. In addition, a buyer is of type i with probability p_i, such that $\sum_{i=1}^{B} p_i = 1$. At each time instant, a buyer arrives independently and identically according to the probability distribution. The seller can take one of these two actions: accept the bid or reject the bid. If the seller accepts the bid then the house is sold at the buyer's bid price and no further bids are possible. If the seller rejects the bids, then the bidding continues. In addition, the seller pays a maintenance cost of C (at each time instant) as longs as he keeps the house.

(a) Formulate the problem as an MDP. Determine the state space, action space, transition probability, and reward.

(b) Write the infinite horizon Bellman dynamic programming equation for the problem.

Before we start analyzing the problem, let us intuitively understand the tradeoffs in this decision-making problem. Obviously, the seller would want to accept the maximum bid possible for the house. But, the seller doesn't know when the maximum bid would be realized, due the randomness in how the buyers arrive. Holding onto the house, in the hopes for accepting the maximum bid, incurs maintenance cost for the seller. However, selling the house too soon (by accepting one of the lower bids) so as to avoid the maintenance cost is also not optimal. Let us now formulate this problem as an infinite horizon MDP.

The state, at any point of time, is the type of buyer (or equivalently, the bid amount). The state space is all possible types of buyer. The decision maker has two actions (action space) either to *Accept* or to *Reject*. The transition probability can be represented using the state transition diagram in Fig. 20.4.

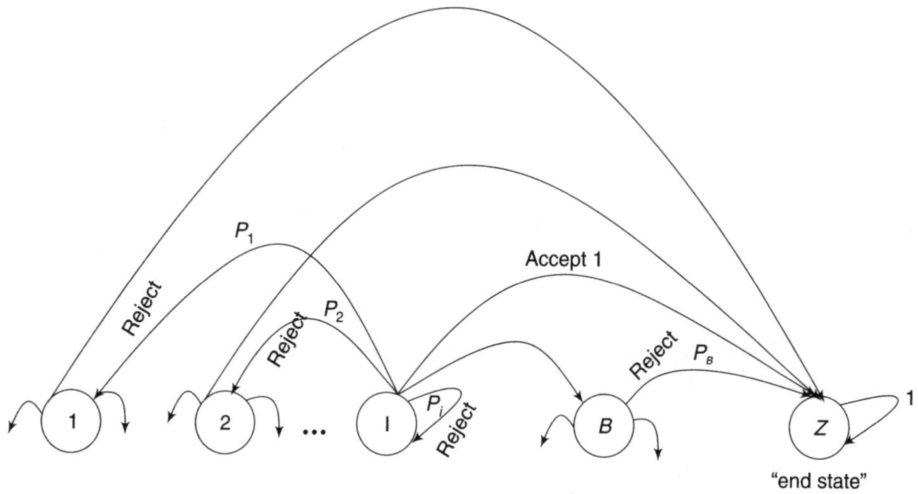

Fig. 20.4 State diagram of the transition probability of the house selling problem in Example 20.4

States 1 to B correspond to the types of buyers. We also introduce an end state Z, which corresponds to the state when the house is sold. Any time a bid is accepted ("Accept" action), the state transitions to Z. Once the state transitions to Z, it remains in Z regardless of the action taken. If the bid is rejected ("Reject" action), then the state transitions to one of the other states corresponding to a new bid being received. Because of the independent and identical nature of how the bids are received, the transition probability doesn't depend on the current state. Hence,

$$P_{i,j}\text{ (Reject)} = \begin{cases} p_j & i \neq Z \\ 0 & i = Z \end{cases}$$

$$P_{i,j}\text{ (Accept)} = \begin{cases} 1 & j = Z \\ 0 & i \neq Z \end{cases}$$

The reward function is straightforward and can be obtained as follows:

$$r\,(i, \text{Accept}) = \begin{cases} 0 & i = Z \\ i & i \neq Z \end{cases}$$

$$r\,(i, \text{Reject}) = \begin{cases} -C & i \neq Z \\ 0 & i = Z \end{cases}$$

Using the transition probability and the reward function above, the Bellman dynamic programming equation can be obtained as follows:

$$V^*(i) = \max\left[i, -C + \gamma \sum_{j=1}^{B} p_j V^*(j)\right] \qquad ...(32)$$

$$\mu^*(i) = \text{argmax}\left[i, -C + \gamma \sum_{j=1}^{B} p_j V^*(j)\right] \qquad ...(33)$$

The next question that we should ask is how to solve the Bellman dynamic programming equations to obtain the optimal policy? For example, how to solve Eqs. (32) to (33) to decide which bids are to be accepted or rejected?

20.4 NUMERICAL METHODS FOR BELLMAN DYNAMIC PROGRAMMING EQUATION

This section deals with numerical methods to solve the dynamic programming equation. For simplicity, we only consider the case of the infinite horizon Bellman dynamic programming equations. The ideas presented in this section, apply equally well to the finite horizon Bellman dynamic programming equations.

The optimal value function $V^*(\cdot)$ of the infinite horizon Bellman dynamic equation is the fixed-point solution of Eq. (21).

20.4.1 Value Iteration (Successive Approximation)

The idea behind value iteration is that we can run the finite horizon Bellman equation for "very large" value of N. The steps for value iteration are shown in Algorithm 1.

$V(s) = 0 \quad \forall s$

For $k = 1, \ldots$ *do*

$$Q_k(s, a) = r(s, a) + \gamma \sum_{s'} P_{s,s'}(a) V_{k-1}(s') \qquad \ldots(34)$$

$$V_k(s) = \max_a Q_k(s, a)$$

$$\mu_k(s) = \text{argmax}_a Q_k(s, a)$$

Algorithm 1: Value iteration algorithm

The critical question is: does the policy obtained as a result of value iteration in Algorithm 1 converge to the infinite horizon policy? The following property guarantees that it does in fact converge.

Property 3: Value iteration algorithm (Algorithm 1) converges geometrically fast to the optimal value function of the infinite horizon Bellman dynamic programming equation.

Here, we skip the proof of Property 3. The proof utilizes the fact that the Bellman operation (the left hand side of Eq. (34)) is a contraction mapping and hence, Algorithm 1 converges to the fixed point of Eq. (11).

Example 20.5 Consider the MDP shown in Fig. 20.5. Assume a discount factor (γ) of 0.9. The reward depends only on the state and is denoted by r. In state S_1, two actions a_1 and a_2 are possible. The numbers next to arrows denote the probability of outcome. Find $V_2(S_1)$.

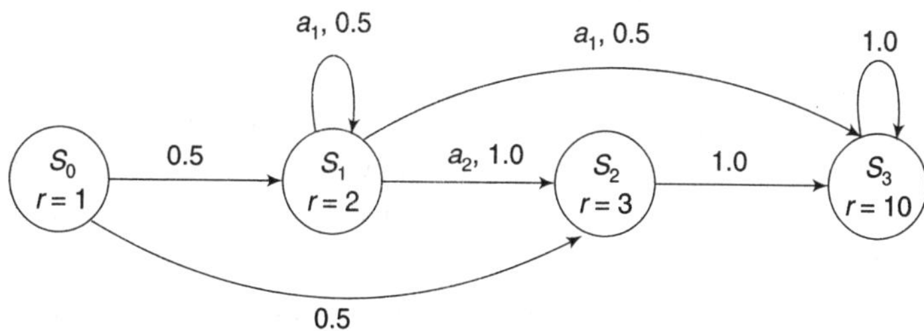

Fig. 20.5 State transition diagram for the MDP in Example 20.5

Consider doing value iteration to find the optimal policy. Let initial value for value iteration be $V_0(S_0) = V_0(S_1) = V_0(S_2) = V_0(S_3) = 0$, where $V_k(s)$ is the value function for iteration k, and state s. Find $V_1(S_1)$, and $V_2(S_2)$.

It is easy to see that $V_1(S_0) = 1$, $V_1(S_1) = 2$, $V_1(S_2) = 3$, and $V_1(S_3) = 10$. To find, $V_2(S_1)$, we apply (34).

$$V_2(S_1) = \text{Max }\{2 + 0.9[0.5 \times 2 + 0.5 \times 10], 2 + 0.9\ [1 \times 3]\} = \text{Max }\{7.4, 4.7\} = 7.4$$

20.4.2 Policy Iteration

In value iteration, we start with some arbitrary value function. As the iterations progress, we refine the value function to be closer to the optimal value function. The policy at each iteration is obtained as a byproduct of value function iterations. In contrast, in policy iteration, we start with some arbitrary policy, and in each iteration, we refine the policy to be closer to the optimal policy. The algorithm for policy iteration is given in Algorithm 2. Policy iteration proceeds in two steps. In Step 1, we find a value function corresponding to a given policy, and in Step 2, we improve the policy.

Start with arbitrary policy μ_0

for $k = 0; \ldots$ do Step 1: Policy evaluation step

$$V_{\mu_k}(s) = r(s, \mu_k(s)) + \sum_{s'} P_{s,s'} V_{\mu_k}(s')$$

Step 2: Policy improvement step

$$\mu_{k+1}(s) = \text{argmax}_a \left[r(s, a) + \gamma \sum_{s'} P_{s,s'} V_{\mu_k}(s') \right]$$

Algorithm 2: Policy iteration algorithm

Step 1 in Algorithm 2 involves solving a set of linear equations of the form $AV_{\mu_k} = b$ and any linear solver (such as linsolve from Matlab) can be used for this purpose.

As in the case of value iteration, policy iteration algorithm is also guaranteed to converge and is given in the following property.

Property 4 Policy iteration algorithm converges to the optimal policy.

20.4.3 Linear Programming

A less used method for solving MDP is the linear programming method, since it tends to be slower compared to specialized versions of policy iteration or value iteration. However, recently, the linear programming method has been used as a basis for approximate solution for large-scale MDPs.

Consider the infinite horizon Bellman dynamic programming equation in (27), reproduced here for convenience:

$$V^*(s) = \max_a \left[r(s, a) + \gamma \sum_{s'} P_{s,s'} V^*(s') \right] \quad \text{...(27)}$$

The idea behind the linear programming formulation is that the above equation can be equivalently represented as follows:

$$V^*(s) \geq r(s, a) + \gamma \sum_{s'} P_{s,s'}(a) V^*(s') \quad \forall a \quad \text{...(35)}$$

Now, consider the following linear programming problem:

$$\text{minimize}_V \sum_s V(s) \qquad \text{...(36)}$$

Such that: $$V(s) \geq r(s,a) + \gamma \sum_{s'} P_{s,s'}(a)V(s')$$

The following property ensures that the solution of (36) is the solution of Bellman dynamic programming equation in (27).

Property 5 The optimal value of the linear program in (36) is V^*.

In (36), we can replace the objective $\sum_s V(s)$ with any positive linear function of $V(s)$, i.e., $\sum_s d(s)V(s)$ with $d(s) > 0$, and the Property 5 still holds.

Conclusion

In this chapter, we described a mathematical framework for modeling sequential decision making problems, namely, the Markov Decision Process (MDP). The optimal policy is obtained as a solution of the Bellman dynamic programming equation. We discussed three numerical methods for the solution of the Bellman equation – value iteration, policy iteration, and linear programming. The examples discussed in the chapter should enable the reader to model any real life sequential decision making problem using MDP and obtain its optimal solution.

Questions

1. Model of disease spread: Suppose there are N individuals in a population, in which some people have a disease and others are healthy. At any time, two individuals are selected at random and assumed to interact with each other. During the interaction, if one of the persons has the disease and other person is healthy, the disease transmission takes place with probability $\alpha = 0.1$. Let X_n denote the number of diseased persons. Does X_n follow a Markov chain? If so, construct the transition probability matrix for $N = 5$.
2. Balls in an urn: An urn contains n white and m black balls. At any time, a ball is selected at random, without replacement. Let $X_k = (w_k, b_k)$ denote the number of white balls and black balls remaining in the urn at time k. Does X_n follow a Markov chain? If so, draw the probability transition diagram when $m = n = 5$.
3. An urn contains n white and m black balls. Balls are selected at random, without replacement. The decision maker wins one dollar when a white ball is selected, and loses one dollar when a black ball is selected. At any point in time, the decision maker is allowed to quit playing.
   (a) Formulate the problem as a MDP. Determine the state space, action space, transition probability, and reward.
   (b) Write the Bellman dynamic programming equation for the problem?
4. Consider a decision maker who can bet any (non-negative) amount, up to his present fortune. The decision maker wins the bet with probability p, and loses the bet with

probability $1 - p$. The reward of the decision maker is given by $\log(x)$, where x is the present fortune of the decision maker. The decision maker is allowed n bets.

(a) Formulate the above problem as a MDP. Determine the state space, action space, transition probability, and reward.

(b) Write the finite horizon Bellman dynamic programming equation for solving the MDP.

5. Consider a simplified model for machine replacement. Suppose that at time, a machine is inspected and its condition and state is noted. States are $\{0, 1, 2, ...\}$ with state 0 being "perfectly new". With each state i, an operating cost of $C(i)$ is incurred at each epoch. After inspecting the state, at each time a decision is made: $a = 0$ (not replace the machine) or $a = 1$ (replace the machine). If the decision is to replace, a cost $R > 0$ is immediately incurred. This then moves the state of the machine to 0 for the next epoch. If the decision is not to replace then the condition of the machine evolves randomly according to the probabilities, $P_{i,j}$.

   Pose the problem as an MDP with infinite horizon and discounted objective. Write the state space, action space, transition probabilities, and reward function. Write the Bellman dynamic programming equation for the MDP.

6. Consider an MDP with four states $\{A, B, C, D\}$ as shown in Fig. 20.6. In each state, we can either perform action a or b. The figure below shows the state transition function and reward (as a function of state and action) obtained by each action. Consider doing value iteration to find the optimal policy. Let initial value for value iteration be $V_0(A) = V_0(B) = V_0(C) = V_0(D) = 0$, where $V_k(s)$ is the value function for iteration k and state s. Find $= V_1(s)$; $s = A, B, C, D$, and $V_2(s)$; $s = A, B, C, D$.

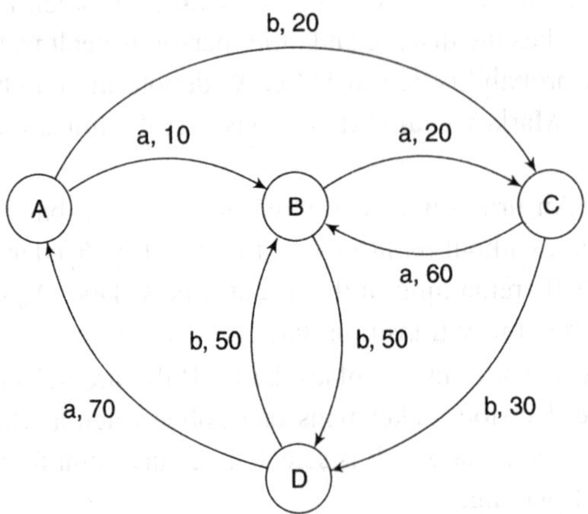

Fig. 20.6 MDP for Qn. 6. The reward as a function of state and action is denoted alongside the arrows.

7. [Programming exercise]: Consider a simplified example of the grid world as shown in Fig. 20.7. A robot placed at any location in this grid world has the goal to reach the reward state (indicated in green, with reward 1), while avoiding traversing through a bad state (indicated in red, with reward –100). The reward in other locations of the grid world is 0. The movement of the robot is inexact (as shown in Fig. 20.7), i.e., the robot moves in the desired direction with probability 0.8 and in one of the other perpendicular locations with probability 0.1. Whenever, the robot moves in the direction that bumps it against a wall, leaves the robot at the same location. Run value iteration, policy iteration and compare the number of iterations required to converge to the optimal solution (optimal solution can be solved using linear programming formulation).

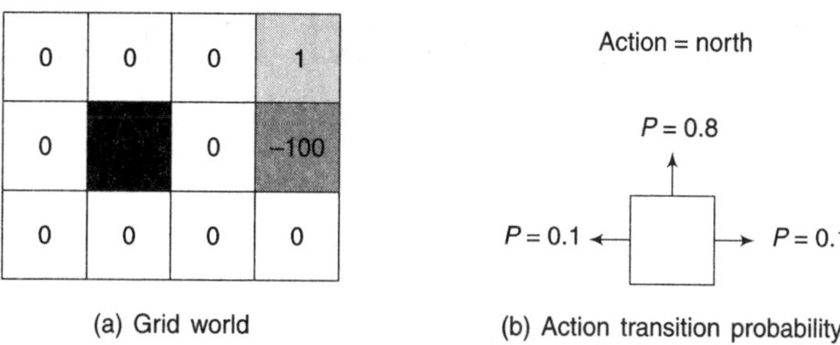

(a) Grid world

(b) Action transition probability

Fig. 20.7 Figure for Qn 7.

8. Consider a Markov decision process where the reward $r(s, a, s')$ depends not only on the current state and action, but the next state as well. Show that the Bellman dynamic programming equations for this MDP can be obtained by replacing $r(s,a)$ by $\bar{r}(s, a) = \sum_{s'} P_{s,s'}(a) r(s, a, s')$.

CHAPTER

21

Reinforcement Learning: Monte Carlo and Temporal Difference Methods

In this chapter

- Discuss key problems associated with reinforcement learning.
- Learn about Q-learning and Deep Q-learning.
- Monte Carlo methods for reinforcement learning.
- TD(0) and its generalization TD(λ).
- Recent advances in deep reinforcement learning.

21.0 INTRODUCTION

In the last chapter, we talked about Markov Decision Processes. The implicit assumptions, in the last chapter, are the state space is known, the transition probability function and the reward function is available to the decision maker before the start of the decision making. These assumptions don't hold in modern practical decision-making systems such as autonomous vehicles, advanced robotics and wireless communication. For example, in an autonomous vehicle it is too complicated to completely characterize the state space and the associated transition probability function. Hence, the idea in reinforcement learning is to apply *machine learning*, i.e., interact with the environment to obtain data which can then be used for learning optimal policies. Based on how machine learning is applied to these tasks, we can divide reinforcement learning into two:

1. **Indirect learning:** In indirect learning or model based learning, a model for the MDP is learnt from samples. Once a model is learnt, we can apply the numerical methods

that we discussed in the previous chapter to obtain the optimal policy. Indirect learning tends to work well when the state space is small.

2. **Direct learning:** In indirect learning, we first learn the model of the environment and then obtain the policy. However, in most situations, it is easier to just learn the optimal policy and bypass the process of learning the MDP model. Direct learning is the only feasible method for large state space decision-making problems.

In this book, we will deal with only direct reinforcement learning methodologies.

21.1 REINFORCEMENT LEARNING: KEY PROBLEM, AND REVIEW OF SOME FUNDAMENTAL IDEAS

21.1.1 Reinforcement Learning: Key Problem

Let us first understand the key problem that we are trying to solve in direct reinforcement learning. For this consider the value iteration algorithm for infinite horizon Bellman dynamic programming equation:

$$Q_k(s, a) = r(s, a) + \gamma \sum_{s'} P_{s,s'}(a) V_{k-1}(s'). \qquad ...(1)$$

Let us rewrite this equation in a slightly different way:

$$Q_k(s, a) = r(s, a) + \gamma \mathbb{E}[V_{k-1}|_{s,a}] \qquad ...(2)$$

In (2), we have rewritten the sum on the right-hand side in (1) as an expectation of the value function, where the expectation is with respect to conditional distribution of the next state given current state is s and action taken is a.

Since, we don't know the transition probability function, we cannot evaluate the expectation in (2). In reinforcement learning, we are interested in approximating this expectation (and other equivalent formulations) using samples as and when the decision maker interacts with the environment.

21.1.2 Review of Some Fundamental Ideas

In this section, let us review some fundamental ideas in probability and in later sections, we will use these ideas to formulate reinforcement learning algorithms.

21.1.2.1 Expectations and Averages

Suppose we want to find the average of a set of numbers $X_1, X_2, ..., X_n$. Then the average can be straightforwardly be obtained as follows:

$$\hat{X} = \frac{X_1 + X_2 + \cdots + X_n}{n} \qquad ...(3)$$

The averaging equation in (3) assumes that we can store the n numbers in memory to obtain the average. However, this may not be possible when n is quite large or the computations are limited. Is there any way to compute averages recursively (or online), i.e., as and when data arrives? Let $\hat{X}_k$ denote the average when k values are available, then $\hat{X}_{k+1}$ can be written recursively as follows:

$$\hat{X}_{k+1} = \frac{X_1 + X_2 + \cdots + X_{k+1}}{k+1} \quad \text{...(4)}$$

$$= \frac{X_1 + X_2 + \cdots + X_k}{k+1} + \frac{1}{k+1} X_{k+1}$$

$$= \frac{X_1 + X_2 + \cdots + X_k}{k} \frac{1}{k+1} + \frac{1}{k+1} X_{k+1}$$

$$= \hat{X}_k \left(1 - \frac{1}{k+1}\right) + \frac{1}{k+1} X_{k+1}$$

$$= \hat{X}_k + \frac{1}{k+1} (X_{k+1}\ \hat{X}_k)$$

$$= \hat{X}_k + \varepsilon_{k+1} (X_{k+1} - \hat{X}_k),$$

where $\varepsilon_k = \frac{1}{k}$, is the step-size.

Equation (4) is of the form:

Updated estimate = Old estimate + step size (New data – Old estimate)	(5)

In all RL algorithms, some version of (5) would be used to update the estimates.

What is the connection of averages with the problem of obtaining expectations mentioned in Section 21.1.2.1. For this, we can use the famous *law of large numbers*, which roughly translates that for random variables, empirical average converges to the expectation of the random variable.

Theorem 1 Strong law of large numbers (SLLN)

Suppose $[X_k]$ is a sequence of independent and identically distributed (i.i.d.) sequence of random variables. Then $\lim_k \widehat{X_k} = \mu$ almost surely iff $\mathbb{E}[|X_1|] < \infty$ and $\mathbb{E}[X_1] = \mu$.

While SLLN in Theorem 1 only applies to i.i.d. case, extensions of SLLN exists for Markov chains (which is what is used in reinforcement learning, however, these are beyond the scope of the current textbook).

21.1.3 Data and Episodes

In reinforcement learning, an agent (or a decision maker) interacts with the environment. A single interaction, referred to as an *episode*, typically consists of sequence of the current state (or observations), the actions that the agent takes (based on a policy), and the reward obtained by the agent. A collection of such episode, referred to as *experience*, is available to the agent for learning, as shown in Fig. 21.1.

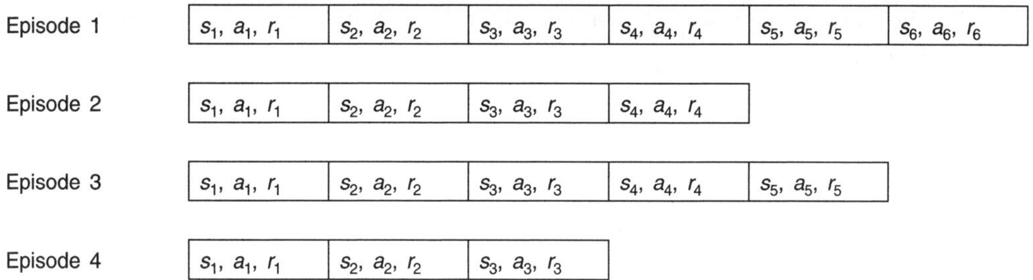

Fig. 21.1 Sample episodes available to the agent

21.1.4 A Note on Notation

In reinforcement learning, we typically have algorithms that learn as a function of episodes. Each episode is a time sequence of state, action and reward obtained as the agent interacts with the environment. For example, in Fig. 21.1, s_6 is the state that the agent observed at time $t = 6$ in Episode 1. Hence, the following notation will be adopted in this chapter and next: s_t refers to the state at time t. In contrast, s, and s' correspond to two states from the agent's state space. Whenever there is ambiguity, $\mathscr{s}$ (script s) would be used to denote a state from the agent's state space. For example, in Example 21.1, the agent's state space consists of $\mathscr{s}_0$, and $\mathscr{s}_1$. Similar notation applies for both the action (a vs $\boldsymbol{a}$) and the reward (r vs $\mathscr{r}$).

21.2 Q-LEARNING

One of the first algorithms to gain popularity is the Q-learning algorithm. Q-learning can be viewed as a reinforcement learning approach to the value iteration algorithm for computing the optimal policy. Consider again the value iteration equations in (1), and rewriting the value function in terms of Q-function and the expectation operator, we have

$$\begin{aligned} Q_k(s, a) &= r(s, a) + \gamma \sum_{s'} P_{s,s'}(a) V_{k-1}(s') \\ &= r(s, a) + \gamma \sum_{s'} P_{s,s'}(a) \max_a Q_{k-1}(s', a) \\ &= \sum_{s'} P_{s,s'}(a)[r(s, a) + \gamma \max_a Q_{k-1}(s', a) \\ &= \mathbb{E}[r(s, a) + \gamma \max_a Q_{k-1}(\cdot, a)|_{s,a}] \end{aligned} \quad ...(6)$$

As before, since we can't compute the expectation in (6), we can compute using iterative averaging, of the form in (5), as follows:

$$\hat{Q}(s_t, a_t) \leftarrow \hat{Q}(s_t, a_t) + \varepsilon_t\left(r_t + \max_a \hat{Q}(s_{t+1}, a) - \hat{Q}(s_t, a_t)\right) \quad ...(7)$$

Using the learnt Q-values, the Q-learning algorithm can be rewritten as follows:

1. Initialize $\hat{Q}(s, a) = 0 \; \forall s, a$.
2. for all episodes do.
3. for $t = 1 \cdots$ do.
4. Obtain (s_t)
5. Obtain greedy policy: $\mu(s) = \max_a \hat{Q}(s, a)$.
6. Take action $a_t : a_t = \mu(s_t)$.
7. Obtain current reward r_t and next state s_{t+1}.
8. $\delta_t = r_t + \gamma \max_a \hat{Q}(s_{t+1}, a) - \hat{Q}(s_t, a_t)$
9. Update Q-values: $\hat{Q}(s_t, a_t) \leftarrow \hat{Q}(s_t, a_t) + \varepsilon_t \delta_t$

Algorithm 1: Q-learning algorithm

Example 21.1 Consider the MDP shown in Fig. 21.2. Assume a discount factor of γ. In state s_1, two actions a_1 and a_2 are possible. The reward depend on both state and action for state s_1 and is given by $r(s_1, a_1) = -1$, and $r(s_1, a_2) = +1$. In state s_2, the reward depends only on state and is given by $r(s_2) = +100$. Suppose we start at $t = 1$ for the episode shown in Fig. 21.3, i.e., we start at state s_1. Compute the optimal policy and the estimated Q-values for $t = 1$ and $t = 2$, assuming the Q-value are initialized to 0. What will happen to the optimal policy at $t = \infty$? Assume a step-size of 1 for this problem.

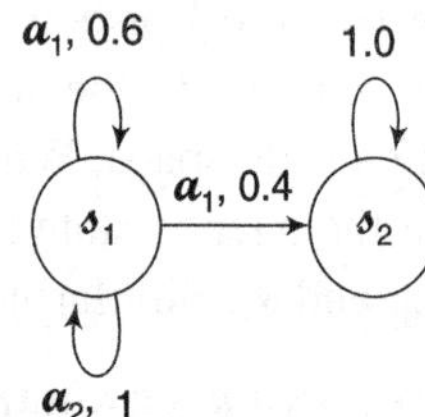

Fig. 21.2 State transition diagram for the MDP in Example 21.1

Before, we start solving the problem, let us intuitively understand how the optimal policy should behave. State s_2 has a reward of 100 compared to state s_1.

$s_1, a_1, -1$	$s_1, a_2, +1$	$s_1, a_2, +1$

Fig. 21.3 Episodes in Example 21.1

Hence, it is straightforward to see that starting from state s_1, an optimal policy should act a_2 incurring a short-term loss of 1 to gain the reward of +100.

However, here we assume that the decision maker does not know the transition probability function. So let, us start at $t = 0$ by initializing the Q-values to 0, i.e., $\hat{Q}(s_1, a_1) = \hat{Q}(s_1, a_2) = 0$. At $t = 1$, we start with state s_1. The greedy policy (using Step 5 in Algorithm 1) is indifferent between a_1 and a_2. Let us arbitrarily choose a_1, and we obtain a reward of -1 as shown in Fig. 21.3. The updated Q-values at the end of $t = 1$ is $\hat{Q}(s_1, a_1) = -1$, $\hat{Q}(s_1, a_2) = 0$. Suppose, on acting a_1 at $t = 1$, we end up in state s_1 again as shown in Fig. 21.3. Now, the greedy algorithm, would choose action a_2, since it's Q-value is higher. On acting a_2, we get an instantaneous reward of +1 as shown in Fig. 21.3. Hence, the Q-values at the end of $t = 2$

is $\hat{Q}(s_1, \boldsymbol{a}_1) = -1$, $\hat{Q}(s_1, \boldsymbol{a}_2) = 1$. Taking action $\boldsymbol{a}_2$, results in the next state being state s_1 with probability 1. Again, action $\boldsymbol{a}_2$ is picked because of it's higher Q-value compared to $\boldsymbol{a}_1$. At $t = \infty$, the Q-values converge to $\hat{Q}(s_1, \boldsymbol{a}_1) = -1$, $\hat{Q}(s_1, \boldsymbol{a}_2) = 1 + \gamma + \gamma^2 + \ldots = \frac{1}{1-\gamma}$.

Notice that, even though the optimal policy is to pick $\boldsymbol{a}_1$ in state s_1, the Q-learning algorithm always picks action $\boldsymbol{a}_2$. This doesn't mean that Q-learning is wrong. The reason this happens is that the initial estimates of Q-function are highly noisy and taking decisions based on these noisy estimates biases our decision strategy. In the next section, we will see one strategy to fix the problem.

21.2.1 Q-learning Algorithm with Exploration

The problem with Q-learning in Example 21.1 is that once we start to greedily select actions based on the estimated Q-function, then we reinforce past errors and end up selecting only a (suboptimal) set of actions. Therefore, *exploration* is required. There are a lot of exploration strategies available in the literature. One of the simplest, but most effective strategy, is the ε–greedy strategy. The idea is that we behave greedily most of the time, but once in a while, i.e., with probability ε, we select randomly from the available actions with equal probability. The Q-learning algorithm with ε-greedy strategy is provided in Algorithm 2.

1. Initialize $\hat{Q}(s, a) = 0 \ \forall s, a$.
2. for all episodes do.
3. for $t = 1 \cdots$ do.
4. Obtain s_t
5. Obtain policy:

$$\mu(s) = \begin{cases} \max_a \hat{Q}(s, a) & \text{with probability } 1-\varepsilon \\ \text{uniform randomly} & a \in A \text{ with probability } \varepsilon \end{cases}$$

6. Take action $a_t : a_t = \mu(s_t)$.
7. Obtain current reward r_t and next state s_{t+1}.
8. $\delta_t = r_t + \gamma \max_a \hat{Q}(s_{t+1}, a) - \hat{Q}(s_t, a_t)$
9. Update Q-values: $\hat{Q}(s_t, a_t) \leftarrow \hat{Q}(s_t, a_t) + \varepsilon_t \delta_t$

Algorithm 2: Q-learning with ε-greedy strategy

The only difference between Algorithm 1 and Algorithm 2 is in Step 5 wherein the greedy selection is replaced by an ε-greedy strategy.

21.3 MONTE CARLO METHODS

The previous section on Q-learning can we viewed as a reinforcement learning approach to value iteration. In this section and next, we focus on reinforcement learning approach to policy iteration. The first approach, based on Monte Carlo method will be presented in this section, while Temporal difference (TD) methods will be presented in Section 21.4.

Recall that policy iteration algorithm proceeds in two steps: policy evaluation and policy improvement. While policy improvement, is relatively straightforward, using the greedy approach, policy evaluation is difficult as it involves the expectation of the value function, which cannot be computed without the complete knowledge of the transition probability function.

The idea behind Monte Carlo methods arises from the definition of the value function as the expected cumulative reward starting from any state, reproduced in Eq. (8) for convenience.

$$V_\mu(s) = \mathbb{E}_\mu [G_t | s_t = s], \qquad ...(8)$$

where G_t is the cumulative reward (in previous chapter, the notation J_t was used instead of G_t), as defined in the previous chapter. Hence, given a policy μ, and episodes generated from the policy μ, an estimate of the value function at any state s can be obtained by averaging the discounted cumulative reward obtained once state s is visited. Based on how the rewards are computed two algorithm can be formulated: Algorithm 3 is the *first visit* Monte Carlo algorithm, where cumulative rewards are computed starting only from the first time a state is visited, Algorithm 4 is the very visit Monte Carlo, where the average involves the cumulative reward every time after a state is visited.

1. Initialize empty list: $V(s)\ \forall s$, CumReturn(s) $\forall s$.
2. for each episode: $s_0, a_0, r_0, s_1, a_1, r_1, ..., s_T, a_T, r_T$ do.
3. $\quad G \leftarrow 0$.
4. $\quad$ for each $t = T - 1, ..., 0$ (starting from end of episode) do.
5. $\qquad G \leftarrow \gamma G + r_{t+1}$.
6. $\qquad$ If s_t doesn't appear in $s_0, s_1, ..., s_{t-1}$ do.
7. $\qquad\quad$ Append G to CumReturn (s_t).
8. $V(s)$ = Average(CumReturn(s)).

Algorithm 3: First visit Monte Carlo

1. Initialize empty list: $V(s)\ \forall s$, CumReturn(s) $\forall s$.
2. for each episode: $s_0, a_0, r_0, s_1, a_1, r_1, ..., s_T, a_T, r_T$ do
3. $\quad G \leftarrow 0$
4. $\quad$ for each $t = T - 1, ..., 0$ (starting from end of episode) do
5. $\qquad G \leftarrow \gamma G + r_{t+1}$
6. $\qquad$ Append G to CumReturn (s_t)
7. $V(s)$ = Average(CumReturn(s))

Algorithm 4: Every visit Monte Carlo

The difference between the two algorithm is that the extra step of checking if a state is visited previously (Step 6 in Algorithm 3) is avoided in Algorithm 4.

However, notice from policy iteration that policy improvement step requires that we compute the Q-function estimates. It is straightforward to estimate the Q-function values instead of value function by keeping track of both the state and action pairs during an episode. Algorithm 5 gives the pseudocode for estimating the Q-function values in a first visit Monte Carlo scenario.

```
Initialize empty list: Q(s, a) ∀s, a CumReturn (s, a) ∀s, a.
for each episode: s_0, a_0, r_0, s_1, a_1, r_1, ..., s_T, a_T, r_T do
    G ← 0
    for each t = T − 1, ··· ; 0 (starting from end of episode) do
        G ← γG + r_{t+1}
        if s_t; a_t doesn't appear in s_0, a_0, s_1, a_1, ..., s_{t−1}, a_{t−1} then
            Append G to CumReturn (s_t; a_t)
Q(s, a) = Average (CumReturn (s, a))
```

Algorithm 5: First visit Monte Carlo-Q values

Finally, we need to answer the question of how to introduce exploration into Monte Carlo algorithms. One option, as discussed in Section 21.2.1, is to use ε-greedy strategy for policy improvement, instead of greedy strategy.

Example 21.2 Consider an MDP as shown in Fig. 21.5(a). For a given policy, one episode was run and the results are as shown in Fig. 21.5(b). For a discount factor of 1, calculate the first-visit and every-visit Monte Carlo estimate of the value function for the states s_1, and s_2.

Monte Carlo estimate for value function for state s_2 is $\hat{V}(s_2) = 10$, and is same regardless of first-visit or every-visit Monte Carlo.

For state (s_1):

First-visit Monte Carlo estimate: $\hat{V}(s_1) = 10 - 1 - 1 - 1 = 7$.

Every-visit Monte Carlo estimate: $\hat{V}(s_1) = \dfrac{9 + 8 + 7}{3} = 8$.

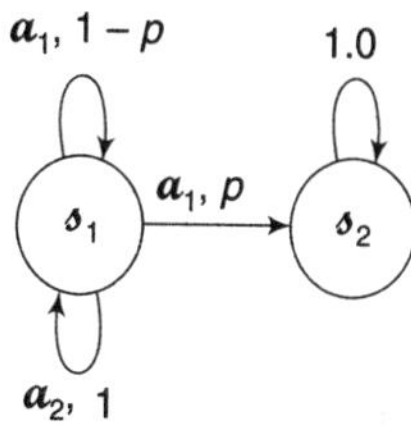

(a) State transition diagram

$s_1, a_1, -1$	$s_1, a_2, -1$	$s_1, a_1, -1$	$s_2, a_1, +10$

(b) Single episode

Fig. 21.4 Example 21.2

21.4 TEMPORAL DIFFERENCE

Temporal difference (TD) algorithm is one of the central and influential ideas in reinforcement learning literature. TD algorithm offer a framework to unify the ideas of Monte Carlo and dynamic programming methods. Even though, in this book, we introduced Q-learning, before this section, in Section 21.2, Q-learning can be viewed in the framework of TD learning. We start with the simple TD(0) learning algorithm in Section 21.4.1 and generalize to TD(λ) algorithm in Section 21.4.2.

21.4.1 TD(0) Algorithm

Consider again the definition of the value function in Eq. (8). The basic idea of TD(0) arises from noticing the following relation:

$$V_\mu(s) = \mathbb{E}_\mu[G_t | s_t = s]$$

$$= \mathbb{E}_\mu [r_t + \gamma V_\mu(s_{t+1}) | s_t = s] \quad ...(9)$$

As in Q-learning, the idea behind TD(0) is given an estimate of value function, the value function can be updated as follows:

$$\hat{V}_\mu(s_t) \leftarrow \hat{V}_\mu(s_t) + \varepsilon_t\left(r_t + \gamma\hat{V}_\mu(s_{t+1}) - \hat{V}_\mu(s_t)\right), \quad ...(10)$$

where, ε_t is the step size at time t. The quantity $r_t + \hat{V}_\mu(s_{t+1})$ is the one-step lookahead estimate for the value function.

The pseudocode for the TD(0) algorithm is shown in Algorithm 6.

1. Initialize: $\hat{V}(s)\ \forall s$.
2. for each episode do.
3. for each step t in the episode do.
4. For state s_t, take action $a_t = \mu(s_t)$, and observe s_{t+1}.
5. $\delta_t = r_t + \gamma \widehat{V_\mu}(s_{t+1}) - \widehat{V_\mu}(s_t)$
6. Update value function: $\widehat{V_\mu}(s_t) \leftarrow \widehat{V_\mu}(s_t) + \varepsilon_t\delta_t$

Algorithm 6: TD (0) algorithm

The quantity δ_t in Step 5 in Algorithm 6, the difference between the current estimate and the one-step lookahead is referred to as the temporal difference, hence the name temporal difference algorithm.

21.4.2 TD(λ) Algorithm

The TD(0) algorithm looks at one-step prediction to update the value function. A natural extension is to look at a n-step prediction algorithm to update the value function.

$$
\begin{aligned}
V_\mu &= \mathbb{E}_\mu[G_t | s_t = s] \\
&= \mathbb{E}_\mu[r_t + \gamma V_\mu(s_{t+1}) | s_t = s] \\
&= \mathbb{E}_\mu[r_t + \gamma r_{t+1} + \ldots + \gamma^n r_{t+n} + \gamma^{n+1} V_\mu(s_{t+n+1}) | s_t = s] \qquad \ldots(11)
\end{aligned}
$$

Notice from (11), that as $n \to \infty$, the n-step prediction converges to the Monte Carlo estimate. Using (11) and replacing the one-step prediction step in (17), we have the following update equation:

$$\hat{V}_\mu(s_t) \leftarrow \hat{V}_\mu(s_t) + \varepsilon_t(r_t + \gamma r_{t+1} + \ldots + \gamma^n r_{t+n} + \gamma^{n+1} \hat{V}_\mu(s_{t+n+1}) - \hat{V}_\mu(s_t)), \qquad \ldots(12)$$

The temporal difference δ_t^n (n in the superscript refers to n-step prediction) can be written as follows:

$$
\begin{aligned}
\delta_t^n &= \sum_{k=0}^{n} \gamma^k r_{t+k} + \gamma^{n+1} \hat{V}(s_{t+n+1}) - \hat{V}(s_t), \\
&= \sum_{k=0}^{n} \gamma^k r_{t+k} + \gamma^{n+1} \hat{V}(s_{t+n+1}) - \hat{V}(s_t) + \sum_{k=0}^{n-1} \gamma^{k+1} \hat{V}(s_{t+k+1}) - \sum_{k=0}^{n-1} \gamma^{k+1} \hat{V}(s_{t+k+1}), \\
&= \sum_{k=0}^{n} \gamma^k r_{t+k} + \sum_{k=0}^{n} \gamma^{k+1} \hat{V}(s_{t+k+1}) - \sum_{k=0}^{n} \hat{V}(s_{t+k}), \qquad \ldots(13) \\
&= \sum_{k=0}^{n} \gamma^k (r_{t+k} + \gamma \hat{V}(s_{t+k+1}) - \hat{V}(s_{t+k})), \\
&= \gamma^k \delta_{t+k'}
\end{aligned}
$$

where, in the second step, we added and subtracted the last two terms and, the third step is obtained by rearranging the terms. The algorithm for n-step TD is exactly the same as in Algorithm 6, except that δ_t^n replaces δ_t in Step 5.

What is the connection of TD(λ) with the n-step prediction? The formal connection is the use of *eligibility traces*; howevever the topic is outside the scope of the current book. The interested reader is referred to Chapter 13 in Reinforcement Learning: An Introduction by Sutton and Barto. In short, in TD(λ) algorithm, temporal difference error δ_t^n (is weighted with $(1 - \lambda)\lambda^n \; \forall n \geq 0$. Hence, the value function update is given by

$$\widehat{V_\mu}(s_t) \leftarrow V_\mu(s_t) + \varepsilon_t \sum_{k=0}^{\infty} (1-\lambda)\lambda^k \delta_t^k = \widehat{V_\mu}(s_t) + \varepsilon_t \sum_{k=0}^{\infty} \gamma^k \lambda^k \delta_{t+k'} \qquad \ldots(14)$$

where the right-hand side is obtained by substituting for δ_t^n from (13). Therefore, $\lambda \to 0$, gives TD(0), and $\lambda \to 1$, gives Monte Carlo.

21.4.2.1 Policy Improvement with TD Learning

TD learning allows for estimating a value function, given a policy. However, notice from the policy iteration algorithm, the policy improvement algorithm requires that we estimate the

Q-function instead of the value function. Estimating the Q-function, is straightforward (as in the case of Monte Carlo), by keeping track of both the state as well as the action pair. For example, the Step 5 in the TD(0) algorithm can be replaced as follows:

1. $\delta t = r_t + \gamma \hat{Q}(s_{t+1}, \mu(s_{t+1})) - \hat{Q}(s_t, a_t)$
2. Update value function: $\hat{Q}(s_t, a_t) \leftarrow \hat{Q}(s_t, a_t) + \varepsilon_t \, \delta_t$

Using the estimated Q-values, the policy iteration algorithm, using greedy policy improvement step is as follows:

1. Start with some intial policy μ^0
2. for $k = 0, 1, 2 \ldots$ do
3. Obtain $\hat{Q}^{\mu^k}$ using any TD algorithm
4. Policy improvement steps: $\mu^{k+1} = \text{argmax}_a \hat{Q}^{\mu^k}$

Algorithm 7: Policy iteration using TD learning

As in Q-learning, the greedy step in Step 4 of Algorithm 8 can be replaced by an ε-greedy strategy.

21.5 DOUBLE LEARNING

The reinforcement learning algorithms we discussed so far (Q-learning, TD learning, Monte Carlo), use maximization (or ε-greedy) approach to policy improvement. This causes significant bias to be introduced in the learning process. For example, consider the MDP as shown in Fig. 21.6. The episodes start from state A, and always terminate in one of the terminal

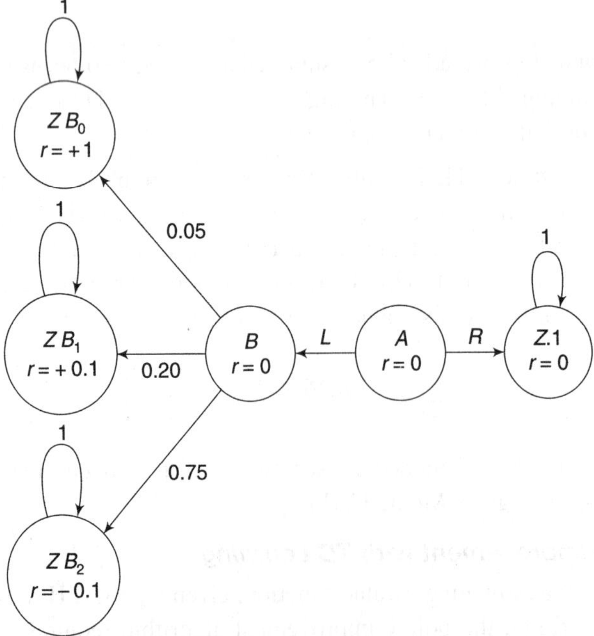

Fig. 21.5 MDP: Example of bias during Q-learning.

states ZA, ZB_0, ZB_1 or ZB_2. Taking action R at A, gives a mean reward of 0. However, taking action L gives a mean reward of -0.05. Hence, the optimal action is to take R at state A. Consider running a Q-learning algorithm, with ε-greedy exploration, for finding the optimal policy. Whenever, action L is taken, with a probability of 0.25, the Q-learning algorithm receives positive reward. This introduces a bias in the learning procedure and we end up selecting the suboptimal action L with a higher probability.

How do we mitigate the effects of bias during the Q-learning procedure? One methodology is to use the idea of *double learning*. In double learning, we learn two independent estimates of the Q-function, say Q_1 and Q_2. One of the estimates, say Q_1, will be used to select actions (either using greedy or ε-greedy strategy), and the other estimate, Q_2 will be update based on the action selected using Q_1. The Q-learning using the double learning strategy is given as follows:

$$a^* = \text{argmax}_a \widehat{Q_1} (s_{t+1}, a)$$

$$\widehat{Q_2} (s_t, a_t) \leftarrow \widehat{Q_2} (s_t, a_t) + \varepsilon_t\left(r_t + \widehat{Q_2} (s_{t+1}, a^*\right) - \widehat{Q_2} (s_t, a_t)) \quad \text{...(15)}$$

Of course, the roles of Q_1 and Q_2 in (15) can be interchanged. However, note that only one estimate is updated at each time step so as to keep the independence between the two estimates. One way to decide is to choose to update only one of them randomly with equal probability. Putting, all this together, the Q-learning algorithm with double learning is shown in Algorithm 8.

Initialize $\hat{Q}_1(s, a) = 0$, $\hat{Q}_2(s, a) = 0$ $\forall s, a$.
for all episodes do
  2 for $t = 0, 1, 2 \ldots$ do.
  Obtain s_t
  Obtain greedy policy: $\mu(s) = \text{argmax}_a \widehat{Q_1} (s, a) + \widehat{Q_2} (s, a)$
  Take action a_t: $a_t = \mu(s_t)$
  Obtain current reward r_t and next state s_{t+1}.
  Obtain $u \sim$ Bernoulli (0:5)
  if $u = 1$ then
    $a^* = \text{argmax}_a \widehat{Q_1} (s_{t+1}, a)$
    $\text{delta}_t = r_t + \widehat{Q_2} (s_{t+1}, a^*) - \widehat{Q_2} (s_t, a_t)$
    Update Q_2-value: $\widehat{Q_2} (s_t, a_t) \leftarrow \widehat{Q_2} (s_t, a_t) + \varepsilon_t \delta_t$
  else
    $a^* = \text{argmax}_a \widehat{Q_2} (s_{t+1}, a)$
    $\delta_t = r_t + \widehat{Q_1}\, s_{t+1}, a^*) - \widehat{Q_1} (s_t, a_t)$
    Update Q_1-value: $\widehat{Q_1} (s_t, a_t) \leftarrow \widehat{Q_1} (st, a_t) + \varepsilon_t \delta_t$

Algorithm 8: Q-learning algorithm with double learning

21.6 LARGE-SCALE LEARNING

The reinforcement learning algorithms we have discussed so far are of *tabular* nature, i.e., the state space has small number of states and it is easy to keep track using a table. However, in many of the practical reinforcement learning problems there are either too many states to keep track off or the state space is continuous, making tabular reinforcement learning algorithms infeasible. Another problem with large state space or continuous state space is that it is unlikely that the same state be visited again, and it is imperative that we learn from "neighbouring" or "similar" states. Learning from similar states is the idea of *generalization* that we encountered before in machine learning literature.

Generalization in RL: Similar to ML algorithms, generalization in reinforcement learning algorithms is achieved by using *function approximators*. In theory, any approximators that we studied in machine learning could be used for reinforcement learning. As an example, the value function, can be approximated using a linear function approximator or a single layer neural network as shown below.

- Linear approximation:

$$\hat{V}_w(s) = w^T\, x(s) = \sum_{i=1}^{d} w_i\, x_i(s),$$

  where w is the weight vector and $x(s)$ is the d-dimensional feature for state s.
- Artificial neural network (ANN): For example, Fig. 21.6 (left figure) shows a single hidden layer neural network and can be written as

$$\hat{V}_{w,b}(s) = \sigma(Wx(s) + b)$$

  where W is the weight matrix, $x(s)$ is the d-dimensional feature for state s, b is the bias vector and $\sigma(\cdot)$ is the non-linear activation function. We can also use a deep neural network for function approximation and can be written as

$$\hat{V}_{\{W_i\},\{b_i\}}(s) = \sigma(W_1\, \sigma(W_2 \ldots \sigma(W_k x(s) + b_k) \ldots + b_2) + b_1),$$

  where W_i, B_i is the weight matrix and bias vector for layer i.

Here on, we will denote by θ, the hyperparameters of the function approximator. For example, for the single layer neural network in Fig. 21.6, the hyperparameters would be the weight matrix and the bias vector, i.e., $\theta = \{W, b\}$, and the value function parameterized by the hyperparameters will be denoted by $\hat{V}_\theta(s)$.

The next component that we require for a function approximator is the loss function. Consider again, the TD learning equation in (9), reproduced here for convenience:

$$V_\mu(s) = \mathbb{E}_\mu[r_t + \gamma V_\mu(s_{t+1}) | s_t = s], \qquad \ldots(16)$$

which, gives the following update of TD algorithm in (17) (again, reproduced here for convenience)

$$\hat{V}_\mu(s_t) \leftarrow \hat{V}_\mu(s_t) + \varepsilon_t(r_t + \gamma \hat{V}_\mu(s_{t+1}) - \hat{V}_\mu(s_t)), \qquad \ldots(17)$$

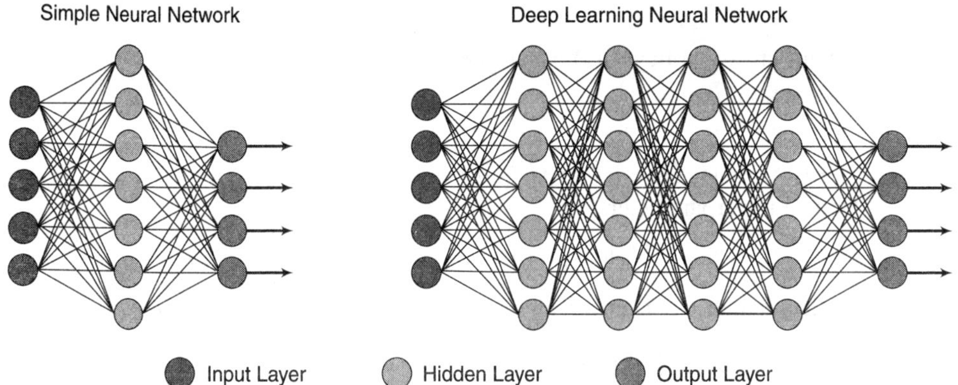

Fig. 21.6 Artificial neural network. The figure on the left shows a single layer neural network and the figure on the right shows a deep neural network.

Equations (16) to (17) can be interpreted as updating the current value function $\hat{V}_\mu(s_t)$ to the "target" $r_t + \gamma\hat{V}_\mu(s_{t+1})$. Hence, the loss function can be defined as

$$\text{loss}_\theta^{\text{TD}}(s, a, s') = (\widehat{V_\mu}(s) - \text{target}(s', a))^2 \qquad ...(18)$$

where, the target (s', a), $= r(s', a) + \gamma \cdot \widehat{V_\mu}(s')$ and θ denotes the hyperparameters of the function approximator. Similary, the loss function of the Q-learing algorithm can be defined as follows:

$$\text{loss}_\theta^Q\,(s, a, s') = \left(Q_\theta(s, a) - (r(s, a) + \gamma \max_a Q_\theta(s', a))\right)^2 \qquad ...(19)$$

The next question, is how do we optimize the hyperparameters to minimize the loss function. We follow ideas from machine learing and choose to optimize the hyperparameters using a gradient based algorithm as follows:

$$\theta \leftarrow \theta - \varepsilon\nabla_\theta \,\text{loss}_\theta\,(s, a, s') \qquad ...(20)$$

where, ε is the step-size parameter of the gradient algorithm. However, as in machine learning, in many applications, we will not be able to compute the exact value of the gradient of loss function. We can, however, use stochastic gradient descent by replacing the gradient by an instantaneous estimate computed using s_t, a_t, s_{t+1}. In addition, we need not limit ourselves to a simple gradient descent algorithm (or stochastic gradient descent) and we can use any of the mordern stochastic gradient algorithm, for example, with momentum strategies such as ADAM.

Putting all this together, the pseudocode for the Q-learning algorithm with function approximator is given in Algorithm 9.

1. Initialize the hyperparameter to θ to arbitrarily value.
2. for all episodes do
3. for $t = 0, 1, 2 \ldots$ do.

4. Obtain s_t
5. Obtain greedy policy: $\mu(s) = \max_a \hat{Q}(s, a)$
6. Take action a_t: $a_t = \mu(s_t)$
7. Obtain current reward r_t and next state s_{t+1}.
8. $\delta_t = r_t + \gamma \max_a \hat{Q}(s_{t+1}, a) - \hat{Q}(s_t, a_t)$
9. Update hyperparameters:

$$\theta_t \leftarrow \theta_t - \varepsilon_t \nabla_\theta \text{loss}_\theta (s_t, a_t, s_{t+1}) = \theta_t - \varepsilon_t \delta_t \nabla Q_\theta(s_t, a_t)$$

Algorithm 9: Q-learning algorithm with function approximation

21.6.1 Deep Q-Network (DQN)

A deep Q-network (DQN) is an algorithm where a deep neural network is used as a function approximator. The algorithm in Algorithm 10 still holds, however a critical question is how to implement the hyperparameter learning step in Step 9. Again, we borrow ideas from machine learning and use the *backpropogation* algorithm to calcuate the gradient of the individual hyperparameters with respect to the loss function.

21.6.1.1 Issues with DQN

Most of these issues are common across schemes that use 'large' function approximator.

1. **Exploration:** In order to achieve the optimal value of hyperparameters all the states and action should be visited 'often'. However, depending on the transition function and the reward function, this may not be always the case. Hence, $Q_\theta(s, a)$ may have varying level of accuracy for each s and a. A classical methodology to alleviate this problem is to introduce exploration strategies such as ε-greedy exploration strategies.
2. **Stability:** When compared to classical supervised learning algorithm, the loss function in, for example in (19), the 'true' label and the target label are functions of the hyperparameters, which could make the training process unstable. There are two procedures to stablize the training process:
   - **Experience replay:** In experience replay, the experiences (the state transitions, rewards and actions) are stored. Then, these experiences are used in mini-batches to update the hyperparameters of the neural networks.
     Suppose the experience is stored as follows: $\mathcal{D}^{\text{exp}} = \{s_t, a_t, r_t, s_{t+1}\}_{t=1}^{N}$. From the "total" experience, obtain a random sample of M (the mini-batch) $\mathcal{D}^{\text{exp (mini)}} \subset \mathcal{D}^{\text{exp}}$. An estimate of gradient of the loss function can be computed as below:

$$\nabla_\theta \text{loss}_\theta = \frac{1}{M} \sum_{\{s_t, a_t, r_t, s_{t+1}\} \in D \exp(mini)} \nabla_\theta \text{loss}(s_t, a_t, r_t, s_{t+1}) \qquad ...(21)$$

This mini-batch gradient reduces correlation between samples used to update the parameters with decisions made from those updates.

   - **Lazy update of target network:** Consider creating a "target Q-network" with parameters ϕ, i.e., $Q_\phi(s, a)$. Then, the loss function in (19), can be replaced by $\text{loss}_\theta^Q (s, a, s') = (Q_\theta(s, a) - (r(s, a) + \gamma \max_a Q(s', a))^2$. The hyperparameters of the "online network" (the original network with hyperparameters θ) is updated as in Step 9 in Algorithm 10. This reduces the instability associated with changing the hyperparameters θ by a small value and causing the loss function to significantly differ from its previous value. In order to remain consistent, $\phi \leftarrow \theta$ every, say thousands of steps.

21.6.2 Recent Advances

In this section, we will discuss some recent advances and extensions to deep Q-network algorithm.

21.6.2.1 Double DQN

In double DQN, the idea is to use double learning along with DQN. It is well known that DQN overestimates the Q-value (due to the maximization bias inherent in reinforcement learning algorithms) and hence, results in sub-optimal policy. Using the double learning idea along with DQN is known to fully solve this issue.

Rather than introduce a new network for double learning, we can reuse the target network in DQN to achieve double learning, as shown below.

$$\text{loss}_{\theta}^{Q}\,(s, a, s') = (Q_{\theta}(s, a) - \left(r(s, a) + \gamma Q_{\phi}(s', \text{argmax}_a\, Q_{\theta}\,(s', a)\right)^2 \qquad ...(22)$$

i.e., using the online network to evaluate the greedy policy but using the target network to estimate its value.

21.6.2.2 Noisy Networks

In the classical DQN architecture that we described in Section 21.6.1, exploration was done using an ε-greedy algorithm. Depending on the size of the state space, this may not be a practical methodology. The following strategies utilize the (deep) neural network in DQN to encourage exploration.

1. **Independent Gaussian noise:** In each iteration, the weights of the neural network are perturbed by a "small" Gaussian noise. Corresponding to each weight, there is a Gaussian random variable, which is sampled to create the perturbation. The parameters of the Gaussian random variable (mean and standard deviation) are trained, as usual, with back propagation.
2. **Factorized Gaussian noise:** Instead of doubling the number of parameters to train (each weight and the associated parameters of the Gaussian random variable) in Independent Gaussian noise case, in factorized approach, for each layer, there is one Gaussian random vector the size of the input of the layer and another Gaussian random vector the size of the output of the layer. The perturbations of the weights are obtained by taking the outer product between these two vectors.

21.6.2.3 Prioritized Experience Replay

In experience replay, we sample uniformly random from the total experience to obtain minibatches. However, some examples are more informative than others. In prioritized experience replay, we sample according to the training error. Let ω_t be the training error corresponding to the tth example $\{s_t, a_t, r_t, s_{t+1}\}$ in the experience dataset,

$$\omega_t = Q_\theta(s_t, a_t) - \left(r_t + \gamma \max_a Q_\phi(s_{t+1}, a)\right). \qquad ...(23)$$

Then, the priority $P(t)$ of the sample t is set as:

$$P(t) = \frac{|\omega_t|^\alpha}{\Sigma_t |\omega_t|^{\alpha'}} \qquad ...(24)$$

where, α is a hyperparameter that controls the sampling. As α goes to 0, we get uniform sampling and as $\alpha \to 1$, more priority is assigned to samples with higher training error (or "more informative" samples). A modified version of prioritized sampling, given in (25), has an extra factor of ε, a small positive constant, ensures that each experience has a non-zero probability of being sampled.

$$P(t) = \frac{(|\omega_t| + \varepsilon)^\alpha}{\Sigma_t (|\omega_t| + \varepsilon)^{\alpha'}} \qquad ...(25)$$

However, prioritized sampling of the experiences introduces bias in the training process. *Importance sampling* can be used to reduce the effects of prioritized sampling; however those are beyond the scope of the current textbook.

21.6.2.4 Dueling DQN

The dueling DQN is based on the observation that in some states action selection is very important, but in some other states, action selection doesn't significantly change the outcome. To express this dependence, we write the Q-function as follows:

$$Q(s, a) = V(s) + A(s, a), \qquad ...(26)$$

where, in (26), the Q-function is written as the sum of the value function and a new function referred to as the *advantage function*. The advantage function characterizes the "advantage" that we get from selecting an action. However, $A(s, a)$ could be either positive or negative. Figure 21.7 shows the architecture of the dueling DQN.

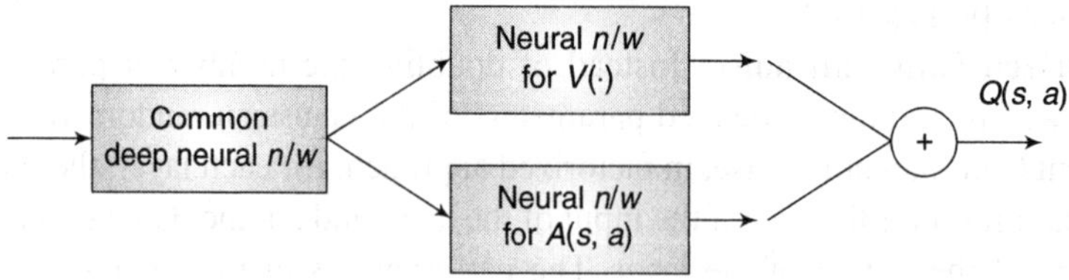

Fig. 21.7 Architecture of the dueling DQN

However, this change in architecture is not sufficient. For example, there is nothing preventing the network from learning $V(s) = 0$, $A(s, a) = Q(s, a)$, which would make the value function network redundant. A "trick" to prevent this from happening is to re-write (8) as follows:

$$Q(s, a) = V(s) + A(s, a) - \frac{1}{|\mathcal{A}|} \sum_{a \in \mathcal{A}} A(s, a). \qquad ...(27)$$

This effectively reduces the mean (across action space) of the advantage function to zero. With these modifications the network obtains faster convergence and performance comparable to a DQN architecture.

Conclusion

In this chapter, we started with the classical ideas of reinforcement learning. The main problem is that in practical decision making problems, the transition probability function is unknown and hence, we cannot compute the expectations. Approximate expectations using empirical averages led us to our first reinforcement learning algorithm: Q learning. We then proceeded to approximate expectation using Monte Carlo simulation (in Monte Carlo learning). Temporal difference (TD) algorithm is one of the most influential ideas in reinforcement learning. The chapter concluded with some recent advances in Q-learning, such as Deep Q-learning and double learning to reduce bias.

Question

1. Consider an MDP with four states $\{A, B, C, D\}$ shown in Fig. 21.8. In each state, we can either perform action a or b. Figure 21.8 shows the state transition function and reinforcement reward obtained by each action. Consider the Q-learning algorithm with $\gamma = 0.9$ (discount factor), and $\alpha = 1$. Find the estimated Q-values, if the MDP begins in state A and performs actions $\{a, a, b, a, b, a\}$. Assume that the Q-learning algorithm is initialized with zero values.

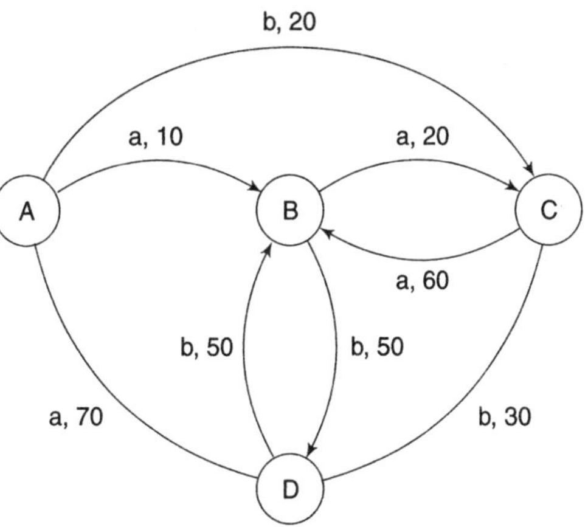

Fig. 21.8 MDP for Qn 1

CHAPTER

22

Reinforcement Learning: Policy Gradient Methods

In this chapter you will

- Define policy gradient and derive policy gradient theorem.
- REINFORCE as a Monte Carlo policy gradient algorithm
- Actor-Critic Algorithm
- Trust region policy gradient algorithm and recent advances such as Natural Policy Gradient (NPG), Trust Region Policy Optimization (TRPO), Proximal Policy Optimization (PPO), Deterministic Policy Gradient (DPG), Soft Q-learning and Soft Actor-Critic.

22.0 INTRODUCTION

In the previous chapter on reinforcement learning, we focused on how to estimate the value function (or the Q-function) given a policy and then the policy was improved using the estimated value function. The process was iterated to compute a "good" policy. In this chapter, we will look at *policy gradient algorithms* that bypass the step of estimating the value function and directly compute the policy.

Before we proceed to discuss the policy gradient algorithms, we need to re-interpret the policy π. In the last two chapters, the policy was treated as a *deterministic function*, i.e., policy is a mapping from the state to action. However, in this chapter, we would treat the policy as a *stochastic function*, i.e., given a state, the policy defines the probability that an action is taken. Hence, we write $\pi(a|s) = \mathbb{P}[a_t = a|s_t = s]$. Of course, the deterministic mapping is a special case where the probability corresponding to the deterministic action is 1, and the rest are assigned to 0.

22.1 POLICY GRADIENT: INTRODUCTION

Recall, from the previous chapter, that the agent learns from experience, where the experience is a series of episodes. Consider an episode as follows: $\tau = s_0, a_0, r_0, s_1, a_1, r_1, \ldots, s_T$. The reader is also referred to notation section in the previous chapter, where we discuss the notation adopted in this chapter.

22.1.1 Recap from Chapter 21: Cumulative Reward

The cumulative return of the episode is given by

$$R(\tau) = \sum_{t=0}^{T-1} \gamma^t r_t. \qquad ...(1)$$

And, the *expected* cumulative return is given by

$$J = \mathbb{E}_\pi\left[\sum_{t=0}^{T-1} \gamma^t r_t\right], \qquad ...(2)$$

where, the expectation is with respect to all the trajectories generated as a result of randomness in the policy, and the dynamics of the MDP.

An optimal policy is one that maximizes the expected cumulative reward in (2), among all policies and all possible starting states, i.e.,

$$\pi^* = \text{argmax}_\pi J \qquad ...(3)$$

22.1.2 Policy Parametrization

We assume that the stochastic policy is implemented by a parametric function, for example, either using the classical soft-max function (Example 22.1) or a modern (deep) neural network. As in Chapter 21, the parameters of the policy are denoted by θ. Hence, we write the policy as $\pi_\theta(a|s)$.

As in the Section 21.6.1 on DQN, we need to tweak the parameters of the policy so that we obtain a good policy. As before, we will adopt a gradient based algorithm, to update the parameters, where one step of the gradient algorithm is given by

$$\theta \leftarrow \theta + \varepsilon \nabla_\theta J(\tau) \qquad ...(4)$$

However, from (4), it looks like finding the gradient of the expected cumulative reward $J(\tau)$ is difficult. Fortunately, the *policy gradient theorem* gives a method to address this problem.

22.1.3 Policy Gradient Theorem

In order to understand the policy gradient theorem, let us consider a one-step MDP, i.e., the decision maker makes only one decision (or in other words, each episode is restricted to one state, action, reward tuple, i.e., $\tau = s_0, a_0, r_0$.). Here the expected cumulative reward can be written as

$$J = \mathbb{E}[r(s, a)] = \sum_s \mu(s)\mathbb{E}_\pi [r(s, a)] = \sum_s \mu(s) \sum_a \pi_\theta (a|s)r(s, a), \quad ...(5)$$

where, $\mu(s)$ is the initial probability distribution of the state given by $\mu(s) = \mathbb{P}[s_0 = s]$. The gradient of the expected cumulative reward can be obtained using (5) as follows:

$$\nabla_\theta J = \nabla_\theta \sum_s \mu(s) \sum_a \pi_\theta (a|s)r(s, a) = \sum_s \mu(s) \sum_a \nabla_\theta \pi_\theta (a|s)r(s, a),$$

$$= \sum_s \mu(s) \sum_a \pi_\theta (a|s) \frac{\nabla_\theta \pi_\theta(a|s)}{\pi_\theta(a|s)} r(s, a), \quad ...(6)$$

$$= \sum_s \mu(s) \sum_a \pi_\theta (a|s) \nabla_\theta \log(\pi_\theta(a|s))r(s, a) = \mathbb{E}_\pi [\nabla_\theta \log(\pi_\theta(a|s))r(s, a)].$$

The second step, above, is obtained by multiplying and dividing by $\pi_\theta(a|s)$, and the last step is obtained by using the '*log-derivative trick*': $\nabla_\theta \log(f(\theta)) = \frac{\nabla_\theta f(\theta)}{f(\theta)}$. The term $\nabla_\theta \log(\pi_\theta))$ is referred to as the *score function.*

Example 22.1 A classical parametrization for discrete state and action spaces is the softmax policy given by

$$\pi_\theta(a|s) = \frac{\exp(\theta^T \phi_{s,a})}{\sum_a \exp(\theta^T \phi_{s,a})}$$

where, $\phi_{s,a}$ is a d-dimensional feature vector for state s and action a, and, $\theta \in \mathbb{R}^d$ are the policy parameters. Then, it is easy to show that:

$$\nabla_\theta \log(\pi_\theta(a|s)) = \phi_{s,a} - \sum_a \phi_{s,a} \pi_\theta(a|s)$$

Example 22.2 (Gaussian function parametrization). Another classical parametrization for continuous action spaces is the Gaussian policies given by

$$\pi_\theta(a|s) = \mathcal{N}(\theta^T \phi_{s,a}, \sigma^2) = \frac{1}{\sqrt{2\pi\sigma^2}} \exp\left(- \frac{(a - \theta^T\phi_{s,a})}{(2\sigma^2}\right)$$

where, as before, $\phi_{s,a}$ is a d-dimensional feature vector for state s and action a, $\theta \in \mathbb{R}^d$ are the policy parameters, and, $\mathcal{N}(\mu, \sigma^2)$ is the Gaussian probability density function with mean μ and σ is the standard deviation. Then, policy gradient can be shown to be equal to

$$\nabla_\theta \log(\pi_\theta(a|s)) = \frac{(a - \theta^T \phi_{s,a})}{2\sigma^2} \phi_{s,a}.$$

Example 22.3 (Deep neural networks). In deep reinforcement learning, the policy function is computed by a multi-layer neural network. The backpropagation algorithm allows the gradient to be computed efficiently.

How does this generalize to general MDP? Let us first consider the finite horizon discounted MDP. Given an episode $\tau = s_0, a_0, r_0, s_1, a_1, r_1, \ldots, s_{T-1}, a_{T-1}, s_T$, starting in state s_0, the cumulative return is given in (1), and the expected cumulative return is given in (2). The expected cumulative return is reproduced here, making explicit the dependence on the starting state and the policy as follows:

$$J_\theta(s_0) = \mathbb{E}[R(\tau)|\pi, s_0] \qquad ...(7)$$

Let $D^{\pi_\theta}(\tau|s_0)$ denote the probability of the episode τ, where the episode starts in state s_0, under policy π_θ. Then, the expected cumulative reward in (7) can be written as:

$$J_\theta(s_0) = \mathbb{E}_{\tau\sim D^{\pi_\theta}}[R(\tau)|s_0] = \sum_{\tau:D^{\pi_\theta}(\tau|s_0)>0} D^{\pi_\theta}(\tau|s_0)R(\tau). \qquad ...(8)$$

Then, the gradient of the expected cumulative reward, using same tricks as for the one-step MDP, is given by

$$\nabla J_\theta(s_0) = \sum_{\tau:D^{\pi_\theta}(\tau|s_0)>0} \nabla_\theta \log(D^{\pi_\theta}(\tau|s_0))R(\tau). \qquad ...(9)$$

The main difference with the one-step MDP, that we considered before, is that we have the gradient $\nabla_\theta \log(D^{\pi_\theta}(\tau|s_0))$ instead of the gradient of the policy. It looks like finding $\nabla_\theta \log(D^{\pi_\theta}(\tau|s_0))$ is quite complicated. Fortunately, we can use the Markov property and simplify $D^{\pi_\theta}(\tau|s_0)$ as follows:

$$D^{\pi_\theta}(\tau|s_0) = \prod_{t=0}^{T-1} \pi_\theta(a_t|s_t)\,\mathbb{P}(s_t, a_t, s_{t+1}). \qquad ...(10)$$

Hence, the gradient $\nabla_\theta \log(D^{\pi_\theta}(\tau|s_0))$, using (10), is given by

$$\nabla_\theta \log(D^{\pi_\theta}(\tau|s_0) = \sum_{t=0}^{T-1} \nabla_\theta \log(\pi_\theta(a_t|s_t)). \qquad ...(11)$$

Notice from (11), that the gradient depends only on the policy. Hence, we can compute the gradient without knowledge of the transition probability function of the MDP!

Theorem 1 Policy gradient theorem (finite horizon discounted MDP): For a finite horizon MDP, let $R(\tau)$ be the total reward for an episode τ, following policy π_θ for T time periods, starting in state s_0. Then,

$$\nabla J_\theta(s_0) = \mathbb{E}_\tau\left[R(\tau)\sum_{t=0}^{T-1} \nabla_\theta \log(\pi_\theta(a_t|s_t))\right] \qquad ...(12)$$

The policy gradient theorem for the infinite horizon MDP case is given in Theorem 2. The proof is somewhat involved and is skipped.

Theorem 2 Policy gradient theorem (infinite horizon discounted MDP): The policy gradient for the infinite horizon discounted MDP is given by

$$\nabla J = \sum_{s} d^{\pi}(s) \sum_{a} \nabla_{\theta} \log (\pi_{\theta}(a|s))Q_{\pi}(s, a) = \mathbb{E}_{\pi}[\nabla_{\theta} \log(\pi_{\theta}(a|s))Q_{\pi}(s, a)] \quad ...(13)$$

Let $\mathbb{P}(s \to s'|k, \pi)$ be the visitation probability, i.e., the probability of going from state s to state s' in k-steps under policy π. Then, $d^{\pi}(s)$ is the discounted visitation probability given by $d^{\pi}(s) = \sum_{k=0}^{\infty} \gamma^{k}\, \mathbb{P}(s_0 \to s|k, \pi)$, and $Q_{\pi}(s, a)$ is the Q-function under policy π.

The connection with the finite horizon case can be seen as follows. Suppose, we run the policy π, starting at some initial state s_0, and assuming a large enough T, then define R_t (similar to Eq. (1)) as

$$R_t = \sum_{t'=t}^{T-1} \gamma^{t'-t} r_t \quad ...(14)$$

Then, it is easy to show that R_t is an unbiased estimator of $Q(s_t, a_t)$. Again, define $F_t = R_t \nabla_{\theta}\pi(a_t|s_t)$, then we can show that $\mathbb{E}[F_t|s_t] = \sum_a Q(s_t, a)\, \nabla_{\theta}\pi(a|s_t)$ (Proof skipped).

22.2 REINFORCE: MONTE CARLO POLICY GRADIENT

The policy gradient theorem (Theorem 1) gives an exact expression for the gradient of the policy. As usual, we will not be able to compute the exact gradient. Instead, we will rely on a stochastic gradient algorithm to optimize the hyperparameters of the policy.

Hence, given an experience containing M episodes, an estimate of the gradient can be obtained as follows:

$$\nabla_{\theta}\hat{J} = \frac{1}{M} \sum_{i=1}^{M} R(\tau^{i}) \sum_{t=0}^{T^{j}-1} \nabla_{\theta}\, \pi_{\theta}(a_t^{j}|s_t^{j}). \quad ...(15)$$

The classical REINFORCE algorithm essentially implements (15) and is given in Algorithm 1.

while not converged do
    Initialize $\nabla_{\theta}J = 0$.
    for episode $i = 1, ..., M$ do
        for $t = 0, ..., T^{j} - 1$ do
        $R_t(\tau) = \sum_{t'=t}^{T^{j}-1} \gamma^{t'-t} r_t$
        $\nabla_{\theta}J = \nabla_{\theta}J + \frac{1}{M} R_t(\tau) \sum_{t'=t}^{T^{j}-1} \pi(a_{t'}|s_{t'})$
    $\theta \leftarrow \theta + \varepsilon\nabla_{\theta}J$

Algorithm 1: REINFORCE: Monte Carlo policy gradient

22.2.1 REINFORCE with Baseline

One disadvantage of the classical REINFORCE algorithm is the high variance caused by Monte Carlo estimation of the expected cumulative reward. One way to reduce the variance is to introduce a function that *only depends on the state*,[1] called a *baseline function*, as follows:

$$\nabla_\theta J = \mathbb{E}_\tau\left[\sum_{t=0}^{T-1}\left(R(\tau)-b(s_t)\right)\nabla_\theta \log(\pi_\theta(a_t|s_t))\right] \quad ...(16)$$

where $b(s)$ is the baseline function which depends only on the state. For an experience with M episodes, an estimate of the gradient with a baseline function is given by

$$\nabla_\theta \hat{J} = \frac{1}{M}\sum_{i=1}^{M}\sum_{t=0}^{T^j-1} R(\tau^i) - b(s_t)\ \nabla_\theta \pi_\theta(a_t^j|s_t^j) \quad ...(17)$$

Note that introducing a baseline function doesn't change the expected value, as seen below:

$$\begin{aligned}
\mathbb{E}_\tau\left[\sum_{t=0}^{T-1} b(s_t)\frac{\partial}{\partial\theta_j}\log(\pi_\theta(a_t|s_t))|s_0\right] &= \mathbb{E}\left[\sum_{t=0}^{T-1}\mathbb{E}\left[b(s_t)\frac{\partial}{\partial\theta_j}\log(\pi_\theta(a_t|s_t))|s_t\right]|s_0\right]\\
&= \mathbb{E}\left[\sum_{t=0}^{T-1} b(s_t)\mathbb{E}\left[\frac{\partial}{\partial\theta_j}\log(\pi_\theta(a_t|s_t))|s_t\right]|s_0\right]\\
&= \mathbb{E}\left[\sum_{t=0}^{T-1} b(s_t)\sum_a \pi_\theta(a|s_t)\frac{\partial}{\partial\theta_j}\log(\pi_\theta(a|s_t))|s_0\right]\\
&= \mathbb{E}\left[\sum_{t=0}^{T-1} b(s_t)\sum_a \frac{\partial}{\partial\theta_j}\pi_\theta(a|s_t)|s_0\right] \quad ...(18)\\
&= \mathbb{E}\left[\sum_{t=0}^{T-1} b(s_t)\frac{\partial}{\partial\theta_j}\sum_a \pi_\theta(a|s_t)|s_0\right]\\
&= \mathbb{E}\left[\sum_{t=0}^{T-1} b(s_t)\frac{\partial}{\partial\theta_j}(1)|s_0\right]\\
&= 0
\end{aligned}$$

Hence, the gradient with baseline function is unbiased. In later sections, we will show how choosing a "good" baseline function reduces the variance of the gradient estimate.

---

1 The baseline function could be time dependent, but we consider the simpler time independent case.

22.3 ACTOR-CRITIC ALGORITHM

In policy gradient algorithm (a.k.a actor-only method), we parameterize the policy and the aim to find optimal hyperparameters that maximizes performance, the expected cumulative reward. An estimate of the performance measure is obtained using simulation, by running the policy and finding the cumulative reward for an episode. One issue, that we alluded before, is that the estimate could have a large variance due to simulation. In addition, as the policy changes, a new gradient is estimated independently, and older information (episodes generated using previous policies) is discarded.

In contrast, critic-only methods (such as Q-learning, TD-learning) rely on value function approximation and use greedy methods to compute a good policy. Such methods are indirect as they first learn a "good" value function approximation, resulting in a "good" policy, rather than optimizing over the policy space as in policy gradient algorithm.

Actor-critic methods combine the advantages of actor-only and critic-only methods.

To understand the actor-critic algorithm, consider again the policy gradient algorithm for infinite horizon (similar argument works for finite horizon, as well).

$$\nabla_{\theta_A} J = \mathbb{E}[Q_\pi(s, a)\nabla_{\theta_A} \log(\pi(a|s))],$$

where, we have used θ_A to denote the hyperparameters of the policy gradient (or the actor). We can also introduce a baseline function, (a function that depends only on the state) as follows:

$$\nabla_{\theta_A} J = \mathbb{E}\left[\left(Q_{\pi_{\theta_A}}(s, a) - b(s)\right) \nabla_\theta \log(\pi(a|s))\right].$$

One particular baseline that is useful is the *value function* of the state. As in the previous chapter, define the advantage function as: $A_\pi(s, a) = Q_\pi(s, a) - V_\pi(s)$.

The first question we need to address is how to estimate the advantage function. Given a policy π, and an estimate of the value function $V_\pi(s)$, the advantage function can be estimated using any of the temporal difference (TD) methods discussed in Section 21.4 in Chapter 21.

$$\text{TD}(0)\text{: } A_\pi(s_t, a_t) = \mathbb{E}[r_t + \gamma V_\pi(s_{t+1})] - V_\pi(s_t) \backsimeq r_t + \gamma V_\pi(s_{t+1}) - V_\pi(s_t) \quad ...(19)$$

$$\text{TD}(n)\text{: } A_\pi(s_t, a_t) = \mathbb{E}[r_t + \gamma r_{t+1} + \ldots + \gamma^n r_{t+n} + \gamma^{n+1} V_\pi(s_{t+n+1})] - V_\pi(s_t)$$

$$\backsimeq r_t + \gamma r_{t+1} + \ldots + \gamma^n r_{t+n} + \gamma^{n+1} V_\pi(s_{t+n+1}) - V_\pi(s_t) \quad ...(20)$$

$$\text{TD}(\lambda)\text{: } A_\pi(s_t, a_t) = \sum_{k=0}^{\infty} (\lambda\gamma)^k \delta_{t+k}, \text{ where } \delta_{t+k} = r_t + V_\pi(s_{t+1}) - V_\pi(s_t) \quad ...(21)$$

In Eqs. (19), (20) and (21), we assumed that an estimate of the value function is available. Let us assume that we generate this estimate using, for example, a neural network with parameters θ_C (the critic hyperparameters). Then, learning the neural network parameters proceed similar to DQN algorithm. For example, consider the simplest TD(0) approach in (19), given value function parameterized by θ_C, we generate $V_{tar}(s_t)$ using episodes generated as follows:

$$V_{tar}(s_t) = r_t + \gamma V_{\theta_C}(s_{t+1}). \quad \text{...(22)}$$

Then using a loss function, for example, the square loss function, we can train the neural network such that the value function $V_\pi(s)$ approaches $V_{tar}(s)$.

Putting all these together the A2C algorithm is shown in Algorithm 2.

0. Randomly initialize the actor and critic hyperparameters, θ_A and θ_C. Select a TD method for advantage estimation and value function target estimation.
1. Randomly initialize the actor and critic hyperparameters, θ_A and θ_C
2. Select a TD method for advantage estimation and value function target estimation.
3. for all episodes do:
4. for $t = 1 \ldots T$ do
5. Obtain estimated value function $V_{\theta_C}(s_t)$
6. Calculate the advantage function $A_{\theta_C}(s_t, a_t)$ using the TD method.
7. Calculate $V_{tar}(s_t)$ using the TD method and trajectory.
8. Calculate the loss function of critic network:

$$\ell(\theta_C) = \frac{1}{T}\Sigma_t\left(V_{tar}(s_t) - V_{\theta_C}(s_t)\right)^2$$

9. Update critic networks using (stochastic) gradient descent:

$$\theta_C \leftarrow \theta_C + \varepsilon\nabla_{\theta_C}\ell(\theta_C)$$

10. Calculate policy gradient:

$$\nabla_{\theta_A} J = \frac{1}{T}\Sigma_t A_{\theta_C}(s_t, a_t)\log\left(\pi_{\theta_A}(a_t|s_t)\right)$$

11. Update actor networks using (stochastic) gradient descent:

$$\theta_A \leftarrow \theta_A + \varepsilon\nabla_{\theta_A} J$$

Algorithm 2: Advantage actor critic (A2C) algorithm

22.3.1 Exploration in Policy Gradient: Entropy Regularization

In earlier chapters, we described the importance of exploration of reinforcement learning algorithms and also proposed ε-greedy method as a simple solution to encourage exploration. Another approach to encourage exploration, which works well with gradient type algorithms, is *entropy regularization*. The idea of entropy regularization is based on the following observation: If $\pi(a|s)$ is uniformly distributed in the action space, then we encourage exploration. A uniform distribution has high entropy $H(\pi) = -\Sigma_a \pi(a|s)\log(\pi(a|s))$. On the other hand, if the distribution is deterministic, then we are exploiting the experience of the agent. The entropy of a deterministic policy is 0. Hence, the entropy characterizes the exploratory behaviour of the policy. We can add the entropy to the loss function of the actor network as follows:

$$\nabla_{\theta_A} J = \mathbb{E}\left[\left(Q_{\pi_{\theta_A}}(s, a) - b(s)\right) \nabla_\theta \log\left(\pi_{\theta_A}(a|s)\right)\right] - \beta \nabla_{\theta_A} H\left(\pi_{\theta_A}(a|s)\right), \quad ...(23)$$

where, β is some weighting constant.

Compared to deep Q-learning architecture, there is no replay buffer, and hence, A2C suffers from training with correlated data. The solution adopted in A2C and A3C (discussed in next section) is to use multiple parallel actors and learners, as shown in Fig. 22.1. The parameters of the actor and critic are stored in a global network. At the beginning of an episode, each worker receives a copy of the actor and critic weights from the global network. Each worker samples an episode (starting from different initial states, so the episodes are uncorrelated), computes the accumulated gradients and sends them back to the global network. The global networks merge the gradients and uses them to update the parameters of the policy and critic networks. The new parameters are sent to each worker again, until it converges. One disadvantage of this approach is that while it is easy to implement parallel learners in a simulation environment, it is much harder to implement in real life, such as in robotic learning.

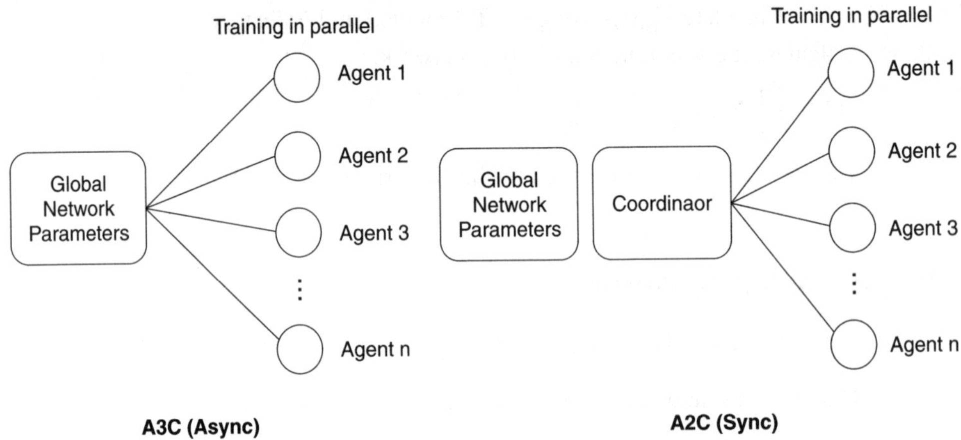

Fig. 22.1 Architecture of A2C and A3C.

22.3.1.1 Asynchronous Advantage Actor-Critic (A3C)

Asynchronous Advantage Actor-Critic extends the approach of A2C by removing the need of synchronization between the workers at the end of each episode before applying the gradients. The rationale behind this is that each worker may need different times to complete its task, so some workers might be idle most of the time, which is a waste of resources.

The solution in A3C is to simply skip the synchronization step: each worker reads and writes the network parameters whenever it wants. Without synchronization, there is a risk that one worker tries to read the network parameters while another writes them: the obtained parameters would be a mix of two different networks. Surprisingly, it does not matter: if the learning rate is small enough, there is anyway not a big difference between two successive versions of the network parameters. This kind of "dirty" parameter sharing is called HogWild! updating and has been proven to work under certain conditions.

22.4 RECENT ADVANCES

22.4.1 Trust Region Policy Gradient Algorithms

One of the main problems of the policy gradient methods is *performance collapse*, wherein the policy improves for some iterations and then drops. Performance collapse can sometimes be very difficult to recover from. The main reason for performance collapse is that while optimizing the parameters of the policy gradient algorithm, small changes in the parameter space (done via gradient algorithm) can cause the policy to change drastically. So, we need a robust methodology of updating the parameters of the policy gradient algorithm which can guarantee monotonic performance improvement.

Suppose we start with a policy π and let π' be the updated policy, then if we ensure that $J(\pi') - J(\pi) \geq 0$, we can always get montonic performance improvement. The quantity $J(\pi') - J(\pi)$, defined as the relative policy performance can be expressed in terms of advantage function as follows.

$$J(\pi') - J(\pi) = \mathbb{E}_{\tau \sim \pi'}\left[\sum_t \gamma^t A_\pi(s_t, a_t)\right] \quad \text{...(24)}$$

Notice that in (24) the expectation is with respect to the new policy, while the advantage function is calculated with respect to the old policy. We now discuss the proof of the relative policy performance. The advantage function can be written in terms of value function (following Eq. (19)) as follows:

$$A_\pi(s_t, a_t) = Q_\pi(s_t, a_t) - V_\pi(s_t) = \mathbb{E}_{s_{t+1}}[r_t + \gamma V_\pi(s_{t+1})] - V_\pi(s_t). \quad \text{...(25)}$$

Next, we manipulate the right-hand side of (24) as follows:

$$\begin{aligned}
\mathbb{E}_{\tau\sim\pi'}\left[\sum_t \gamma^t A_\pi(s_t, a_t)\right] &= \mathbb{E}_{\tau\sim\pi'}\left[\sum_t \gamma^t(\mathbb{E}_{s_{t+1}}[r_t + \gamma V_\pi(s_{t+1})] - V_\pi(s_t))\right], \\
&= \mathbb{E}_{\tau\sim\pi'}\left[\sum_t \gamma^t r_t + \gamma^{t+1} V_\pi(s_{t+1}) - \gamma^t V_\pi(s_t)\right], \\
&= \mathbb{E}_{\tau\sim\pi'}\left[\sum_t \gamma^t r_t\right] + \mathbb{E}_{\tau\sim\pi'}\left[\sum_t \gamma^{t+1} V_\pi(s_{t+1}) - \gamma^t V_\pi(s_t)\right], \\
&= J(\pi') - \mathbb{E}_{\tau\sim\pi'}[V_\pi(s_0)] = J(\pi') - J(\pi),
\end{aligned}$$

where, the first equality is obtained by substituting Eq. (25) and the second equality comes from the fact that once the trajectory is fixed $\tau \sim \pi'$, the second expectation is constant. The remaining equalities arise from the definition of the value function and the cumulative expected reward.

However, there is one problem preventing us from using Eq. (24) as an objective function. Notice in the expression $\mathbb{E}_{\tau\sim\pi'}[\sum_t \gamma^t A_\pi(s_t, a_t)]$, the trajectories need to be sampled from π' which is unknown. To overcome this, we can use importance sampling[2] as follows:

$$\begin{aligned}\mathbb{E}_{\tau\sim\pi'}\left[\sum_t \gamma^t A_\pi(s_t,a_t)\right] &= \sum_t \mathbb{E}_{s_{t+1}|\pi',s_t}\, \mathbb{E}_{a_t|\pi',s_t} \gamma^t A_\pi(s_t,a_t) \\ &= \sum_t \mathbb{E}_{s_{t+1}|\pi',s_t}\, \mathbb{E}_{a_t|\pi,s_t} \gamma^t A_\pi(s_t,a_t)\frac{\pi'(a_t|s_t)}{\pi(a_t|s_t)}, \\ &\simeq \sum_t \mathbb{E}_{s_{t+1}|\pi,s_t}\, \mathbb{E}_{a_t|\pi,s_t} \gamma^t A_\pi(s_t,a_t)\frac{\pi'(a_t|s_t)}{\pi(a_t|s_t)}, \\ &= \mathbb{E}_{\tau\sim\pi}\left[\sum_t \gamma^t A_\pi(s_t,a_t)\frac{\pi'(a_t|s_t)}{\pi(a_t|s_t)}\right] \triangleq J_\pi^{\text{CPI}}(\pi').\end{aligned} \quad ...(26)$$

where in the third step, we have approximated the expectation of the next state under policy π' as the expectation under policy π. We will shortly see how good this approximation is. We will use the objective in Eq. (26) to do policy iteration, referred to as *conservative policy iteration* (CPI). The advantage of using J_π^{CPI} is that it can be estimated from the samples of the policy π.

22.4.2 Policy Gradient in Conservative Policy Iteration

What is the policy gradient of the objective in Eq. (26)? Suppose that the policy π and π' are parameterized by θ and θ', respectively.

$$\begin{aligned}\nabla_\theta J_\theta^{\text{CPI}}(\theta')\big|_{\theta'=\theta} &= \nabla_{\theta'}\mathbb{E}_{\tau\sim\pi_\theta}\left[\sum_t \gamma^t A_{\pi_\theta}(s_t,a_t)\frac{\pi_{\theta'}(a_t|s_t)}{\pi_\theta(a_t|s_t)}\right]_{\theta'=\theta} \\ &= \mathbb{E}_{\tau\sim\pi_\theta}\left[\sum_t \gamma^t A_{\pi_\theta}(s_t,a_t)\frac{\nabla_{\theta'}\pi_{\theta'}(a_t|s_t)}{\pi_\theta(a_t|s_t)}\right]_{\theta'=\theta} \\ &= \mathbb{E}_{\tau\sim\pi_\theta}\left[\sum_t \gamma^t A_{\pi_\theta}(s_t,a_t)\frac{\nabla_\theta\pi_{\theta'}(a_t|s_t)}{\pi_{\theta'}(a_t|s_t)}\bigg|_{\theta'=\theta}\right] \\ &= \mathbb{E}_{\tau\sim\pi_\theta}\left[\sum_t \gamma^t A_{\pi_\theta}(s_t,a_t)\nabla_{\theta'}\log(\pi_{\theta'}(a_t|s_t))\big|_{\theta'=\theta}\right] \\ &= \nabla_{\theta'}J(\theta')\big|_{\theta'=\theta}\end{aligned} \quad ...(27)$$

[2] Suppose our goal is to find $\mathbb{E}[f(X)] = \int f(x)p(x)\,dx$, where $p(\cdot)$ is the probability density of X. Then, assuming $p(x) > 0\ \forall x$, we can write $\mathbb{E}[f(X)] = \int f(x)p(x)\,dx = \int f(x)\frac{p(x)}{q(x)}q(x)\,dx = \mathbb{E}_q\left[\frac{f(X)p(X)}{q(X)}\right]$, where $q(\cdot)$ is an arbitrarty probability density.

Hence, the gradient of the objective in conservative policy iteration is same as the "original" policy gradient.

22.4.2.1 Bound on the Error

(This section can be skipped without any loss of continirty). What is error in the approximation of using J_{π}^{CPI} instead of $J(\pi') - J(\pi)$? It is intutive that if π and π' are relatively "close" to each other then this error should be small. How to measure the distance between two policies? Notice that, given a state s, the $\pi(a|s)$ and $\pi'(a|s)$ are probability distributions. One measure of relative distance between probability measures is given by *Kullback–Leibler divergence* (KL) distance. The KL distance between two probability distributions π and π' is defined as follows:

$$D_{KL}(\pi \| \pi') = \sum_{x} \pi(x) \log\left(\frac{\pi(x)}{\pi'(x)}\right). \qquad ...(28)$$

It can be shown that the approximation error can be bounded using the KL distance between the two policies (the proof is involved and is beyond the scope of the current book) as follows.

$$\text{Approximation error } |(J(\pi') - J(\pi)) - J_{\pi}^{CPI}| \leq C\sqrt{\mathbb{E}_{s\sim d^{\pi}(s)} D_{KL}(\pi(s) \| \pi'(s))}, \qquad ...(29)$$

where $d^{\pi}(s)$ is the discounted visitation probability defined in (15). Using the bound, we have $J(\pi') - J(\pi) \geq J_{\pi}^{CPI} + C\sqrt{\mathbb{E}_{s\sim d^{\pi}(s)} D_{KL}(\pi(s) \| \pi'(s))}$. Hence, maximizing $J_{\pi}^{CPI} + C\sqrt{\mathbb{E}_{s\sim d^{\pi}(s)} D_{KL}(\pi(s) \| \pi'(s))}$ leads to a policy π' that is an improvement over π, i.e., a *monotonic* improvement. However, it is difficult to optimize right hand side of (29), mainly due to the presence of a constant which depends on the MDP parameters. Hence, we formulate an approximate monotonic improvement problem.

$$\text{Approximate monotonic improvement } \pi' = \text{argmax}_{\hat{\pi}} J_{\pi}^{CPI}(\hat{\pi}) \qquad ...(30)$$

$$\text{such that } \mathbb{E}_{s\sim d^{\pi(s)}} D_{KL}(\pi(s) \| (\hat{\pi}(s)) \leq \delta$$

In the approximate policy improvement in (31), the penalization term is replaced by a constraint. Intuitively, δ limits the optimization choice to only nearby policies. The "policy region", defined by the constraint $\mathbb{E}_{s\sim d^{\pi}(s)} D_{KL}(\pi(s) \| \hat{\pi}(s)) \leq \delta$, is referred to as *trust region* and, hence, the optimization problem in (31) is referred to as a *trust region policy optimization*. In the following, we will see various algorithms on how to solve this trust region policy optimization problem. Before that, let us rewrite the optimization problem in terms of policy parameters, for example the hyperparameters of the neural network implementing the policy.

$$\text{Trust region policy optimization } \theta' = \text{argmax}_{\hat{\theta}} J_{\pi_{\theta}}^{CPI}(\pi_{\hat{\theta}}) \qquad ...(31)$$

$$\text{(in terms of parameters)} \qquad \text{such that } \mathbb{E}_{s\sim d^{\pi(s)}} D_{KL}(\pi_{\theta}(s) \| (\pi_{\hat{\theta}}(s)) \leq \delta$$

22.4.3 Natural Policy Gradient

In natural policy gradient, we approximate the trust region policy optimization as follows:

1. Linear approximation of the objective: $J_{\pi_\theta}^{\text{CPI}}(\pi_{\hat{\theta}}) \backsimeq J_{\pi_\theta}^{\text{CPI}}(\pi_\theta) + g^T(\hat{\theta} - \theta)$, where g is the gradient given by $g = \nabla_{\hat{\theta}} J_{\pi\theta}^{\text{CPI}}(\pi_{\hat{\theta}})\big|_{\hat{\theta}=\theta}$.
2. Quadratic approximation of the constraint:
   $\mathbb{E}_{s\sim d^\pi(s)}\, D_{\text{KL}}(\pi_\theta(s) \| (\pi_{\hat{\theta}}(s)) \backsimeq f + \hat{g}(\hat{\theta} - \theta) + \frac{1}{2}(\hat{\theta} - \theta)^T H(\hat{\theta} - \theta)$,
3. where, $f = \mathbb{E}_{s\sim d^\pi(s)}\, D_{KL}(\pi_\theta(s) \| (\pi_{\hat{\theta}}(s)))|_{\hat{\theta}=\theta} = 0$, $\hat{g}$ is the first order derivate given by $\hat{g} = \nabla_{\hat{\theta}}\, \mathbb{E}_{s\sim d^\pi(s)}\, D_{KL}(\pi_\theta(s) \| \pi_{\hat{\theta}}(s))|_{\hat{\theta}=\theta}$, and H is the second order derivate (or Hessian) given by $H = \nabla_{\hat{\theta}}^2\, \mathbb{E}_{s\sim d^\pi(s)}\, D_{KL}(\pi_\theta(s) \| (\pi_{\hat{\theta}}(s)) \|_{\hat{\theta}=\theta}$. A simple manipulation shows that $\hat{g} = 0$. The KL-divergence Hessian H is a special matrix called the *Fisher information matrix.*

$$H = \mathbb{E}_{s,a\sim\pi_{\hat{\theta}}}\left[(\nabla_{\hat{\theta}} \log(\pi_{\hat{\theta}})|_{\hat{\theta}=\theta})(\nabla_{\hat{\theta}} \log(\pi_{\hat{\theta}})|_{\hat{\theta}=\theta})^T\right] \quad \text{...(32)}$$

The optimization problem can now be written as follows:

$$\theta' = \text{argmax}_{\hat{\theta}}\; g^T(\hat{\theta} - \theta) \quad \text{...(33)}$$

$$\text{such that } \frac{1}{2}(\hat{\theta} - \theta)^T H (\hat{\theta} - \theta) \le \delta$$

The optimization problem in (33) is a linear objective with a quadratic constraint. The solution is available in closed form and is given by

$$\theta' = \theta + \sqrt{\frac{2\delta}{g^T H^{-1} g}}\, H^{-1} g \quad \text{...(34)}$$

The natural policy gradient algorithm is given in Algorithm 3.

1. Initialize policy parameters $\theta_0 = 0$.
2. for $k = 0, 1 \ldots$ do
3. Collect episode on policy π_{θ_k}.
4. Estimate advantage $\hat{A}_{\pi_{\theta_k}}$.
5. Estimate policy gradients $\hat{g}_k$
6. Estimate Fisher information matrix $\hat{H}_k$
7. Update policy parameters using Eq. (34) as:

$$\theta^{k+1} = \theta_k + \sqrt{\frac{2\delta}{\hat{g}_k^T \widehat{H}_k^{-1} \hat{g}_k}}\, \widehat{H}_k^{-1} \hat{g}_k$$

Algorithm 3: Natural policy gradient

Remark 1 For a deep neural network, the number of parameters could be quite large. Hence, inverting the Hessian is computationally challenging. One proposed solution is to approximately compute $H^{-1}g$ by running the Conjugate Gradient algorithm for a fixed number of iterations; the algorithm is referred to as *Truncated natural policy gradient* (TNPG).

22.4.4 Trust Region Policy Optimization (TRPO)

The natural policy gradient, because of its approximation to the objective and the constraints, might cause the K-L constraint to be violated; if δ is too large, the performance can degrade. The solution is to treat the update given by the natural policy gradient algorithm as a proposal and search along the proposal direction such that both the monotonic improvement and K-L constraint are satisfied. This search can be done using a *backtracking* line search with exponential decay. Algorithm 4 shows the backtracking line search.

1. At each iteration k, and backtracking parameter α.
2. Obtain proposal: $\Delta\theta_k = \sqrt{\dfrac{2\delta}{\hat{g}_k^T \hat{H}_K^{-1} \hat{g}_k}}\, \widehat{H_k^{-1}}\, \hat{g}_k$.
3. for $l = 0, 1, \ldots$ do
4. Compute proposed update: $\hat{\theta} = \theta_k + \alpha^l \Delta\theta_k$
5. if $J_{\pi_\theta}^{\text{CPI}}(\pi_{\hat{\theta}}) \geq 0$ and $\mathbb{E}_{s\sim d^\pi(s)}\, D_{KL}(\pi(s)||(\pi_{\hat{\theta}}(s))) \leq \delta$ then
6. Accept the update: $\theta_{k+1} = \hat{\theta}$.
7. break

Algorithm 4: Back tracking line search for TRPO

The TRPO algorithm is simply a TNPG algorithm with a backtracking line search. The TRPO algorithm is provided in Algorithm 5.

1. Initialize policy parameters $\theta_0 = 0$.
2. for $k = 0, 1, \ldots$ do
3. Collect episode on policy π_{θ_k}
4. Estimate advantage $\hat{A}_{\pi_{\theta_k}}$
5. Estimate policy gradients $\hat{g}_k$
6. Estimate Fisher information matrix $\hat{H}_k$
7. Obtain $\widehat{H_k^{-1}}\, \widehat{g_k}$ using conjugate gradient algorithm (with fixed number of iterations).
8. Obtain proposed update $\Delta\theta_k$ from Eq. (34)
9. Perform backtracking line search to obtain Δ_{k+1} using Algorithm 4.

Algorithm 5: Trust region policy optimization

22.4.5 Proximal Policy Optimization (PPO)

Proximal policy optimization (PPO) takes a different approach to solving the trust region optimization problem. PPO modifies the objective to add the K-L constraint as a penalty to obtain a surrogate objective as follows:

$$J^{KLPEN}(\hat{\theta}) = J^{CPI}_{\pi_\theta}(\pi_{\hat{\theta}}) - \beta\, \mathbb{E}_{s\sim d^{\pi}(s)}\, D_{KL}(\pi_\theta(s) \| (\pi_{\hat{\theta}}(s)), \qquad ...(35)$$

where, β is a coefficent that controls the importance of the K-L penalty; smaller values of β correspond to a larger trust region, while larger values correspond to smaller trust region. However, β cannot be kept fixed since the trust region changes during the policy iteration. In PPO algorithm, β is changed in a heuristic way to approximately enforce the K-L constraint. The intution is that if the K-L constraint is "highly" violated, we increase the penalization, and if the K-L constraint is "tight" we relax (decrease) the penalization. The PPO algorithm with "adaptive penalization" is shown in Algorithm 6.

1. Initialize policy parameters $\theta_0 = 0$, and penalty β.
2. for $k = 0, 1, \ldots$ do
3. Collect episode on policy π_{θ_k}.
4. Estimate advantage $\hat{A}_{\pi_{\theta_k}}$
5. Update the policy parameters: $\theta_{k+1} = \text{argmax}_\theta\, J^{KLPEN}(\theta)$.
6. if $\mathbb{E}_{s\sim d^{\pi_{\theta_k}}} D_{KL}\left(\pi_{\theta_k}(s) \| (\pi_{\theta_{k+1}}(s)\right) \geq 1.5\, \delta$ then
7. $\beta \leftarrow 2\beta$
8. else
9. if $\mathbb{E}_{s\sim d^{\pi_{\theta_k}}} D_{KL}\left(\pi_{\theta_k}(s) \| (\pi_{\theta_{k+1}}(s)\right) \leq \delta/1.5$ then
10. $\beta \leftarrow \beta/2$

Algorithm 6: Proximal policy optimization (PPO) with adaptive penalty

The numbers 1.5 and 2 in Steps 6 to Steps 10 in Algorithm 6 determining the degree of penalization and constraint violation are chosen empirically. However, the algorithm is not very sensitive to the choice of these numbers. Because of the approximate way in which the K-L constraint is enforced, occasionally the K-L constraint is violated but the algorithm adapts quickly. The adaptive penalty approach has the advantage of being simple to implement, however, it could be expensive to calculate the K-L constraint in each iteration.

The disadvantages of adaptive penalty can be overcome with PPO with clipped objective. Let $r_t(\hat{\theta}) = \dfrac{\pi_{\hat{\theta}}(a_t|s_t)}{\pi_\theta(a_t|s_t)}$. Then, the clipped objective function (a surrogate of $J^{CPI}_{\pi_\theta}$) can be defined as

$$J^{CLIP}_{\pi_\theta}(\hat{\theta}) = \mathbb{E}_{\tau\sim\pi_\theta} \sum_{t=0}^{T} [\min\,(r_t\,(\hat{\theta})\hat{A}^{\pi_\theta}_t,\ \text{clip}(r_t(\hat{\theta}),\ 1-\varepsilon,\ 1+\varepsilon)\hat{A}^{\pi_\theta}_t)] \qquad ...(36)$$

where ε is a hyperparameter that needs to be tuned. The second term inside the min operation, i.e., the clip operation limits the term to be between (1 – ε) and (1 + ε). When r_t is between (1 – ε) and (1 + ε) both the terms inside the min are the same. This clipping operation disincentives the parameter updates from causing large and "risky" changes to the parameters, i.e., the new policy is in the neighbourhood of the old policy. The biggest advantage of the clipped PPO algorithm is that the clipping operation is relatively cheap to compute, and very easy to understand. In addition, the clipped version performs as well as the adaptive penalized version and hence, is preferred. Putting, all this together the clipped PPO algorithm is shown in Algorithm 7.

1. Initialize policy parameters $\theta_0 = 0$, and clipping threshold, ε.
2. for $k = 0, 1, \ldots$ do
3. Collect episode on policy π_{θ_k}.
4. Estimate advantage $\hat{A}_{\pi_{\theta_k}}$.
5. Update the policy parameters: $\theta_{k+1} = \text{argmax}_{\hat{\theta}}\, J^{CLIP}(\hat{\theta})$.

Algorithm 7: Proximal policy optimization (PPO) with clipping

22.4.6 Deterministic Policy Gradient (DPG)

In this chapter, we have been working with stochastic policies where given a state s, the policy $\pi(a|s)$ is a distribution over the action space. However, in many Q-learning type algorithms that we have seen before, the policy is deterministic. For example, in Chapter 21, the policy was obtained as a greedy maximization of the Q-values as follows: $\pi^*(s) = Q(s, a)$. In this section, we will now assume that, instead of a stochastic policy, we are intersted to learn a deterministic policy $\pi_\theta(s)$.

As in the previous chapter, let $\mathbb{P}(s \to s'|k, \pi)$ be the visitation probability of going from state s to s' in k-steps under the policy π. The discounted state distribution can be defined as $\rho^\pi(s_0) = \Sigma_s \sum_{k=1}^{\infty} \gamma^{k-1}\, \mathbb{P}(s_0)\mathbb{P}(s_0 \to s\,|\,k, \pi)$. Then, the expected cumulative reward of the MDP can be rewritten as follows: $J(\theta) = \mathbb{E}_{s\sim\rho^\pi} Q_\pi(s, \pi_\theta(s))$. Using this we can derive an equivalent gradient theorem for the deterministic policy.

Deterministic policy gradient theorem:

$$\nabla_\theta J(\theta) = \mathbb{E}_{s\sim\rho^\pi}[\nabla_a Q(s, a)\nabla_\theta \pi_\theta(s)|_{a=\pi_\theta(s)}]. \qquad \ldots(37)$$

The proof of the deterministic policy gradient theorem is straightforward from the chain rule. We see an actor-critic algorithm here with $\nabla_\theta \pi_\theta(s)$ depending on only the actor and the $\nabla_a Q(s, a)$ acting as a critic.

Looking at the deterministic policy gradient theorem in Eq. (37), it is easy to compute the gradient of the policy with respect to the parameters, the difficulty is in computing the gradient of the Q-function. Suppose, we replace the Q-function gradient in Eq. (37) by a function approximator, parameterized by ψ, (such as a neural network or linear approximation) the gradient of which is easy to obtain, then we can rewrite Eq. (37) as follows:

$$\nabla_\theta J(\theta) = \mathbb{E}_{s\sim\rho^\pi}[\nabla_a Q_\psi(s, a)\nabla_\theta \pi_\theta(s)|_{a=\pi_\theta(s)}]. \quad ...(38)$$

The function approximation, in turn, has to minimize the following loss function (as a function of the parameters-ψ):

$$\ell(\psi)\ \mathbb{E}_{s\sim\rho^\pi}[Q_\pi(s, \pi_\theta(s)) - Q_\psi(s, \pi_\theta(s))]. \quad ...(39)$$

One method is using a Q-learning type error to tune the parameters of the Q-function, given

$$\delta_t = r_t + Q_\psi(s_{t+1}, a_{t+1}) - Q_\psi(s_t, a_t), \quad ...(40)$$

$$\psi_{t+1} \leftarrow \psi_{t+1} + \text{step-size}_t\ \delta_t\ \nabla_\psi\ Q_\psi\ (s_t, a_t). \quad ...(41)$$

What function estimators can be used for approximating Q? Unfortunately, not all function estimators can be used for this purpose. The function estimators should be *compatible*[3], one such example is the linear approximation.

Exploration: One problem associated with having a deterministic policy is the issue of exploration, we cannot do entropy regularization as we do in the case of stochastic policy. In the Q-learning type algorithms that we have discussed before, we solved the exploration problem by using ε-greedy type algorithm. Another option, in the case of continuous action spaces, is to add small exploratory noise in the DPG policy as shown below.

$$a_t \leftarrow \pi(a_t|s_t) + \mathcal{N}_t, \quad ...(42)$$

where, $\mathcal{N}_t$ is the standard Gaussian noise.

22.4.6.1 Deep Deterministic Policy Gradient (DDPG)

Deep Deterministic Policy Gradient (DDPG) extends the DPG algorithm to non-linear function approximator, specifically using deep neural networks. The DDPG algorithm uses the following ideas from DQN architecture:

- Actor and critic target networks.
    (a) Let θ' and ψ' be the parameters of the target actor and critic algorithm.
    (b) Actions are selected using critic network with parameters θ, i.e., $a_t = \pi_\theta(a|s_t)$.
    (c) Loss for the Q-learning algorithm using the target networks: loss = $\left(\left(r_t + Q_{\psi'}(s_{t+1}, \pi_{\theta'}(a_{t+1}|s_{t+1}))\right) - Q_\psi(s_t, a_t)\right)$.
    (d) "Soft" update of both actor and critic target networks:

$$\theta' \leftarrow \tau\theta + (1 - \tau)\theta'$$
$$\psi' \leftarrow \tau\psi + (1 - \tau)\psi'$$

- Experience replay: In experience replay, the experiences (the state transitions, rewards and actions) are stored. Then, these experiences are used in mini batches to update the hyperparameters of the neural networks.

---

[3] Discussion on compatible function approximator is outside the scope of the current textbook.

Putting all these together the DDPG algorithm is shown in Algorithm 8.

1. Initialize critic network Q_ψ and critic target network $Q_{\psi'}$ with $\psi' \leftarrow \psi$.
2. Initialize actor network π_θ and actor target network $\pi_{\theta'}$ with $\theta' \leftarrow \theta$.
3. Initialize replay buffer R.
4. for episode in 0, 1, … do
5. for $t = 0, 1, \ldots$ do
6. Select action according to current policy and exploration noise: $a_t = \pi_\theta(s_t) + \mathcal{N}_t$
7. Execute action a_t, observe the current reward r_t, the next state s_{t+1}.
8. Save (s_t, a_t, r_t, s_{t+1}) to the replay buffer R.
9. Sample N data from the replay buffer.
10. for $n = 1, \ldots$ do
11. $y_n = r_t + Q_{\psi'}(s_{t+1}, \pi_{\theta'}(a_{t+1} | s_{t+1}))$; (s_t, a_t, r_t, s_{t+1}) in replay buffer
12. $\text{loss}_N \leftarrow \text{loss}_N + \frac{1}{N}(y_n - Q_\psi(s_t, a_t))^2$
13. Update the critic policy parameters (ψ) by minimizing$_N$.
14. Update the actor policy parameters using the policy gradient $\nabla_\theta J \simeq \frac{1}{N} \Sigma_t \nabla_a Q_\theta(s, a)|s_t, a_t \; \nabla_{\theta_\pi}(s)|_{s_t}$
15. Soft update of policy parameters: $\theta' \leftarrow \tau\theta + (1 - \tau)\theta'$, $\psi' \leftarrow \tau\psi + (1 - \tau)\psi'$

Algorithm 8: DDPG algorithm

22.4.7 Soft-Q Learning and Soft Actor-Critic

Earlier in this chapter, we have used entropy regularization to encourage exploration. Soft-Q learning generalizes this idea so that the policy selects states with high uncertainty, thus ensuring efficient exploration. In Soft-Q learning, we incorporate entropy directly in the reward to encourage exploration, i.e., policy is trained to maximize the expected return and the entropy. Hence, the expected accumulated reward is as shown below.

$$J = \mathbb{E} \sum_{t=0}^{\infty} [r(s_t, a_t) + \beta H(\pi(\cdot | s_t))]. \quad \ldots(43)$$

The Bellman equations for the objective in (43) is given below (proof skipped)

$$Q_{\text{soft}}(s_t, a_t) = r(s_t, a_t) + \mathbb{E}[V_{\text{soft}}(s_{t+1})], \quad \ldots(44)$$

where, V_{soft} is defined as

$$V_{\text{soft}}(s_t) = \mathbb{E}_{a \sim \pi}[Q_{\text{soft}}(s_t, a) - \log(\pi(a|s_t))]. \quad \ldots(45)$$

It can be shown, similar to the classical Bellman equations, the value iteration algorithm (based on Equations (44) and (45)) converges to the soft Q-value of the optimal policy. The policy is obtained as a softmax over the soft Q-values as follows:

$$\pi_{soft} = \frac{1}{Z_{\pi_{soft}}} \exp(Q_{soft}(s, a)/\beta) \propto \exp(Q_{soft}(s, a)/\beta), \qquad ...(46)$$

where, $Z_{\pi_{soft}}$ is a normalization factor. Hence, in tabular form, the soft Q-learning algorithm can be summarized as in Algorithm 9.

1. Initialize $Q_{soft}(s, a)$, and obtain initial policy $\pi_{soft}(s, a)$.
2. Initialize replay buffer R.
3. While not converged do
4. for $t = 0, 1, \ldots T^{j-1}$ do
5. For current state s_t, take action according to π^t_{soft}.
6. Obtain current reward r_t, and next state s_{t+1}.
7. Store the transition in a replay buffer: $R = R \cup (s_t, a_t, r_t, s_{t+1})$.
8. Obtain N samples randomly from the buffer: $R_N \subset R$.
9. For each transition (s, a, r, s') in R_N do.
10. Update $Q_{soft}(s, a)$ using (44).
11. Estimate $V_{soft}(s)$ using (45).
12. Update the policy using (46).

Algorithm 9: Soft Q-learning-Tabular

Algorithm 9 is difficult to implement for continuous action spaces, since several actions need to be sampled to estimate (45). One option is to look for parameterized classes of policy functions, for example, the Gaussian distributions. However, in this case, the policy update (Step 5 in Algorithm 9) need not correspond to a distribution in the parameterized class. This can be approximated by projecting the updated policy into the parameterized class using the K-L divergence as the criteria as follows:

$$\pi^{new} = \underset{\pi' \in \Pi}{\arg\min}\, KL\left(\pi'(\cdot|s_t) \,\middle\|\, \frac{\exp(\pi_{old}(s_t, .)/\beta)}{Z_{\pi_{old}}}\right), \qquad ...(47)$$

where, Π is the parameterized class of policies.

An advantage of soft Q-learning algorithm is that it is effective in multi-goal environment. Traditional RL algorithm would find one of the goals and exploit the rewards available from one of the goals after convergence. However, because of the soft nature of the policy, the algorithm remains stochastic and can exploit rewards from multiple goals even after convergence.

22.4.7.1 Soft Actor-Critic (SAC)

The soft actor-critic algorithm extends the Q-learning to an actor-critic framework. The SAC algorithm learns the following three (approximate) functions:

1. soft value function $V_\eta(s)$,
2. soft Q-value function $Q_\psi(s, a)$,
3. stochastic policy: π_θ.

Soft value function: The value function is trained by turning (45) into a loss function as follows:

$$\mathcal{L}(\eta) = \mathbb{E}_s\left[V_\eta(s) - \mathbb{E}_{a\sim\pi}\left[Q_\psi(s, a) - \log(\pi_\theta(a|s))\right]\right]^2. \quad ...(48)$$

The approximate gradient is given by

$$\nabla\mathcal{L}(\eta) = \nabla V_\eta(s_t)\left[V_\eta(s_t) - \left[Q_\psi(s_t, a') - \log(\pi_\theta(a'|s_t))\right]\right], \quad ...(49)$$

where, we have replaced the expectations with noisy version by using only the current state s_t and an action a'. As usual the Q-values are trained using the TD error and using the replay memory R as follows:

$$\mathcal{L}(\psi) = \mathbb{E}_{(s_t, a_t, r_t, s_{t+1})\sim R}\left[r_t + \gamma V_\eta(s_t) - Q_\psi(s_t, a_t)\right]^2. \quad ...(50)$$

Finally, the policy π_θ is trained using the KL criteria as follows:

$$\mathcal{L}(\theta) = \mathbb{E}_s\left[\mathrm{KL}(\pi'(\cdot|s)\|\frac{\exp(Q_\psi(s,\cdot)/\beta)}{Z_s}\right], \quad ...(51)$$

where, as before, Z_s is a normalization constant. The difficulty lies in training the policy parameters θ using the K-L criteria. We skip the details and refer the reader to the orginal paper for more details[4].

Conclusion

In this chapter, we considered a reinforcement learning approach referred to as policy gradient. The idea is to directly optimize policy, instead of learning the value function or Q-function as we have done in Chapter 21. A classical algorithm, REINFORCE uses Monte Carlo method to compute the policy gradient. The important Actor-Critic algorithm uses the value function as a baseline for the REINFORCE algorithm. The Actor-Critic method merges the ideas in Chapter 21 and this chapter and is the basis for all modern reinforcement learning algorithms. Finally, we looked at some extensions of policy gradient algorithm which guarantee monotonic improvements and leading to some state-of-the-art algorithms such as Natural Policy Gradient (NPG), Trust Region Policy Optimization (TRPO), Proximal Policy Optimization (PPO), Deterministic Policy Gradient (DPG), Soft Q-learning and Soft Actor-Critic.

4 Haarnoja, T., Zhou, A., Abbeel, P. & Levine, S. (2018, July). Soft actor-critic: Off-policy maximum entropy deep reinforcement learning with a stochastic actor. In International Conference on Machine Learning (pp. 1861-1870). PMLR.

CHAPTER

23

Partially Observable Markov Decision Process (POMDP)

In this chapter you will

- Introduction to the POMDP framework as a generalization of MDP framework
- Classical solutions of POMDP where the model is fully known
- Reinforcement algorithms for POMDP

23.0 INTRODUCTION

In this chapter we see a generalization of the Markov decision process considered in Chapter 21.

Consider the following situations:

1. **Wireless transmission:** Consider the problem of packet transmission in a wireless channel. The packets undergo errors depending on the wireless channel and the power at which they are transmitted. If the wireless channel is estimated (using pilot packets) before information packet transmission then the problem of allocating power to reduce long-term packet transmission error can be formulated as a Markov decision process. However, in some situations, such as in edge computing, or computing with renewable energy resources it might be quite expensive to estimate the channel before information packet transmission, and decision making has to proceed without channel information. In such cases, the "state" of the wireless system is not "fully observable". Some information about the state of the channel can be obtained from the packet layer. How to design power management algorithms to reduce long-term packet transmission error?

2. **Advertisement scheduling:** In social media, advertisement is a major source of revenue. Strategically placing advertisement so that it coincides with regions of interesting content is found to improve the effectiveness of the advertisement. A problem of particular interest in social media is to schedule advertisement in regions of high interesting content. The "live" nature of several social media platforms, such as Facebook Live, compounds to this already difficult problem. However, not everything is lost. In social media, comments, and likes give an "indication" of the "average" interest in the content. Hence, an estimate of the interest, at any time, can be obtained using comments and likes. Using such information, the interest "state" of the social media content is "partially observable".

Partially Observable Markov Decision Process (POMDP) is a mathematical framework for decision making under such partially observable constraints. Compared to MDP, the framework of POMDP is much more general, but, nevertheless, quite complicated.

This chapter on POMDP is discusses only a few selected algorithms for POMDP.

23.1 POMDP FRAMEWORK

In this section, we introduce the POMDP framework. For simplicity, we introduce only the framework with finite state space and observation space. The POMDP framework consists of the following components.

State-Space

The finite set of states is denoted by $\mathcal{S}$. Unlike the MDP framework, in POMDP, the state at any time is not fully observable by the decision maker.

Observation Space

The observation space $\mathcal{O}$ is the finite set of observations. The observations are "correlated" with the state (to be made precise later). Since the state is not fully observable in a POMDP, the decision maker relies on the observations to make inferences about the unobservable state.

Action-Space

Similar to the MDP framework, the action-space is the set of possible actions, and is denoted by $\mathcal{A}$.

State Transition Function

Let two arbitrary states in $\mathcal{S}$ be s and s'. As in MDP, the state transition function $P_{s,s'}(a)$ is the probability of starting in state s, taking an action a, and landing up in state s'.

Observation Function

The observation function $B_{s,a}(o)$ is the probability of observing $o \in \mathcal{O}$ given the current state s and action a.

Reward

As in MDP, we define the reward $r(s, a)$ as a function of state s and action a. The reward could be time dependent, in which case we denote the reward function as $r_k(s, a)$.

Objective

The goal here, as in MDP, is to find the optimal policy that maximizes the expected long-term reward of the decision maker. In the finite horizon case (for a horizon of length N), the expected cumulative reward is given by

$$J_\mu(x) = \mathbb{E}\left[\sum_{k=0}^{N-1} r_k(s_k, a_k) + r_N(s_N) | s_0 = x\right] \quad ...(1)$$

and, for the infinite horizon case it is given by

$$J_\mu(x) = \mathbb{E}\left[\sum_{k=0}^{\infty} \gamma^k r(s_k, a_k) | s_0 = x\right], \quad ...(2)$$

where, as in MDP, γ is the discount factor, and the expectation is taken with respect to the state distribution, the observation distribution and the policy μ. Notice that in (1) or (2), the actions a_k depend on the policy μ chosen (though, we have not specified how). The optimal policy μ^* is the one that maximizes the expected cumulative reward in (1) or (2).

23.2 BELIEF AND BELIEF STATE FORMULATION

Since the current state is not observable in a POMDP, an optimal Bayesian approach is to infer the state through the history of observations and actions available to the decision maker.

Denote by $\mathcal{J}_k$, the history of actions and observations available to the decision maker, i.e., $\mathcal{J}_k = \{a_0, y_1, a_1, \ldots, y_k\}$. The information available to the decision maker in terms of the history of actions and observations can be encoded into a posterior probability as follows:

$$\pi_k(s) = \mathcal{P}(s_k = s | \mathcal{J}_k). \quad ...(3)$$

The $[S]$-dimensional distribution $\pi_k = [\pi_k(s_1), \pi_k(s_2), \ldots, \pi_k(s_{|S|}]$ is referred to as the *belief state* or the information state at time k.

The belief can be obtained using a Hidden Markov Model (HMM) as follows:

$$\begin{aligned}\pi_{k+1}(s) &= P(s_{k+1} = s|\mathcal{J}_{k+1}) \propto P(s_{k+1} = s, \mathcal{J}_{k+1}) = P(s_{k+1} = s, \mathcal{J}_k, a_k, o_{k+1}) \\ &= P(\mathcal{J}_k)P(s_{k+1} = s, a_k, o_{k+1}|\mathcal{J}_k) \propto P(s_{k+1} = s, a_k, o_{k+1}|\mathcal{J}_k) \\ &= \sum_{s'} P(s_{k+1} = s, s_k = s', a_k, o_{k+1}|\mathcal{J}_k) \\ &= \sum_{s'} P(s_k = s'|\mathcal{J}_k)P(s_{k+1} = s|s_k = s')\, P(o_{k+1}|s, a_k) \\ &= B_{s,a_k}(o_{k+1}) \sum_{s'} \pi_k(s')P_{s',s},\end{aligned} \quad ...(4)$$

where, we have used the Markov property and the fact that the observation depends only on the state and action. Please note that in (4), the posterior probability is unnormalized. The normalized posterior probability can be obtained by dividing the unnormalized posterior with the sum taken over all possible states. Hence, given the belief state at time k, the belief state at time $k + 1$ is obtained using the recursive relation in (4). We will adopt the following notation for the HMM belief space update:

$$\pi_{k+1} = T(\pi_k, o_{k+1}, a_k), \text{ where}$$

$$T(\pi, o, a)[s] = \frac{B_{s,a}(o)\sum_{s'}\pi(s')P_{s',s}(a)}{\sigma(\pi, o, a)}, \; \sigma(\pi, o, a) = \sum_s B_{s,a}(o)\sum_{s'} \pi(s')P_{s',s}(a) \qquad ...(5)$$

In matrix form, Eq. (5) can be rewritten as

$$T(\pi, o, a) = \frac{B_o(a)P'(a)\pi)}{\sigma(\pi, o, a)} \quad \text{where, } \sigma(\pi, o, a) = 1' B_o(a)P'(a)\pi$$

and $\quad B_o(a) = \text{diag}(B_{s_1,a}(o), \ldots \ldots, B_{|S|,a}(o)).$ ...(6)

Since we encode all the history into the belief, then the POMDP policy takes can be defined as a mapping from the belief state into an action:

$$\text{POMDP policy: } \mu_k : \pi_k \to \mathcal{A}. \qquad ...(7)$$

Hence, the POMDP controller can be described by the block diagram in Fig. 23.1.

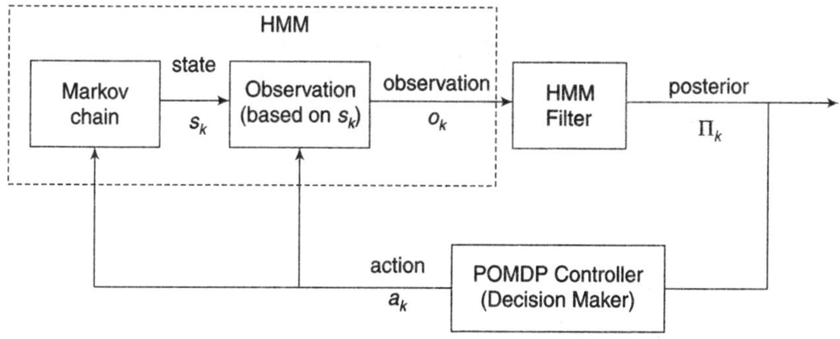

Fig. 23.1 POMDP controller

23.3 FINITE HORIZON POMDP

Consider the finite horizon objective in (1):

$$J_\mu(\pi_0) = \mathbb{E}\left[\sum_{k=0}^{N-1} r_k(s_k, a_k) + r_N(s_N)\middle|\pi_0\right], \qquad ...(8)$$

$$= \mathbb{E}\left[\sum_{k=0}^{N-1} \mathbb{E}[r_k(s_k, a_k)\,|\,\mathcal{I}_k] + \mathbb{E}[r_N(s_N)\,|\,\mathcal{I}_n]\middle|\pi_0\right] \qquad ...(9)$$

$$= \mathbb{E}\left[\sum_{k=0}^{N-1}\sum_s \pi_k(s)r_k(s,a_k) + \sum_s \pi_N(s)r_N(s)\middle|\pi_0\right].$$

Notice that in Eq. (8), we write the expected cumulative reward as a function of the starting belief π_0. The second equation follows from iterated expectations, and the third equation from the fact that the history of the actions and observations up to any time k can be summarized by the belief state at time k. Using the following vector notation: $r_{a_k} = [r(s_0, a_k), \ldots, r(s_N, a_k)]$, and $r_N = [r_N(s_0), \ldots, r(s_N)]$, (9), can be written as

$$J_\mu(\pi_0) = \mathbb{E}\left[\sum_{k=0}^{N-1} \pi_k^T r_{a_k} + \pi_N^T r_N \middle| \pi_0\right]. \quad ...(10)$$

Comparing this with the finite horizon MDP objective in Chapter 21, we notice the following:

1. The belief π_k takes the place of the state s_k.
2. Instead of the immediate rewards $r_k(s_k, a_k)$ we have $\pi_k^T r_{a_k}$ in (10).
3. The belief state π_k evolves according to the HMM equation in (4), instead of s_k evolving according to a Markov chain in MDP.

23.3.1 Dynamic Programming for Finite Horizon POMDP

Having noticed the similarity with the finite horizon MDP objective, it would come as no surprise that there exists a dynamic programming equation for the finite horizon POMDP. The following theorem provides the dynamic programming solution to finite horizon POMDP.

Dynamic programming equation for finite horizon POMDP

Theorem 1. The optimal policy $\mu^* = (\mu_0^*, \mu_1^*, \ldots, \mu_N^*)$ for a finite horizon POMDP is the solution of the following Bellman dynamic programming backward recursion, with the initialization $J_N(\pi) = r_N^T \pi$, and for $k = N - 1, \ldots, 0$.

$$J_k(\pi) = \max_a r_a^T \pi + \Sigma_o J_{k+1}(T(\pi, o, a))\, \sigma(\pi, o, a) \quad ...(11)$$

$$\mu_k(\pi) = \text{argmax}_a r_a^T \pi + \Sigma_o J_{k+1}(T(\pi, o, a))\, \sigma(\pi, o, a). \quad ...(12)$$

The proof of Theorem 1 is obtained by noticing the similarities of the belief state formulation with the finite horizon MDP framework. Notice that the dynamic programming recursions is with respect to the belief state. The belief state is continous and hence, the above recursion does not transalate into a practical solution methodology. However, the following theorem (Theorem 2) says that the value function $J_k(\pi)$ has a finite dimensional charachterization, when the observation space is finite.

Theorem 2. Consider a POMDP with finite state and finite observation space. At each time k, the value function $J_k(\pi)$ and the optimal policy $\mu_k(\pi)$ have the following finite dimensional characterization.

$$J_k(\pi) = \max_{\gamma \in \Gamma_k} \gamma^T \pi \quad ...(13)$$

where, Γ_k at each time k is a finite set of vectors.

Theorem 2 states that the value function $J_k(\pi)$ is a piecewise linear function. In addition, it can also be shown that the value function is convex. Figure 23.2 shows the piecewise linear and convex characterization of the value function. In Figure 23.2, there are 5 line segements (with slopes $\gamma_1, \ldots, \gamma_5$) characterizing the value function. Notice in Fig. 23.2 that the line segement using γ_5 is redundant. The idea behind the proof of Theorem 2 is provided by the incremental pruning algorithm discussed in the next section.

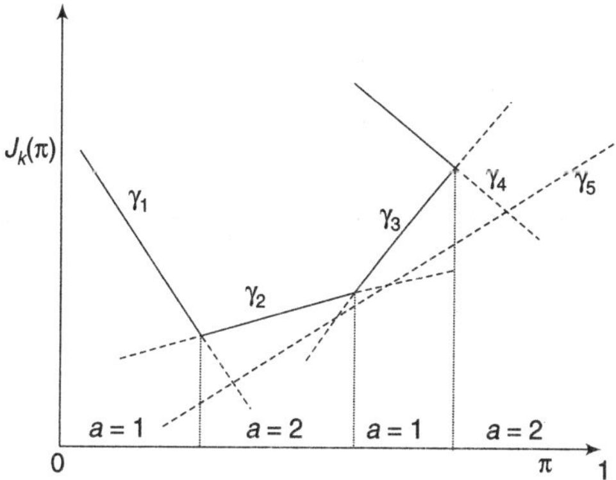

Fig. 23.2 Finite dimensional characterization of the finite horizon POMDP

The finite dimensional characterization is the basis of many exact algorithms for solving finite horizon POMDP.

23.3.2 Exact Algorithms for Finite Horizon POMDP

Let us first rewrite the equations in Theorems 1 and 2 as follows:

$$J_k(\pi) = \max_a Q_k(\pi, a)$$

$$Q_k(\pi, a) = \Sigma_o Q_k(\pi, a, o)$$

$$Q_k(\pi, a, o) = \frac{r_a^T \pi}{|\mathcal{O}|} + J_{k+1}(T(\pi, a, o))\,\sigma(\pi, a, o) \quad \ldots(14)$$

where, in the last equation we have taken a summation with respect to the observations for the first term $r_a^T \pi$ (which doesn't depend on the observations); hence the normalization. Assume $J_{k+1}(\pi)$ is piecewise linear and concave and given by $J_{k+1}(\pi) = \max_{\gamma \in \Gamma_{k+1}} \hat{\gamma}^T \pi$. Substituting in (14),

$$Q_k(\pi, a, o) = \frac{r_a^T \pi}{|\mathcal{O}|} + \max_{\hat{\gamma} \in \Gamma_{k+1}} \hat{\gamma}^T \frac{B_{s,a}(o) \Sigma_{s'} \pi(s') P_{s',s}}{\sigma(\pi, o\, a)} \sigma(\pi, a, o) \quad \ldots(15)$$

Rearranging term in (15), we have

$$Q_k(\pi, a, o) = \max_{\hat{\gamma} \in \Gamma_k} \left[\frac{r_a}{|\mathcal{O}|} + P(a) B_o(a) \hat{\gamma} \right]^T \pi. \quad \ldots(16)$$

Hence, the value function $J_k(\pi)$ can be seen to be piecewise linear and concave and given by the following equations:

$$\Gamma_k(a, o) = \left\{\frac{r_a}{|\mathcal{O}|} + P(a)B_o(a)\hat{\gamma} \,|\, \hat{\gamma} \in \Gamma_{k+1}\right\}$$

$$\Gamma_k(a) = \bigoplus_a \Gamma_k(a, o)$$

$$\Gamma_k = \bigcup_a \Gamma_k(a)$$

$$J_k(\pi) = \min_{\gamma \in \Gamma k} \gamma^T \pi \qquad ...(17)$$

where, ⊕ denotes the cross-sum operation on sets.

This leads us to the first algorithm called the Incremental Pruning algorithm given in Algorithm 1.

1. Given set Γ_k from Γ_{k+1} as follows, with $\Gamma_N = r_n$.
2. Initialize $\Gamma_k(a, o)$, $\Gamma_k(a)$, Γ_k.
3. for a do
4. for $o \in \mathcal{O}$ do
5. $\Gamma_k(a, o) = \text{prune}\left(\left\{\frac{r_a}{|\mathcal{O}|} + P(a)B_o(a)\hat{\gamma} \,|\, \hat{\gamma} \in \Gamma_{k+1}\right\}\right)$
6. $\Gamma_k(a) \leftarrow \text{prune}\left(\Gamma_k(a) \oplus_a \Gamma_k(a, o)\right)$
7. $\Gamma_k \leftarrow \text{prune}(\Gamma_k \cup \Gamma_k(a))$

Algorithm 1: Incremental pruning algorithm

Algorithm 1 summarizes equations in (17), except for the prune (·) function in Steps 5 to 7. For example, in Fig. 23.2 γ_5 is never active and, hence, can be removed from Γ_k. This happens when a vector dominates every other vector in Γ_k; the prune (·) function removes all those vectors. One possible implementation of prune (·) is through the following linear program (18).

$$\begin{aligned} &\max x \\ &\text{subject to } (\gamma - \bar{\gamma})^T \pi \geq x \quad \bar{\gamma} \in \{\Gamma - \gamma\} \\ &p(s) \geq 0, \qquad \sum_s \pi(s) = 1 \end{aligned} \qquad ...(18)$$

Monahan's algorithm, a variant of Incremental pruning algorithm omits the prune operation in Steps 5 and 6 in Algorithm 1.

Approximate algorithms for finite horizon POMDPs: Here we discuss some algorithms for approximate computation of the value function for finite horizon POMDPs.

1. *Lovejoy's suboptimal algorithm*: The algorithm operates by computing an upper bound and a lower bound on the piecewise linear segments. The upper bound can be obtained by considering only a subset of piecewise linear segments. The lower bound can be obtained by a linear interpolation of the convex function.

2. *Point based value iteration*: In point based value iteration, instead of computing the value function for all the beliefs, we compute beliefs only at a subset: either those beliefs that are encountered during POMDP simulation, or some discretization of the continuous belief space. Point based value iteration is the basis of SARSOP algorithm, one of the most popular approximate solver for POMDP.
3. *Belief compression*: In order to accommodate value iteration on high dimensional spaces, belief compression methods "project" the higher dimensional belief into a lower dimensional belief. Suppose, during a POMDP simulation, we obtain n high dimensional beliefs. Consider forming a matrix of size $|S| \times n$ by stacking the high dimensional beliefs. Using SVD (see the chapter on dimensionality reduction), the belief space is reduced to $k << |S|$ dimension. The value iteration is done in this lower dimension.
4. *Open loop feedback control (OLFC) algorithm*: Open loop feedback control is a sub-optimal method where at each time k, the decision maker generates a sequence of open loop actions $a^*_k, \ldots, a^*_N$ such that the expected reward starting from time k is maximized. At time k, the first action a^*_k is executed and the belief is updated based on the received observation. The entire decision making is repeated again at time $k + 1$.

23.4 DISCOUNTED INFINITE HORIZON POMDPs

So far, we have considered only finite horizon POMDP. This section considers infinite horizon POMDPs.

The discounted infinite horizon objective is as follows:

$$J_\mu(x) = \mathbb{E}\left[\sum_{k=0}^{\infty} \gamma^k r(s_k, a_k) \middle| s_0 = x\right], \qquad \text{(2) revisited}$$

We can express the above objective in terms of the belief state as

$$J_\mu(\pi_0) = \mathbb{E}\left[\sum_{k=0}^{\infty} \gamma^k r^T_{\mu(\pi_k)} \middle| \pi_0\right], \qquad \text{...(19)}$$

Using the dynamic programming recursion for the finite horizon (assuming $N \to \infty$), we have

$$J_k(\pi) = \max_a \left[\gamma^{N-k} r_a^T \pi + \sum_o J_{k+1}\big(T(\pi, o, a)\big)\sigma(\pi, o, a)\right] \qquad \text{...(20)}$$

with, $J_N(\pi) = 0$. As in MDP, for the infinite horizon problems, we will work with the 'V' notation, by mapping as follows:

$$V_k(\pi) = \gamma^{N-k} J_{N-k}(\pi) \qquad \text{...(21)}$$

Then, the dynamic programming in (20) can be written as:

$$V_k(\pi) = r_a^T \pi + \gamma \sum_o V_{k-1}(T(\pi, o, a))\, \sigma(\pi, o, a), \qquad \text{...(22)}$$

where, $V_0(\pi) = 0$.

This is summarized in the following theorem.

Theorem 3 (Dynamic programming equation for infinite horizon POMDP)

1. The optimal expected cumulative reward is achieved by a stationary deterministic policy μ^*.
2. The optimal policy $\mu^*(\pi)$ and value function $V(\pi)$ satisfy the following Bellman dynamic programming equation:

$$\mu^*(\pi) = \text{argmax}_a\, Q(\pi, a),\ J_{\mu*}(\pi_0) = V(\pi_0), \quad \text{...(23)}$$

$$V(\pi) = \max_a Q(\pi, a),\ Q(\pi, a) = r_a^T \pi + \gamma \textstyle\sum_o V(T(\pi, o, a))\, \sigma(\pi, o, a)$$

3. The value function $V(\pi)$ is continuous and convex in π.

The intuition behind Statement 2 in Theorem 3 is that (22) converges to a stationary function $V(\cdot)$ as the number of iterations goes to infinity. The proof for the existence and uniqueness of the stationary function $V(\cdot)$ is beyond the scope of the current textbook. Hence, we can write a "value iteration" algorithm for the infinite horizon POMDP in Algorithm 2.

1. $Q_0(\pi, a) = 0\ \forall \pi, a$
2. for $k = 1, \ldots$ do
3. $\quad Q_k(\pi, a) = r_a^T \pi + \gamma \sum_o V_{k-1}(T(\pi, o, \mu_{k-1}(\pi)))\, \sigma(\pi, o, \mu_{k-1}(\pi))$
4. $\quad V_k(\pi) = \max_a Q_k(\pi, a)$
5. $\quad \mu_k(\pi) = \text{argmax}_a Q_k(\pi, a)$

Algorithm 2: Value iteration algorithm for infinite horizon POMDP

The POMDP value iteration algorithm is essentially same as the MDP value iteration algorithm. If the observations set is finite, then at each iteration, the number of piecewise linear segments can be computed using, for example, Algorithm 1. However, the number of piecewise linear segments grow exponentially, and, hence, the value iteration algorithm may be computationally feasible only when the state, observation and action spaces are relatively small.

23.5 REINFORCEMENT LEARNING IN POMDP

In this section, we discuss reinforcement learning approaches to POMDP, where we assume that the transition probability function, the observation probability function and the reward function is not known. Without the knowledge of transition function and the observation function, we cannot compute the belief state. Hence, classical reinforcement learning algorithms rely on approximating the belief state. Once, the belief state is approximated, reinforcement learning approaches for MDP can be modified for POMDP. To avoid redundancy, we discuss only the policy gradient approaches to POMDP, and extensions of deep reinforcement learning techniques to POMDP.

23.5.1 Policy Gradient Algorithms for POMDP

Consider the following approach of approximating the belief using a sliding window, of size Δ, consisting of Δ past actions and observations, i.e.

$$\mathcal{J}_k^{\Delta} = \{a_{k-\Delta}, o_{k-\Delta}, \ldots, a_{k-1}, o_k\} \quad \text{...(24)}$$

Then, the POMDP policy ψ, as a function of $\mathcal{J}_k^{\Delta}$ with parameters θ can be written as

$$\psi_\theta(\mathcal{J}_k^{\Delta}) = P[a_k = a|\mathcal{J}_k^{\Delta}]. \quad \text{...(25)}$$

The expected cumulative reward, using the policy ψ_θ can be obtained as

$$J(\theta) = \sum_s \sum_a \sum_{\mathcal{J}_k^{\Delta}} \pi_\theta (s, a, \mathcal{J}_k^{\Delta}) r(s, a), \quad \text{...(26)}$$

where, $\pi_\theta(s, a, \mathcal{J}_k^{\Delta})$ is the probability distribution induced by the policy ψ_θ.

In order to find the policy gradient with respect to the policy parameters θ, consider the augmented process $z_k = (s_k, a_k, \mathcal{J}_k^{\Delta})$. It is easy to see that z_k is a Markov process with probability transition function given by

$$\begin{aligned} P(s_{k+1}, o_{k+1}, \mathcal{J}_{k+1}^{\Delta} | s_k, o_k, \mathcal{J}_k^{\Delta}) &= P(s_{k+1}|s_k, a_k) P(o_{k+1}|s_{k+1}, a_k)\, P(a_{k+1}| \mathcal{J}_k^{\Delta}), \\ &= P(s_{k+1}|s_k, a_k) P(o_{k+1}|s_{k+1}, a_k)\, \psi_\theta(\mathcal{J}_k^{\Delta}) \end{aligned} \quad \text{...(27)}$$

Using the policy gradient theorem in Chapter 22, we have

$$\nabla_\theta P(s_{k+1}, o_{k+1}, \mathcal{J}_{k+1}^{\Delta} | s_k, o_k, \mathcal{J}_k^{\Delta}) = P(s_{k+1}|s_k, a_k) P(o_{k+1}|s_{k+1}, a_k)\, \nabla_\theta \psi_\theta(\mathcal{J}_k^{\Delta}). \quad \text{...(28)}$$

The score function is given by

$$\frac{\nabla_\theta P(s_{k+1}, o_{k+1}, \mathcal{J}_{k+1}^{\Delta} | s_k, o_k, \mathcal{J}_k^{\Delta})}{P(s_{k+1}, o_{k+1}, \mathcal{J}_{k+1}^{\Delta} | s_k, o_k, \mathcal{J}_k^{\Delta})} = \frac{\nabla_\theta \psi_\theta(\mathcal{J}_k^{\Delta})}{\psi_\theta(\mathcal{J}_k^{\Delta})}. \quad \text{...(29)}$$

Hence, the score function doesn't depend on the transition and the observation probability.

Algorithm 3 details the policy gradient algorithm for the case $\Delta = 0$. When $\Delta = 0$, $\mathcal{J}_k = o_k$.

1. for episode $i = 1, 2, \ldots$ do
2. for $k = 1, 2, \ldots N$ do
3. Update score: $S_{k+1} = \dfrac{\nabla_\theta \psi_\theta(\mathcal{J}_k^{\Delta})}{\psi_\theta(\mathcal{J}_k^{\Delta})} + \beta S_k.$
4. Evaluate the gradient estimate: $\nabla_\theta J = \dfrac{1}{N} \sum_{k=1}^{N} r_k S_k$
5. Update parameters of the policy $\theta \leftarrow \theta + \in \nabla_\theta J$

Algorithm 3: Policy gradient algorithm for POMDP

In Step 3 in Algorithm 3, we have used a factor of $\beta \in (0, 1)$ to reduce the variance of the score estimator. For example, if we use the exponential parameterization for the case $\Delta = 0$, i.e.,

$$\psi_\theta(o_k) = \frac{\exp(\theta_{a,o_k})}{\sum_o \exp(\theta_{a,o})} \qquad ...(30)$$

then, the score function update in Step 3 in Algorithm 3 can be shown to be equal to

$$\frac{\nabla_\theta \psi_\theta(\mathcal{J}_k^\Delta)}{\psi_\theta(\mathcal{J}_k^\Delta)} = \begin{cases} 1-\theta_{a_{k+1},y_{k+1}} & \text{if } a = a_{k+1},\ y = y_{k+1} \\ -\theta_{a,y_{k+1}} & \text{if } a \neq a_{k+1},\ y = y_{k+1} \\ 0 & \text{else} \end{cases} \qquad ...(31)$$

23.5.2 Deep Learning Approaches: Deep Recurrent Q-Network (DRQN)

Recall that Q-learning for MDPs is given by

$$Q(s_t, a_t) = r_t + \mathbb{E}[\gamma \max_a Q(s_{t+1}, a)]$$

Compared to the MDP framework, in POMDP, we cannot observe the state directly. We can, however, compute the belief state. However, that would require the knowledge of the dynamics (the state transition probability and the observation probability). Notice that the belief state can be written as $\pi_t = f(\pi_{t-1}, o_t)$, i.e., as a function of the current observation, the past belief and the dynamics (which are hidden in the equation). The idea in recurrent Q-learning is to learn the non-linear mapping, using a neural network. Neural networks of the form where the output is dependent on a delayed version of itself is known as recurrent neural network and was covered in Part II of this book. The orginal DQRN formulation used a special recurrent neural network known as LSTM (refer to Chapter 12). Denote by h_t, the hidden state, a proxy for the belief state, which is updated as follows: $h_t = \text{LSTM}(h_{t-1}, o_t)$. Instead of $Q(s_t, a_t)$, the DQRN network uses $Q(h_t, a_t)$. Figure 23.3 shows the comparison between DQN and DRQN architecture for the problem of learning to play in Atari games.

The architecture in Fig. 23.3 is relatively straightforward. A deep CNN architecture extracts features from the frames of the Atari Games. The CNN features, in the case of DQN, are fed into a dense neural network layer which approximates the Q-values based on the CNN features and the action taken. In the case of DQRN, the CNN features are fed into an LSTM layer. The hidden state in the LSTM acts as a proxy for the belief and the LSTM neural network approximates the Q-function as a function of the hidden state and the action of the player.

As in DQN, DQRN training is done through either

- **Bootstrapped sequential updates:** Episodes are selected randomly and LSTM updates start from the beginning of the episode and continue till the conclusion of the episode. The target network provides the target for the mean squared error criteria at each time.
- **Bootstrapped random updates:** *Episodes are selected randomly from the memory, and LSTM updates begins from random points in the episode, and only for a fixed number of*

iterations. Again, the target for the mean squared error criteria are provided by the target network. The advantage of this approach is the lower complexity and better sampling of random episodes.

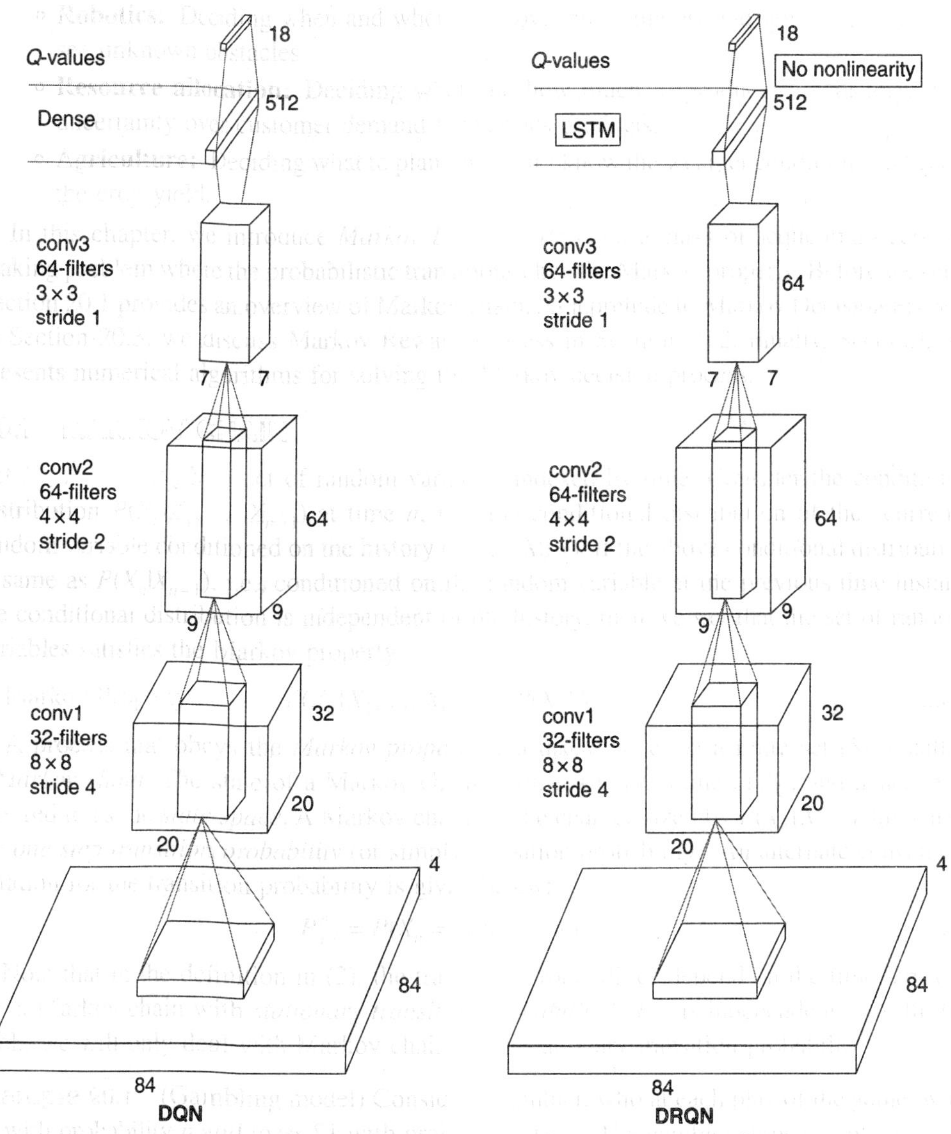

Fig. 23.3 Deep recurrent Q-network (DQRN) in comparison with DQN architecture. The key difference is that in the DQRN an LSTM layer is used to capture the time dependent belief state.

23.5.3 Deep Learning Approaches: Recent Advances

The DRQN can be extended to include double learning or other variants discussed in chapters 21 and 22. The state-of-the-art reinforcement learning algorithm is MERLIN proposed by DeepMind. The architecture combines many existing ideas and emulates animal learning in the sense that it learns to process high-dimensional sensory streams, compress and store them, and recall events with less dependence on task reward. In contrast to an LSTM network, the MERLIN architecture consists of a memory-based predictor (MBP) and a policy. The memory-based predictor is responsible for compressing observations into low-dimensional state representations and storing them in memory. The state variables, in memory, in turn, are used by the MBP to make predictions guided by past observations. Compressing the observations is achieved through an encoder, a probability distribution, known as the prior, predicts the next state variable conditioned on a history maintained in memory of the previous state variables and actions. Another probability distribution, the posterior, corrects this prior based on the new observations to form a better estimate of the state variable. The MBP is trained by optimizing the variational lower bound. We skip the details and refer the reader to the original paper: Unsupervised Predictive Memory in a Goal-Directed Agent.

Conclusion

In this chapter, we discussed POMDP as a framework for decision making under partial observability. The POMDP can be written as a MDP in the belief state. The optimal policy can be found as the solution to the Bellman equation in the belief state. However, because the belief state is continuous, solving the Bellman equation is not a computationally feasible solution. Finally, we considered practical reinforcement learning algorithms in POMDP.

Questions

1. Consider the following simplified version of the machine replacement problem. A machine can be one of two states: either brand new and working perfectly or working poorly and needs replacement. The decision maker (who owns the machine) can decide either to continue using the machine or replace it with a brand new one. The state of the machine is observable based on the quality of the goods produced. Formulate the problem as a POMDP with appropriate choice of state transition, observation distribution, and cost[1]. Find the finite horizon policy given a time horizon of N.
2. A target moves in a grid of K cells according to a Markov chain with transition matrix P. At each time k a searcher (for the target) must choose either to search a particular cell or not. If the searcher decides to search cell k, then the actual search is executed with probability $1 - q(k)$. When the actual search happens, if the target is in the selected cell, then the target is detected with probability $1 - \beta(k)$. Set up this problem, using appropriate choice of the transition matrix and find the search order so to minimize expected effort for finding the target for a given time horizon.

[1] Here, it is appropriate to use the Cost function, defined as the negative of reward, instead of the reward function

APPENDIX

A

Linear Algebra

A.0 VECTORS

A vector is a quantity or phenomenon that has two independent properties: magnitude and direction. An n-dimensional column vector ($\boldsymbol{x}$) and its transpose ($\boldsymbol{x}^T$) can be written as

$$\boldsymbol{x} = \begin{bmatrix} x_1 \\ x_2 \\ x_3 \\ \vdots \\ x_n \end{bmatrix} \qquad \boldsymbol{x}^{\mathrm{T}} = \begin{bmatrix} x_1 & x_2 & x_3 & \cdots & x_n \end{bmatrix} \qquad \text{...(1)}$$

$$\forall x_i \in \mathbb{R}$$

A.1 VECTOR SPACE

A vector space is a set (**V**) of elements called vectors, having operations of vector addition and scalar multiplication defined on it that satisfies the following conditions. ($\boldsymbol{u}$, $\boldsymbol{v}$ and $\boldsymbol{w}$ are arbitrary elements of **V**, and c and d are scalars.)

Closure Axioms

1. The sum ($\boldsymbol{u} + \boldsymbol{v}$) exists and is an element of **V**. (**V** is closed under addition.)
2. $c\,\boldsymbol{u}$ is an element of **V**. (**V** is closed under scalar multiplication.)

Addition Axioms

1. $\boldsymbol{u} + \boldsymbol{v} = \boldsymbol{v} + \boldsymbol{u}$ (commutative property)
2. $\boldsymbol{u} + (\boldsymbol{v} + \boldsymbol{w}) = (\boldsymbol{u} + \boldsymbol{v}) + \boldsymbol{w}$ (associative property)
3. There exists an element of **V**, called a zero vector, denoted by **0**, such that $\boldsymbol{u} + \mathbf{0} = \boldsymbol{u}$, $\forall \boldsymbol{u} \in \mathbf{V}$.
4. For every element $\boldsymbol{u}$ of **V** there exists an element called a negative of $\boldsymbol{u}$, denoted by $-\boldsymbol{u}$, such that $\boldsymbol{u} + (-\boldsymbol{u}) = \mathbf{0}$.

Scalar Multiplication Axioms

1. $c(\boldsymbol{u} + \boldsymbol{v}) = c\boldsymbol{u} + c\boldsymbol{v}$
2. $(c + d)\boldsymbol{u} = c\boldsymbol{u} + d\boldsymbol{u}$
3. $c(d\boldsymbol{u}) = (cd)\boldsymbol{u}$
4. $1\boldsymbol{u} = \boldsymbol{u}$

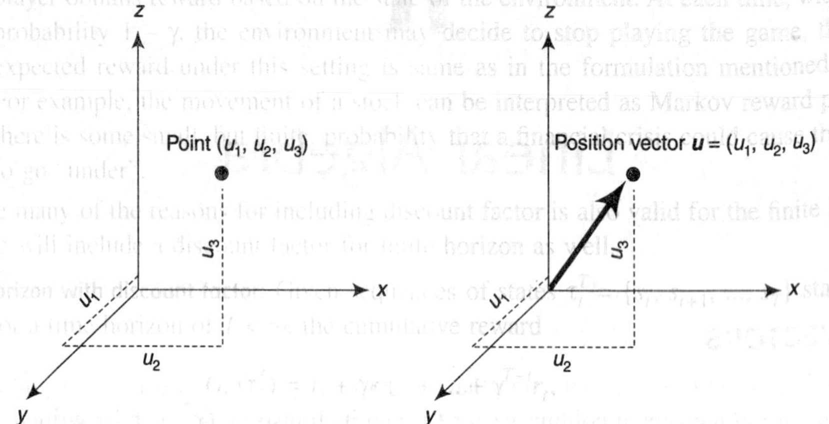

Fig. 1 Representing the vector $\boldsymbol{u}$ in the space $\mathbb{R}^3$

Let $(u_1, u_2, ..., u_n)$ be a sequence of n real numbers. The set of all such sequences is called n-space and is denoted by $\mathbb{R}^n$. u_1 is the first component of $(u_1, u_2, ..., u_n)$, u_2 is the second component, and so on. The elements of $\mathbb{R}^n$ can, however, be interpreted as points in n-space or as position vectors in n-space. $\mathbb{R}^n$ is closed under addition and under scalar multiplication.

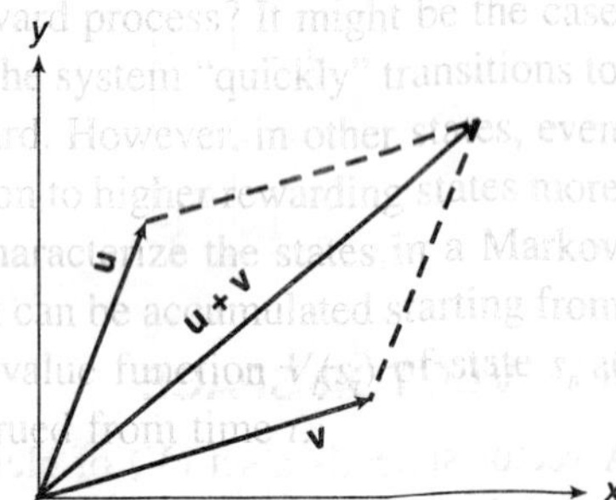

Fig. 2 Vector addition (geometrical representation) in $\mathbb{R}^2$ space

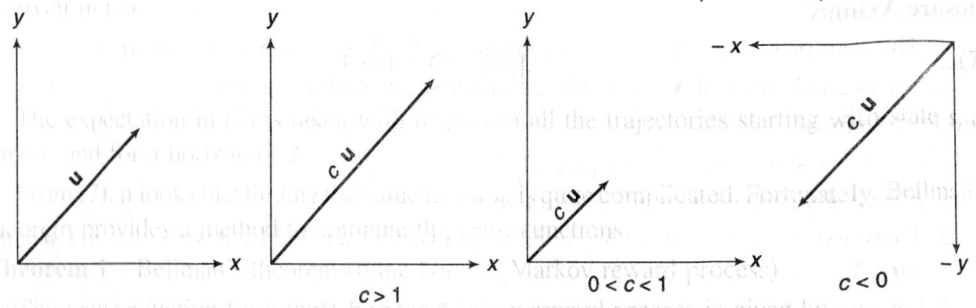

Fig. 3 Scalar multiplication (geometrical representation) in $\mathbb{R}^2$ space

A.1.1 Subspace

Let **V** be a vector space, then the subset **U** of **V** is said to be subspace or linear subspace if,

- If $u, v \in$ U, then $u + v \in$ U, $\forall u, v$
- $\alpha\, u \in$ U, $\forall \alpha \in \mathbb{R}$ and $\forall u \in$ U.

Example: W = $(a, b, a + b)$ is a subspace of $\mathbb{R}^3$.

Proof:

Let $u = (u_1, u_2, u_1 + u_2)$ and $v = (v_1, v_2, v_1 + v_2)$ be any arbitrary element in **W**.

- $u + v = (u_1 + v_1, u_2 + v_2, u_1 + u_2 + v_1 + v_2)$

  The third element is the sum of first two elements. Hence, $u + v$ is an element of **W**. That is closed under addition.

- $cu = (cu_1, cu_2, c(u_1 + u_2))$

The third element is the sum of first two elements. Hence, cu is an element of **W**. That is closed under scalar multiplication.

A.1.2 Linear Combination of Vectors

Let $v_1, v_2, \ldots, v_n$ be any n vectors in a vector space v. The vector v in **V** is a linear combination of $v_1, v_2, \ldots, v_n$ if there exists scalars $c_1, c_2, \ldots, c_n$ such that **v** can be expressed as

$$v = L(v_1, v_2, \ldots, v_n) = c_1 v_1 + c_2 v_2 + \ldots + c_n v_n \sum_{i=1}^{n} c_i v_i \qquad \ldots(2)$$

Example: Express (4, 5, 5) as the linear combination of (1, 2, 3), (−1, 1, 4) and (3, 2, 2).

$$(4, 5, 5) = c_1 (1, 2, 3) + c_2 (-1, 1, 4) + c_3 (3, 2, 2)$$

On solving,

$$(4, 5, 5) = (-2r + 3)(1, 2, 3) + (r - 1)(-1, 1, 4) + r(3, 2, 2)$$

By letting r take on different values, we get specific combinations.

A.1.3 Linear Span of Vectors

Let S be a non-empty subset of a vector space **V**. Then, the set of all linear combinations of finite sets of all elements of S is called the linear spans of S, $L(S)$

$$L(S) = \left\{ \sum_{i=1}^{n} \alpha_i v_i,\ \forall\ v_i \in S \right\} \qquad \ldots(3)$$

$L(S)$ is a subspace of **V**.

Let **V** be a vector space and **W** be any subset of **V**. Then, **W** is known as the spanning set of **V** if L(**W**) = **V**. **W** will span the vector space **V**.

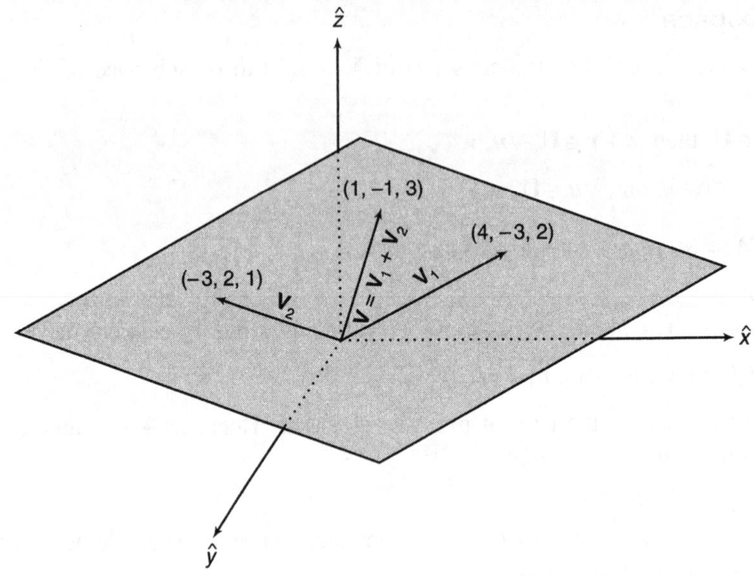

Fig. 4 Span of (4, −3, 2) and (−3, 2, 1) as (1, −1, 3)

A.1.4 Linear Independence of Vectors

A set of vectors ($\mathbf{x}_1, \mathbf{x}_2, \ldots, \mathbf{x}_n$) is said to be linearly independent, when the following condition is satisfied.

$$\alpha_1\mathbf{x}_1 + \alpha_2\mathbf{x}_2 + \cdots . + \alpha_n\mathbf{x}_n = \mathbf{0}, \quad \text{only if } \alpha_i = 0 \ \forall i \qquad \ldots(4)$$

The concept of linear dependency has significant part to play in defining the basis for a vector space.

Example:

$$\mathbf{x}_1 = \begin{bmatrix} 1 \\ 2 \\ 0 \end{bmatrix} \qquad \mathbf{x}_2 = \begin{bmatrix} 0 \\ 1 \\ -1 \end{bmatrix} \qquad \mathbf{x}_3 = \begin{bmatrix} 1 \\ 1 \\ 2 \end{bmatrix}$$

$$\alpha_1\begin{bmatrix} 1 \\ 2 \\ 0 \end{bmatrix} + \alpha_2\begin{bmatrix} 0 \\ 1 \\ -1 \end{bmatrix} + \alpha_3\begin{bmatrix} 1 \\ 1 \\ 2 \end{bmatrix} = \begin{bmatrix} 0 \\ 0 \\ 0 \end{bmatrix}$$

The identity leads to the following system of linear equations,

$$\alpha_1 + \alpha_3 = 0, \qquad 2\alpha_1 + \alpha_2 + \alpha_3 = 0, \qquad -\alpha_2 + 2\alpha_3 = 0$$

This system has the unique solution, $\alpha_1 = 0$, $\alpha_2 = 0$ and $\alpha_3 = 0$,

Hence, the set is linearly independent.

The set of vectors $\{\mathbf{x}_1, \mathbf{x}_2, \ldots\ldots \mathbf{x}_n\}$ in a vector space X is said to be linearly dependent if there exists scalars $\alpha_1\ \alpha_2, \ldots\ \alpha_n$, not all zero, such that $\alpha_1\mathbf{x}_1 + \alpha_2\mathbf{x}_2 + \cdots . + \alpha_n\mathbf{x}_n = \mathbf{0}$, i.e., one vector can be represented in terms of the remaining vectors.

A.1.5 Basis of a Vector Space

Let the vectors $v_1, v_2, \ldots, v_n$ span a vector space **V**. Each vector in **V** can be expressed uniquely as a linear combination of these vectors if and only if the vectors are linearly independent. A set of vectors $v_1, v_2, \ldots, v_n$ } is called a basis for a vector space **V** if the set spans **V** and is linearly independent. Each vector in **V** can be expressed uniquely as a linear combination of the vectors in a basis.

Example: $\mathcal{S} = \{(1, 0, 0), (0, 1, 0), (0, 0, 1)\}$ in $\mathbb{R}^3$. $\mathcal{S}$ is the standard basis of $\mathbb{R}^3$.

The number of vectors in any basis of the vector space **V** is known as dimension of **V** and is denoted as $dim\mathbf{V}$.

Let **V** be a vector space of dimension n. Then, if $\mathcal{S} = \{v_1, v_2, \ldots, v_n\}$ is a set of n linearly independent vectors in **V**, then $\mathcal{S}$ is a basis for **V**.

A.1.6 Inner Product Space

An inner product on a real vector space **V** is a function that associates a number, denoted as $\langle u, v\rangle$ with each pair of vectors of u and v of **V**. This function must satisfy the following conditions.

1. $\langle u, v\rangle = \langle v, u\rangle$ (Symmetry axiom)
2. $\langle u + v, w\rangle = \langle u, w\rangle + \langle v, w\rangle$ (Additive axiom)
3. $\langle cu, v\rangle = c\langle u, v\rangle$ (Homogeneity axiom)
4. $\langle v, v\rangle \geq 0$ and $\langle v, v\rangle = 0$ if and only if $v = \mathbf{0}$ (Positive definite axiom) where, $u, v, w \in \mathbf{V}$ and $c \in F$ (field).

Any vector space **V** on which an inner product is defined is known as inner product space. Simplest inner product is dot product.

A.1.7 Normed Vector Space

l_2-Norm of a vector is defined as the Euclidean length of the vector. It's given by,

$$\|\mathbf{u}\| = \sqrt{\Sigma u_i^2} = \langle u, u\rangle^{1/2} \qquad \ldots(5)$$

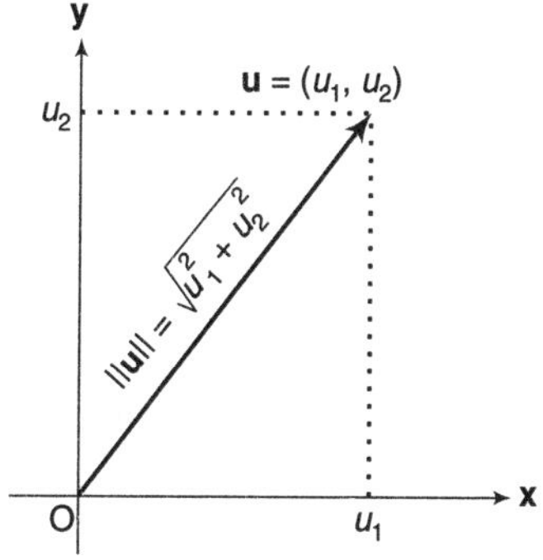

Fig. 5 Norm of a vector

Example:

$$u = \begin{bmatrix} 2 \\ 3 \\ 4 \\ 5 \end{bmatrix}$$

$$\|u\| = \sqrt{2^2 + 3^2 + 4^2 + 5^2}$$
$$= 54$$

Suppose $x \in \mathbb{R}^N$, then l_p norm (generalization) is defined as

$$\|x\|_p = \begin{cases} \left\{ \sum_{i=1}^{N} |x_i|^p \right\}^{\frac{1}{p}}, & p \in [1, \infty) \\ \underbrace{\max}_{i=1,2,\ldots,N} |x_i|, & p = \infty \end{cases} \tag{6}$$

A.1.8 Angle between Two Vectors

We have the dot product between two vectors X and Y is given as

$$\mathbf{u}.\ \mathbf{v} = \|\mathbf{u}\|\ \|\mathbf{v}\| \cos\theta \tag{7}$$

where θ is the angle between the vectors **u** and **v**. Then we have,

$$\theta = \cos^{-1}\left(\frac{\mathbf{u}.\ \mathbf{v}}{\|\mathbf{u}\|\ \|\mathbf{v}\|}\right) \tag{8}$$

$$= \cos^{-1}\left(\frac{\langle \mathbf{u}, \mathbf{v} \rangle}{\langle u, u \rangle^{1/2}\ \langle v.\ v \rangle^{1/2}}\right)$$

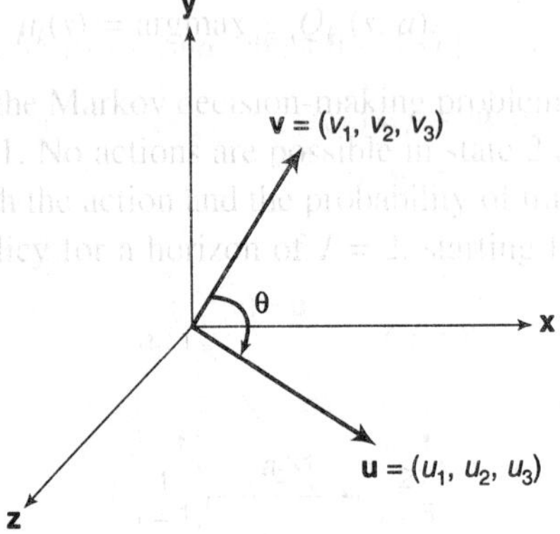

Fig. 6 Angle between the vectors *u* and *v*

A.1.9 Orthogonality

Two vectors **u** and **v** are said to be orthogonal if the inner product between them is zero. In that case, there won't be any component of **u** along **v** or vice versa.

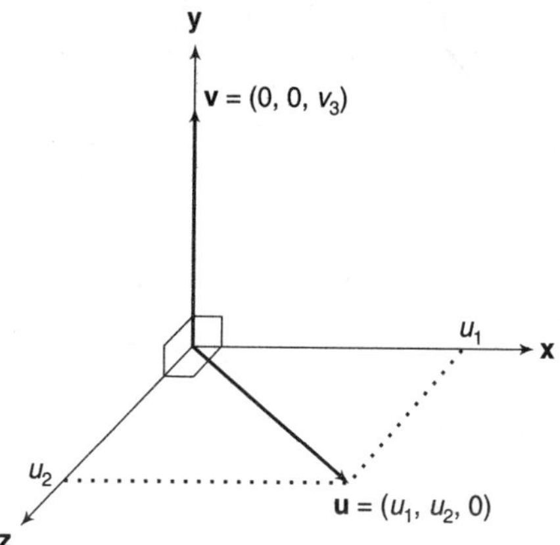

Fig. 7 Orthogonal vectors. Vectors **u** and **v** are orthogonal to each other.

A list of vectors is called *orthonormal*, if the vectors in it are pairwise orthogonal and each vector has norm one.

For orthonormal vectors $(\boldsymbol{e}_1, \boldsymbol{e}_2, ..., \boldsymbol{e}_n)$,

$$\langle \boldsymbol{e}_i, \boldsymbol{e}_j \rangle = \begin{cases} 0, & \text{if } i \neq j \\ 1, & \text{if } i = j \end{cases} \qquad ...(9)$$

A.1.10 Projection of One Vector onto Another Vector

Let $\boldsymbol{v}$ and $\boldsymbol{u}$ be vectors in $\mathbb{R}^n$ with angle α between them. The vector $\overrightarrow{OA}$ tells us "how much" of $\boldsymbol{v}$ is pointing in the direction of $\boldsymbol{u}$. We call $|\overrightarrow{OA}|$ the projection of $\boldsymbol{v}$ onto $\boldsymbol{u}$.

$$\begin{aligned} Proj_u\, \boldsymbol{v} &= |\overrightarrow{OA}| = |\overrightarrow{OB}| \cos \alpha \\ &= \|\boldsymbol{v}\| \cos \alpha \qquad ...(10) \\ &= \frac{\langle \boldsymbol{u}, \boldsymbol{v} \rangle}{\|\boldsymbol{u}\|} \end{aligned}$$

Now, the component of $\boldsymbol{v}$ along $\boldsymbol{u}$ is the vector $\overrightarrow{OA}$, which is obtained as the vector with magnitude $Proj_u\, \boldsymbol{v}$ in the direction of $\boldsymbol{u}$. That is,

$$\begin{aligned} Comp_u\, \boldsymbol{v} &= (Proj_u\, \boldsymbol{v}) \frac{\boldsymbol{u}}{\|\boldsymbol{u}\|} \qquad ...(11) \\ &= \frac{\langle \boldsymbol{u}, \boldsymbol{v} \rangle}{\|\boldsymbol{u}\|^2} \boldsymbol{u} \end{aligned}$$

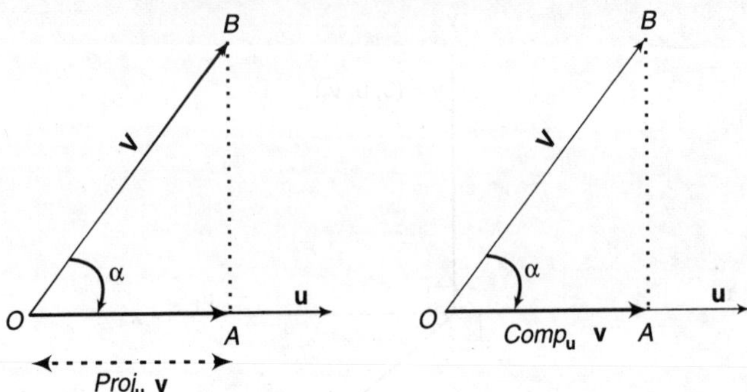

Fig. 8 Projection and component

A.2. LINEAR TRANSFORMATION

Let $\mathbb{R}^n$ and $\mathbb{R}^m$ be two vector spaces. Let $\boldsymbol{u}$ and $\boldsymbol{v}$ be vectors in $\mathbb{R}^n$ and c be a scalar. Then, a transformation $T : \mathbb{R}^n \rightarrow \mathbb{R}^m$ is called a linear transformation if,

- $T(\boldsymbol{u} + \boldsymbol{v}) = T(\boldsymbol{u}) + T(\boldsymbol{v})$; (preserves addition)
- $T(c\boldsymbol{v}) = cT(\boldsymbol{v})$; (preserves scalar multiplication)

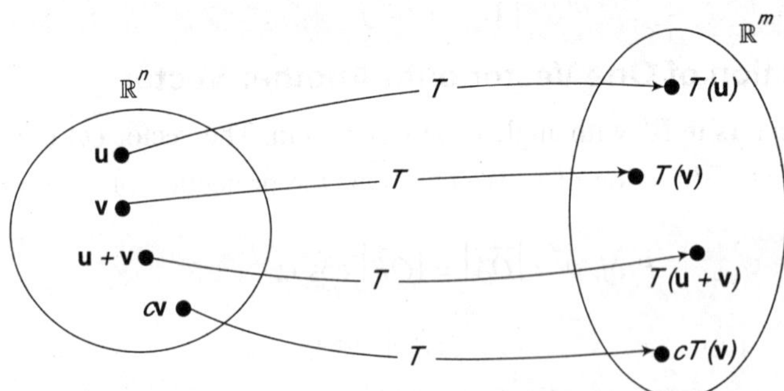

Fig. 9 $\mathbb{R}^n \rightarrow \mathbb{R}^m$

Let T be a linear transformation on $\mathbb{R}^n$.

Let $(\boldsymbol{e}_1, \boldsymbol{e}_2, \ldots, \boldsymbol{e}_n)$ be the standard basis of $\mathbb{R}^n$ and $\boldsymbol{u}$ be an arbitrary vector in $\mathbb{R}^n$. Then, the linear transformation $\boldsymbol{T}$ is defined by the matrix,

$$\boldsymbol{A} = [T(\boldsymbol{e}_1)\ T(\boldsymbol{e}_2)\ \ldots\ T(\boldsymbol{e}_n)] \tag{12}$$

with order, $m \times n$

$\boldsymbol{A}$ is called standard matrix of $\boldsymbol{T}$.

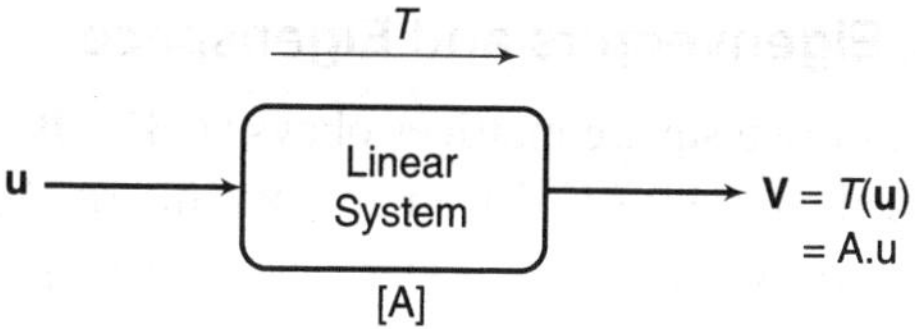

Fig. 10 Linear transformation T

$$T : \mathbb{R}^n \to \mathbb{R}^m \text{ and } \boldsymbol{u} \in \mathbb{R}^n;\ \boldsymbol{v} \in \mathbb{R}^m$$

A defines the system.

A.2.1 Image or Range of Transformation T

Let $T : \boldsymbol{U} \to \boldsymbol{V}$ be a linear mapping, then the range of T is defined as

$$lm\ T = \{T(x)/x \in \boldsymbol{U}\} \quad \text{...(13)}$$

It is a subspace of $\boldsymbol{V}$.

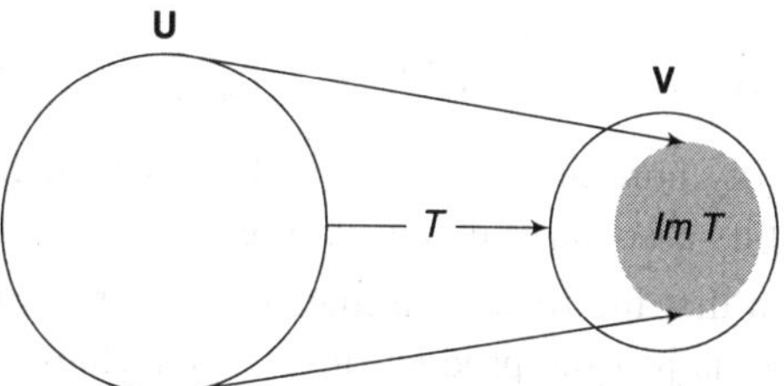

Fig. 11 Range or image of the transformation T

A.2.2 Kernel or Null Space of Linear Mapping

Let $T : \boldsymbol{U} \to \boldsymbol{V}$ be a linear mapping, the kernel of T is defined as

$$Ker\ T = \{x \in \boldsymbol{U}/T(x) = \boldsymbol{0}\} \quad \text{...(14)}$$

$Ker\ T$ is a subspace of $\boldsymbol{U}$

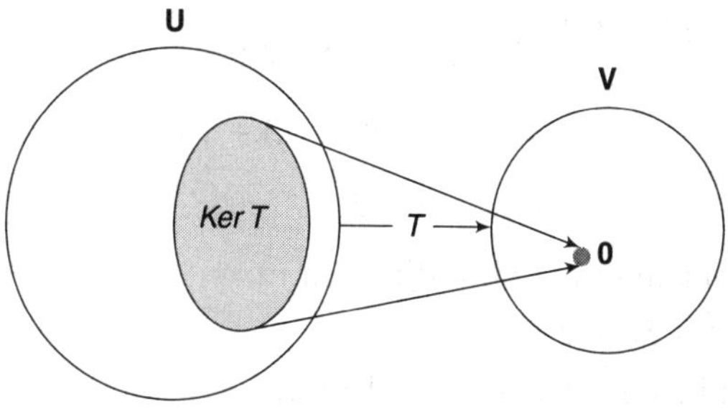

Fig. 12 Kernel of the transformation T

A.2.3 Eigenvalues, Eigenvectors and Eigenspace

The inverse of the product of two square matrices obeys $[\mathbf{AB}] = \mathbf{B}^{-1}\mathbf{A}^{-1}$, as can be verified by multiplying on the right or the left by AB. Given an $n \times n$ matrix **A**, a very important class of linear equations is of the form where λ is a scalar. The above equation may be rewritten as

$$(\mathbf{A} - \lambda\mathbf{I})\mathbf{x} = \mathbf{0} \quad \text{...(15)}$$

where **I** is the identity matrix and **0** is the zero vector. The solution vector $\mathbf{x} = \mathbf{e}_i$ and the corresponding scalar $\lambda = \lambda_i$ are called the eigenvector and associated eigenvalue, respectively. If **A** is real and symmetric, there are n (possibly nondistinct) solution vectors $\{\mathbf{e}_1, \mathbf{e}_2, ..., \mathbf{e}_n\}$, each with an associated eigenvalue $\{\lambda_1, \lambda_2, ..., \lambda_n\}$. Under multiplication by **A** the eigenvectors are changed only in magnitude, not direction:

$$\mathbf{Ae}_j = \lambda_j\mathbf{e}_j \quad \text{...(16)}$$

If **A** is diagonal, then the eigenvectors are parallel to the coordinate axes.

One method of finding the eigenvectors and eigenvalues is to solve the characteristic equation,

$$|\mathbf{A} - \lambda\mathbf{I}| = \lambda^n + a_1\lambda^{n-1} + \cdots a_{n-1}\lambda + a_n = 0 \quad \text{...(17)}$$

For each of its n (possibly non-distinct) roots λ_j. For each such root, we then solve a set of linear equations to find its associated eigenvector $\mathbf{e}_j$.

Finally, it can be shown that the trace of a matrix is just the sum of the eigenvalues and the determinant of a matrix is just the product of its eigenvalues:

$$\text{tr}(\mathbf{A}) = \sum_{i=1}^{n} \lambda_i \quad \text{and} \quad |\mathbf{A}| = \prod_{i=1}^{n} \lambda_i \quad \text{...(18)}$$

If the matrix is diagonal, then its eigenvalues are simply the nonzero entries on the diagonal, and the eigenvectors are the unit vectors parallel to the coordinate axes.

Example:

$$\mathbf{A} = \begin{bmatrix} -4 & -6 \\ 3 & 5 \end{bmatrix}$$

$$[\mathbf{A} - \lambda\mathbf{I}] = \begin{vmatrix} -4-\lambda & -6 \\ 3 & 5-\lambda \end{vmatrix}$$

$$= (-4-\lambda)(5-\lambda) + 18$$

$$= \lambda^2 - \lambda - 2$$

The characteristic equation $|\mathbf{A} - \lambda\mathbf{I}| = 0$ is then,

$$\lambda^2 - 5\lambda - 2 = 0$$

The eigenvalues can be obtained as $\lambda = -1$ or 2.

Substituting the values for λ in equation (15) results in eigenvectors.

For $\lambda = -1$,

$$(\mathbf{A} + 1\mathbf{I})\mathbf{x} = \mathbf{0}$$

$$\begin{bmatrix} -3 & -6 \\ 3 & 6 \end{bmatrix}\begin{bmatrix} x_1 \\ x_2 \end{bmatrix} = \begin{bmatrix} 0 \\ 0 \end{bmatrix}$$

Solving for x_1 and x_2, the eigenvectors are of the form,

$$\begin{bmatrix} x_1 \\ x_2 \end{bmatrix} = r\begin{bmatrix} -2 \\ 1 \end{bmatrix}$$

For $\lambda = 2$

$$(\mathbf{A} + 1\mathbf{I})\mathbf{x} = \mathbf{0}$$

$$\begin{bmatrix} -6 & -6 \\ 3 & 3 \end{bmatrix}\begin{bmatrix} x_1 \\ x_2 \end{bmatrix} = \begin{bmatrix} 0 \\ 0 \end{bmatrix}$$

Solving for x_1 and x_2, the eigenvectors are of the form,

$$\begin{bmatrix} x_1 \\ x_2 \end{bmatrix} = s\begin{bmatrix} -1 \\ 1 \end{bmatrix}$$

r and s are some arbitrary scalars.

Eigenspace: Let $\boldsymbol{A}$ be an $n \times n$ matrix and λ be an eigenvalue of $\boldsymbol{A}$. Then, the set of all eigenvectors corresponding to λ together with a zero vector is known as eigenspace.

APPENDIX

B

Python Programming

Python is the most popular language for AI and ML. The advantages are many, e.g.,

(i) It is a free and open source language and is supported by Windows, Linux and MacOS.

(ii) It has a large set of libraries using which programming can be done easily.

(iii) Resources are available in plenty as many people are doing innovative work and bringing in more improvements.

(iv) A number of IDEs (Integrated Development Environments) are available for it.

(v) Google Colab is an online IDE using which one can get access to GPUs as well.

B.0 GETTING STARTED

The simplest way to get started is to install the Anaconda Navigator. This can be obtained from https://www.anaconda.com/. Once that is done, we can work using the IDLE editor, Jupyter Notebook or Spyder.

Jupyter Notebook is very popular. It is possible to run code as a single line or small chunks, observe the results and then do the remaining code in such tiny steps. Plots and arithmetic results are obtained inline.

Before going on to machine learning codes using Python, it would be best to understand some fundamentals of Python as it has relatively simple syntax compared to C and C++. Only a few aspects will be discussed here.

B.1 PYTHON FUNDAMENTALS

Here we will take a look at the syntax of some commonly used programming constructs.

B.1.1 The Print Statement

To print a character string, embed it with quotes and enclose it in brackets. To print a number, it is enough to use brackets for the number which is to be printed.

In the following, we see the print statements as used inline in the IDLE editor.

```
>>> print('Hi')
Hi
>>> print (45)
45
>>>
```

Next we save programs in a file and execute them.

B.1.2 Code-1

#add two integers entered from the keyboard on being prompted by the program.

```
print('Please enter an integer value:')
a = input()
print('Please enter another integer value:')
b=input()
z=a+b
x=int(a)
y=int(b)
z=x+y
print('a + b', '=', z)
print(z)
+++++++++++++++++++++++++++
```

OUTPUT:

Please enter an integer value:

78

Please enter another integer value:

89

a + b = 167

167

===

B.1.3 Code 2

#Using an 'If -else ' control structure.

Note that the 'body of the if control structure has to be **indented to the right. A colon is used as shown.**

```
d1 = 1.11 - 0
d2 = 3.2 - 2.1
print('d1 =', d1, ' d2 =', d2)
if d1 == d2:
print('Same')
```

```
else:
print('Different')
++++++++++++++++++++++++++++++++++++++++++++++++++++++++++++++++
OUTPUT:
d1 = 0.21000000000000008 d2 = 1.1
Different
++++++++++++++++++++++++++++++++++++++++++++++++++++++++++++++++
```

B.1.4 Code 3

 # nested if

#The 'eval' command permits the data to be taken as a float/integer/string depending on what the user has typed it as.

```
value = eval(input("Please enter an integer value in the range 0...10:"))
if value >= 0:                     # First check
 if value <= 10:                   # Second check
 print("In range")
print("Done")
++++++++++++++++++++++++++++++++++++++++++++++++++++++++++++++++
OUTPUT (CASE 1)
Please enter an integer value in the range 0...10: 7
In range
Done
>>>
OUTPUT (CASE 2)
Please enter an integer value in the range 0...10: 23
Done
================================================================
```

B.1.5 Code 4

#The For statement Note that the 'body of the **For** control structure has to be **indented to the right**

```
for n in range (1,7):
  print(n)
++++++++++++++++++++++++++++++++++++++
OUTPUT
1
2
3
4
```

5
6
>>>
Note: The numbers excluding the upper limit is the range
==

B.1.6 Code 5

```
#steps in the for statement.
for n in range(16, 0, -2):
print(n, '', end='')
++++++++++++++++++++++++++++
OUTPUT
16 14 12 10 8 6 4 2
>>>
```

==

B.1.7 Code 6

```
# Counter. Note the Indentation to the right, of the body of the while loop.
count = 1 # Initialize counter
while count <= 10:
   print(count)      # print count values, then increment counter
   count += 1
+++++++++++++++++++++++++++++
OUTPUT
1
2
3
4
5
6
7
8
9
10
>>>
```

==

B.2 PYTHON LIBRARIES FOR MACHINE LEARNING

The list shown below are the popular libraries which are useful for machine learning. Some of them (Numpy, Pandas, Matplotlib) are pre-installed in Anaconda. Others may be easily installed by going to the Anaconda prompt and typing 'pip install ----'.

- Numpy
- Scipy
- Scikit-learn
- Theano
- TensorFlow
- Keras
- PyTorch
- Pandas
- Matplotlib
- OpenCV

Now a few short programs showing the use of some of these libraries is discussed with examples.

B.2.1 The Numpy Library

Numpy stands for 'Numeric Python'. It is a library which has multidimensional array objects and a set of routines for managing arrays. Mathematical and logical operations on arrays can be performed using Numpy.

B.2.1.1 Numpy 1

```
import numpy as np
x=np.array([10,20,30])          # defines an array x with three elements
print(x)                        # prints the array x
++++++++++++++++++++++++++++++
OUTPUT
[10 20 30]
==================================================================
```

B.2.1.2 Numpy 2

```
import numpy as np
a=np.array([(200,4,4,400),(2,100,3,600)])  # define a two-dimensional array
print(a)
print(a.ndim)                   #dimension
print(a.itemsize)               #no. of bytes
print(a.dtype)                  # type
print(a.shape)                  # shape of the array
```

```
print(a.size)                  # number of elements in the array
y=a.reshape(4,2)               # reshapes from 2×4 to 4×2
print(y)
++++++++++++++++++++++++++++++++++++++++++++++++++++++++++++++++
OUTPUT
[[200 4   4  400]
[   2 100 3  600]]
2
4
int32
(2, 4)
8
[[200   4]
 [ 4  400]
 [ 2  100]
 [ 3  600]]
================================================================
```

B.2.1.3 Numpy 3

```
import numpy as np
a=np.array([(6,7,8,9),(3,4,5,6)])
print (a)
print(a[0,1])                  # prints element with index (0,1)
print(a[0,2]                   # prints only the second column
+++++++++++++++++++++++++++++++++++
OUTPUT
[[6  7  8  9]
[3  4  5  6]]
7
[8  5]
================================================================
```

B.2.1.4 Numpy 4

```
import numpy as np
a = np.array([[6, 9, 9], [3, 9, 6]], dtype = 'float')  # creates array from list with type float
print (a)
+++++++++++++++++++++++++
OUTPUT
[[6.  9.  9.]
 [3.  9.  6.]]
================================================================
```

B.2.1.5 Numpy 5

```
import numpy as np
b = np.array((5, 6, 7, 8))          # creating array from tuple
print (b)
++++++++++++++++++++++++
OUTPUT
[5 6 7 8]
```

==

B.2.1.6 Numpy 6

```
import numpy as np
e = np.random.random((3, 4))   # create an array with random values
print ("\nA random array:\n", e)
 f = np.arange(0, 40, 4)          # create a sequence of integers from 0 t0 40 in steps of 4
print ("\nA sequential array with steps of 4:\n", f)
++++++++++++++++++++++++++++++++++++++++++
OUTPUT
A random array:
 [[0.99041186 0.78145793 0.36733996 0.62533127]
 [0.18517327  0.86047831 0.71034946 0.79650764]
 [0.8643608   0.94775369 0.53368559 0.69026684]]
A sequential array with steps of 4:
 [ 0  4  8 12 16 20 24 28 32 36]
```

==

B.2.1.7 Numpy 7

```
import numpy as np
arr = np.array([[5, 6, 7, 8],
 [9, 8, 7, 6],
 [0, 2, 1, 1]])
new = arr.reshape(2, 2, 3)          # Reshaping 3×4 array to 2×2×3 array
print ("\nOriginal array:\n", arr)
print ("Reshaped array:\n", new)
arr = np.array([[3, 4, 3], [5, 7, 6]])
flatt = arr.flatten()                    # Flatten array
print ("\nOriginal array:\n", arr)
print ("Fattened array:\n", flatt)
++++++++++++++++++++++++++++++++++++++++++++++++
```

```
OUTPUT
Original array:
 [[5 6 7 8]
 [9 8 7 6]
 [0 2 1 1]]
Reshaped array:
 [[[5 6 7]
 [8 9 8]]

 [[7 6 0]
 [2 1 1]]]

Original array:
 [[3 4 3]
 [5 7 6]]
Fattened array:
 [3 4 3 5 7 6]
=================================================================
```

B.2.2 Pandas

This is a library used for data analysis and manipulation of tabular data in 'Dataframes'.It is built on top of the Numpy library. A Pandas DataFrame is a two-dimensional data structure, the same as a 2-dimensional array. It may be visualized as a table with rows and columns.

B.2.2.1 Pandas 1

```
import pandas as pd
import numpy as np
# makes a table using the data given
data = {'year': [2011, 2012, 2013, 2014, 2015, 2016, 2017, 2018, 2019],
 'team': ['Team1', 'Team2', 'Team3', 'Team4', 'Team5', 'Team6', 'Team7',
 'Team8', 'Team9'],
 'wins': [32, 20, 15, 26, 12, 16, 11, 15, 18],
 'draws': [8, 7, 3, 5, 3, 7, 9, 10, 6],
 'losses': [4, 5, 2, 4, 2, 5, 7, 10, 11]
 }
football = pd.DataFrame(
 data, columns=['year', 'team', 'wins', 'draws', 'losses'])
print(football)
++++++++++++++++++++++++++++++++++++++++++++++++++++++++++
```

```
OUTPUT
  year  team  wins draws losses
0 2011  Team1  32    8     4
1 2012  Team2  20    7     5
2 2013  Team3  15    3     2
3 2014  Team4  26    5     4
4 2015  Team5  12    3     2
5 2016  Team6  16    7     5
6 2017  Team7  11    9     7
7 2018  Team8  15   10    10
8 2019  Team9  18    6    11
```

==

B.2.3 Matplotlib

This is a library to do plotting in various forms, such as X-Y plot, scatter plot, bar chart, histogram, pi chart, etc.

B.2.3.1 Plot 1

```
From matplotlib import pyplot as plt
plt.plot([1,2,3],[4,5,1])          # data for an x-Y plot
plt.show()                         #Show(display) the plot
```

++

OUTPUT

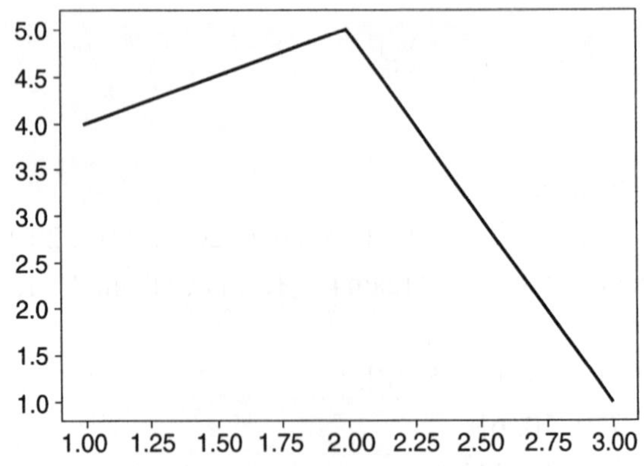

==

B.2.3.2 Plot 2

 # plot with labelled axes

```
From matplotlib import pyplot as plt
x = [5,2,7]
```

```
y = [2,16,4]
plt.plot(x,y)
plt.title('Info')
plt.ylabel('Y axis')
plt.xlabel('X axis')
plt.show()
++++++++++++++++++++++++++++++++++++++++++++++++++++
OUTPUT
```

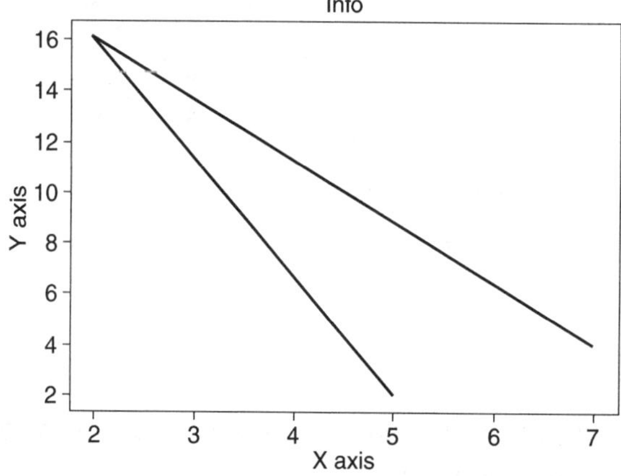

Fig. AB.1 Output from the code Plot 2

```
==================================================================
```

B.2.3.3 Plot 3

```
# shows a scatterplot with legend, label and color
From matplotlib import pyplot as plt
x = [1,1.5,2,2.5,3,3.5,3.6]
y = [7.5,8,8.5,9,9.5,10,10.5]
x1=[8,8.5,9,9.5,10,10.5,11]
y1=[3,3.5,3.7,4,4.5,5,5.2]
plt.scatter(x,y,label='variation',color='r')
plt.scatter(x1,y1,label='living',color='b')
plt.xlabel('saving*100')
plt.ylabel('income*1000')
plt.title('Scatter Plot')
plt.legend()
plt.show()
++++++++++++++++++++++++++++++++++
```

OUTPUT

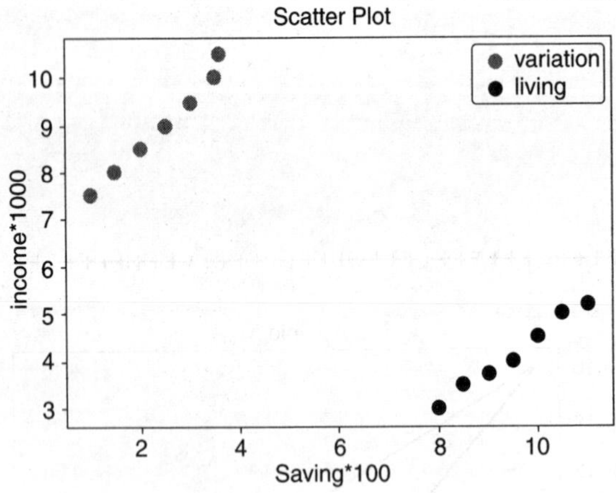

Fig. AB.2 Output of code 'Plot 3'

==

B.2.3.4 Plot 4

```
# plots a histogram
From matplotlib import pyplot as plt
age=[10,15,30,25,45,89,12,13,45,67,89,90,78,100,9098,67,54,45,34,56,78,23,14,25,]
bins=[10,20,30,40,50,60,70,80,90,100,110]
plt.hist(age, bins, histtype='bar', rwidth=0.8,color='g')
plt.title('age vs people')
plt.xlabel('age')
plt.ylabel('frequency')
plt.show()
```

++++++++++++++++++++++++++++++++++++++

OUTPUT

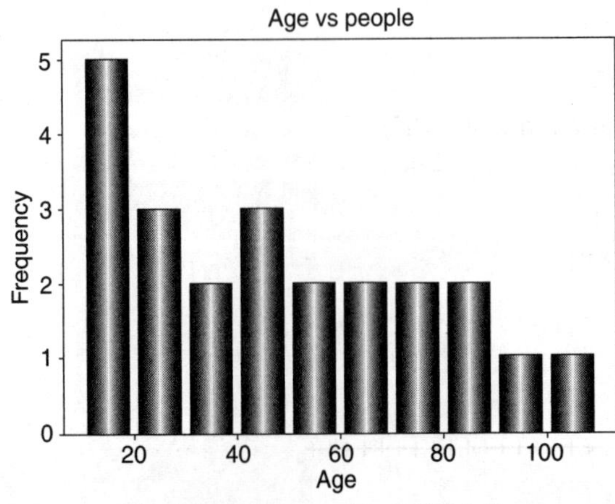

Fig. AB.3 Output of code 'Plot 4'

==

B.2.3.5 Plot 5

```
# this shows a bar chart with colors, labels and legend
From matplotlib import pyplot as plt
plt.bar([0.25,1.25,2.25,3.25,4.25],[50,40,70,80,20],
label="BMW",width=.5)
plt.bar([.75,1.75,2.75,3.75,4.75],[80,20,20,50,60],
label="Audi", color='r',width=.5)
plt.legend()
plt.xlabel('Days')
plt.ylabel('Distance (kms)')
plt.title('Information')
plt.show()
++++++++++++++++++++++++++++++++++++++
OUTPUT
```

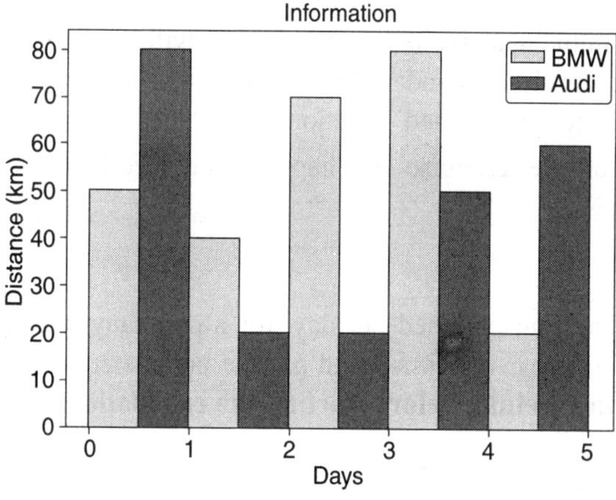

Fig. AB.4 Output of code 'Plot 5'

==

B.2.3.6 Plot 6

```
# this plots a sine wave defined by numpy
Import numpy as np
Import matplotlib.pyplot as plt
x= np.arange(0,3*np.pi,0.1)
y=np.sin(x)
plt.plot(x,y)
plt.show()
+++++++++++++++++++++++++++++++++++++++++++++
```

OUTPUT

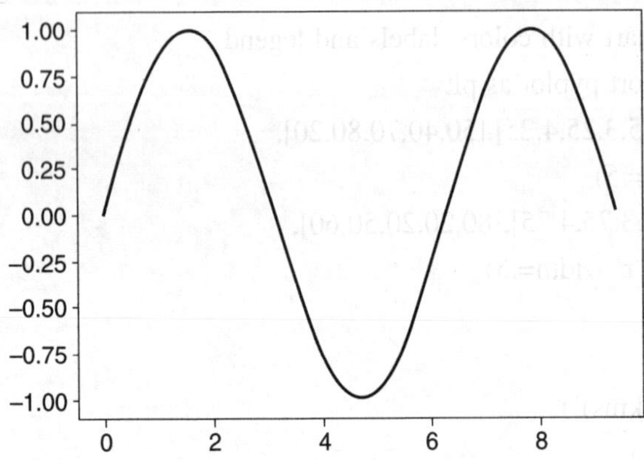

Fig. AB.5 Output of code 'Plot 6'

B.3 MACHINE LEARNING

Now some short and simple machine learning programs will be shown here. In Python, there are functions available for all the standard ML algorithms. But some simple calculation may be done without using the 'pre-defined' functions.

Question 3 of 'end chapter Exercise' of Chapter 3 is copied here and the code and results are shown.

B.3.1

This is tabulation of the rent obtained per day, for a company that has different types of rooms. Use this data in linear regression and get the parameters of the line used to fit the data. **Observe the data carefully before starting the calculations.**

Table AB.1

Store No	*No. of rooms (x)*	*Rent per day (rupees) (y)*
1	17	3680
2	15	3990
3	28	6655
4	35	9540
5	12	3310
6	22	5560
7	13	4500
8	**3**	**35650**

In this dataset, entry no. 8 is not used as it seems to be an 'outlier'.

- This program runs Linear Regression for the data given as x and y.
- It uses a test data of $x = 35$ and calculates the parameters β_1 and β_0.
- It also finds the value of y for $x = 35$ using the equation $y = \beta_0 + \beta_x x$.

CODE

```
Import numpy as np
Import matplotlib.pyplot as plt
Import pandas as pd
x = np.array([12,13,15,17,22,28])
y = np.array([3310,4500,3990,3680,5560,6655])
x = x.reshape(-1,1)
from sklearn.linear_model import LinearRegression
regressor = LinearRegression()
regressor.fit(x, y)
y_pred = regressor.predict(x)
plt.scatter(x, y, color='red')
plt.plot(x, regressor.predict(x), color='blue')
plt.title('Visualizing the results')
plt.xlabel('No. of days')
plt.ylabel('Rent/day')
plt.show()
# testing
regressor.predict([[35]])
regressor.intercept_
regressor.coef_
print(regressor.intercept_)
print(regressor.coef_)
y=regressor.coef_*35 +regressor.intercept_
print(y)
++++++++++++++++++++++++++++++++++++++++
==================================================================
```

OUTPUT

```
1237.2836752899202      # value of β0
[189.45138269]          # value of β1
[7868.08206958]         #value of y
```

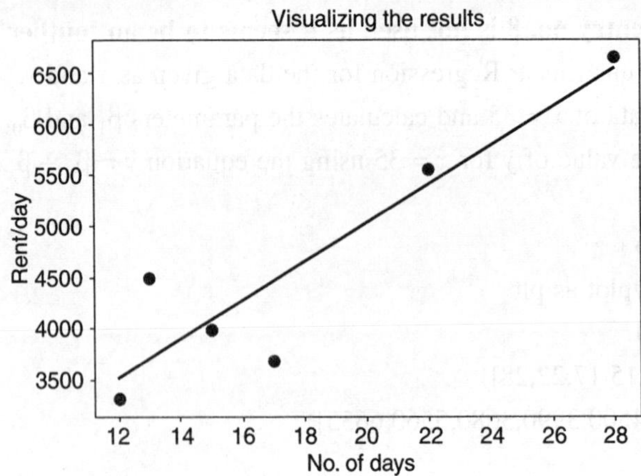

Fig. AB.6 Plot of the linear regression data

Conclusion

With this, we come to the end of a short introduction to Python and three basic libraries. Since there are many libraries which are useful and because many codes may be long, it is not useful when available in print form. **A soft version of a 'Coding Manual' (QR code) is included as one of the 'online resources' of the book.**

Bibliography

1. Nair Vinod and Hinton, Geoffrey E. *Rectified linear units improve restricted Boltzmann machines,* Proceedings of the 27th International Conference on Machine Learning, ICML, pp. 807–814, 2010.
2. Srivastava, Nitish, Hinton, Geoffrey, Krizhevsky, Alex, Sutskever, Ilya, and Salakhutdinov, Ruslan. *Dropout: A simple way to prevent neural networks from overfitting*. J. Mach. Learn. Res., 15(1): 1929–1958, January 2014.
3. G.D. Suriya Prasath, M.K. Rahgul Poopathi, P. Sarvesh and A. Samuel *Application of Machine Learning Algorithms in Autonomous Vehicles Navigation System,* IOP Conference Series: Materials Science and Engineering, Volume 912, Multidisciplinary, 2020.
4. Biggi, Gianluca and Stilgoe, Jack, *Artificial Intelligence in Self-Driving Cars Research and Innovation: A Scientometric and Bibliometric Analysis*, https://ssrn.com/abstract=3829897, April 2021.
5. Kritika Rana and Parampreet Kaur, *Review on machine learning based algorithms used in autonomous cars*, JETIR, Volume 5, Issue 10, October 2018, pp. 114-118.
6. Chenyi Chen, Princeton Autonomous Vehicle Engineering, Ebook on *Deep Learning for Self-driving Car*, 2021.
7. Der-Hau Lee, Kuan-Lin Chen, Kuan-Han Liou, Chang-Lun Liu and Jinn-Liang Liu, *Deep Learning and Control Algorithms of Direct Perception for Autonomous Driving*, Springer, 2021.
8. Jianfeng Zhao, Bodong Liang and Qiuxia Chen, *The key technology toward the self-driving car*, International Journal of Intelligent Unmanned Systems, 6 (1): 2-20, 2018.
9. Andrew NG, *Machine Learning Yearning-Draft E-book*, 2018.
10. Chigozie Enyinna Nwankpa, Winifred Ijomah, Anthony Gachagan, and Stephen Marshal, *Article on Activation Functions: Comparison of Trends in Practice and Research for Deep Learning*, Cornell University, 2018.
11. Sergey Ioffe and Christian Szegedy, *Batch Normalization: Accelerating Deep Network Training by Reducing Internal Covariate Shift*, Proceedings of the 32nd International Conference on Machine Learning, Lille, JMLR: W&CP, Volume 37, France, 2015.
12. Josh Patterson and Adam Gibson, *Deep Learning: A Practitioner's Approach*, Published by O'Reilly Media, Inc., 2017.
13. Yann LeCun, Yoshua Bengio and Geoffrey Hinton, *Deep Learning*, Macmillan Publishers Limited, 2015.
14. Ronen Eldan and Ohad Shamir, *The Power of Depth for Feedforward Neural Networks*, JMLR: Workshop and Conference Proceedings, Volume 49: 1–34, 2016.

15. Mohit Deshpande, *Ebook on Deep Learning for Human Beings: Understand How Deep Neural Networks work,* 2018.
16. Nitish Srivastava, Geoffrey Hinton, Alex Krizhevsky, Ilya Sutskever and Ruslan Salakhutdinov, *Dropout: A simple way to prevent neural networks from overfitting*, Journal of Machine Learning Research 15, 2014, pp. 1929-1958.
17. Geoffrey E. Hinton, Nitish Srivastava, Alex Krizhevsky, Ilya Sutskever and Ruslan R. Salakhutdinov, *Improving neural networks by preventing co-adaptation of feature*, arXiv:1207.0580, 2012.
18. Simon Haykins, *Neural Networks and Learning Machines,* Third Edition, Pearson Education, 2008.
19. Daniel Jurafsky and James H. Martin, *Speech and Language Processing: An Introduction to Natural Language Processing, Computational Linguistics, and Speech Recognition*, Third Edition draft, 2021.
20. Jingzhao Zhang, Tianxing He, Suvrit Sra and Ali Jadbabaie, *Why gradient clipping accelerates training: A theoretical justification for adaptivity,* International Conference on Learning Representations, ICLR 2020.
21. Alex Krizhevsky, Ilya Sutskever and Geoffrey E. Hinton, *ImageNet Classification with Deep Convolutional Neural Networks*, Conference on Advances in Neural Information Processing Systems 25 (NIPS 2012).
22. Sergey Ioffe and Christian Szegedy, *Batch normalization: accelerating deep network training by reducing internal covariate shift*, Proceedings of the 32nd International Conference on International Conference on Machine Learning, ICML'15, Volume 37, Pages 448-456, July 2015.
23. L. Bottou, *Stochastic Gradient Learning in Neural Networks*, 1991. Proceedings of Neuro Nimes 91(8), p. 12.
24. Xavier Glorot, Antoine Bordes and Yoshua Bengio, *Deep Sparse Rectifier Neural Networks*, Proceedings of the 14th International Conference on Artificial Intelligence and Statistics (AISTATS) 2011, Volume 15 of JMLR: W&CP 15, 2011.
25. Ross Girshick, *Fast R-CNN*, Proceedings of the IEEE International Conference on Computer Vision (ICCV), 2015.
26. Ross Girshick, Jeff Donahue, Trevor Darrell and Jitendra Malik, *Rich feature hierarchies for accurate object detection and semantic segmentation Tech report (v5)*, IEEE Conference on Computer Vision and Pattern Recognition, CVPR, Pages 580-587, June 2014.
27. Ross Girshick, Jeff Donahue, Trevor Darrell and Jitendra Malik, *Region-based Convolutional Networks for Accurate Object Detection and Segmentation*, IEEE Transactions on Pattern Recognition and Machine Intelligence, 2015.
28. Shaoqing Ren, Kaiming He, Ross Girshick, and Jian Sun, *Faster R-CNN: Towards Real-Time Object Detection with Region Proposal Networks*, NIPS'15: Proceedings of the 28th International Conference on Neural Information Processing Systems, Volume 1, Pages 91-99, December 2015.
29. Baoyuan Liu, Min Wang, Hassan Foroosh, Marshall Tappen and Marianna Penksy, *Sparse Convolutional Neural Networks,* Proceedings of the IEEE Conference on Computer Vision and Pattern Recognition (CVPR), 2015.
30. Dharampal and Vikram Mutneja, *Methods of image edge detection: A review*, Journal of Electrical & Electronic Systems, 2015.

31. Markus Thom and Günther Palm, *Sparse activity and sparse connectivity in supervised learning*, Journal of Machine Learning Research 14, 2013.
32. Asifullah Khan, Anabia Sohail, Umme Zahoora and Aqsa Saeed Qureshi, *A Survey of the Recent Architectures of Deep Convolutional Neural Networks*, Artificial Intelligence Review, 2019.
33. Karen Simonyan and Andrew Zisserman, *Very Deep Convolutional Networks for Large Scale Image Recognition*, Proceedings of the International Conference on Learning Representations (ICLR), 2015.
34. K.G. Shreyas Dixit, Mahima Girish Chadaga, Sinchana S. Savalgimath, G. Ragavendra Rakshith and Naveen Kumar M.R., *Evaluation and evolution of object detection techniques YOLO and R-CNN*, International Journal of Recent Technology and Engineering (IJRTE) 2277-3878, Volume 8, Issue 2S3, July 2019, pp. 824-829.
35. Farida Kachapova, *Representing Markov chains with transition diagrams*, Journal of Mathematics and Statistics 9(3): 149-154, 2013.
36. Atsuhiko Kai, Yoshifumi Hirose and Seiichi Nagagawa, *Dealing with out-of-vocabulary words and speech disfluencies in an n-gram based speech understanding*, 5th International Conference on Spoken Language Processing (ICSLP 98), 1998.
37. Eric Brille, *A simple Rule Based Part of Speech Tagger,* Proceedings of the Third Conference of Applied Computational Linguistics, 1992.
38. Anirudh Goyal, Alex Lamb, Ying Zhang, Saizheng Zhang, Aaron Courville and Yoshua Bengio, *Professor Forcing: A New Algorithm for Training Recurrent Networks*, 30th Conference on Neural Information Processing Systems, NIPS 2016.
39. Kyunghyun Cho, Dzmitry Bahdanau, Fethi Bougares, Holger Schwenk and Yoshua Bengio, *Learning Phrase Representations using RNN Encoder–Decoder for Statistical Machine Translation,* Proceedings of the Conference on Empirical Methods in Natural Language Processing (EMNLP), 2014.
40. EMC Educational Services, *Data Science & Big Data Analytics: Discovering, Analyzing, Visualizing and Presenting Data,* John Wiley and Sons, Inc. 2015.
41. Rachel Schutt and Cathy O'Neil, *Doing Data Science, Straight Talk from the Frontline*, O'Reilly, 2011.
42. Alexander Clark, Chris Fox and Shalom Lappin, *The Handbook of Computational Linguistics and Natural Language Processing*, Wiley Blackwell, 2010.
43. Aditya Gupta, Khatri Mrunal Mohan and Sushila Shidnal, *Spam filter using Naïve Bayesian technique*, International Journal of Computational Engineering Research (IJCER), 8(6): pp. 26-32, June 2018.
44. Shruti Bajaj Mangal,Vishal Goyal, *Text news classification system using Naïve Bayes classifier*, International Journal of Engineering Sciences, Issue December, Vol. 3: pp. 1-5, 2014.
45. Tutorials Point, *Tutorial on Natural Language Processing*, 2019.
46. Ronan Collobert, Jason Weston, L´eon Bottou, Michael Karlen, Koray Kavukcuoglu and Pavel Kuksa, *Natural language processing (almost) from scratch*, Journal of Machine Learning Research 12, 2011, pp. 2493-2537.
47. Gabriel Recchia and Michael N. Jones, *More data trumps smarter algorithms: Comparing pointwise mutual information with latent semantic analysis,* Journal of The Psychonomic Society, Inc. Behavior Research Methods 2009, pp. 647-656.

48. Noam Shazeer, Ryan Doherty, Colin Evans and Chris Waterson, *Swivel: Improving Embeddings by Noticing What's Missing*, CoRR abs/1602.02215,2016.
49. Tapas Nayak, Hwee Tou Ng, *Effective Modeling of Encoder-Decoder Architecture for Joint Entity and Relation Extraction,* Association for the Advancement of Artificial Intelligence (www.aaai.org), 2020.
50. Ilya Sutskever Google, Oriol Vinyals Google vinyals and Quoc V. Le, *Sequence to Sequence Learning with Neural Networks*, Proceedings of the conference Advances in Neural Information Processing Systems (NeurIPS), 2014.
51. Bowen Liu, Fengjiao Lyu and Rajarshi Roy, *Natural Language Question-Answering using Deep Learning,* Article in Stanford University Archive, 2017.
52. Yoav Goldberg and Omer Levy, word2vec Explained: Deriving Mikolov et al.'s Negative-Sampling Word-Embedding Method, CoRR abs/1402.3722, 2014.
53. Ian Goodfellow, Yoshua Bengio and Aaron Courville, *Deep Learning*, MIT Press, 2017.
54. Zhang Jian and Wang Xue Wu, *The application of feed-forward neural network for the X-ray image fusion*, J. Phys.: Conf. Ser. 312 0620052011.
55. Luong MT, Sutskever I, Le Quoc V, Vinyals O, Zaremba W. *Addressing the Rare Word Problem in Neural Machine Translation*, Proceedings of the 53rd Annual Meeting of the Association for Computational Linguistics and the 7th International Joint Conference on Natural Language Processing, 2015.
56. Divya Saxena and Jiannong Cao, *Generative Adversarial Networks (GANs): Challenges, solutions, and future directions,* ACM Computing Surveys, Volume 54, Issue 3, April 2022, pp. 1-42.
57. Ricard Durall, Kalun Ho, Franz-Josef Pfreundt and Janis Keuper, *Latent Space Conditioning on Generative Adversarial Networks*, Proceedings of the 16th International Joint Conference on Computer Vision, Imaging and Computer Graphics Theory and Applications (VISIGRAPP 2021) - Volume 4: VISAPP, pages 24-34, 2021.
58. Ian J. Goodfellow, Jean Pouget-Abadie, Mehdi Mirza, Bing Xu, David Warde-Farley, Sherjil Ozair, Aaron Courville and Yoshua Bengio, *Generative Adversarial Nets*, Proceedings of the Conference on Advances in Neural Information Processing Systems 27 (NIPS 2014).
59. Zhiyong Cui, Ruimin Ke, Ziyuan Pu and Yinhai Wang, *Stacked Bidirectional and Unidirectional LSTM Recurrent Neural Network for Network-wide Traffic Speed Prediction*, Proceedings of Transportation Research Part C Emerging Technologies, 2018.
60. Junyoung Chung, Caglar Gulcehre, KyungHyun and Yoshua Bengio, *Empirical Evaluation of Gated Recurrent Neural Networks on Sequence Modeling,* Proceedings of the NIPS Deep Learning and Representation Learning Workshop, 2014.
61. J. Seberry, B.J. Wysocki and T.A. Wysocki - Metrika, *On Some Applications of Hadamard Matrices*, Springer, 2005.
62. Cem Subakan; Mirco Ravanelli; Samuele Cornell; Mirko Bronzi and Jianyuan Zhong, *Attention Is All You Need In Speech Separation*, Proceedings of the IEEE International Conference on Acoustics, Speech and Signal Processing (ICASSP), 2021.
63. Ashish Vaswani and Noam Shazeer, Niki Parmar, Jakob Uszkoreit, Llion Jones, Aidan N. Gomez, Łukasz Kaiser and Illia Polosukhin, *Attention is All you Need*, Proceedings of the Conference on Advances in Neural Information Processing Systems 30 (NIPS 2017).

64. Cho, K., Van Merriënboer, B., Gulcehre, C., Bahdanau, D., Bougares, F., Schwenk, H. and Bengio, Y. *Learning phrase representations using RNN encoder-decoder for statistical machine translation. arXiv preprint arXiv:1406.1078*, 2014.

65. Bobin, Jérôme, Jean-Luc Starck, Jalal M. Fadili, Yassir Moudden and David L. Donoho, *Morphological component analysis: An adaptive thresholding strategy*." IEEE Transactions on Image Processing 16, no. 11, 2675-2681, 2007.

66. Duda, Richard O. and Peter E. Hart. *Pattern Classification*. John Wiley & Sons, 2006.

67. Leung, K. Ming. *"Naive Bayesian classifier."* Polytechnic University Department of Computer Science/Finance and Risk Engineering (2007): 123-156.

68. Izenman, Alan Julian. *"Linear discriminant analysis." Modern Multivariate Statistical Techniques*. Springer, New York, 2013. 237-280.

69. Balakrishnama, Suresh and Aravind Ganapathiraju. *"Linear discriminant analysis-a brief tutorial."* Institute for Signal and Information Processing, 18 (1998): 1-8.

70. Li, Ming, and Baozong Yuan. "2D-LDA: *A statistical linear discriminant analysis for image matrix."* Pattern Recognition Letters 26.5 (2005): 527-532.

71. Lam, Wai and Fahiem Bacchus. *"Learning Bayesian belief networks: An approach based on the MDL principle."* Computational Intelligence 10.3 (1994): 269-293.

72. Bishop, Christopher M. and Nasser M. Nasrabadi. *Pattern Recognition and Machine Learning*. Vol. 4. No. 4. New York: Springer, 2006.

73. Moeyaert, Mariola, et al. *"Multilevel modeling of single-case data: A comparison of maximum likelihood and Bayesian estimation."* Psychological Methods 22.4 (2017): 760.

74. Babich, Gregory A. and Octavia I. Camps. *"Weighted Parzen windows for pattern classification."* IEEE Transactions on Pattern Analysis and Machine Intelligence 18.5 (1996): 567-570.

75. Zhang, Min-Ling and Zhi-Hua Zhou. *"ML-KNN: A lazy learning approach to multi-label learning."* Pattern Recognition 40.7 (2007): 2038-2048.

76. Zhang, Hao, et al. *"SVM-KNN: Discriminative nearest neighbor classification for visual category recognition."* 2006 IEEE Computer Society Conference on Computer Vision and Pattern Recognition (CVPR'06). Vol. 2. IEEE, 2006.

77. Burges, Christopher JC. *"A tutorial on support vector machines for pattern recognition."* Data Mining and Knowledge Discovery 2.2 (1998): 121-167.

78. Smola, Alex J. and Bernhard Schölkopf. *"A tutorial on support vector regression."* Statistics and Computing 14.3 (2004): 199-222.

79. Xu, Rui and Donald Wunsch. *"Survey of clustering algorithms."* IEEE Transactions on Neural Networks 16.3 (2005): 645-678.

80. Hartigan, John A. and Manchek A. Wong. *"Algorithm AS 136: A k-means clustering algorithm."* Journal of the Royal Statistical Society. Series c (Applied Statistics) 28.1 (1979): 100-108.

81. Likas, Aristidis, Nikos Vlassis and Jakob J. Verbeek. *"The global k-means clustering algorithm."* Pattern Recognition 36.2 (2003): 451-461.

82. He, Xiaofei, et al. *"Laplacian regularized gaussian mixture model for data clustering."* IEEE Transactions on Knowledge and Data Engineering 23.9 (2010): 1406-1418.

83. Uykan, Zekeriya. *"Fusion of centroid-based clustering with graph clustering: An expectation-maximization-based hybrid clustering."* IEEE Transactions on Neural Networks and Learning Systems (2021).
84. Vidal, René. *"Subspace clustering."* IEEE Signal Processing Magazine 28.2 (2011): 52-68.
85. Elhamifar, Ehsan and René Vidal. *"Sparse subspace clustering: Algorithm, theory, and applications."* IEEE Transactions on Pattern Analysis and Machine Intelligence 35.11 (2013): 2765-2781.
86. Francis, Jobin, M. Baburaj and Sudhish N. George. *"An l ½ and Graph Regularized Subspace Clustering Method for Robust Image Segmentation."* ACM Transactions on Multimedia Computing, Communications, and Applications (TOMM) 18.2 (2022): 1-24.
87. Abdi, Hervé and Lynne J. Williams. *"Principal Component Analysis."* Wiley Interdisciplinary Reviews: Computational Statistics 2.4 (2010): 433-459.
88. Wold, Svante, Kim Esbensen and Paul Geladi. *"Principal component analysis."* Chemometrics and Intelligent Laboratory Systems 2.1-3 (1987): 37-52.
89. Belhumeur, Peter N., Joao P. Hespanha and David J. Kriegman. *"Eigenfaces vs. fisherfaces: Recognition using class specific linear projection."* IEEE Transactions on Pattern Analysis and Machine Intelligence 19.7 (1997): 711-720.
90. Li, Ming and Baozong Yuan. "2D-LDA: *A statistical linear discriminant analysis for image matrix."* Pattern Recognition Letters 26.5 (2005): 527-532.
91. Shijila, B., Anju Jose Tom and Sudhish N. George. *"Moving object detection by low rank approximation and l1-TV regularization on RPCA framework."* Journal of Visual Communication and Image Representation 56 (2018): 188-200.
92. Li, Cheng and Bingyu Wang. *"Fisher linear discriminant analysis."* CCIS Northeastern University (2014).
93. Frank, Ronald E., William F. Massy, and Donald G. Morrison. *"Bias in multiple discriminant analysis."* Journal of Marketing Research 2.3 (1965): 250-258.
94. Huberty, Carl J. *"Discriminant analysis."* Review of Educational Research 45.4 (1975): 543-598.
95. Stewart, Gilbert W. *"On the early history of the singular value decomposition."* SIAM Review 35.4 (1993): 551-566.
96. Baker, Kirk. *"Singular Value Decomposition Tutorial."* The Ohio State University 24 (2005).
97. Wall, Michael E., Andreas Rechtsteiner and Luis M. Rocha. "Singular value decomposition and principal component analysis." *A Practical Approach to Microarray Data Analysis*. Springer, Boston, MA, 2003. 91-109.
98. Klema, Virginia, and Alan Laub. *"The singular value decomposition: Its computation and some applications."* IEEE Transactions on Automatic Control 25.2 (1980): 164-176.
99. *Reinforcement Learning: An Introduction* (Second Edition). R. Sutton and A. Barto. MIT Press, 2018.
100. *Algorithms for Reinforcement Learning.* C. Szepesvari. Morgan and Claypool Publishers, 2010.
101. *Reinforcement Learning: State-of-the-Art.* M. Wiering and M. van Otterlo. Springer, 2012
102. Krishnamurthy, V., *Partially Observed Markov Decision Processes.* Cambridge University Press, 2016.

103. Mnih, V., Badia, A. P., Mirza, M., Graves, A., Lillicrap, T., Harley, Silver, D. and Kavukcuoglu, K. (2016, June). *Asynchronous methods for deep reinforcement learning.* In International Conference on Machine Learning (pp. 1928-1937). PMLR.

104. Silver, D., Lever, G., Heess, N., Degris, T., Wierstra, D. and Riedmiller, M. (2014, January). *Deterministic policy gradient algorithms.* In International Conference on Machine Learning (pp. 387 395). PMLR.

105. Lillicrap, T. P., Hunt, J. J., Pritzel, A., Heess, N., Erez, T., Tassa, Y., Silver D. and Wierstra, D. (2015). Continuous control with deep reinforcement learning. arXiv preprint arXiv:1509.02971.

106. Barth-Maron, Gabriel, Matthew W. Hoffman, David Budden, Will Dabney, Dan Horgan, Dhruva Tb, Alistair Muldal, Nicolas Heess and Timothy Lillicrap. "Distributed distributional deterministic policy gradients." arXiv preprint arXiv:1804.08617 (2018).

107. Schulman, J., Levine, S., Abbeel, P., Jordan, M. and Moritz, P. (2015, June). *Trust region policy optimization.* In International Conference on Machine Learning (pp. 1889-1897). PMLR.

108. Schulman, J., Wolski, F., Dhariwal, P., Radford, A. and Klimov, O. (2017). Proximal policy optimization algorithms. arXiv preprint arXiv:1707.06347.

109. Haarnoja, T., Zhou, A., Abbeel, P. and Levine, S. (2018, July). Soft actor-critic: *Off-policy maximum entropy deep reinforcement learning with a stochastic actor.* In International Conference on Machine Learning (pp. 1861-1870). PMLR.

Websites (Accessed during the period from May 2021 to May 2022)

1. https://www.visteon.com/machine-learning-algorithms-in-autonomous-cars/
2. https://intellias.com/how-machine-learning-algorithms-make-self-driving-cars-a-reality/
3. https://www.kdnuggets.com/2017/06/machine-learning-algorithms-used-self-driving-cars.html
4. https://www.thinkautonomous.ai/blog/?p=deep-learning-in-self-driving-cars
5. https://www.sciencedirect.com/science/article/pii/S2666827021000827
6. https://bdtechtalks.com/2020/07/29/self-driving-tesla-car-deep-learning/
7. https://towardsdatascience.com/self-driving-cars-past-present-and-future-71532430346
8. https://www.synopsys.com/automotive/what-is-autonomous-car.html
9. https://www.landmarkdividend.com/self-driving-car/
10. https://victorzhou.com/blog/intro-to-neural-networks/
11. https://www.neuraldesigner.com/blog/perceptron-the-main-component-of-neural-networks
12. https://dustinstansbury.github.io/theclevermachine/a-gentle-introduction-to-neural-networks
13. https://dustinstansbury.github.io/theclevermachine/derivation-backpropagation
14. https://machinelearningmastery.com/dropout-for-regularizing-deep-neural-networks/
15. https://towardsdatascience.com/simplified-math-behind-dropout-in-deep-learning-6d50f3f47275
16. https://ml-cheatsheet.readthedocs.io/en/latest/optimizers.html#adamoptimisers
17. https://machinelearningmastery.com/rectified-linear-activation-function-for-deep-learning-neural-networks/
18. http://colah.github.io/posts/2015-09-Visual-Information/
19. https://neptune.ai/blog/cross-entropy-loss-and-its-applications-in-deep-learning
20. https://towardsdatascience.com/perplexity-in-language-models-87a196019a94

21. https://gist.github.com/aparrish/2f562e3737544cf29aaf1af30362f469
22. http://www.nlp.town/blog/sentence-similarity/
23. https://wiki.pathmind.com/word2vec#:~:text=The%20purpose%20and%20usefulness%20of,the%20context%20of%20individual%20words.
24. https://medium.com/inside-machine-learning/what-is-a-transformer-d07dd1fbec04
25. https://nlp.seas.harvard.edu/2018/04/03/attention.html#prelims
26. Chris McCormick, *Ebook on The Inner Workings of Word2Vec*,2019.

Index